Communications
in Computer and Information Science 1904

Rationale

The CCIS series is devoted to the publication of proceedings of computer science conferences. Its aim is to efficiently disseminate original research results in informatics in printed and electronic form. While the focus is on publication of peer-reviewed full papers presenting mature work, inclusion of reviewed short papers reporting on work in progress is welcome, too. Besides globally relevant meetings with internationally representative program committees guaranteeing a strict peer-reviewing and paper selection process, conferences run by societies or of high regional or national relevance are also considered for publication.

Topics

The topical scope of CCIS spans the entire spectrum of informatics ranging from foundational topics in the theory of computing to information and communications science and technology and a broad variety of interdisciplinary application fields.

Information for Volume Editors and Authors

Publication in CCIS is free of charge. No royalties are paid, however, we offer registered conference participants temporary free access to the online version of the conference proceedings on SpringerLink (http://link.springer.com) by means of an http referrer from the conference website and/or a number of complimentary printed copies, as specified in the official acceptance email of the event.

CCIS proceedings can be published in time for distribution at conferences or as post-proceedings, and delivered in the form of printed books and/or electronically as USBs and/or e-content licenses for accessing proceedings at SpringerLink. Furthermore, CCIS proceedings are included in the CCIS electronic book series hosted in the SpringerLink digital library at http://link.springer.com/bookseries/7899. Conferences publishing in CCIS are allowed to use Online Conference Service (OCS) for managing the whole proceedings lifecycle (from submission and reviewing to preparing for publication) free of charge.

Publication process

The language of publication is exclusively English. Authors publishing in CCIS have to sign the Springer CCIS copyright transfer form, however, they are free to use their material published in CCIS for substantially changed, more elaborate subsequent publications elsewhere. For the preparation of the camera-ready papers/files, authors have to strictly adhere to the Springer CCIS Authors' Instructions and are strongly encouraged to use the CCIS LaTeX style files or templates.

Abstracting/Indexing

CCIS is abstracted/indexed in DBLP, Google Scholar, EI-Compendex, Mathematical Reviews, SCImago, Scopus. CCIS volumes are also submitted for the inclusion in ISI Proceedings.

How to start

To start the evaluation of your proposal for inclusion in the CCIS series, please send an e-mail to ccis@springer.com.

Marie-Luce Bourguet · Jule M. Krüger ·
Daniela Pedrosa · Andreas Dengel ·
Anasol Peña-Rios · Jonathon Richter
Editors

Immersive Learning Research Network

9th International Conference, iLRN 2023
San Luis Obispo, USA, June 26–29, 2023
Revised Selected Papers

 Springer

Editors
Marie-Luce Bourguet ⓘ
Queen Mary University of London
London, UK

Jule M. Krüger ⓘ
University of Potsdam
Potsdam, Germany

Daniela Pedrosa ⓘ
University of Aveiro
Aveiro, Portugal

Andreas Dengel
Goethe University Frankfurt
Frankfurt am Main, Germany

Anasol Peña-Rios ⓘ
British Telecom Research Labs
Ipswich, UK

Jonathon Richter ⓘ
University of Montana
Missoula, MT, USA

ISSN 1865-0929   ISSN 1865-0937 (electronic)
Communications in Computer and Information Science
ISBN 978-3-031-47327-2   ISBN 978-3-031-47328-9 (eBook)
https://doi.org/10.1007/978-3-031-47328-9

This Springer imprint is published by the registered company Springer Nature Switzerland AG
The registered company address is: Gewerbestrasse 11, 6330 Cham, Switzerland

Paper in this product is recyclable.

Preface

2023 marks the 9th edition of the annual International Conference of the Immersive Learning Research Network. iLRN has hosted a hybrid conference in Vienna (2022), two entirely online and in-VR conferences in 2021 and 2020, and in-person editions in London, UK (2019), Missoula, Montana, USA (2018), Coimbra, Portugal (2017), Santa Barbara, California, USA (2016), and Prague, Czech Republic (2015). The iLRN conference has become the premier scholarly event focusing on advances in immersive learning to support learners across the entire span of learning—from K-12 through higher education to work-based, informal, and lifelong learning contexts.

The 9th annual International Conference of the Immersive Learning Research Network (iLRN 2023) continued to push the boundaries of immersive learning, offering a hybrid experience that combined a virtual campus experience on the iLRN Virtual Campus (powered by ©Virbela) and Zoom meetings in May, followed by on-location events in June at the California Polytechnic State University (CalPoly) campus, in San Luis Obispo (SLO), California. This year's conference brought together an international community of scholars, practitioners, and innovators to explore the theme of *"Learning Across the Metaverse: Building an Evidence-based Framework through Science, Community, Vision, & Adventure!"*

Building on the success of our past conferences, iLRN 2023 showcased cutting-edge research that explored the transformative potential of immersive learning to create more inclusive, engaging, and effective learning experiences for diverse populations. The conference also provided a platform for attendees to network, connect, and contribute to the growing area of immersive learning. In addition, the iLRN 2023 keynote and featured speakers represented diverse backgrounds and perspectives, including experts worldwide, contributing to the discussion of applications of Immersive Learning in different domains.

In keeping with our commitment to innovation and inclusion, iLRN 2023 featured a range of exciting events, including the Metaverse Adventures series, which brought together experts and thought leaders worldwide to explore the latest developments in the metaverse. We hosted eleven academic tracks, including the special track *"Immersive Learning across Latin America"*, which explored state-of-the-art research, use cases, and projects specifically for the Latin America region. In collaboration with Hitcher Encounters, we organized our first alternate reality game (ARG) for all registered attendees, highlighting the potential of collaborative social learning.

Three hundred thirty authors from 169 different academic institutions, research centers and companies in thirty-one countries submitted publications to the Academic and Practitioner tracks. Countries included Australia, Austria, Belgium, Brazil, Canada, China, Colombia, Cyprus, Denmark, Finland, France, Germany, Greece, Ireland, Italy, Japan, Latvia, Malawi, Mexico, The Netherlands, Portugal, Puerto Rico, Russia, Singapore, South Korea, Turkey, UK, and USA.

One hundred and ten submissions were received for the Academic track. Every submission underwent a rigorous review by at least three members of the Program Committee to maintain high scientific and quality standards. All contributions were evaluated in a double-blind review process and checked for plagiarism to ensure authors submitted original work. After the peer-review process, all authors were given meaningful feedback on their submissions.

After a rigorous review process and based on the peer-review results, the editorial board decided to accept thirty-nine papers for the Springer proceedings (44.32% acceptance rate). The papers are arranged into ten main Immersive Learning areas of application (iLRN Branch Houses) and an additional one for our special track. iLRN Branch Houses work as umbrellas for each application area towards the systematization of research, design, and practice of immersive learning experiences. These are part of the Immersive Learning Knowledge Tree initiative, aiming to bridge their different epistemological landscapes to combine their efforts and develop the field of immersive learning research.

We are pleased to partner with Springer's Communications in Computer and Information Science (CCIS) series to publish all accepted and registered full and short papers in the Academic Stream presented at iLRN 2023. All work-in-progress poster papers, doctoral colloquium papers, and practitioner papers were published with an individual DOI in the iLRN online proceedings.

This was only possible due to authors submitting their novel research, peer-reviewers providing expertise to suggest improvements and recommendations, and volunteers donating their time to our conference. We sincerely thank those involved who volunteered their time to make this an unforgettable event and attendees for joining us and sharing their excellent work with the iLRN community.

We hope this publication will be a valuable resource for scholars, practitioners, and researchers in immersive learning and inspire future discoveries and innovations in our exciting and rapidly evolving field.

If you are not already involved, we invite you to read these proceedings and join us in our subsequent events and ongoing initiatives.

July 2023

Anasol Peña-Rios
Andreas Dengel
Daniela Pedrosa
Marie-Luce Bourguet
Jule M. Krüger
Jonathon Richter

Organization

Steering Committee

Leonel Morgado — iLRN Vice President for Scientific Quality, Universidade Aberta & INESC TEC, Portugal

Daphne Economou — iLRN Director of Conferences, University of Westminster, UK

Christian Gütl — iLRN Scientific Advisory Board Chair, Graz University of Technology, Austria

Dennis Beck — iLRN Knowledge Tree Director, University of Arkansas, USA

Anasol Peña-Rios — iLRN Director of Publications, BT Research Labs, UK

Andreas Dengel — IEEE Technical Committee on Immersive Learning Environments, Goethe Universität Frankfurt am Main, Germany

Jonathon Richter — iLRN President and Chief Executive Officer, University of Montana, USA

General Chairs

Anasol Peña-Rios — BT Research Labs, UK

Andreas Dengel — Goethe Universität Frankfurt am Main, Germany

Academic Program Committee Chairs

Marie-Luce Bourguet — Queen Mary University of London, UK

Jule M. Krüger — University of Duisburg-Essen, Germany

Practitioner Stream Chairs

Paula MacDowell — University of Saskatchewan, Canada

Jewoong Moon — University of Alabama, USA

Douglas Wilson — George Mason University, USA

Publication Chair

Daniela Pedrosa   University of Aveiro, Portugal

Publication Co-editor Assistants

Maria Castelhano   University of Porto, Portugal
Carolin Zierer   Goethe Universität Frankfurt am Main, Germany
Diana Almeida   University of Aveiro, Portugal

Doctoral Colloquium Chair

Noah Glaser   University of Missouri, USA

Local Chairs

Christian Eckhardt   California Polytechnic State University, USA
April Grow   California Polytechnic State University, USA
Rodrigo Canaan   California Polytechnic State University, USA

Administration and Operations Chair

Jonathon Richter   University of Montana, USA

Virtual Campus and Technical Chairs

Michael Hamaoka   OMAX Corporation, USA
Genevieve Smith-Nunes   University of Cambridge, UK

Videos, Posters, and Exhibitions Chairs

Aliane Krassmann   Instituto Federal Farroupilha, Brazil
Pamela Rabin   San Diego State University, USA

Registration Chairs

Alec Bodzin   Lehigh University, USA
Muhammad Zahid Iqbal   Teesside University, UK

Finance Chair

Patrick O'Shea   Appalachian State University, USA

Session Chair Director

Laurissa Tokarchuk   Queen Mary University of London, UK

Awards Chairs

Daphne Economou   University of Westminster, UK
Filippo Gabriele Prattico   Politecnico di Torino, Italy

Evaluation Chair

Sarah Ramaiah   University of Alabama, USA

iLRNFuser Game Jam Series Chair

Markos Mentzelopoulos   University of Westminster, UK

Opportunity and Inclusion Chair

Sarune Savickaite   University of Glasgow, UK

Special Track LATAM Chairs

Jorge Bacca-Acosta   Fundación Universitaria Konrad Lorenz,
                                   Colombia

Cecilia Avila-Garzon	Fundación Universitaria Konrad Lorenz, Colombia
Jennifer Samaniego	Universidad Técnica Particular de Loja, Ecuador

Volunteer Coordinators

Charlene Hardin	Embry-Riddle Aeronautical University, USA
Chioma Udeozor	Newcastle University, UK

Volunteers (Online Conference Information Desk)

Anisa Bora	Barnard College, USA
Farah Akbar	Columbia University, USA

International and Publicity Chairs Coordinators

Stylianos Mystakidis	Hellenic Open University, Greece
Mengjie Huang	Xi'an Jiaotong-Liverpool University, China
Jorge Bacca-Acosta	Fundación Universitaria Konrad Lorenz, Colombia

International Co-chairs (The Americas)

USA

Minjuan Wang	San Diego State University, IEEE-TLT Journal Editor-in-Chief, USA

Latin America and the Caribbean

Romero Tori	University of São Paulo, Brazil
Eliane Schlemmer	Universidade do Vale do Rio dos Sinos, Brazil
Jorge Bacca-Acosta	Fundación Universitaria Konrad Lorenz, Colombia

International Co-chairs (Europe)

UK and Ireland

Eleni Mangina   University College Dublin, Ireland
Fridolin Wild   Oxford Brookes University, UK
Daniel Livingstone   Glasgow School of Art, Scotland

Northern Europe

Mikhail Fominykh   Norwegian University of Science and Technology,
                               Norway
Ekaterina Prasolova-Førland   Norwegian University of Science and Technology,
                               Norway

Western Europe and Italy

Sébastien George   Le Mans Université, France

Central Europe

Michael Kickmeier-Rust   St.Gallen University of Teacher Education,
                               Switzerland
Fabrizio Lamberti   Politecnico di Torino, Italy
Krzysztof Walczak   Poznań University of Economics and Business,
                               Poland
Mohamed Yassine Zarouk   University of Potsdam, Germany

Southeastern Europe

Andri Ioannou   Cyprus University of Technology and CYENS
                               Centre of Excellence, Cyprus
Ioannis Kazanidis   International Hellenic University, Kavala, Greece
Fotis Liarokapis   Cyprus University of Technology and CYENS
                               Centre of Excellence, Cyprus
Tassos Mikropoulos   University of Ioannina, Greece
Ioana-Andreea Stefan   Advanced Technology Systems, Romania

International Co-chairs (Middle East)

Malek Alrashidi	University of Tabuk, Saudi Arabia
Mohammad Al-Smadi	Qatar University, Qatar
Elhanan Gazit	Ono Academic College & Tel-Aviv University, Israel

International Co-chair (Africa)

Koos de Beer	University of Pretoria, South Africa

International Co-chairs (Asia Pacific)

Greater China

Su Cai	Beijing Normal University, China
Morris S. Y. Jong	Chinese University of Hong Kong, China
Fengfeng Ke	Florida State University, USA

South Asia (incl. Indian subcontinent)

Ramesh C. Sharma	Dr. B. R. Ambedkar University Delhi, India

Japan and Korea

Jeeheon Ryu	Chonnam National University, South Korea

Southeast Asia

Yiyu Cai	Nanyang Technological University, Singapore
Jolanda G. Tromp	Duy Tân University, Vietnam
Kenneth Y. T. Lim	National Institute of Education, Singapore
Noor Dayana Abd Halim	Universiti Teknologi Malaysia, Malaysia

International Co-chair (Oceania)

Erica Southgate   University of Newcastle, Australia

Program Committee

Samuel Acosta Ortiz	Universidad EAFIT, Colombia
Salah Ahmed	Shaanxi Normal University, China
Panagiotis Antoniou	Aristotle University of Thessaloniki, Greece
Antonio Araujo	Universidade Aberta, Portugal
Jyoti Arora	Independent consultant, India
Cecilia Avila	Fundación Universitaria Konrad Lorenz, Colombia
Jorge Bacca-Acosta	University of Girona, Italy
Alex Barrett	Florida State University, USA
Thayna Bertholini	Independent Consultant, Brazil
Nitesh Bhatia	Imperial College London, UK
Alec Bodzin	Lehigh University, USA
Carl Boel	Thomas More University of Applied Sciences + Ghent University, Belgium
Aymeric Bouchereau	Université Paris-Est Créteil, France
Pamela Buñay Guisñan	Universidad Nacional de Chimborazo, Ecuador
Pedro Cardoso	University of Aveiro / DigiMedia, Portugal
Hubert Cecotti	Fresno State, USA
Huseyin H. Cetinkaya	Başkent University, Turkey
Hua Chai	University of New South Wales, Australia
Yan-Ming Chiou	University of Delaware, USA
Xiaoyan Chu	Zhejiang University, China
Prathamesh Churi	Narsee Monjee Institute of Management Studies, India
Radu Comes	Technical University of Cluj-Napoca, Romania
José Cravino	UTAD, Portugal
Drew Davidson	Carnegie Mellon University, USA
Federico De Lorenzis	Politecnico di Torino, Italy
João Luis de Miranda	ESTG/IPP, CERENA/IST, Portugal
José J. de Moura Ramos	Universidade da Coruña, Spain
Jorge Delgado Altamirano	Universidad Nacional de Chimborazo, Ecuador
Andy Dengel	Goethe University Frankfurt, Germany
Irwin Devries	Thompson Rivers University, Canada
Michele Dickey	Miami University, USA
Fahima Djelil	IMT Atlantique, France

Parisa Meisami	University of Maryland, USA
Alexander Mikroyannidis	Open University, UK
Lee Mitchell	Florida State University, USA
Thomas Moser	St. Pölten University of Applied Sciences, Austria
Stylianos Mystakidis	University of Patras, Greece
Kayoko Nakamura	Keio University, Japan
Leticia Neira	Universidad Autónoma de Nuevo León, Mexico
Anastasija Nikiforova	University of Tartu, Estonia
Mohammad F. Obeid	Shenandoah University, USA
Dorothy Ogdon	University of Alabama at Birmingham, USA
Brent Olson	University of Saskatchewan, Canada
Daniela Pedrosa	University of Aveiro, Portugal
Nikolaos Pellas	University of Western Macedonia, Greece
Lance Peng	University of Cambridge, UK
Lisbeth Pérez Martínez	Universidad Espíritu Santo, Ecuador
Sharon Pisani	University of St Andrews, UK
David Plecher	Technical University of Munich, Germany
Yannick Prie	Nantes University, France
Andres Quevedo	Escuela Politécnica del Litoral, Ecuador
Sarah Ramaiah	University of Alabama, USA
Luis E. Ríos Castillo	Universidad Técnica Particular de Loja, Ecuador
Sandra Roa Martinez	Universidad del Cauca, Colombia
Sonia Sahli	Higher Institute of Technological Studies of Kairouan, Tunisia
Jennifer Samaniego	Universidad Técnica Particular de Loja, Ecuador
Saba Saneinia	University of Science and Technology of China, China
Robin Schramm	Mercedes-Benz Tech Motion GmbH, Germany
Andrés Sebastián Quevedo	Universidad Católica de Cuenca, Ecuador
Jun Shen	University of Wollongong, Australia
Sung Shim	Seton Hall University, USA
Genevieve Smith-Nunes	University of Cambridge, UK
Francesco Strada	Politecnico di Torino, Italy
Sayuri Tanabashi	University of Tokyo, Japan
Rachel Tatro-Duarte	California State University of Bakersfield, USA
Hendrys Tobar-Muñoz	Centro de Desarrollo Tecnológico CreaTIC, Colombia
Yi-Chou Tsai	Cardinal Tien Junior College of Healthcare and Management, Taiwan
Chioma Udeozor	Newcastle University, UK
Alonso E. Veloz Arce	Universidad Católica de Santiago de Guayaquil, Ecuador

Inés C. Villamagua Jiménez   Universidad Técnica Particular de Loja, Ecuador
Alessandro Visconti   Politecnico di Torino, Italy
Quincy Wang   Simon Fraser University, Canada
Wenting Weng   Johns Hopkins University, USA
Junjie Gavin Wu   City University of Hong Kong, China
Lili Yan   Utah State University, USA

Contents

Assessment and Evaluation (A&E)

Galleries, Libraries, Archives and Museums (GLAM)

Inclusion, Diversity, Equity, Access, and Social Justice (IDEAS)

STEM Education (STEM)

Foundations in Immersive Learning Research and Theory

The Role of Context and Interaction When Learning With Augmented 360° Photos

Jule M. Krüger(✉) ⓘ, Mariam Koch, and Daniel Bodemer ⓘ

University of Duisburg-Essen, Duisburg, Germany
`jule.krueger@uni-due.de`

Abstract. 360° photos can be used to place learners into different environments augmented with additional information in the form of virtual overlays. This way, more information can be provided than usually, resembling context-based augmented reality (AR). Both contextuality and interactivity are important aspects when it comes to AR- and 360° photo-based learning environments. To find out more about the specific impact context and interaction with the learning material have in an augmented 360° photo environment, we conducted an experimental 2 × 2 between-subjects design with the factors context (visible vs. non visible) and interaction (learner vs. system control) with N = 138 participants. We examined variables concerning immersion, motivation and learning outcome. Concerning immersion, we found a large positive main effect of learner control. Concerning motivation, we found positive main effects of context visibility and learner control. For a subfactor of motivation, satisfaction, we found an interaction effect showing a disadvantage of non-visible context and system control in comparison to all other conditions. We found no effects on learning outcome. We discuss the limitations and implications of the study considering the theoretical background.

Keywords: Context · Interaction · 360° Photo · Augmented · Immersion · Motivation

1 Introduction

360° media like photos and videos offer a potential way of immersing learners in different environments that are otherwise not easily accessible. They have been applied in many different educational areas like science education, health sciences, environmental education, arts and humanities, or teacher education [1–5]. Variables that are often examined in these settings include engagement, usability, immersion, motivation, attentiveness, knowledge retention and knowledge transfer [1, 5]. Studies have shown mixed results of the effectiveness concerning learning outcomes, including positive effects of learning with a 360° video in comparison to conventional studying [6] and similar learning outcomes with 360° as with normal videos [2]. Results may thus differ with environment design, and to get a more detailed picture of learning with 360° environments, a closer look into the effect of specific design decisions may be necessary.

In comparison to being in the real environment, 360° media offer an easy possibility to enrich them with additional virtual information like annotations or interactive media.

© The Author(s), under exclusive license to Springer Nature Switzerland AG 2024
M.-L. Bourguet et al. (Eds.): iLRN 2023, CCIS 1904, pp. 3–21, 2024.
https://doi.org/10.1007/978-3-031-47328-9_1

This enables a form of freely creatable and manipulatable augmented reality (AR) that is in the physical world only possible with complex technological devices for visual overlay. Eiris and colleagues, for example, annotated 360° panoramas for construction safety training [7], whereas Choi and colleagues developed layered 360° experiences, including a combination of photos, videos and interactive elements [8]. Milgram and colleagues [9] define not only live but also stored video images of the real world that are digitally overlaid with computer generated information as monitor-based AR. In contrast to AR from live images, stored images do not offer the full amount of interactive and spatial potential. Still the three AR-specific characteristics contextuality, interactivity and spatiality as described by Krüger and colleagues [10] can become relevant in the context of augmented 360° media, as will be described in the following sections. For a more systematic examination of the influence of specific characteristics of those environments, in the current study we focus on the characteristics contextuality and interactivity in the environment design instead of comparing them to more traditional settings. Here, we decided to focus on 360° photos, as the addition of interactive elements in 360° video increased negative affect, decreased positive affect, and added tension in one study, potentially evoked by the combination of dynamic video material and many interactive possibilities [11]. The goal of the current study is to gain insights into the influence that design decisions concerning contextuality and interactivity in augmented 360° photos has on learning processes and outcomes.

2   Theoretical Background

2.1   Contextuality in Augmented 360° Photos

Contextuality describes the parallel and integrated perception of virtual and real elements in AR environments [10]. In augmented 360° photos, the real elements are presented by the photo, which displays a panorama view of a real-world location including the general environment and potentially physical objects that are part of the learning material. The virtual elements can be different enriching media, for example text, pictures, or videos that are overlayed onto the real-world recording. Those virtual elements are thus contextualized within the (image of the) real world, which is an integral part of this medium. Examples for contexts which have been displayed in 360° media are settings in nature like marine environments [4], cultural settings like cultural heritage sites [12], and settings for specific training, like an operation area during a surgery [6]. In the study by Arvaniti and Fokides [4] including a marine environment, children had better learning outcomes and felt higher immersion in a 360° video than with printed material or webpages. They also had more fun and enjoyed the 360° video more than printed material but not more than information on web pages. However, it is not clear which role the displayed environment had on these outcomes. In the current study, the role of the context for learning outcomes, immersion, and motivation in augmented 360° photos will be examined systematically.

As stated above, the real-world elements in a learning environment can include both objects that are part of the learning material and a surrounding environment for relevant contextualization. For example, an augmented 360° photo that is used for instruction about trees can include both the trees that are part of the learning material and the surrounding forest in the image. While the trees have an obvious direct influence on learning, the forest environment may only contextualize without providing additional information. In the current study, we want to examine which role the visibility of the contextualizing environment plays for learning processes and outcomes in an educational augmented 360° environment.

2.2 Interactivity in Augmented 360° Photos

Interactivity describes the combined and integrated interaction with physical and virtual elements in AR-based environments [10]. In augmented 360° photos, the interaction with the physical environment is limited to the possibility to move and turn around so that the perspective on the surroundings can be changed. On the virtual level, different forms of interaction with the augmenting virtual elements are possible, depending on the kind of elements that are added. Examples for forms of interaction are a free navigation through a bigger 360° environment including the option to walk around [12] or the possibility to turn around in the environment [7]. Also, virtual elements can be actively retrieved and more complex media like videos or quizzes can be embedded and interacted with [4, 11]. In their study, Torres and colleagues [11] found higher usability scores for the non-interactive video and higher negative affect and tension for the interactive video. However, this design included a dynamic video, which may have interacted negatively with the possibilities of interaction, and no learning outcomes or other variables related to learning were assessed. In the current study, the role of interactivity for learning outcomes, immersion, and motivation in augmented 360° photos will be examined systematically.

One form of interaction with the real-world environment is the learner-controlled navigation including turning around in the environment. The learner control principle in multimedia learning states that learner control supports learning by enabling active and constructive information processing [13]. Learner control can include control of content selection and progress pacing and is differentiated from system control. In the current study, we want to examine which role learner control in comparison to system control plays for learning processes and outcomes in an educational augmented 360° environment.

While there are many constructs that play a role in immersive learning environments, the feelings of immersion (sometimes described as presence, which is for the current study defined as only a part of immersion, see Sect. 2.3) and motivation have been identified as two central variables for learning with immersive media (see, for example, models in [14, 15]). Both immersion, or sense of presence, and motivation have been found to be positively influenced by 360° environments in multiple studies [5]. In the current study, we focus on these two variables, examining how they are influenced by context visibility and interaction control in a 360° environment, and how they in turn influence learning outcomes.

2.3 Immersion

Immersion can be defined from a psychological [16] or a technological [17] perspective. Psychological immersion is the subjective sense of actually being inside an environment sometimes referred to as sense of presence [18]. In the augmented reality immersion (ARI) framework, Georgiou and Kyza (2017) describe three levels of immersion: 1) engagement, including *interest* for the activity and *usability* of the application; 2) engrossment, including *emotional attachment* to and *focus of attention* during the activity; 3) total immersion, including *presence*, the feeling of being surrounded by the environment, and *flow*, the full absorption into the activity [18].

Immersive learning has been "defined as learning with artificial experiences that are perceived as non-mediated" (p.1) [19]. While research on immersive multimedia learning environments often shows positive effects on enjoyment and motivation in more immersive environments, results on learning outcomes are mixed showing both positive and negative relations [20]. In game-based learning, for example, game immersion experience has been identified as being related to in-game performance, with the sub-factor of engagement having a positive effect on science learning outcomes [21]. In location-based AR environments, learners with high levels of immersion were also found to display different learning behaviors [22] and have higher learning outcomes [23, 24]. On the other hand, the immersion principle from the Cognitive Theory of Multimedia Learning describes that immersive environments do not necessarily promote learning but can lead to distractions and cognitive overload due to the many displayed elements that are not directly related to the content of the learning material [25]. Based on the theoretical and empirical connection of immersion and motivation, we still expect immersion to have a positive influence on motivation, which in turn should have a positive influence on learning.

In augmented 360° environments, immersion in the displayed real-world location is possible. Three dimensions of immersion are defined as system immersion, narrative immersion and challenge immersion [26]. In the current study, the visibility of context is expected to lead to increased technological immersion, because more visual cues are available to place oneself into the environment and simulating the physical world was classified as a system immersion theme [26]. We thus propose that the visibility of the environment is important for the feeling of immersion – if the environment of the location-based learning material is not visible, immersion within the location is hindered. The possibilities of learner- instead of system-controlled perspective changing including spatial orientation and interactive exploration, which have also been classified as important for system immersion [26], are also expected to increase immersion. These forms of learner control including interactive manipulation/exploration and engagement with higher attention focus through content selection [26] (also a factor in the ARI framework [18]) have furthermore also been classified as factors of challenge immersion, so that learner control should have an even increased influence on immersion.

2.4 Motivation

Motivation generally describes the reasons behind people's actions, with research on motivation often looking at beliefs, values and goals that drive action [27]. Motivation is still not very often examined in the context of multimedia learning [28]. From a design-based perspective, the ARCS (attention – relevance – confidence – satisfaction) model by Keller describes how learning material design can increase learners' motivation to learn [29]. It defines four major dimensions of learning motivation that are proposed to build upon each other. *Attention* is described as the interest capturing and curiosity stimulation of learners. *Relevance* involves the fit for personal goals and value for positive attitude evolvement. *Confidence* includes learners' belief that they succeed and are in control, and *satisfaction* describes the general positive attitude towards the learning material, which can be reinforced.

Increased motivation is often mentioned to be an advantage of learning with AR (see [30, 31]). Concerning the visibility of the context, it is expected that especially learners' perceived relevance, which is one of the ARCS-variables [29], can be increased by embedding information into their real-world context and thus showing their real-world application. Concerning learner or system control of interaction with a 360° environment, the INTERACT model suggests an influence of learner interaction on cognitive and motivational variables [32]. Furthermore, personal control is one of the factors that is proposed to influence the ARCS-variable confidence [29] and so in general should have an influence on motivation.

In addition to the proposed direct influence of context visibility and learner control on motivation, this effect is expected to be even increased by an indirect effect through immersion. The Cognitive Affective Model of Immersive Learning (CAMIL), for example, predicts an influence of the feeling of immersion (here called presence) on motivational factors, and in turn an influence on learning outcomes [15]. Concerning learning outcomes, motivation is expected to increase learners' engagement with the learning material and the effort that they put into learning with the material, as has been proposed by Mayer [33] and Paas and colleagues [34]. In the current study, we thus also assume that the increase in motivation proposed for visible context and learner control lead to a higher learner effort, which in turn leads to improved learning outcomes.

3 Research Questions and Hypotheses

Based on the literature showing a more general and less specific research on 360° media, the goal of the current study is to draw a more detailed picture concerning the specific influence of different characteristics of the environment. Here, the focus on the two characteristics contextuality and interactivity that define the research question: "Which role do the visibility of context and learner-controlled interaction with an educational augmented 360° photo play for immersion, motivation and learning outcomes?".

In the first set of hypotheses (H1), positive effects of visible context and learner control on *immersion* are hypothesized based on their potential influence on system and challenge immersion described in Sect. 2.3. The hypotheses are:

H1a: Learning with a visible context in an augmented 360° photo environment leads to higher immersion than learning with a non-visible context.

H1b: Learning with learner control in an augmented 360° photo environment leads to higher immersion than learning with system control.

H1c: Learning with a combined visible context and learner control in an augmented 360° photo environment leads to higher immersion than only one or none of those features.

In addition to the hypotheses concerning immersion in general, the nuances of group differences concerning the six subconstructs (1) interest, (2) usability, (3) emotional attachment, (4) focus of attention, (5) flow and (6) presence will be explored, expecting the same pattern as the one hypothesized for general immersion in H1a – H1c.

In the second set of hypotheses (H2), positive effects of perceivable context and learner control on *motivation* are hypothesized, based on their potential influence especially on relevance and confidence described in Sect. 2.4. The hypotheses are:

H2a: Learning with a visible context in an augmented 360° photo environment leads to higher motivation than learning with a non-visible context.

H2b: Learning with learner control in an augmented 360° photo environment leads to higher motivation than learning with system control.

H2c: Learning with a combined visible context and learner control in an augmented 360° photo environment leads to higher motivation than only or none of those features.

In addition to the hypotheses concerning motivation in general, the nuances of group differences concerning the four subconstructs (1) attention, (2) relevance, (3) confidence, (4) satisfaction will be explored, expecting the same pattern as the one hypothesized for general motivation in H2a – H2c.

In the third set of hypotheses (H3), positive effects of visible context and learner control on *knowledge* are hypothesized. This is based on the assumption that motivation, which is expected to be influenced positively by the two factors (see H2), influences the effort learners apply to the learning task, which in turn improves learning outcomes, as described in Sect. 2.4. The hypotheses are:

H3a: Learning with a visible context in an augmented 360° photo environment leads to a better learning outcome than learning with a non-visible context.

H3b: Learning with learner control in an augmented 360° photo environment leads to a better learning outcome than learning with system control.

H3c: Learning with a combined visible context and learner control in an augmented 360° photo environment leads to a better learning outcome than only or none of those features.

4 Method

4.1 Design

The following study was executed in summer 2020 as an online study due to the globally prevalent COVID-19 pandemic. A 2 × 2 between-subjects design with the factors *context visibility* (visible c+ vs. non-visible c−) and *interaction control* (learner control i+ vs. system control i−) was applied. For visible context (c+) the full 360° photo was shown, including the background of the relevant objects, while for non-visible context (c−) the background was removed. Learner control (i+) included navigation of an augmented 360° photo with freely retrievable additional virtual information, while for system control (i−) a video recording of the environment was shown. The dependent variables were immersion (H1a − H1c), motivation (H2a − H2c), and learning outcome (H3a − H3c).

4.2 Participants

$N = 138$ participants remained in the data set after five participants who indicated that they had problems with the application and one participant who gave the same answer for every item were filtered out. The participants were aged 18 to 58, with a mean of $M = 26.36$ ($SD = 9.61$). In total, 42 indicated to be male, 93 to be female, 2 to be diverse and 1 did not indicate. 101 of the participants (73%) were students, 21 where employed (15%) and the rest (12%) were a mix of pupils, trainees, civil servants, self-employed or had no job. In Table 1, the characteristics of the sample are shown split by condition. Due to the random assignment, the size of the groups and characteristics are not evenly distributed. To participate in the study, participants were required to be at least 18 years of age and to conduct the study on a laptop computer of at least 13 inches screen diagonal. The study with ID psychmeth_2021_AR15_18 was approved by the departments' ethics committee.

Table 1. Participant characteristics per condition.

Group	N	Age	Gender				Students
		M (SD)	m	f	d	n	%
c+/i+	39	23.90 (6.85)	5	33	1	0	80
c+/i−	38	26.92 (9.94)	15	22	1	0	68
c−/i+	27	27.74 (12.25)	10	16	0	1	67
c−/i−	34	27.47 (9.48)	12	22	0	0	65

4.3 360° Learning Environment

The augmented 360° environment was based on a 360° photo of a spot in a local botanical garden. It was taken and automatically processed with the Google Street View application (https://streetviewstudio.maps.google.com/) and imported as a 360° virtual tour into the program Klapty (https://www.klapty.com/). Here, buttons to retrieve additional information were added to augment the photo with virtual elements. Specifically, textual and pictorial information about the different plants that were visible around the learner were added.

Concerning context visibility, the 360° photo was left as it was, including the surrounding background of the plants for the visible context conditions (s. Fig. 1). For the non-visible context conditions the background was removed and replaced with a gray area including a drawn-on horizon for better orientation, so that only the plants to be learned were visible (s. Fig. 2). Concerning interaction control, for learner control navigation in the form of looking around the panorama view was enabled. Furthermore, the information buttons could be hovered over for the plant name and clicked on for additional information retrieval (s. Fig. 3). For system control, the usage of the 360° environment was filmed through a screen-recording. A pre-test with four students was executed to make sure that all information was shown long enough for learners to view the images and read the textual information. In the end, it was decided to show the additional information about the plants twice, once for 50 s (textual) plus 10 s (close-up picture) and in a second round for 25 plus 5 s. The 360° web applications are available from Klapty (links in figure captions).

Fig. 1. 360°-application with visible context: https://www.klapty.com/tour/G3F05v7VZn

Fig. 2. 360°-application with non-visible context: https://www.klapty.com/tour/GhF05v7VZn

Fig. 3. Interactive features: (1) hovering over i-button shows plant name and (2) clicking on i-button opens pop-up window with information about the plant.

4.4 Instruments

Immersion. Immersion was measured with a translated version of the Augmented Reality Immersion (ARI) questionnaire by Georgiou & Kyza [18]. This questionnaire is divided into engagement, engrossment, and total immersion. Engagement is further divided into the *interest* and *usability* subscales, each containing four items. Engrossment is divided into the subscales *emotional attachment* and *focus of attention*, each with three items. Total immersion is again divided into the two subscales *presence*, with four items, and *flow*, with three items. The individual items were rated in a seven-point format from "totally disagree" (1) to "totally agree" (7). Means were calculated for each individual subscale, which were then averaged for the immersion score. To answer the hypotheses, the averaged immersion score was used, and the subscales were used for exploring the subconstruct patterns. McDonald's omega, measuring internal consistency of the scale was excellent for the complete scale ($\omega = 0.90$), and high for interest ($\omega = 0.84$), focus of attention ($\omega = 0.81$), presence ($\omega = 0.89$) and flow ($\omega = 0.86$). It was acceptable for usability ($\omega = 0.72$), but questionable for emotional attachment ($\omega = 0.62$). Results concerning emotional attachment should thus be interpreted with care.

Motivation. Motivation was measured with a translated version of the Instructional Materials Motivation Survey (IMMS) [35], which measures the four subconstructs of the ARCS model [29]. Attention (12 items), relevance (9 items), confidence (9 items) and satisfaction (6 items) were rated in a five-point format from "not true" (1) to "very true" (5). Means were calculated for each individual subscale, which were then averaged for the motivation score. To answer the hypotheses, the averaged motivation score was used, and the subscales were used for exploring the subconstruct patterns. McDonald's omega, measuring internal consistency of the scale was excellent for the complete scale ($\omega = 0.93$). It was high for attention ($\omega = 0.88$) and satisfaction ($\omega = 0.85$), and acceptable for relevance ($\omega = 0.71$) and confidence ($\omega = 0.76$).

Knowledge. Learning outcome was measured through a knowledge test with 15 multiple choice questions, which was developed based on the learning material. 12 items included a fully textual question, while three items also including a picture of a plant in the question. All items had only one correct answer, with four choices available for 13, and three choices for the other 2 items. The difficulty of the items varied from a 99% answer correctness to a 7% answer correctness ($M = 0.55$, $SD = 0.27$).

4.5 Procedure

During the study, participants were randomly assigned to one of the four conditions. The investigator was available to the participants via video and voice chat for the duration of the study, so that questions could be asked at any time. In this way, the situation resembled a remote laboratory study rather than a standard online survey. After the participants were welcomed and informed about the study by an investigator, they gave their consent for data collection. Subsequently, the participants received links to the 360° application or video, depending on their condition, which they were instructed to learn with for 15 min. After that, the questionnaires about immersion and motivation were answered, followed by the knowledge test. Finally, the demographical data were collected, and the participants were debriefed by the investigator.

5 Results

In the following sections, the results concerning the hypotheses on immersion (H1a, H1b, H1c), motivation (H2a, H2b, H2c) and knowledge (H3a, H3b, H3c) will be tested through 2 × 2 ANOVAs with context visibility and interaction control as factors and the respectively relevant variable as outcome variable.

5.1 Immersion

In H1a, immersion was hypothesized to be increased for the visible in comparison to the non-visible context, and in H1b, it was hypothesized to be increased for learners in comparison to system control. Furthermore, H1c predicts an interaction effect showing that especially the combination of visible context and learner control would lead to increased immersion. For immersion averaged from all subscales, the c−/i+ and c+/i+ conditions had the two very similar highest scores and c−/i− had the lowest score, while c+/i− had a score in between (s. Table 2 and Fig. 4). A 2 × 2 ANOVA was executed with the averaged immersion score as outcome variable. No main effect was found for context visibility, $F(1) = 0.87$, $p = 0.352$, $\omega2 < 0.00$, thus not supporting H1a with descriptively very similar immersion scores for visible ($M_{c+} = 4.09$, $SE_{c+} = 0.09$) and non-visible context ($M_{c-} = 3.96$, $SE_{c-} = 0.10$). Concerning H1b, higher immersion for learner control ($M_{i+} = 4.37$, $SE_{i+} = 0.10$) than system control ($M_{i-} = 3.68$, $SE_{i-} = 0.10$) was found, showing a large main effect for interaction control, $F(1) = 16.16$, $p < 0.001$, $\omega2 = 0.15$. The interaction effect was also not significant, $F(1) = 1.21$, $p = 0.273$, $\omega2 < 0.01$, so that H1c was rejected.

Exploring the effect of the two factors and their interaction on the six immersion subconstructs, the means per subscale can also be found in Table 2, generally showing the lowest score in the c−/i− condition, and the highest score in the c+ /i+ condition (interest, usability, and presence) or the c−/i+ condition (emotional attachment, focus of attention, and flow). The main effect for interaction control was also found for all subscales: *interest*, $[F(1) = 5.58, p = 0.020, \omega2 = 0.03]$, *usability*, $[F(1) = 4.90, p = 0.029, \omega2 = 0.03]$, *emotional attachment*, $[F(1) = 14.94, p < 0.001, \omega2 = 0.09]$, *focus of attention* $[F(1) = 19.42, p < 0.001, \omega2 = 0.12]$, *presence* $[F(1) = 9.57, p = 0.002, \omega2 = 0.06]$, and *flow* $[F(1) = 11.43, p < 0.001, \omega2 = 0.07]$. Furthermore, main effects for context visibility were found for *interest* $[F(1) = 19.49, p < 0.001, \omega2 = 0.11]$ and *presence* $[F(1) = 5.18, p = 0.024, \omega2 = 0.03]$. No interaction effects were found for the subconstructs of immersion either. An overview of all effects can be found in Table 4.

Table 2. Descriptives of immersion variables.

M and *SD* per variable[a]	Conditions			
	c+/i+	c+/i−	c−/i+	c−/i−
	M (SD)	M (SD)	M (SD)	M (SD)
Immersion	4.36 (0.79)	3.82 (0.83)	**4.38 (0.76)**	*3.53 (0.84)*
· Interest	**5.72 (0.90)**	5.04 (1.13)	5.44 (1.14)	*4.41 (1.30)*
· Usability	**5.84 (0.78)**	5.37 (1.16)	5.56 (1.09)	*5.26 (1.01)*
· Emo. Atta	3.74 (1.05)	3.27 (0.84)	**4.04 (0.89)**	*3.22 (1.05)*
· Focus of at	4.11 (1.18)	3.49 (1.31)	**4.65 (0.98)**	*3.39 (1.41)*
· Presence	**3.37 (1.42)**	2.86 (1.48)	2.67 (1.61)	*2.09 (1.02)*
· Flow	3.36 (1.33)	2.87 (1.36)	**3.93 (1.35)**	*2.84 (1.38)*

a. Note: Highest mean per subscale in **bold**, lowest mean per subscale in *italic*

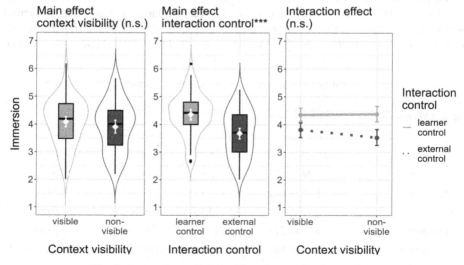

Fig. 4. Interaction and main effects concerning immersion.

5.2 Motivation

In H2a, motivation was hypothesized to be increased for the visible in comparison to the non-visible context, and in H2b, it was hypothesized to be increased for learners in comparison to system control. Furthermore, H2c predicts an interaction effect showing that especially the combination of visible context and learner control would lead to increased motivation. For motivation averaged from all subscales, the c+ /i+ condition had the highest score and c−/i− had the lowest score, while c−/i+ and c+ /i− had very similar scores in between, (s. Table 3 and Fig. 5). A 2 × 2 ANOVA was executed with the averaged motivation score as outcome variable. A small to medium main effect was found for context visibility, $F(1) = 7.36$, $p = 0.008$, $\omega 2 = 0.04$, supporting H1a with higher motivation for visible context ($M_c = 3.28$, $SE_{c+} = 0.07$) than non-visible context ($M_{c-} = 3.00$, $SE_{c-} = 0.08$). Concerning H1b, higher motivation for learner control ($M_{i+} = 3.29$, $SE_{i+} = 0.07$) than system control ($M_{i-} = 3.00$, $SE_{i-} = 0.07$) was found, showing a small to medium main effect for interaction control, $F(1) = 8.12$, $p = 0.005$, $\omega 2 = 0.05$. The interaction effect was not significant, $F(1) = 2.85$, $p = 0.094$, $\omega 2 = 0.01$, so that H2c was rejected.

Exploring the effect of the two factors and their interaction on the four motivation subconstructs, the means per subscale can also be found in Table 3, generally showing the lowest score in the c−/i− condition, and the highest score in the c+ /i+ condition except for relevance, where c+ /i− has the highest score. The main effect for interaction control was found for *attention* [$F(1) = 13.29$, $p = < .001$, $\omega 2 = 0.07$], *relevance* [$F(1) = 5.21$, $p = 0.024$, $\omega 2 = 0.03$], and *satisfaction* [$F(1) = 4.93$, $p = 0.028$, $\omega 2 = 0.03$]. Furthermore, main effects for context visibility were found for *attention* [$F(1) = 15.10$, $p = < .001$, $\omega 2 = 0.09$], *confidence* [$F(1) = 7.39$, $p = 0.007$, $\omega 2 = 0.04$], and *satisfaction* [$F(1) = 7.46$, $p = 0.007$, $\omega 2 = 0.04$]. Furthermore, main effects for context visibility were found for. Also, an interaction effect was found for *satisfaction* [$F(1) = 4.19$, $p = 0.043$, $\omega 2 = 0.02$]. In post hoc paired comparisons with holm corrected p-values, *satisfaction* in the c−/i− group was significantly lower than c+/i+ [$t(134) = 4.08$, $p < 0.001$, $d = 0.96$], c+/i− [$t(134) = 3.21$, $p = 0.008$, $d = 0.76$] and c−/i+ [$t(134)$

Table 3. Descriptives of motivation variables.

M and SD per variable[a]	Conditions			
	c + /i +	c + /i−	c−/i +	c−/i−
	M (SD)	M (SD)	M (SD)	M (SD)
Motivation	**3.34 (0.55)**	3.22 (0.68)	3.23 (0.60)	*2.77 (0.55)*
· Attention	**3.69 (0.64)**	3.38 (0.83)	3.41 (0.75)	*2.75 (0.65)*
· Relevance	3.01 (0.57)	**3.13 (0.75)**	2.90 (0.63)	*2.75 (0.53)*
· Confidence	**3.71 (0.53)**	3.52 (0.65)	3.70 (0.53)	*3.33 (0.68)*
· Satisfaction	**2.94 (0.85)**	2.85 (0.89)	2.92 (0.87)	*2.24 (0.71)*

[a.] Note: Highest mean per subscale in **bold**, lowest mean per subscale in *italic*

$= 3.03$, $p = 0.012$, $d = 0.78$], while there were no significant differences between the other groups (s. Figure 6). An overview of all effects can be found in Table 4.

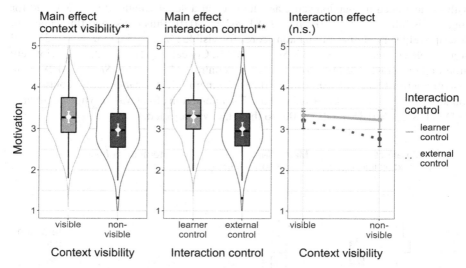

Fig. 5. Interaction and main effects concerning motivation.

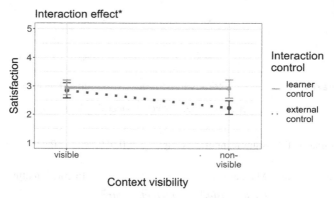

Fig. 6. Interaction effect concerning satisfaction.

5.3 Knowledge

In H3a, knowledge was hypothesized to be increased for the visible in comparison to the non-visible context, and in H3b, it was hypothesized to be increased for learners in comparison to system control. Furthermore, H3c predicts an interaction effect showing that especially the combination of visible context and learner control would lead to increased knowledge. Descriptively, the c−/i + condition had the highest knowledge test score ($M_{c-/i+} = 8.78$, $SD_{c-/i+} = 2.64$), c+/i+ the second ($M_{c+/i+} = 8.44$, $SD_{c+/i+} = 2.12$) and c + /i− the third highest ($M_{c+/i-} = 8.18$, $SD_{c+/i-} = 1.97$), while c−/i− ($M_{c-/i-} = 7.82$, $SD_{c-/i-} = 2.29$) had the lowest score (s. Figure 7). A 2x2 ANOVA was executed with the averaged immersion score as outcome variable. No main effect was found for context visibility, $F(1) < 0.01$, $p = 0.981$, $\omega2 = -0.01$, thus not supporting H3a with descriptively very similar immersion scores for visible ($M_{c+} = 8.31$, $SE_{c+} = 0.25$) and non-visible context ($M_{c-} = 8.30$, $SE_{c-} = 0.29$). Concerning H3b, with a descriptively little higher knowledge test score for learner control ($M_{i+} = 8.61$, $SE_{i+} = 0.28$) than system control ($M_{i-} = 8.00$, $SE_{i-} = 0.26$), no main effect for interaction control was found, $F(1) = 2.46$, $p = 0.119$, $\omega2 = 0.01$. The interaction effect was also not significant, $F(1) = 0.84$, $p = 0.362$, $\omega2 < 0.00$, so that H3c was rejected.

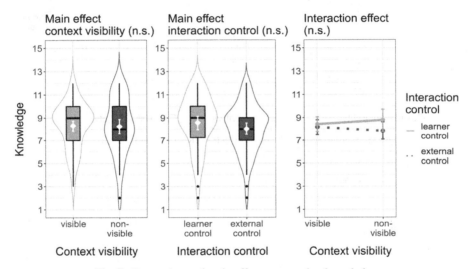

Fig. 7. Interaction and main effects concerning knowledge.

Table 4. Summary of the significant effects (sig: * $p < 0.050$, ** $p < 0.010$, *** $p < 0.001$).

Sig. Effects per variable	Main effects		Interaction effect
	context visib.[a]	*interact. Contr.*[b]	
Immersion	n.s	learn > ext ***	n.s
· Interest	vis > n-vis *	learn > ext ***	n.s
· Usability	n.s	learn > ext *	n.s
· Emo. Atta	n.s	learn > ext ***	n.s

(*continued*)

Table 4. (*continued*)

Sig. Effects per variable	Main effects		Interaction effect
	context visib.[a]	*interact. Contr.*[b]	
• Focus of at	n.s	learn > ext ***	n.s
• Presence	vis > n-vis **	learn > ext *	n.s
• Flow	n.s	learn > ext ***	n.s
Motivation	vis > n-vis **	learn > ext **	n.s
• Attention	vis > n-vis ***	learn > ext ***	n.s
• Relevance	vis > n-vis *	n.s	n.s
• Confidence	n.s	learn > ext **	n.s
• Satisfaction	vis > n-vis *	learn > ext **	c−/i− sig. Lower than other groups *
Knowledge	n.s	n.s	n.s

[a] factor context visibility, two levels: visible ("vis") and non-visible ("n-vis")
[b] factor interaction control, two levels: learner control ("learn") and system control ("ext")

6 Discussion

The goal of the current study is to examine the role of context visibility and interaction control on immersion, motivation and learning outcomes in an augmented 360° environment. We found positive main effects of the visibility of the context on motivation, especially attention, relevance, and satisfaction, supporting H2a. While we did not find this effect concerning immersion in general, thus rejecting H1a, we did find it concerning its subconstructs interest and presence. Moreover, a large positive main effect of learner control on immersion in general revealed, supporting H1b, and including positive effects on all the subconstructs: interest, usability, emotional attachment, focus of attention, presence, and flow. This positive main effect was also found in support of H2b concerning motivation, with positive effects the subconstructs attention, confidence, and satisfaction. No interaction effects were found, rejecting H1c and H2c. We also did not find any effects on knowledge as the learning outcome, rejecting H3a, H3b and H3c. Descriptively, all immersion, motivation and knowledge variables show the pattern that the condition with non-visible context and system control has the lowest score. Concerning the motivational subconstruct satisfaction, a significant interaction effect and post hoc paired comparisons even showed significant increases in satisfaction for the other three conditions in comparison to the non-visible context and system control condition.

As expected, learner control had a large positive effect on immersion, including all immersion related subconstructs, which suggests an influence on system and challenge immersion [26]. The specific differentiation between system and challenge immersion has not been made in the data collection, so that we do not know which immersion was mainly supported through learner control. Context visibility, on the other hand, did not have the expected effect on general immersion, although it did positively influence interest and presence. For the other subconstructs, context visibility and its potential effect on system immersion may not be big enough, although this may be different in an immersive headset. The missing interaction effect supports that concerning immersion, only learner control was relevant in the current educational setting. Also as expected, motivation was positively influenced by both context visibility and learner control. When looking closer into the subconstructs on motivation, it is striking that relevance is only positively affected by context visibility, while confidence is only positively affected by learner control. This is in accordance with our assumptions on the design choices based on the ARCS model [29], where we proposed that feelings of relevance are affected by showing the relevant real-world context of the learning material, and confidence is proposed to be dependent on learner control. The missing interaction effect might show that the effects of context visibility on relevance and learner control on confidence are only additive. Concerning the missing effects on knowledge there could be different explanations. On one hand, the increased motivation may not have been strong enough to lead to more effort put into the learning activity. Furthermore, concerning immersion it needs to be considered that when the context is invisible, a focus on the learning material is easier (see immersion principle [25], so that positive effects of immersion may have been cancelled out by negative effects of distraction when the context was visible. Descriptively, the condition with invisible context and learner control scored the highest, which might suggest the positive influence of this combination.

During the study, there were some technical challenges as some participants had problems with viewing the application. Furthermore, some participants assumed that the grey background in the invisible context conditions was a display error. It is also obvious that the gray background is not a realistic environment. These limitations might have had an influence on some of the participants' immersion and motivation.

In general, the results show an inferiority of learning environments in which both visual context and learner control are removed concerning immersion, motivation and descriptively even learning outcomes. Specifically, learner control seems to be a very important factor for immersion and motivation, while context visibility is mainly important for motivation. For the design of immersive environments that have the goal to support motivation and feelings of immersion, this means that the placement in a relevant, visible context and giving learners control should be considered. Although we described that the current augmented 360° photo is a specific form of AR, it is not sure if and how these results can be transferred onto AR-based learning with a live-view set-up of the real, physical world. In further research, these results need to be transferred. However, the invisibility of the context and the system control are harder to implement in a live AR application, so that the current implementation may be a good way to manipulate and test very specific characteristics of AR-based environments in a controlled setting.

In conclusion it can be said that the effects of context immersion and learner control on the feeling of immersion and motivation found in the current study show an exciting basis for more specific research concerning learning-related variables and should be considered in 360° media design.

Acknowledgments. We thank Maren Wodara for material creation and data collection in collaboration with co-author Mariam Koch as part of their bachelor's theses.

References

1. Ranieri, M., Luzzi, D., Cuomo, S., Bruni, I.: If and how do 360° videos fit into education settings? Results from a scoping review of empirical research. J. Comput. Assist. Learn. **38**, 1199–1219 (2022). https://doi.org/10.1111/jcal.12683

2. Ulrich, F., Helms, N.H., Frandsen, U.P., Rafn, A.V.: Learning effectiveness of 360° video: experiences from a controlled experiment in healthcare education. Interact. Learn. Environ. **29**, 98–111 (2021). https://doi.org/10.1080/10494820.2019.1579234

3. Kosko, K.W., Ferdig, R.E., Zolfaghari, M.: Preservice teachers' professional noticing when viewing standard and 360 video. J. Teach. Educ. **72**, 284–297 (2021). https://doi.org/10.1177/0022487120939544

4. Arvaniti, P.A., Fokides, E.: Evaluating the effectiveness of 360 videos when teaching primary school subjects related to environmental education. JPR. **4**, 203–222 (2020). https://doi.org/10.33902/JPR.2020063461

5. Pirker, J., Dengel, A.: The potential of 360° virtual reality videos and real VR for education—a literature review. IEEE Comput. Graph. Appl. **41**, 76–89 (2021). https://doi.org/10.1109/MCG.2021.3067999

6. Arents, V., de Groot, P.C.M., Struben, V.M.D., van Stralen, K.J.: Use of 360° virtual reality video in medical obstetrical education: a quasi-experimental design. BMC Med. Educ. **21**, 202 (2021). https://doi.org/10.1186/s12909-021-02628-5

7. Eiris, R., Gheisari, M., Esmaeili, B.: PARS: using augmented 360-degree panoramas of reality for construction safety training. Int. J. Environ. Res. Public Health. **15**, 2452 (2018). https://doi.org/10.3390/ijerph15112452

8. Choi, K., Yoon, Y.-J., Song, O.-Y., Choi, S.-M.: Interactive and immersive learning using 360° virtual reality contents on mobile platforms. Mob. Inf. Syst. 1–12 (2018). https://doi.org/10.1155/2018/2306031

9. Milgram, P., Takemura, H., Utsumi, A., Kishino, F.: Augmented reality: a class of displays on the reality-virtuality continuum. In: SPIE 2351: Telemanipulator and Telepresence Technologies, pp. 282–292. Boston, MA, USA (1994)

10. Krüger, J.M., Buchholz, A., Bodemer, D.: Augmented reality in education: three unique characteristics from a user's perspective. In: Chang, M., So, H.-J., Wong, L.-H., Yu, F.-Y., Shih, J.L. (eds.) Proceedings of the 27th International Conference on Computers in Education, pp. 412–422. Asia-Pacific Society for Computers in Education, Taiwan (2019)

11. Torres, A., et al.: A 360 video editor framework for interactive training. In: 2020 IEEE 8th International Conference on Serious Games and Applications for Health (SeGAH), pp. 1–7. IEEE, Vancouver, BC, Canada (2020)

12. Harun, N.Z., Mahadzir, S.Y.: 360° virtual tour of the traditional malay house as an effort for cultural heritage preservation. IOP Conf. Ser.: Earth Environ. Sci. **764**, 012010 (2021). https://doi.org/10.1088/1755-1315/764/1/012010

13. Scheiter, K.: The learner control principle in multimedia learning. In: Fiorella, L., Mayer, R.E. (eds.) The Cambridge Handbook of Multimedia Learning, pp. 418–429. Cambridge University Press, Cambridge (2021)

14. Dengel, A., Mägdefrau, J.: Immersive learning explored: subjective and objective factors influencing learning outcomes in immersive educational virtual environments. In: Lee, M.J.W., et al. (eds.) 2018 IEEE International Conference on Teaching, Assessment, and Learning for Engineering (TALE), pp. 608–615 (2018)

15. Makransky, G., Petersen, G.B.: The cognitive affective model of immersive learning (CAMIL): a theoretical research-based model of learning in immersive virtual reality. Educ. Psychol. Rev. **33**, 937–958 (2021). https://doi.org/10.1007/s10648-020-09586-2

16. Witmer, B.G., Singer, M.J.: Measuring presence in virtual environments: a presence questionnaire. Presence: Teleoperators Virtual Environ. **7**, 225–240 (1998). https://doi.org/10.1162/105474698565686

17. Slater, M., Wilbur, S.: A framework for immersive virtual environments (FIVE): speculations on the role of presence in virtual environments. Presence: Teleoperators Virtual Environ. **6**, 603–616 (1997). https://doi.org/10.1162/pres.1997.6.6.603

18. Georgiou, Y., Kyza, E.A.: The development and validation of the ARI questionnaire: an instrument for measuring immersion in location-based augmented reality settings. Int. J. Hum.-Comput. St. **98**, 24–37 (2017). https://doi.org/10.1016/j.ijhcs.2016.09.014

19. Dengel, A.: What is immersive learning? In: Dengel, A., et al. (eds.) 2022 8th International Conference of the Immersive Learning Research Network (iLRN), pp. 1–5 (2022)

20. Makransky, G.: The immersion principle in multimedia learning. In: Fiorella, L., Mayer, R.E. (eds.) The Cambridge Handbook of Multimedia Learning, pp. 296–303. Cambridge University Press, Cambridge (2021)

21. Cheng, M.-T., She, H.-C., Annetta, L.A.: Game immersion experience: its hierarchical structure and impact on game-based science learning. J. Comput. Assist. Learn. **31**, 232–253 (2015). https://doi.org/10.1111/jcal.12066

22. Georgiou, Y., Kyza, E.A.: Investigating immersion in relation to students' learning during a collaborative location-based augmented reality activity. In: Smith, B.K., Borge, M., Mercier, E., Lim, K.Y. (eds.) 12th International Conference on Computer Supported Collaborative Learning (CSCL) 2017, vol. 1, pp. 423–430. International Society of the Learning Sciences, Philadelphia, PA (2017)

23. Georgiou, Y., Kyza, E.A.: Relations between student motivation, immersion and learning outcomes in location-based augmented reality settings. Comput. Hum. Behav. **89**, 173–181 (2018). https://doi.org/10.1016/j.chb.2018.08.011

24. Georgiou, Y., Kyza, E.A.: A design-based approach to augmented reality location-based activities: investigating immersion in relation to student learning. In: Proceedings of the 16th World Conference on Mobile and Contextual Learning, pp. 1–8. Association for Computing Machinery, New York, NY, USA (2017)

25. Mayer, R.E.: 18 Immersion principle. In: Multimedia Learning. Cambridge University Press, Cambridge (2020)

26. Beck, D., Morgado, L., Shea, P.: Finding the gaps about uses of immersive learning environments: a survey of surveys. JUCS – J. Univ. Comput. Sci. **26**(8), 1043–1073 (2020). https://doi.org/10.3897/jucs.2020.055

27. Eccles, J.S., Wigfield, A.: Motivational beliefs, values, and goals. Annu. Rev. Psychol. **53**, 109–132 (2002). https://doi.org/10.1146/annurev.psych.53.100901.135153

28. Schrader, C., Kalyuga, S., Plass, J.L.: Motivation and affect in multimedia learning. In: Mayer, R.E., Fiorella, L. (eds.) The Cambridge Handbook of Multimedia Learning. pp. 121–131. Cambridge University Press, Cambridge (2021)

29. Keller, J.M.: Motivational Design for Learning and Performance. Springer, Boston (2010)

30. Garzón, J., Pavón, J., Baldiris, S.: Systematic review and meta-analysis of augmented reality in educational settings. Virtual Reality **23**, 447–459 (2019). https://doi.org/10.1007/s10055-019-00379-9

31. Akçayır, M., Akçayır, G.: Advantages and challenges associated with augmented reality for education: a systematic review of the literature. Educ. Res. Rev. **20**, 1–11 (2017). https://doi.org/10.1016/j.edurev.2016.11.002

32. Domagk, S., Schwartz, R.N., Plass, J.L.: Interactivity in multimedia learning: an integrated model. Comput. Hum. Behav. **26**, 1024–1033 (2010). https://doi.org/10.1016/j.chb.2010.03.003

33. Mayer, R.E.: Incorporating motivation into multimedia learning. Learn. Instr. **29**, 171–173 (2014). https://doi.org/10.1016/j.learninstruc.2013.04.00

34. Paas, F., Tuovinen, J.E., van Merriënboer, J.J.G., Aubteen Darabi, A.: A motivational perspective on the relation between mental effort and performance: optimizing learner involvement in instruction. ETR&D. **53**, 25–34 (2005). https://doi.org/10.1007/BF02504795
35. Loorbach, N., Peters, O., Karreman, J., Steehouder, M.: Validation of the instructional materials motivation survey (IMMS) in a self-directed instructional setting aimed at working with technology. Br. J. Educ. Technol. **46**, 204–218 (2015). https://doi.org/10.1111/bjet.12138

Failure Stories and Surprising Findings: Learning from When VR Did Not Work

Xichen Li[(⊠)] [iD] and Joey J. Lee[iD]

Teachers College, Columbia University, New York, NY 10027, USA
XL3197@tc.columbia.edu

Abstract. It is easy to assume that virtual reality will naturally lead to improved learning outcomes, as there is a tendency to view VR, as an exciting new technology, as a "silver bullet" that can dramatically enhance learning. However, several research studies reveal surprising or counter-intuitive findings – for example, when low-immersion media led to better learning outcomes than VR. We provide a systematic review and discuss specific cases in which results were not as expected. Factors that adversely affect learning include novelty effects, VR sickness, low interaction fidelity, cognitive overload, or other environmental or classroom factors. Through this study, we argue that designers and educators can avoid pitfalls by studying the times when VR did not work as expected. We also provide recommendations based upon these findings. In this way, we can gain insights on how to actually obtain desirable outcomes from the new technology.

Keywords: Virtual Reality · Educational VR · Multimedia Learning · Systematic Review

1 Introduction

It is easy to assume that virtual reality (VR) will naturally lead to improved learning outcomes, as there may be a tendency to view it as a "silver bullet" that can dramatically enhance learning. Despite enthusiasm for the technology, however, several research studies have actually revealed surprising or counter-intuitive findings - for example, times when the use of low-immersion media led to better learning outcomes compared to VR [1, 2]. Research is still inconclusive on the impact of different levels of immersion for performance on various cognitive and functional tasks [3, 4].

Despite relatively limited evidence supporting its learning effectiveness, VR-based instruction has flourished due partly to lower cost and commercial interest [5]. Some off-the-shelf educational simulations used by teachers are meant to be entertaining interactive experiences rather than learning materials designed carefully with instructional principles in mind [6].

This can be problematic if VR experiences are sometimes found to be ineffective for learning -- or even detrimental. We need to carefully consider the nuance of how learning takes place and identify design principles supported by empirical findings. If not, we may lose opportunities to effectively support students and even readily harm

M.-L. Bourguet et al. (Eds.): iLRN 2023, CCIS 1904, pp. 22–36, 2024.
https://doi.org/10.1007/978-3-031-47328-9_2

students' comprehension and development [5, 7]. Schools with limited resources may invest heavily in VR technology and subsequently realize that it fails to deliver on its promised benefits [8].

We provide a systematic review and discuss specific cases in which results were not as expected. Many existing review studies focus on the positive effects of VR for learning, encompassing enhanced student engagement, constructivist learning, and authentic experiences [9]. While this is helpful, we believe it can be even more beneficial to focus on surprising moments or failure stories and understand why things turned out differently than expected.

It can be hard to define VR concisely due to its fast and ever-changing development. In general, VR is expected to be immersive and create a sense of presence for the participants in the virtual space. VR should also provide a level of interactivity for users to manipulate and interact with objects [1].

Different educational mediums provide learners with different levels of immersion. According to Cummings and Bailenson [10], immersion is an objective measure that reflects the level of vividness created and the extent to which a medium shuts out the outside world.

Text-based instruction typically offers little to no immersion. Media involving both video and sound creates low immersion, such as desktop VR supported by conventional PC monitors. High immersion is when the learner experiences the situation in question in a way that surrounds them [11]. Immersive VR (I-VR) provided by a head-mounted display (HMD) or Cave Automatic Virtual Environment (CAVE), provides high immersion. It usually features better graphic fidelity and a higher sense of presence [6].

This study focuses on the effectiveness of I-VR supported by HMD or CAVE compared to other low-immersion mediums, such as desktop VR and slideshow presentation. We explore the following research questions in this study: *RQ1:* What are examples of research studies in which immersive virtual reality had a negative effect on learning? *RQ2:* What can we learn from these cases?

2 Methodology

We conducted a Scopus query to gather systematic review and meta-analysis journal articles on virtual reality for the K-12 and higher education context. From our systematic literature review, we identified research studies where VR produced worse learning outcomes than low-immersion mediums for closer examination. As the space has matured and many rapid developments have occurred (including the proliferation of lower cost, wireless headsets), we limited the search to the last three years (i.e., after 2019). This decision was to ensure the research studies included were timely, relevant, responsive to current opportunities, and usable and useful for classrooms.

Our initial query process (see Fig. 1), which targeted the keywords "virtual reality," "VR," and "systematic review" within the last three years, yielded 1,190 results. To ensure the results were relevant to the K-12 or higher education context or classroom teaching, we added "k-12 OR 'higher-education' OR pedagogic*," which reduced the number of findings to 37. We then excluded seven articles that focused on clinical psychology and healthcare applications of VR, leading to 30 results (see Fig. 2). 13

articles were manually excluded as irrelevant or off-topic, as they focused on topics other than education or technologies other than virtual reality. This process resulted in a total of 17 papers that met the final inclusion criteria.

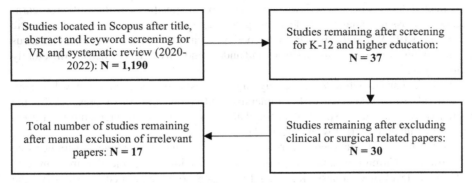

Fig. 1. Stage-by-stage selection process for systematic literatures.

TITLE-ABS-KEY (("virtual reality" OR vr OR i-vr OR ivr) AND ("systematic review" OR "meta-analysis") AND (k-12 OR "higher-education" OR pedagogic*) AND NOT clinical AND NOT autism AND NOT "healthcare" AND NOT health) AND PUBYEAR > 2019)

Fig. 2. Scopus query.

Of this sample of articles, 9 discussed VR but offered little to no analysis of learning outcomes. Most systematic literature focused on VR in K-12 and higher education in the past decade. Only two focused on specific subject areas, one in chemical education [12] and one in foreign language study [13].

To gain a deeper understanding of surprising or counter-intuitive results, we closely examined the studies that reported adverse effects from the pool of studies analyzed within the 17 systematic literature reviews. The selected systematic literature suggested 35 publications with detrimental or mixed results. We excluded 9 duplicate studies and ten that used AR, desktop VR, or learning tools other than I-VR. We also removed five studies that focused on education areas other than K-12 and higher education, such as professional training and surgery training. In the end, 11 publications met all the criteria (see Fig. 3).

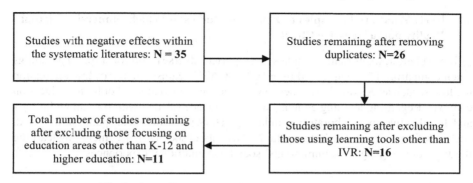

Fig. 3. Stage-by-stage selection process for case studies.

3 Analysis of Adverse Learning Outcomes

While most of the systematic reviews acknowledged the learning benefits of VR, the three meta-analyses all found that the overall effect size on the learning outcomes of I-VR was small [4, 14], or even negative [15].

To dive deeper into adverse learning outcomes, we calculated the percentage of studies in the systematic literature where more immersive technology failed to deliver better learning outcomes than more traditional instructional methods. We found that each systematic review or meta-analysis reported that 13% to 38% of I-VR or VR-based instruction studies had no effect or adverse effects [1, 12–18].

Considering the fair proportion of studies that reported no learning enhancement for VR-based instruction, many reviews suggested some recommendations or comments on how to use the new technology. With 34% of the studies showing no improved learning results using I-VR, Wu et al. [18] concluded that HMDs are more likely to complement rather than replace traditional instructions as the internet and mobile devices were once predicted to be [19]. As non-HMD interventions yielded a much larger effect size than HMD interventions, Luo et al. [15] concluded that new tools do not guarantee improved comprehension, and the decision to adopt the technology should be based on an assessment of learning domains and tasks; e.g. VR seems to more ideal for "teaching abstract concepts, procedural knowledge, affect, attitude, and authentic problem solving and more… [ideal for teaching] subjects such as chemistry, geology, astronomy, surgery, history, culture, and safety education" (p. 897) [15].

Systematic literatures provided an overview of our research questions. Among the pool of studies analyzed within these systematic literatures, we then looked closely at the cases where VR failed to deliver better learning outcomes to answer our questions in depth.

3.1 RQ1: What are Examples of Research Studies in Which Immersive Virtual Reality had a Negative Effect?

In Table 1 below, we present 11 studies that reported adverse results or surprising findings when comparing I-VR supported by HMD or CAVE against a range of low immersion mediums, such as desktop VR, slideshow, movie, and video in K-12 or higher education contexts. Regarding learning content, six were science related, with four about biology and the other two about laboratory simulations. Three were motion or spatial skill related, such as safety training. The last two studies were about social science, including learning the Japanese language and immigrants' social and emotional experiences.

Table 1. Studies with negative learning effects using I-VR.

ID	Citation	Study focus	Participant details	Media in comparison	Surprising findings
1	[20]	Motion training for Chinese Taichi	18 students	CAVE, HMD, PC	HMD enhanced the learning experience but generated worse learning outcomes than CAVE or PC. CAVE had the highest learning efficiency.
2	[21]	Japanese language	68 participants from the university community	HMD, desktop VR	I-VR's impact on language acquisition was inconclusive.
3	[22]	Chemistry laboratory	40 graduate students majoring in education and the arts	HMD, real-life chemistry laboratory	I-VR was comparable to a real-life lab in most aspects, but clean-up behaviors were less frequent in VR.
4	[23]	Safety training	High school students Study 1 (N = 53) Study 2 (N = 68)	CAVE, PPT	The PPT procedure with vivid film scenes was not significantly worse than I-VR concerning changes in risk perception, learning outcomes, or decision-making, and is less costly.
5	[6]	Biology laboratory	52 university students	HMD, PC	I-VR was more motivating than PC, but resulted in less learning and a higher cognitive load.
6	[2]	Science knowledge about cells	118 university students	HMD, video	There is an interaction between media and method. Pre-training with I-VR positively affected knowledge, transfer, and self-efficacy, while pre-training with video had no such effect.

(*continued*)

Table 1. (*continued*)

ID	Citation	Study focus	Participant details	Media in comparison	Surprising findings
7	[24]	Biology knowledge of how the body works	55 college students	HMD, self-directed PPT	The VR cohort had worse post-test performance than the slideshow cohort, but adding a written summary to VR improved performance without decreasing interest, engagement, and motivation.
8	[25]	Difficulties faced by new immigrants	178 seventh and eighth graders	HMD, movie	The movie was more effective than I-VR in raising native-born students' awareness of a teen immigrant's social and emotional difficulties.
9	[26]	Spatial learning	40 undergraduate and graduate students	HMD, desktop VR	After accounting for motion sickness and workload effort, walk-restrictive IVR resulted in similar or even poor performance on learning tasks compared to desktop VR.
10	[27]	Anatomy knowledge	52 s-year medical students	MR, 3DM, textbook	The MR group showed poorer performance on nominal questions after the learning session, but better retention of both nominal and spatial information for at least a month, compared to the other groups.
11	[28]	Biology knowledge of what is inside a human body	75 college students	VR, interactive video	VR increased participants' motivation but did not affect comprehension. Summarizing significantly reduced learners' perceived effort for both conditions.

We coded and summarized the factors raised in these 11 studies, which could explain their surprising results. Among them, VR sickness and difficulty in handling novelty effects (described in the following section) were the top reasons why a less immersive medium could be more effective in learning. How VR is implemented, low interactive fidelity, ineffectiveness in delivering certain types of knowledge, extraneous information, and students' misperception have also been raised as factors influencing I-VR's effectiveness in facilitating learning (see Table 2).

Table 2. Summary of factors that explain why VR failed.

ID	VR sickness	Novelty effect	Poor integration of instructional strategies	Low interactive fidelity	Worse at basic or factual knowledge	Extraneous information	Student misperception
1	✓			✓			
2	✓	✓		✓			
3					✓		✓
4				✓			
5		✓			✓	✓	✓
6	✓		✓		✓	✓	
7			✓		✓	✓	
8	✓	✓					✓
9		✓		✓			
10	✓	✓	✓				
11			✓				

3.2 RQ2: What Can We Learn from These Cases?

Immersive VR Simulation has Significantly Higher Negative Symptoms of Discomfort and Dizziness. VR sickness is defined as motion sickness resulting from the immersivity of a computer-generated virtual space [29, 30]. 45% of our selected studies reported simulator sickness as a primary factor that decreased learning performances in I-VR. Meyer et al. [2] found that participants using immersive VR experienced more simulator sickness than those watching a video. In their study, general discomfort, nausea, and stomach awareness level were significantly different between the groups [2]. Chen et al. [20] also suggested that comfortability issues affect learning quality.

Participants also reported other physical discomforts, like the weight of the device and the requirement of orientation [27]. According to Cheng et al. [21], 27.9% participant comment and feedback were related to user interface and gameplay, such as difficulty reading words in the inventory, sense of disorientation, or counter-intuitive interaction mode.

VR designers must create a more comfortable, intuitive VR experience by enabling movement without sickness and natural user input in the virtual environment. Cheng et al. [21] retained the original drag-and-drop UI when adapting a desktop game to VR. The interaction was not ideal for a natural VR experience and received negative participant feedback. They suggested that significant efforts are needed to create a natural VR experience.

It is worth noting that learners' positive or negative experiences might be more vivid in I-VR because I-VR can provide a higher sense of presence and higher levels of extraneous load simultaneously [2]. Therefore, designing VR experiences free of motion sickness is challenging but critical for VR designers and educators.

The Novelty of Technology Can Hurt Learning Due to Over-Excitement or Unfamiliarity with the VR Learning Tool. In our sample, 45% reported challenges in handling novelty effects as the main reason immersive VR yields worse learning outcomes than conventional instructional materials. Many suggested that a lack of time, orientation, and being too excited and fascinated by the unfamiliar new technology might have negatively affected learning with I-VR.

Makransky et al. [6] found that some students were overwhelmed by the excitement and fun of being in immersive VR for the first time. They suggested that a lack of familiarity may increase students' extraneous workload. Similarly, Passig et al. [25] pointed out that the VR group might not have had the experience they expected due to unfamiliarity with solving problems using HMD and feeling disoriented using the new device. Wang et al. [27] indicated that students carried away by the new tool could not focus on learning. In their study, participants commented that the learning session was too pressured as they were still understanding how to use the tool and did not have enough time to study satisfactorily [27].

To reduce the novelty effect, the researchers suggested that teachers introduce the head-mounted device as a learning tool before presenting the main instructional content. In this way, students understand how the novel tool integrates with their learning and do not become distracted by the fascination but still feel excited about the new tool [27]. Zhao et al. [28] pointed out that researchers could also have learners experience a longer time in the VR environment.

Learning Effectiveness also Depends on Instructional Strategies and How Teachers Teach with VR, not just VR as a Standalone Technology for Learning. Several studies have shown that VR alone does not guarantee deep engagement or active processing of the learning materials [6, 24]. Poor integration of instructional strategies might also explain why VR might fail in education. When VR did not deliver desired outcomes, some researchers tried to improve VR's learning effectiveness by applying conventional instructional strategies, such as adding written summaries or pre-training the main knowledge concepts. Among Our selected case studies, 36% recognized instructional strategies as practical solutions to improve VR learning results.

Other key learning activities, such as debriefing and reflection prompts outside the VR environment, can greatly improve the learning benefits of a VR experience as a scaffolding strategy [20]. Parong and Mayer [24] found that adding written summaries at various points significantly improved students' test performance without hurting their interest or motivation. This finding is based on generative learning theory, which posits that people learn better when they can select, organize, and integrate new information into their existing knowledge structures [24].

Interestingly, certain conventional instructional methods might be even more effective in I-VR than less immersive media. Meyer et al. [2] found that adding a pre-training that debriefs the main concepts yielded more significant learning outcomes and higher self-efficacy in the VR group than in the video group. This is also the only occasion where the VR cohort learned better than the video cohort. As a part of the Cognitive

Theory for Multimedia Learning (CTML), the pre-training principle suggests that people learn better with multimedia information when they have a basic understanding of the main concepts and lower intrinsic cognitive load during the lesson [2].

Some of these instructional strategies may have the potential for generalization across different disciplines in VR-based instruction. Meyer et al. [2] proposed that pre-training could be included as part of regular classroom teaching, regardless of subject, as long as students learn complex or abstract information in VR. Pre-training can also be built into a VR simulation and presented before the primary learning experience begins. In addition, instructional strategies that reduce intrinsic cognitive load can achieve similar results as pre-training in their study [2].

Low Interaction Fidelity Might Harm Learning. One of the critical objectives of immersive technology is to increase fidelity and the degree of similarity between the virtual and real world [26]. According to Srivastava et al [26], fidelity consists of interaction fidelity and virtual display fidelity. In our sample, 36% of studies emphasized the importance of interaction fidelity as a potentially significant advantage of VR over traditional instructional forms. Many found that the absence of interaction fidelity may harm learning, while virtual display fidelity or vividness has little effect on learning and transfer [23, 26].

Srivastava et al. [26] noted that HMD had an advantage over desktop VR in spatial skill training when learners can walk freely in I-VR [11]. However, if walking is restricted in HMD, I-VR had no or even worse effect on spatial learning performance than desktop VR, controlling for motion sickness and workload. The researchers suggested that it is interaction fidelity rather than visual fidelity that played the crucial role in improving spatial learning performance. It's probably because ego-centric locomotion matched the navigation experience in the natural environment in a better way. On the other hand, vividness or higher visual fidelity may not be necessary for facilitating meaningful learning. These may be viewed as seductive details that create extraneous overload and interfere with reflection [26].

Leder et al. [23] had similar findings in their safety training experiments. Differences in learning were insignificant between the I-VR and PPT conditions immediately after the training, in the replicate study, and six months after the learning session. Surprisingly, participants in the I-VR condition made more risk-seeking choices than those in the PPT condition in one of the studies [23].

A noticeable commonality between these two studies is that they both carefully designed the two media in comparison to having similar affordances except for the level of immersion. As mentioned before, Srivastava et al. [26] designed the I-VR experience to be non-ambulatory. To test solely for the effects of immersion, Leder et al. [23] designed I-VR to be non-interactive while PPT contained filmed VR sequences so that PPT presentation was also vivid and differed from the VR condition only by the fact that it was not immersive.

Many VR designs shut out the physical reality of users to enhance inclusiveness. In a motion skill learning study, Chen et al. [20] found the HMD condition had the best user experience and fastest learning process but the lowest learning quality compared to the CAVE and PC conditions because HMD was "over immersive." In other words, students could not see their bodies or movement. As a result, some students were unaware that their motion was distorted and had relatively low quality [20].

VR designers should consider incorporating embodiment and natural body movements into the virtual environment to facilitate motion, spatial skills-related learning, or even cultural studies. In a virtual laboratory study, Hu-Au and Okita [22] suggested that better quality and motion of virtual gestures and the realistic function of the existing tools enhanced learning in the virtual lab. Cheng et al. [21] also found using head motions to mimic bowing effective in teaching participants the Japanese language and culture. Using natural movements in the learning environment can help form strong knowledge concepts and memories [31]. These gestures could reduce the cognitive load and enable learners to process more new information readily.

VR May Be Worse Than a Traditional Lesson in Delivering Certain Types of Knowledge, Such as Factual Knowledge and Basic Knowledge. VR may be good at teaching certain types of knowledge and behavior over others [15]. In our selected studies, 36% found that VR may be worse than traditional instructional forms in delivering declarative or factual knowledge and teaching basic concepts while better at teaching abstract and procedural knowledge.

Several researchers have concluded that VR does not show an apparent advantage in teaching declarative knowledge [6, 32]. Parong and Mayer [24] found that VR is less effective in teaching scientific information than equivalent slideshows, where students spent less time on the lesson but scored significantly higher in the post-test. The researchers pointed out that VR animations add distracting extraneous visual input rather than really enhancing basic factual knowledge. In contrast, slideshows can deliver factual knowledge more focused and straightforwardly. Similarly, Passig et al. [25] found that film was more effective in raising students' awareness of immigrants' difficulties because it spoke more openly and straightforwardly about complex issues. However, in the VR simulation, learners were immigrants and had to discover and make inferences about what immigrants felt as immigrants were not explicitly mentioned [25].

Many studies indicated that immersive VR is neither an optimal medium for learning basic concepts. However, once they have a basic understanding of the material, learners might benefit from interactions enabled by VR [6]. In a virtual chemistry lab experiment, Hu-Au and Okita [22] found that VR effectively taught application knowledge but had no effect on basic or inference questions compared to real-life laboratory environments.

Discovery-based multimedia instruction, like VR-based learning, has been speculated to only benefit experts or students with a relatively solid foundation in the field being learned. Clark et al. [33] argued that exploring complex knowledge in a discovery process requires much unproductive mental effort. Beginners or students with limited prior knowledge benefit most from fully guided instruction [8]. This finding also supports offering pre-training, which may decrease cognitive load and equip students with crucial fundamental knowledge of the content before entering an immersive VR environment.

Designs that Add Motivation May Interfere with Reflection and Result in Worse Learning. In cases where I-VR generates no better learning results than low immersion medium, a distraction from extraneous information may have had a more significant negative effect than potential positive effects brought by increased interest [24]. 27%

of our sample reported extraneous information from instructional design as one major factor for how a VR experience could be worse than traditional methods of instruction.

According to interference theory, providing extraneous material to motivate students will interfere with necessary processing [34]. Distractions such as music, animation, and pedagogy agents have been recognized as significant drawbacks of multimedia instruction [33]. The extraneous cognitive load caused by poor instructional design may decrease learning as learners need to make an effort to ignore irrelevant contextual information to identify and learn essential information [6].

Makransky et al. [6] found that studying in simulations, regardless of the immersive level, was a difficult learning task for most students. In their study, they used EEG to measure workload scores and found that students were overloaded 47.78% of the time on average during the two 15-min interventions (students include participants in both the PC and I-VR conditions).

To achieve a higher level of immersion, I-VR often has more seductive details which are interesting but irrelevant to learning and result in higher cognitive overload than desktop VR and other conventional media [6]. In one of their two interventions, Makransky et al. [6] found that the VR group was overloaded significantly more than the PC group. Parong and Mayer [24] also observed that in the immersive biology lesson, learners' attention may have diverted from listening to the core narrations to the animation of blood cells constantly moving past and the ability to look at them in all directions at the same time.

Seductive details in I-VR can interfere with reflection by distracting students from building a cause-and-effect schema from the material [24]. In addition, if students use the time to absorb the seductive details, they do not have enough time and capacity for cognitively assimilating new information to existing schemas. According to CTML's coherence principle, people learn better when extraneous information is excluded rather than included [6]. Seductive details are also a concern for gamification in education and game-based learning.

There may be ways to design VR experiences that increase motivation and learning effect at the same time. For example, according to self-efficacy theory, providing appropriate feedback when learners progress in the VR experience can immediately boost their self-efficacy and enhance their motivation for the class. Immediate and adaptive feedback VR could provide has an advantage over feedback in traditional lessons because it boosts students' self-efficacy instantly [24]. There still needs to be more generalized principles for I-VR. Evidence-based design principles will be valuable future guidelines for VR designers and educators [8].

Learning Decreases When Students Perceive or Expect the VR Experience to be Entertainment or Game-Like Simulation. Unlike traditional learning materials, which learners know are learning resources, students view VR learning in various ways, such as entertainment, unreal simulation, or games, and form expectations around these perceptions. 27% of our sample found that students' misperceptions or expectations affect VR learning results.

Makransky et al. [6] suggested that students using VR likely learned less because they have focused their cognitive effort on the gameplay, which is not part of the instructional goal. Since the distinction between utilitarian and hedonic information processing is not always clear [35], Makransky et al. [6] pointed out that a highly immersive environment may mislead students to treat them as hedonic systems.

Similarly, Passig et al. [25] found that unrealistic expectations of the technology and wrong focus on the gameplay were potential reasons why the rise of awareness for immigrants' difficulties was less noticeable in the VR cohort than the film cohort. Students had high expectations of VR, where they performed tasks that could not be solved because they were immigrants in the game. Four immigration issues experts validated the VR design as an authentic representation of immigrants' experiences. However, students might not have attributed their failure to immigration-related difficulties, but to the way or strategy they used to carry out the task. By failing the tasks and other usability reasons, the VR group might not have gotten the expected experience [25].

Viewing the virtual learning space as an unrealistic, game-like simulation may also decrease learning. Students may believe that achievements in a game will not transfer to real-life academic achievements [36]. For example, Passig et al. [25] also found that the unreal perception of VR made it less effective in raising awareness than a movie. Contrary to seeing young immigrant actors in the film speak in their own voices, sometimes with foreign accents, computerized graphic figures talking about their feelings and difficulties were less effective in creating personal identification [25].

One study also found that students show subversive or unconventional behavior in a less-consequential virtual space [22]. In a virtual chemistry laboratory, students tend to behave more recklessly (e.g. breaking a glass beaker) or take more risks, which would be taboo or dangerous if transferred to a real-life situation. In a related study, Hu-Au and Okita [22] observed that although participants in the VR condition scored higher on laboratory safety knowledge, they performed fewer actual laboratory safety behaviors than those in the real lab condition. Therefore, we can conclude that managing students' perceptions and expectations of immersive technology are critical for the success of VR-based instruction.

4 Discussion and Conclusion

Although it is common to assume that VR technologies will impact education significantly in beneficial ways, we have shown that many studies on the effectiveness of VR-based learning have produced mixed or even negative results. In our systematic review, we identified 11 research studies from 17 systematic reviews and meta-analysis that reported adverse learning outcomes or other counter-intuitive and surprising results concerning VR-based instruction compared to less immersive mediums, such as slideshow and videos. A range between 13% to 38% of studies gathered by each systematic review and meta-analysis reported no effect or adverse effects of I-VR or VR-based instruction [1, 12–18].

It is noteworthy that mediating certain problems in media comparison studies is complex, and the actual likelihood of getting no effect or negative results with VR-based instruction may be larger than we see. Media in comparison are not only different instructional mediums but also different in their instructional method and learning content. Clark et al. [8] thus suggested that when studies found the advantages of VR over more conventional instructional methods, it may be because of poor experimental design where VR provides extra instructional content and functionalities that are missing in the low-immersion form. Considering huge variances in affordances, media comparison studies need careful design to align learning experiences across all mediums, including words, graphics, vividness, and interaction, among many other things [26].

By coding and analyzing the 11 case studies where VR produced no effect or adverse effects, we identified a list of factors that may explain why VR may deliver worse learning outcomes. We provide the following recommendations for VR learning designers, educators, and researchers to enhance learning:

- Design VR experiences free of motion sickness
- Take advantage of increased motivation and interest, but also reduce the unfamiliarity and overexcitement of novelty effects
- Bring learners' attention to core instructional materials, while reducing cognitive overload and unnecessary seductive details
- Focus less on vividness and more on the educational opportunities and benefits of natural body movements
- Manage students' expectations and perception of learning in I-VR to bring out the best learning potential
- Assess whether the learning goals leverage VR's strengths (e.g., teaching abstract concepts and procedural knowledge)
- Consider non-VR aspects in the classroom (e.g. pre-training, reflection, discussion) and pedagogical strategies or models to scaffold, supplement and obtain the most benefit from the use of VR experiences
- Target subject areas that are more suitable to teach using VR

There are several limitations of our findings. First, we should be cautious with generalizing these findings to different subjects. Various types of knowledge would require different VR designs and instructional strategies [26, 27]. Second, some papers that are not experimental in nature (for example do not have a control group) might not appear in systematic literature reviews or meta-analysis and these papers may have been excluded from this review. Since almost all included research studies were conducted in laboratories, many classroom problems and teacher considerations were not captured in this study, such as how to transition into and out of the devices [37]. They are equally important when considering VR's potential in learning, as teachers provide important scaffolding and opportunities for reflection.

In this study, we have provided several case studies with negative learning outcomes; clearly education technology advancements do not always guarantee better learning [15]. As headsets supporting immersive virtual experiences become more prevalent, we must be careful with overenthusiasm and ensure empirical evidence guides a more nuanced understanding of optimal design. This paper is only a starting point; future research is needed to determine additional design principles and effective instructional strategies for formal and informal learning environments, especially those with generalizable potential across different subjects and disciplines.

References

1. Hamilton, D., McKechnie, J., Edgerton, E., Wilson, C.: Immersive virtual reality as a pedagogical tool in education: a systematic literature review of quantitative learning outcomes and experimental design. J. Comput. Educ. **8**(1), 1–32 (2021)
2. Meyer, O.A., Omdahl, M.K., Makransky, G.: Investigating the effect of pre-training when learning through immersive virtual reality and video: a media and methods experiment. Comput. Educ. **140**, 103603 (2019)
3. Slater, M., Usoh, M., Steed, A.: Depth of presence in virtual environments. Presence. **3**, 130–144 (1994)
4. Wilson, C.J., Soranzo, A.: The use of virtual reality in psychology: a case study in visual perception. Comput. Math. Meth. Med. **2015**, 151702 (2015)
5. Clark, R.E.: When teaching kills learning: research on mathemathantics. In: Mandl, H., De Corte, E., Bennett, N., Friedrich, H.F. (eds.) Learning and Instruction. European Research in an International Context, vol. II. Pergamon, Oxford (1989)
6. Makransky, G., Terkildsen, T.S., Mayer, R.E.: Adding immersive virtual reality to a science lab simulation causes more presence but less learning. Learn. Instr. **60**, 225–236 (2019)
7. Lohman, D.F.: Predicting mathemathantic effects in the teaching of higher-order thinking skills. Educ. Psychol. **21**(3), 191–208 (1986)
8. Clark, R.E., Feldon, D.F., Jeong, S.: Fifteen common but questionable principles of multimedia learning. In: Mayer, R.E. (ed.) The Cambridge Handbook of Multimedia Learning (Chapter 3). Cambridge University Press, New York (In Press)
9. Hu-Au, E., Lee, J.J.: Virtual reality in education: a tool for learning in the experience age. Int. J. Innov. Educ. **4**(4), 215–226 (2017)
10. Cummings, J.J., Bailenson, J.N.: How immersive is enough? A meta-analysis of the effect of immersive technology on user presence. Media Psychol. **19**(2), 272–309 (2016)
11. Murcia-López, M., Steed, A.: The effect of environmental features, self-avatar, and immersion on object location memory in virtual environments. Front. ICT **3**, 24 (2016)
12. Chiu, W.K.: Pedagogy of emerging technologies in chemical education during the era of digitalization and artificial intelligence: a systematic review. Educ. Sci. **11**(11), 709 (2021)
13. Peixoto, B., Pinto, R., Melo, M., Cabral, L., Bessa, M.: Immersive virtual reality for foreign language education: a prisma systematic review. IEEE Access. **9**, 48952–48962 (2021)
14. Coban, M., Bolat, Y.I., Goksu, I.: The potential of immersive virtual reality to enhance learning: a meta-analysis. Educ. Res. Rev. **36**, 100452 (2022)
15. Luo, H., Li, G., Feng, Q., Yang, Y., Zuo, M.: Virtual reality in K-12 and higher education: a systematic review of the literature from 2000 to 2019. J. Comput. Assist. Learn. **37**(3), 887–901 (2021)
16. Di Natale, A.F., Repetto, C., Riva, G., Villani, D.: Immersive virtual reality in K-12 and higher education: a 10-year systematic review of empirical research. Br. J. Edu. Technol. **51**(6), 2006–2033 (2020)
17. Pellas, N., Mystakidis, S., Kazanidis, I.: Immersive virtual reality in K-12 and higher education: a systematic review of the last decade scientific literature. Virtual Reality **25**(3), 835–861 (2021)
18. Wu, B., Yu, X., Gu, X.: Effectiveness of immersive virtual reality using head-mounted displays on learning performance: a meta-analysis. Br. J. Edu. Technol. **51**(6), 1991–2005 (2020)
19. Spector, J.M.: Trends and research issues in educational technology. Malays. Online J. Educ. Technol. **1**(3), 1–9 (2013)
20. Chen, X., et al.: ImmerTai: immersive motion learning in VR environments. J. Vis. Commun. Image Represent. **58**, 416–427 (2019)

21. Cheng, A., Yang, L., Andersen, E.: Teaching language and culture with a virtual reality game. In: Proceedings of the 2017 CHI Conference on Human Factors in Computing Systems, pp. 541–549 (2017)
22. Hu-Au, E., Okita, S.: Exploring differences in student learning and behavior between real-life and virtual reality chemistry laboratories. J. Sci. Educ. Technol. **30**(6), 862–876 (2021)
23. Leder, J., Horlitz, T., Puschmann, P., Wittstock, V., Schütz, A.: Comparing immersive virtual reality and powerpoint as methods for delivering safety training: impacts on risk perception, learning, and decision making. Saf. Sci. **111**, 271–286 (2019)
24. Parong, J., Mayer, R.E.: Learning science in immersive virtual reality. J. Educ. Psychol. **110**(6), 785–797 (2018)
25. Passig, D., Eden, S., Heled, M.: The impact of virtual reality on the awareness of teenagers to social and emotional experiences of immigrant classmates. Educ. Inf. Technol. **12**(4), 267–280 (2007)
26. Srivastava, P., Rimzhim, A., Vijay, P., Singh, S., Chandra, S.: Desktop VR is better than non-ambulatory HMD VR for spatial learning. Front. Robot. AI **6**, 50 (2019)
27. Wang, C., Daniel, B.K., Asil, M., Khwaounjoo, P., Cakmak, Y.O.: A randomised control trial and comparative analysis of multi-dimensional learning tools in anatomy. Sci. Rep. **10**(1), 1–10 (2020)
28. Zhao, J., Lin, L., Sun, J., Liao, Y.: Using the summarizing strategy to engage learners: empirical evidence in an immersive virtual reality environment. Asia Pac. Educ. Res. **29**(5), 473–482 (2020)
29. Roettl, J., Terlutter, R.: The same video game in 2D, 3D or virtual reality-how does technology impact game evaluation and brand placements? PLoS ONE **13**, e0200724 (2018)
30. Sharples, S., Cobb, S., Moody, A., Wilson, J.R.: Virtual reality induced symptoms and effects (VRISE): comparison of head mounted display (HMD), desktop and projection display systems. Displays **29**, 58–69 (2008)
31. Brown, J.S., Collins, A., Duguid, P.: Situated cognition and the culture of learning. Educ. Res. **18**(1), 288–305 (1989)
32. Moreno, R., Mayer, R.E.: Learning science in virtual reality multimedia environments: role of methods and media. J. Educ. Psychol. **94**(3), 598–610 (2002)
33. Clark, R.E., Yates, K., Early, S., Moulton, K.: An analysis of the failure of electronic media and discovery-based learning: evidence for the performance benefits of guided training methods. In: Handbook of Improving Performance in the Workplace, vol. 1–3, pp. 263-297 (2009)
34. Dewey, J.: Interest and Effort in Education. Houghton Mifflin, Cambridge (1913)
35. Van Der Heijden, H.: User acceptance of hedonic information systems. MIS Q. **28**(4), 695–704 (2004)
36. Itō, M.: Hanging Out, Messing Around, and Geeking Out: Kids Living and Learning With New Media. MIT Press, MIT Press (2010)
37. Castaneda, L., Pacampara, M.: Virtual reality in the classroom-an exploration of hardware, management, content and pedagogy. In: Society for Information Technology & Teacher Education International Conference, pp. 527–534. Association for the Advancement of Computing in Education (AACE) (2016)

Learning Analytics and Classroom Management in Specialized Environments: Enhancing the VR Classroom for CS Teacher Education

Birte Heinemann[(✉)] [iD] and Ulrik Schroeder [iD]

Learning Technologies Research Group, RWTH Aachen University, Aachen, Germany
{heinemann,schroeder}@cs.rwth-aachen.de
https://learntech.rwth-aachen.de/

Abstract. The teachers' attention is an important factor in managing a classroom effectively. It affects students' learning outcomes and is different for novice and experienced teachers. However, teaching classroom management, especially for specialized subjects like computer science where specific equipment is necessary, can be challenging. Moreover, it is difficult to provide real-life training opportunities as lessons cannot be repeated and experimentation time is very limited. This is particularly problematic for novice teachers and teacher students. To address this and support this issue, virtual reality and immersive learning can be used to simulate classroom scenarios and provide (data-driven and personal) feedback to pre-service teachers. In this paper, the subject-specific dimensions of computer science classroom management are discussed and a virtual computer lab for training purposes is proposed. Additionally, the potential of learning analytics to help learners reflect on their experiences is theory-led derived. The developments presented can be used to examine subject-specific differences between computer science and other subjects, as well as cultural differences between teachers around the world and differences between novices and more experienced teachers.

Keywords: Computer science education · Teacher training · Virtual reality · Classroom management · Learning analytics · Eye-tracking

1 Introduction

The VR classroom is an open-source simulation in which prospective teachers can practice various classroom situations [45]. One of the main learning objectives is the training and reflection of classroom management skills, which is too often neglected in teacher training [11]. Other learning objectives for the virtual reality (VR) teacher training include impulse-driven dialogue [24], the first few minutes of the lesson, or safety in specialist rooms, using chemistry as an example [46].

The simulation builds on various other research, for example on the topic of classroom management without the use of VR. One way to teach classroom management is by using recordings of real classroom events or extracurricular activi-

© The Author(s), under exclusive license to Springer Nature Switzerland AG 2024
M.-L. Bourguet et al. (Eds.): iLRN 2023, CCIS 1904, pp. 37–52, 2024.
https://doi.org/10.1007/978-3-031-47328-9_3

ties. Eisenmann et al. [11] compared five activities to address classroom management: analyzing movies, microteaching, creating an animated video, using observation protocols, and developing a personal management system. They promote effective learning environments, which fit the teaching philosophy and reflect on the teachers' management models [11]. Additionally, they show different starting points and the importance of interventions, without drawing a quantitative conclusion. The range of interventions does not end with the five activities by Eisenmann et al. [11], e.g. another activity is acting to learn about classroom management strategies.

Immersive learning in virtual reality can be an extension of these teaching methods, offering various advantages - for example, through the use of technology, scripts can be used that control the flow of the teaching scenes and make them repeatable; on the other hand, so-called coaches can control the virtual students and thus adapt the scene to the person in VR [45]. VR lets you experience the process instead of just observing it, and when training safety aspects, no real student is in danger. The potential of VR for education, in general, is manifold and many researchers have shown positive effects on learning, e.g. [2,27,32,51]. For some subject areas and purposes, like using VR in language classes, there are recommendations for the educational design [37]. Still, the potential, e.g. in integrating eye-tracking, has not yet been exhausted. Eye-tracking in VR allows researchers to gather data in a controlled environment [19], in which we know or can determine the position of the objects at any time. An introduction to the combination of eye-tracking and VR is done by [8].

It is at this intersection that this paper explores the limits and possibilities of immersive learning in combination with learning analytics in a concrete example. Within the example, eye-tracking can improve the application itself but also support reflection on what has been learned and offer real added value to learners. But not only the integration of learning analytics can improve the learning experience, but also the integration of special teaching situations is essential to be able to train subject-specific features. For this reason, we have extended an existing VR classroom application with two computer science (CS) rooms, primarily to prepare CS teachers for teaching, but also to prepare other teachers for the special features of media and technology-supported teaching.

Thus, the paper helps to answer two questions; first, is there a difference in classroom management between CS and other subjects, and if so, what makes the difference? This answers the question of whether there should be dedicated training rooms in VR. And the second question is, what is the added value of integrating learning analytics, especially eye tracking, to investigate the differences in classroom management in a structured and systematic way?

2   Background

In this section, we first go into special features of CS classrooms, excluding a discussion about the pros and cons of teacher training in VR, which the interested reader can find in various sources using various applications: [13,24,25,40,44,50]. An overview for the last years is given by Huang et al. [23].

Some arguments named in the mentioned related work are for example repeatable and rare situations, a protected training space, possible early usage, free for experimentation, and others. O'Connor and Wiepke et al. [31,45] provide suggestions for assessment and research in VR applications as well as VR teacher training. Yang et al. [50] conclude after testing their simulation with the in-service teachers that various types of interaction between the virtual student and the learner are important for a natural classroom environment. All in all the aforementioned research shows the potential and effectiveness of VR in teacher training, next step is to review if the extension for a computer room is a meaningful feature for such applications. To investigate this question, different search engines (google scholar, IEEE, ACM) were searched with different keywords: ('computer science' AND ('teacher' OR ('Computer classroom' OR 'Laboratory')) in connection with ('Classroom management' OR 'teaching strategies OR 'Challenges' OR 'Competency' OR 'Teaching Methods'...), but due to the large number and the ambiguity of keywords, the searches became more and more refined and were extended to the method of concentric circles. After the literature review of CS classroom management, we provide an overview of the current state of research for eye-tracking with teachers. In the last part, we present information about visualization and evaluation methods connected with the given use case. The only connection between both topics: Eye tracking in the classroom and teacher education in virtual reality, is [19], which is a poster contribution, whose paper shortly presents the motivation to systematically investigate eye movements in teachers using VR to illustrate the effects of professionalization.

2.1   The Computer Classroom

Is there a difference in classroom management and teaching strategies in computer rooms to other rooms and subjects, and if so, what makes the difference? To answer this question this section describes what typical topics are to be taught in computer rooms and discusses specific conditions and requirements for it. Labs and special rooms are also part of other STEM disciplines, but teaching in a computer room is different, not only because of the different equipment [18].

Using computers and technology in teaching needs strategies, not only for computing classes [7,38,43]. Another factor requiring strategies is the number of students in a computer classroom and the classroom organization [38]. Prospective CS teachers need to learn how to deal with heterogeneous prior knowledge among their learners (e.g., by choosing good teams [5,38]). Additionally, computing is well suited to interdisciplinary teaching, e.g. by integrating data science and mathematics [20], drama [28] or music, sports, and others (all [14]). Greifenstein et al. [16] connect specifically the subject of programming with many other subjects, this not only interdisciplinary but often also playful and cognitively reduced approach, can also be a chance for teachers.

Another aspect typically part of CS teacher training is gender disbalance, a topic that connects to classroom management and teaching methods [5,16].

Best practices and research in integrating women and underrepresented minorities show for example, that it's helpful to reduce competition and to include opportunities for exchange [5]. Greifenstein et al. [16] collected challenges and opportunities of teachers in the context of programming at primary schools. The results show, that we could prepare teachers in different dimensions, not only heterogeneity [16]. 30,5% of teachers in practice rank didactic considerations as one of the top challenges for teachers in training. The example they gave is to "master looking after each student and their individual programming issues" [16]. Another factor special for the computer classroom and in line with the challenge of didactic considerations is the software time factor [38]. One opportunity of computing classes is to teach project-based, hands-on and with a constructivist approach [18]. A lab-based teaching method changes the traditional teaching approaches. Yadav et al. [49] did a study on teachers' self-efficacy after a two-week professional development program for CS. They explained their mixed results on the self-efficacy that teachers may feel confident in the CS content, but lack confidence regarding pedagogical aspects [49]. Recently Dengel & Gehrlein [9] replicated a study to investigate teaching methods in CS comparing experienced with preservice teachers. They conclude that practical training in teaching methods should be integrated early in the (CS) teacher education [9]. This implication and the need for critical reflection on teaching methods strengthens the argument of why there should be an additional CS room in VR training. Margaritis & Magenheim [26] collected data about pedagogical content knowledge, where some data points reflect the subject-specific teaching concept, the specific teaching elements and the use of media. The measurement of these competencies for teaching CS, especially of some aspects of the pedagogical content knowledge is supported in virtual reality. As Yadav & Berges [48] suggest, teachers with low experience need to handle 20–25 students and strategies like code execution for debugging, might be challenging. Additionally, the feedback created with learning analytics could be integrated into preservice teachers' training.

Summarising all the factors and aspects presented above, it is clear that teaching in a computer lab requires special skills in classroom management and didactic methods, and these requirements affect not only CS teachers but also other teachers who use computers (or use technology) in their teaching. Therefore, adding CS and media to the existing simulations is a sensible step.

2.2 Eye-Tracking in Classroom Situations

Eye-tracking has already been used by several research groups to better understand the complexities of classrooms and determine important factors for good teaching.

Santini et al. [35] did research on the student's attention. They show that student attention is an important aspect of classroom learning and feedback for the teacher can be a supportive tool for teachers. The difficulty is that for live feedback and improvement of classroom management, a lot of technical equipment is needed to map the whole class.

One study that also uses eye-tracking glasses to track teacher attention is [42]. In this study, 15 to 20-minute-long videos of standardized small-group situations were used, with data analyzed using computer vision.

The result, attention maps, show the distribution of the teacher's focus but were not analyzed more deeply with dialectical questions. They found a relation between the teacher's focus and some facial attributes, e.g. gender. These findings could be verified using virtual simulations like the VR classroom. Wolff [47] has conducted studies comparable to Sumer's and presents them in her dissertation, in which sixty-seven teachers (35 experienced, 32 inexperienced) participated in a study. These teachers were presented with two different types of video recordings of classroom situations. The evaluation showed that novices spread their visual attention throughout the room and focused on issues of behavior and discipline, while experienced teachers focused more on the interesting parts of the classroom. A connection between didactic goals and a teacher's gaze can also be demonstrated by [17], who in addition to the gaze video recorded the teaching situation and evaluated an interview on the scaffolding events.

. Two larger-scale studies describe [22] in her dissertation, in which she studied 50 and 10 teachers. She could show, that experts' and novice teachers' eye movements differ and first classifications for the person- and subject-specific gaze patterns. The differences found in both young and experienced teachers and in gaze patterns offer research opportunities for the VR classroom, as they can be systematically investigated further there. A similar field experiment, but with a different research question was done in [29]. They analyzed the gaze proportions of teachers and were able to show that teachers from different cultures show different distributions of attention in relation to, for example, teaching materials versus learners. At the same time, they found that inexperienced teachers pay more attention to non-instructional regions. Experienced teachers have a stronger focus on students, regardless of cultural background. With their study of 40 teachers in 2 locations with 10 experts and novices per location, the researchers were able to show that the data recorded with real students and eye-tracking glasses reveal some differences. In an earlier investigation [30] found coherent results in the differences between expert teachers, for which the data suggest a more strategic use of gaze.

Connecting learning analytics with the background of teachers and classroom management is also explored by Dessus et. a.l [10]. Four teachers taught wearing eye-tracking equipment during an entire lesson. The results of the data analysis show for example the distribution of visual attention by determining for each student how often he/she was looked at by the teacher. A correlation between expertise and gazes was established in this study. The dashboards were used to be able to explore the data in more depth. The classroom situation was quantified using the classroom assessment scoring system.

In conclusion, the preliminary work shows that the recording of teachers' eye movements can offer interesting insights into classroom management and teacher training. Weaknesses of previous studies include the often very small numbers of participants and, and the difficulty in standardizing real classroom situations.

Both weaknesses can be addressed through the use of VR, because in VR we can pre-script situations and can overcome hurdles of real-life investigations, such as consultation with schools and privacy.

2.3   Evaluations and Visualisations for Gaze Data

Eye movement data can be analyzed in a variety of ways. Besides statistical quantities presented in diagrams, e.g. the bar plot showing the teacher's attention for each student in [10], a typical form of evaluation is the heat map. Stickler and Shi [41] describe the power of the visual nature of eye-tracking data: "but eye tracking has specific advantages over other visual data: (a) it adds a layer of information to a simple recording of screen interactions, and (b) it can cluster this information [...] showing cumulative attention focus points".

Specifically looking at visualization and data collection in VR, [8] shows that eye-tracking in VR offers interesting possibilities due to the ability to move relatively freely in an environment allowing a sense of presence while still providing a controllable environment. Another promising option might be representing the gaze points as spheres that mark the hitpoints of the gaze vectors, see [8].

Integrating learning analytics and eye-tracking with different visualizations could help learners reflect on their own behavior in class - which is especially helpful for teacher students in their professional development [17]. Seeing Visualisations of experts' gaze is also identified as helpful for learning in different contexts, so-called eye movement modeling examples (EMME) [1,3,12]. For the teacher training context, it still needs to be identified how to create effective EMME, but the effectiveness of EMME is a promising educational tool in the context of programming [12].

In summary, the integration of eye-tracking and various visualizations as an impetus for deeper reflection is a sensible step based on theory. In combination with other feedback from learning analytics, for example, the position data, it should be easier to analyze the own experience and to discuss it with the coach and fellow students.

3   Integrating Computing in the VR Classroom

The first part of this section briefly presents the simulation we build upon, then the results of the investigation of the two computer rooms, and some development details.

3.1   The VR Classroom Simulation

The VR classroom is an application that can be used for teaching various purposes, such as and especially classroom management. The avatars could act through a mixture of human control (the so-called coach) and specific programming depending on the intended use. There is a range of good behaviors (like writing), behaviors that are inattentive (like playing with own school material), and disruptive behaviors (like talking to the neighbor). The possibility to script certain behaviors of the virtual students beforehand allows for repeating the same teaching situations several times. An overview picture of some of the components is shown in Fig. 1. On the left is the user interface for the coach to control the virtual students, in the middle is the current view of the learner and on the right is the test person. The typical didactic setup of the VR classroom includes the coach, who operates the user interface (with an additional view of the learner) on a normal computer, and optionally other students, who can observe the learning opportunity on another screen. Didactically, the intention is to use the VR classroom as a supplement to other methods in teacher education. A simulation brings certain possibilities, e.g. repeatable, dangerous or rare situations, controllable content, a safe place to practice, and the systematic integration of learning analytics and feedback, but it can not replace a real teaching practice.

Fig. 1. Setup with three components of a VR classroom experience. Left: user interface for the coach. Middle: VR View (cutout). Right: Learner.

Certain classroom configurations can also be varied, so the appearance and the table arrangement can be adapted (see [45]). For learners, teachers, and researchers, this scenario offers the advantages already mentioned. The classroom offers the chance to try out teaching methods and to be able to repeat teaching situations, while the coach benefits from the controllable settings and the situations that specifically match the current learning objective. The use of VR allows the transfer of the real-life experiments described in the previous section to a more controlled experimental environment to push along the results and explore the differences between inexperienced and experienced teachers, cultural factors, and others in more depth.

3.2   A Room for Computer Science

The room setup was the first decision that had to be made in developing the computer lab. For this, we interviewed several CS teachers and found a thin theoretical foundation for the different classroom setups. Signorelli et al. propose a "campfire-style computer room" [39], which was not used due to the structural conditions of most German schools. Instead, we first created the structure using two prototypical templates, one of them showing the current shift to partially mobile devices, as shown in Fig. 2.

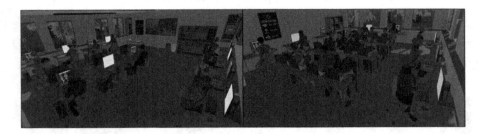

Fig. 2. Left: Computer Science Room with Desktop PCs. Right: Computer Science Room with a Mix of Mobile and Desktop PCs.

The next step was to create the room-specific animations - students in a computer room need to operate the computer. The first attempt with Inverse Kinematics (IK) in Unity gave good results, but could not be transferred easily to other virtual students because you would have had to set the targets (to be followed in IK) for each student. Rebuilt animations in Blender were not transferred to Unity without problems, probably due to scaling issues. We ended up using animations from Mixamo, which we customized for a typing animation. We used targets in the keyboards, which are followed by the fingers using IK.

In contrast to other rooms, it is more difficult to place name tags in computer rooms (compare Fig. 1 and 2). The solution is an automatically generated seating plan, see Fig. 3.

In order to have as many options as possible for teacher training, the screen contents of the virtual PCs can be added and manipulated by coaches even without a technical background by including small videos and screen captures. This way, the screen contents of the virtual students are not static and could display content in line with the objectives. Furthermore, built-in projectors allow one to personalize the learning scenario. The blackboard, which can also be replaced with a whiteboard, can be used by learners for their VR lessons.

4   Integrating Eye-Tracking in the VR Classroom

In this section, we present the results of integrating eye-tracking and the first visualizations. The first step to reach this goal is to integrate eye-tracking in the

Fig. 3. Seating plan in first person view (in a room variant with fewer computers).

VR classroom, the second is to include the evaluation methods and to create the data visualization. The VR classroom is developed for different VR Headsets; for this extension, we used the HTC Vive Pro Eye, which is used with a Schenker Compact 15 notebook with an Intel Core i7-8750H CPU, 64 GB RAM, NVIDIA GeForce RTX 2070, and Windows 10 Education 64-bit. The development is done in Unity with Microsoft Visual Studio 2019 for C# code using the HTC SRanipal SDK (for gaze data). The project is open available[1].

The following design decisions were made during the development of the data visualizations. Only data (fixations) related to the virtual students are analyzed, i.e. for the heatmap visualization, other objects like chairs, tables, the blackboard, and the whiteboard are neglected. More possibilities of eye tracking, like regions of interest, and features of gaze data, are discussed in various sources [10, 21, 41]. They also present more details on the computation of this data, e.g. the algorithmic idea of how to calculate intersections between gaze and objects [10, 21]. By concentrating on fixations on students, the focus on reflection and the self or co-regulated learning process should be directed to the part that is needed for the learning goal to analyze the own attention distribution between the virtual students. Two versions of a heatmap have been created. The first version shows semi-colored students; see left Fig. 4. In the second version, which was implemented based on feedback, the coloring is a lot easier to recognize, but the features of the virtual students are lost. Recognizing who has not been looked at is intuitive in the second representation. Testing of both variants is planned for the summer term of 2023.

In addition to the easily accessible heatmap visualizations, there are other ways to use the gaze data. For example, the desire was expressed to be able to analyze the gaze data in relation to the behavior of the students. For this purpose, the gaze data were connected with the log data of the student behavior in a diagram. In Fig. 5 it can be seen that the frequency of viewing is not necessarily related to the amount of disruptive behavior. For example, Steffi, a

---

[1] https://gitup.uni-potsdam.de/mm_vr/vr-klassenzimmer, accessed 27.04.23.

student who was not particularly disruptive, was looked at more frequently than Moritz, a student who spent a long time in the various behaviors classified as disruptive, like throwing paper balls or talking to the neighbor. The data for Fig. 5 visualization were collected with the task of supervising and keeping the virtual students quiet during a class assignment. The data for the other two visualizations Fig. 4 were collected without a specific task, during this recording, the exclamation of a test subject who has known the VR classroom for some time occurred: "I never saw this student", which led to interesting ideas presented in the future research part. The participants were CS students who already have experience with VR and have some background on the topic of didactics and teaching, e.g., by being tutors in university courses, teaching school students in the university's student laboratory, or having had other teaching experience. A tutorial helps to reduce the novelty effect or some kind of overload because the participants had no time to adjust to the situation. All presented visualizations are taken -as the first purpose- in the seminar or course to discuss the results live with the students and reinforce reflection occasions.

Fig. 4. Highlighted virtual students according to the teacher's gaze, second version. The colours are in the spectrum blue/green (a little looked at) to red (a lot looked at). Virtual students who have not been looked at are not coloured. (Color figure online)

5   Future Work, Discussion, and Limitations

Eye-tracking, in addition to the possibilities of integrating learning analytics and improving feedback and reflections, also provides the opportunity to make interaction in the VR classroom even more natural. For example, the method presented by Schweigert et al. could improve non-verbal communication between virtual students and the learner [36]. The technique builds on the gaze creating a ray cast to identify an object, while a pointing gesture leads to a selection. In the case of the VR classroom, students selected in this way could automatically respond to the gesture and, depending on the context, could respond automatically or be highlighted for the coach to select a response.

Another opportunity that integrating eye-tracking offers, in addition to further supporting the coach, is the gradual automation of virtual students. They

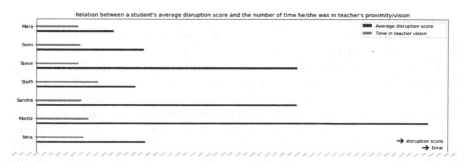

Fig. 5. Connection between duration of disruptive behavior (blue - lower bar) and the total amount of time they were looked at by the teacher (green - upper bar). Subsequently, the x-Axis presents the average disturbance level and the accumulated time. Data only from a single test person. (Color figure online)

can automatically stop (or reduce) disturbing when the teacher looks at them. The first steps towards automation have already been taken so that the VR classroom can also be used for self-regulated learning in the future [45]. The heatmap presented in this paper is -due to first informal evaluations- an intuitive tool to stimulate and support reflection on the experience alone, with the coach, or with peers. The pilot also raised the question of what effect it would have to replace the heat map with a transparency map so that virtual students who were never fixated or fixated too briefly would disappear from the class. Would such a type of visualization have an impact on learner acceptance? Could it trigger feelings of guilt/increase the learning effect? Learning analytics focusing on the aspect of visual attention should be investigated further.

Another variable that is not currently used but can further stimulate reflection on instructional design and classroom management is "time to the first fixation," a metric that, among others, can improve the analysis of visual attention in VR [6]. Rahman et al. [34] compared different techniques for the visualization of gaze data, they did not find statistically significant differences in performance between the techniques. However, the subjective rating of the 26 subjects, who were asked to monitor the attention of learners in the role of assistant teachers, showed a clearly favored technique: gaze trails. This technique, in which data are aggregated with 3-second windows and displayed as a moving particle beam, was favored by the subjects. This technique could be very useful for more detailed viewing of individual snapshots in the VR classroom while probably not suitable for looking at the collected data of a longer session.

A side effect that early exposure of student teachers to technology could have is that they gain greater confidence in using media. So that challenges like those found by Pirker et al. [33] can be reduced in the future. They found in a study that teachers in the STEM field would use VR, but the technology is not yet suitable for everyday school life because they expect long setup times [33]. Grassinger et al. [15] have extended the question of digital media-related competencies to students of all disciplines and proposed a process to support learning. One support structure could be the VR classroom fulfilling ideas they had, e.g. blended learning and learning analytics.

This work has potential limitations. A limiting factor for the initial results shown here is that these are not solely undergraduate student teachers. Evaluation and comparison are in the process. However, student teachers who were asked about the effect of the visualizations showed interest that reduced concerns about data generation. Moreover, prior research studies that are relevant to special features of teaching in computer rooms are very limited. Bringing together different perspectives it's possible to argue for the special features of teaching CS, but this is hard to research. An approximation is brought by competency models for CS teachers such as the competency model for teaching CS by Bender et al. [4] and recent CS-associated models, like the framework for digital media-related competencies [15]. In conclusion, our work is based on the theoretically justified assumption that VR can also be helpful for the specifics of CS teaching and in the media didactic training of teachers. A detailed investigation with comparison groups, e.g. between different subjects, expertise levels or cultures (like done by McIntyre et al. [29]), or other study designs is still open.

6   Conclusion

This paper presents why VR training is suitable for CS teacher students and which particular aspects of teaching can be addressed in a simulation and the associated lecture/seminar, see Sects. 2.1 and 3.2. Additionally, a new theory-based visualization technique and the possibilities of extending VR with eye-tracking were presented. A distinctive feature of this work is that the visualizations should not only be used by researchers or teachers alone but also actively support the self and co-regulated learning process. The learning experience in the computer room could not only be used to train CS teachers but also others using technology in their classes. The learning analytics feedback and the experiences are to be evaluated by the learners (together with the teachers/coaches or peers) and stimulate reflection on the own classroom management and the integration of all students in the CS room. Initial informal test runs with the learning analytics visualizations during iterative development indicate that teachers and students are interested in the visualizations, an approach that is also suitable for teaching digital media-related competencies [15]. The discussion presents different perspectives on technical implementation, opportunities for future research, and limitations of the current implementation, and discusses the goals enabled by VR teacher training. The next steps are to use the visualizations with learners in teaching situations, to sharpen the CS-specific aspects in classroom management, and to evaluate if the visualizations promote self- and co-regulated learning.

References

1. Alemdag, E., Cagiltay, K.: A systematic review of eye tracking research on multimedia learning. Comput. Educ. **125**, 413–428 (2018)
2. Asad, M., Naz, A., Churi, P., Tahanzadeh, M.: Virtual reality as pedagogical tool to enhance experiential learning: a systematic literature review. Educ. Res. Int. **2021**, 1–17 (2021). https://doi.org/10.1155/2021/7061623
3. Bednarik, R., Schulte, C., Budde, L., Heinemann, B., Vrzakova, H.: Eye-movement modeling examples in source code comprehension: a classroom study. In: Proceedings of the 18th Koli Calling International Conference on Computing Education Research, pp. 2:1–2:8. Koli Calling 2018, ACM, New York, NY, USA (2018). https://doi.org/10.1145/3279720.3279722
4. Bender, E., et al.: Towards a competency model for teaching computer science. Peabody J. Educ. **90**(4), 519–532 (2015). https://doi.org/10.1080/0161956X.2015.1068082
5. Buhnova, B., Happe, L.: Girl-friendly computer science classroom: Czechitas experience report. In: Muccini, H., et al. (eds.) ECSA 2020. CCIS, vol. 1269, pp. 125–137. Springer, Cham (2020). https://doi.org/10.1007/978-3-030-59155-7_10
6. Cardoso da Silva, A., Sierra-Franco, C., Silva-Calpa, G., Carvalho, F., Raposo, A.: Eye-tracking data analysis for visual exploration assessment and decision making interpretation in virtual reality environments. In: 22nd Symposium on Virtual and Augmented Reality (SVR), pp. 39–46 (2020). https://doi.org/10.1109/SVR51698.2020.00022
7. Clark-Wilson, A., Robutti, O., Thomas, M.: Teaching with digital technology. ZDM **52**(7), 1223–1242 (2020). https://doi.org/10.1007/s11858-020-01196-0
8. Clay, V., König, P., Koenig, S.: Eye tracking in virtual reality. J. Eye Mov. Res. **12**(1) (2019). https://doi.org/10.16910/jemr.12.1.3
9. Dengel, A., Gehrlein, R.: Comparing teachers' and preservice teachers' opinions on teaching methods in computer science education. In: Proceedings of the 17th WiPSCE, pp. 1–4. Association for Computing Machinery, New York, NY, USA (2022)
10. Dessus, P., Cosnefroy, O., Luengo, V.: "Keep your eyes on 'em all!": a mobile eye-tracking analysis of teachers' sensitivity to students. In: Verbert, K., Sharples, M., Klobučar, T. (eds.) EC-TEL 2016. LNCS, vol. 9891, pp. 72–84. Springer, Cham (2016). https://doi.org/10.1007/978-3-319-45153-4_6
11. Eisenman, G., Edwards, S., Cushman, C.A.: Bringing reality to classroom management in teacher education. Prof. Educ. **39**(1) (2015)
12. Emhardt, S., Jarodzka, H., Brand-Gruwel, S., Drumm, C., van Gog, T.: Introducing eye movement modeling examples for programming education and the role of teacher's didactic guidance. In: ACM Symposium on Eye Tracking Research and Applications, pp. 1–4. ETRA 2020 Short Papers, Association for Computing Machinery, New York, NY, USA (2020). https://doi.org/10.1145/3379156.3391978
13. Fukuda, M., Huang, H.H., Nishida, T.: Investigation of class atmosphere cognition in a VR classroom. In: Proceedings of the 6th International Conference on Human-Agent Interaction, pp. 374–376. HAI 2018, Association for Computing Machinery (2018). https://doi.org/10.1145/3284432.3287191
14. Goldschmidt, D., MacDonald, I., O'Rourke, J., Milonovich, B.: An interdisciplinary approach to injecting computer science into the K-12 classroom. J. Comput. Sci. Coll. **26**(6), 78–85 (2011)

15. Grassinger, R., et al.: Fostering digital media-realted competences of student teachers. SN Comput. Sci. **3**(4), 258 (2022). https://doi.org/10.1007/s42979-022-01135-8
16. Greifenstein, L., Graßl, I., Fraser, G.: Challenging but full of opportunities: teachers' perspectives on programming in primary schools. In: 21st Koli Calling International Conference on Computing Education Research, pp. 1–10. Koli Calling 2021, Association for Computing Machinery (2021). https://doi.org/10.1145/3488042.3488048
17. Haataja, E., Garcia Moreno-Esteva, E., Salonen, V., Laine, A., Toivanen, M., Hannula, M.S.: Teacher's visual attention when scaffolding collaborative mathematical problem solving. Teach. Teach. Educ. **86**, 102877 (2019). https://doi.org/10.1016/j.tate.2019.102877
18. Hazzan, O., Ragonis, N., Lapidot, T.: Lab-based teaching. In: Guide to Teaching Computer Science, pp. 221–249. Springer, Cham (2020). https://doi.org/10.1007/978-3-030-39360-1_11
19. Heinemann, B., Hennig, D., Ismail, A., Schroeder, U.: Das VR Klassenzimmer als Experimentallabor für die systematische Erforschung der Blickbewegungen von Lehrkräften. In: 20. Fachtagung Bildungstechnologien (DELFI). Gesellschaft für Informatik e.V., Bonn (2022)
20. Heinemann, B., et al.: Drafting a data science curriculum for secondary schools. In: Proceedings of the 18th Koli Calling International Conference on Computing Education Research, pp. 17:1–17:5. Koli Calling 2018, ACM (2018). https://doi.org/10.1145/3279720.3279737
21. Holmqvist, K., Nystrom, M., Andersson, R., Dewhurst, R., Jarodzka, H., Weijer, J.: Eye Tracking: A Comprehensive Guide to Methods and Measures. 1 edn. Oxford University Press, Oxford (2012)
22. Huang, Y.: Learning from teacher's eye movement: expertise, subject matter and video modeling. Ph.D. thesis, University of Michigan, Michigan (2018)
23. Huang, Y., Richter, E., Kleickmann, T., Richter, D.: Virtual reality in teacher education from 2010 to 2020: a review of program implementation, intended outcomes, and effectiveness measures. In: Scheiter, K., Gogolin, I. (eds.) Edition ZfE [Journal of Educational Science Edition]. Bildung für eine digitale Zukunft [Education for a Digital Future], vol. 15, pp. 399–441. Springer, Wiebsaden (2023). https://doi.org/10.1007/978-3-658-37895-0_16
24. Huang, Y., Richter, E., Kleickmann, T., Wiepke, A., Richter, D.: Classroom complexity affects student teachers' behavior in a VR classroom. Comput. Educ. **163**, 104100 (2021). https://doi.org/10.1016/j.compedu.2020.104100
25. Latoschik, M.E., Lugrin, J.L., Habel, M., Roth, D., Seufert, C., Grafe, S.: Breaking bad behavior: immersive training of class room management. In: Proceedings of the 22Nd ACM Conference on Virtual Reality Software and Technology, pp. 317–318. VRST 2016, ACM, New York, NY, USA (2016). https://doi.org/10.1145/2993369.2996308
26. Margaritis, M., Magenheim, J.: Pedagogical content knowledge a comparative study between CS pre-service teachers and experienced teachers. In: 2015 IEEE Global Engineering Education Conference (EDUCON), pp. 102–111 (2015). https://doi.org/10.1109/EDUCON.2015.7095958
27. Martín-Gutiérrez, J., Mora, C.E., Añorbe-Díaz, B., González-Marrero, A.: Virtual technologies trends in education. EURASIA J. Math. Sci. Technol. Educ. **13**(2), 469–486 (2017). https://doi.org/10.12973/eurasia.2017.00626a
28. McGuffee, J.W.: Drama in the computer science classroom. J. Comput. Sci. Coll. **19**(4), 292–298 (2004)

29. McIntyre, N.A., Jarodzka, H., Klassen, R.M.: Capturing teacher priorities: using real-world eye-tracking to investigate expert teacher priorities across two cultures. Learn. Instr. **60**, 215–224 (2019). https://doi.org/10.1016/j.learninstruc.2017.12.003

30. McIntyre, N.A., Mainhard, M.T., Klassen, R.M.: Are you looking to teach? Learn. Instr. **49**, 41–53 (2017). https://doi.org/10.1016/j.learninstruc.2016.12.005

31. O'Connor, E.: Virtual reality: bringing education to life. In: Bradley, E. (ed.) Games and Simulations in Teacher Education. AGL, pp. 155–167. Springer, Cham (2020). https://doi.org/10.1007/978-3-030-44526-3_11

32. Papanastasiou, G., Drigas, A., Skianis, C., Lytras, M., Papanastasiou, E.: Virtual and augmented reality effects on K-12, higher and tertiary education students' twenty-first century skills. Virtual Reality **23**(4), 425–436 (2019). https://doi.org/10.1007/s10055-018-0363-2

33. Pirker, J., Holly, M., Almer, H., Gütl, C.: Virtual reality STEM education from a teacher's perspective. In: Proceedings from the Fifth Immersive Learning Research Network Conference (iLRN). Verlag der Technischen Universität Graz, London (2019). https://doi.org/10.3217/978-3-85125-657-4-14

34. Rahman, Y., Asish, S.M., Fisher, N.P., Bruce, E.C., Kulshreshth, A.K., Borst, C.W.: Exploring eye gaze visualization techniques for identifying distracted students in educational VR. In: IEEE Conference on Virtual Reality and 3D User Interfaces (VR), pp. 868–877 (2020). https://doi.org/10.1109/VR46266.2020.00009

35. Santini, T., et al.: Automatic mapping of remote crowd gaze to stimuli in the classroom. In: Eye Tracking Enhanced Learning (ETEL2017), p. 9 (2017)

36. Schweigert, R., Schwind, V., Mayer, S.: EyePointing: a gaze-based selection technique. In: Proceedings of Mensch Und Computer 2019, pp. 719–723. MuC 2019, Association for Computing Machinery, New York, NY, USA (2019). https://doi.org/10.1145/3340764.3344897

37. Scrivner, O., Madewell, J., Buckley, C., Perez, N.: Best practices in the use of augmented and virtual reality technologies for SLA: design, implementation, and feedback. In: Carrió-Pastor, M.L. (ed.) Teaching Language and Teaching Literature in Virtual Environments, pp. 55–72. Springer, Singapore (2019). https://doi.org/10.1007/978-981-13-1358-5_4

38. Sharp, V.F.: Computer Education for Teachers: Integrating Technology into Classroom Teaching, 6th edn. Wiley, Hoboken (2009)

39. Signorelli, V., Ekrem, E., Overin, L., Lim, C., Muirhead, N., Demetriou, A.: Visualising transformative spaces for education: a focus on lecture halls, computer rooms and studios. JUICE: J. Useful Invest. Creative Educ. **3** (2020)

40. Stavroulia, K.E., Baka, E., Lanitis, A., Magnenat-Thalmann, N.: Designing a virtual environment for teacher training: enhancing presence and empathy. In: Proceedings of Computer Graphics International 2018, pp. 273–282. ACM, New York, USA (2018). https://doi.org/10.1145/3208159.3208177

41. Stickler, U., Shi, L.: Eyetracking methodology in SCMC. ReCALL **29**(2), 160–177 (2017). https://doi.org/10.1017/S0958344017000040

42. Sümer, Ö., et al.: Teachers' perception in the classroom. In: Proceedings of the IEEE Conference on Computer Vision and Pattern Recognition (CVPR) Workshops (2018)

43. Terzieva, V., Paunova-Hubenova, E., Dimitrov, S., Boneva, Y.: ICT in STEM education in Bulgaria. In: Auer, M.E., Tsiatsos, T. (eds.) ICL 2018. AISC, vol. 916, pp. 801–812. Springer, Cham (2020). https://doi.org/10.1007/978-3-030-11932-4_74

44. Vince Garland, K., Garland, D.: TeachLivE^{TM} and teach well: simulations in teacher education. In: Bradley, E. (ed.) Games and Simulations in Teacher Education. AGL, pp. 183–195. Springer, Cham (2020). https://doi.org/10.1007/978-3-030-44526-3_13

45. Wiepke, A., Heinemann, B., Lucke, U., Schroeder, U.: Jenseits des eigenen Klassenzimmers: Perspektiven & Weiterentwicklungen des VR-Classrooms. Gesellschaft für Informatik e.V. (2021). Accessed 25 Aug 2021. ISSN: 1617–5468

46. Wiepke, A., Hildebrandt, C., Hagen, N., Krüger, A.S., Lucke, U., Banerji, A.: Das VR-Labor-Klassenzimmer zur Professionalisierung von Lehramtsstudierenden der Chemie. In: 20. Fachtagung Bildungstechnologien (DELFI) (2022). https://doi.org/10.18420/delfi2022-030. iSBN: 9783885797166 Publisher: Gesellschaft für Informatik e.V

47. Wolff, C.E.: Revisiting 'withitness': differences in teachers' representations, perceptions, and interpretations of classroom management. Ph.D. thesis, Open University of the Netherlands, Heerlen (2016)

48. Yadav, A., Berges, M.: Computer science pedagogical content knowledge: characterizing teacher performance. ACM Trans. Comput. Educ. **19**(3), 1–24 (2019). https://doi.org/10.1145/3303770

49. Yadav, A., Lishinski, A., Sands, P.: Self-efficacy profiles for computer science teachers. In: Proceedings of the 52nd ACM Technical Symposium on Computer Science Education, pp. 302–308. SIGCSE 2021, Association for Computing Machinery, New York, NY, USA (2021). https://doi.org/10.1145/3408877.3432441

50. Yang, E., Kim, C., Ryu, J.: Work-in-progress-effects of interactive conversation on in-service teacher experience in classroom simulation for teacher training. In: 7th International Conference of the Immersive Learning Research Network (iLRN), pp. 1–3 (2021). https://doi.org/10.23919/iLRN52045.2021.9459359

51. Zender, R., Knoth, A.H., Fischer, M.H., Lucke, U.: Potentials of virtual reality as an instrument for research and education. i-com **18**(1), 3–15 (2019). https://doi.org/10.1515/icom-2018-0042

Immersive Learning Research from the Perspective of Its Researchers and Practitioners: Questionnaire Validation and Early Results from a Survey on a Conceptual Framework for the Field

Leonel Morgado[1,6(✉)] [iD], Dennis Beck[2] [iD], Christian Gütl[3] [iD], Teresa Oliveira[1,7] [iD], and Jonathon Richter[4,5] [iD]

[1] Universidade Aberta, Coimbra, Lisbon, Portugal
Leonel.Morgado@uab.pt
[2] University of Arkansas, Fayetteville, AR, USA
[3] Graz University of Technology, Graz, Austria
[4] Immersive Learning Research Network, Missoula, MT, USA
[5] University of Montana, Missoula, MT, USA
[6] INESC TEC, Porto, Portugal
[7] CEAUL, Lisbon, Portugal

Abstract. Immersive learning research is a field of study that emphasizes diversity of scholarship and subject areas. This diversity presents a challenge for understanding the breadth and depth of the field of immersive learning, a challenge that led to the Immersive Learning Research Network's call for the community of immersive learning researchers to develop a conceptual framework supporting a common understanding of this diverse field - The Immersive Learning Knowledge Tree. However, this structure has not had its underlying assumptions validated by the larger, diverse community of immersive learning researchers and practitioners. Thus, we developed, validated, and disseminated across associations of the field a questionnaire for analyzing the assumptions, structure, and relevance of the Knowledge Tree proposal. Early results point towards overwhelming agreement from the community on the premise that the field of immersive learning research is muddled/fragmented, the current knowledge partially disjointed, specifically among different disciplines (Q3), due to its interdisciplinary nature. There are also strong indications supporting the premise that researchers active in the field of immersive learning research desire to combine their efforts with others.

Keywords: Survey · Questionnaire · Immersive Learning · Knowledge Tree · iLRN

1 Introduction

The immersive learning research field of study emphasizes diversity of scholarship. Researchers hail from traditional academics and from private industry; they also originate from a veritable cornucopia of subject areas, including (but not limited to): Educational

M.-L. Bourguet et al. (Eds.): iLRN 2023, CCIS 1904, pp. 53–69, 2024.
https://doi.org/10.1007/978-3-031-47328-9_4

technology, computer science, game design, learning sciences, psychology, biomedical sciences, narrative studies, arts, design, media studies, communication sciences, and the multitude of disciplinary and occupational content areas wherein immersive learning and training may be relevant. Each researcher approaches their study of immersive learning with a unique combination of knowledge development, assumptions, theories, practices, and methodological means. This diversity is, indeed, a strength of the field as the overall spectrum of research is less likely to find itself dwelling on a small number of definitions or lenses for interpreting data. However, it may be likewise a weakness, as it presents a challenge for understanding the breadth and depth of the field of immersive learning. Beyond field-specific preferences for how to do qualitative and quantitative research, differences include distinct definitions of "immersion", "learning", and "environment", or varying methods in accomplishing literature reviews and meta-analyses. This has been discussed in the Immersive Learning Research Network (iLRN) community for several years, most notably by Jonathon Richter in his paper about the Immersive Learning Quadrivium [1]. Building on this, iLRN launched a call for the community of immersive learning researchers for the development of a conceptual framework supporting a common understanding of this diverse field - The Immersive Learning Knowledge Tree initiative [2].

The Immersive Learning Knowledge Tree (ILKT) conceptual framework is based on a few premises its proponents consider essential (ibid.). First, the premise of the importance of developing a common language. Confusion and frustration ensue if the individuals in a room only speak and write different languages. Unfortunately, similar conditions often exist when groups of immersive learning researchers meet at conferences or regional meetings, because they are speaking different "languages", as shown in a recent analysis of the thin theoretical grounding of recent surveys in the field [3]. Second, the premise of the importance of not only using similar terminology as other researchers, but also having a deep understanding of how the methods researchers utilize in their own research are similar or different from those used by others. Some similar methodologies used in the field go by completely different names, while others use similar names but vary widely in their specifics of application. The third and final premise of the ILKT conceptual framework is the importance of advancing the use of common theoretical approaches and models. The stated rationale for this is to enable researchers to do better work by building their research upon the work of others and not simply attempting to do the same research that has already been accomplished by others with whom they are not familiar. The ILKT proposal contends that the current state of adoption of these three premises in the field of immersive learning is "muddled, the current knowledge partially disjointed, specifically among different disciplines" [2].

The ILKT's several premises may or may not be consensual among the community of immersive learning researchers and practitioners. We sought to analyze their validity, conducting a questionnaire-based survey of the community. This paper presents that questionnaire's validation and early survey outcomes. It is structured as follows: background and related work, questionnaire development and validation, application of the questionnaire, analysis of early results, and conclusions regarding the validation of the ILKT conceptual framework.

2 Background and Related Work

2.1 The Concept of Immersive Learning

The field of immersive learning is faced with a paradox of terminology differences. It is understood as the process of employing immersion as "a theoretical lens to analyze, interpret, and shape" the context of learning and teaching [3]. However, the clarity of that depends on how researchers interpret "immersion" as a theoretical lens. The terms "immersion" and "immersive" are used so widely that literature surveys often do not cite a definition or employ very distinct meanings (ibid.). Technology-based researchers often consider Murray's intuitive "sensation of being surrounded by a completely other reality" [4], Slater's perspective of immersion as a quality of technology [5] or Witmer & Singer's view of immersion as a subjective user experience [6]. Researchers in other fields, such as psychology, literature studies, the arts, etc., view it from perspectives of narrative, engagement, and psychological flow [7]. An example of this is Agrawal et al.'s proposal p. 6 [8] of an objective, interdisciplinary definition of immersion from the literature: "a phenomenon experienced by an individual when (…) in a state of deep mental involvement in which (…) cognitive processes (…) cause a shift in (…) attentional state such that one may experience disassociation from the awareness of the physical world." A second example would be Nilsson et al.'s framework of breaking down the perspective into three aspects: system, narrative, and challenge [7]. Such a framework enables clear interpretation of an immersive learning experience as the phenomenon emerging from the conceptual interconnection of system, narrative, and challenge aspects of immersion. System immersion reflects Slater's or Murray's perspective, Narrative immersion reflects mental absorption with a story and its characters, and Challenge immersion reflects mental absorption dealing with agency: tasks, problems, activities. Unfortunately, the use of this or other broader, interdisciplinary conceptual tools is not commonplace. Consequently, literature reviews are hard to compare/contrast, and outcomes research is prey to misunderstandings, or other ontological inconsistencies: a fragmentation of the field of immersive learning research, isolated and blunted in impact.

2.2 The Immersive Learning Knowledge Tree

The Immersive Learning Knowledge Tree conceptual framework (ILKT) is an iLRN initiative endorsed by the IEEE Education Society Technical Committee on Immersive Learning Environments (TC-ILE). It was launched as an appeal to the community of immersive learning researchers and practitioners to achieve better conceptual under-standing and developed solid bases for cooperation and engagement. To communicate intuitively, iLRN adopted the metaphor of a tree, grounded in soil by its roots, growing into leaves and populated by birds [2]. The roots of the ILKT are common definitions, methods, and research instruments. Just as roots hold the soil together and protect from erosion, so also do common definitions, methods, and instruments provide stability to the "soil", composed of elements such as ontologies, taxonomies, and conceptual data models. Together, the roots and the soil set the stage for the growth of the trunk of the tree: the structural knowledge of the field of immersive learning. This comprises things like scoping reviews and systematic literature reviews; classified collections of facts, like expert input from the field of immersive learning (e.g., the iLRN State of XR and Immersive Learning Report) and evidence repositories; and the awareness of the networked knowledge of the community researching and applying immersive learning, provided by Scientometrics and other network mapping instruments.

The structural knowledge trunk sprouts initiatives and knowledge towards outcomes. These are branches sprouting from the trunk: fields of inquiry and intertwined research priorities/agendas. The outcomes shooting from the branches are leaves, such as exemplars (e.g., practitioner accounts, usage cases), instruments (e.g., templates for practice and research), and tools. Birds represent the community of immersive learning researchers and practitioners, employing these leaves in their work, creating, combining efforts, e.g., "crowdsourcing efforts like tagging and reporting" [2].

3   Validation of the ILKT Conceptual Framework

3.1   Research Questions and Questionnaire Development

While the informed argument for the ILKT is compelling [2] it lacks any confirmation of whether the community of immersive learning researchers and practitioners acknowledges its assumptions. Thus, our analysis of those assumptions is targeting this community. Also, we seek to evaluate the structure of the framework itself, determining the community's views on the relevance of its elements. Finally, we seek to identify other aspects of the status of the field which may be relevant for the ILKT framework.

From the above rationale, our research questions were as follows:

RQ1. How do the assumptions of the ILKT align with the community of immersive learning researchers and practitioners?
RQ2. What are the community of immersive learning researchers and practitioners' views on the structure of the ILKT's framework and its elements?
RQ3. What other aspects of the field of immersive learning are relevant for the ILKT framework?

We are addressing these RQs via a survey, based on a questionnaire. To develop the questionnaire, we employed empirical data [9], by analyzing the exact phrasings of the arguments published in the seminal ILKT paper [2], and identifying their assumptions. Each assumption was rendered as a statement following the phrasing published in that paper. For each assumption we created a matching question. When assumptions were presented as fact, we asked for agreement positioning (Strongly Disagree-Strongly Agree) using 5-point Likert scales, e.g. "The field of 'immersive learning research' is muddled/fragmented due to its interdisciplinary nature." When assumptions employed intensity, we asked for viewpoints on level. For instance, "How strong do you find the theoretical grounding for the field of immersive learning research?" from "Very Weak" to "Very Strong". All these questions were followed by open-ended question items for respondents to explain their viewpoints, to attain better qualification of the evaluations. The final items in the assumptions were the actual phrasing of the ILKT proposal, presented as an idea, questioning its relevance, and asking for viewpoint explanation: "A conceptual framework for building a common and agreed understanding as well as for mapping knowledge, tools and services in the field of immersive learning research, combining both scholarly and practical knowledge."

To evaluate the ILKT structure, we also extracted from its paper the phrasing of the ILKT stated components, organized as categories, which were also as phrased in the paper itself ("research sources", "disciplinary and interdisciplinary areas and processes", "practical knowledge sources", "community participation and application"). For each component in each category, we created a matching question, and included an open-ended question item in each category for respondents to suggest other relevant components.

Finally, to minimize agreement bias, we did not provide the respondents with a link to the ILKT paper, nor did we employ either the term "Knowledge Tree" or its metaphors (roots, soil, trunk, branches, leaves, birds). Instead, only the actual assumptions and components were employed in the questions.

3.2 Questionnaire Validation

The tentative questionnaire was subjected to expert review [9], for which we sought out experts in immersive learning. We did this in two iterative cycles. In iteration 1, we sent the questionnaire to the boards of the two immersive learning research and practice organizations associated with the ILKT proposal: IEEE TC-ILE and iLRN, comprising a total of 14 different experts (paper authors not included). We received qualitative feedback via email as well as trial responses from six experts.

Feedback centered around issues related to navigation, data privacy, grammar, and interpretation of questions. Navigational feedback recommended adding a back button on each page of the survey, not requiring participants to answer all questions on a page to move to the next survey page, adding a progress bar, and flow between questions and sections. Data privacy feedback suggested including further statements on how the data would/would not be used and disposed of. Interpretation-related recommendations focused on proper grammar, the meaning of specific terminology, and cases where certain items should be split into multiple questions for clarity.

Trial responses were analyzed for consistency between Likert scale questions and the associated open text explanations. Some cases were identified where the open text responses revealed that the respondents had interpreted the question differently from its intent, thus revealing ambiguity or equivocal aspects that were corrected. One example was the phrasing "struggle to combine their efforts with others". This phrasing had trial responses on the Likert scale disagreeing with the existence of "struggle to combine", explained in the open text responses that researchers wanted to combine efforts, but had difficulty comparing them due to differences in terminology or conceptual models. This led us to divide the question into two, addressing both aspects: one inquiring about the desire to cooperate with others, and the original one changing in phrasing into "struggle to compare/contrast efforts with others".

During iteration 2 we again sent the questionnaire to the 8 experts from the TC-ILE and iLRN boards who had not replied with feedback during the first iteration, plus an author of the original ILKT proposal who is not a member of either board. We received 1 qualitative feedback via email and trial responses from 6 experts. Mostly, responses were consistent between Likert scale and open text questions, pointing towards adequacy of the survey instrument. There was a single conceptual misunderstanding: an incorrect interpretation of theoretical grounding as meaning, "grounded in data." As a result, we rephrased it to read, "theoretical background". The remaining feedback was a clarification for the informed consent and proposed additions to options of the ILKT framework elements. These were: clarifying "classified collections of facts" as "classified collections of facts and/or research results"; adding "review of reviews" to the same question as an option; adding "Metaphors and models for expressing interdisciplinary connections between areas" to the "Disciplinary and interdisciplinary areas and processes" as a question option; and rephrasing "community participation and application" as "community participation methods" and altering wording of one of the question options to emphasize analysis as a process.

3.3   Final Questionnaire

The validated questionnaire is included in the appendix, and its structure is presented as a scheme in Fig. 1. It is structured as follows: the first part of the questionnaire (topic T0, questions Q1-Q2) presents the purpose of the study and provides the informed consent form; the rest of the questionnaire covers topics T1 through T5. These are:

T1: The need for the conceptual framework
T2: The theory, methods, and collaboration in the field
T3: Framework structure
T4: Demographics
T5: Interview request

The questions under topics T1 and T2 address RQ1 ("How do the assumptions of the ILKT align with the community of immersive learning researchers and practitioners?"). The questions under topic T3 address RQ2 ("What are the community of immersive learning researchers and practitioners' views on the structure of the ILKT's framework and its elements?"). In T3 questions, we included open-ended question items labeled as "Others (please specify)" to Q23–Q26, which enabled us to address RQ3 ("What other aspects of the field of immersive learning are relevant for the ILKT framework?").

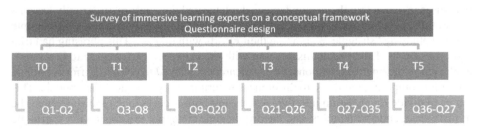

Fig. 1. Questionnaire structure.

In topic T1, we asked respondents to evaluate assumptions about the need for the ILKT framework on a five-point scale: Strongly Disagree (1), Disagree (2), Neither Agree nor Disagree (3), Agree (4), Strongly Agree (5).

The first addressed premise was:

Q3: The perspective of the field of 'immersive learning research' status is muddled/fragmented, the current knowledge partially disjointed, specifically among different disciplines.

Respondents which agreed or strongly agreed with this assumption were presented with follow-up questions on its three different aspects, Q4–Q6, shown below. All other respondents would be directed to question Q7.

Q4: The field of 'immersive learning research' is muddled/fragmented due to its interdisciplinary nature.
Q5 Other: the field of immersive learning research is muddled/fragmented for a different reason. (open-ended answer)
Q6: Researchers who are working in the field of immersive learning research desire to combine their efforts with others.

The second addressed premise was:

Q7: Researchers struggle to compare/contrast efforts with others from different fields of activity within immersive learning.

Respondents which agreed or strongly agreed with this assumption were presented with the follow-up question Q8, shown below. All other respondents would be directed to the following topic (T2, question Q9).

Q8: Please explain your point of view (open-ended answer)

In topic T2, we asked respondents to evaluate each assumption of the ILKT framework on the strength of theories and definitions in the field of immersive learning on a five-point scale for Q9, Q11, and Q13: Very Weak (1), Weak (2), Neither Weak nor Strong (3), Strong (4), Very Strong (5). We also asked for the reasons behind those evaluations (Q10, Q12, Q14).

Q9: How strong do you find the theoretical background for the field of immersive learning research?
Q10: Please indicate the reasons for such a status of theoretical background.
Q11: How strong do you find the consensus on the definition of immersion?
Q12: Please explain your point of view.
Q13: How strong do you find the consensus on the definition of learning?
Q14: Please explain your point of view.

Also, within topic T2, we then addressed assumptions of the ILKT framework on the strength of collaboration and methods in the field of immersive learning, by providing a range of possibilities from 0 to 10 (Q15, Q17, Q19), with follow-up open-ended questions asking for the reasons for those assessments (Q16, Q18, Q20).

Q15: On a scale of 0 to 10, how strong is collaboration across the disciplines in the field of immersive learning research:
Q16: Please explain your point of view.
Q17: On a scale of 0 to 10, how strong are methods used to analyze immersion in the field of immersive learning research:
Q18: Please explain your point of view.

Q19: On a scale of 0 to 10, how strong are methods used to analyze learning in the field of immersive learning research:
Q20: Please explain your point of view.

Within topic T3, related to the community's view on the structure of the ILKT framework, we first address the relevance of the framework itself on a five-point scale (Irrelevant, Slightly Relevant, Moderately Relevant, Relevant, Very Relevant) and then provided an open-ended follow-up question:

Q21: A conceptual framework for building a common and agreed understanding as well as for mapping knowledge, tools, and services in the field of immersive learning research, combining both scholarly and practical knowledge.
Q22: Please explain your point of view.

We then address the relevance of each of the framework's components, using the same range of possibilities: the research sources (Q23), the disciplinary and interdisciplinary areas and processes (Q24), the practical knowledge sources (Q25), and the community participation methods (Q26). For each, an open-ended option "Others (please specify)" was included. The various options for these questions are provided in the appendix.

Q23: Please evaluate the relevance of the following research sources for the proposed framework.
Q24: Please evaluate the relevance of the following disciplinary and interdisciplinary areas and processes for the proposed framework.
Q25: Please evaluate the relevance of the following practical knowledge sources for the proposed framework.
Q26: Please evaluate the relevance of the following community participation methods for the proposed framework.

Topic T4 (Q27–Q35) surveyed the respondents' personal context and information, including their personal perspective in the research-practice continuum (five options), years of experience in the field doing research (seven options) and practice (seven options), their field of activity (27 options), country, age (eight classes), gender (six classes), academic qualifications (six options), and professional affiliations (17 options).

Topic 5 inquired on respondents' availability for a follow-up interview (Q36, Yes/No answer options) and on whether to receive the results of the survey (Q37 Yes/No answer options, plus Q38 email field for 'yes' responses).

4   Data Collection Procedures

4.1   Survey Process

We selected a wide range of researcher and practitioner organizations whose members may be working in the field of immersive learning (see Table 1). We first created a potential list from our own contacts and professional networks, and then presented the resulting list to colleagues on the iLRN and IEEE EdSoc TC-ILE boards, updating the list from their inputs. We then e-mailed each organization stating the purpose of our questionnaire and why we thought that their organization might have some members who worked in immersive learning, asking them to consider distributing the questionnaire link to their membership. For example, we sent an e-mail to the Association for Educational Computing & Technology (AECT) suggesting that the purpose of our questionnaire tightly aligned with their mission of providing, "international leadership by promoting scholarship and best practices in the creation, use, and management of technologies for effective teaching and learning." Initially, 29 organizations from Table 1 were contacted and asked to distribute the survey. Two of these organizations responded positively, with iLRN and IEEE EdSoc TC-ILE agreeing to distribute our questionnaire. We also sent out two subsequent reminders to these organizations, requesting for a reminder to be distributed to their members. Further, we spread the questionnaire to individual researchers we had identified as having publicly contributed to past iLRN conferences in an earlier survey [9], also asking for subsequent dissemination to other researchers. A total of 47 participants have completed the survey.

4.2 Respondents

Of the 47 respondents, women comprised 27%, 70% were men, and 3% preferred not to answer. They were mostly 45–64 years old (57%), with age classes represented from 26–34 to 75–84. Their qualifications were essentially at doctoral level (81%), with some representation at master level (14%) or short-cycle tertiary (5%). Geographically, roughly a third stemmed from the USA (34%), followed by Portugal (9%), and the UK and Greece (9% each), Norway and Romania (6%), and other countries (3% each): Austria, Brazil, Canada, Colombia, Estonia, Israel, Japan, New Zealand, and Pakistan. They mainly listed their fields of activity as Multidisciplinary (32%) and Computer Science (30%), followed by Social Sciences and Engineering (14% each), with lower participation of other fields (3% each): Arts and Humanities, Environmental Science, Mathematics, and Medicine. Mostly, they described their perspective in the Research-Practice continuum as Balanced (50%), with contributions from Mostly Practice and Mostly Research (22% each), and Research (6%). Respondents participated in multiple professional organizations each, most mentioned being iLRN (26%), then EATEL (10%), iED (8%), VRARA (7%), AACE (6%), EDEN (6%), IEEE Education Society (5%), IEEE EdSoc TC-ILE (4%), OLC (4%), AECT (3%), ISTE (3%), Games for Change (3%), DiGRA (2%), and SEGAN (2%). Others (8%) were mentioned (one mention each): ACM, AERA, AREA, ASEE, CEC, CSEDU, Gesellschaft für Informatik, IEEE TALE, ISI, LORNET, and SCMS.

In terms of experience, the largest class was that of 3–5 years of experience in the field (42%), followed by 11–15 years of experience (17%), then 1–2 years (11%), and 6–10 year of experience, over 20 years of experience, or no experience (each 8%). With less participation we had the class with 16–20 years of experience (6%).

Table 1. List of organizations to whom we sent the questionnaire.

Organizations
Academy of International Extended Reality
Association for the Advancement of Computing in Education (AACE)
Association for Educational Computing & Technology (AECT)
Consortium for School Networking (CoSN)
Creative Science Foundation (CSf)
Digital Games Research Association (DIGRA)
Ecocity Builders
Educators in VR
EDUCAUSE
eLearning Guild
European Association of Technology-Enhanced Learning (EATEL)
European Distance and E-learning Network (EDEN)
European Edtech Alliance
Games for Change
IEEE EdSoc TC-ILE
IEEE Education Society
Immersive Education Initiative (iED)
Immersive Learning Research Network (iLRN)
Institute for Learning Innovation
International Game Developers Association (IGDA)
International Society for Technology in Education (ISTE)
Online Learning Consortium (OLC)
Serious Games Network (SEGAN)
Serious Play Conference
VR/AR Association
VRDays
XR Association (XRA)
IEEE ICICLE
AGORA - EIT Manufacturing

5   Preliminary Results

As the questionnaire includes Likert scale items and open-ended questions, we combine qualitative and quantitative analysis. 28 Likert scale-based items have been answered completely by 38 respondents. The evaluation of the Cronbach's Alpha coefficient [10] is 0.77. It reveals a relatively high internal consistency reliability, meaning that response values for each participant across the questionnaire set of questions are consistent, and the developed questionnaire is acceptable for applied scenarios. Table 2 gives an overview about respondents' average opinion (mean values) and discrepancies (standard deviation) of the Likert scale items, with the notation "Qx_y" denoting sub-question y of question x (for instance in Q23, there is a different response for each research source). A notable high disagreement "(!!)" can be found for the group of items Q15, Q17 and Q19, but also items Q4, Q13, Q23_7, Q24_1 and Q25_1 exceed the standard deviation "(!)" of the other items. While questions Q21-Q26 are not discussed further, their mean values and standard deviations are presented in Table 2 as they are part of the overall internal consistency reliability.

Table 2. Mean values and standard deviations of the Likert scale items.

Item	Mean	Std. Dev	Item	Mean	Std. Dev.
Q3	3.93	0.759	Q23_4	3.92	0.818
Q4	3.69	1.022(!)	Q23_5	3.92	0.85
Q6	4.12	0.88	Q23_6	3.95	0.941
Q7	3.66	0.938	Q23_7	3.30	1.077(!)
Q9	3.22	0.962	Q23_8	4.05	0.911
Q11	3.33	0.982	Q24_1	3.80	1.095(!)
Q13	3.95	1.011(!)	Q24_2	4.17	0.845
Q15	5.95	2.253(!!)	Q24_3	3.75	0.806
Q17	5.40	2.158(!!)	Q25_1	3.78	1.017(!)
Q19	6.32	2.069(!!)	Q25_2	3.00	0
Q21	4.11	0.894	Q25_3	4.39	0.766
Q23_1	4.34	0.669	Q25_4	4.56	0.652
Q23_2	4.32	0.739	Q26_1	4.42	0.692
Q23_3	4.05	0.868	Q26_2	4.39	0.728

Respondents provided information on RQ1 (assumptions of the ILKT), on RQ2 (relevance of the ILKT framework and its components) and on RQ3 (other aspects potentially relevant for the ILKT framework). Questionnaire items based on 5-point Likert ratings were analyzed quantitatively. Open response items were subjected to thematic analysis [11]. Here we provide preliminary results for RQ1 in Table 3.

Table 3. Preliminary survey results on RQ1.

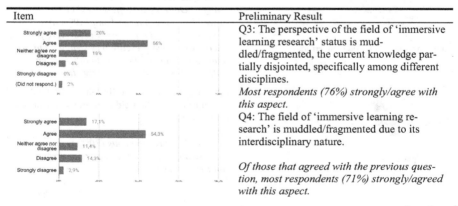

Item	Preliminary Result
	Q3: The perspective of the field of 'immersive learning research' status is muddled/fragmented, the current knowledge partially disjointed, specifically among different disciplines. *Most respondents (76%) strongly/agree with this aspect.* Q4: The field of 'immersive learning research' is muddled/fragmented due to its interdisciplinary nature. *Of those that agreed with the previous question, most respondents (71%) strongly/agreed with this aspect.*

(continued)

Table 3. (*continued*)

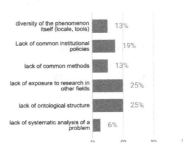

(Sum is not 100 due to rounding errors.)

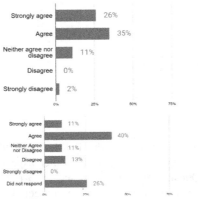

(Sum is not 100 due to rounding errors.)

(Sum is not 100 due to rounding errors.)

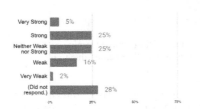

(Sum is not 100 due to rounding errors.)

Q5: Other: the field of immersive learning research is muddled/fragmented for a different reason.

Thematic analysis of open-ended answers showed that the most prevalent reasons (25% each) were the lack of exposure to research in other fields and the lack of ontological structure in the field. 19% considered either lack of common institutional policies, while 13% mentioned either the diversity of the phenomenon itself (locale, tools) or lack of common methods. Also mentioned (6%) was the lack of a systematic analysis of a problem.

Q6: Researchers who are working in the field of immersive learning research desire to combine their efforts with others.

Of those that agreed with Q3, the majority of respondents (61%) strongly/agree with this aspect. 11% neither agree or disagree, and 2% strongly/disagree.

Q7: Researchers struggle to compare/contrast efforts with others from different fields of activity within immersive learning.

Most respondents (51%) strongly/agreed with this aspect. 11% neither agreed or disagreed, and 13% strongly/disagree.

Q8: Please explain your point of view.

Thematic analysis showed that 32% of respondents did not explain their point of view on Q7. 'Ontological differences' (14%), followed by 'Lack of a road map' (9%) and 'epistemological differences' (7%) were pointed out as for why researchers struggled to compare/contrast efforts with others from different fields within immersive learning.

Q9: How strong do you find the theoretical background for the field of immersive learning research?

A minority of respondents (30%) found it very/strong. 25% neither weak nor strong, and 18% very/weak.

(*continued*)

Table 3. (*continued*)

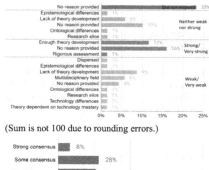

(Sum is not 100 due to rounding errors.)

Q10: Please indicate the reasons for such a status of theoretical background:

Thematic analysis showed that 30% of those responding (10%+16%+4%) did not explain their point of view on Q9. There was a split with 15% indicating 'lack of theory development' while 12% said there was sufficient theory development. The multidisciplinary nature of the field was the reason for 4% of respondents.

Q11: How strong do you find the consensus on the definition of immersion?

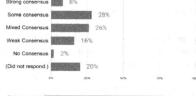

There is predominance for strong/some consensus (36%), with similar amount of mixed consensus (26%) and less respondents asserting weak/no consensus (18%).

Q12: Please explain your point of view.

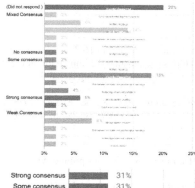

Thematic analysis showed 46% of respondents did not explain their point of view on Q11. 'Multiple meanings' of immersion and 'Confusion with other important concepts' accounted for 16% of explanations. 6% pointed a split of psychological and sensorial meanings, and 8% because of technology-dependent definitions.

Q13: How strong do you find the consensus on the definition of learning?

Strong consensus	31%
Some consensus	31%
Mixed Consensus	20%
Weak Consensus	4%
No Consensus	2%
(Did not respond.)	11%

(Sum is not 100 due to rounding errors.)

Most respondents (62%) found consensus to be strong/some. Only 6% found consensus to be weak or none.

Q14: Please explain your point of view

Thematic analysis showed 53% of respondents did not explain their point of view on Q14. Major reasons given for strong consensus were 'common understandings based on experience', 'decades of research on learning', and 'mature learning theories' all at 4%. The single reason given for weak consensus (2%) was 'mature methods in educational science, disregarded in technology/design'.

(*continued*)

Table 3. (*continued*)

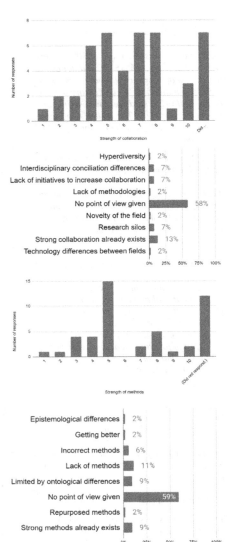

Q15: On a scale of 0 to 10, how strong is collaboration across the disciplines in the field of immersive learning research:

Some respondents (11) rated collaboration across the disciplines as an 8, 9, or 10. More rated it as a 5, 6, or 7 (18). Some respondents rated it as a 1, 2, 3, or 4 (10).

Q16: Please explain your point of view.

Thematic analysis showed that 58% of respondents did not explain their point of view on Q15. 13% said that it was strong because strong collaboration already exists in the field of immersive learning.

Q17: On a scale of 0 to 10, how strong are methods used to analyze immersion in the field of immersive learning research:

The most common response was 5 (15 responses) with 10 responses below and 10 responses above.

Q18: Please explain your point of view.

Thematic analysis showed that 59% of respondents did not explain their point of view on Q17. 9% indicated that methods used to analyze immersion are strong because 'strong methods already exist' and 2% because the field of immersive learning has repurposed methods from other fields. The rest of the respondents disagreed, stating their reasons that methods used to analyze immersion are weak or mixed due to ontological differences (9%), incorrect methods or 'getting better' (8%), and epistemological differences (2%).

(*continued*)

Table 3. (*continued*)

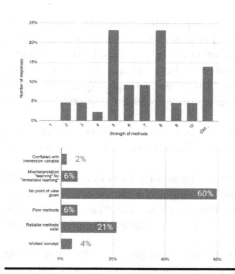

Q19: On a scale of 0 to 10, how strong are methods used to analyze learning in the field of immersive learning research:

Strengths 5 and 8 stood out with 23% of responses each. At a second tier, responses 6 & 7 combined 19% of responses. Below 5 there were 12%, and above 8, 9% of responses.

Q20: Please explain your point of view.

No point of view was given by 60% of respondents. The prevalent reason was the existence of reliable methods (21%), with 6% disagreeing and referring poor methods. 6% misinterpreted 'learning' for 'immersive learning', 4% referred its nature of wicked concept, and 2% mentioned conflating with the immersion variable.

6 Discussion

As put forward in section III.C, the questions under topics T1 and T2 address RQ1, "How do the assumptions of the ILKT align with the community of immersive learning researchers and practitioners?". These are Q3.Q20, with early results presented in Table III. The questions addressing RQ2 and RQ3 are still under analysis. These are early results because the responses are still being tallied.

The early results point towards overwhelming agreement from the community on the premise that the field of immersive learning research is muddled/fragmented, the current knowledge partially disjointed, specifically among different disciplines (Q3), due to its interdisciplinary nature (Q4). There are also strong indications supporting the premise that researchers who are working in the field of immersive learning research desire to combine their efforts with others (Q6) but that the struggle to compare/contrast efforts with others from different fields of activity (Q7).

The strength of the theoretical background for the field presented responses centered around the middle point (Q9), while there were indications of consensus on the definition of immersion (Q11) and learning (Q13). Methods for analyzing immersion seem to be average in strength (Q17), while methods to analyze learning are seen in a somewhat stronger status (Q18). The strength of current collaboration seems to point towards above average (Q15), but with a dispersion of responses.

7 Conclusions

The questionnaire validation results support its applicability. The early results of the survey indicate that the assumptions of the ILKT align with the community of immersive learning researchers and practitioners, by supporting several premises. Firstly, the field of immersive learning research is muddled/fragmented due to its interdisciplinary nature, with large majorities of subjects responding "Agree" or "Strongly Agree". Secondly, there is the desire of the immersive learning research community to collaborate but struggling to compare or contrast results.

The questions regarding the theoretical background point towards some development but also struggle since a tendency for consensus on definitions is perplexingly combined with lack of strength on methods for their analysis.

We acknowledge the limitations of this study. The small number of respondents (47) limit the generalizability of this validation study to a broader audience of scholars. Also, 44% respondents indicated experience from computer science and engineering, with low participation from several academic fields, putting the generalizability of these results in question.

Next steps in this research study include 1) Analyzing questions that were not yet analyzed in this paper; and 2) Implementing the questionnaire on a wider basis as a means for better understanding the breadth and depth of immersive learning researchers and practitioners.

Acknowledgments. This work was supported by the National Funds through the Portuguese funding agency, FCT – Fundação para a Ciência e a Tecnologia, within project LA/P/0063/2020 (INESC TEC), and partially financed within the project UIDB/00006/2020 (CEA/UL).

References

1. Richter, J.: Immersive learning research: a proposed design for an open networked global community effort. In: iLRN 2017 Coimbra - Workshop, Long and Short Paper, and Poster Proceedings from the Third Immersive Learning Research Network Conference, pp. 15–16. Verlag der Technischen Universität Graz, Graz (2017). https://doi.org/10.3217/978-3-85125-530-0-08
2. Beck, D., et al.: Towards an immersive learning knowledge tree - a conceptual framework for mapping knowledge and tools in the field. In: 2021 7th International Conference of the Immersive Learning Research Network (iLRN), Eureka, CA, USA, pp. 1–8. IEEE (2021). https://doi.org/10.23919/iLRN52045.2021.9459338
3. Morgado, L., Beck, D.: Unifying protocols for conducting systematic scoping reviews with application to immersive learning research. In: 2020 6th International Conference of the Immersive Learning Research Network (iLRN), San Luis Obispo, CA, USA, pp. 155–162. IEEE (2020). https://doi.org/10.23919/iLRN47897.2020.9155093
4. Murray, J.H.: Hamlet on the Holodeck: The Future of Narrative in Cyberspace. Free Press, New York (1997)
5. Slater, M.: Place illusion and plausibility can lead to realistic behaviour in immersive virtual environments. Philos. Trans. R. Soc. B Biol. Sci. **364**, 3549–3557 (2009). https://doi.org/10.1098/rstb.2009.0138

6. Witmer, B.G., Singer, M.J.: Measuring presence in virtual environments: a presence questionnaire. Presence Teleoperators Virtual Environ. **7**, 225–240 (1998). https://doi.org/10.1162/105 474698565686
7. Nilsson, N.C., Nordahl, R., Serafin, S.: Immersion revisited: a review of existing definitions of immersion and their relation to different theories of presence. Hum. Technol. **12**, 108–134 (2016). https://doi.org/10.17011/ht/urn.201611174652
8. Agrawal, S., Simon, A., Bech, S.: Defining immersion: literature review and implications for research on immersive audiovisual experiences. In: 147th AES Pro Audio International Convention, p. 14. Audio Engineering Society, New York (2019)
9. Hyrkäs, K., Appelqvist-Schmidlechner, K., Oksa, L.: Validating an instrument for clinical supervision using an expert panel. Int. J. Nurs. Stud. **40**, 619–625 (2003). https://doi.org/10.1016/S0020-7489(03)00036-1
10. Cronbach, L.J.: Coefficient alpha and the internal structure of tests. Psychometrika **16**, 297–334 (1951). https://doi.org/10.1007/BF02310555
11. Vaismoradi, M., Jones, J., Turunen, H., Snelgrove, S.: Theme development in qualitative content analysis and thematic analysis. J. Nurs. Educ. Pract. **6**, 100 (2016). https://doi.org/10.5430/jnep.v6n5p100

Trial Assessment of Online Learners' Engagement with 360-Degree Architecture Videos

Fengyuan Liu[1], May Kristine Jonson Carlon[1] , Mohamed Rami Gaddem[2] ,
and Jeffrey S. Cross[1(✉)]

[1] Tokyo Institute of Technology, 2-12-21 Ookayama, Meguro-ku, Tokyo, Japan
`ideale816@gmail.com, mcarlon@acm.org, cross.j.aa@m.titech.ac.jp`
[2] The University of Tokyo, Hongo, Bunkyo-ku, Tokyo, Japan
`gaddem@pse.t.u-tokyo.ac.jp`
`https://www.clab-tokyotech.org/`

Abstract. In recent years, with the development of massive open online courses (MOOCs) and extended reality (XR), the use of XR within MOOCs is becoming more feasible. Aside from making simulations possible, XR can support learning in domains where spatial awareness can be critical, such as in architecture. An intermediate technology to XR is 360-degree videos embedded in MOOCs that can be rendered in two-dimensional view (2D) via web browsers or in three-dimensional (3D) view (i.e., volumetric) with the use of a head-mounted display (HMD). When rendered in 3D, a more immersive learning environment may be achieved as the field of view restrictions in 2D format are removed. However, whether the additional dimension can enhance the learning experience, may it be in performance or satisfaction, is yet to be investigated. This study used a short learning module using contents from an existing edX architecture MOOC in a pre-test/post-test randomized mixed methods experiment where learners watch 360-degree videos via a web browser or with an HMD while being observed. Results indicate that while HMD usage may appear to elicit more engagement, the measured learned outcomes between the two groups do not significantly differ. Since purchasing an HMD for online learning is an expense, suggestions for improving the 3D experience were derived from learner interviews. These include better scrutiny of the purpose and alignment of 360-degree video content with the lessons and more robust beta-testing before course release to the public.

Keywords: 360-degree video · Volumetric video · 3D video · Massive open online course · Head-mounted display · Architecture

1 Introduction

Massive open online courses (MOOCs) are internet-based courses designed to cater to thousands of learners simultaneously. Short video lectures typically deliver the content by the instructor and the learners learn through quiz completion, reading materials, and discussions, among others [14]. MOOCs had been

M.-L. Bourguet et al. (Eds.): iLRN 2023, CCIS 1904, pp. 70–83, 2024.
https://doi.org/10.1007/978-3-031-47328-9_5

created for various topics such as chemistry, computer science, and business, among many others. In this research, an architecture edX MOOC developed by the Tokyo Institute of Technology's (Tokyo Tech) Online Education Development Office (now Online Content Research and Development Section) was used as the basis of the investigation[1].

In face-to-face classes, especially for courses such as architecture where the in-person experience can magnify learning, the instructor will organize some activities such as field trips to visit buildings and immerse learners in the targeted architectural environment [10]. Learners can observe the buildings visually (e.g., get the impression of the real size of the buildings) and exchange ideas with each other, which leads to a better learning experience. However, when the course is offered online, the learners can only see buildings on their mobile device display or computer monitor, losing some of the critical immersiveness for learning. To simulate an online architecture course to have similar functionality as a face-to-face class, 3D 360-degree videos were introduced into the said MOOC. Unlike regular 2D videos, 3D 360 videos have full 360 degrees view and depth of field that can be experienced through rendering devices such as head-mounted displays (HMD) for virtual reality (VR) applications. This provides learners with an immersive learning environment, giving them a sense of presence in the course and its 3D environment.

Recently, 360-degree videos and VR were used in education for different domains. In physics education, learners described their experiences with VR as highly engaging, making VR a valuable tool to increase motivation in classrooms [16]. In system modeling education, learners could be immersed in the learning material by using 360-degree video with VR headsets, which leads to enhanced motivation and active engagement [12]. The use of visualization tools such as 360-degree videos has many merits, such as the cost-effective delivery of an integrated educational environment. Finally, a 360-video virtual reality application was also used in nursing education [19], where elevated levels of engagement and satisfaction from the participants were observed.

2   Related Works

Noting that most MOOCs present the majority of their content in the form of videos [3], many research works discuss the importance of videos in improving learner engagement. For instance, short videos are found to be much more engaging in the online setting than long recorded lectures [8]. Additionally, compared to traditional lecture styles such as PowerPoint slides or code screencasts, Khan-style videos are more favorable. Due to the prevalence of (or lack thereof) technology, the research on videos for learner engagement in online education is mostly on 2D videos.

With VR techniques, 360-degree videos can be utilized in applications to help learners learn what they want, such as foreign language learning. VR headsets

---

[1] This course is still available on https://www.edx.org/course/japanese-architecture-and-structural-design.

were used to allow learners to visualize and interact using voice commands with the virtual world so that learners are provided an opportunity to experience the target language in a real-world situation [2]. Aside from language learning, VR was also used in education for nursing and midwifery. Implementing immersive 3D visualization as a teaching strategy is an innovative move to improve and expand the curriculum by providing new opportunities for learning [9]. In a specific learning environment that is difficult to access physically, utilizing 360-degree videos together with an HMD can provide an immersive learning experience that is not possible otherwise [1]. However, paying more attention to the novelty of the VR experience may distract learners from the content of the video. Learners with greater VR expectations may perform worse than when watching regular 2D videos [18].

Many research works have reported on MOOC learning outcomes and advised how to improve the MOOC learning experience. For instance, when creating or redesigning a MOOC, practitioners should consider the teaching and learning environment that might affect engagement multidimensionally [6]. Multidimensionality is person-centered approach catering to behavioral, cognitive, emotional, and social engagement. Of these aspects, it has been proven that emotional engagement contributed to learner satisfaction more than any other engagement dimension [5]. As such, it is important to assess learner impression and engagement with new technologies. This is particularly critical when considering an understudied technology to be used in a learning setting, such as the employment of VR combined with MOOC-based lessons via videos.

3   About the Course

Titled Japanese Architecture and Structural Design (JASD), learners can learn about design concepts such as seismic isolation through the MOOC used as the basis for this research (teaser image in Fig. 1). A comprehensive overview of the evolution of structural design from traditional timber buildings to steel structures is covered along with a discussion on the development of the architectural metabolism movement and modern spatial structures in Japan. A particular emphasis was put on the combination of seismic performance with both environmental performance and aesthetics of the structural design. Sustainability considerations are presented by using videos of the Tokyo Tech architecture faculty-designed campus buildings as design examples.

The first version of the course was released in May 2021 for 6 months on the learning management system (LMS). Several thousand learners enrolled in the first release of the course. The edX course was accompanied by a post-course survey to collect anonymous information about learners' satisfaction. In the post-course survey, answers rating the course as "Excellent" and "Good" were 52% and 34% of the total answers respectively. The positive reception of the course was due to the presence of concrete examples along with detailed diagrams and figures that explain theoretical concepts. The post-course survey also showed that learners are interested in seeing more drawings and details

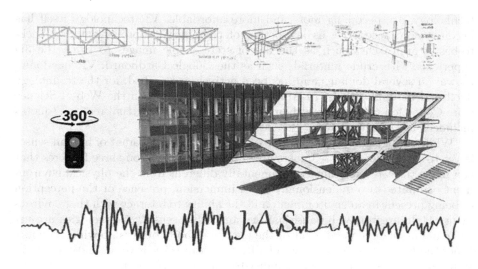

Fig. 1. Image used for the promotion of the course.

about the discussed structures and also animations and 3D renderings instead of plain 2D drawings and maps.

To improve the quality of the content and make it more engaging for learners, 360-degree videos of the discussed buildings were shot and included in the second release of the course. The videos were processed to add visual cues that help the learner focus on important details in the building. The course was re-released in December 2021. A playlist of the filmed videos is made available for all learners with a short instruction on how to watch the 360-degree video with a headset[2].

By using 360-degree videos to cater to learner feedback on the revised course, it is hoped that the multidimensionality is improved in several ways. First is by providing a potentially better way to engage with content. Second is by magnifying the learning by simulating the field trip experience with immersive technologies. Finally, the introduction of this new technology enables testing of the theoretical learning advantages of VR in a more incremental and controlled setting.

4   Theoretical Framework

In 1965, Ivan Sutherland, a pioneer of graphical user interfaces, posed the notion of an **ultimate display** that will allow humans to realize concepts not possible in the physical world by serving as many senses as possible [21]. This notion of a **looking glass**, which is later on referred to as **virtual reality**, has become more than a concept. HMDs, which had been critical in the acceptance of VR

---

[2] A playlist of the 360-degree videos can be found in this URL: https://www.youtube.com/playlist?list=PLA-JBrgwfYIfqrlK82QY6IPwMmStfJ0Ba.

technology, are becoming more and more affordable. VR technology itself has become more accessible, as a function of technology improvement and back-to-basics approaches such as the use of stereoscopic images to bring the 3D experience with crude materials such as the Google Cardboard. VR has found its way in several domains and has been actively researched, for the technology itself and its applications. In April 2023, a quick search on the Web of Science Core Collection returns more than 67, 500 results with "virtual reality" (quotes included) as the search key.

While a VR technology that uses and triggers the full gamut of human senses is yet to be developed, researchers are starting to hone in on three features that can make the VR experience fundamentally different from the physical environment or limited two-dimensional worlds: immersion, presence or the perception of being present in an environment, and the ability to interact with that environment [4]. Interestingly, because haptics and other sensory technologies are yet to be mainstream, embodiment or the illusion of body ownership which is sometimes thought of as the advantage of VR, is a feature that is yet to make headway. Immersion refers to the system's ability to make the user deeply engrossed in the task at hand. Presence refers to the psychological feeling of being in the world. Finally, interaction refers to the affordance provided by the system for the user to affect their environment.

Volumetric 360-degree videos are a step toward VR that taps into all three features immersion, presence, and interaction. Arguably, immersion is achievable even in conventional user interfaces, specifically with gamification, potentially to a better extent [7]. However, with VR, particularly through stereoscopic experience, immersion can be an artifact of stimulating senses in novel ways. Having a 360-degree view, where the user can be within the environment in whichever direction they look at, contribute to the feeling of presence. Finally, even with the simplest configuration of just having annotations, the user's ability to change their environment through head movements renders interactivity despite user manipulation not being baked into the system.

How then can these VR features contribute to the learning experience? Firstly, the three-dimensional and 360-degree view can improve visual modality. While the Learning Styles myth has long been debunked, the benefit of presenting information in different modalities remains to be grounded in neuroscience research where it is proven on several occasions that catering to multiple senses can have additive effects [15]. In the mini-lesson created for this research, several similar pieces of information are presented in different formats as illustrated in Fig. 2. Secondly, VR features were shown to enable engagement, empathy, and embodied cognition which all contribute to a more holistic take on the lessons learned [20]. This is especially important for architecture courses which can have implications in the physical and social world. Finally, the added freedom of movement and sense of presence can increase self-efficacy or a learner's belief in their capacity to achieve desired results [17].

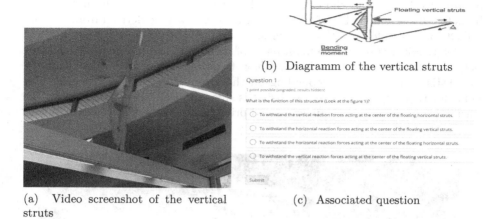

(b) Diagramm of the vertical struts

(a)   Video screenshot of the vertical struts

(c) Associated question

Fig. 2. The mini-lesson created for this research included a video (screenshot on (a)) featuring vertical struts as shown in (b). Text materials were added to allow learners to answer the associated quiz question (c).

5 Methodology

A mixed-methods approach was used for data analysis. Quantitative data included quiz scores, Likert scale responses, and quantification of behavior observations. Qualitative data included analysis of open-question responses and follow-up interviews. By looking at different measures for similar concepts, we enable our experiments to make their validity evident or even potentially arrive at divergent results that could lead to other important research questions that are not previously raised.

An online learning module derived from the architecture MOOC was created for this study using the Open edX learning management system. Before the experiment, the participants were asked to look through the outline of the research, objectives, methods, storage of data, and other relevant matters to obtain their consent to participate in this human subjects' ethical research which was approved by the institution. They then answered a pre-course survey that includes filtering criteria for further analysis (e.g., whether or not they have studied the course before). They also answered a pre-test to evaluate their knowledge levels before they read the materials and watch the videos.

After the pre-test, the participants were asked to read the materials and watch the 360-degree videos. The 20 participants were divided into two separate groups: namely, the treatment group in which participants watched 360-degree videos through an HMD, and the control group in which participants watched the 360-degree videos through a web browser on a laptop delivered via YouTube. The participants were exposed to three architectural concepts in the online module: spatial structures, integrated façade engineering, and grid-skin structures. All these concepts were demonstrated in the 360-degree videos of buildings taken within the campus and showcased in the MOOC used as the basis for this research. The reading materials were likewise derived from the said MOOC and the aforementioned topics.

Before going through the main parts of the online learning module, the participants were given instructions on how to watch 360-degree videos through the HMD or the browser depending on the group they were assigned in. The video for this tutorial, whose screenshot is shown in Fig. 3, was not used for the learning module to prevent unwarranted prior knowledge before the experiment.

Fig. 3. Screenshot of 360-degree video used before the formal experiment.

After the necessary instruction, the participants were asked to go through the online learning module. There was a time limit of 10 min for each quiz and 45 min for the reading and video materials. Participants were instructed to inform the observing researchers every time they finish a portion of the module. The researchers conduct quantitative field observation based on the Baker Rodrigo Ocumpaugh Monitoring Protocol (BROMP) 2.0 [13] while the participants are going through the module. In this observation method, the researchers assess and record the participants' behavior while studying the online module individually in a pre-determined order. The behavior and affect coding schemes used in this research are detailed in Table 1 and Table 2 respectively.

Two researchers observed the participants in real time while they are going through the video and reading materials to increase the coding reliability. The inter-rater reliability between the two coders was checked afterward. Observation codes for both affect and behavior are taken every twenty seconds. Images depicting setups for both conditions are shown in Fig. 4.

After going through the course content, the participants once again answered the same questions from the pre-test, this time as a post-test. The participants

Table 1. Behavior coding scheme based on the work by Pittsburgh Science of Learning Center (PSLC).

Description (code)	Details
On task (ONT)	The student is doing what he or she is supposed to be doing
On-task conversation (ONTC)	The student is working towards the online learning module while having a conversation with two researchers about the learning task etc
Off task (OFT)	The student is not working on the educational task assigned by the researcher
Gaming the system ($)	The student is still engaged with the online learning module but is not engaged with learning. Instead, they are attempting to advance through the system without actually learning the material
Other (?)	If none of the above codes apply to the participant

Table 2. Affect coding scheme based on the work by PSLC.

Description (code)	Details
Boredom (B)	The student appears to find the activity they are engaged with dull or tedious (e.g., yawning)
Confusion (C)	The student looks like they are having difficulty understanding the class materials
Engaged concentration (EC)	The student is paying focused attention to their current task
Frustration (F)	This affect is coded when the student shows expressions or feelings of distress or annoyance
Other (?)	If none of the above codes apply to the participant

Fig. 4. Setup for HMD (left) and web browser (right) group experiments.

were also asked to write about their learning experiences by studying this online learning module. Questions probed the participants' satisfaction levels and perceptions of their learning achievement in the short module. Additionally, the evaluation of the video viewing experience between the HMD group and the browser group was investigated. The participants were given the opportunity to share their opinions about the online learning module through open-response questions.

After analyzing the quiz questions and post-survey results, some participants were invited for an interview to discuss their results. Since the research is about knowing the potential of watching videos through HMDs, everyone in the HMD group (ten participants) was asked about how to improve the 360-degree videos used in this research for learning and engagement. Six participants from the browser group were also invited for an interview to clarify their opinions about the use of 360-degree videos for learning they expressed in the survey.

6 Results and Discussions

Convenience sampling was conducted for this research by inviting volunteers from the researchers' social circles and encouraging the participants to invite others as well. A minimal amount of remuneration was provided which was approved by the university's human subjects research review board. Demographic details about the participants are shown in Table 3.

Table 3. Participant details.

Variables	Items	Number	Percentage
Gender	Male	15	75
	Female	5	25
Age	21 to 23	12	60
	24 to 26	6	30
	27 to 29	2	10
Educational level	Bachelors	7	35
	Masters	9	45
	PhD	4	20
MOOC experience	None	4	20
(How many courses taken)	1 to 3	10	50
	4 to 6	4	20
	7 or more	2	10
Architecture MOOC	No	20	100
(Have taken or not)	Yes	0	0

None of the participants had taken the edX architecture MOOC which was used as the basis for preparing this module before and most of them did not know the concepts introduced in the learning module. Most of the participants also indicated openness to learning via this online module. The specific information is summarized in Fig. 5. No statistically significant difference was detected when the differences in the post-test and pre-test scores were compared between the HMD group and the browser group ($p - value > 0.05$). Some participants mentioned they got all the important information from the reading materials, not from the 360-degree videos. This might be the reason why the experimental treatment was not instrumental to increase their learning performance.

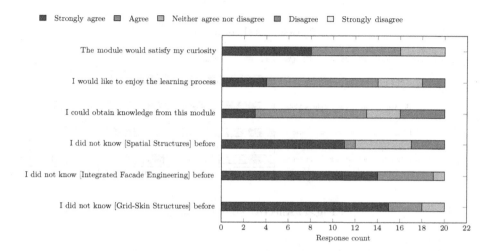

Fig. 5. Likert scale responses from pre-survey.

The interrater reliability was calculated for both affect and behavior schemes using Cohen's Kappa coefficient. The resulting values are more than 0.9 for both schemes, indicating almost perfect agreement [11]. Figure 6 shows the distribution of recorded behaviors for each group. On-task refers to observations where the participant is doing what they are expected to (e.g., watching videos) while on-task conversation refers to behaviors where the participants engage with the researchers while being on task. Recorded observations for on-task conversation showed that participants in the HMD group tended to express themselves more when watching videos and participants in the browser group tended to express themselves more when reading the materials. Figure 7 shows the distribution of recorded affects for each group. From these results, it can be seen that participants in the browser group expressed more signs of boredom.

Their responses on the post-surveys were likewise tested for statistical significance using a t-test, to which no statistical difference was observed ($p - value > 0.05$). The responses to the open-ended questions in the survey were also analyzed.

For the post-survey, participants were asked to answer the following questions in free format:

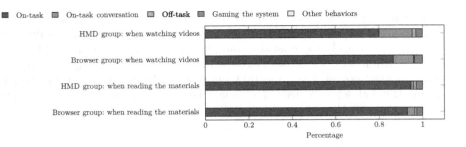

Fig. 6. Behavioral coding results.

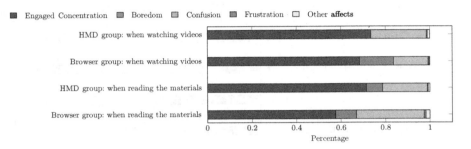

Fig. 7. Affective coding results.

– What do you think about this online learning module?
– Please give more details about your learning experience (good points and bad points).

Manual inspection of the responses to these questions was conducted. Both groups mentioned that giving more time would be helpful in terms of watching the 360-degree videos. Of particular interest are the points that are discussed by one group but not by the other. For instance, participants in the HMD group mentioned issues related to motion sickness, eye fatigue, and the disproportionate size of text used for annotation. Participants in the browser group mentioned missing annotations as a result of their trying to manipulate their 360-degree view and not having enough time to read the annotations. Select participants were interviewed to clarify the group responses in the survey.

The participants agreed that the videos helped in visualizing the concepts being discussed in the lesson. However, because the learners have the freedom to change their view either by moving their heads with the HMD or mouse-dragging, it is easy to miss critical information. Adding audio cues was suggested to redirect the learner to the target focal area just in case they had been exploring a different part of the world. The amount of time needed for reading through annotations is suspected to vary between browser-based and HMD-based navigation and should additionally be considered during video production. Finally, while HMDs are expected to have improved software to prevent eye fatigue and motion sickness, these concerns should be considered as well during video production for the time being.

Considering both the post-survey results and interview results, the recommendations when considering utilizing 360-degree videos can be summarized as follows:

- The information in the videos should be easy to watch.
- Learners should feel that watching the videos is worth their time and effort.
- Audio/visual cues should be added in the video.
- The view change should be natural, not something like a presentation slide.
- The length of the video should be well considered (motion sickness, eye fatigue).
- The speed of the video should be well considered (motion sickness).

7 Conclusion and Future Work

Although the use of HMDs in online courses has merits when watching video lectures such as the realization of the visualization or immersion, which can enhance the motivation and concentration of learners, there were much more opinions about the improvement points of the 360-degree videos than originally expected. From this research, recommendations for editing 360-degree videos and their usage for learning such as the appropriate placing of video text/graphic annotations and additional audio explanations were obtained. The results of this research will serve as a foundation when designing future online courses that make use of 360-degree videos.

An immediate potential future work is to have a revision of the course applying the recommendations gathered from this research. It may also be worthwhile to consider other courses that may benefit from the use of similar technology. The role of this technology should be clarified before putting it into use in future course releases. Will it be used for content edification, increased appreciation, or simply for the fun factor?

This research only looked into comparing two different groups when using 360-degree videos in an online learning module. Another comparison that can be made is the difference in experience between learners who used 360-degree videos versus the typical (2D) videos. Although this was beyond the scope of the present study, it may also be worthwhile to study the effect of using online learning modules versus having the learners directly go to see the actual architectural structures onsite within the campus.

Acknowledgement. This work was supported by the Japan Society for the Promotion of Science (JSPS) via the Grants-in-Aid for Scientific Research (Kakenhi) Grant Number JP20H01719. The authors thank Tokyo Tech Professor Toru Takeuchi and retired Professor David Stewart for their advice regarding this research project, which helped determine the direction and generated important ideas for further study. The authors also thank Tokyo Tech students in the Cross lab Dongzi Hu and Abraham Castro Garcia for their contribution to the experiments. This work was made possible by the support of Tokyo Tech's Online Content Research and Development Section in the Center for Innovative Teaching and Learning.

References

1. Atkins, A., Charles, F., Adjanin, N.: A new realm for distance and online learning: 360-degree VR. Teach. Journal. Mass Commun. **10**(2), 51–54 (2020)
2. Berns, A., Mota, J.M., Ruiz-Rube, I., Dodero, J.M.: Exploring the potential of a 360 video application for foreign language learning. In: Proceedings of the Sixth International Conference on Technological Ecosystems for Enhancing Multiculturality, pp. 776–780 (2018)
3. Carlon, M.K.J., Keerativoranan, N., Cross, J.S.: Content type distribution and readability of MOOCs. In: Proceedings of the Seventh ACM Conference on Learning@ Scale, pp. 401–404 (2020)
4. Cipresso, P., Giglioli, I.A.C., Raya, M.A., Riva, G.: The past, present, and future of virtual and augmented reality research: a network and cluster analysis of the literature. Front. Psychol. **9**, 2086 (2018)
5. Deng, R.: Emotionally engaged learners are more satisfied with online courses. Sustainability **13**(20), 11169 (2021)
6. Deng, R., Benckendorff, P., Gannaway, D.: Linking learner factors, teaching context, and engagement patterns with MOOC learning outcomes. J. Comput. Assist. Learn. **36**(5), 688–708 (2020)
7. Goethe, O.: Immersion in games and gamification. In: Gamification Mindset. HIS, pp. 107–117. Springer, Cham (2019). https://doi.org/10.1007/978-3-030-11078-9_10
8. Guo, P.J., Kim, J., Rubin, R.: How video production affects student engagement: an empirical study of MOOC videos. In: Proceedings of the First ACM Conference on Learning@ Scale, pp. 41–50 (2014)
9. Hanson, J., Andersen, P., Dunn, P.K.: Effectiveness of three-dimensional visualisation on undergraduate nursing and midwifery students' knowledge and achievement in pharmacology: a mixed methods study. Nurse Educ. Today **81**, 19–25 (2019)
10. Kerr, J., Lawson, G.: Augmented reality in design education: landscape architecture studies as AR experience. Int. J. Art Des. Educ. **39**(1), 6–21 (2020)
11. McHugh, M.L.: Interrater reliability: the kappa statistic. Biochem. Medica **22**(3), 276–282 (2012)
12. Muñoz-Carpio, J.C., Cowling, M., Birt, J.: Doctoral colloquium-exploring the benefits of using 360 video immersion to enhance motivation and engagement in system modelling education. In: 2020 6th International Conference of the Immersive Learning Research Network (iLRN), pp. 403–406. IEEE (2020)
13. Ocumpaugh, J.: Baker Rodrigo Ocumpaugh Monitoring Protocol (BROMP) 2.0 technical and training manual. New York, NY and Manila, Philippines: Teachers College, Columbia University and Ateneo Laboratory for the Learning Sciences, p. 60 (2015)
14. O'Malley, P.J., Agger, J.R., Anderson, M.W.: Teaching a chemistry MOOC with a virtual laboratory: lessons learned from an introductory physical chemistry course. J. Chem. Educ. **92**(10), 1661–1666 (2015)
15. Papadatou-Pastou, M., Touloumakos, A.K., Koutouveli, C., Barrable, A.: The learning styles neuromyth: when the same term means different things to different teachers. Eur. J. Psychol. Educ. **36**, 511–531 (2021)
16. Pirker, J., Holly, M., Gütl, C.: Room scale virtual reality physics education: use cases for the classroom. In: 2020 6th International Conference of the Immersive Learning Research Network (iLRN), pp. 242–246 (2020). https://doi.org/10.23919/iLRN47897.2020.9155167

17. Qian, J., Ma, Y., Pan, Z., Yang, X.: Effects of virtual-real fusion on immersion, presence, and learning performance in laboratory education. Virtual Real. Intell. Hardw. **2**(6), 569–584 (2020)

18. Rupp, M.A., Kozachuk, J., Michaelis, J.R., Odette, K.L., Smither, J.A., McConnell, D.S.: The effects of immersiveness and future VR expectations on subjective-experiences during an educational 360 video. In: Proceedings of the Human Factors and Ergonomics Society Annual Meeting, vol. 60, pp. 2108–2112. SAGE Publications Sage CA, Los Angeles, CA (2016)

19. Seo, J.H., Kicklighter, C., Garcia, B., Chun, S.W., Wells-Beede, E.: Work-in-progress-design and evaluation of 360 VR immersive interactions in nursing education. In: 2021 7th International Conference of the Immersive Learning Research Network (iLRN), pp. 1–3. IEEE (2021)

20. Shin, D.H.: The role of affordance in the experience of virtual reality learning: technological and affective affordances in virtual reality. Telemat. Inform. **34**(8), 1826–1836 (2017)

21. Sutherland, I.E., et al.: The ultimate display. In: Proceedings of the IFIP Congress, vol. 2, pp. 506–508. New York (1965)

Are Students Ready to Be Immersed? Acceptance of Mobile Immersive Virtual Reality by Secondary Education Students

Carl Boel[1,2]([✉]) [iD], Tijs Rotsaert[2] [iD], Martin Valcke[2] [iD], Yves Rosseel[2] [iD], Alexander Vanhulsel[1] [iD], and Tammy Schellens[2] [iD]

[1] Thomas More University of Applied Sciences, Raghenoplein 21 bis, 2800 Mechelen, Belgium
carl.boel@thomasmore.be
[2] Ghent University, Henri Dunantlaan 2, 9000 Ghent, Belgium

Abstract. As immersive virtual reality (iVR) is gaining popularity, interest from education and educational research is growing likewise. As such, it is of interest to investigate which factors thrive and inhibit acceptance of this iVR technology in education. In this study we investigated the perceptions of 2,640 Flemish secondary education students on iVR as an instructional tool. As a theoretical framework, we adopted the UTAUT2 model extended with the factor of personal innovativeness in the domain of information technology. Students watched a video with several examples of iVR educational experiences. Next, their perceptions on iVR as an instructional method were measured using an online survey. To test the several hypotheses, we applied general linear modelling. The results account for 50% of variance in behavioral intention to use. These findings help to understand which factors contribute to the acceptance of iVR in secondary education and might guide the design of evidence-informed implementation plans by school managers and teachers.

Keywords: Mobile Immersive Virtual Reality · Secondary Education · Acceptance · UTAUT2 · Personal Innovativeness

1 Introduction

Immersive virtual reality (iVR) is gaining popularity, as the iVR head-mounted displays (HMDs) are becoming more user-friendly and more affordable [1]. The iVR technology is also increasingly being used in the educational field as it holds several benefits. These benefits, commonly indicated as affordances [2], have been studied quite extensively, and include: no risk of harm, no risk of causing damage, unlimited learning opportunities, experiencing what is otherwise too expensive or even impossible, enhancing understanding through 3D-visualisation and so on [3–5]. Several meta-analyses have indicated that learning with iVR outperforms less immersive learning experiences [6, 7]. Although the effect size is higher in K-12 settings [7], this educational level is underrepresented in research, as most studies focus on higher education [3, 7].

© The Author(s), under exclusive license to Springer Nature Switzerland AG 2024
M.-L. Bourguet et al. (Eds.): iLRN 2023, CCIS 1904, pp. 84–95, 2024.
https://doi.org/10.1007/978-3-031-47328-9_6

1.1   Research on Acceptance of Immersive Virtual Reality

This includes the investigation of the acceptance of iVR technology in secondary edu-cation. However, it is of great importance to study which factors guide and inhibit the acceptance of immersive virtual reality in secondary education as it can inform design guidelines for implementation [8, 9]. Especially, as the iVR technology has some distinc-tive features, which makes it hard to transfer insights from other technology acceptance studies [10]. However, studying individual acceptance of use of technology is one of the most mature streams in information systems research [11] with several acceptance models having been developed. One of the most comprehensive models is the second version of the Unified Theory of Acceptance and Use of Technology (UTAUT2; see Fig. 1), as it has incorporated several predicting factors and moderators from previous research on user acceptance of technology [11].

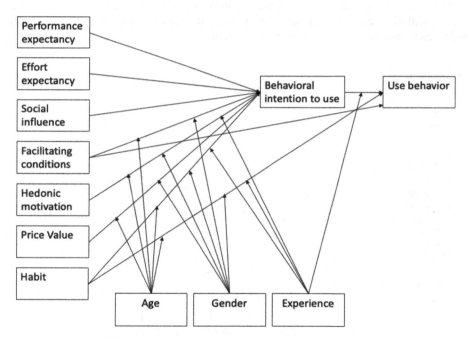

Fig. 1. Original UTAUT2 model (adapted from [11]).

Moreover, UTAUT2 can account for 70% of variance in behavioral intention to use and 50% of variance in the actual use of the technology. This model also served as an initial framework for the present study. Several studies have already investigated stu-dents' perceptions on immersive virtual reality as an instructional tool. However, apart from [12] none focused on secondary education. There are several other limitations of the existing literature: the studies often involved small sample sizes [8, 12–15], several studies used non-validated measuring instruments [16–19] and there is a lack of gener-alizability as the studies were often aimed at testing usability and user satisfaction of one specific iVR learning instrument [19–23]. The present study aims to address these research gaps by investigating which factors contribute to the acceptance of immersive virtual reality in secondary education students, using an elaborated UTAUT2 model via a large-scale survey study.

1.2   Research Model and Hypotheses

Building upon insights from literature, while addressing the research gaps, we constructed a research model (see Fig. 2). Our model consists of 5 out of the 7 factors of the UTAUT2 model, leaving out price value and habit. Evaluating the cost and return on investment of iVR technology is not of concern to students, but to teachers and school management. Hence, price value was dropped. Second, as we predicted only few students would have already some iVR experience in an educational setting, it would therefore be very hard for the students to indicate to which extent they perceive iVR technology to fit in with their current learning habit. As such, the factor of habit was also dropped, and likewise use behavior as an outcome variable.

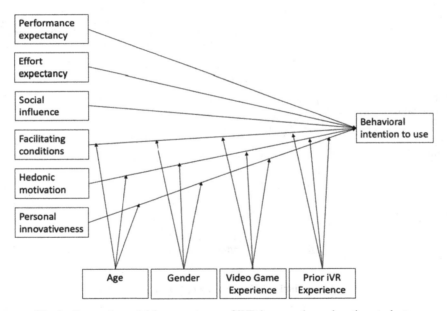

Fig. 2. Research model for acceptance of iVR in secondary education students.

Therefore, we hypothesized:

- H1. Performance expectancy has a significant effect on behavioral intention to use;
- H2. Effort expectancy has a significant effect on behavioral intention to use;
- H3. Social influence has a significant effect on behavioral intention to use;
- H4. Facilitating conditions has a significant effect on behavioral intention to use;
- H5. Hedonic motivation has a significant effect on behavioral intention to use.

Apart from leaving out two factors, we added a new one: personal innovativeness in the domain of information technology which was defined as "the willingness of an individual to try out any new information technology" by (p.206) [24]. As related research has shown, this factor also contributes to the adoption of iVR technology [22, 25, 26]. We therefore hypothesize:

- H6. Personal innovativeness has a significant effect on behavioral intention to use.

Finally, four moderating elements were identified: age, gender and prior experience [11] and video gaming experience [19] resulting in these three (sub) hypotheses:

- H7a. Age, gender, prior iVR experience and video gaming experience moderate the association between facilitating conditions and behavioral intention to use;
- H7b. Age, gender, prior iVR experience and video game experience moderate the association between hedonic motivation and behavioral intention to use;
- H7c. Age, gender, prior iVR experience and video game experience moderate the association between personal innovativeness and behavioral intention to use.

2 Methodology

2.1 Participants and Data Collection

The present study is the counterpart on the students' perspective and was run in parallel with a study on teachers' perceptions [25]. Participating schools were recruited via social media, the personal network of the researchers, a technology-oriented educational e-zine in Flanders and several educational organizations. Following the ethical procedures as defined in the General Ethical Protocol of the Faculty of Psychology and Educational Sciences of Ghent University, all students, their legal representatives, teachers involved and the management of schools interested to take part in the study, were presented an information letter on the procedure of the study. In addition, all students were asked active informed consent prior to the actual study. In total 2,640 students from 23 schools were involved.

2.2 Instruments

All students were presented an online survey using Qualtrics. First, they were asked some demographic variables, which are synthesized in Table 1.

Next, they had to watch a tailor-made video on the nature of mobile iVR technology and on possible applications of iVR for secondary education classes. This approach, resembling [9] offers the possibility for a large-scale study such as the current study, but can also be seen as a means to investigate acceptance of iVR to a more generalized extent. The students were shown how a student puts on a mobile iVR HMD and starts an application. Next, they are presented 20 examples of iVR applications in secondary education, such as biology, language teaching, history, engineering, nursing, artistry, chemistry and so on. As such, we provided the students with a broad view on the affordances of iVR for secondary education, instead of aiming at a single iVR experience. In this way, we were able to address the lack of generalizability of previous studies. The video duration is 4 min 39 s, and the video could not be skipped by the respondents. Captions were added in Dutch, matching the mother tongue of the participants. Some screenshots were added in Fig. 3.

Table 1. Demographic overview of participants.

Variable	Value	Frequency	%
Gender	Male	1,505	57.0
	Female	1,104	41.8
	Undefined	31	1.2
Age (year of education)	1st year	636	24.1
	2nd year	660	25.0
	3rd year	397	15.0
	4th year	344	13.0
	5th year	295	11.2
	6th year	260	9.8
	7th year	48	1.8
Experience with iVR	No experience	1,695	64.2
	Very little experience	240	9.1
	Little experience	204	7.7
	Some experience	318	12.0
	Moderate experience	109	4.1
	A lot of experience	39	1.5
	Extensive experience	35	1.3
Experience with video gaming	No experience	203	7.7
	A few times a year	217	8.2
	A few times a month	320	12.1
	A few times a week	747	28.3
	Daily, less than 2 h	482	18.3
	Daily, more than 2 h	671	25.4

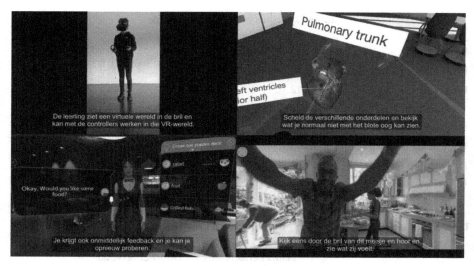

Fig. 3. Screenshots taken from the video shown to the participants.

2.3 Measures

After having watched the video, the students were asked about their perceptions on immersive virtual reality as an instructional tool in secondary education courses. These perceptions were investigated, using a survey consisting of 23 items on a 7-point Likert scale ranging from 1 – "Completely disagree" to 7 – "Completely agree". The 23 items included performance expectancy (3 items), effort expectancy (4 items), social influence (3 items), facilitating conditions (3 items), hedonic motivation (3 items), personal innovativeness (4 items) and finally behavioral intention to use (3 items). All items were randomly presented to the participants.

3 Results

Data were analyzed using the SPSS28 (IBM) package. First, we wanted to check the unidimensionality of the measurement instruments by running exploratory factor analyses. Except for one item in personal innovativeness, all scale items had satisfactory factor loadings for their respective construct. The reverse item in personal innovativeness (PI3, "In general, I am hesitant to try out new information technologies") was below the threshold of .50 and was excluded for further analysis. Next, we checked the scales for reliability by calculating Cronbach's alpha (see Table 2). All scales had high to very high reliability scores, except for facilitating conditions which reflected a moderate reliability.

To test the hypotheses of our research model, we carried out general linear modelling analyses (Table 3). First, we investigated the main effects between the predicting factors and the outcome variable of behavioral intention to use. Second, we also added the moderators of gender, age, prior iVR experience, and video gaming experience.

Table 2. Results of reliability analysis.

Scale	Cronbach's alpha	Means	Standard Deviation
Performance expectancy	0.868	5.12	1.30
Effort expectancy	0.812	5.19	1.14
Social influence	0.722	3.61	1.34
Facilitating conditions	0.620	4.40	1.10
Hedonic motivation	0.849	5.40	1.21
Personal innovativeness	0.762	4.59	1.26
Behavioral intention	0.909	4.10	1.55

Table 3. Results of regression models with behavioral intention to use as the dependent variable.

	Direct effects only	Direct effects and interactions
	Parameter estimates	Parameter estimates
Performance expectancy (PE)	0.109**	0.111**
Effort expectancy (EE)	0.148**	0.148**
Social influence (SI)	0.301**	0.301**
Facilitating conditions (FC)	0.196**	0.365
Hedonic motivation (HM)	0.089*	−0.008
Personal Innovativeness (PI)	0.281**	−0.175
Age (year of education)	−0.025	−0.169*
Gender	Female: 0.0370[a]; Male: 0.048[a]	Female: −0.901[a]; Male: −0.786[a]
Prior iVR experience	0.041*	0.013
Video gaming experience	−0.015	−.109
R^2	0.499	
FC × Age (year of education)		0.010
FC × Gender		Female: −0.198[a]; Male: 0.198[a]
FC × Prior iVR experience		−0.023
FC × Video gaming experience		0.010
HM × Age (year of education)		−0.001
HM × Gender		Female: 0.087[a]; Male: 0.087[a]
HM × Prior iVR experience		0.021

(continued)

Table 3. (*continued*)

	Direct effects only	Direct effects and interactions
HM × Video gaming experience		−0.004
PI × Age (year of education)		0.024
PI × Gender		Female: 0.289[a]; Male: 0.337[a]
PI × Prior iVR experience		0.004
PI × Video gaming experience		0.015
R^2		0.503

a To test interaction with gender, *undefined* is used as a comparison base with value 0.
* p <0.05; ** p <0.001.

When looking at the results of the main effects analyses, all predicting factors have a significant effect on behavioral intention to use. Therefore, H1 to H6 were confirmed. When adding interaction effects of age (year of education), gender, prior iVR experience, and video gaming experience, no significant effects could be identified. So H7a, H7b and H7c were all rejected. The proportion of variance which could be explained in behavioral intention to use was 49.9% for the main effects and 50.3% when adding indirect effects.

4 Discussion

The present study aims to identify which factors contribute and inhibit the acceptance of immersive virtual reality by secondary education students in Flanders. To this end, we developed a survey, building upon the UTAUT2 framework [11] and added personal innovativeness [24] as a factor and video gaming experience as a moderator. 2,640 students from 23 schools were involved. Results of general linear modelling analyses indicate all predicting factors were significantly associated with behavioral intention to use, confirming H1 to H6. No significant moderating effects could be identified, rejecting H7a, H7b and H7c. Our analyses were able to account for 50% of variance in behavioral intention to use. We will now discuss the results in greater detail.

Performance expectancy is significantly associated with behavioral intention to use (H1 accepted). This is in line with other research [9, 12, 13, 17–19, 21–23, 27, 28]. Even though the students were not immersed in an actual iVR learning experience, they could perceive iVR as a valuable instructional tool for their learning process.

Similar results were found for effort expectancy (H2 accepted). Students perceived immersive virtual reality as easy to use, which is in line with previous studies [12, 13, 23, 27, 28]. However, several other studies have reported on participants struggling with navigating in and interacting with the iVR learning environment [8, 18, 21, 22]. Nevertheless, effort expectancy only plays a minor role in the UTAUT2 model [29]. Future research should investigate to which extent effort expectancy does or does not have a significant effect on the behavioral intention to use iVR in education.

Social influence seems to play the most important role in the acceptance of iVR by secondary education students (H3 accepted), which is in line with previous studies [9, 23, 28]. A possible explanation is the lack of choice students have on the use of technology in class, as this is mainly initiated by the teacher. However, this result indicates students feel a tendency and urge to use iVR in class.

Consequently, it is not surprising to see facilitating conditions to be significantly associated with behavioral intentions to use (H4 accepted). Students indicate the boundary conditions for the implementation of iVR in secondary education, such as technical and pedagogical support, affect the adoption of iVR technology, which resembles previous findings [9, 21].

The students participating in this study were not actually immersed in an iVR learning experience. Nevertheless, hedonic motivation was significantly associated with behavioral intention to use (H5 accepted). This reaffirms the hedonic value of iVR technology [2] and other research on iVR acceptance [13, 15, 21, 28, 30].

Finally, also personal innovativeness was identified as being significantly associated with behavioral intention to use (H6 accepted), reaffirming previous research [22, 26]. However, these studies also see an indirect, significant effect of personal innovativeness on perceived usefulness, which can be linked to performance expectancy in our research model. Future research should further investigate this double link.

When adding moderators to our analyses, no significant effect of age (year of education), gender, video gaming experience, nor of prior iVR experience could be identified. This is again in line with other research such as [21, 23, 31]. H7a, H7b and H7c were thus rejected.

These results can have both theoretical and practical implications. First, future research might use the extended UTAUT2 model as a basis to further investigate the acceptance and use of immersive virtual reality by students, and apply this model in studies involving other educational levels and in other countries. Especially, adding the construct of personal innovativeness proved valuable, as this is the second most important factor in predicting behavioral intention in secondary education students. It is therefore suggested to integrate this factor in future research models on iVR acceptance in education.

From a more practical perspective, the identified factors might guide school managers in designing evidence-informed programs on how to implement iVR into their schools successfully. Results indicated a significant effect of social influence on behavioral intention to use. As such, when introducing immersive virtual reality in students' curricula, it seems important to provide for a sound pedagogical vision on how this technology fits the current educational policy of the schools. When students notice a belief in and a stress on iVR by the school management, they are seemingly more likely to accept iVR as a valuable instructional method. Second, as personal innovativeness plays such an important role in the acceptance, it is suggested to start with students and classes who are innovation- and technology minded. Instead of implementing immersive virtual reality at the whole school level at once, it might be a better strategy to first address students who show an interest for this technology. Finally, when designing the implementation strategies, there is no value to take into account differences in gender, age, prior iVR experience or video gaming experience, as their moderating effects proved not to be of significance. This might simplify the design of the targeted iVR implementation program.

5 Conclusion

In this study we investigated which factors contribute to and inhibit the acceptance of immersive virtual reality by secondary education students. Results indicate all hypothesized factors, including performance expectancy, effort expectancy, social influence, facilitating conditions, hedonic motivation and personal innovativeness are significantly associated with behavioral intention to use. No moderating effects of age (year of education), gender, prior VR experience or video gaming experience could be identified. Looking at the relatively high mean scores for the different factors, we might conclude by answering our title question positively. Secondary education students apparently are ready for the use of immersive virtual reality in their curriculum.

Although we were successful in explaining 50% of variance in behavioral intention to use and we were able to confirm 6 of our 7 hypotheses, our study is not without limitations. First, our participants were not immersed into an actual iVR learning experience. As such, variables such as immersion, realism, interactivity, which have shown to be of importance to user satisfaction [2] were not taken into account. Although our findings were consistent with studies in which participants were immersed in an iVR experience, a follow-up or replication study, involving an actual iVR experience is suggested. Second, [11] suggest to run the UTAUT test several times over a longer period. We were only able to run one test. As such, we could not confirm nor refute the hypothesis of a novelty effect as expressed by [32]. Last, we only used a quantitative approach. As mobile immersive virtual reality in education still is fairly new and not yet a wide-spread phenomenon, adding qualitative research to investigate the underlying motivations and perceptions in a greater detail could further our understanding of this topic [10].

These findings, together with the insights from the parallel study on teachers' perceptions [25], help to understand which factors come into play in the acceptance of iVR in secondary education and might guide the design of evidence-informed implementation strategies. As such, our results both have theoretical and practical implications.

Acknowledgments. The authors would like to thank all the students, their parents, school managers, and teachers for their willingness to collaborate in this study.

References

1. Yu, Z., Xu, W.: A meta-analysis and systematic review of the effect of virtual reality technology on users' learning outcomes. Comput. Appl. Eng. Educ. **30**(5), 1470–1484 (2022). https://doi.org/10.1002/cae.22532
2. Makransky, G., Borre-Gude, S., Mayer, R.E.: Motivational and cognitive benefits of training in immersive virtual reality based on multiple assessments. J. Comput. Assist. Learn. **35**(6), 691–707 (2019). https://doi.org/10.1111/jcal.12375

3. Hamilton, D., McKechnie, J., Edgerton, E., Wilson, C.: Immersive virtual reality as a pedagogical tool in education: a systematic literature review of quantitative learning outcomes and experimental design. J. Comput. Educ. **8**(1), 1–32 (2021). https://doi.org/10.1007/s40 692-020-00169-2

4. Luo, H., Li, G., Feng, Q., Yang, Y., Zuo, M.: Virtual reality in K-12 and higher education: a systematic review of the literature from 2000 to 2019. J. Comput. Assist. Learn. **37**(3), 887–901 (2021). https://doi.org/10.1111/jcal.12538

5. Maas, M.J., Hughes, J.M.: Virtual, augmented, and mixed reality in K–12 education: a review of the literature. Technol. Pedagog. Educ. **29**(2), 231–249 (2020). https://doi.org/10.1080/1475939X.2020.1737210

6. Kaplan, A.D., Cruit, J., Endsley, M., Beers, S.M., Sawyer, B.D., Hancock, P.A.: The effects of virtual reality, augmented reality, and mixed reality as training enhancement methods: a meta-analysis. Hum. Factors **63**(4), 706–726 (2021). https://doi.org/10.1177/001872082090 4229

7. Wu, B., Yu, X., Gu, X.: Effectiveness of immersive virtual reality using head-mounted displays on learning performance: a meta-analysis. Br. J. Edu. Technol. **51**(6), 1991–2005 (2020). https://doi.org/10.1111/bjet.13023

8. Han, I.: Immersive virtual field trips and elementary students' perceptions. Br. J. Edu. Technol. **52**(1), 179–195 (2021). https://doi.org/10.1111/bjet.12946

9. Shen, C.W., Ho, J.T., Ly, P.T.M., Kuo, T.C.: Behavioural intentions of using virtual reality in learning: perspectives of acceptance of information technology and learning style. Virtual Reality **23**(3), 313–324 (2019). https://doi.org/10.1007/s10055-018-0348-1

10. Mütterlein, J., Hess, T.: Immersion, presence, interactivity: Towards a joint understanding of factors influencing virtual reality acceptance and use. In: 23rd Americas Conference on Information Systems (AMCIS), pp. 1–10. Assoc Information Systems, Boston (2017)

11. Venkatesh, V., Thong, J.Y.L., Xu, X.: Consumer acceptance and use of information technology: extending the unified theory of acceptance and use of technology. MIS Q. **36**(1), 157–178 (2012). https://doi.org/10.2307/41410412

12. Bodzin, A., Junior, R.A., Hammond, T., Anastasio, D.: Investigating engagement and flow with a placed-based immersive virtual reality game. J. Sci. Educ. Technol. **30**(3), 347–360 (2021). https://doi.org/10.1007/s10956-020-09870-4

13. Al-Azawei, A., Baiee, W.R., Mohammed, M.A.: Learners' experience towards e-assessment tools: a comparative study on virtual reality and moodle quiz. Int. J. Emerg. Technol. Learn. **14**(5), 34–50 (2019). https://doi.org/10.3991/ijet.v14i05.9998

14. Zorzal, E.R., Paulo, S.F., Rodrigues, P., Mendes, J.J., Lopes, D.S.: An immersive educational tool for dental implant placement: a study on user acceptance. Int. J. Med. Inform. **146**, 104342 (2021). https://doi.org/10.1016/j.ijmedinf.2020.104342

15. Cheng, K.H., Tsai, C.C.: Students' motivational beliefs and strategies, perceived immersion and attitudes towards science learning with immersive virtual reality: a partial least squares analysis. Br. J. Edu. Technol. **51**(6), 2139–2158 (2020). https://doi.org/10.1111/bjet.12956

16. Kluge, M.G., Maltby, S., Keynes, A., Nalivaiko, E., Evans, D.J.R., Walker, F.R.: Current state and general perceptions of the use of extended reality (XR) Technology at the university of Newcastle: interviews and surveys from staff and students. Sage Open **12**(2) (2022). https://doi.org/10.1177/21582440221093348

17. Taçgın, Z.: The perceived effectiveness regarding immersive virtual reality learning environments changes by the prior knowledge of learners. Educ. Inf. Technol. **25**(4), 2791–2809 (2020). https://doi.org/10.1007/s10639-019-10088-0

18. Baxter, G., Hainey, T.: Student perceptions of virtual reality use in higher education. J. Appl. Res. High. Educ. **12**(3), 413–424 (2020). https://doi.org/10.1108/JARHE-06-2018-0106

19. Madden, J., Pandita, S., Schuldt, J.P., Kim, B., Won, A.S., Holmes, N.G.: Ready student one: exploring the predictors of student learning in virtual reality. PLoS ONE **15**(3), 1–26 (2020). https://doi.org/10.1371/journal.pone.0229788
20. Botha, B.S., de Wet, L., Botma, Y.: Undergraduate nursing student experiences in using immersive virtual reality to manage a patient with a foreign object in the right lung. Clin. Simul. Nurs. **56**, 76–83 (2021). https://doi.org/10.1016/j.ecns.2020.10.008
21. Bracq, M.S., et al.: Learning procedural skills with a virtual reality simulator: an acceptability study. Nurse Educ. Today **79**, 153–160 (2019). https://doi.org/10.1016/j.nedt.2019.05.026
22. Sagnier, C., Loup-Escande, E., Lourdeaux, D., Thouvenin, I., Valléry, G.: User acceptance of virtual reality: an extended technology acceptance model. Int. J. Human-Comput. Interact. **36**, 1–15 (2020). https://doi.org/10.1080/10447318.2019.1708612
23. Noble, S.M., Saville, J.D., Foster, L.L.: VR as a choice: what drives learners' technology acceptance? Int. J. Educ. Technol. High. Educ. **19**(1), 6 (2022). https://doi.org/10.1186/s41239-021-00310-w
24. Agarwal, R., Prasad, J.: A conceptual and operational definition of personal innovativeness in the domain of information technology. Inf. Syst. Res. **9**(2), 204–215 (1998). https://doi.org/10.1287/isre.9.2.204
25. Boel, C., Rotsaert, T., Valcke, M., Rosseel, Y., Struyf, D., Schellens, T.: Are teachers ready to immerse? Acceptance of mobile immersive virtual reality in secondary education teachers. Res. Learn. Technol. **31** (2023). https://doi.org/10.25304/rlt.v31.2855
26. Fagan, M., Kilmon, C., Pandey, V.: Exploring the adoption of a virtual reality simulation: the role of perceived ease of use, perceived usefulness and personal innovativeness. Campus-Wide Inf. Syst. **29**(2), 117–127 (2012). https://doi.org/10.1108/10650741211212368
27. Liu, R., Wang, L., Lei, J., Wang, Q., Ren, Y.: Effects of an immersive virtual reality-based classroom on students' learning performance in science lessons. Br. J. Edu. Technol. **51**(6), 2034–2049 (2020). https://doi.org/10.1111/bjet.13028
28. Udeozor, C., Toyoda, R., Russo Abegão, F., Glassey, J.: Perceptions of the use of virtual reality games for chemical engineering education and professional training. High. Educ. Pedagogies **6**(1), 175–194 (2021). https://doi.org/10.1080/23752696.2021.1951615
29. Tamilmani, K., Rana, N.P., Dwivedi, Y.K.: Consumer acceptance and use of information technology: a meta-analytic evaluation of UTAUT2. Inf. Syst. Front. **23**(4), 987–1005 (2021). https://doi.org/10.1007/s10796-020-10007-6
30. Bower, M., DeWitt, D., Lai, J.W.M.: Reasons associated with preservice teachers' intention to use immersive virtual reality in education. Br. J. Edu. Technol. **51**(6), 2214–2232 (2020). https://doi.org/10.1111/bjet.13009
31. Ciftci, O., Berezina, K., Kang, M.: Effect of personal innovativeness on technology adoption in hospitality and tourism: meta-analysis. In: Wörndl, W., Koo, C., Stienmetz, J.L. (eds.) Information and Communication Technologies in Tourism 2021, pp. 162–174. Springer, Cham (2021). https://doi.org/10.1007/978-3-030-65785-7_14
32. Hill, T., du Preez, H.: A longitudinal study of students' perceptions of immersive virtual reality teaching interventions. In: Proceedings of 2021 7th International Conference of the Immersive Learning Research Network (iLRN), pp. 1–7. IEEE, Eureka, CA, USA (2021). https://doi.org/10.23919/iLRN52045.2021.9459334

Framework of Pedagogic and Usability Principles for Effective Multi-user VR Learning Applications

Anna Ansone, Lana Franceska Dreimane[✉], and Zinta Zalite-Supe

Faculty of Pedagogy, Psychology and Art, University of Latvia, Riga 1083, Latvia
{a.ansone,lana.dreimane,zinta.zalite-supe}@lu.lv

Abstract. Education and learning continue to evolve as a result of the rapid speed of technological advancement in the 21st Century. The growing presence of emerging technologies increases the potential of an innovative environment that can promote and facilitate learning. The impact of immersive technology in the field of learning has been widely discussed and studied by the scientific community in the first two decades of the 21st Century. This is especially true with the advent of the ambition for the unified and fluid multi-user virtual world - Metaverse and the limiting realities of the COVID-19 pandemic - where new modes of virtual interaction are in the spotlight, including the field of education. The success of VR educational content, especially multi-user educational content, depends, in large part, on how usable and adaptable it is for learning purposes. This study investigates pedagogic and usability principles for effective multi-user VR learning applications based on the Technology Enhanced Learning approach, Gagne's Nine Events of Instruction model and Nielsen's usability heuristics and analyses survey data collected during multi-user VR content testing. The study used a mixed-methods approach involving multi-user VR environment testing with a group of Higher Education students. This study tested three different VR multi-user learning applications to evaluate them from various pedagogical and usability perspectives and collected survey data to gain a deeper understanding of the students' experience. This study proposes a framework of pedagogic and usability principles for developing effective multi-user VR learning applications.

Keywords: Multi-user VR · Usability · Instructional design · Higher Education

1 Introduction

Recent technological developments, as well as the affordable costs of Virtual Reality (VR), have brought an unprecedented variety to applications of VR technology in the second decade of the 21st Century. Using computer and simulation technologies, the emerging VR technology can create an immersive, interactive environment with features that replicate the real or imagined world or objects and present them to the user [1].

These hardware developments and new online-accessible applications allow VR to be integrated into all areas of teaching and learning, creating new synergies with

© The Author(s), under exclusive license to Springer Nature Switzerland AG 2024
M.-L. Bourguet et al. (Eds.): iLRN 2023, CCIS 1904, pp. 96–110, 2024.
https://doi.org/10.1007/978-3-031-47328-9_7

different methodologies and pedagogies, as well as teaching and learning methods, where the students can develop knowledge and skills and be at the forefront of the learning process [2]. Education and learning continue to evolve because of the rapid speed of technological advancement in the 21st Century. The growing presence of emerging technologies increases the potential for innovative applications that can promote and facilitate learning. The impact of immersive technology in the field of learning has been widely discussed and studied by the scientific community in the first two decades of the 21st Century. This is especially true with the advent of the ambition for the unified and fluid multi-user virtual world - Metaverse and the limiting realities of the COVID-19 pandemic - where new modes of virtual interaction are in the spotlight, including in the field of education. The success of VR educational content, especially multi-user content for education, depends on how usable and adaptable it is for learning purposes.

This study investigates pedagogic and usability principles for effective multi-user VR learning applications. The objectives of the study were: 1) to identify what pedagogic and usability principles support the effectiveness of multi-user VR learning applications; and 2) to propose a framework of pedagogic and usability principles for effective multi-user VR learning applications based on the Technology Enhanced Learning (TEL) approach [3, 4]; Gagne's Nine Events of Instruction model [5]; Nielsen's Usability Heuristics [6]; and survey data analysis.

The study used a mixed-methods approach involving the multi-user VR environment testing of three VR learning applications with a group of Higher Education students. This study contributes to the expanding body of research on the use of VR in education by proposing a framework of pedagogic and usability principles to develop and evaluate multi-user VR learning applications, emphasising the significance of pedagogic alignment and usability in the design and development of VR educational applications.

The following sections provide a review of the relevant literature on pedagogic approaches, as well as instructional design and usability principles including Gagne's Nine Events of Instruction model and TEL approach, describe the applied research methods and participants, and finally present the results of the study while discussing the practical implications and limitations of the study.

2   Literature Review

2.1   Multi-user VR in Education

This study is based on the Constructivist [7, 8]; Constructionist [9] and Connectivist [10, 11] learning approaches. Each of these presents significant elements that can explain the value of interactive learning applications and technology in education and may be used to support the choice of a particular digital tool and the creation of a particular instructional design. According to the Constructivist learning paradigm, knowledge is created based on prior experience, and learning is an active process [9]. This approach helps educators to understand how people learn through technology [12]. Constructionism, created by Papert, is another key paradigm outlining the potential advantages of utilising immersive technology [9]. This approach emphasises the opportunity for practical exercises or learning by experience [9]. By mixing technology with traditional Constructivist activities, it was believed that students would create new experiences and ways of thinking

[9]. Since the beginning of the 21st Century, online interactive learning has become a more significant component of contemporary education. According to Siemens [10], Connectivism is a learning theory for the digital century that clarifies the essential elements of learning in a digital setting [10] and learning, itself, is evolving into a process of knowledge creation in which the human and information networks serve as generators of new knowledge.

To effectively use VR in the teaching and learning process, it is essential to assess the provided technological possibilities, limitations, and to understand how specific learning objectives will be attained. A VR learning environment can assist in the attainment of learning objectives across all cognitive processes and knowledge dimensions of Bloom's Taxonomy [13]. Chen et al. [14] emphasise VR as a suitable collaborative tool for educational applications because it enables more natural and immersive social interactions and experiential learning. In addition, according to Dieterle [15]; multi-user VR allows multiple users to a) access virtual contexts, b) interact with digital artefacts, c) represent themselves with "avatars", d) talk to other participants, and e) take part in experiences [15].

Although all multi-user VR content shares some common characteristics, even when analysing closed VR multi-user applications, several sub-categories can be distinguished:

1) Social VR,
2) Remote work and
3) Simulated environments.

Social VR (examples include *VR Chat, Altspace, Rec Room*) distinguishes itself by allowing users to interact simultaneously with users from various devices and locations in real-time [16]. Remote work applications (examples include Horizon Workrooms, Immersed), are carried out by providing synchronous working possibilities and these enable groups of users to hold virtual meetings, collaborate and co-create regardless of their physical location [17]. Simulated environments (examples include *TribeXR, Engage XR*) offer users a realistic and immersive multi-user environment that enables them to practise and apply their knowledge in a safe and controlled setting [18].

2.2 Pedagogic Perspective

Gagne's Nine Events of Instruction model reinforces the roots of Instructional design [19], both as a concept and a practice, reaching from cognitive and behavioural psychology through Constructivism, Constructionism and TEL [13]. "Instructional design is intended to be an iterative process of planning outcomes, selecting effective strategies for teaching and learning, choosing relevant technologies, identifying educational media, and measuring performance" (p. 77) [19]. Gagne's Nine Events of Instruction [5] is an instructional model developed in the 1980s that describes the stages that must be followed to properly transfer knowledge from the instructor to the student. The nine teaching events that Gagne suggested are:

1) Gaining attention;
2) Informing learners of the objective;

3) Stimulating recall of prior learning;
4) Presenting the stimulus;
5) Providing learning guidance;
6) Eliciting performance;
7) Providing feedback;
8) Assessing performance; and
9) Enhancing retention and transfer [20].

The objective of these events is to stimulate internal cognitive processes and not to replace them; therefore, not all of them need to be present for learning to occur [21]. Gagne is regarded as one of the most influential pioneers of the systematic approach to instructional design [22]. He stated that an educator's learning planning should focus on how students learn, adding that through comprehending facets of student learning, the specified learning objectives will be met [5]. Therefore, when planning the work for each session, the educator must evaluate what he or she intends to teach as well as how to organise the work in a way that encourages and supports students' learning [5]. One of the key benefits of implementing Gagne's Nine Events of Instruction model in VR content creation is to help facilitate an intentional and purposeful learning process.

The 1980s also marked a turning point in the history of digital technology when the fundamentals of the World Wide Web were established [23]. In parallel, research in the education sciences had begun to place a greater emphasis on Technology Enhanced Learning (TEL) [13, 24, 25]. Since the concept of TEL first came into use, researchers have applied the term to describe the role of technology in education and learning, emphasising several aspects, including learning flexibility and the fundamentals of using ICT (information and communication technology) applications to teach and learn [26, 27]. Daniela [23] emphasises that the growth of digital pedagogy (Smart Pedagogy), in which the educator makes use of readily available technologies to assist students and learners in the learning process, is driven by TEL [23]. Daniela [3] emphasises that educators must take precautions when using technology. First, these learning activities must be evaluated in light of the specified learning outcomes to be attained before technology may be incorporated into the training process. Secondly, before being applied as a learning resource or tool, for instance, digital and virtual solutions must be thoroughly assessed to ensure that their aim is not restricted to the principle of amusement [23]. Thirdly, the educator must possess the instructional knowledge and skills necessary to select the technology or digital tool that is most appropriate for the defined learning objective.

2.3 Usability

In the 1980s, as a result of more attainable market prices, personal computers became more accessible to people without professional technical backgrounds. This, in turn, signalled the need to design software in a way that made it accessible to a wider user audience, not just those trained in computer sciences [28]. To accomplish this, it was essential that digital products were not only functional but also "user-friendly" from their targeted user audience's perspective.

The International Organisation for Standardisation (ISO) describes usability as 'the extent to which a product can be used by specified users to achieve specified goals with effectiveness, efficiency, and satisfaction in a specified context of use' [29]. Nevertheless, the same idea of a user-friendly system should be applied to the development of the VR industry. Because of such factors as motion sickness, technological limitations, device restrictions, and a lack of universal standards, usability is an essential aspect of VR [30].

Usability testing is a critical component of determining the efficacy of software, including multi-user VR learning apps [31]. Usability testing usually includes representative users trying representative tasks in representative applications, on early prototypes or working versions of computer interfaces, with the objective of improving the quality of an interface by identifying flaws, or areas of the interface that require improvement [32]. To evaluate the usability of these apps, several commonly used usability testing methods can be used. Observational usability testing involves watching users interact with software in a laboratory setting. Researchers can observe users' actions and note any difficulties or errors that occur during the interaction. This method can provide rich, qualitative data. Surveys and questionnaires can also be used to collect feedback from users about their experience using VR applications, for example System Usability Scale (SUS) or custom survey, specifically tailored for evaluating different usability aspects, such as ease of use, learnability, satisfaction and efficiency [33].

Other usability testing methods include heuristic evaluations, which involve comparing the app to a set of pre-defined usability principles. Usability Heuristics, introduced by Nielsen [6] are among the widely used strategies for identifying product and design usability issues. By analysing a system, whether it is a website or VR content, heuristics may serve as a guide for identifying usability issues and influencing design choices to enhance a product's usability. Selecting a team of evaluators with experience in the interface or usability domain is a necessary step in the process. Each evaluator examines the interface independently making a note of any usability problems they find and then assigning a severity rating to each problem identified. The results are compiled and analysed to find common problems and areas for improvement after all evaluators have finished their reviews.

As a result of the special challenges and opportunities this technology presents, it is crucial to use a variety of usability methods when assessing virtual reality (VR) applications. Users' comfort, engagement, and performance may be impacted by VR because it is an immersive and interactive medium that calls for users to interact physically with the environment. Designers and developers can gain a more complete understanding of the user experience in VR by utilising a variety of usability methods. Usability testing is especially important for the field of education regarding immersive technologies because it helps to.

1) identify issues with the VR learning environment;
2) identify areas for improvement; and
3) discover the preferences and behaviours of the students.

Although a range of usability assessment tools, methodologies, and approaches exist for the evaluation of digital learning tools, this is not the case with VR content. Thus, this study uses Gagne's Nine Events of Instruction model, Nielsen's Usability Heuristics, and the pedagogical principles of TEL as a combined and more thorough approach for assessing multi-user VR content for learning from both educational alignment and usability perspectives (see Fig. 1).

1. Technology Enhanced Learning approach

1. Technology must be assessed in the light of the defined learning outcomes
2. VR learning environment must be carefully evaluated before use as a learning resource
3. The educator needs the knowledge and expertise to choose the most relevant VR learning environment

2. Gagne's Nine Events of Instruction model

1. Gaining attention
2. Informing learners of the objective
3. Stimulating recall prior to learning
4. Presenting the stimulus
5. Providing learning guidance
6. Eliciting performance
7. Providing feedback
8. Assessing performance
9. Enhancing preparation and transfer

3. Nielsen's Usability heuristics

1. Visibility of system status
2. Match between system and the real world
3. User control and freedom
4. Consistency and standards
5. Error prevention and recovery
6. Recognition rather than recall
7. Flexibility and efficiency of use
8. Aesthetic and minimalist design
9. Help users recognize, diagnose and recover from errors
10. Help and documentation

Fig. 1. Combined theoretic approach for assessing multi-user VR learning content adapted from [3–6].

This approach is based on the recognition that multi-user VR learning environments require a thorough evaluation from both educational alignment and usability perspectives. Gagne's Nine Events of Instruction model provides a comprehensive framework for designing and evaluating instructional content, ensuring that it is aligned with specific learning objectives. Meanwhile, Nielsen's Usability Heuristics offer a set of guidelines for assessing the usability of digital interfaces, which is particularly important in multi-user VR environments where intuitive and user-friendly design is essential. In addition, incorporation of pedagogical principles of TEL into this model further emphasises the importance of creating engaging and interactive learning experiences that are relevant to learners' needs and preferences. Thus, a combination of these theoretical frameworks provides a more thorough and comprehensive approach for assessing the quality and effectiveness of multi-user VR learning environments.

3   Methodology

This study was conducted over a period of three months at the XR educational laboratory in a university setting from November 2022 until January 2023 (user and expert testing). To assess the usability of multi-user VR learning applications for learning purposes, this study used a mixed-methods approach that included multi-user VR content testing and survey data collection. The study involved a sample of twelve Higher Education students, nine females and three males, with different backgrounds, and ages ranging from 24 to 35. Students were chosen from a variety of professional backgrounds. In addition, three experts with experience in digital design and VR technologies were involved in VR application usability evaluation.

This study tested three different multi-user VR applications for evaluation from pedagogical alignment and usability perspectives. Two surveys were developed to collect data on students' experiences and perceptions of multi-user VR content. The study collected qualitative and quantitative survey data, first, to gain a deeper understanding of the students' experience, containing general questions about their prior experience with VR technology, while the second survey included more specific questions regarding the learning process in VR and feedback about their subjective experiences while testing content.

The first survey (before VR content testing) contained general questions about the students' experience with VR technology, including the types of VR devices they have used and the frequency of use. Although all students stated that they had experience with VR technologies, when asked about their experience with VR technologies for learning, only five students from the entire sample had some prior experience; however, three students stated that they would like to use this technology in the learning process.

The second survey (after VR application testing) raised more specific questions about the learning process in VR, including the students' perceptions of the usability and design aspects of the tested VR learning applications. A more detailed overview of the collected data from student surveys is discussed in Sect. 4: Findings.

VR learning applications were analysed using the VR learning experience evaluation tool developed by Dreimane [13]; where specific criteria related to multi-user interaction were added. There were four criteria groups:

1) Purpose of the learning experience;
2) Instructional strategy;
3) The design of the experience; and
4) Multi-user interaction, for a total of twenty criteria and eighty-eight sub-criteria.

As a result, fifty VR learning applications were analysed, but for user testing, only three VR learning applications were chosen in accordance with the defined different sub-categories of VR multi-user applications: 1) Social VR *(Altspace)*; 2) Remote Work *(Noda);* and 3) Simulated Environments *(Tribe XR).*

The user testing involved a series of identical tasks that the students were asked to complete using the multi-user VR applications. The tasks were designed to simulate real-world scenarios and were based on the objectives of the VR learning applications. The tests included

1) Social VR *(Altspace):* edit your avatar; create a shared room and invite others to join; create a group picture;
2) Remote Work: *Noda:* create a shared room and invite others to join; create a mind map of your preferred movies; and
3) Simulated Environments - *Tribe XR:* try the "Basics" tutorial; create a shared room; try to play something you learned for other participants.

In addition, experts tested VR applications, completing the same tasks. Afterwards each expert evaluated applications individually by using Nielsen's Usability Heuristics as a guideline.

The testing was conducted using the Varjo-V3 head-mounted display (HMD), which allowed additional tracking of the students' eye movements. Gagne's Nine Events of Instruction model, Nielsen's Usability Heuristics, and TEL principles were combined to analyse survey response data.

The study was conducted in accordance with the ethical guidelines of the University of Latvia Research Ethics Committee (Ethics Committee Permit Number 30-47/1). Informed consent was obtained from all participants, and their privacy was protected. All data were collected anonymously and kept confidential. The main limitations of this study include comparatively small number of participants and short term testing, which highlight the further need for larger scale and longitudinal studies to be conducted to further inform the topic. Each participant tested a total of three different applications, which took an average of twenty minutes for each application. The time participants spent doing the tasks in the VR app does not necessarily reflect the ease of learning and using the VR app. These tasks did not represent a particular lesson plan, but rather activities and actions characteristic to learning activities in Higher Education, such as personalization of the chosen avatar, creating a virtual meeting and completing the in-app tutorials. When surveying students (post-testing surveys) about their opinions on the usability of the tested VR applications, user bias or personal preferences should be considered.

4 Findings

The purpose of this study was to examine the effectiveness of multi-user VR applications for learning purposes and to propose a framework of pedagogic and usability principles for the development of effective multi-user VR learning applications (see Fig. 2). To gain a deeper understanding of the student's experience, a mixed-methods approach was employed, which included usability testing of three different VR multi-user learning applications and two student surveys.

The previous section, (see Fig. 1) provided a theoretical insight into the framework for evaluating VR applications based on pedagogical and usability aspects. However, Fig. 2 gives a more practical compilation of pedagogic and usability principles for the development of effective multi-user VR learning applications. In parallel, this framework can be used as a tool for educators for evaluating VR multi-user applications, both from the pedagogical and the usability perspectives.

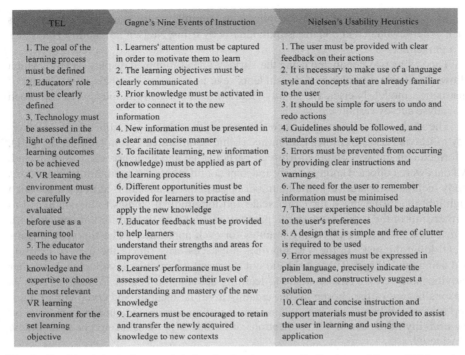

TEL	Gagne's Nine Events of Instruction	Nielsen's Usability Heuristics
1. The goal of the learning process must be defined 2. Educators' role must be clearly defined 3. Technology must be assessed in the light of the defined learning outcomes to be achieved 4. VR learning environment must be carefully evaluated before use as a learning tool 5. The educator needs to have the knowledge and expertise to choose the most relevant VR learning environment for the set learning objective	1. Learners' attention must be captured in order to motivate them to learn 2. The learning objectives must be clearly communicated 3. Prior knowledge must be activated in order to connect it to the new information 4. New information must be presented in a clear and concise manner 5. To facilitate learning, new information (knowledge) must be applied as part of the learning process 6. Different opportunities must be provided for learners to practise and apply the new knowledge 7. Educator feedback must be provided to help learners understand their strengths and areas for improvement 8. Learners' performance must be assessed to determine their level of understanding and mastery of the new knowledge 9. Learners must be encouraged to retain and transfer the newly acquired knowledge to new contexts	1. The user must be provided with clear feedback on their actions 2. It is necessary to make use of a language style and concepts that are already familiar to the user 3. It should be simple for users to undo and redo actions 4. Guidelines should be followed, and standards must be kept consistent 5. Errors must be prevented from occurring by providing clear instructions and warnings 6. The need for the user to remember information must be minimised 7. The user experience should be adaptable to the user's preferences 8. A design that is simple and free of clutter is required to be used 9. Error messages must be expressed in plain language, precisely indicate the problem, and constructively suggest a solution 10. Clear and concise instruction and support materials must be provided to assist the user in learning and using the application

Fig. 2. Combined theoretic approach for the development of effective multi-user VR learning applications adapted from [3–6].

4.1 Pedagogic Perspective

Constructivism, Constructionism and TEL emphasise the importance of a learner-centred approach to learning, where the learner takes an active role in the learning process. In addition, when combined, these learning approaches provide a valuable theoretical framework for comprehending the learning principles governing learning in VR. In addition to pedagogical alignment, in order to achieve effective instructional design, before utilising or integrating educational technologies in any learning processes, these approaches must be assessed and evaluated from their usability perspective.

Despite engaging visuals and interactive elements, none of the VR multi-user applications presented an introductory module that could introduce students to the environment, capture students' attention, or provide additional motivation for learning. In addition, none of the applications was aimed at a specific learning objective. This suggests that before utilising any of the tested VR applications in the learning process, educators should clearly define the learning objective(s), in accordance with Gagne's principles, when utilising VR multi-user applications. According to the survey results, most of Gagne's principles were never met in the tested VR applications. The most frequently implemented of Gagne's Events of Instruction were numbers Four – 'providing stimuli' and Six – 'eliciting performance'. Most users (79%) agreed that VR applications present content in a clear and concise manner by presenting concepts or by providing practice opportunities with mastered tasks, activities, or skills.

4.2 Usability

The usability of the VR multi-user learning applications was positively evaluated by 59% of the participants. 41% of the surveyed students stated that the usability concerns they encountered might be resolved by providing clearer instructions and user assistance materials. Although tested VR applications supplied guides and instructions, there were still issues, which raises the question of whether the instructions are helpful and how they should be communicated. For instance, *Altspace* made use of a virtual room that guided users through fundamental interaction modes and principles, while *Noda* environment provided textual or video guides. Only two of the twelve users were observed to have carefully read the written instructions. Users were also confused by the fact that *Altspace* and *Tribe XR* instructions presented different controllers from the ones the user was holding. *Tribe XR* did not provide any onboarding guides or instructions, which led to some misunderstandings over VR environment navigation.

Another usability problem that emerged was the compatibility of VR with the real world (Nielsen's second heuristic). Obviously, VR is a medium in which not only is the content shown in a full three-dimensional (3D) environment, but the user also loses the ability to immediately monitor input devices, such as the mouse and keyboard. Although VR content varies from desktop-based apps, it is crucial to use concepts that users are familiar with, such as visual elements (symbols, icons), natural motions, and controls, in order to ensure Nielsen's second. Heuristic – a match between the system and the real world. It was observed that the evaluated VR multi-user learning applications provided the user with few opportunities to personalize their experience and did not mention accessibility settings.

To gain a deeper understanding of the usability characteristics that students encountered during multi-user VR learning environment testing, the study compiled and calculated student average evaluations (1- disagree, 5 - agree) of the identified usability characteristics for each VR application that they tested (see Table 1).

According to the data, users apparently found multi-user VR environment *Noda* to be the easiest VR experience to use overall, giving it the highest rating of 4.30 as opposed to 3.30 for *Altspace* and 3.56 for Tribe XR. Tribe XR had the highest ratings for text readability, controller usability and visual design, while *Noda* had the highest ratings for completing tasks quickly and easily and having clear instructions.

In terms of safety and comfort, all three experiences received relatively high ratings, with *Altspace* and Tribe XR receiving the highest ratings for feeling safe and *Noda* receiving the highest rating for comfort. However, users of all three experiences reported some discomfort with movement, with *Altspace* receiving the highest rating of 4.20 for this criterion.

Further analysis of the data shows that users of *Altspace* and *Noda* reported higher levels of doing things by accident with ratings of 3.60, respectively, compared to *Tribe XR's* rating of 4.56. In addition, users of *Noda* reported the highest rating for mistake resolution, with a score of 3.50, compared to *Altspace's* rating of 2.70 and *Tribe XR's* low rating of 1.56.

Table 1. Usability characteristics identified by users.

Usability characteristic	VR application name		
	Altspace	Noda	Tribe XR
Overall, I'm pleased with how easy it is to use this VR experience	3.3	4.3	3.5
I was able to complete the tasks quickly and easily	2.7	4.0	3.3
I found it easy to read the text	4.5	3.8	3.4
I got enough support from the instructions in the experience to know how to use it	4.7	4.4	4.6
It was easy for me to understand how the controllers work	3.6	4.2	4.3
I often did things by accident	3.6	3.6	4.5
If I made a mistake, I was able to solve it easily and quickly	2.7	3.5	1.5
I liked the visual design of the experience	3.1	3.5	4.0
I felt safe	4.7	4.1	4.6
Moving made me feel uncomfortable	4.2	4.6	4.4

It is important to consider that the user usability evaluation results are in any instance subjective and that the evaluations are subject to personal preferences, past experiences and the user's prior experience with VR technology. Therefore, it is very valuable to gather feedback from a diverse group of users in order to get a more truthful picture of the overall users' experience. The inevitable subjectivity of user evaluations is precisely the reason why this research additionally incorporated design and usability expert evaluations, by using Nielsen's Usability Heuristics (see Table 2.). Usability experts completed the same tasks as students, after individually evaluating each application using Nielsen's Usability Heuristics as guidelines. The heuristics were rated on a scale of 1 to 5, with a lower score indicating a better result – score of 1 indicated "no problems identified", while a score of 5 indicated a "usability catastrophe".

The results of the evaluations allowed for a comparison of the relative strengths and weaknesses of each of the tested applications.

Tribe XR received an average score of 1.4, making it the application with the highest expert usability rating, specifically for heuristics such as "User control and freedom" and "Recognition rather than recall". These findings suggest that *Tribe XR* has a more user-friendly and intuitive design than the other two tested applications. The experts rated *Altspace* and *Noda* as having more usability problems, although the severity varied across heuristics; for instance, "Match between system and the real world", "Consistency and standards", and "Help users recognize, diagnose, and recover from errors".

The heuristic - "Error prevention" - received the highest scores, indicating the severity of usability problems with regard to error prevention, across all three tested VR applications indicating that this is the area that designers and developers should explore more thoroughly, by incorporating better support and instruction methods. The heuristic

Table 2. Expert evaluation in accordance with Nielsen's Usability Heuristics.

Nielsen's Usability Heuristics	VR application name		
	Altspace	Noda	Tribe XR
1. Visibility of system status	2.3	2	1.3
2. Match between system and the real world	3.3	3	1.3
3. User control and freedom	2.3	3	1
4. Consistency and standards	3	2	1.6
5. Error prevention	4	4	2.6
6. Recognition rather than recall	2	3	1.3
7. Flexibility and efficiency of use	2	2	1
8. Aesthetic and minimalist design	3	1.6	1.6
9. Help users recognize, diagnose, and recover from errors	2.3	2.3	2.3
10. Help and documentation	2.3	1.3	1.3
Average evaluation score	2.6	2.7	1.4

- "Match between system and the real world" - which refers to the idea that the application should use language and concepts that are familiar to the user, was also poorly rated across all of the tested applications. The compiled expert suggestions noted that this area can be improved by incorporating objects, concepts and interaction methods that are intuitive and more familiar to users. The suggested improvements can include using gestures and natural movements to interact with objects, as well as providing visual cues and feedback to help the user understand how to interact with objects in VR application.

4.3 Technology Enhanced Learning Perspective

Constructivism, Constructionism and TEL emphasise the importance of a learner-centred approach to learning, where the learner takes an active role in the learning process. In addition, when combined, these learning approaches provide a valuable theoretical framework for comprehending the learning principles governing learning in VR. In addition to pedagogical alignment, in order to achieve effective instructional design, before utilising or integrating educational technologies in any learning processes, they must be assessed and evaluated from their usability perspective.

5 Conclusions

VR is rapidly gaining traction in many fields, including education, necessitating usability testing for VR applications. The combination of Gagne's Nine Events of Instruction, aspects of TEL, and Nielsen's Usability Heuristics provides a more thorough approach to evaluating the usability and effectiveness of multi-user VR learning applications. Usability is one of the major considerations for the effective adoption of technology and the perceived usefulness of technology systems significantly affects the learning experience. To successfully incorporate VR in education, there must be a synergy between usability and instructional focus.

By considering both the pedagogical and usability aspects, this framework can help to identify areas for improvement and ultimately lead to the creation of more effective and engaging VR learning applications that support the learning process. This framework was devised based on theoretical literature analysis [3–6, 13, 23, 30], user testing results, and respective student survey responses. The findings of the study provide valuable insights for the design and development of multi-user learning environments for VR in education.

This study was focused on exploring the potential of a new framework for evaluating multi-user VR content for learning, rather than on drawing definitive conclusions about the usability and effectiveness of specific multi-user VR applications for learning. As such, this study was intended to serve as a preliminary investigation that could inform future more focused research in this area. Further research validating the proposed framework is recommended, including longer-term framework testing and validation with larger and more diverse educator and learner groups in order to increase the statistical power of the results. This subsequent phase of the study should include a validation of the framework with education and VR technology experts, as well as defining specific examples of how to achieve each principle defined in the framework of usability principles for effective multi-user VR learning content. Focus of this study was on exploring the usability of multi-user VR learning applications, rather than on assessing the effectiveness of specific learning objectives, thus an important direction for future research is to incorporate concrete learning objectives in order to better understand the impact of the proposed approach on student learning outcomes.

References

1. Ding, Y., Li, Y., Cheng, L.: Application of Internet of Things and virtual reality technology in college physical education. IEEE Access **8**, 96065–96074 (2020)
2. González-Zamar, M.-D., Abad-Segura, E.: Implications of virtual reality in arts education: research analysis in the context of higher education. Educ. Sci. **10**, 225 (2020)
3. Daniela, L.: Smart pedagogy for technology-enhanced learning. In: Daniela, L. (eds.) Didactics of Smart Pedagogy, pp. 3–21. Springer, Cham (2019). https://doi.org/10.1007/978-3-030-01551-0_1
4. Dreimane, L.F., Zalite-Supe, Z.: Teaching interior design in augmented reality. In: Proceedings of the Human, Technologies and Quality of Education, pp. 169–180 (2022)
5. Gagné, R.M., Briggs, L.J., Wager, W.W.: Principles of Instructional Design, 4th edn. Harcourt Brace Jovanovich College Publishers, San Diego (1992). https://www.scribd.com/document/387651918/Principles-of-Instructional-Design-4th-Edition. Accessed 23 Apr 2023
6. Nielsen, J.: Enhancing the explanatory power of usability heuristics. In: Adelson, B., Dumais, S., Olson, J. (eds.) Conference on Human Factors in Computer Systems 1994, CHI, vol. 94, pp. 152–158. Association for Computing Machinery, Boston, Massachusetts, USA (1994)
7. Piaget, J., Cook, M., et al.: The origins of intelligence in children. International Universities Press, New York (1952). https://www.pitt.edu/~strauss/origins_r.pdf. Accessed 19 Apr 2023
8. Vygotsky, L.S., Cole, M.: Mind in Society: Development of Higher Psychological Processes. Harvard University Press, Cambridge (1978)

9. Papert, S.: Microworlds: incubators for knowledge. Mindstorms-Children, Computers and Powerful Ideas, pp. 120–134 (1980)
10. Siemens, G.: Connectivism: A Learning Theory for the Digital Age (2005). http://www.itdl. org/Journal/Jan_05/article01.htm. Accessed 19 Apr 2023
11. Downes, S.: An introduction to connective knowledge. In: Media, Knowledge & Education: Exploring new Spaces, Relations and Dynamics in Digital Media Ecologies, pp. 77–102 (2007). https://www.downes.ca/cgi-bin/page.cgi?post=33034. Accessed 21 Apr 2023
12. Garzón, J., Baldiris, S., Gutiérrez, J., Pavón, J., et al.: How do pedagogical approaches affect the impact of augmented reality on education? A meta-analysis and research synthesis. Educ. Res. Rev. **31**, 100334 (2020)
13. Dreimane, L.F.: Taxonomy of Learning in Virtual Reality. PhD dissertation, Dept. Peda., Psy., Art., University of Latvia., Riga, Latvia (2020). https://ieej.lv/YHehm. Accessed 21 Apr 2023
14. Chen, L., Liang, H.-N., Lu, F., Wang, J., Chen, W., Yue, Y.: Effect of collaboration mode and position arrangement on immersive analytics tasks in virtual reality: a pilot study. Appl. Sci. **11**, 10473 (2021)
15. Dieterle, E.: Multi-user virtual environments for teaching and learning. In: Encyclopedia of Multimedia Technology and Networking, Second Edition, pp. 1033–1041. IGI Global (2009)
16. Ning, H., et al.: A Survey on Metaverse: the State-of-the-art, Technologies, Applications, and Challenges. arXiv preprint arXiv:2111.09673. (2021)
17. Pidel, C., Ackermann, P.: Collaboration in virtual and augmented reality: a systematic overview. In: De Paolis, L., Bourdot, P. (eds.) Augmented Reality, Virtual Reality, and Computer Graphics. AVR 2020. LNCS, vol. 12242, pp. 141–156. Springer, Cham (2020). https:// doi.org/10.1007/978-3-030-58465-8_10
18. Ke, F., Dai, Z., Pachman, M., Yuan, X.: Exploring multiuser virtual teaching simulation as an alternative learning environment for student instructors. Instr. Sci. **49**, 831–854 (2021)
19. Branch, R.M., Kopcha, T.J.: Instructional design models. In: Spector, J., Merrill, M., Elen, J., Bishop, M. (eds.) Handbook of Research on Educational Communications and Technology, pp. 77–87. Springer, New York, NY (2014). https://doi.org/10.1007/978-1-4614-3185-5_7
20. Driscoll, M.P., Burner, K.J.: Psychology of learning for instruction, pp. 341–472 (2005)
21. McNeill, L., Fitch, D.: Microlearning through the lens of Gagne's nine events of instruction: a qualitative study. TechTrends, pp. 1–13 (2022)
22. Khadjooi, K., Rostami, K., Ishaq, S.: How to use Gagne's model of instructional design in teaching psychomotor skills. Gastroenterol. Hepatol. Bed Bench **4**, 116–119 (2011)
23. Daniela, L.: Concept of smart pedagogy for learning in a digital world. In: Epistemological Approaches to Digital Learning in Educational Contexts, pp. 1–16. Routledge (2020)
24. Laurillard, D.: Technology enhanced learning as a tool for pedagogical innovation. J. Philos. Educ. **42**, 521–533 (2009)
25. Daniela, L.: Smart pedagogy as a driving wheel for technology-enhanced learning. Technol. Knowl. Learn. **26**, 711–718 (2021)
26. Kirkwood, A., Price, L.: Technology-enhanced learning and teaching in higher education: what is 'enhanced' and how do we know? A critical literature review. Learn. Media Technol. **39**, 6–36 (2014)
27. Zhu, Z.-T., Yu, M.-H., Riezebos, P.: A research framework of smart education. Smart Learn. Environ. **3**, 1–17 (2016)
28. Kamińska, D., Zwoliński, G., Laska-Leśniewicz, A.: Usability testing of virtual reality applications—the pilot study. Sensors **22**, 1342 (2022)
29. ISO.: Ergonomics of human-system interaction — Part 11: Usability: Definitions and concepts. iso.org/obp, Homepage. https://www.iso.org/obp/ui/#iso:std:iso:9241:-11:ed-2:v1:en. Accessed 19 Jan 2023
30. Hillmann, C.: The History and Future of XR. In: UX for XR. Design Thinking, pp. 17–72. Apress, Berkeley, CA (2021). https://doi.org/10.1007/978-1-4842-7020-2_2

31. Riihiaho, S.: Usability Testing. In: Wiley Handbook of Human-Computer Interaction, Norman, K.L., Kirakowski, J. (eds.), pp. 255–275. John Wiley & Sons, Ltd., Hoboken (2017)
32. Lazar, J., Feng, J.H., Hochheiser, H.: Usability testing. Research Methods in Human Computer Interaction, pp. 263–298 (2017)
33. Vlachogianni, P., Tselios, N.: Perceived usability evaluation of educational technology using the System Usability Scale (SUS): a systematic review. J. Res. Technol. Educ. **54**, 392–409 (2022)

Teachers' Experience When Using Interactive Applications with Augmented Reality Glasses

George Koutromanos[1] , Ioannis Vrellis[2(✉)] , Tassos A. Mikropoulos[2] ,
and Tryfon Sivenas[1]

[1] Department of Primary Education, National and Kapodistrian University of Athens, Athens,
Greece
{koutro,sivenastrif}@primedu.uoa.gr
[2] University of Ioannina, Ioannina, Greece
{ivrellis,amikrop}@uoi.gr

Abstract. The emerging technology of Augmented Reality (AR) is expected to
have a significant impact on education. The most frequently studied implementation of this technology concerns applications based on widespread mobile devices.
These applications usually enrich the real world with virtual educational multimedia content that users can view, but not interact with. Wearable devices like AR
glasses allow users to be better immersed in and more effectively interact with the
virtual content since their hands are free for handling controllers or hand tracking. Nevertheless, relevant literature indicates that there is a limited amount of
research on teachers' experience when using interactive educational applications
with wearable AR glasses. The aim of this study was to investigate teachers' experience when using interactive educational applications with AR glasses. The sample
consisted of 46 primary and secondary school teachers with previous experience
in using mobile-based AR applications. The participants used three interactive
applications on the Magic Leap 1 AR glasses for 40–45 min and were then asked
to evaluate their levels of spatial presence, simulator sickness, usability, and workload. The results support that the use of educational interactive applications with
AR glasses was a positive experience and that this is a promising technology for
educational uses.

Keywords: Augmented Reality · AR Glasses · Teachers · Educational
Interactive Applications · User Experience

1 Introduction

Augmented reality (AR) is an emerging technology that seems to have great potential in
education [1]. According to Azuma, [2] this technology allows (a) virtual objects to be
integrated into the real world (b) be interactive in real-time and (c) be registered in three
dimensions. More recently AR "…regarded as a type of Mixed Reality (MR) with more
weight and focus on the real-world environment, such as incorporation of virtual objects
overlaid on the real-world environment" [1]. Some of the benefits of AR in educational
settings include the observation of invisible phenomena, the conceptual understanding

© The Author(s), under exclusive license to Springer Nature Switzerland AG 2024
M.-L. Bourguet et al. (Eds.): iLRN 2023, CCIS 1904, pp. 111–123, 2024.
https://doi.org/10.1007/978-3-031-47328-9_8

of abstract concepts, increased interactivity, increased motivation and attention, information accessibility, increased creativity, improved development of spatial abilities, and long-term memory retention [1, 3–5].

AR can be implemented in various ways. The most mainstream implementation, which allowed this technology to be widely accessible in educational settings, is based on mobile devices, especially smartphones [3, 6]. Smartphone-based AR applications allow users to view the augmented real world through the screen of their mobile device. Nevertheless, smartphones provide limited levels of interactivity with the virtual content and immersion in this content [5].

Interactivity is considered an important feature of AR technology and is essential for the engagement of students in knowledge construction through "learning by doing" according to constructivism [7]. For example, physically immersive AR experiences, where users interact with virtual content using their bodies and limbs, can lead to enhanced memory encoding and knowledge transfer to the real world [5]. Nevertheless, interaction is not usually realized with the conventional technology of smartphones [1].

Immersion is the extent to which the user's senses are exposed to the virtual content [8] and is also considered important in creating a more realistic and situated learning experience with AR [4, 9]. Again, smart mobile devices provide minimal levels of immersion since the user must view the virtual content through the small non-stereoscopic screen of the smartphone or tablet. The above limitations of smartphone-based AR applications can be alleviated using head-mounted displays (HMD) or AR glasses. These wearable devices are more technologically advanced and expensive and usually have transparent stereoscopic displays that allow users to be more immersed in the virtual content [2] while freeing their hands to interact with it using controllers or hand tracking [5, 10].

Although there is a substantial amount of research regarding AR in education, most of it refers to mobile-based applications [3]. This study focuses on wearable AR glasses, which, due to their advanced technology, maximize the features of immersion and interaction that are essential in creating effective AR learning applications [6, 9]. In order for AR glasses to be integrated into classroom settings, teachers must be able to use them easily and effectively and have a positive attitude towards them before employing them in their teaching. According to Fullan [11, pp. 115], any "educational change depends on what teachers do and think". So, this study aims at investigating the user experience of teachers when using immersive interactive applications with AR glasses. The objectives of the study were to investigate teachers' a) spatial presence, b) simulator sickness, c) usability and d) workload of immersive interactive applications through AR glasses.

2   Previous Work

User experience is considered a prerequisite for the acceptance of new technology and its effectiveness in educational settings. Factors that affect user experience in immersive AR applications are presence, simulator sickness, usability, and workload. Presence and usability are considered positive factors, while simulator sickness and workload are negative factors [5, 10, 12]. Presence is a key concept in virtual and augmented environments and can be defined as the feeling of "being there" with or in the virtual content [13]. Higher levels of immersion usually tend to induce higher levels of presence [12], which is considered a prerequisite for the learning benefits of virtual environments [14]. Sometimes the virtual content of an AR application can cause sensory stimulation, which mismatches the stimulation expected from real-world experiences (e.g., the feeling of moving although being still). This mismatch can cause a form of motion sickness called simulator sickness [10]. Although the symptoms of simulator sickness are usually milder in AR applications compared to VR applications, nevertheless they can negatively affect user experience and learning outcomes [10, 12].

Usability is a measure of how effective, efficient, and satisfactory a system is [15]. There is conflicting evidence about the usability of AR applications. Although ease of use is reported as an advantage [6], there is also evidence of technical problems, lack of stability, and complicated interfaces that require time for familiarization [3, 4, 6].

The workload is a measure of the cost for the human operator when accomplishing a task using a system [16]. AR applications have the potential to reduce the cognitive workload on the learner due to integrating multiple sources of information [6]. Nevertheless, the empirical evidence is also conflicting with some studies suggesting that AR lowers cognitive load compared to other technologies [5], while others indicate that AR applications induce cognitive overload and a feeling of being overwhelmed or confused [3, 4, 6].

Some indicative studies regarding user experience with AR glasses are presented below. Vovk et al. [10] conducted a study with 142 subjects investigating the level and causes of simulator sickness induced by the Microsoft HoloLens AR glasses when used in three different industries: aviation, medical, and space. They used the Simulator Sickness Questionnaire (SSQ) [17] which categorizes symptoms into three clusters: Oculomotor (eyestrain, difficulty focusing, blurred vision, headache), Disorientation (dizziness, vertigo), and Nausea (nausea, stomach awareness, increased salivation, burping). Their results suggest that Microsoft HoloLens causes only negligible symptoms of simulator sickness, with the main symptom being eyestrain.

Beckmann et al. [12] proposed a holistic evaluation for the development of their VR/AR learning system for vocational training in the Heating, Ventilation and Air Conditioning Industry. They followed a human-centered interaction design focusing on users' interactive experience. They hypothesized that a better interactive experience leads to higher learning outcomes. To evaluate the interactive experience, they suggested presence and usability on the positive side, and simulator sickness on the negative side. Their proposed instruments were composed of: Presence Questionnaire [18], System Usability Scale (SUS) [15], and Simulator Sickness Questionnaire (SSQ) [17]. Nevertheless, no empirical data were reported regarding interactive experience.

Vrellis et al. [19] created a simple activity with Magic Leap 1 AR glasses to visualize electromagnetic fields emitted by various everyday devices (cell phone, DECT phone, laptop, and router) for science literacy purposes. The activity did not involve any interaction with the virtual content. The authors evaluated user experience in terms of presence, simulator sickness, and satisfaction among university students (N = 154). They used the Spatial Presence (SP) dimension of the Temple Presence Inventory (TPI) [8] and the Simulator Sickness Questionnaire (SSQ) [17]. The results showed moderate spatial presence, low simulator sickness, and high levels of satisfaction.

The above studies indicate that the evaluation of user experience in AR applications is important for their effectiveness in educational settings. Nevertheless, these studies were performed on users from industry, vocational training, or university students. There is a lack of empirical data regarding teachers' experience when using interactive educational applications with AR glasses. These data could give insights for better classroom integration of this emerging technology. Therefore, the aim of this study was to investigate teachers' experience when using interactive educational applications with AR glasses in terms of presence, simulator sickness, usability, and workload.

3 Method

3.1 Sample

The sample featured voluntary participants consisting of 46 teachers who had attended a course on immersive technologies and AR in education within the framework of their post-graduate university studies. Of these, 41 (89.1%) were women and 5 (10.9%) were men. 25 (54.3%) teachers worked at the primary school level and 21 (45.7%) at the secondary school level. Teachers' years of teaching experience ranged from 1 to 33 and their ages from 25 to 60. Furthermore, teachers' average computer, AR/VR and smart glasses experience was 5.57, 3.89 and 2.24, respectively (Likert scale: 1 = no experience to 7 = high experience).

3.2 Data Collection

In this study, we used an online questionnaire (Google Forms) consisting of two parts. The first part included questions regarding demographic information of the teachers (i.e., gender, age, experience in teaching, computers, VR/AR, and smart glasses). The second part asked teachers about their perceptions regarding presence, sickness, usability, and workload related to the use of AR glasses. Presence was measured using the Spatial Presence dimension of the Temple Presence Inventory (TPI) [8], which uses 7 questions with a 7-point Likert scale. The phrasing of TPI was modified to match the context of the AR applications used: (a) the references to "people" were removed, (b) the references to "objects" were renamed "Augmented Reality objects", and (c) the scale of the last question that evaluates the resemblance of the virtual experience to looking at a screen or through a window was replaced with the dipole "screen/reality" (Cronbach's Alpha: .736). Sickness was measured using the items from the Simulator Sickness Questionnaire (SSQ) [17]. SSQ consists of 16 items which measure three categories of symptoms: nausea (i.e., stomach awareness, burping), oculomotor (i.e., eyestrain, headache) and disorientation (i.e., dizziness, vertigo). The 16 items were measured using a 4-point Likert scale, with answer choices ranging from "No symptoms" (0) to "Severe symptoms" (7).

Usability of AR applications through the AR glasses was measured using the System Usability Scale (SUS) [15], which was adapted into the Greek language by Katsanos et al. [20]. A 5-point Likert scale was used to collect the data. In this scale, the word "system" was replaced with the words "applications with AR glasses" (Cronbach's Alpha: .756). The NASA TLX [16] which is composed of six items, was used to measure workload.

3.3 Procedure

This study was carried out in January 2023 in three phases by the Informatics Laboratory of the Department of Primary Education at the National and Kapodistrian University of Athens, Greece. In Phase 1, each teacher was informed about the aim of the study and how the AR Magic Leap 1 glasses operate. In Phase 2 (Fig. 1), the teachers wore the glasses and were asked to use three existing interactive educational applications that had been pre-installed on the glasses. The first application was "Dinosaur Kit" related to the assembly of a dinosaur skeleton. Teachers used the Magic Leap controller to drag and drop scattered bones at their correct places to construct the skeleton of a Velociraptor (Fig. 2). The second application was "Figmin XR", an art program, where teachers used the controller to select various brushes, colors, and 3D shapes to create virtual drawings or holograms (Fig. 3). The third application was "Museum Alive" that displayed animations of three extinct prehistoric animals. The interaction was based on hand tracking and participants could select an animal by placing their hand inside the corresponding virtual sphere, without using the controller. Then, they watched the selected extinct animal come to life and move around the room while listening to a narration about its characteristics (Fig. 4). In Phase 3, each teacher completed the research questionnaire. All three phases lasted between 40–45 min for each teacher.

3.4 Analysis

Data were coded and analyzed using SPSS (version 29). Initially, Cronbach's alpha was calculated for the sections on TPI and SUS. Afterwards, the mean, standard deviation, and minimum and maximum value for each item of the questionnaire were calculated. Finally, the total score of the TPI, SSQ, SUS, and workload items were computed following the directions of Lombard et al. [8], Kennedy et al. [17], Brooke [15], and Hart [16], respectively.

4 Results

Descriptive statistics (minimum [Min], maximum [Max] values, means [M] and standard deviations [SD]) of spatial presence, simulator sickness, usability and workload for the AR glasses were shown in the following four tables. Table 1 shows that the overall mean score (M = 5.75, SD = .808) of teachers' spatial presence was relatively high. Inspection of the means and standard deviations of this table indicate that teachers in this study scored highly on most questions, reflecting the relatively high degree of presence they felt when using the AR glasses. Questions 1 (M = 6.28) and 2 (M = 6.35) had the highest mean scores, which were related to teachers' perception that the AR objects they saw using the AR glasses were in the same place as they were and that they could reach out and touch them. On the contrary, Question 3, which was related to teachers' sense that they had to get out of the way of an AR object when it seemed to be headed toward them, had the lowest relative mean score. This is likely due to the fact that teachers only had the ability to see virtual objects (i.e., animals) move around the room in the third application that was used in this study.

Fig. 1. Teachers using the interactive applications with the AR glasses.

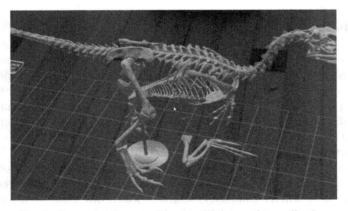

Fig. 2. Screenshot from the Dinosaur Kit interactive application.

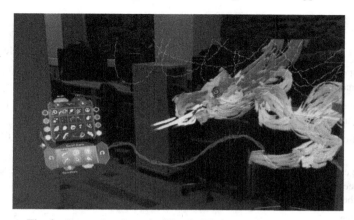

Fig. 3. Screenshot from the Figmin XR interactive application.

Fig. 4. Screenshot from the Museum Alive interactive application.

Table 1. Spatial Presence (TPI).

	Min	Max	Mean	SD
Q1. How much did it seem as if the AR objects you saw/heard had come to the place you were?	3	7	6.28	.911
Q2. How much did it seem as if you could reach out and touch the AR objects you saw/heard?	3	7	6.35	.822
Q3. How often when an AR object seemed to be headed toward you did you want to move to get out of its way?	1	7	4.41	1.962

(*continued*)

Table 1. (*continued*)

	Min	Max	Mean	SD
Q4. To what extent did you experience a sense of being there inside the environment you saw/heard?	1	7	6.02	1.341
Q5. To what extent did it seem that sounds came from specific different locations?	1	7	5.17	1.450
Q6. How often did you want to or try to touch something you saw/heard?	3	7	6.02	1.085
Q7. Did the experience seem more like looking at the events/people through screens (i.e., computer monitor, tablet, etc.) or more like looking at the events/people in reality?	2	7	6.00	1.174
Overall score	3	7	5.75	.808

Table 2 presents the results of the simulator sickness questionnaire (SSQ). The scores were low, which means that the use of the interactive applications with AR glasses did not induce significant discomfort in the participants. The scores were similar to the results of Vrellis et al. [19], who used the same AR system, except for the oculomotor cluster, which was reported lower, perhaps due to the simplicity of their virtual content (visualization of electromagnetic waves with expanding concentric spheres).

Nevertheless, SSQ scores were higher than those reported by Vovk et al. [10], who used the Microsoft HoloLens HMD in three different training settings: aviation, medical, and space. This difference could be attributed to the technical characteristics of the headsets, or possibly the specific settings of their training activities (sitting in front of medical equipment or moving in confined spaces like an airplane cockpit/space vehicle). One common finding is that the symptom with the highest intensity was "eye strain".

Table 2. Simulator Sickness Questionnaire (SSQ).

	Min	Max	Mean	SD
General discomfort	0	2	.35	.640
Fatigue	0	2	.41	.617
Headache	0	3	.20	.619
Eye strain	0	3	.61	.881
Difficulty focusing	0	3	.54	.836
Salivation increasing	0	0	.00	.000
Sweating	0	2	.09	.354
Nausea	0	1	.02	.147

(*continued*)

Table 2. (*continued*)

	Min	Max	Mean	SD
Difficulty concentrating	0	2	.26	.491
Fullness of the Head	0	3	.48	.752
Blurred vision	0	2	.41	.686
Dizziness with eyes open	0	1	.13	.341
Dizziness with eyes closed	0	1	.02	.147
Vertigo	0	1	.02	.147
Stomach awareness	0	0	.00	.000
Burping	0	1	.02	.147
Nausea	.00	38.16	7.05	9.091
Oculomotor	.00	83.38	21.09	23.965
Disorientation	.00	83.52	22.69	24.962
Total Score	.00	71.06	19.27	20.725

High values of standard deviation were measured in all symptom clusters and the total SSQ score. These high SD values are also reported in similar studies [10, 19] and could be attributed to the fact that most users felt no symptoms while few of them reported intense symptoms may be due to their age or lack of experience. The increased variability of each symptom was then amplified by the scoring procedure of the SSQ which is based on weighted sums [17].

Table 3 shows that the total score for the usability of AR glasses was 80.38%. This result shows that teachers found the three interactive AR applications very easy to learn and use. In general, the mean for each item indicates teachers' positive views regarding the usability of interactive AR applications with AR glasses.

Table 3. System Usability Scale (SUS).

	Min	Max	Mean	SD
1. I think that I would like to use the applications with the AR glasses frequently	1	5	4.30	.963
2. I found the applications with the AR glasses unnecessarily complex	1	5	1.39	.802
3. I thought the applications with the AR glasses were easy to use	1	5	4.15	.965
4. I think that I would need the support of a technical person to be able to es the applications with the AR glasses	1	5	2.30	1.209
5. I found the various functions in the applications with the AR glasses well integrated	1	5	4.20	.910

(*continued*)

Table 3. (*continued*)

	Min	Max	Mean	SD
6. I thought there was too much inconsistency in the applications with the AR glasses	1	5	1.43	.910
7. I would imagine that most people would learn to use the applications with the AR glasses very quickly	1	5	3.85	.988
8. I found the applications with the AR glasses to be very cumbersome to use	1	5	1.33	.818
9. I felt very confident using the applications with the AR glasses	1	5	3.85	1.115
10. I needed to learn a lot of things before I could get going with applications with the AR glasses	1	5	1.74	1.144
SUS Score	28	100	80.38	13.864

More specifically, the very high mean for items 1 (M = 4.30) and 3 (M = 4.15) respectively, shows that using interactive AR applications with AR glasses was considered particularly easy and that the sample would like to use them again. The usability and functionality of interactive AR applications are also apparent from the sample's responses to items 5 (M = 4.20) and 6 (M = 1.43), as well as the mean score for items 2 (M = 1.39) and 8 (M = 1.33).

Furthermore, the confidence felt by the sample while using the applications with the AR glasses is noteworthy (see item 9, M = 3.85). The teachers in this study rated the ease of learning how to use the interactive AR applications with the AR glasses equally positively. As evidenced by the mean scores for items 4 (M = 2.30) and 10 (M = 1.74), the sample felt that it did not need to receive technical support while using the applications for the AR glasses and that it was not necessary to learn a lot of things prior to their use.

Table 4 shows the workload experienced by the teachers during the use of the interactive AR applications with the AR glasses. The results indicate that both for the six sub-categories for workload and for the overall workload, the mean score was low. It is

Table 4. Workload (NASA-TLX).

	Min	Max	Mean	SD
Mental Demand	0	70	29.13	20.529
Physical Demand	0	70	28.48	21.906
Temporal Demand	0	70	22.39	20.568
Performance	0	80	20.87	21.273
Effort	0	70	16.09	17.698
Frustration	0	80	6.74	15.210
Overall Workload	0	53	20.62	13.316

important to note that the values for standard deviation in these six sub-categories were high. Generally, the results of mean scores are satisfactory compared to those found in previous studies regarding workload associated with immersive technologies [21, 22].

5 Discussion

This study investigated in-service teachers' experience when using educational interactive applications with AR glasses. The applications used provide increased levels of interactivity and immersion compared to smartphone-based AR applications. Through these applications, teachers had the opportunity to interact with the virtual content using a controller or their hands in order to assemble AR objects or create their own augmented artefacts. At the same time, they were immersed in the virtual content via the see-through stereoscopic screens of the AR glasses, while moving freely around the physical environment.

User experience was assessed through both presence which is considered a positive factor, and simulator sickness which is considered negative factor [12, 18]. The results of the study indicated that teachers experienced a relatively high degree of presence which is considered important for spatial knowledge representation, contextual learning, and engagement [14]. Simulator sickness levels were generally low like in other similar studies [9, 10], which means that the participants felt minimal discomfort. It seems that AR glasses tend to create less simulator sickness than VR glasses because they allow users to receive orientation cues from the real world [10]. The low levels of simulator sickness also seem to allow participants to be focused on learning material and not be distracted by discomfort [12, 18].

Moreover, user experience was assessed through usability and workload. Results suggest that the specific interactive applications used with the AR glasses were very usable and did not induce high workload to the users.

This empirical study pointed out two main issues as far as it concerns the use of AR applications in educational settings. First, teachers can very easily use AR glasses and interact with their applications. This means that educational applications have to be interactive, as expected. On the contrary, concerning applications with which teachers do not interact, it is likely that they will remain mere spectators to the augmentation thus offering a rather behaviorist pedagogical approach. Second, AR applications with the use of AR glasses contribute to high degree of sense of presence, as indicated by the results of this study as well. In this instance, there is a greater possibility that teachers will prefer to utilize the applications using AR glasses in their teaching, compared to mobile phones and tablets, where the sense of presence is lower.

6 Conclusion

This study showed that interactive applications on AR glasses can very easily be used by teachers. Furthermore, they can contribute to a high degree of presence, a low degree of sickness, and a low workload. To the best of our knowledge, this study is the first to examine user experience with interactive applications on AR glasses using teachers as the sample. Future studies should consider the following limitations. First, the sample in this study had prior experience using AR applications on mobile devices. Second, the sample was convenient. Last, future studies need to examine user experience with AR glasses and interactive educational applications in real teaching conditions, both for teachers and students.

References

1. Chang, H.-Y., et al.: Ten years of augmented reality in education: a meta-analysis of (quasi-) experimental studies to investigate the impact, vol. 191 (2022). https://doi.org/10.1016/j.com pedu.2022.104641
2. Azuma, R.T.: A survey of augmented reality. Presence Teleoperators Virtual Environ. **6**, 355–385 (1997)
3. Akçayır, M., Akçayır, G.: Advantages and challenges associated with augmented reality for education: a systematic review of the literature. Educ. Res. Rev. **20**, 1–11 (2017). https://doi. org/10.1016/j.edurev.2016.11.002
4. Wu, H.-K., Lee, S.W.-Y., Chang, H.-Y., Liang, J.-C.: Current status, opportunities and challenges of augmented reality in education. Comput. Educ. **62**, 41–49 (2013). https://doi.org/10.1016/j.compedu.2012.10.024
5. Radu, I.: Augmented reality in education: a meta-review and cross-media analysis. Pers. Ubiquitous Comput. **18**(6), 1533–1543 (2014). https://doi.org/10.1007/s00779-013-0747-y
6. Khan, T., Johnston, K., Ophoff, J.: The impact of an augmented reality application on learning motivation of students. Adv. Hum.-Comput. Interact. **2019**, 1–14 (2019). https://doi.org/10.1155/2019/7208494
7. Ertmer, P.A., Newby, T.J.: Behaviorism, cognitivism, constructivism: comparing critical features from an instructional design perspective. Perform. Improv. Q. **26**, 43–71 (2013). https://doi.org/10.1002/piq.21143
8. Lombard, M., Ditton, T.B., Weinstein, L.: Measuring (Tele) presence: the temple presence inventory. In: Twelfth International Workshop on Presence (2009)
9. Di Serio, Á., Ibáñez, M.B., Kloos, C.D.: Impact of an augmented reality system on students' motivation for a visual art course. Comput. Educ. **68**, 586–596 (2013). https://doi.org/10.1016/j.compedu.2012.03.002
10. Vovk, A., Wild, F., Guest, W., Kuula, T.: Simulator sickness in augmented reality training using the Microsoft HoloLens. In: Proceedings of the 2018 CHI Conference on Human Factors in Computing Systems (2018). https://doi.org/10.1145/3173574.3173783
11. Fullan, M.: The New Meaning of Educational Change. Teachers College Press, New York (2016)
12. Beckmann, J., Menke, K., Weber, P.: Holistic evaluation of AR/VR-trainings in the Arul-Project. In: INTED2019 Proceedings (2019). https://doi.org/10.21125/inted.2019.1079
13. Heeter, C.: Being there: the subjective experience of presence. Presence Teleoperators Virtual Environ. **1**, 262–271 (1992). https://doi.org/10.1162/pres.1992.1.2.262
14. Dalgarno, B., Lee, M.J.: What are the learning affordances of 3-D virtual environments? Br. J. Edu. Technol. **41**, 10–32 (2009). https://doi.org/10.1111/j.1467-8535.2009.01038.x
15. Brooke, J.: SUS: A 'Quick and Dirty' Usability Scale. Taylor & Francis, London (1996)
16. Hart, S.G.: NASA-task load index (NASA-TLX); 20 years later. In: Proceedings of the Human Factors and Ergonomics Society Annual Meeting, vol. 50, pp. 904–908 (2006). https://doi.org/10.1177/154193120605000909
17. Kennedy, R.S., Lane, N.E., Berbaum, K.S., Lilienthal, M.G.: Simulator sickness questionnaire: an enhanced method for quantifying simulator sickness. Int. J. Aviat. Psychol. **3**, 203–220 (1993). https://doi.org/10.1207/s15327108ijap0303_3

18. Witmer, B.G., Singer, M.J.: Measuring presence in virtual environments: a presence questionnaire. Presence Teleoperators Virtual Environ. **7**, 225–240 (1998). https://doi.org/10.1162/105 474698565686
19. Vrellis, I., Delimitros, M., Chalki, P., Gaintatzis, P., Bellou, I., Mikropoulos, T.A.: Seeing the unseen: user experience and technology acceptance in augmented reality science literacy. In: 2020 IEEE 20th International Conference on Advanced Learning Technologies (ICALT) (2020). https://doi.org/10.1109/ICALT49669.2020.00107
20. Katsanos, C., Tselios, N., Xenos, M.: Perceived usability evaluation of learning management systems: a first step towards standardization of the system usability scale in Greek. In: 2012 16th Panhellenic Conference on Informatics (2012). https://doi.org/10.1109/PCi.2012.38
21. Tang, A., Owen, C., Biocca, F., Mou, W.: Comparative effectiveness of augmented reality in object assembly. In: Proceedings of the SIGCHI Conference on Human Factors in Computing Systems (2003). https://doi.org/10.1145/642611.642626
22. Papachristos, N.M., Vrellis, I., Mikropoulos, T.A.: A comparison between oculus rift and a low-cost smartphone VR headset: immersive user experience and learning. In: 2017 IEEE 17th International Conference on Advanced Learning Technologies (ICALT) (2017). https://doi.org/10.1109/ICALT.2017.145

Teachers' Perceptions Towards the Use of Augmented Reality Smart Glasses in Their Teaching

Georgia Kazakou [ID] and George Koutromanos[(✉)] [ID]

Department of Primary Education, National and Kapodistrian University of Athens, Athens, Greece
{gkazakou,koutro}@primedu.uoa.gr

Abstract. The purpose of this study was the investigation of teachers' perceptions towards the use of Augmented Reality Smart Glasses (ARSGs) in their teaching and the pilot testing of a questionnaire regarding the factors that influence the intention to use those glasses. The theoretical framework of the questionnaire was based on the variables of the Mobile Augmented Reality Acceptance Model (MARAM) as well as on the variable of the social influence of UTAUT. The sample consisted of 45 in-service primary and secondary education teachers who interacted with Augmented Reality (AR) applications through the Magic Leap 1 device. The results of this pilot study showed that teachers were positive about viewing the AR with the ARSGs, and that all variables of the model were evaluated positively. In addition, the results showed that further research is needed to enhance Cronbach's alpha in the intention and facilitating conditions variables. Future research will be re-implemented with a larger sample in order to draw conclusions that are expected to have significant implications to researchers, practitioners, and education policymakers.

Keywords: Augmented Reality Smart Glasses · MARAM · Education · Pilot Study

1 Introduction

Augmented reality (AR) is one of the emerging technologies in teaching and learning [1]. Nowadays viewing AR is more immersive and interactive through AR glasses. These have unique characteristics such as presence, the hand free feature and first-person view, which differentiate them from other mobile devices (i.e., smartphones, tablets). Although Augmented Reality Smart Glasses (ARSGs) are used in many fields of activity (e.g., medicine, industry 4.0) [2–5] however in education their use is limited [6, 7]. So far research shows that AR has added value in learning outcomes, student motivation, attitudes toward learning [8, 9]. As education enters the Metaverse era it is expected that teachers will increasingly use immersive technologies in the educational process. This means that ARSGs are expected to provide new immersive and interactive experiences within the Metaverse era in the coming years. That's because ARSGs and

© The Author(s), under exclusive license to Springer Nature Switzerland AG 2024
M.-L. Bourguet et al. (Eds.): iLRN 2023, CCIS 1904, pp. 124–137, 2024.
https://doi.org/10.1007/978-3-031-47328-9_9

the Metaverse share the same technological affordances and features such as immersion, embodiment, and presence. Therefore, their value and importance in education increases and consequently the need to investigate them.

Although research activity has addressed the issue of the acceptance of ARSGs in education [10], it is nevertheless limited. In fact, the research conducted so far has not enabled participants to interact with ARSGs and their applications. Teachers are among the most important stakeholders for the successful integration of ARSGs in the education of the future as they are for any other technology [11]. In order to investigate the factors that can influence the intention of teachers to use ARSGs, a model of their acceptance in the context of formal and informal learning needs to be developed and measured. To the best of our knowledge this study is the first that investigates teachers' perceptions towards the use of ARSGs in the educational process by giving them the opportunity to interact with them.

This study is a pilot one and is part of a broader research aimed at the formation of an acceptance model for the ARSGs by primary and secondary education teachers. More specifically, the specific objectives of this study were: (1) the examination of teachers' perceptions regarding the use of ARSGs in teaching and (2) the pilot implementation of a questionnaire for the acceptance of ARSGs.

2 Theoretical Framework

The research community in the field of educational technology has used a variety of theories and models in order to explain the acceptance of technology. The Theory of Reasoned Action (TRA) [12] is the first acceptance theory which formed the basis for the next ones. It consisted of the variables "attitude toward behavior" and "subjective norm". Attitude is associated with positive or negative feelings that derive from a targeted behavior [12]. Subjective norm refers to a user's perception of whether "important others" expect him/her to behave in a certain way [12]. TRA was expanded by [13] with the addition of the "perceived behavioral control" variable and became a new, autonomous model, the Theory of Planned Behavior (TPB). Another extension of the TRA was the Decomposed Theory of Planned Behavior (DTPB) [14] which decomposes the variables "attitude toward behavior", "subjective norm" and "perceived behavioral control" in the context of accepting a technology. One of the most well-known and widespread models in the field of educational technology is Technology Acceptance Model (TAM) [15] which according to the meta-analyses of [16, 17] is a valid model for explaining the acceptance of technology by teachers. Its main variables are "intention", "attitude", "perceived usefulness", and "perceived ease of use". Perceived usefulness is associated with an individual's beliefs that using a system will make him/her more efficient in his/her job [15]. Perceived ease of use is defined by [15] as the extent to which an individual believes that using a system is effortless or not.

Extensions of TAM are TAM 2 [18] and TAM 3 [19]. TAM 2 modifies the first TAM by integrating social factors into it. According to TAM 2, variables associated with social processes, such as the subjective norm of TRA, voluntariness, and image as well as variables associated with cognitive instrumental processes, such as job relevance, output quality, result demonstrability, and perceived ease of use, affect PEOU and intention

[18]. Voluntariness is related to the perception that the user of a system has, as to the obligatory use of that system [20]. Image refers to the fact that the use of a system enhances a person's social status [20]. Whether a system is applicable or not to a user's job goals is defined by [18] as job relevance. Whether a system can perform tasks well or not is defined by [18] as output quality. Finally, whether a system's results are tangible or not is defined by [20] as result demonstrability. TAM 3 [19] is a combination of TAM 2 and its model [20] on determinants of "perceived ease of use". In TAM 3, the variables that affect PEOU are the computer self–efficacy, perception of external control, computer anxiety, computer playfulness, perceived enjoyment, and objective usability.

UTAUT [21] consists of four direct determinants of intention and use (i.e., performance expectancy, effort expectancy, social influence, facilitating conditions) and four moderators of the above variables (i.e., gender, age, experience, voluntariness of use). The extent to which a person believes that using a system will benefit his or her job performance is defined as performance expectancy by [21]. Effort expectancy is defined as the extent to which a person believes that using a system is easy or complex. According to UTAUT, behavioral intention and facilitative conditions affect use behavior while performance expectancy, effort expectancy, and social influence affect behavioral intention. Performance expectancy is influenced by the moderators: gender and age. Effort expectancy is influenced by the moderators: gender, age, and experience. Social influence, which is represented as subjective norm of TRA, is affected not only by the above the moderators but also by voluntariness of use. Facilitating conditions, i.e., the existing organizational and technical infrastructure, are influenced by the moderators: age and experience.

Later, three variables i.e., "hedonic motivation", "habit", and "price value" were added by [22] to UTAUT forming UTAUT2. Hedonic motivation refers to positive situations or feelings, such as the fun or pleasure that the use of a specific technology can provide [22]. Habit is associated with the automaticity of an individual's behavior and price value refers to the financial burden that a consumer will bear to purchase a device [22]. According to UTAUT 2, hedonic motivation, habit, performance expectancy, effort expectancy, and social influence, which influence behavioral intention, are moderated by age, gender, and experience. Also, price value and facilitating conditions affect behavioral intention while moderated by age and gender.

3   Previous Empirical Research on ARSGs and Mobile AR Acceptance in Education

Regarding the acceptance of ARSGs in the field of education, four studies have been conducted. Of these, three concerned the tertiary education and were quantitative [24–26] while the fourth concerned in-service primary and secondary education teachers and was qualitative [10].

In particular, [23] conducted a quantitative study with a sample of 968 students from universities in the Persian Gulf countries. Their purpose was to propose a model for the adoption of Google Glass by higher education students in their learning. They were based on the theoretical framework of TAM, which they expanded with the variables "motivation", "functionality", and "trust and privacy". Motivation is associated by [23] with the extent to which students engage in various tasks when using the Google Glass. Functionality is the degree of attraction, complexity, and practicality of the Google Glass device. Trust and privacy are considered by Al-Marrof et al. [23] as the degree to which a student trusts the Google Glass device to share his/her data with others. It was found that "perceived usefulness" and "perceived ease of use" are positively influenced by the variables "motivation", "functionality", and "trust and privacy". The acceptance of Google Glass by higher education students was also addressed by AlHamad et al. [24]. The model they propose is based on TAM and is being expanded with the variables "functionality", and "trust and privacy". Four hundred twenty-nine students from universities in the United Arab Emirates (UAE) participated in the study. According to the results of the study, "functionality", "trust and privacy" positively influence "perceived usefulness" and "perceived ease of use", which in turn have an influence on the intention to use Google Glass. Similarly, Alfaisal et al. [25] conducted a quantitative study using the Google Glass device. The purpose of their research was to measure an acceptance model of Google Glass by teachers and students. Five hundred twenty-eight students from UAE universities participated in the study. These researchers also relied on TAM which they expanded with the variables of "motivation", "functionality", and "trust and privacy". In this study it was found that "perceived usefulness", "perceived ease of use", "motivation", "functionality", and "trust and privacy" variables positively affect the intention variable.

The study of [10] is qualitative and was based on the theoretical framework of the variables of TAM. The purpose of the study was to investigate the perceptions of 91 in-service primary and secondary education teachers regarding the factors that may influence their intention to use ARSGs in teaching. According to the results of the study, teachers intend to use ARSGs if they are convinced of their usefulness in the educational process. Also, the factors that were found to affect the intention to use them are "perceived usefulness", "compatibility", "facilitating conditions" (i.e., technical and pedagogical training, supply of educational material, infrastructure, and school equipment), "privacy risk", and "potential health risk". Compatibility is defined by [10] as the extent to which a teacher believes that using ARSGs is compatible with their teaching style and experience and meets their needs during teaching. Privacy risk includes teachers' concerns about the security of personal data collected by ARSGs while health risk includes their concerns about potential damage to their health.

The aforementioned studies concerning the acceptance of ARSGs in the field of education have two common characteristics. The first is that they base their theoretical framework on the TAM which they are expanding. The second is that participants in these studies did not have the opportunity to interact with the device of ARSGs. In the study of [10] teachers were given a presentation about the glasses and their functions and then they were asked to answer a questionnaire. In the [24–26] studies it is only reported that the questionnaire was sent electronically to the participants.

Similar research has been conducted in the context of the acceptance of mobile AR applications by teachers which propose acceptance models for this technology. Some of them are theoretically based on UTAUT such as [26, 27]. More research is based on TAM variables which they expand by adding variables such as [29–33]. For example, the [31] who formed the Mobile Augmented Reality Acceptance Model (MARAM) based on the core variables of TAM (i.e., intention, attitude, perceived usefulness, perceived ease of use) to which they added four more (i.e., perceived enjoyment, facilitating conditions, perceived relative advantage, mobile self-efficacy).

Taking into account the aforementioned empirical studies, both those on the acceptance of ARSGs in the field of education and those on the acceptance of mobile AR, it was deemed necessary to base the questionnaire of the present study on the MARAM of [31] and the social influence variable of UTAUT [22]. The MARAM was chosen because it was found to be valid for predicting the acceptance of AR by pre-service and in-service teachers [31, 32]. The addition of the social influence variable was made because an individual's beliefs are shaped by both individual and social factors [33]. Social influence is defined as "the degree to which an individual perceives that important others believe he or she should use the new system" [22]. It is a variable corresponding to the subjective norms proposed by TRA, TAM2, TPB/DTPB, and combined TAM-TPB and to the image of Innovation Diffusion Theory (IDT) [34].

4   Research Methodology

4.1   Sample

The sample of the study consisted of 45 Greek in-service primary (N = 28, 62.2%) and secondary education teachers (N = 17, 37.8%). Forty of them (88.9%) were women and five (11.1%) were men. Teachers' years of service ranged from one to 33 years. These teachers were postgraduate students at the Department of Primary Education of the National and Kapodistrian University of Athens and had experience in using AR through smartphones and tablets.

4.2   Data Collection Instrument

The data collection instrument was a questionnaire consisted of validated items derived from MARAM [31, 32] and the social influence variable of UTAUT [22]. The items were verbally adapted to refer to the ARSGs. This questionnaire was pilot tested by four in-service teachers. It was created online (Google Forms) and consisted of two sections. The first concerned the demographics of the participants, i.e., gender, age, level of education, years of teaching service and teaching subject. The second section consisted of 33 items for the nine variables of the research model. Participants were asked to respond in a 5-point Likert scale. The items per variable are presented in Table 2.

4.3   Procedure

The study took place in January 2023 during the winter semester. For the purposes of the research, the Magic Leap 1 device was used. As soon as teachers wore the ARSGs, they were asked to freely browse various applications in order to familiarize themselves with their use (Fig. 1). Of those applications they then used three interactive ones. The first involved assembling the skeleton of a dinosaur. By using the glasses' controller, participants dragged and dropped the bones of the skeleton in a specific position in order to assemble it (see Fig. 2).

Fig. 1. Teachers interacting with the ARSGs.

Upon completion of the skeleton, participants were able to watch the assembled dinosaur move around while listening to a narrative with information about this animal. The second application had artistic content since by using it, it was possible to create virtual drawings. Specifically, participants using the glasses' controller were able to choose brushes, colors, and three-dimensional objects to create their virtual drawings (see Fig. 2). The third application was related to the animations of three extinct prehistoric animals. Participants interacted with the application only by using their hands (i.e., without using the controller) which they placed on each of the three virtual spheres. Each sphere featured one of the three extinct prehistoric animals. Then, the sphere was activated, causing the disappeared animal to come alive and move around while the participant listened to a narrative with information about this animal (see Fig. 3). In the end, each teacher was asked to answer the online questionnaire. The process lasted 40 min for each teacher.

4.4 Analysis

SPSS 26 was used to code and analyze the data. In order to examine the internal consistency of the 33 items, Cronbach's coefficient alpha was used (see Table 1). Subsequently, a descriptive analysis of the data was conducted, i.e., mean (M) and standard deviation (SD) were calculated for each of the 33 items (see Table 2).

Fig. 2. Screenshot from the first application.

Fig. 3. Screenshot from the second application.

Fig. 4. Screenshot from the third application.

5 Results

Table 2 presents the results of Cronbach's coefficient alpha for each of the nine variables in the questionnaire. Its values range from .614 (intention) to .966 (perceived enjoyment). The majority of variables have values above 0.70 which is considered satisfactory [35] with the exception of intention (.615) and facilitating conditions (.614).

Table 1. Cronbach alpha of items.

Variables	Number of items	Cronbach alpha
Intention (I)	3	.615
Attitude (Att)	3	.963
Perceived ease of use (PEOU)	3	.803
Perceived usefulness (PU)	3	.963
Perceived relative advantage (PRA)	5	.894
Facilitating Conditions (FC)	4	.614
Perceived enjoyment (PE)	4	.966
Mobile Self-Efficacy (MSE)	5	.714
Social Influence (SI)	6	.924

Table 2 presents descriptive statistics, i.e., mean (M) and standard deviation (SD) for the nine variables and the 33 items of the questionnaire. The values of the overall mean scores range from 3.40 (facilitating conditions) to 4.75 (attitudes). Most variables had on average relatively high means (above 4) meaning that the teachers of the study had positive scores for these variables. Although the values of the means of facilitating conditions (M = 3.40), mobile self-efficacy (M = 3.89) and social influence (M = 3.42) are lower, these results show that teachers are still relatively positive towards these variables.

More specifically, the teachers of this study had a positive intention (M = 4.38, SD = .480) to use ARSGs in their teaching. Their attitudes towards the use of ARSGs (M = 4.75, SD = .636) in teaching were also very positive. Also, teachers had a very positive perception of ease of use (M = 4.59, SD = .492) and usability (M = 4.33, SD = .865) of ARSGs in their teaching as well as of the enjoyment (M = 4.69, SD = .689) from their use. Although teachers' perception of the relative advantage of ARSGs over other mobile devices is positive (M = 4.23, SD = .689), they have a lower score on the question "Overall, ARSGs are better than existing mobile devices (smartphone, tablet)". This is probably because they are more familiar with the use of smartphones and tablets in their teaching. Regarding the facilitating conditions variable, they may feel that they have the necessary resources to use the ARSGs in their teaching (M = 4.02, SD = 1.076), but they do not have the knowledge (M = 3.44, SD = 1.216), the time (M = 3.36, SD = 1.048) nor the necessary support from the school (M = 2.78,

Table 2. Means (M) and standard deviations (SD) for the variables of the research model.

Variables	M	SD
Intention (I)	4.38	.480
I intent to use ARSGs in my future teaching	4.53	.588
I plan to use ARSGs in my future teaching	4.24	.679
I predict to use ARSGs in my future teaching	4.36	.645
Attitude (Att)	4.75	.636
Using ARSGs is a good idea	4.73	.580
I like using ARSGs	4.76	.712
It is desirable to use ARSGs	4.76	.679
Perceived ease of use (PEOU)	4.59	.492
My interaction with ARSGs is clear and understandable	4.62	.535
It is easy for me to become skillful at using ARSGs	4.60	.580
I find ARSGs easy to use	4.56	.624
Perceived usefulness (PU)	4.33	.865
Using ARSGs enhances my teaching effectiveness	4.36	.883
ARSGs are useful for my teaching	4.33	.879
Using ARSGs increases my teaching productivity	4.31	.925
Perceived relative advantage (PRA)	4.23	.694
ARSGs would be more advantageous in my teaching than other mobile devices (smartphone, tablet)	4.27	.939
ARSGs would make my teaching more effective than other mobile devices (smartphone, tablet)	4.18	.886
ARSGs are relatively efficient in my teaching compared to other mobile devices (smartphone, tablet)	4.13	.869
The use of ARSGs offers new learning opportunities compared to other mobile devices (smartphone, tablet)	4.58	.583
Overall, ARSGs are better than existing mobile devices (smartphone, tablet)	3.98	.812
Facilitating Conditions (FC)	3.40	.798
I have the resources (e.g., Internet connection) necessary to use ARSGs in my teaching	4.02	1.076
I have the knowledge needed to use ARSGs in my teaching	3.44	1.216
I have the time needed to use ARSGs in my teaching	3.36	1.048
I have the necessary support from my school (e.g., headmaster, colleagues) to use ARSGs in my teaching	2.78	1.330

(*continued*)

Table 2. (*continued*)

Variables	M	SD
Perceived enjoyment (PE)	4.69	.689
Using ARSGs is truly fun	4.73	.618
I know using ARSGs to be enjoyable	4.71	.727
The use of ARSGs gives me pleasure	4.69	.763
The use of ARSGs makes me feel good	4.64	.773
Mobile Self-Efficacy (MSE)	3.89	.703
I could complete a task (e.g., activity) using ARSGs	4.33	.905
I could complete a task using ARSGs if someone showed me how to do it	4.40	.837
I was fully able to use ARSGs before I began using AR applications	3.22	1.277
I am confident that I can effectively use AR applications using ARSGs	3.80	1.014
I believe I can use ARSGs even if I have never used a similar technology before	3.71	1.058
Social Influence (SI)	3.42	.993
People who are important to me think that I should use ARSGs	3.36	1.111
People who influence my behavior think that I should use ARSGs	3.29	1.058
People whose opinions that I value prefer that I use digital ARSGs	3.62	1.029

SD = 1.330) to use them eventually. Teachers' perception of their self-efficacy about using ARSGs in their teaching is relatively positive (M = 3.89, SD = .703). In terms of social influence, teachers do not seem to feel strong pressure from significant others to use ARSGs in their teaching (M = 3.42, SD = .993).

6 Discussion

One of the objectives of this study was to investigate teachers' perceptions regarding the use of ARSGs in teaching. For this investigation, the MARAM variables (i.e., intention, attitude, perceived usefulness, perceived ease of use, perceived enjoyment, facilitating conditions, perceived relative advantage, mobile self-efficacy) and the UTAUT social influence variable were used. The results of the study showed that teachers had positive perceptions towards the majority of variables. Similar results were found in the studies of [31] and [32] who used MARAM to investigate the mobile augmented reality acceptance of in-service and pre-service teachers relatively. This means that teachers are positive about the use of ARSGs in their teaching. On the contrary, they had fewer positive perceptions towards facilitating conditions. This fact reveals that in order for teachers to use ARSGs in their teaching in the future, they need to have all those conditions that can facilitate them to do so. Given that ARSGs are still an expensive technology, schools need to be equipped with these devices. Also, teachers need education and training on how to pedagogically use ARSGs as well as support from the school environment (e.g., headmaster, colleagues). Previous studies in the field of mobile augmented reality showed that these facilitating conditions could enable in-service teachers to use it in their teaching [37–39]. The results also showed that teachers had a low mean in social influence. This finding means that they do not feel pressured by their environment to use ARSGs. Perhaps, due to the fact that this technology is still new, the teachers' environment does not perceive its value.

The second objective of this study was the pilot implementation of the questionnaire. The examination of Cronbach's coefficient alpha showed that the reliability of the majority of variables was high and acceptable. In contrast, the value of Cronbach's coefficient alpha for intention was low. Meaning that future research will have to examine whether the three items of intention (i.e., I intent to use… I plan to use… and I predict to use…) that have so far been used for the acceptance of many technologies through TAM, are suitable for research on the acceptance of ARSGs in the field of education. One possible solution is for the intention variable to be examined by adopting appropriately other items that have been used in more recent research with immersive technologies e.g., [24, 40, 41]. For example, items as the following could provide with different results in measuring teachers' intention to use the glasses in their teaching compared to the items that have been used in this study: "I will use the … [ARSGs] in the future" [41], "I am interested in … [using ARSGs in my teaching]" and "I would use the … [ARSGs] … again if given the opportunity" [40].

Cronbach's coefficient alpha was also low in the variable of facilitating conditions. The teachers of this study come from two different levels of education: primary and secondary. Greek schools, where the sample originates, have different characteristics between education levels (e.g., in secondary education there are various teaching subjects taught by different teachers) and different computer equipment and technology. Also, the purchase of infrastructure depends to a large extent on the centralized education system and less on the initiatives of teachers, parents, local government, or other bodies. Therefore, teachers might have perceived facilitating conditions to varying degrees. Probably these differences explain the low Cronbach's coefficient alpha. In any case, future research should consider how to enhance the reliability of the facilitating conditions variable.

7   Limitations and Future Research

The present study is the first to use a sample of teachers who interacted with AR applications through ARSGs. However, it's limitations are twofold. First, for the purposes of the research, a specific smart glasses device, the Magic Leap 2, was used. It may be that using another device would lead to different results. Second, the sample had experience in using AR via mobile devices.

Further research is needed to enhance Cronbach's alpha in the intention and facilitating conditions variables. Moreover, this study needs to be extended by measuring the proposed questionnaire to larger and more representative teacher samples to develop an acceptance model for ARSGs by primary and secondary education teachers. It will be useful to include in this model variables that will measure the affordances of ARSGs and to whether they affect teachers' intention. Such affordances include immersion, presence, interaction, and engagement.

Acknowledgments. Authors would like to thank the teachers that participated in this pilot study.

References

1. Vuorikari, R., Punie, Y., Cabrera Giraldez, M.: Emerging technologies and the teaching profession. EUR 30129 EN, Publications Office of the European Union, Luxembourg (2020). https://doi.org/10.2760/46933, JRC120183
2. Munzer, B., Khan, M., Shipman, B., Mahajan, P.: Augmented reality in emergency medicine: a scoping review. J. Med. Internet Res. **21**(4), Art no. 12368 (2019). https://doi.org/10.2196/12368
3. Romare, C., Skär, L.: Smart glasses for caring situations in complex care environments: scoping review. JMIR mHealth uHealth **8**(4), Art no. 6055 (2020). https://doi.org/10.2196/16055
4. Danielsson, O., Holm, M., Syberfeldt, A.: Augmented reality smart glasses in industrial assembly: current status and future challenges. J. Ind. Inf. Integr. **20**, Art no. 100175 (2020). https://doi.org/10.1016/j.jii.2020.100175
5. Reljić, V., Milenković, I., Dudić, S., Šulc, J., Bajči, B.: Augmented reality applications in industry 4.0 environment. Appl. Sci. **11**(12), 5592 (2021). https://doi.org/10.3390/app11125592
6. Havard, B., Podsiad, M.: A meta-analysis of wearables research in educational settings published 2016–2019. Educ. Tech. Res. Dev. **68**, 1829–1854 (2020). https://doi.org/10.1007/s11423-020-09789-y
7. Koutromanos, G., Kazakou, G.: The use of smart wearables in primary and secondary education: a systematic review. Themes eLearn. **33**, 33–53 (2020). https://www.earthlab.uoi.gr
8. Mazzuco, A., Krassmann, A.L., Reategui, E., Salcedo Gomes, R.: A systematic review of augmented reality in chemistry education. Rev. Educ. **10**, Art no. 3325 (2022). https://doi.org/10.1002/rev3.3325
9. Cai, Y., Pan, Z., Liu, M.: Augmented reality technology in language learning: a meta-analysis. J. Assist. Learn. 1–17 (2022). https://doi.org/10.1111/jcal.12661
10. Kazakou, G., Koutromanos, G.: Augmented reality smart glasses in education: teachers' perceptions regarding the factors that influence their use in the classroom. In: Auer, M.E., Tsiatsos, T. (eds.) New Realities, Mobile Systems and Applications. IMCL 2021. LNNS, vol. 411, pp. 145–155. Springer, Cham (2022). https://doi.org/10.1007/978-3-030-96296-8_14
11. Fullan, M.: The New Meaning of Educational Change. Routledge Falmer, London (2001)
12. Fishbein, M., Ajzen, I.: Belief, Attitude, Intention, and Behavior: An Introduction to Theory and Research. Reading, Addison-Wesley, MA, USA (1975)
13. Ajzen, I.: The theory of planned behavior. Organ. Behav. Hum. Decis. Process. **50**(2), 179–211 (1991). https://doi.org/10.1016/0749-5978(91)90020-T
14. Taylor, S., Todd, P.A.: Understanding information technology usage: a test of competing models. Inf. Syst. Res. **6**, 144–176 (1995). https://doi.org/10.1287/isre.6.2.144

15. Davis, F.D.: Perceived usefulness, perceived ease of use, and user acceptance of information technology. MIS Q. **13**(3), 319–340 (1989). https://doi.org/10.2307/249008
16. Scherer, R., Siddiq, F., Tondeur, J.: The technology acceptance (TAM): a meta-analytic structural equation modeling approach to explaining teachers' adoption of digital technology in education. Comput. Educ. **128**, 13–35 (2019). https://doi.org/10.1016/j.compedu.2018.09.009
17. Scherer, R., Teo, T.: Unpacking teachers' intentions to integrate technology: a meta-analysis. Educ. Res. Rev. **27**, 90–109 (2019). https://doi.org/10.1016/j.edurev.2019.03.001
18. Venkatesh, V., Davis, F.D.: A theoretical extension of the technology acceptance model: four longitudinal field studies. Manag. Sci. **46**(2), 186–204 (2000). https://www.jstor.org/stable/2634758
19. Venkatesh, V., Bala, H.: Technology acceptance model 3 and a research agenda on interventions. Decis. Sci. **39**(2), 273–312 (2008). https://doi.org/10.1111/j.1540-5915.2008.00192.x
20. Moore, G.C., Benbasat, I.: Development of an instrument to measure the perceptions of adopting an information technology innovation. Inf. Syst. Res. **2**(3), 192–222 (1991). https://doi.org/10.1287/isre.2.3.192
21. Venkatesh, V., Morris, M.G., Davis, G.B., Davis, F.D.: User acceptance of information technology: toward a unified view. MIS Q. **27**(3), 425–478 (2003). https://doi.org/10.2307/30036540
22. Venkatesh, V., Thong, J.Y.L., Xu, X.: Consumer acceptance and use of information technology: extending the unified theory of acceptance and use of technology. Manag. Inf. Syst. Q. **36**(1), 157–178 (2012). https://doi.org/10.2307/41410412
23. Al-Maroof, R.A., Alfaisal, A.M., Salloum, S.A.: Google glass adoption in the educational environment: a case study in the Gulf area. Educ. Inf. Technol. (2020). https://doi.org/10.1007/s10639-020-10367-1
24. AlHamad, M.A.Q., Akour, I., Alshurideh, M., Al-Hamad, A.Q., Kurdi, B.A., Alzoubi, H.: Predicting the intention to use google glass: a comparative approach using machine learning models and PLS-SEM. Int. J. Data Netw. Sci. **5**, 311–320 (2021). https://doi.org/10.5267/j.ijdns.2021.6.002
25. Alfaisal, R., et al.: Predicting the intention to use google glass in the educational projects: a hybrid SEM- ML approach. Acad. Strateg. Manag. J. **21**(6), 1–13 (2022)
26. Mohd Nizar, N.N., Rahmat, M.K., Maaruf, S.Z., Damio, S.M.: Examining the use behaviour of augmented reality technology through Marlcardio: adapting the UTAUT model. Asian J. Univ. Educ. **15**(3), 198 (2019). https://doi.org/10.24191/ajue.v15i3.7799
27. Ning, F., Yang, Y., Zhu, T., Bayarmaa, T.-I., Ma, N.: Influence of pre- service and in-service teachers' gender and experience on the acceptance of AR Technology. In: Chang, M., et al. (eds.) Foundations and Trends in Smart Learning, pp. 125–134. LNET. Springer, Singapore (2019). https://doi.org/10.1007/978-981-13-6908-7_18
28. Ibili, E, Resnyansky, D., Billinghurst, M.: Applying the technology acceptance model to understand maths teachers' perceptions towards an augmented reality tutoring system. Educ. Inf. Technol. **24**(5), 2653–2675 (2019). https://doi.org/10.1007/s10639-019-09925-z
29. Rahmat, M.K., Mohamad, N.: Modelling the successful integration of mobile augmented reality technology (MART) among Malaysian pre- service teachers. Int. J. Educ. Psychol. Couns. **6**(38), 57–65 (2021). https://doi.org/10.35631/IJEPC.638006
30. Jang, J., Ko, Y., Shin, W.S., Han, I.: Augmented reality and virtual reality for learning: an examination using an extended technology acceptance model. IEEE Access **9**, 6798–6809 (2021). https://doi.org/10.1109/access.2020.3048708
31. Koutromanos, G., Mikropoulos, T.A.: Mobile augmented reality applications in teaching: a proposed technology acceptance model. In: 7th International Conference of the Immersive Learning Research Network (iLRN) (2021). https://doi.org/10.23919/iLRN52045.2021.9459343

32. Mikropoulos, T.A., Delimitros, M., Koutromanos G.: Investigating the mobile augmented reality acceptance model with pre-service teachers. In: 8th International Conference of the Immersive Learning Research Network (iLRN) (2022). https://doi.org/10.23919/iLRN55037.2022.9815972

33. Bozan, K., Parker, K., Davey, B.: A closer look at the social influence construct in the UTAUT model: an institutional theory based approach to investigate health IT adoption patterns of the elderly. In: 49th Hawaii International Conference on System Sciences (HICSS), pp. 3105–3114, Koloa, HI, USA (2016). https://doi.org/10.1109/HICSS.2016.391

34. Rogers, E.M.: Diffusion of Innovations, 3rd edn. The Free Press, New York (1983)

35. DeVellis, R.: Scale Development: Theory and Applications: Theory and Application. Sage, Thousand Okas, CA (2003)

36. Koutromanos, G., Jimoyiannis, A.: Augmented reality in education: exploring greek teachers' views and perceptions. In: Reis, A., Barroso, J., Martins, P., Jimoyiannis, A., Huang, R.Y.M., Henriques, R. (eds.) Technology and Innovation in Learning, Teaching and Education. TECH-EDU 2022. CCIS, vol. 1720, pp. 31–42. Springer, Cham (2022). https://doi.org/10.1007/978-3-031-22918-3_3

37. Alalwan, N., Cheng, L., Al-Samarraie, H., Yousef, R., Alzahrani, A.I., Sarsam, S.M.: Challenges and prospects of virtual reality and augmented reality utilization among primary school teachers: a developing country perspective. Stud. Educ. Eval. **66**, 100876 (2020). https://doi.org/10.1016/j.stueduc.2020.100876

38. Arici, F., Yilmaz, R.M., Yilmaz, M.: Affordances of augmented reality technology for education: views of secondary school students and science teachers. Hum. Behav. Emerg. Technol. (2021). https://doi.org/10.1002/hbe2.310

39. Rauschnabel, P.A., Brem, A., Ivens, B.S.: Who will buy smart glasses? Empirical results of two pre-market-entry studies on the role of personality in individual awareness and intended adoption of Google Glass wearables. Comput. Hum. Behav. **49**, 635–647 (2021). https://doi.org/10.1016/j.chb.2015.03.003x

40. Barrett, A.J., Pack, A., Quaid, E.D.: Understanding learners' acceptance of high-immersion virtual reality systems: insights from confirmatory and exploratory PLS-SEM analyses. Comput. Educ. **169**, Art no. 104214 (2021). https://doi.org/10.1016/j.compedu.2021.104214

41. Holdack, E., Lurie-Stoyanov, K., Fromme, H.F.: The role of perceived enjoyment and perceived informativeness in assessing the acceptance of AR wearables. J. Retail. Consum. Serv. **65**, 102259 (2022). https://doi.org/10.1016/j.jretconser.2020.102259

Exploring the Needs and Preferences of Autistic Users in Extended Reality: A Participatory and Human-Centered Approach

Jie Lu$^{(\boxtimes)}$ ⓘ and Matthew Schmidt ⓘ

University of Florida, Gainesville, FL 32601, USA
`jie.lu@ufl.edu`

Abstract. Virtual reality (VR) has been widely applied as a promising technology for individuals with autism spectrum disorder (ASD). However, most studies in the literature have been conducted by researchers who are not disabled or autistic, resulting in products that are less user-centered. To address this issue, Project PHoENIX is initiated to gather information from stakeholders, including autistic people, caregivers, and parents, about their needs and preferences when using VR. Throughout the development cycle, a variety of user-centered learning experience design methods and process were employed. To assess the usability and user experience of Project PHoENIX, a formative evaluation with multiple usability sessions was conducted across two phases: Phase I Usability Testing and Phase II Pilot Testing. In this paper, we present the co-design process of Project PHoENIX with autistic stakeholders, followed by the results of a formative evaluation on the VR environments in Project PHoENIX. Multiple usability evaluation methods were utilized in both phases. The quantitative and qualitative findings suggest that utilizing co-design and user experience design methods, Project PHoENIX was designed using an innovative approach and is perceived as a highly usable, relevant, and satisfying VR technology, with the potential to scale to serve a broader community of individuals with autism.

Keywords: Virtual Reality (VR) for Autism · User Experience Design · Usability Evaluation

1 Introduction

Virtual Reality (VR) is considered an advanced evolution of human-computer interaction [1] and is one of the immersive technologies used as a learning aid in various fields, including special education, industry, and higher education [2–5]. Specifically, VR is believed to offer benefits in neurorehabilitation, including the treatment for autism spectrum disorder (ASD), a developmental disorder that poses everyday challenges for individuals with autism [6]. Over the years, a cadre of VR programs and interventions have been designed and implemented to address the primary challenges faced by autistic people, including social and communication challenges [7], emotional skills [8], and daily living challenges [9]. However, VR interventions addressing these challenges that involve autistic users in the design process exist but are limited [10, 11], resulting in less user-centered products and potentially increasing the abandonment rate. To address this issue, we designed and developed a virtual environment using a user-centered methodology to explore the needs and preferences of autistic people. Specifically, we conducted empathy interviews with stakeholders (i.e., autistic people, caregivers, parents) before ideation and continuously involved them in the design, development, and evaluation process.

This paper is structured as follows: Sect. 2 presents related work on how VR applications have been applied to the field of Autism research and practice, and how such applications have been evaluated in the literature. A brief description is also provided for Project PHoENIX and the VR environments. Section 3 details the iterative design, development, and evaluation processes. The results of usability testing are presented in Sect. 4. This paper concludes with a discussion centered around the usability and feasibility of Project PHoENIX.

2 Related Work

2.1 VR for Autism Spectrum Disorder

ASD is a complex, lifelong developmental disorder that can cause significant social, behavioral, and communication challenges [12]. In accordance with the research of [13], we thereby refer to individuals with ASD as autistic people, a term highly endorsed across community groups. Although the challenges experienced by autistic people vary, they generally encounter difficulties in social communication [14] and exhibit repetitive behaviors and interests [15]. Various interventions have been developed and implemented in different formats (i.e., face-to-face therapy, technology-mediated intervention) to address such difficulties, and most of them were found to be effective [16].

In the literature, the effectiveness of VR for autistic people has been discussed with great detail [17–19]. The visually stimulating nature of the technology can be intrinsically reinforcing for the target population. However, most efforts in the literature tend to apply VR applications as a cure to ameliorate the broad range of challenges [20] identified by non-autistic and non-disabled researchers, which may differ from what is needed and preferred by the autistic community. For instance, as in [21], issues related to lifespan, transition from one stage of life to another, and well-being are prioritized by the autistic people, whereas clinical research has primarily centered around social skills and emotional skills [18].

2.2 Evaluation of VR Applications for Autism

Research on how autistic people perceive VR technology as stakeholders is surprisingly limited. While substantial efforts have been made in the literature to evaluate the impact and effectiveness of VR interventions on learning outcomes [18, 22–24], limited attention has been paid to the system usability and user experience of the programs themselves. Therefore, we argue that along with the emerging advancements of VR interventions, there is an increasing need to evaluate such learning technologies in terms of effectiveness, efficiency, and satisfaction [25]. While both formative and summative evaluations are critical and commonly used in formal evaluation, usability evaluation is gaining substantial attention as a multidimensional methodological approach to address the need [26].

3 Project Description

Project PHoENIX (Participatory, Human-centered, Equitable, Neurodiverse, Inclusive, eXtended Reality) was initiated to solicit voices of the autistic community in terms of needs and preferences regarding the use of VR, with a focus on autistic adolescents who are transitioning from secondary education into adult life. In particular, we were interested in the types of reality that autistic people have used or plan to use, the reasons for their use, and how they wish to use it more. The project was conducted in a developed VR environment by inviting the target population, as well as other stakeholders such as their parents and caregivers, to experience this desktop-based VR and participate in designed activities. The VR environment was designed with user-centered methods (i.e., empathy interview, empathy mapping, personas).

Project PHoENIX consists of three individual spaces, namely, the Training Space, Gallery 1 VR for Autism, and Gallery 2 Social VR Tools. Each space has its unique features and objectives and is designed with a number of interactive activities. For example, the Training Space is designed to train users in navigating a desktop-based virtual environment. A variety of activities were designed to teach and reinforce the skills needed in the rest of the spaces. Gallery 1 is designed as a virtual museum addressing multiple aspects of VR, from its general use to specific use (for autistic people), from lab to the real world, and from the past to the future. It also includes a 360-degree video that demonstrates how to navigate to a bus stop from a specific location on a university campus. In Gallery 2, we present users with a variety of social VR software developed by different companies. Participants are able to learn about features and affordances of each social VR tool and then rate them on a scale of one star to three stars, designed as a drag-and-drop activity. Both gallery spaces have a designated area for group discussion.

4 Methods

4.1 Design Approach

Co-design and participatory design are a widely applied user-centered innovation methodologies that values the involvement of end users and associated stakeholders in the design process [27]. In Project PHoENIX, a range of user experience design methods such as design thinking methods were used to ensure the participation of end users as well as stakeholders, and to gather information about participants' prior experiences in research studies and with VR technology. In the following, we provide a brief introduction to the design thinking methods and discuss their benefits.

Design Thinking Methods. User experience design research and methodologies highlight the users. To approach potential target users, we applied widely used design thinking methods, including a three-stage process of empathy interviews, empathy mapping, and persona development. Empathy interviews [28] are one-on-one conversations that help designers understand how potential users feel about the central problem and how they might perceive designed solutions. Unlike other types of interviews, empathy interviews aim to promote empathy and require interviewers to immerse, observe, and engage during the interviews [28]. To systematically extract information from empathy interviews, we generate empathy maps by categorizing interview notes based on what interviewees say, do, think, and feel. Empathy maps help designers understand the interviewee's emotions and experiences, which are priorities of Project PHoENIX. Empathy maps are particularly informative in creating user personas, which are fictional archetypes of users who might use the designed technology within their specific usage context. Each persona represents a fictional user who shares the same or similar characteristics as a group of learners. Personas guide and inform design decisions and help examine them. To this end, personas should be updated if learner needs and challenges change. Taken together, we used empathy methods to learn what is important to autistic people, to reveal emotional and perhaps tacit insights, to explore behaviors, needs, and challenges, and ultimately to develop a deep understanding of their daily lived experiences [29, 30].

Four autistic participants were invited to participate in the empathy interviews, resulting in the development of four user personas. These participants were invited back to review the personas and to share their thoughts and opinions on colors, themes, objects, etc. of the design of any VR space. Information collected from the second round of interviews resulted in the development of two gallery spaces (Fig. 1). Additionally, a Training Space (Fig. 2) was developed to help participants navigate the VR space and complete interactive tasks.

Fig. 1. An overview of the initial design of Gallery 1.

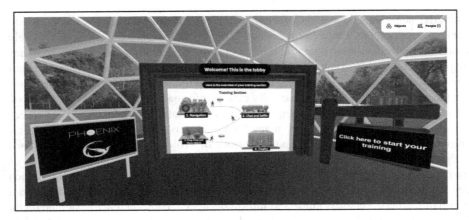

Fig. 2. An overview of the Training Space.

4.2 Phase I Usability Testing

To assess the usability and user experience of the spaces, we recruited five autistic people who had not participated in previous studies. Each participant completed two usability sessions on different days. In Session 1, each participant evaluated the Training Space and Gallery 1, while only Gallery 2 was evaluated on the second session. Each session was facilitated by a trained researcher under the supervision of a university professor and lasted about an hour. The facilitator adhered to a pre-developed protocol throughout each session, and at least two observers were present to take field notes. Participants were asked to think out loud in all testing sessions, which were recorded with video and audio with their consent.

Instruments used in this phase include the Computer System Usability Questionnaire (CSUQ) [31], a self-developed social validity questionnaire, and four open-ended questions. The CSUQ is a standardized self-reported questionnaire designed to assess the perceived usability of a given software, project, or application [31]. Specifically, it evaluates a given technology along four factors, namely, overall, system usefulness, information quality, and interface quality. The social validity questionnaire was internally developed by the lead researcher and reviewed by experts for content validity, aiming to assess the research procedures, goals, and participants' experience. As a critical concept in the field of applied behavior analysis [32], social validity tends to be overlooked in research that involved autistic people. This could potentially affect the effectiveness of evidence-based intervention [33], including applications used for autism research.

The three instruments were input in a Qualtrics survey distributed to participants at the end of Session 2. Participants' responses were exported from Qualtrics and imported into spreadsheet software for analysis. Following guidelines by [34], CSUQ data were analyzed by first calculating individual scores and then averaging them across all items. Additionally, data were analyzed along the reported factor structure [34]. Data from the social validity questionnaire were quantitatively analyzed by computing the mean score of all individuals across all items. Video recordings from each session were processed

(Fig. 3) and analyzed using a coding scheme adapted from [35]. Finally, content analysis was conducted on responses from the four open-ended questions.

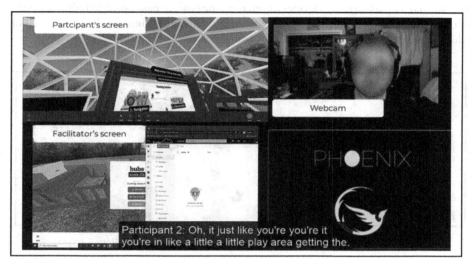

Fig. 3. A screenshot that illustrates how videos were combined, synchronized, and closed-captioned for video analysis.

4.3 Phase II Pilot Testing

In order to assess the feasibility of conducting research studies within Project PHoENIX the VR environments, a pilot testing was carried out with a focus group of four autistic participants. All participants were invited to campus. Upon arrival, they were first greeted by the research team in the research lab, and then placed in four different rooms. Note that all participants had completed the training prior to the pilot testing session. Participants completed Gallery 1 and Gallery 2 as a group within one day with multiple breaks. Research procedures, instruments, and data analysis techniques used in this phase were identical to those used in Phase I.

5 Results

5.1 Design Revisions

Design revisions were iteratively and instantly implemented between sessions in the two phases. The most salient change was the structure of Gallery 1 and Gallery 2. Initially, an open-space structure with an un-curated experience was employed, allowing participants to visit any station in any order at any time before being called to gather in the gathering area. However, after the first two usability testing sessions in Phase I, participants experienced technical issues, such as slow loading speed, blurry graphics, and delayed motion responses. After an investigation into such issues, it was discovered that these issues could be due to the participants' internet, device models, and the fact that our designed spaces contained too many three-dimensional objects. Given the lack of control over participants' devices or internet, the design team opted to reduce the size of each gallery by breaking the entire space with four stations into smaller spaces, all of which were still connected to the gallery using a directory map (Fig. 4).

Fig. 4. An overview of the final design of Gallery 1 (left) and Gallery 2 (right).

5.2 Qualitative Results of Phase I and Phase II

In Phase I, a spreadsheet was used to record usability issues identified by observers or directly captured by participants during the testing sessions, with severity levels noted [37]. A total of 58 usability problems were identified, of which 52 were resolved (Fig. 5). Of the remaining six unresolved issues, three were not considered usability issues and the rest were related to cosmetic preferences, which varied by participant. In Phase II, no usability issues were identified by observers or participants.

The four open-ended questions asked participants to provide feedback on what they liked the best, what they liked the least, what they would change, and any additional comments (optional). Participants generally appreciated the atmosphere in all three spaces and described it as "nice and calming". Acknowledgement of the contents presented in the stations was observed, as multiple participants indicated they enjoyed "learning about different VR technologies and how they might be applied to autism research", and "seeing the different programs". Such perspectives aligned exceptionally well with our design intentions, which were drawn from the empathy interviews and personas in terms of autistic users' preferences and needs.

In this phase, participants' responses to the question regarding what they liked the least and what they would change emphasized technical difficulties encountered during the testing sessions, such as "The volume needs a toggle", "The rating system was a bit difficult to use", and "Improve the drag and drop of the rating system". All of these issues were addressed by the research team before Phase II. Responses to these two questions after Phase II Pilot Testing were far less critical, with some participants indicating that

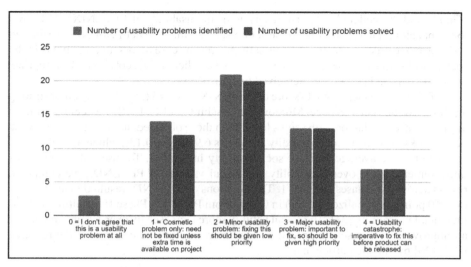

Fig. 5. Total number of usability issues identified and resolved, stratified by priority.

they were "not sure" or providing comments unrelated to the VR environment or research procedures, such as a lunch order.

Results from the video analysis in both phases support the quantitative findings and were consistent with responses from the open-ended questions. In Phase I, fewer usability problems and more recognition of the design were identified by participants as the study progressed. In Phase II, the primary focus was on examining the feasibility of Project PHoENIX and its potential to scale for use in an authentic research context. The nature of the user experience was broadly exposed as participants initiated and engaged in a variety of conversations around VR for autistic people ("It's nice to know we're being thought of"). The usefulness and relevance of the program were highlighted throughout both phases. For instance, three participants took turns sharing their personal experiences on social anxiety at a station in Gallery 1, "What VR helps with is that it's not a place where people would be watching you specifically, because you can mess up all you want in VR", "There won't be consequences if they mess up in VR", "It would have really helped me out", etc.

5.3   Quantitative Results of Phase I and Phase II

In Phase I, the mean CSUQ score for overall performance of PHoENIX was 1.98 (sd = 0.53), indicating an above average performance according to the benchmarks established by [31]. It is important to note that the CSUQ scale was designed using a 7-point Likert scale ranging from strongly agree to strongly disagree, where a smaller rating represents better performance. To obtain a more concrete understanding of how PHoENIX performed, we converted the traditional score from the historical 7-point scale to a 0–100-point scale to use the Curved Grading Scale (CGS) [31], which has been shown as valid and reliable convention method [31]. A mean score of 81.79 was obtained, falling within the 90–95 percentile range on the CGS, indicating acceptable usability between

"Good" and "Excellent" [31]. The analysis of the usability of PHoENIX's VR environments along the reported factor structure showed that Project PHoENIX performed above average on every factor. Additionally, the mean score across all eight items in the social validity questionnaire was 5.88 (sd = 0.98), indicating acceptable and appropriate research goals and procedures perceived by autistic users.

In Phase II, the mean CSUQ score of PHoENIX was 1.45 (sd = 0.57), demonstrating an above average performance. Moreover, the usability of PHoENIX's VR environments improved on every factor, with scores lower than those obtained in Phase I and below the benchmarks. The mean social validity score was 6.94 (sd = 0.13), which also improved compared to the average score of social validity in Phase I. To assess the continuous improvement of the overall usability and social validity of PHoENIX, we compared results across two phases in Table 1. The iterations of PHoENIX resulted in an increase over 10 points (normalized scores) in CSUQ from Phase I to Phase II, resulting in "best imaginable" usability [31]. The social validity score increased by over 1 point, indicating an improvement in research procedures and more positive perceptions of the research goals [36] by autistic participants.

Table 1. Comparison of results from two stages of usability testing.

Study Phases	CSUQ Scores (normalized)	Social Validity Scores
Phase I Usability Testing	m = 81.79 (sd = 11.79)	m = 5.88 (sd = 0.98)
Phase II Pilot Testing	m = 92.53 (sd = 9.45)	m = 6.94 (sd = 0.13)

6 Discussion

The present study aimed to solicit voices of the autistic community in terms of needs and preferences regarding the use of VR. To achieve this goal, we utilized a participatory design approach along with a range of user-centered learning experience design methods (e.g., empathy interviews, personas) to co-develop an inclusive VR technology with autistic participants that caters to their needs and preferences. Participation of autistic people throughout the entire process of design, development, implementation, and evaluation was integral to ensuring that project PHoENIX fulfilled its intended purpose. Specifically, the design decisions, including colors, themes, and objects used in the final version, were directly informed by participants' inputs. Furthermore, the specific content of the VR application was developed by considering the features that autistic users were seeking to help them with autism.

A formative evaluation of the project was performed across two phases in multiple sessions, with findings from such sessions being used to iteratively improve the overall design of the VR environments. Specifically, the use of multiple usability evaluation methods, such as think-aloud protocol and self-reported questionnaires, resulted in multiple sources of qualitative and quantitative data, ensuring the validity and reliability of the findings. In this study, data sources include video recordings of each testing session, individual responses to open-ended questions, and individual responses to questionnaires.

Taken together, our qualitative and quantitative findings suggest that Project PHoENIX achieves high system usability, fulfills satisfactory user experience, and is relevant for autistic stakeholders. The rigorous formative evaluation demonstrates an example of how researchers and practitioners can assess educational technologies to ensure stakeholders' voices are heard. Our approach to co-design and participatory design underscores the mission of Project PHoENIX and takes the initiative towards promoting a more inclusive future for research in this area.

References

1. Pantelidis, V.: Reasons to use virtual reality in education and training courses and a model to determine when to use virtual reality. Themes Sci. Technol. Educ. **2**(1–2), 59–70 (2010)
2. Jeffs, T.: Virtual reality and special needs. Themes Sci. Technol. Educ. **2**(1–2), 253–268 (2010)
3. Ma, D., Gausemeier, J., Fan, X., Grafe, M.: Virtual Reality & Augmented Reality in Industry. Springer, Berlin (2011). https://doi.org/10.1007/978-3-642-17376-9
4. Radianti, J., Majchrzak, T., Fromm, J., Wohlgenannt, I.: A systematic review of immersive virtual reality applications for higher education: design elements, lessons learned, and research agenda. Comput. Educ. **147**, 103778 (2020)
5. Raskind, M., Smedley, T., Higgins, K.: Virtual technology: bringing the world into the special education classroom. Interv. Sch. Clin. **41**(2), 114–119 (2005)
6. DeLuca, R., et al.: Innovative use of virtual reality in autism spectrum disorder: a case-study. Appl. Neuropsychol. Child **10**(1), 90–100 (2021)
7. Cheng, Y., Huang, C.L., Yang, C.S.: Using a 3D immersive virtual environment system to enhance social understanding and social skills for children with autism spectrum disorders. Focus Autism Other Dev. Disabil. **30**(4), 222–236 (2015). https://doi.org/10.1177/108835761 5583473
8. Lorenzo, G., Lledó, A., Pomares, J., Roig, R.: Design and application of an immersive virtual reality system to enhance emotional skills for children with autism spectrum disorders. Comput. Educ. **98**, 192–205 (2016)
9. Cox, D.J., et al.: Can youth with autism spectrum disorder use virtual reality driving simulation training to evaluate and improve driving performance? An exploratory study. J. Autism Dev. Disord. **47**(8), 2544–2555 (2017). https://doi.org/10.1007/s10803-017-3164-7
10. Dahlstrom-Hakki, I., et al.: Inclusive VR through inclusive co-design with neurodiverse learners. In: 7th International Conference of the Immersive Learning Research Network (iLRN), pp. 1–5 (2011). https://doi.org/10.23919/iLRN52045.2021.9459322
11. Economou, D., Russi, M., Doumanis, I., Mentzelopoulos, M., Bouki, V., Ferguson, J.: Using serious games for learning British sign language combining video, enhanced interactivity, and VR technology. J. Univ. Comput. Sci. **26**(8), 996–1016 (2020). https://doi.org/10.3897/jucs.2020.053
12. Barahona-Corrêa, J., Velosa, A., Chainho, A., Lopes, R., Oliveira-Maia, A.: Repetitive transcranial magnetic stimulation for treatment of autism spectrum disorder: a systematic review and meta-analysis. Front. Integr. Neurosci. **12**, 27 (2018)
13. Kenny, L., Hattersley, C., Molins, B., Buckley, C., Povey, C., Pellicano, E.: Which terms should be used to describe autism? Perspectives from the UK autism community. Autism **20**(4), 442–462 (2016)

14. Lord, C., et al.: Autism spectrum disorder. Nat. Rev. Disease Primers **6**(1), 1–23 (2020)
15. Zhou, M., Nasir, L., Farhat, M., Kook, B., Artukoglu, B., Bloch, M.: Meta-analysis: pharmacologic treatment of restricted and repetitive behaviors in autism spectrum disorders. J. Am. Acad. Child Adolesc. Psychiatry **60**(1), 35–45 (2021)
16. Soares, E., Bausback, K., Beard, C., Higinbotham, M., Bunge, E., Gengoux, G.: Social skills training for autism spectrum disorder: a meta-analysis of in-person and technological interventions. J. Technol. Behav. Sci. **6**(1), 166–180 (2021)
17. Karami, B., Koushki, R., Arabgol, F., Rahmani, M., Vahabie, A.: Effectiveness of virtual/augmented reality-based therapeutic interventions on individuals with autism spectrum disorder: a comprehensive meta-analysis. Front. Psychiatry **12**, 887 (2021)
18. Mesa-Gresa, P., Gil-Gómez, H., Lozano-Quilis, J., Gil-Gómez, J.: Effectiveness of virtual reality for children and adolescents with autism spectrum disorder: an evidence-based systematic review. Sensors **18**(8), 2486 (2018)
19. Parsons, S.: Authenticity in Virtual Reality for assessment and intervention in autism: a conceptual review. Educ. Res. Rev. **19**, 138–157 (2016)
20. Schmidt, M., Glaser, N.: Investigating the usability and learner experience of a virtual reality adaptive skills intervention for adults with autism spectrum disorder. Educ. Tech. Res. Dev. **69**(3), 1665–1699 (2021). https://doi.org/10.1007/s11423-021-10005-8
21. Harris, L., Gilmore, D., Longo, A., Hand, B.: Patterns of US federal autism research funding during 2017–2019. Autism **25**(7), 2135–2139 (2021)
22. Josman, N., Ben-Chaim, H., Friedrich, S., Weiss, P.: Effectiveness of virtual reality for teaching street-crossing skills to children and adolescents with autism. Int. J. Disabil. Hum. Dev. **7**(1), 49–56 (2008)
23. Kandalaft, M., Didehbani, N., Krawczyk, D., Allen, T., Chapman, S.: Virtual reality social cognition training for young adults with high-functioning autism. J. Autism Dev. Disord. **43**(1), 34–44 (2013)
24. Parsons, S., Cobb, S.: State-of-the-art of virtual reality technologies for children on the autism spectrum. Eur. J. Spec. Needs Educ. **26**(3), 355–366 (2011)
25. Honebein, P.C., Honebein, C.H.: Effectiveness, efficiency, and appeal: pick any two? The influence of learning domains and learning outcomes on designer judgments of useful instructional methods. Educ. Tech. Res. Dev. **63**(6), 937–955 (2015). https://doi.org/10.1007/s11423-015-9396-3
26. Lu, J., Schmidt, M., Lee, M., Huang, R.: Usability research in educational technology: a state-of-the-art systematic review. Educ. Technol. Res. Dev. **70**(6), 1951–1992 (2022). https://doi.org/10.1007/s11423-022-10152-6
27. Rosenzweig, E.: Successful User Experience: Strategies and Roadmaps. Morgan Kaufmann, Waltham, Maryland (2015)
28. Nelsestuen, K., Smith, J.: Empathy interviews. Learn. Prof. **41**(5), 59 (2020)
29. Gray, C., Yilmaz, S., Seifert, C., Gonzalez, R.: Idea generation through empathy: reimagining the cognitive walkthrough. In: 2015 ASEE Annual Conference & Exposition, pp. 26.871.1–26.871.29 (2015)
30. Strobel, J., Hess, J., Pan, R., Wachter Morris, C.: Empathy and care within engineering: qualitative perspectives from engineering faculty and practicing engineers. Eng. Stud. **5**(2), 137–159 (2013)
31. Sauro, J., Lewis, J.: Quantifying the User Experience: Practical Statistics for User Research. Morgan Kaufmann, Cambridge, Maryland (2016)
32. Foster, S., Mash, E.: Assessing social validity in clinical treatment research: issues and procedures. J. Consult. Clin. Psychol. **67**(3), 308 (1999)
33. Park, E., Blair, K.: Social validity assessment in behavior interventions for young children: a systematic review. Top. Early Child. Spec. Educ. **39**(3), 156–169 (2019)

34. Lewis, J.: Psychometric evaluation of the PSSUQ using data from five years of usability studies. Int. J. Hum.-Comput. Interact. **14**(3–4), 463–488 (2002). https://doi.org/10.1080/104 47318.2002.9669130

35. Kushniruk, A., Borycki, E., Kitson, N., Kannry, J.: Development of a video coding scheme focused on socio-technical aspects of human-computer interaction in healthcare. Stud. Health Technol. Inf. **257**, 236–243 (2019)

36. Common, E., Lane, K.: Social validity assessment. In: Applied Behavior Analysis Advanced Guidebook, pp. 73–92. Academic Press (2017)

37. Nielsen Norman Group Articles Page. https://www.nngroup.com/articles/how-to-rate-the-sev erity-of-usability-problems/. Accessed 01 Feb 2023

Outdated or Not? A Case Study of How 3D Desktop VR Is Accepted Today

Hao He[1]([✉]) [iD], Xinhao Xu[2] [iD], Jhon Bueno-Vesga[3] [iD], Shangman Li[2] [iD], and Yuanyuan Gu[2] [iD]

[1] Emporia State University, Emporia, KS 66801, USA
hhe1@emporia.edu
[2] University of Missouri, Columbia, MO 65202, USA
[3] Pennsylvania State University, University Park, PA 16802, USA

Abstract. Virtual reality (VR) is believed to be a beneficial medium for teaching and learning. While many researchers are pursuing more advanced VR technologies, devices, or systems to provide users or learners with more immersive and interactive VR learning experiences, many people have not even experienced some basic VR systems. In this paper, we investigated a straightforward question, "How do learners perceive their learning experience in a legacy VR system?" using OpenSimulator to host a VR online orientation. The results indicate that it was many participants' first-time experiencing VR. Even if the VR system we used might seem outdated using today's criteria, most enjoyed it very much and felt immersed in the VR world. The results implied that, though advanced immersive VR technology provides a better experience, a legacy VR system such as OpenSimulator may still be helpful in particular learning activities for specific learning populations.

Keywords: Virtual Reality · Legacy System · OpenSimulator · Learning Experience

1 Introduction

A 3D interactive or virtual reality learning environment (VRLE) is deemed a tool that brings changes to online learning [1]. Many researchers have applied 3D interactive or virtual reality (VR) technology in educational research. For example, using VR, Gerry [2] explored creativity and empathy in painting. El-Mounayri et al. [3] created a VRLE to teach computer major students machine learning. Yeh and Lan [4] studied learner autonomy by allowing students to create in a VRLE. The VRLEs in these studies, and many others, were created using immersive VR technology, which required high-performance computers or VR headsets to view or interact in the VR world. This limitation may require higher affordability for learners, which makes it harder for home-based online students to experience VR-enabled learning and thus fails to scale up the use of a VRLE.

3D desktop-based VR platforms/systems have been existing for decades. An early example of using 3D desktop VR systems for research was Robertson's and colleagues' [5] study on immersion in desktop VR in 1997. Compared to the more immersive VR

M.-L. Bourguet et al. (Eds.): iLRN 2023, CCIS 1904, pp. 150–160, 2024.
https://doi.org/10.1007/978-3-031-47328-9_11

technologies (e.g., a head-mounted display (HMD) VR) nowadays, 3D desktop-based VR technology provides users with easy access by using keyboards, mouses, joysticks, or touch screens [6], which may make some people think such kind of interaction outdated. However, the disadvantages in some people's eyes may be the advantages over the limitations of the more immersive VR technologies mentioned above. For example, a 3D desktop-based VR system can run on a regular personal computer without spending extra money purchasing an HMD device or upgrading the CPU, memory, or graphics card. To make a VRLE more affordable and accessible, we created a Virtual Reality Online Orientation (VRO2) using OpenSimulator [7] (see Figs 1, 2, 3 and 4). As an open-source VR platform launched in 2007, OpenSimulator can run on a personal desktop computer or laptop without additional external devices. Considering the release year, the graphics quality, and the functions and interactions it supports, we consider OpenSimulator a legacy platform. We have oriented online students using the VRO2 since August 2019. Compared to more and more immersive VR platforms and tools nowadays, OpenSimulator is a VR platform with some history. While many VR researchers pursue a visually highly immersive experience in VR systems, in this short paper, we are curious about whether VR learning scenarios enabled by a platform such as OpenSimulator would still be feasible and effective by studying how our students would perceive and be interested in using an "old" VR system for learning. In other words, we are mainly interested in one research question: How did users/learners perceive a legacy VR learning system within which they were exploring?

2   Literature Review

2.1   The Evolution of VR Types

Almost 30 years ago, Loeffler & Anderson [8] and Moore [9] categorized VR into four types: text-based VR (e.g., online chat rooms or multi-user dungeon (MUD) games), desktop-based VR (e.g., most 3D video games today), Sensory-immersive VR (e.g., a 4D movie theater in an amusement park), and fully-immersive VR (e.g., a game using a VR headset). Unlike today's VR environments with appealing graphics or interactivity, a text-based VR environment needs users to type in text or commands to interact [10]. Though simple and crude, text-based VR has already shared many social interaction features that can be found in today's more immersive VR platforms [11, 12]. Therefore, text-based VR was used in some education fields, such as language education [13].

Unlike text-based VR, desktop-based VR added more graphical elements to attract users [14]. A desktop-based VR could be 2D or 3D, depending on what graphic elements are developed in the VR environment. The desktop-based VR is still in use today and generates significant findings. For example, researchers used a desktop-based VR system and found that learners' cognitive load would predict their engagement in a VRLE [15]. Using a desktop-based VR system, Liu et al. [16] investigated how self-regulation skills impact learner satisfaction and learning intention.

Sensory-immersive VR has become increasingly popular in recent years due to technological advancement and lower device prices [17]. Many sensory-immersive VR systems and platforms were designed for leisure or entertainment purposes [18]. Another example of sensory-immersive VR is CAVE (Cave Automatic Virtual Environment)

[19]. However, the device for sensory-immersive VR, such as CAVE or a 4D movie theater, could be very costly [20], restricting their accessibility and affordability.

Finally, fully-immersive VR allows users to view a computer-generated 3D virtual world with an HMD [18]. Used in education, a fully-immersive VRLE enhances learners' learning motivation and develops their competencies [21]. Therefore, in recent years, fully-immersive VR technology has been widely used in education, especially in various disciplines in higher education [22].

2.2 Impact of Different VR Types on User/Learners

Early text-based VR environments might provide users with some social interaction [11] and relatively enhance users' or learners' self-efficacy [23] in a virtual space, but they were far from being considered immersive using today's criteria. As technology advances, desktop-based VR emerged and provided a better learning experience [6]. By displaying a 3D virtual environment on a desktop device's (e.g., a computer, a laptop, or a tablet) screen [24], desktop-based VR systems provide users with a 3D computer-generated virtual world where the latter can interact and explore in real-time [25]. Many 3D video games, such as Tomb Raider, Dark Souls, or the Call of Duty, are examples of desktop-based VR systems. Desktop-based VR systems improve learners' learning outcomes [26] and enhance their learning experience [27].

In recent years, new types of VR devices (such as HMDs) have become the main types of VR devices that users or learners would prefer to use in their VR experience [28], which provides greater availability, improved safety, and convenient data provision for users or learners [29]. These devices make VRLEs fully immersive, which enhances learners' learning experience [30], helps them quickly get into their roles in the learning process [31], strengthens their collaboration skills [32], and improves their learning outcomes [33]. In addition to learning improvement, immersive VR is also used in other areas, such as the hospital to help relieve patients' perceived pain [34].

3 Methodology

3.1 Participants

Our participants were 27 students (10 male and 17 female) registered in a Learning Technologies program (online) at an R1 university in the Mid-west United States. These students were located around the States and had few chances to visit the university campus for the face-to-face program orientation. Their careers included students (pre-service teachers), school teachers, corporate trainers, and instructional designers.

3.2 Data Collection

The data collection was from fall 2019 to fall 2021 (five 16-week semesters). Throughout these semesters, we invited more than 100 active online students who were new to the online program or had not experienced the VRO2 to interact with it. All students received tutorial materials on how to set up and attend the VRO2. If a student chose to participate in the VRO2, they could quit anytime if they wanted.

During the VRO2, students walked around the building and found different rooms (Fig. 1) to complete a series of activities, including visiting professors and students (Fig. 2), locating devices (see Fig. 3), finding learning resources (see Fig. 4), and gaining learning tips. In this way, they became familiar with the building, the program, and the people in the program.

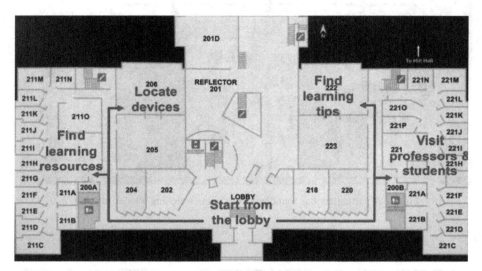

Fig. 1. The floor plan and orientation activities.

Fig. 2. A participant is visiting a professor.

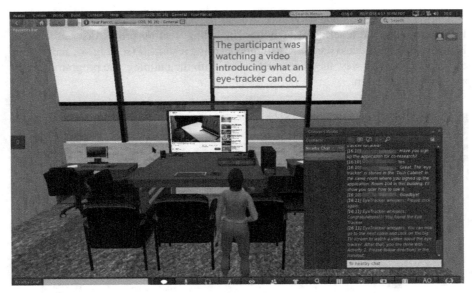

Fig. 3. A participant has found a device and is watching a video about it.

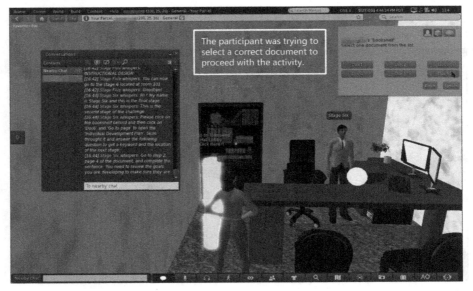

Fig. 4. A participant first clicked on the bookshelf; on the pop-up blue dialog box, they chose the correct document to proceed with.

At the end of the VRO2, each participant was prompted with three interview questions: (1) Overall, what do you think about the VRO2? (2) What was something that did not work for you? (3) How would you suggest improving the VRO2? Each interview was around 3 to 5 min. All interviews were audio recorded for data analysis purposes.

3.3 Data Analysis

Since this is an in-progress study, only 27 interviews were analyzed when we wrote this paper. The interview recordings were transcribed by an AI-based automatic transcription tool [35] and then proofread and updated by native English speakers. NVivo [36] was used for data analysis. Braun and Clarke's [37] six-step thematic analysis process was adopted to code the data. We first read through the transcription. Then we coded on sentences. We assigned sentences expressing the same meaning to the same code. All codes were based on the data instead of pre-determined. Sample codes include "enjoyed," "interesting," "informative," "eye-opening," etc. for participants' overall impression and "need more maps," "improve the movement," "more practice activities," etc. for issues or improvement. These codes were later clustered to themes such as "Like" or "Dislike" for the overall impression and "Environment," "Navigation," or "Guidance" for the improvement. In this preliminary study, only one researcher coded the data, but the coding results were discussed with the entire research team to reach a consensus.

4 Results

We present the results from three aspects: (1) Overall impression, (3) issues and difficulties, and (2) improvement. These results indicate participants' perceptions of the VRO2 and the VR system.

4.1 Overall Impression

Theme 1: Like. Overall, our participants (25 out of 27) liked the VRO_2. For example, "(P082) *I think it's kind of interesting. It was definitely different than anything I've ever done before. I'm not really like a gamer, or, like I don't use virtual reality tools … but I think it was, it was interesting.*" Many of them mentioned they "(P100) *have never done something like this*" or "(P99) *have never really used virtual reality or augmented reality until having a chance to do it [VRO$_2$].*" Some found VRO_2 very eye-opening, "(P088) *I've taught for 22 years. When I first started teaching, there were no computers, and we were very excited when we got a cart with a TV strapped on top of it. Oh, this [VRO$_2$] is amazing. So that's why I decided to get into this program as to learn more.*" Some believed that VRO_2 "(P057) *made me feel like I could kind of know my way around the department building.*"

Theme 2: Dislike. Of course, some participants (six out of 27 and 4 out of the six expressed likeness simultaneously) did not like the VRO_2. For example, one participant (P076) complained that VRO_2 was too lengthy (set to 1.5 h). Other participants were "(P052) *kind of anxious and kind of frustrated … because I'm not a gamer. I don't really have experience with this [VRO$_2$] … so I was super slow, and I'm not normally slow at things.*"

4.2   Issues and Difficulties

Though very few (5 out of 27), some participants still encountered issues or difficulties when experiencing VRO_2.

Theme 1: Navigation. The most reported difficulty was navigation in the VR world. Some found that "(P062) *it's hard to like, initially orient yourself of like, specifically where am I in the building? Especially since you've never been there.*" Some others, on the other hand, complained about the difficulty of controlling the avatar "(P006) *I'm not very good at coordinating the movement of the avatar. To me, to navigate the avatar was the hardest part of the whole thing.*"

Theme 2: Technical Issues. Other issues were mainly technical, such as "(P069) *the connection was slow,*" "(P057) *lost the Internet connection,*" and "(P030) *computer processing is not very fast.*"

4.3   Improvements

Theme 1: Guidance. As for improvement, many participants made suggestions for better tutorials and guidance. For example, some of them suggested "(P007) *a little miniature activity that could kind of warm people up to kind of give them an idea of what to expect*" or "(P069) *activities for practice so that the learner can be familiar with what's going on around and how to use the keys and everything.*" Others recommended some "(P052) *videos about changing your avatars' clothes, and move your avatar, or something like that, for us to watch.*"

Theme 2: Environment. Some participants proposed to change part of the VR world, such as "(P088) *add more maps, like, if there's a way to like, show where you are all the time (P078)*" or "*making sure that things are easily not too close to other things that need to be.*"

Theme 3: Activities. Others suggested redesigning the orientation activities, for instance, "(P063) *Maybe [add] some help things that you can click on like if you get stuck or maybe like a walkthrough video.*" Some individual participants preferred creation or free exploration, such as "(P078) *like being creative, and like exploring myself,*" or group interaction, such as "(P046) *it'd be cool if like other students could just like meet in the VR, too.*"

Theme 4: Navigation. More other participants expected that we could "(P089) *improve the walking*" or "(P030) *do the first-person view*" to help them navigate better in the virtual world.

Theme 5: Length. Still, other participants hoped that we could "(P063) *condense it [VRO_2] based on the amount of information*" or "(P069) *separate it [VRO_2] into two parts.*"

5   Discussion

From the results, many participants mentioned that they had never experienced such a VR learning experience. Even if the VR system (OpenSimulator) we used seems outdated in some researchers' or developers' eyes, it did not demotivate our participants. Rather, upon discovering that they could move, view, and interact within the VR environment, they found the experience captivating, informative, and eye-opening. Their positive reactions meant that, even if virtual reality has emerged for about half a century [38], many people still have not experienced their first-time VR trip yet; even if researchers or developers might have been familiar with VR in learning and now pursuing more realistic immersive VR learning experience, many people still regard the technology as very new to them; even if the platform seems outdated, we could still bring students an amazing experience. These findings imply that despite the effort or concentration on making a VR environment more visually immersive, which may not always be necessary [39], a more practical application of VR is to fulfill learners' actual learning needs. Even if the practice runs on a VR system that appears "outdated," it would still be valuable and effective.

Many of our participants were first-timers to a VRLE. Experiencing a visually realistic VRLE was not their top need. Instead, they were more interested in what a VRLE looked like and what they could do inside it. They cared more about how the VRLE was designed and how they could easily get along with the system. In summary, they paid more attention to the activities and interaction, which would contribute to their presence in the VRLE [11]. Therefore, to engage these novice learners in a VRLE for extended hours (say, in a two-hour VR experience or class), providing them with more activities to do and making the environment appropriately interactive and user-friendly is more important than being merely visually immersive. Such presence and agency design requires more effort to consider better activities, usability, and user experience.

In addition, using a seemingly "outdated" VR platform allows learners to experience a VRLE on a regular-performance computer such as a MacBook Air. The low system requirements increase the accessibility and affordability of the VR learning experience. Home-based online learners do not need to upgrade their devices or purchase any external devices, which may otherwise escalate their financial burden and discourage their acceptance of VR learning. Though an immersive VRLE enhances learners' immersion [39], such an environment requires higher investment in hardware, faster Internet connection, and more effort to set up and learn how to use that VRLE, which would pose more challenges to learners and steepen their learning curve.

Finally, we believe it is essential to provide different learners with VRLEs of different levels of fineness depending on their varied VR experiences. For novice or first-time learners (e.g., learners who have limited VR or 3D gaming experience), the VRLE does not necessarily have to be highly realistic because, as we stated above, their major focus will be how they can interact with the VRLE, what levels of control they have, and what they can do in the VRLE. For experienced learners (e.g., learners with sufficient VR experience or frequent 3D video gamers), a realistic VRLE with multi-sensory (e.g., visual, auditory, or even haptic) immersion features might be more helpful to improve their senses of immersion, presence, and agency. Such a bifurcate design may allow VRLE educators, researchers, and developers to fulfill learners' needs better.

6   Conclusion

In conclusion, a legacy VR platform still possesses some values. It is especially helpful in making VR-based learning more accessible and affordable. In addition, different learning activities may apply to different VR platforms. Though the VR platform we used might have been in the market for a while, it is still very suitable for learning activities for first-time VR participants to experience VR learning. Furthermore, from a practical perspective, the content design (what we want learners to do) in a VRLE tops everything. In future research, we will dive into how home-based online students perceive our learning activity or task design.

Acknowledgements. The VRO2 project discussed in this paper was funded by the University of Missouri Richard Wallace Faculty Incentive Grant. We appreciate Dr. Gayathri Sadanala's contribution to the construction of the VRO_2.

References

1. Dickey, M.D.: Teaching in 3D: pedagogical affordances and constraints of 3D virtual worlds for synchronous distance learning. Dist. Educ. **24**(1), 105–121 (2003). https://doi.org/10.1080/01587910303047
2. Gerry, L.J.: Paint with me: stimulating creativity and empathy while painting with a painter in virtual reality. IEEE Trans. Vis. Comput. Graph. **23**(4), 1418–1426 (2017). https://doi.org/10.1109/TVCG.2017.2657239
3. El-Mounayri, H., Rogers, C., Fernandez, E., Satterwhite, J.C.: Assessment of STEM e-Learning in an immersive virtual reality (VR) environment. In: 2016 ASEE Annual Conference Content Access Proceedings, ASEE Conferences, p. 12 (2016). https://doi.org/10.18260/p.26336
4. Yeh, Y.-L., Lan, Y.-J.: Fostering student autonomy in English learning through creations in a 3D virtual world. Educ. Technol. Res. Dev. **66**(3), 693–708 (2018). https://doi.org/10.1007/s11423-017-9566-6
5. Robertson, G., Czeminski, M., van Dantzich, M.: Immersion in desktop virtual reality. In: Proceedings of the 10th Annual ACM Symposium on User Interface Software and Technology, in UIST - Symposium on User Interface Software and Technology. Banff, Alberta, Canada: ACM Press, pp. 11–19 (1997). https://doi.org/10.1145/263407.263409
6. Ai-Lim Lee, E., Wong, K.W., Fung, C.C.: How does desktop virtual reality enhance learning outcomes? A structural equation modeling approach. Comput. Educ. **55**(4), 1424–1442 (2010). https://doi.org/10.1016/j.compedu.2010.06.006
7. OpenSimulator Community, OpenSimulator. http://opensimulator.org/wiki/Main_Page. Accessed 09 Aug 2019
8. Loeffler, C.E., Anderson, T.: The Virtual Reality Casebook. Van Nostrand, New York (1994)
9. Moore, P.: Learning and teaching in virtual worlds: implications of virtual reality for education. Australas. J. Educ. Technol., **11**(2) (1995). https://doi.org/10.14742/ajet.2078
10. Jin, Q., Yano, Y.: Design issues and experiences from having lessons in text-based social virtual reality environments. In: Computational Cybernetics and Simulation 1997 IEEE International Conference on Systems, Man, and Cybernetics, vol. 2, pp. 1418–1423 (1997). https://doi.org/10.1109/ICSMC.1997.638175

11. Jacobson, D.: Presence revisited: imagination, competence, and activity in text-based virtual worlds. Cyberpsychol. Behav. **4**(6), 653–673 (2001). https://doi.org/10.1089/109493101753 376605

12. Kiesler, S.: Culture of the Internet. Psychology Press (1997)

13. Schwienhorst, K.: The state of VR: a meta-analysis of virtual reality tools in second language acquisition. Comput. Assist. Lang. Learn. **15**(3), 221–239 (2002). https://doi.org/10.1076/ call.15.3.221.8186

14. Ioannou-Georgiou, S.: Constructing meaning with virtual reality. TESOL J. **11**(3), 21–26 (2002)

15. Bueno-Vesga, J.A., Xu, X., He, H.: The effects of cognitive load on engagement in a virtual reality learning environment. In: Proceedings of 2021 IEEE Virtual Reality and 3D User Interfaces (VR), pp. 645–652. IEEE, Lisboa, Portugal (2021). https://doi.org/10.1109/VR5 0410.2021.00090

16. Liu, Z., Yu, P., Liu, J., Pi, Z., Cui, W.: How do students' self-regulation skills affect learning satisfaction and continuous intention within desktop-based virtual reality? A structural equation modelling approach. Br. J. Educ. Technol. **54**, 667–685 (2022). https://doi.org/10.1111/ bjet.13278

17. Muñoz-Saavedra, L., Miró-Amarante, L., Domínguez-Morales, M.: Augmented and virtual reality evolution and future tendency. Appl. Sci., **10**(1), (2020). https://doi.org/10.3390/app 10010322

18. Huang, L.-L., Lin, C.-W., Liao, C.-M., Yang, T.: Research on Upper Extremity Rehabilitation Product Use Needs and Development Suggestions. In: Rau, P.-L. (ed.) HCII 2021. LNCS, vol. 12771, pp. 340–350. Springer, Cham (2021). https://doi.org/10.1007/978-3-030-77074-7_27

19. Cruz-Neira, C., Sandin, D.J., DeFanti, T.A.: Surround-screen projection-based virtual reality: the design and implementation of the CAVE. In: Proceedings of the 20th Annual Conference on Computer Graphics and Interactive Techniques, Anaheim, CA, USA, pp. 135–142 (1993). https://doi.org/10.1145/166117.166134

20. Halarnkar, P., Shah, S., Shah, H., Shah, H., Shah, A.: A review on virtual reality. Int. J. Comput. Sci. Issues IJCSI **9**(6), 325–330 (2012)

21. Sattar, M.U., Palaniappan, S., Lokman, A., Hassan, A., Shah, N., Riaz, Z.: Effects of virtual reality training on medical students' learning motivation and competency. Pak. J. Med. Sci. **35**(3), 852–857 (2019). https://doi.org/10.12669/pjms.35.3.44

22. Radianti, J., Majchrzak, T.A., Fromm, J., Wohlgenannt, I.: A systematic review of immersive virtual reality applications for higher education: design elements, lessons learned, and research agenda. Comput. Educ. **147**, 103778 (2020). https://doi.org/10.1016/j.compedu.2019.103778

23. Lee, K.M: MUD and self efficacy. Educ. Media Int. **37**(3), 177–183 (2000). https://doi.org/ 10.1080/09523980050184745

24. Nesamalar, E.K., Ganesan, G.: An introduction to virtual reality techniques and its applications. Int. J. Comput. Algorithm **1**(2), 59–62 (2012). https://doi.org/10.20894/IJCOA.101. 001.002.001

25. Blach, R.: Virtual reality technology - an overview. In: Talaba, D., Amditis, A. (eds.) Product Engineering: Tools and Methods Based on Virtual Reality, pp. 21–64. Springer, Dordrecht (2008). https://doi.org/10.1007/978-1-4020-8200-9_2

26. Merchant, Z., Goetz, E.T., Cifuentes, L., Keeney-Kennicutt, W., Davis, J.T.: Effectiveness of virtual reality-based instruction on students' learning outcomes in K-12 and higher education: a meta-analysis. Comput. Educ. **70**, 29–40 (2014). https://doi.org/10.1016/j.compedu.2013. 07.033

27. Chuah, K.-M., Chen, C.J.: Unleashing the potentials of desktop virtual reality as an educational tool: a look into the design and development process of ViSTREET. In: Proceedings

of the 2nd International Malaysian Educational Technology Convention, Kuantan, Pahang, Malaysia (2008).https://www.researchgate.net/profile/Kee-Man-Chuah/publication/200803 587_Unleashing_the_Potentials_of_Desktop_Virtual_Reality_as_an_Educational_Tool_A_ Look_into_the_Design_and_Development_Process_of_ViSTREET/links/546a93ff0cf2397 f78301ab9/Unleashing-the-Potentials-of-Desktop-Virtual-Reality-as-an-Educational-Tool-A-Look-into-the-Design-and-Development-Process-of-ViSTREET.pdf

28. Kim, Y.M., Rhiu, I., Yun, M.H.: A systematic review of a virtual reality system from the perspective of user experience. Int. J. Hum.-Comput. Interact. **36**(10), 893–910 (2020). https://doi.org/10.1080/10447318.2019.1699746

29. Rebelo, F., Noriega, P., Duarte, E., Soares, M.: Using virtual reality to assess user experience. Hum. Factors **54**(6), 964–982 (2012). https://doi.org/10.1177/0018720812465006

30. Georgiou, Y., Tsivitanidou, O., Ioannou, A.: Learning experience design with immersive virtual reality in physics education. Educ. Technol. Res. Dev. **69**(6), 3051–3080 (2021). https://doi.org/10.1007/s11423-021-10055-y

31. Kilmon, C.A., Brown, L., Ghosh, S., Mikitiuk, A.: Immersive virtual reality simulations in nursing education. Nurs. Educ. Perspect. **31**(5), 314 (2010)

32. Jackson, R.L., Fagan, E.: Collaboration and learning within immersive virtual reality. In: Proceedings of the Third International Conference on Collaborative Virtual Environments, in CVE 2000, pp. 83–92. Association for Computing Machinery, New York (2000). https://doi.org/10.1145/351006.351018

33. Hamilton, D., McKechnie, J., Edgerton, E., Wilson, C.: Immersive virtual reality as a pedagogical tool in education: a systematic literature review of quantitative learning outcomes and experimental design. J. Comput. Educ. **8**(1), 1–32 (2021). https://doi.org/10.1007/s40 692-020-00169-2

34. Theingi, S., Leopold, I., Ola, T., Cohen, G.S., Maresky, H.S.: Virtual reality as a non-pharmacological adjunct to reduce the use of analgesics in hospitals. J. Cogn. Enhanc. **6**(1), 108–113 (2022). https://doi.org/10.1007/s41465-021-00212-9

35. Otter.ai (2020). https://otter.ai/

36. QSR International Pty Ltd, "NVivo qualitative data analysis software." QSR International Pty Ltd (2020). https://www.qsrinternational.com/nvivo/home

37. Braun, V., Clarke, V.: Using thematic analysis in psychology. Qual. Res. Psychol. **3**(2), 77–101 (2006). https://doi.org/10.1191/1478088706qp063oa

38. Slater, M., Sanchez-Vives, M.V.: Enhancing our lives with immersive virtual reality. Front. Robot. AI **3** (2016). https://doi.org/10.3389/frobt.2016.00074

39. Bowman, D.A., McMahan, R.P.: Virtual reality: how much immersion is enough? Computer **40**(7), 36–43 (2007). https://doi.org/10.1109/MC.2007.257

Research Agenda 2030: The Great Questions of Immersive Learning Research

Andreas Dengel[1]([✉])(iD), Alexander Steinmaurer[2](iD), Lea Marie Müller[3](iD),
Melanie Platz[3](iD), Minjuan Wang[4](iD), Christian Gütl[2](iD), Andreas Pester[5](iD),
and Leonel Morgado[6,7](iD)

[1] Goethe University Frankfurt, Frankfurt (Main), Germany
dengel@uni-frankfurt.de
[2] Graz University of Technology, Graz, Austria
{alexander.steinmaurer,c.guetl}@tugraz.at
[3] Saarland University, Saarbrücken, Germany
{leamarie.mueller,melanie.platz}@uni-saarland.de
[4] San Diego State University, San Diego, USA
mwang@sdsu.edu
[5] British University of Egypt, Cairo, Egypt
andreas.pester@bue.edu.eg
[6] Universidade Aberta, Coimbra, Lisbon, Portugal
Leonel.Morgado@uab.pt
[7] INESC TEC, Porto, Portugal

Abstract. The research areas of the Immersive Learning community cover many different interests and perspectives on teaching and learning with immersive technologies. Based on existing efforts to map the field of research, we gathered 35 participants at the iLRN 2022 conference during an open hybrid workshop. These volunteers formed expert groups focusing on five possible perspectives on Immersive Learning. The expert groups gathered and summarized possible research questions with regards to an "Agenda 2030", meaning the most intriguing questions that should be addressed during the years to come. We let all participants vote on these research endeavors regarding their academic value and importance for the community. As a results, we gathered a total of 23 ranked questions. These questions were subsumed into ten topics forming a Research Agenda for Immersive Learning 2030 (RAIL.2030).

Keywords: Immersive learning · Expert panel · Immersive education

1 Introduction

The research field of Immersive Learning can be considered as multi- and transdisciplinary [2,12] with perspectives and research interests coming from various disciplines. Formulating and investigating research questions for the years to come is an important task for the Immersive Learning research community.

M.-L. Bourguet et al. (Eds.): iLRN 2023, CCIS 1904, pp. 161–172, 2024.
https://doi.org/10.1007/978-3-031-47328-9_12

Ranging from technological developments [8], questions on predictors of learning outcomes in immersive experiences [7], authoring toolkits for designing such experiences [5,9], industrial uses [24], questions of assessment/evaluation [22], and standardizations [2], to questions of the ethical concerns [23]. Structuring all these research interests is difficult, but having common goals for the development of the field could help fostering connections between the perspectives on education with immersive media.

During a workshop at the 2022 International Conference of the Immersive Learning Research Network (iLRN) in Vienna, a group of 35 experts from various research fields worked on the identification of the most pressing questions in Immersive Learning. The research questions for this study include:

1. *What research questions do experts identify within different areas of Immersive Learning?*
2. *How important are these questions for the research community in Immersive Learning?*

2   Research on Teaching and Learning with Immersive Technologies: An Overview

Immersive Learning is a term that can be used and understood in different ways, as demonstrated in a recent survey on the theoretical stance of the literature on the concept [16]. A possible definition of Immersive Learning when focusing on intentionally designed educational settings is learning with artificial experiences that are perceived as non-mediated [6], where the artificial experiences can be transported through a certain technology or through a physical setting. Perspectives of Immersive Learning could be differentiated in

- the research area Immersive Learning (sometimes called Immersive Education), which investigates educational benefits provided by such experiences,
- the internal process Immersive Learning, as the active construction and adaption of cognitive, affective, and psychomotor models through these experiences, and
- the educational method of Immersive Learning (also called Immersive Teaching) that uses these experiences as a learning supply [6].

A broader vision on the phenomenon of immersion includes also naturally occuring physical experiences from two additional aspects: psychological absorption with the narrative and with one's agency, i.e., challenges/engagement/collaboration [19]. The Immersive Learning Research Network has embraced this wider understanding of immersion to define Immersive Learning in its Network Knowledge Tree initiative as the application of immersion "as a lens and instrument to investigate, understand, and manipulate" learning contexts [2]. In this view, immersive learning "addresses not only the learning outcomes, but also the mutual relationship between the provided educational medium, the learners' perception and cognitive processes as well as their motivational and affective states and traits, among other topics, including organizational and social aspects" (ibid.).

In addition to these understandings of the term "Immersive Learning", different technological developments are involved: From virtual environments consisting of only simulated components to mixed environments where a real environment is augmented with virtual objects (augmented reality) or a virtual environment that is enriched with real components (augmented virtuality) [15]. When considering the entire mixed reality spectrum as immersive technologies, researchers and practitioners might find different approaches, each with its pros and cons depending on a variety of factors [17]. A third way to distinguish efforts in immersive learning is by topics of the provided immersive experiences. Results from different subjects show that learning in such settings can be enhanced through using realistic visualization, abstractions, or even metaphorical representations [1,21], kinesthetic learning supported by haptic feedback [21], communication and collaboration as a team in instructional settings [4,21], higher motivation, induced emotions, and satisfaction through the use of XR [4,10,20], using narratives and game-based learning [1,4,10] as well as situating the content in a realistic context [10,20]. However, achieving solid repeatable research outcomes in live educational setting has been plagued by replication difficulties, due to often poor details on the educational practices and strategies being employed - a state of affairs to which Beck et al.'s [3] recent framework and mapping of the field seeks to contribute, by enabling researchers and practitioners to more clearly situate their settings, practices, and strategies.

The Immersive Learning Research Network's "State of XR Report" investigated the field's needs, opportunities, barriers, and transformation potentials of learning with XR. Lee et al. [13] conducted expert panels regarding the greatest needs and most promising opportunities in learning with XR. The results show that XR can help facilitate authentic learning experiences, empower learners as creative designers and makers, and integrate immersive storytelling in learning. A particular opportunity was seen in integrating immersive learning in STEM Education. Social VR and other XR technologies have the potential to foster collaboration, to cultivate immersive and blended-reality learning spaces and laboratories, and to develop the capabilities of the future workforce. The second research question asked about the barriers for institutions towards adopting immersive learning technologies. Access, limited affordability, limited or inadequate XR teacher training programs, lacking interoperability, the lack of content and the lack of infrastructure were listed as major barriers. The third research question asked about potential catalysts, technologies and digital developments. The report lists flexible and Open XR resources as a first catalyst. Technological developments have the potential to strengthen Immersive Learning research and practice. XR games as well as Artificial Intelligence (AI) and Machine Learning (ML) in XR are suggested as big research opportunities in the future. As a last catalyst, the report lists the evidence based XR learning and program design as an important aspect of the next three years.

The Knowledge Tree project is described as a systematization effort for the research field of Immersive Learning, integrating scholarly and practical knowledge [2]. In this stead, Morgado & Beck [16] discuss how scholars from different academic fields often approach their research with extremely differing methods and terminology. Using the analogy of a physical tree, the purpose of the Knowledge Tree is to cultivate a robust and ever-growing knowledge base and to provide a methodological toolbox for immersive learning, aimed at promoting evidence-informed practice and guiding future research in the field. For the *Roots*, research should focus on finding a common language regarding definitions, methods, and instruments. The *Soil* describes all investigations of the ontological and epistemological terrain in which academics should shape their research. The *Trunk* of the Knowledge Tree represents the structural knowledge formed from scoping and systematic literature reviews on topics related to immersive learning, classified collections of facts like expert input from the field of immersive learning, evidence repositories, and Scientometrics (self-awareness among the community). The *Branches* consist of fields of inquiry extending from the *Trunk* leading to specific outcomes and "the research priorities and agendas of the field, intertwined with the fields of inquiry" [2].

These selected perspectives of published reviews and meta-reviews on Immersive Learning can give first insights into the diversity of the field. These insights were used to form the expert groups regarding the technology, the methods, the educational purposes, the human factors, and the standardization efforts in Immersive Learning.

3   Method

During the iLRN conference 2022 in Vienna, we organized a workshop with the objective to gather potential scientific questions within different areas in Immersive Learning research. In our endeavors to map the research efforts in Immersive Learning, we asked 35 participants to form five expert groups and discuss possible research questions.

3.1   Sample

35 people participated in the workshop (17 male, 14 female, 4 unknown genders, age between 27–70). As all of them were also participants or presenters at the iLRN conference, we considered them as being experienced in the research field of Immersive Learning. The participants came from at least 15 different countries. 73% worked in academia, 9% in industry, 3% in K-12 Education, and 15% in other sectors. 26% had their main research area in Computer Science, 3% in Cognitive Science, 19% in Game Design and Development, 24% in Pedagogy, and 28% in other areas.

3.2 Instruments

We used interactive collaborative software tools to receive information about the participants, for brainstorming on the research questions and to vote for their importance with the other participants. The research questions were conceived within five expert groups using a virtual whiteboard inserted into five slides (one for each group) so that all questions belonging to a certain topic were visible at the same time. All questions were assessed on 7-point Likert scales ranging from *1: strongly disagree* to *7: strongly agree* using the participants' smartphones. Besides collecting research questions in Immersive Learning we asked for basic demographic data such as gender, age, and country of origin.

3.3 Procedure

The workshop took place as a hybrid event between iLRN participants on Zoom and in person. First, the five groups and their aims were introduced and afterward the people could choose a group to participate based on their experience and interest. The five expert groups comprised *Technology and Metaverse in XR*, *AI/ML in Immersive Learning*, *Immersive Learning in Education*, *Human Factors in Immersive Learning*, and *Standardization in Immersive Learning*. Each group had 25 min to discuss possible research questions of their specific area and gather three to five questions which they were asked to present to the audience afterward. Due to the hybrid setup of the workshop, each group collaboratively worked on a Mural board[1] to brainstorm and collect all information. After the brainstorming sessions, everyone in the audience, including the presenters, assessed the importance of each of these questions using Mentimeter.

3.4 Results

The groups collected 23 research questions (A.1–E.5). The research questions of the *Technology and Metaverse in XR* group comprised ethical issues, pedagogical approaches, various barriers, issues on communication and collaboration as well as questions regarding assessment methods in the Metaverse. The *AI/ML in Immersive Learning* group gathered only three potential questions on potential use cases, testing, and mastery learning supported through AI/ML. The *Immersive Learning in Education* group focused on uses, practices, strategies, accessibility, and differences in learning with immersive experiences as well as barriers and strategies regarding the integration in the everyday classroom. For the *Human Factors in Immersive Learning*, intersections between cognition and learning, disabilities, cultural appropriateness, learning assessment, and human perception are all of interest. The *Standardization in Immersive Learning* group gathered five questions on interoperability for collaborative learning, classifications for qualitative learning experiences, terminologies and ontologies, and security concerns. Three overarching themes become apparent: The issue of pedagogical strategies for Immersive Learning can be found in three out of five

---

[1] https://www.mural.co/.

Table 1. Research questions derived from the five expert groups

#	Question	M	Std
A. Technology and Metaverse in XR (4 experts)			
A.1	What are the ethical issues of Edu Metaverse: the divide, code of conduct, avatar presence etc.?	5.5	1.77
A.2	What are the pedagogy associated with Edu Metaverse?	4.7	2.19
A.3	What are the barriers (technologic, cultural, societal) that researchers should address?	5.3	1.51
A.4	How do we people communicate and collaborate in Edu Metaverse? What are the diverse aspects of these?	4.9	1.73
A.5	How do we assess learning in Edu-M? Including both learning process and outcomes?	5.3	1.80
B. AI/ML in Immersive Learning (5 experts)			
B.1	What's the ideal use case for AI on Immersive Learning?	5.4	1.56
B.2	Has AI (ML) been tested on ILE?	4.5	1.94
B.3	Mastery of learning from the pedagogical aspect?	4.7	2.23
C. Immersive Learning in Education (10 experts)			
C.1	What are the best uses, practices and strategies in immersive learning environments?	5.5	1.70
C.2	How can immersive experiences be accessible and how can they support accessibility?	5	1.45
C.3	How do immersive learning experiences differ from other learning processes?	4.6	1.89
C.4	How can immersive learning experiences be integrated in the overall teaching/be combined with other pedagogical methods?	5.1	1.79
C.5	What are the barriers to classroom integration, teaching?	5.4	1.46
D. Human Factors in Immersive Learning (7 experts)			
D.1	What is the intersection between cognition and learning in XR environments?	5.5	1.60
D.2	How to address sensing disabilities in XR settings intersecting learning?	5.1	1.45
D.3	How would non-educational XR platforms be used safely in different cultures in terms of appropriateness, age, and cultural appropriateness?	4.2	1.75
D.4	How can learning processes in XR be measured?	5.3	2.05
D.5	How to prioritize the full spectrum of sensors for human learning?	5.2	1.73
E. Standardization in Immersive Learning (3 experts)			
E.1	What interoperability is needed to realise/hybrid spaces/that link AR/VR, real/virtual for collaborative synchronous learning? Requirements?	5.6	1.09
E.2	What makes quality XR learning? How to classify/categorize/describe educational activities at strategic/tactical/operational levels?	5.3	1.74
E.3	What level of interoperability is desired and required, so educational information systems communicate and interlink with ILEs?	5	1.46
E.4	What is the terminology/ontology of ILE concepts?	5.1	2.11
E.5	What are the security concerns of ILE?	5.6	1.41

working groups. Communication can be found in two groups and three groups are concerned with acccessibility. Three groups address assessment in one way or another.

The research questions were then rated by all participants (see Table 1). All research questions received a rather moderate to high score, ranging from 4.2 to 5.6. For *Technology & Metaverse in XR*, the highest ranked question was *A.1: What are the ethical issues of the Edu Metaverse: the divide, code of conduct, avatar presence, etc.* (M = 5.5, SD = 1.77). In the *AI/ML in Immersive Learning* group, *B.1: What is the ideal use case for AI on Immersive Learning?* received the highest score (M = 5.4, SD = 1.56). In *Immersive Learning in Education*, the highest ranked question was *C.1: What are the best uses, practices, and strategies in immersive learning environments?* (M = 5.5, SD = 1.70). For the group *Human Factors in Immersive Learning*, the question *D.1: What is the intersection between cognition and learning in XR environments?* scored highest (M = 5.5, SD = 1.60). In *Standardization in Immersive Learning*, the two highest ranked questions were *E.1: What interoperability is needed to realise hybrid spaces that link AR/VR, real/virtual for collaborative synchronous learning?* (M = 5.6, SD = 1.09) and *E.5: What are the security concerns of Immersive Learning Environments?* (M = 5.6, SD = 1.41).

A summarizing content analysis [14] was used to collate the research questions into topics. Even though most suggested research questions might affect more than one topics, we tried to distinguish them into only one topic per question to generate a landscape of distinct topics. After formulating the categories in a first step of the analysis, two raters reached an agreement coefficient (Cohen's Kappa) of .847 (almost perfect agreement [11]) for allocating the research questions to these ten categories:

1. *Communication & Collaboration*: research efforts investigating ways to communicate and collaborate in immersive settings (1 mention; A.4; M = 4.9).
2. *Interoperability*: questions regarding technological developments, interfaces, and software factors required to create interoperability between virtual/virtual and real/virtual environments (2 mentions; E.1, E.3; M = 5.3).
3. *Use Cases*: actual use cases of immersive experiences in education, entertainment, and industry (3 mentions; B.1, B.2, C.1; M = 5.1).
4. *Assessment*: efforts to investigate ways to test and evaluate immersive experiences but also to assess learning outcomes and changes of learning relevant factors (2 mentions; A.5, D.4; M = 5.3).
5. *Cognition*: characteristics of cognitive processes in immersive learning (3 mentions; C.3, D.1, D.5; M = 5.1).
6. *Standards & Terminology*: theoretical approaches to identify standards and establish common terminologies within the area of Immersive Learning (2 mentions; E.2, E.4; M = 5.2).
7. *Ethics*: questions on ethical issues, cultural appropriateness and socio-economical perspectives (2 mentions; A.1, D.3; M = 4.8).
8. *Security*: questions on security regarding data and privacy as well as physical and mental health related to immersive experiences (1 mention; E.5; M = 5.6).

9. *Barriers & Accessibility*: questions on how barriers regarding the adoption of immersive technologies can be removed and how immersive contents can become more accessible (4 mentions; A.3, C.2, C.5, D.2; M = 5.2).
10. *Pedagogy*: questions regarding pedagogical approaches, implementation in the everyday classroom, and correlates of immersive learning processes with other factors relevant for learning (3 mentions; A.2, B.3, C.4; M = 4.8).

Regarding the averaged scores of the research questions for each of the ten topics, the *Security* topic shows the highest, *Ethics* the lowest rating. All topics are "agreed" or "strongly agreed" upon to become an important part of future Immersive Learning research and consist of one to four research questions.

4   Discussion and Limitations

For the first question, *What research questions do experts identify within different areas of Immersive Learning?*, we see that there is a broad variety of topics that is of interest for the different perspectives on Immersive Learning. Using the content analysis approach, it was possible to subsume the 23 different research questions under 10 topics. Even though we used two raters who achieved high agreement regarding the categorization, there might be other useful ways to structure the named research efforts. Also, the sample size was limited to 35 experts, who, even though from very different fields of expertise, can only give limited insights into the questions related to their area. Still, we believe that the 10 topics retrieved from these expert opinions might give a good overview of current interests in the research community.

Regarding the second question, *How important are these questions for the research community in Immersive Learning?*, the answer is twofold: Within the groups, the highest ranked individual questions were A.1 (*What are the ethical issues of Edu Metaverse: the divide, code of conduct, avatar presence etc.?*), B.1 (*What's the ideal use case for AI on Immersive Learning?*), C.1 (*What are the best uses, practices and strategies in immersive learning environments?*), D.1 (*What is the intersection between cognition and learning in XR environments?*), and E.5 (*What are the security concerns of ILE?*), where E.5 received the highest score. It is not surprising that for four out of five groups, the first question was selected as these might be the first ones that came to mind in the expert groups, indicating that those are already the research focus points of the participants. When merging the research questions to topics, the topic that subsumes the most questions is *Barriers & Accessibility*, followed by *Use Cases, Cognition*, and *Pedagogy*. Regarding their combined overall ratings, the topic *Security* with its single research question E.5 again received the highest score, meaning that efforts regarding data security, privacy, but also physical and mental health seem to lead the field of upcoming research.

5 Agenda 2030: Implications for Future Research

For a research agenda towards 2030, we summarize the questions to 10 over-arching topics related to current Immersive Learning research. Similar to other projects that suggest future agendas, such as the completed EU funding program Horizon 2020, these research questions should not be understood "to be solved" until 2030, but should rather be dedicated to exploring and creating approaches and technologies which might be able to tackle the grand challenges lying behind these questions [25].

Doing so, we present a potential Research Agenda for Immersive Learning 2030 (RAIL.2030). The ten topics subsume the research questions from the various perspectives gathered throughout this study and can help steering current and future research within the research field of Immersive Learning (Fig. 1):

Fig. 1. Research Agenda Immersive Learning 2030.

1. *Communication & Collaboration*: How should people communicate and collaborate in educational immersive experiences and how can it be achieved?
2. *Interoperability*: What interoperability between physical elements, traditional information systems, and virtual components is needed for educational immersive experiences and how can it be achieved?
3. *Use Cases*: What are the current use cases for educational immersive experiences?

4. *Assessment*: How can we assess learning, learning-relevant factors, and content quality in and of educational immersive experiences?
5. *Cognition*: What are the cognitive processes in immersive experiences and how do they influence learning?
6. *Standards & Terminology*: Which terminologies and standards should we use in Immersive Learning and how should they be defined?
7. *Ethics & Culture*: Which ethical and cultural issues need to be solved to design and use appropriate educational immersive experiences and how can they be addressed?
8. *Security*: What are concerns regarding data, privacy, and physical/mental health and how can they be resolved?
9. *Barriers & Accessibility*: What are current barriers to adopting educational immersive experiences and how can we make them accessible for everyone?
10. *Pedagogy*: How do we integrate immersive experiences in the classroom and what are pedagogical approaches that can be used in and around these experiences?

6 Conclusion

Immersive Learning is a transdisciplinary research field: Its researchers come from heavily differing disciplines, each with its own questions, terminologies, and methodologies. This study gathered expert opinions from these different fields in Immersive Learning regarding future research directions. By letting the audience vote on these research questions and their importance for Immersive Learning in general, we gathered first insights into the of question how future research has to be shaped to foster collaborations between these different disciplines. After presenting the results and implications for each perspective, we subsumed the suggested research questions into a Research Agenda for Immersive Learning 2030 (RAIL.2030). This agenda can be used to situate future research and developed tools. In the time since Vienna's 2022 workshop was held, progress has been reported in various of these challenges, e.g. Beck et al.'s [3] educational practices and strategies framework or Mystakidis et al. [18] summary on Immersive Learning. In a next step, we plan on setting up an open web page to build a community-wide knowledge base of research.

References

1. Argyriou, L., Economou, D., Bouki, V.: 360-degree interactive video application for cultural heritage education. In: 3rd Annual International Conference of the Immersive Learning Research Network. Verlag der Technischen Universität Graz (2017)
2. Beck, D., et al.: Towards an immersive learning knowledge tree-a conceptual framework for mapping knowledge and tools in the field. In: 2021 7th International Conference of the Immersive Learning Research Network (iLRN), pp. 1–8. IEEE (2021)

3. Beck, D., Morgado, L., O'Shea, P.: Educational practices and strategies with immersive learning environments: mapping of reviews for using the metaverse. IEEE Trans. Learn. Technol. (2023)
4. Challenor, J., Ma, M.: A review of augmented reality applications for history education and heritage visualisation. Multimodal Technol. Interact. **3**(2), 39 (2019)
5. Dengel, A., Iqbal, M., Grafe, S., Mangina, E.: A review on augmented reality authoring toolkits for education. Front. Virtual Real. **3**, 798032 (2022). https://doi.org/10.3389/frvir
6. Dengel, A.: What is immersive learning? In: 2022 8th International Conference of the Immersive Learning Research Network (iLRN), pp. 1–5. IEEE (2022)
7. Dengel, A., Mägdefrau, J.: Immersive learning predicted: presence, prior knowledge, and school performance influence learning outcomes in immersive educational virtual environments. In: 2020 6th International Conference of the Immersive Learning Research Network (iLRN), pp. 163–170. IEEE (2020)
8. Gaspar, H., Morgado, L., Mamede, H., Oliveira, T., Manjón, B., Gütl, C.: Research priorities in immersive learning technology: the perspectives of the iLRN community. Virtual Reality **24**, 319–341 (2020)
9. Horst, R., Naraghi-Taghi-Off, R., Rau, L., Dörner, R.: Bite-sized virtual reality learning applications: a pattern-based immersive authoring environment. J. Univ. Comput. Sci. **26**(8), 947–971 (2020)
10. Kavanagh, S., Luxton-Reilly, A., Wuensche, B., Plimmer, B.: A systematic review of virtual reality in education. Themes Sci. Technol. Educ. **10**(2), 85–119 (2017)
11. Landis, J.R., Koch, G.G.: The measurement of observer agreement for categorical data. Biometrics, 159–174 (1977)
12. Lee, M.J., Georgieva, M., Alexander, B., Craig, E., Richter, J.: The state of XR and immersive learning outlook report: 2020 edition-executive summary. Immersive Learn. Res. Netw. (2020)
13. Lee, M.J., Georgieva, M., Alexander, B., Craig, E., Richter, J.: State of XR & immersive learning outlook report 2021. Immersive Learning Research Network, Walnut (2021)
14. Mayring, P.: Qualitative content analysis. Companion Qual. Res. **1**(2), 159–176 (2004)
15. Milgram, P., Takemura, H., Utsumi, A., Kishino, F.: Augmented reality: a class of displays on the reality-virtuality continuum. In: Telemanipulator and Telepresence Technologies, SPIE, vol. 2351, pp. 282–292 (1994)
16. Morgado, L., Beck, D.: Unifying protocols for conducting systematic scoping reviews with application to immersive learning research. In: 2020 6th International Conference of the Immersive Learning Research Network (iLRN), pp. 155–162. IEEE (2020)
17. Morgado, L., et al.: Recommendation tool for use of immersive learning environments. In: 2022 8th International Conference of the Immersive Learning Research Network (iLRN), pp. 1–8. IEEE (2022)
18. Mystakidis, S., Lympouridis, V.: Immersive learning. Encyclopedia **3**(2), 396–405 (2023)
19. Nilsson, N.C., Nordahl, R., Serafin, S.: Immersion revisited: a review of existing definitions of immersion and their relation to different theories of presence. Hum. Technol. **12**(2), 108–134 (2016)
20. Peixoto, B., Pinto, R., Melo, M., Cabral, L., Bessa, M.: Immersive virtual reality for foreign language education: a prisma systematic review. IEEE Access **9**, 48952–48962 (2021)

21. Pellas, N., Dengel, A., Christopoulos, A.: A scoping review of immersive virtual reality in stem education. IEEE Trans. Learn. Technol. **13**, 748–761 (2020)

22. Queiroz, A.C.M., Nascimento, A.M., Tori, R., da Silva Leme, M.I.: Immersive virtual environments and learning assessments. In: Beck, D., et al. (eds.) iLRN 2019. CCIS, vol. 1044, pp. 172–181. Springer, Cham (2019). https://doi.org/10.1007/978-3-030-23089-0_13

23. Southgate, E., et al.: Embedding immersive virtual reality in classrooms: ethical, organisational and educational lessons in bridging research and practice. Int. J. Child-Comput. Interact. **19**, 19–29 (2019)

24. Tan, Y., Xu, W., Li, S., Chen, K.: Augmented and virtual reality (AR/VR) for education and training in the AEC industry: a systematic review of research and applications. Buildings **12**(10), 1529 (2022)

25. Veugelers, R., et al.: The impact of horizon 2020 on innovation in Europe. Intereconomics **50**(1), 4–30 (2015)

Exploring Data Visualization in Mixed Reality Simulations to Measure Teacher Responsiveness

Rhonda Bondie[1]([⊠]) [iD], Zid Mancenido[2], Happi Adams[2], and Chris Dede[2]

[1] Hunter College, New York, USA
rb4016@hunter.cuny.edu
[2] Harvard University, Cambridge, USA
Zid.Mancenido@edresearch.edu.au, chris_dede@gse.harvard.edu

Abstract. A growing body of research begins to illustrate how mixed reality simulation (MRS) based on digital puppeteering (e.g., Mursion) may be used to provide practice-based opportunities in teacher education. Ironically, current research of this new technology often uses historic measures and conventional data analytics to measure teacher learning, such as holistic rubrics of qualities that describe an average or overall teacher performance or frequency counts of teaching behaviors. What is missing from the literature are novel approaches to measures, data collection and analyses that leverage the digital data available through MRS to explore new dynamic and responsive measures of teaching. For example, measurement of teacher growth could shift from focusing on teacher performance and behaviors to measuring teacher responsiveness to student variances. Rather than just measuring the extent to which a teacher can implement a specific teaching practice, researchers could examine the extent that the teacher adapted the teaching practice or selected appropriate teaching strategies based on qualities perceived in student responses. Now more than ever, we need innovation in teaching, especially developing teacher capacity to perceive and respond to student diversity in real time as learning unfolds. This study explored possible MRS measures and data analytics that examine teaching as a dynamic process responsive to student diversity. We found that specific elements of simulation design and implementation can generate data that measures indicators of teacher responsiveness to student variance.

Keywords: Immersive Learning · Teacher Education · Mixed Reality Simulation · Data Analysis · Virtual Performance Simulations

1 Introduction

Increasingly, teacher education programs have explored mixed-reality simulations (MRS) as a means for teaching practice [1]. Figure 1 illustrates a MRS, using Mursion software, where a trained actor-coach digitally puppets student avatars in a 3D virtual classroom accessed by teachers through Zoom. This software is referred to as mixed reality because there is an unseen human being controlling the avatars in the virtual world. The realistic practice environment may create a strong sense of presence and focus, and potentially increase near transfer [6]. Teacher education research has demonstrated that rehearsals, such as MRS, can develop teachers' ambitious instructional practices [9, 11]. However, Philip et al. [12] criticized teaching rehearsals arguing that "decontextualized moves" and technical efficiency are gained at the expense of responsiveness to student needs as learning unfolds (see also [15]). Teaching rehearsals may not provide "the stable groundwork within which rich responses to student performances can be improvised" [11]. Rather, these "rigid conceptualizations of practice and prescriptiveness [separate] the teachers' social and cultural identities from what they are able to actually do in a classroom: how they can respond, what they can convey, and to whom" [12]. Given this debate, more empirical research is necessary that explores the extent that teaching rehearsals can promote teachers' responsiveness to their students' diverse and spontaneous needs.

Educators find that adjusting teaching in response to the wide range of student reading strengths is challenging [4]. Rigorous academic discussions in early elementary grades support literacy growth through vocabulary development, comprehension, and engagement in academic tasks. Therefore, our MRS aimed at improving teacher ability to adjust peer discussion directions to increase the quality of student responses and equity in participation when avatar students were given a task of discussing a comparison of two photographs.

Previous MRS studies have described learning growth through frequencies of desired teacher actions [5–8]. However, MRS studies have not measured the extent that teachers adjust their practice in response to diverse learner needs. Addressing this void, this exploratory study examined how teaching was adjusted in response to digital puppeteering of avatar students during multiple MRS trials. Two research questions guided our exploration:

1. How do teachers' adjustments to peer discussion directions align with avatar student demonstrated learning needs regarding response quality and equity in participation?
2. How do simulation design features of a) coaching versus self-reflection time and b) multiple trials impact teaching adjustments?

2 Methods

2.1 Participants

The study recruited seven teachers engaged in an alternative secondary certification graduate teacher education program in the Northeast United States. All participants were undertaking their first practicum in the same summer high school. Participants were recruited in person by one of the authors during a compulsory teaching methods course; there were no benefits or requirements in engaging in the study. The treatment group consisted of four teachers, two identified as male teaching math and two as female teaching science and social studies. The control group had three participants, two identified as female teaching social studies and science, and one as male teaching social studies. Participants were not explicitly told that they were in a particular treatment group.

2.2 Procedure

Teachers were provided with preparation materials for the peer-to-peer discussion task used during the simulation and specific strategies to adjust directions in response to student learning needs (see https://wke.lt/w/s/OSIEuF). Each teacher completed the MRS individually via Zoom. (see Fig. 1). The treatment group received coaching from an avatar coach that was controlled by the simulation specialist. The control group received individual planning time in an empty virtual classroom with no coaching from the simulation specialist during the simulation. The white female simulation specialist was highly skilled with MRS and had P-12 teaching experience. The simulation specialist completed the script development, rehearsal, and seven simulations in 12 h. The researchers developed the script collaboratively with the simulation specialist to rehearse if-then responses to possible direction elements for the avatar student pair discussions. The avatars were both controlled by the software and the simulation specialist used voice morphing software and equipment to capture the simulation specialists movement. Because one simulation specialist controlled the class of students, only one student could speak at one time.

Fig. 1. Mursion Virtual Classroom.

2.3 Data Sources and Analysis

Automated transcripts generated from Zoom were cleaned, then analyzed using constant comparison analysis and in vivo using a line by line approach to examine each utterance during the simulation [14]. Three coders independently coded all transcripts, then the research team discussed the codes and reduced them into specific elements for adjusting directions [13]. The researchers were two US white women; one, a faculty member with more than twenty years of teaching experience and the other, a graduate student who currently teaches high school English, and an Australian male who was also an experienced teacher. Throughout the process, the team evaluated personal assumptions and biases that influenced perceptions of the data collected and analysis. Member checks were completed with four participants to ensure coding accuracy.

3 Results

The first research question explored how teachers' directions aligned with the avatar students discussions. In Fig. 2, the shade of each box illustrates the presence of specific qualities in teacher directions across three trials. Starting from the center moving left across Fig. 2, shaded cells represent each trial and indicate teachers' explicit attention to specific elements of high quality student responses (i.e., evidence, academic language, and compare and contrast thinking) and, toward the right, we see equity in discussion participation (i.e., tools for supporting student social regulation including teacher artic-ulation of student discussion roles, rules, turn taking, and time). For example, teachers could use the equity elements in their directions to address challenges such as one student dominating the conversation.

Each row in the figure represents a different teacher; the treatment coaching group are above the center row of compare and contrast thinking and, toward the right, we see equity in discussion participation (i.e., tools for supporting student social regulation including teacher articulation of student discussion roles, rules, turn taking, and time). For example, teachers could use the equity elements in their directions to address challenges such as one student dominating the conversation. A plus (+) sign means the element was added from the previous trial and a negative (−) symbol means the teacher direction element had been present in the previous trial, but was not present in the next trial.

The red circle indicates that at least one avatar student responded to the teacher directions by including that element in their response (e.g., the teacher gives examples of academic vocabulary that can be used and then the avatar students used those words in their peer discussion). When a box is white, not shaded, but has a circle, it means that the avatar students had the element in their discussions; however, the teacher did not specifically ask for the element in the teacher directions. An X in a box identifies an element that was present in student responses; however, the students were incorrect (e.g. students using vocabulary incorrectly or used background knowledge instead of evidence from the photographs to support an inference). The frequency of each element by individual participant is shown in the numbers along the end vertical columns. For example, Teacher 1 included 4 high quality elements in their directions and 8 equitable student participation elements. The total number of elements for each treatment group is shown in the corner and by each trial along the top for the coaching-treatment group and along the bottom for the control – self-reflection group. The key at the bottom of the figure identifies each symbol.

The second research question explored how the MRS design features of coaching versus self-reflection time and multiple trials shaped teaching adjustments. Frequency counts along the outside of Fig. 2 reveal that the coaching group implemented 28 out of 36 or 75% of the possible teacher direction elements aimed at increasing the quality of student responses. The control group implemented 18 out of 27 possible elements across three trials or 67%. There were four equity elements for each of three trials for each teacher in the treatment (48 total elements) and control (36 total elements). The treatment group used 28 elements or 56% and the self-reflection group used 25 elements or 69%. Teachers in the treatment group seemed to focus more on high quality responses than equitable participation in their discussion directions. The teachers assigned to self-reflection included about equally elements focused on academic quality and equitable

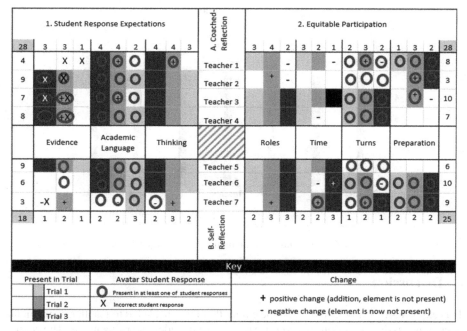

Fig. 2. Teacher direction elements and avatar responses match by teacher and trial.

participation. Figure 3 displays the total number of elements used in teacher directions by trial and coaching versus the self-reflection group. Surprisingly, teacher use of the direction elements did not increase in a linear manner over the three trials. Instead most teachers increased the number of elements in their directions from trial 1 to trial 2, but decreased their use of direction elements in trial 3. No teacher included all 7 direction elements.

Taken together, Fig. 2 and Fig. 3 demonstrate how the elements in teacher directions may vary. For example, Fig. 3 shows that Teacher 1 and Teacher 2 both had 3 elements in their trial 1 directions. However, when investigating the three elements using Fig. 2, we see that Teacher 1 focused on equitable participation elements while Teacher 2 focused on the high quality responses without attention to equity in participation. Another example, when looking at Teacher 7 in Fig. 3, we see the fewest elements in trial 1 directions and the greatest growth in trial 2 by adding four elements. However, when investigating specific changes we see that the teacher focused almost exclusively on student participation with little attention to the quality of what students were saying in their discussion. Visualizing the elements of the complex teaching practice of giving directions with the impact of those directions on student responses illuminates the diversity in teacher learning and how growth in one aspect of the practice (e.g. equitable participation) does not necessarily lead to higher quality in student responses.

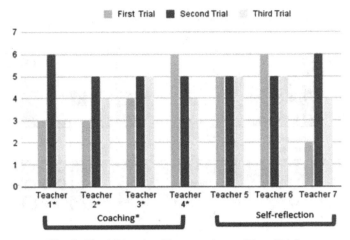

Fig. 3. Total Direction Elements Across Three Trials.

4 Discussion

This exploratory study investigated the extent that three trials led to teacher adjustments of peer discussion directions in response to perceived student learning needs. The central contribution of this small study is the exploration of visualizing teacher learning in MRS as dynamic and related to student learning needs versus a decontextualized count of teaching behaviors. This study employed qualitative line by line coding of teacher and avatar student utterances. The analysis approach used in this exploratory study of qualitatively coding language at the utterance level and then visualizing responsiveness to student demonstrated needs holds the potential for examining teaching as interaction versus a static implementation process. Further, this study demonstrates that professional learning within MRS moves forward and backward as well as remaining constant. Most importantly, visualizing both the teacher and the avatar student responses together, we can see how the simulation specialist may influence teacher experiences and learning within MRS. When examining each row in Fig. 2 representing a teacher direction element across three trials separated by elements promoting high quality student responses and equitable student participation, teaching appears more like a dance than an assembly line.

In summary, our results illustrated changes in teaching practices across a repeated practice model. We observed that repeated practice did not lead to continuous growth in teacher direction elements. In fact, teacher use of the discussion direction elements generally rose and then fell, with fewer elements used in the final trial. This may have been a result of the simulation specialist needing more challenges in the script for avatar discussions, teachers may have become tired, or the repeated practice of the same task may have lost cognitive interest for teachers. This exploratory study illuminates questions regarding the number of trials needed for mastery of teaching practices and the concern about repeated practice when an appropriate challenge isn't present in student response or when teachers are tired from the effort required to sustain focus in the MRS may lead to the rehearsal of less effective teaching practices. Our analyses suggest that both planned and improvised avatar responses and interactions may influence the growth of teaching practices.

5 Implications

5.1 MRS Designers

The contributions of this short paper are the innovative use of avatar puppeteering for the orchestration of realistic teacher training simulations and the proposed visual data coding method. More specifically, our exploration surfaces four important factors that impact MRS design. First, to promote teacher responsiveness, the simulation should begin with the teacher listening to students and then adjusting teaching in response. This centers responding to student variation in learning as the goal of teaching. Second, MRS practice should be personalized. For example, during the third trial teachers could have been given a choice to restart the MRS from the beginning, continue where they had left off in trial 2, or move on to a transfer task of giving directions for a new pair discussion. Offering personalized practice leverages the affordances of MRS versus real-life rehearsals in schools and provides optimal challenge so that teachers benefit from each MRS trial. Third, the number of trials and length of MRSs needs further exploration about what is effective. Fourth, research is needed on how MRS learning can be tailored to teacher needs and the MRS conditions that promote effective coaching.

5.2 Simulation Specialists

By analyzing avatar responses, this study lifts up the importance of a simulation specialist fully understanding the task and specific vocabulary that students might use in their responses based on age level and experiences. Simulation specialists must understand the ways that student thinking and responding might vary. MRS designers and simulation specialists should try the MRS tasks with real students in schools to gain insight into possible student responses. It is important to plan not only standard challenges in the script, but the extent to which avatar students will persist with incorrect ideas or offer mistakes to increase the complexity of the teacher's task. Simulation specialists need to be well versed in the elements of complex teaching practices. For example, coaching in this study did not lead to teachers increasing teaching elements focused on equitable participation, however, teachers given self-reflection increased equity elements. This could be that the simulation specialist was not familiar with the teaching elements and did not recognize when the teacher used the elements in their discussion directions. Being able to not only puppet the students, but recognize the presence and absence of discussion direction elements was essential for both coaching and avatar responses to teacher directions.

5.3 Teachers, Teacher Educators, and Researchers

The Xs in Fig. 2 illustrate opportunities for teachers to correct a student mistake. We observed no teachers correcting mistakes. Even in the virtual classroom, teachers did not draw student attention to errors. Future studies should explore why teachers correct students or ignore student errors. Further, research might investigate how teachers adjust when the avatar student does not follow their directions. For example, does the teacher repeat the directions, ask for questions, or embellish the directions with more information?

5.4 Limitations

The small sample size limits any generalizations beyond the current study. A larger sample in a replication study would increase the number of utterances examined and may reveal additional codes. There was no pre-post measurement limiting information on pre-simulation participant equivalence. Within these limits, this exploratory study illuminated specific simulation design elements and provided evidence of the potential insights gained from analyzing simulation interactions that can inform future simulation design and research.

6 Conclusion

Now more than ever, we need innovation in teaching, especially developing teacher capacity to perceive and respond to student diversity in real time as learning unfolds [3]. This study explored possible ways to visualize teacher learning in MRS as interactions with students. This approach supports the future work of technologists, teacher educators, and educational researchers in transforming teacher professional learning from an industrialized machine-like approach to teaching to instead a dynamic process responsive to student diversity. Specifically, this study illuminates MRS design choices, such as the importance of personalized practice and use of coaching and self-reflection that leverage the MRS technology affordances. This exploratory study sets the stage for further research aimed at transforming standard teacher professional development (PD) to experiences that nurture responsive and improvisational aspects of teaching necessary to meet the diverse learning needs of students by providing PD that also responds to the individual learning needs of teachers [2].

Acknowledgements. This research was part of the Reach Every Reader initiative supported by the Chan Zuckerberg Foundation.

References

1. American Association of Colleges of Education (AACTE, Producer) (2020). Let's test drive classroom simulation. [Webinar Series]
2. Bondie, M, Dede, C.: Redefining and transforming field experiences in teacher preparation through personalized mixed reality simulations. In: Ferdig, R.E., Pytash, K.E. (eds.), What Teacher Educators Should Have Learned from 2020. Association for the Advancement of Computing in Education (AACE) (2021)
3. Bondie, M., Dede, C.: Principles for designing virtual humans to develop teachers' responsiveness towards diverse learners. J. Res. Technol. Educ. **53**(1), 107–123 (2021)

4. Bondie, R., Zusho, A.: Differentiating Instruction Made Practical: Engaging the Extremes Through Classroom Routines. Routledge, New York (2018)
5. Dawson, M.R., Lignugaris/Kraft, B.: Meaningful practice: generalizing foundation teaching skills from TLE TeachLivETM to the classroom. Teach. Educ. Spec. Educ. **40**(1), 26–50 (2017)
6. Dede, C.J., Jacobson, J., Richards, J.: Introduction: virtual, augmented, and mixed realities in education. In: Liu, D., Dede, C., Huang, R., Richards, J. (eds.) Virtual, augmented, and mixed realities in education. SCI, pp. 1–16. Springer, Singapore (2017). https://doi.org/10.1007/978-981-10-5490-7_1
7. Dieker, L.A., Rodriguez, J.A., Lignugaris/Kraft, B., Hynes, M.C., Hughes, C.E.: The potential of simulated environments in teacher education: current and future possibilities. Teach. Educ. Spec. Educ. **37**(1), 21–33 (2014)
8. Kannan, P., Zapata-Rivera, D., Mikeska, J., Bryant, A., Long, R., Howell, H.: Providing formative feedback to pre-service teachers as they practice facilitation of high-quality discussions in simulated mathematics and science methods classrooms. In: Langran, E., Borup, J. (Eds.) Proceedings of Society for Information Technology & Teacher Education International Conference, pp. 1570–1575. Association for the Advancement of Computing in Education (AACE), Chesapeake (2018)
9. Kavanagh, S.S., Rainey, E.C.: Learning to support adolescent literacy: teacher educator pedagogy and novice teacher take up in secondary English language arts teacher preparation. Am. Educ. Res. J. **54**(5), 904–937 (2017)
10. Lampert, M., Graziani, F.: Instructional activities as a tool for teachers' and teacher educators' learning. Elementry Sch. J. **109**(5), 491–509 (2009)
11. Loewenberg Ball, D., Forzani, F.M.: The work of teaching and the challenge for teacher education. J. Teach. Educ. **60**(5), 497–511 (2009)
12. Philip, T.M., et al.: Making justice peripheral by constructing practice as "core": how the increasing prominence of core practices challenges teacher education. J. Teach. Educ. **70**(3), 251–264 (2019)
13. Saldaña, J.: The qualitative coding manual (2009)
14. Strauss, A., Corbin, J.M.: Grounded Theory in Practice. Sage, Thousand Oaks (1997)
15. Zeichner, K.: The turn once again toward practice-based teacher education. J. Teach. Educ. **63**(5), 376–382 (2012)

A Portable Multi-user Cross-Platform Virtual Reality Platform for School Teaching in Malawi

Francis Kambili-Mzembe[1]($\boxtimes$) and Neil A. Gordon[2]

[1] Department of Computing, University of Malawi, P.O. Box 280, Zomba, Malawi
kambilimzembefrancis@gmail.com
[2] School of Computer Science, University of Hull, Cottingham Road, Hull HU6 7RX, UK
n.a.gordon@hull.ac.uk

Abstract. This paper discusses and evaluates a self-contained portable multi-user cross-platform Virtual Reality (VR) setup that was devised and configured using off the shelf technologies and devices. This paper exemplifies how some fundamental challenges like those faced in Malawi in relation to technology use, can be addressed, to allow for the use of VR technology as a potential solution to improving the quality of secondary school education in situations where the challenges in question are faced. This paper explains how the proposed VR setup was evaluated, where the results of that evaluation indicate that the proposed portable multi-user cross-platform VR setup is viable and can potentially be used for secondary school teaching. This is a follow-up to previous work that outlined the design and implementation of a VR software application to showcase the capabilities and functionality of this "Synchronous Multi-User Cross-Platform Virtual Reality for School Teachers", which consisted of using questionnaire data collected from school educators in England and it was part of a larger study. Whilst the challenges addressed are those that are faced in Malawi, the platform has more general applicability to a range of teaching contexts.

Keywords: Virtual Reality · Education · Technology · Malawi

1 Introduction

Virtual Reality is seen to eventually become an important part of education [1]. However, at present VR is not widely prevalent in education [2], but VR is gradually gaining traction in education [3]. VR is perceived to be beneficial to education. For instance, according to Kumar et al. [1], when applied to practical based subjects in education, VR has potential benefits such as allowing for repeated learning for students [1]. In this regard, Kwon [4] suggests that VR allows for students to engage in experiences that would otherwise not be possible for them.

The work presented in this paper is a follow-up to our previous work in which the implementation of a VR software application which was developed to showcase the functionality and capabilities of a multi-user cross-platform VR setup, was discussed [5]. The previous work in question highlighted a cross-platform VR setup which consisted

M.-L. Bourguet et al. (Eds.): iLRN 2023, CCIS 1904, pp. 182–192, 2024.
https://doi.org/10.1007/978-3-031-47328-9_14

of a Head Mounted Display (HMD) VR device and desktop VR devices [5]. In this regard, this paper discusses the configuration and evaluation of the VR setup that was highlighted in our previous work, in which case the focus of the work presented in this paper is on configuration of the hardware used to run the application discussed in our previous work, which focused on the prototype VR software application highlighted in this paper. The Malawi Government [6] has indicated that there is a need for "improved quality of secondary school education" [6] in Malawi. Therefore, as discussed in our previous work, taking into account the perceived benefits of VR, VR was proposed as a potential solution to improving the quality of secondary school education in Malawi [5]. However, as highlighted in our previous work, information regarding the use of VR technology within education in Malawi, could not found [5]. Therefore, the VR setup discussed in this paper was devised to showcase how the technologies highlighted in our previous work can be configured into a VR platform that can potentially be used by VR application developers, researchers and possibly educators in Malawi, in the process of assessing the feasibility and benefits of applying VR for secondary school teaching in Malawi.

2   Related Work

A multi-user VR application developed for the purpose of aiding surgeons in collaboratively planning for surgeries, is presented by Chheang et al. [7]. According to Chheang et al. [7], their application was developed using the Unity game engine and it utilises the HTC Vive HMD VR device [7]. Furthermore, multi-user functionality is enabled via a network [7], in which both "asynchronous (sequential) and synchronous (simultaneous)" [7] functionality between users is supported. According Chheang et al. [7], experts who evaluated their VR application considered the application helpful for training purposes. Marks and White [8] discuss a multi-user mixed reality system that utilises both VR and Augmented Reality (AR) [8]. According to Marks and White [8], this system consists of an HMD VR device and a tablet, enabling a user on each device to collaborate within the same virtual environment [8]. In this regard, the user on the HMD VR device is responsible for navigation within the virtual environment, while the user on the tablet, which serves as the AR device, is responsible for user interface functionality [8]. Furthermore, Marks and White [8] state that their mixed reality application utilises a network for multi-user functionality. In addition Marks and White [8] state that their application has been used within an education setting, and that feedback from learners suggested that the learners considered the system beneficial [8].

3   Considerations

The technologies and devices comprised in the proposed VR setup were chosen to account for some of the technology usage related challenges faced in Malawi, as well as the fact that the proposed VR setup is intended for a classroom setting.

3.1 Technology Usage Related Challenges Faced in Malawi

As discussed in our previous work [5], Malawi is a very underdeveloped country [6], which is echoed by the National Planning Commission in Malawi [9], which states that "poverty" [9] is the biggest challenge faced in Malawi, where according to the Malawi Government [6], "the majority" [6] of the population in Malawi resides in poverty stricken areas. Furthermore, the National Planning Commission [9] states that one of the challenges faced is costly Information Communication Technology (ICT) services, which according to the National Planning Commission [9], negatively affects "technology adoption" [9] in Malawi. This is echoed by Hettinger et al. [10] who indicate that the cost of services such as the internet is a challenge in Malawi. In addition, adequate availability of and access to electricity is also a challenge for many in Malawi [6, 11], including schools where for instance "18%" [12] of secondary schools in Malawi have no access to electricity. However, the National Planning Commission in Malawi also states that interest in the use of technology has improved in Malawi, particularly "mobile phone technology" [9].

3.2 The Education Context

Hmelo-Silver [13] suggests that collaboration is an important component of education, and in this regard, Cooper et al. [14] state that the "collaborative potential" [14] of VR should be accounted for when considering VR for educational purposes. Furthermore, Garcia-Bonete et al. [15] state that if educational VR applications can only be utilized on a "specific device" [15], this can result in limiting the number of people that can use the applications, thereby potentially introducing accessibility and inclusion challenges, where in this regard accessibility refers to how the VR applications in question, are "accessible by as many people as possible" [16], and inclusion refers to how accommodating the VR applications in question are to "the widest possible number of people" [16].

4 The Proposed VR Setup

The technologies and devices used to configure the proposed VR setup, take into consideration the context of Malawi as well as the educational context in which these technologies are being proposed for. Therefore, as shown in Fig. 1, to account for accessibility and inclusion, the proposed VR setup was devised as a cross-platform setup consisting of an Oculus Quest VR device, which is an HMD VR platform, as well as a Windows tablet, and an Android tablet, both of which are used as desktop VR platforms. Garcia-Bonete et al. [15] suggest that "cross-platform technologies" [15] should be preferred to ensure accessibility of VR content used for educational purposes. As shown in Fig. 1, each of the devices consist of different input and output functionalities, where the Windows tablet uses a mouse and keyboard for input; the Android tablet uses touch screen functionality for input; and the Oculus Quest HMD uses motion controllers for input. Sharp et al. [16] state that allowing for different ways of interaction for users enables those that might otherwise have difficulties with a specific way interacting with the product, to have an alternative means of interaction. Therefore, by providing support for different VR platforms with different methods of input and output, the proposed VR setup not only accounts for accessibility, but also considers inclusion. Furthermore, to account for cost related challenges, the proposed VR setup was devised to be flexible, in that if specific type of VR devices were not available (for instance HMDs), then it can still be used with the devices that are available.

Fig. 1. The proposed portable multi-user cross-platform VR setup, with the Oculus Quest HMD on the top left, the router on the top right, the Windows tablet on the bottom left and the Android tablet on bottom right.

To account for synchronous multi-user functionality, which enables collaborative VR experiences, the proposed VR setup utilises Wireless Local Area Network (WLAN) technology. According to Yadav et al. [17], WLAN technology is appropriate in situations where network infrastructure is a challenge. In addition, WLAN technology is thought to be simple to use and cost effective [17]. Therefore, the proposed VR setup consists of an off the shelf Wi-Fi capable network router, which was used for multi-user functionality, of which Wi-Fi is WLAN based "network communication" [18] technology. In this regard, an existing network infrastructure, or the internet, is not required. Therefore, all network communication between the VR devices is facilitated by the router, on which a local network is configured and used.

To account for electricity access challenges, all the devices used in the proposed VR setup do not rely on a persistent supply of electricity for power. Therefore, the VR devices that were used, are all battery powered mobile devices. Furthermore, as shown in Fig. 2, for power, the Wi-Fi router uses an off the shelf portable rechargeable power bank, which is a device that is usually used as a portable charger for mobile devices like a phone [19]. In this regard, the power bank that was used to power the router has a battery capacity of 24800 milliampere-hour, and in our experience it would last for an entire evaluation session (discussed in the sections to follow) lasting at least an hour in length, without needing to be recharged. In the proposed setup, only the router was connected to the power bank as a power source, and the other devices utilised their internal batteries. Using battery powered devices ensures that even areas with no access to electricity can use the proposed VR setup.

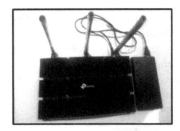

Fig. 2. Wi-Fi router and power bank used as part of the VR setup.

5   Evaluation of the VR Setup

Evaluation can be carried out for the purpose of determining the suitability of a given design of a product [16]. In this regard, the proposed VR setup was evaluated using heuristic evaluation, which is an established and commonly employed evaluation method [20, 21]. The purpose of the evaluation was not to compare each of the 3 devices, but to get feedback on the experience on each device.

5.1   Heuristic Evaluation

Heuristic evaluation belongs to a category of evaluation methods referred to as "inspection methods" [16], which can be employed to identify "usability problems" [16] without the involvement of intended users [16]. In this regard, heuristic evaluation involves experts carrying out an evaluation by using a set of guidelines known as "heuristics" [16]. Between three and five evaluators is regarded as appropriate for heuristic evaluation [16], and between five and ten items in regard to heuristics, is considered adequate for heuristic evaluation [16].

5.2   Data Collection

Although there is an established set of heuristics referred to as "Nielsen's heuristics" [22], Nielsen's heuristics are not always adequate for the evaluation of domain specific aspects [22] due to the notion that domain specific factors could be overlooked [23]. Therefore, a number of heuristics have been developed to cater to specific domains [22, 23], some of which were developed by adapting Nielsen's heuristics [22]. In this regard, this study adopted without modification, some of the 16 usability heuristics proposed by Muñoz and Chalegre [21]. In this regard, our study did not make use of all the proposed 16 heuristics. Sharp et al. [16], state that the heuristics that are to be chosen depend on what is being evaluated. In addition, as previously stated, between "5 and 10" [16] heuristic items are considered adequate for heuristic evaluation [16]. In this regard, our study adopted 10 of the heuristics presented by Muñoz and Chalegre [21], listed in Table 1, that were regarded as the ones corresponding the most to the features and functionality implemented in our proposed VR setup. Furthermore, as detailed by Muñoz and Chalegre [21], each of the heuristics is defined by items which correspond to a particular heuristic. Therefore, some of the items within each chosen heuristic were used as the item to evaluate against a given heuristic. In total, 26 items belonging to the heuristics listed in Table 1 were adopted for use in our study. Details of the 26 items used were discussed in the study by Kambili-Mzembe [24], of which our study is part of. Each item was given a rating from a 4 point rating scale, by an evaluator, as a rating of their experience on each platform in relation to the item in question. According to Herr et al. [25], one of the objectives of heuristic evaluation is the quantification of identified usability problems, in regard to severity [25]. A five point severity scale, which is considered as an "established" [25] scale, was proposed by Nielsen [26], and ranges from "0 = I don't agree that this is a usability problem at all" [26], to "4 = Usability catastrophe: imperative to fix this before product can be released" [26]. However, Herr et al. [25] propose that Nielsen's severity scale can be used without the zero scale rating, since according to Herr et al. [25], the zero point rating scale can lead to "biases" [25] in the results, among other drawbacks [25]. In this regard, as previously stated, our study made use of a 4 point rating scale as an adaptation of Nielsen's severity scale without the zero rating scale, as shown in Table 2.

Table 1. 10 of the 16 usability heuristics proposed by Muñoz & Chalegre [21] and used in our study.

Serial number	Heuristic
1	Feedback
2	Clarity
3	Consistency
4	Simplicity
5	Orientation and Navigation
6	Control camera and Visualization
7	Communication between avatars
8	Sense of ownership
9	Interaction with the Virtual World
10	Error Prevention

Heuristic evaluation of the proposed VR setup was carried out in England by 4 evaluators, all of whom were academics from a university in England, with expertise in domains such as software development; Virtual Reality; computer graphics; and computer games. Evaluations were carried out separately on different occasions with each evaluator, where an evaluator would in turn make use of each device while executing the VR application presented in our previous work [5], as shown in Fig. 3. In this regard, an evaluator would start with the Android tablet, initiated as the server on which the other devices would connect to for a multi-user experience. The evaluator would then transition to using the Windows tablet by connecting to the session that was initiated on the Android tablet, at which point the session would now consist of two connected devices, of which the Android tablet is the server and the Windows tablet is connected

Table 2. Adaptation of Nielsen's severity scale as used in our study.

Rating value	Value meaning	Details of scale
1	Cosmetic problem	Need not be fixed unless extra time is available
2	Minor usability problem	Fixing the problem should be given lower priority
3	Major usability problem	Important to fix, should be given high priority
4	Usability catastrophe	Imperative to fix before release

as the client. Finally the evaluator would then join the session using an Oculus Quest HMD, at which point the session would consist of all three devices, of which the Oculus Quest and Windows tablet are clients connected to the multi-user session executing on the Android tablet as the server. The evaluator would then provide ratings against the 26 items belonging to the heuristics listed in Table 1, based on their experience with the VR application on each of the three devices.

Fig. 3. The same synchronous multi-user cross-platform VR scene, showing from the perspectives of the Android tablet user on the top left, the Windows tablet user on the top right and the Oculus Quest HMD VR user at the bottom.

5.3 Data Analysis

Data collected from the heuristic evaluation activity was numerically analysed using a method known as Content Validity Index (CVI). According to Polit et al. [27], CVI can be used to measure how much experts agree on the rating of specified items in regard to how relevant those items are [27]. In this regard, Motlagh Tehrani et al. [28] used CVI to analyse heuristic evaluation data for a virtual museum smartphone application. A four point ordinal scale can be used with CVI [29], of which items are rated from "1 = not relevant" [27], to "4 = highly relevant" [27]. According to Polit and Beck [29], a CVI value can be calculated for each item by categorising the four point expert ratings into dichotomous ratings of either "not relevant" [29] for ratings of 1 or 2, and "relevant" [29] for ratings of 3 or 4. In this regard, Polit and Beck [29] state that by only considering ratings that are within the relevant category (ratings of 3 or 4), the item CVI or "I-CVI" [29] can be calculated by identifying the number of times an item has been rated as relevant and then dividing that number by the number of experts [29]. Furthermore, the CVI value for all available items, which Polit and Beck [29] refer to as the "S-CVI" [29] can be calculated by obtaining the mean of all I-CVI values [29], resulting in what Polit and Beck [29] refer to as "S-CVI/Ave" [29]. In this regard, Polit and Beck [29] recommend that if the number of experts is between three and five, then an I-CVI value of 1 should be regarded as relevant, and a S-CVI/Ave value greater than or equal to "0.90" [29] should be regarded as relevant. To align the four point ratings used in our study with the I-CVI calculation presented by Polit and Beck [29], ratings of 1 or 2 were categorized as minor usability problem, akin to not relevant, and ratings of 3 or 4 were categorized as major usability problem, akin to relevant. In this regard, Table 3 shows the total number of major usability problems on each device as rated by each evaluator, out of the 26 items. Table 4 shows the S-CVI/Ave value that was calculated for each of the three devices that were used. More detailed values of data collected from all evaluators is provided in the study by Kambili-Mzembe [24], of which our study is a part of.

Table 3. The total number of major usability problems indicated by the evaluators.

Device name	Evaluator A	Evaluator B	Evaluator C	Evaluator D
Android tablet	0	0	23	1
Windows tablet	4	0	8	3
Oculus Quest HMD	0	1	0	3

Table 4. The highest observed I-CVI and the S-CVI/Ave for each device.

Device name	Highest observed I-CVI	S-CVI/Ave
Android tablet	0.5	0.23
Windows tablet	0.5	0.14
Oculus Quest HMD	0.25	0.04

6 Discussion and Conclusion

As shown in Table 3, the device with the highest total number of major usability problems based on the evaluator ratings, was the Android tablet, of which Evaluator C had identified 23 major usability problems, in that the evaluator in question had given 23 out of the 26 items, a rating of either 3 or 4. The 23 items will need to be taken into consideration in future. The evaluation scores of the 23 items in question are listed in the study by

Kambili-Mzembe [24], of which our study is a part of. However, as shown in Table 3, two out of the four evaluators (A and B) found no major usability problems with the Android tablet, with the other remaining evaluator (D) finding only 1 major usability problem. This supports the notion that cross-platform VR applications are needed for accessibility and inclusion purposes, since, as suggested by these results, some individuals could face challenges making use of a particular device and/or platform, of which one of the evaluators identified problems when using the android tablet. However, overall, when taking into consideration all four evaluators, as shown in Table 4, the highest observed I-CVI value on the Android tablet is 0.5. The I-CVI value in this case is less than 1, therefore, in accordance to what was previously discussed, this item cannot be considered as a major usability problem on the Android tablet. As shown in Table 4, both the Windows tablet and Oculus Quest HMD devices also have highest observed I-CVI values of less than 1. Furthermore, as shown in Table 4, all three devices have an observed S-CVI/Ave value of less than 0.9, with 0.23 for the Android tablet being the highest observed S-CVI/Ave value out of the three devices. Therefore, in accordance to what was previously discussed, this indicates that overall, in terms of usability, according to the expert evaluation, the highlighted multi-user VR software application experience on the proposed VR setup, cannot be considered a major usability problem on any of the featured devices.

Considering that the results of the heuristic evaluation showed that overall, there were no major usability problems identified by the evaluators on all devices comprised in the proposed VR setup, the data indicates that the proposed portable multi-user cross platform VR setup is viable for use by VR application developers; researchers; and possibly even educators, to deploy VR applications within a school environment in which challenges such as availability of electricity; or access to an existing network and/or internet infrastructure; availability of adequate dedicated physical space for VR, are a concern. In addition, the cross-platform nature of the proposed VR setup highlights that accessibility and inclusion are taken into consideration, while also allowing for flexibility in terms of how the proposed VR setup can be configured, since any of the proposed VR devices can be used with this setup, without the need to have all of them available, thereby also addressing cost related challenges.

7   Limitations and Future Development

A major limitation of the study was that the data collection activity did not involve educators from Malawi. Considering that the study was carried out during the COVID-19 pandemic, travel to Malawi from England was a challenge during this period, therefore educators from Malawi could not physically take part in any evaluation activities.

Considering that educators in Malawi were not able to evaluate the proposed VR setup, as previously stated, in future, the study will focus on further developing the proposed VR setup in collaboration with educators in Malawi in which they will be able to evaluate the proposed VR setup, as well provide input for further improvements.

Acknowledgments. We would like to acknowledge the Commonwealth Scholarship Commission in the UK for supporting the research that this paper is based on. We would like to thank the Faculty of Science and Engineering and the School of Computer Science at the University of Hull for their support. We would also like to thank Dr Mike Brayshaw for his support and feedback. Finally, we would like to thank all the research participants and anyone who contributed and assisted in any way to the study discussed in this paper.

References

1. Kumar, V., Gulati, S., Deka, B., Sarma, H.: Teaching and learning crystal structures through virtual reality based systems. Adv. Eng. Inform. **50**, 101362 (2021). https://doi.org/10.1016/j.aei.2021.101362
2. Southgate, E., et al.: Embedding immersive virtual reality in classrooms: ethical, organisational and educational lessons in bridging research and practice. Int. J. Child-Comput. Interact. **19**, 19–29 (2019). https://doi.org/10.1016/j.ijcci.2018.10.002
3. McGovern, E., Moreira, G., Luna-Nevarez, C.: An application of virtual reality in education: can this technology enhance the quality of students' learning experience? J. Educ. Bus. **95**, 490–496 (2020). https://doi.org/10.1080/08832323.2019.1703096
4. Kwon, C.: Verification of the possibility and effectiveness of experiential learning using HMD-based immersive VR technologies. Virtual Reality **23**(1), 101–118 (2018). https://doi.org/10.1007/s10055-018-0364-1
5. Kambili-Mzembe, F., Gordon, N.A.: Synchronous multi-user cross-platform virtual reality for school teachers. In: 2022 8th International Conference of the Immersive Learning Research Network (iLRN), pp. 1–5 (2022)
6. Malawi Government: The Malawi Growth and Development Strategy III (2018). https://www.mw.undp.org/content/malawi/en/home/library/the-malawi-growth-and-development-strategy-iii-.html
7. Chheang, V., et al.: A collaborative virtual reality environment for liver surgery planning. Comput. Graph. **99**, 234–246 (2021). https://doi.org/10.1016/j.cag.2021.07.009
8. Marks, S., White, D.: Multi-device collaboration in virtual environments. In: Proceedings of the 2020 4th International Conference on Virtual and Augmented Reality Simulations, pp. 35–38. Association for Computing Machinery, New York (2020)
9. National Planning Commission: Malawi Vision 2063: An Inclusively Wealthy and Self-reliant Nation (2021). https://malawi.un.org/en/108390-malawi-vision-2063-inclusively-wealthy-and-self-reliant-nation
10. Hettinger, P.S., Mboob, I.S., Robinson, D.S., Nyirenda, Y.L., Galal, R.M.A., Chilima, E.Z.: Malawi Economic Monitor: Investing in Digital Transformation (2021). https://documents1.worldbank.org/curated/en/131501624458623473/pdf/Malawi-Economic-Monitor-Investing-in-Digital-Transformation.pdf
11. Pankomera, R., Van Greunen, D.: An ICT model to enhance teaching and learning in a resource constrained setting: a case of Malawi. In: Brinda, T., Mavengere, N., Haukijärvi, I., Lewin, C., Passey, D. (eds.) Stakeholders and Information Technology in Education, pp. 163–173. Springer, Cham (2016). https://doi.org/10.1007/978-3-319-54687-2_16
12. Malawi Ministry of Education: 2021 Malawi Education Statistics Report (2022). https://www.education.gov.mw/index.php/edu-resources/category/10-reports
13. Hmelo-Silver, C.E.: Problem-based learning: what and how do students learn? Educ. Psychol. Rev. **16**, 235–266 (2004). https://doi.org/10.1023/B:EDPR.0000034022.16470.f3
14. Cooper, G., Park, H., Nasr, Z., Thong, L.P., Johnson, R.: Using virtual reality in the classroom: preservice teachers' perceptions of its use as a teaching and learning tool. Educ. Media Int. **56**, 1–13 (2019). https://doi.org/10.1080/09523987.2019.1583461

15. Garcia-Bonete, M.-J., Jensen, M., Katona, G.: A practical guide to developing virtual and augmented reality exercises for teaching structural biology. Biochem. Mol. Biol. Educ. **47**, 16–24 (2019). https://doi.org/10.1002/bmb.21188

16. Sharp, H., Preece, J., Rogers, Y.: Interaction Design: Beyond Human-Computer Interaction. Wiley-Blackwell, Indiana (2019)

17. Yadav, P., Agrawal, R., Kashish, K.: Performance evaluation of ad hoc wireless local area network in telemedicine applications. Procedia Comput. Sci. **125**, 267–274 (2018). https://doi.org/10.1016/j.procs.2017.12.036

18. Zhang, R., et al.: A new environmental monitoring system based on WiFi technology. Procedia CIRP **83**, 394–397 (2019). https://doi.org/10.1016/j.procir.2019.04.088

19. Zheng, T., et al.: A portable, battery-powered photoelectrochemical aptasesor for field environment monitoring of E. coli O157:H7. Sens. Actuators B: Chem. **346**, 130520 (2021). https://doi.org/10.1016/j.snb.2021.130520

20. Inostroza, R., Rusu, C., Roncagliolo, S., Rusu, V.: Usability heuristics for touchscreen-based mobile devices: update. In: Proceedings of the 2013 Chilean Conference on Human - Computer Interaction, pp. 24–29. Association for Computing Machinery, New York (2013)

21. Muñoz, R., Chalegre, V.: Defining virtual worlds usability heuristics. In: 2012 Ninth International Conference on Information Technology - New Generations, pp. 690–695 (2012)

22. Quiñones, D., Rusu, C.: How to develop usability heuristics: a systematic literature review. Comput. Standards Interfaces **53**, 89–122 (2017). https://doi.org/10.1016/j.csi.2017.03.009

23. Quiñones, D., Rusu, C., Rusu, V.: A methodology to develop usability/user experience heuristics. Comput. Standards Interfaces **59**, 109–129 (2018). https://doi.org/10.1016/j.csi.2018.03.002

24. Kambili-Mzembe, F.: Investigating virtual reality for secondary school teaching in Malawi. Ph.D. thesis. University of Hull, United Kingdom (2022)

25. Herr, S., Baumgartner, N., Gross, T.: Evaluating severity rating scales for heuristic evaluation. In: Proceedings of the 2016 CHI Conference Extended Abstracts on Human Factors in Computing Systems, pp. 3069–3075. Association for Computing Machinery, New York (2016)

26. Nielsen, J.: Severity Ratings for Usability Problems. https://www.nngroup.com/articles/how-to-rate-the-severity-of-usability-problems/

27. Polit, D.F., Beck, C.T., Owen, S.V.: Is the CVI an acceptable indicator of content validity? Appraisal and recommendations. Res. Nurs. Health **30**, 459–467 (2007). https://doi.org/10.1002/nur.20199

28. Motlagh Tehrani, S.E., Zainuddin, N.M.M., Takavar, T.: Heuristic evaluation for virtual museum on smartphone. In: 2014 3rd International Conference on User Science and Engineering (i-USEr), pp. 227–231 (2014)

29. Polit, D.F., Beck, C.T.: The content validity index: are you sure you know what's being reported? Critique and recommendations. Res. Nurs. Health **29**, 489–497 (2006). https://doi.org/10.1002/nur.20147

Assessment and Evaluation (A&E)

Assessment Framework for Immersive Learning: Application and Evaluation

Chioma Udeozor[1] (ID), Jessica Lizeth Dominguez Alfaro[2], and Jarka Glassey[1]([✉])

[1] School of Engineering, Newcastle University, Newcastle Upon Tyne NE17RU, UK
Jarka.glassey@newcastle.ac.uk
[2] Department of Chemical Engineering, KU Leuven, Leuven, Belgium

Abstract. Technological advances, changing demands of students and employers as well as the stiff competition among higher education (HE) institutions are leading to the exploration and adoption of innovative learning technologies in HE. The use of immersive technologies for education is rising given their potential to complement current methods of delivering learning content to students. Among the benefits of these technologies to education is their ability to promote active, experiential and higher-order learning. However, what is still unclear to educators is how to measure learning in immersive environments. This paper proposes a framework developed to guide educators through the process of designing and implementing assessments when using immersive technologies. The assessment framework presented in this paper builds upon the principle of Constructive Alignment (CA) and the Evidence-Centered Design (ECD) framework. A qualitative evaluation of the proposed framework was conducted to evaluate how easy it is for educators to understand and use it for assessment design around immersive learning activities. The framework was found to provide familiar and user-friendly assessment design guidelines for educators. Lastly, this paper also presents a suggestion for the application of the proposed assessment framework to the design of assessments for an augmented reality game. It also outlines best practices when considering immersive technologies for assessments in HE.

Keywords: Assessment · Evaluation · Assessment Framework · Augmented Reality · Immersive Technologies

1 Introduction

Technologies play important roles in many educational institutions today. Recently, interest in immersive technologies such as virtual reality (VR) and augmented reality (AR) is on the rise following the changes in learning and teaching (L&T) that took place during the Covid-19 pandemic. In higher education (HE), technological advances, changing demands of students and employers as well as the competition among these institutions have led to the exploration and adoption of immersive technologies for L&T. Given their ability to promote active, experiential and higher-order learning, immersive technologies are increasingly being used to complement current methods of delivering

M.-L. Bourguet et al. (Eds.): iLRN 2023, CCIS 1904, pp. 195–208, 2024.
https://doi.org/10.1007/978-3-031-47328-9_15

learning content to students [1–3]. One challenge with their use for formal classroom teaching, however, is the lack of a structured method for the measurement of learning in the immersive environments afforded by these technologies[4–6]. So far, there are limited established assessment design strategies targeted at educators interested in using immersive technologies in classrooms. This paper introduces a game-based assessment framework developed to guide educators through the design of appropriate assessment tasks to measure learning in immersive environments.

2 Conceptual Background

The game-based assessment framework (GBAF) proposed in this paper is grounded in the Constructive Alignment (CA) principle [7] and the Evidence-Centered Design (ECD) framework [8]. The ECD framework is commonly used for designing assessments for measuring performance in game-based environments. It consists of models that define the operational elements of an assessment and these are the Student models, the Evidence models, Task models, Assembly model and Presentation model. The Student models specify the variables associated with the skills, knowledge and abilities to be measured. The Evidence models provide proof of the competencies of students by linking their actions to the measured proficiencies. The Task model specifies the group of tasks or activities that would be performed by students to elicit observable evidence of the unobservable competencies defined in the Student models [8]. Lastly, the Assembly and Presentation models describe how much evidence or tasks are needed to make valid inferences about the proficiencies of students, and how the assessment tasks are presented to students. The ECD framework recommends the use of Bayesian inferential networks for updating information about the competencies of students at every point in time and for building evidentiary arguments of what they know [8, 9]. The ECD framework has been used to design stealth assessments [1] and other games/simulation-based assessments [10–12]. Although the ECD provides a systematic process of assessment design for measuring competencies in complex learning environments, the process is often considered tedious and time-consuming and requires expertise in advanced statistics [13–15].

The CA principles on the other hand are based on the idea that students learn by constructing knowledge through active participation. Popularly used in HE [16], CA recommends adequate alignment between intended learning outcomes (ILOs), learning activities and assessment tasks [7]. The four steps proposed by Biggs to ensure the alignment of these components is to first define the ILOs following appropriate taxonomies such as Bloom's taxonomy or the structure of observed learning outcomes taxonomy (SOLO) [17]. Secondly, Biggs recommends active and engaging pedagogical activities over passive learning activities. Finally, assessment tasks should be designed to align with one or more of the pre-defined ILOs. The CA principles provide logical steps for assessment designs that have been widely used in classrooms for conventional assessments. While the CA principles have not been used for the design of assessments for measuring learning in immersive environments, these principles could potentially be used for this purpose. Both the ECD and the CA principles provide useful considerations for the design of games/simulation-based assessments. Whereas the ECD framework highlights the necessary models for assessment design, the CA emphasizes the connections between the ILOs, the assessment tasks and the learning activities. The CA principles offer educators familiar guidelines while the ECD has a wider application in the field of game-based assessment.

3   The Game-Based Assessment Framework

The GBAF was developed to guide the design assessments for measuring learning when using VR, AR and serious digital games (DGs) for L&T. Founded in the constructivist learning theory, CA recommends starting from intended learning outcomes (ILOs) when designing assessments, ensuring that the ILOs, assessment tasks and the L&T activities of choice are aligned [17]. The GBAF provides a simple, logical and structured process of assessment design for DGs, VR and AR learning environments. It consists of five components necessary for assessments in immersive environments: the overall objective, learning outcomes, game tasks, scoring metrics, and grading methods. As illustrated in Fig. 1, these components must be adequately aligned when designing assessments.

3.1   Overall Objectives

Immersive learning environments are often designed to teach certain subjects, skills or competencies. In order to identify relevant pre-existing immersive learning environments or to begin the design of a new environment, it is necessary to first outline broadly the learning objective in connection to the curriculum. Clearly articulating this would enhance the identification and/or design of appropriate learning environments.

3.2   Learning Outcomes

The next step involves the drafting of the ILOs. The ILOs should follow a structured approach such as those provided by the SOLO taxonomy [18] or Bloom's taxonomy [19] to describe specific measurable competencies that students would learn and demonstrate knowledge of in the learning environment. The ILOs for immersive environments should focus on what students are expected *to do* to demonstrate mastery of the desired knowledge and skills. The statements of learning outcomes should also guide the choice of an immersive learning environment to adopt. When designing a new environment, the ILOs should inform the learning activities or game tasks to be embedded in the environment.

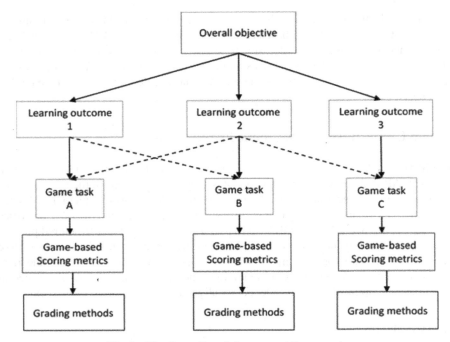

Fig. 1. The Game-Based Assessment Framework.

3.3 Game Tasks

Game tasks constitute the group of activities that students would have to perform in the environment. With the possibility of simulating real-world tasks in immersive environments, complex competencies and higher-order cognitive processes of students can be assessed in these environments. A single task in an immersive learning environment could elicit more than one competence and is thus useful for measuring more than one ILO. For a pre-existing learning environment, the available tasks should be useful for assessing all or most of the desired ILOs.

3.4 Scoring Metrics

Another important factor to consider in the design of assessments for measuring learning in immersive environments is the scoring metrics to use. Scoring metrics here refer to those game metrics that are relevant for providing evidence of the competencies of students on the desired ILOs. In pre-existing environments, the collected data on the activities of students should be sufficient to measure desired ILOs in the environment. When designing a new environment, real-time data on relevant metrics should be collected and stored. Scoring metrics could be as general as "completion time", "tasks completed" or "correct/incorrect responses", or more refined and grain-sized metrics such as "locations visited", "path taken" or "errors made".

3.5 Grading Methods

It is good practice to establish appropriate grading techniques and scoring schemes to enhance the objectivity and reliability of the grading process [20, 21]. The grading method should specify the formula and weighting to be used to determine the grades of students based on their performance on the scoring metrics. The scheme should show the scoring strategies and quality criteria for different performance ratings of students. This can be incorporated into the immersive learning environment so that grades are automatically generated and presented to students upon completing the assigned tasks.

Another important element to consider in the assessment of learning in immersive environments is how to deliver feedback to students. Feedback can be immediate and integrated into the environment or delayed, provided during debriefing sessions. Although relevant to assessment implementation, feedback does not have to be aligned with the five components described above. All five components must be closely aligned. It is also crucial to identify and use only relevant learning environments, particularly when considering carrying out assessments. While there is less flexibility for assessments when using a pre-existing environment, a useful decision-making process map for choosing an appropriate pre-existing environment is presented in [22].

4 Application of the GBAF to the Design Assessment for an AR Game

To demonstrate how the GBAF can be applied to the design of assessments for immersive learning environments, its application to the design of assessments for an AR titration game is described. The mobile AR (MAR) game adopted here and presented in Fig. 2 is a markerless titration application that was developed to teach students the basics of the titration process [23]. Using the GBAF, the assessment components and their interrelationships are presented in Fig. 3.

4.1 Assessment Design Components for the MAR Game

The assessment design process took place during the development of the game. The overall objective of the AR game as illustrated in Fig. 3 is to teach and assess the knowledge and skills of students on titration. The ILOs of interest, the cognitive process levels and the knowledge dimensions following Bloom's taxonomy are respectively outlined below.

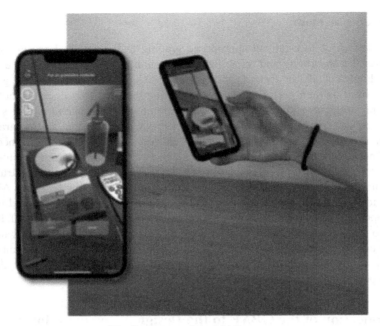

Fig. 2. Picture of the MAR game.

During the AR gameplay, students should be able to correctly:

1) Set up the titration equipment - *Apply, Procedural*
2) Assess the nature of the chemicals [acid and base] used for titration - *Evaluate/Understand; Procedural*
3) Calculate the pH of a mixture of acid and base - *Apply; Procedural*
4) Observe safety protocols in the lab - *Apply; Procedural*

To assess the proficiencies of students on these ILOs, titration tasks were designed on three levels of the game with increasing difficulties. Students are expected to perform titration experiments using the correct instruments, identify and use relevant acids and bases, and log titration readings. The choices made, and errors and successes achieved by students were collected as scoring metrics for the assessment. Additionally, multiple-choice questions (MCQs) were incorporated into the game levels and presented to students at specific times to assess their knowledge of different chemicals and their pH levels as illustrated in Fig. 3. ILO 1 and ILO 2 are assessed by the number of errors made by students. Furthermore, ILO 2 and ILO 3 are assessed by the answers to some conceptual MCQs. Lastly, ILO 4 is assessed by the number of hints students received on the personal protective equipment (PPE) to use for the experiment.

The formulas for grading the performance of students on the game are as follows:

$$\textbf{\textit{Level 1}} = \textit{Assembly of equipment} \times 0.4 + \textit{Distinction of chemicals} \\ \times 0.2 + \textit{pH identification} \times 0.1 + \textit{safety awareness} \times 0.3 \quad (1)$$

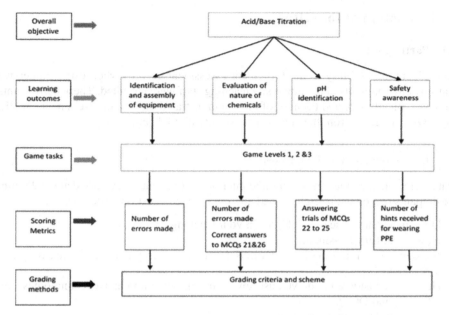

Fig. 3. Assessment design framework for the MAR game based on the GBAF.

$$\textbf{Level 2} = \textit{Assembly of equipment} \times 0.2 + \textit{Distinction of chemicals}$$
$$\times\ 0.3 + \textit{pH identification} \times 0.4 + \textit{safety awareness} \times 0.1 \qquad (2)$$

$$\textbf{Level 3} = \text{Assembly of equipment} \times 0.1 + \text{Distinction of chemicals}$$
$$\times\ 0.4 + \text{pH identification} \times 0.4 + \text{safety awareness} \times 0.1 \qquad (3)$$

At Level 1, the students are just familiarizing themselves with the application, the materials and the procedures. Therefore, the "assembly of equipment" is weighted higher. The weightings are adjusted in Levels 2 and 3 to emphasise the competencies of focus. The grading methods developed for this assessment are presented in Table 1 and outline three performance ratings that will be awarded to students given their scores in all three levels of the MAR game.

Table 1. Scoring scheme for MAR game.

	Performance rating		
	Novice	Competent	Expert
Level 1	0–40%	41–80%	81–100%
Level 2	0–40%	41–80%	81–100%
Level 3	0–40%	41–80%	81–100%

5 Evaluation of the GBAF

5.1 Participants

To evaluate the usability of the GBAF for assessment designs when using immersive learning environments, three university teaching staff were recruited. These participants were specifically selected because of their demonstrated interest in assessments in HE. They were lecturers from the engineering faculty of a UK university.

5.2 Data Collection and Analyses

Data were collected via semi-structured interviews. Each interview lasted about 25 min. Participants responded to eight closed and open-ended questions listed below:

1. Do you currently use technologies in your teaching?
2. How about for assessment?
3. In your opinion, are there any barriers to the use of technologies for teaching and assessments?
4. Have you considered or do you use any of the emerging immersive technologies, e.g. VR, AR, and DGs?
5. What would make you use those?
6. How about for assessments, would you consider these for assessment?
7. Would this assessment framework help? Without an explanation of how it works, do you understand the framework?
8. Can you describe how you can apply it to a hypothetical/previously mentioned immersive learning environment?

The collected data were descriptively analysed on Microsoft Word. The responses noted during the interviews were first reviewed and then answers provided by participants to each question were collated. The main points in the responses were highlighted and similar points were summarised.

5.3 Results

For the first six questions that are not directly linked to the GBAF, the points made by the participants are outlined in Table 2. All the participants reported using technology for teaching. The technologies mentioned include videos, learning management systems (LMS), interactive apps and open-source programming environments. They also reported using similar technologies for assessments.

The barriers to the use of technologies for teaching and assessments identified in their responses can be grouped as differences in the preferences of students, lack of necessary technological resources, the usability of the provided technological applications and accessibility of relevant technologies as shown in Table 2. One participant stressed the need for unified but relevant technologies across institutions. They emphasised that educators often have to adapt each time they move from one institution to another and that in most cases, the necessary technologies are not always available. They recommended the use of open-source technologies that are easily accessible across institutions and geographies. Another participant explained how the LMS used in some universities makes it difficult for students to access feedback after an assessment. The participant discussed the need for more efficient educator-and student-friendly technologies that would enhance L&T.

For questions four to eight, the discussions were focused on immersive learning technologies. Although one participant reported playing games in VR, none of the participants had used immersive technologies for teaching or assessments. Nonetheless, they all had positive perceptions of the potential of immersive technologies to improve learning experiences. In all three interviews, there were major discussions about the challenges of adopting immersive technologies for education. The participants all highlighted the time and skills requirements for designing relevant applications for classroom use. They considered this as the biggest barrier to using these technologies for teaching. When asked about their use for assessment, the participants did not show the same level of positive views as they did with immersive technologies for teaching. They seemed open to the idea but also showed some reservations. This did not come as a surprise particularly because none of these educators has or is currently applying these technologies to their teaching. Conceptualising the practicalities of assessing in immersive environments would be challenging for anyone with similar limited experience.

All participants agreed that a framework and guidelines useful for assessments in immersive environments would certainly enhance their adoption. When presented with the GBAF, each participant took about a minute to look through it while describing how they think it works. One participant thought it was intuitive and easy to understand. Another agreed that all the components were indeed necessary for assessment but described the development of the immersive learning environment as the bottleneck. This participant showed much more interest in the design of the learning environments than in their use for assessment:

> "... I think this is easy to understand and implement for assessment design. [pointing at the 'task' component of the GBAF 2] this is the biggest problem...How do we design this environment? If you can tell me or give me a framework like this, that will make it easier..."

The third participant was also able to explain the assessment framework. He described it to be useful for any assessment. This participant also recommended having an additional arrow going from "grading methods" to "learning outcomes". This, in their opinion, would indicate whether the learning outcomes are met given the performance of students.

Table 2. Key points from the interview.

Interviews Questions	Points	Summary
Do you currently use technologies in your teaching?	Yes; canvas, videos, board games Yes; Blackboard, Slido, Canvas, Google Colab	N/A
How about for assessment?	Yes; quizzes and mini-projects Yes; easy for assessments [implementation], collaboration and feedback Definitely; enhances formative assessments and feedback	N/A
Any barriers to the use of technologies for teaching and assessments?	Not [suitable] for all students. Variety of assessment types necessary Lack of relevant technological resources and applications; differs from institution to institution. More open-source applications needed One-size-fits-all applications that are not useful. Usability and accessibility	Students' preferences Lack of resources Technology usability Accessibility
Have you considered or do you use any of the emerging immersive techs, e.g. VR, AR, DGs?	No. Designing these is time-consuming but I would adopt one if I find one No. But should be engaging and interesting to students Not personally as I do not teach at the moment, but I will recommend it to the teaching staff	Positive perceptions
What would make you use these?	If I find a suitable one for my module and student cohort, of course, I will use it It must be useful for my module and interesting to the students Relevant. Accessible	Relevance to module Accessibility
How about for assessments?	Yes. If the environment allows it Possibly. Can be used for assessment if properly developed I would want to explore it	Openness to explore

6 Assessment Best Practices

The GBAF provides a useful guide for the design and implementation of assessments for complex learning environments. The assessment design considerations proposed by this framework offer important guidance to educators. An outline of best practices when considering teaching and assessments with immersive learning technologies would however provide holistic guidelines for educators. Based on research and experiences gained developing the GBAF, the following best practices are proposed when implementing game-based assessments in HE:

1. A chosen immersive learning environment must be engaging. HE students expect any immersive environment given to them to be fun and engaging [24].

   It is not enough for it to replicate existing systems; it should promote experimentation and manipulation of variables. A boring educational game or simulation might not only fail to engage students in the learning activities but could result in invalid assessment outcomes.

2. *An immersive learning environment identified for educational use must be aligned with curriculum outcomes.*

   HE students expect that any innovative learning technology given to them must be relevant to their learning goals [24]. Carrying out assessments in immersive environments that are not well-linked to the curriculum will result in a waste of time for both students and the educator.

3. *Immersive environments should be used for formative rather than summative assessments.*

   These environments provide excellent opportunities to assess and improve the learning of students using real-time process data of their interactions in the immersive learning environment.

4. *Allow plenty of gameplay time before assessing learning in a new immersive environment.*

   The interactions and behaviours of students in unfamiliar immersive learning environments have been shown to be erratic or exploratory at the beginning with more strategic behaviours after some time [25]. Allowing some time before assessment ensures that valid inferences are made about the proficiencies of students. It also minimises the resistance of students toward a new form of assessment as it is often the case that changes to the ways things are normally done are not always welcomed [26].

5. *Gauge the levels of experience of students with any immersive environment when considering them for assessments.*

   It has been found that the gameplay experiences of students might have some influence on their performance in educational games [27]. Understanding the experiences of students and accounting for the differences in levels of experience by ensuring that all students reach similar levels of confidence and comfort using the technology prior to assessments, would enhance the validity, reliability and fairness of the assessment outcomes.

6. *Alternative assessment arrangements should be made to accommodate every learner when considering measuring learning gains in immersive environments.*

Immersive technologies, particularly VR, may not be suitable for every learner because of the risks of triggering motion sickness and epilepsy in some learners. It is important to consider alternative assessment forms for students who may need them. This could be the use of traditional assessment methods. It could mean using group assessments where students can work in groups in different capacities to complete tasks in immersive environments.

7. *For a valid assessment design when using immersive learning environments, an established framework or methodology should be used.*

The GBAF provides a structured and user-friendly assessment framework for educators designing game-based or simulation-based assessments.

7 Conclusions and Limitations

This paper presents a newly developed game-based assessment framework (GBAF), highlighting five components of the framework. The GBAF offers a simple, structured and logical process of designing assessments of learning with VR, AR and DGs. The application of the GBAF to the design of assessment for an AR game demonstrates that the framework is easy to use compared to the ECD and Stealth Assessment [24] which uses the ECD framework. To use the ECD framework to design stealth assessments for measuring the competencies addressed in this paper, a Bayesian Network for the competencies in the statements of learning outcomes would be created for each level of the game. This would often require the use of advanced software such as Netica [25]. To infer the proficiency levels of students based on their actions in the game environment, probability models would have to be created. The prior probabilities or initial values of the inferred competencies of the students would be automatically updated as each student progresses through the game. This process of assessment design and implementation is complex, time-consuming and requires advanced statistical skills which many educators lack. Nonetheless, the strength of the ECD framework lies in its ability to automatically update information on the proficiencies of learners based on their actions over time. This particular attribute is highly relevant in large-scale testing where hundreds or thousands of players or students are assessed. For small scale classroom assessments which is the focus of this paper, designing and implementing assessments using the ECD framework would require extensive amounts of time with little or no added benefits to educators. The GBAF provides a simpler and more educator-familiar alternative to the ECD framework for classroom assessments. It offers guidelines for designing and implementing small to medium sized assessments for research or classroom learning purposes.

Although limited by the sample size and experiences of the evaluators in immersive technologies, the outcome of the evaluation of the framework shows that it is easy to understand and apply to assessment designs. In the future, a more robust evaluation of the GBAF will need to be carried out with at least seven experienced academics to evaluate its usability. Furthermore, the application of the GBAF to the design of assessments for different immersive environments is needed to demonstrate its wider application.

Acknowledgement. This project has received funding from the European Union's EU Framework Programme for Research and Innovation Horizon 2020 under Grant Agreement No [812716].

References

1. Shute, V., Rahimi, S., Emihovich, B.: Assessment for learning in immersive environments. In: Liu, D., Dede, C., Huang, R., Richards, J. (eds.) Virtual, Augmented, and Mixed Realities in Education, pp. 71–87. Springer, Singapore (2017). https://doi.org/10.1007/978-981-10-5490-7
2. Plass, J.L., Homer, B.D., Kinzer, C.K.: Foundations of game-based learning. Educ. Psychol. **50**, 258–283 (2015). https://doi.org/10.1080/00461520.2015.1122533
3. Squire, K.: Video games in education. Int. J. Intell. Games Simul. **2** (2003). https://doi.org/10.4018/978-1-61520-781-7.ch020
4. de Freitas, S.: Learning in immersive worlds: a review of game-based learning. JISC e-Learn. Innov. **3**, 73 (2006)
5. Razak, A.A., Connolly, T., Hainey, T.: Teachers' views on the approach of digital games-based learning within the curriculum for excellence. Int. J. Game-Based Learn. **2**, 33–51 (2012). https://doi.org/10.4018/ijgbl.2012010103
6. Routledge, H.: Games-based learning in the classroom and how it can work! In: Connolly, T., Stansfield, M., and Boyle, L. (eds.) Games-Based Learning Advancements for Multi-Sensory Human Computer Interfaces, pp. 274–286. IGI Global, Pennsylvania (2009)
7. Biggs, J.: Aligning teaching for constructing learning. High. Educ. Acad. **1**, 1–4 (2003)
8. Mislevy, R., Steinberg, L.S., Almond, R.G.: Focus article: on the structure of educational assessments. Meas. Interdiscip. Res. Perspect. **1**, 3–62 (2003). https://doi.org/10.1207/s15366359mea0101_02
9. Behrens, J.T., Mislevy, R.J., Dicerbo, K.E., Levy, R.: Evidence centered design for learning and assessment in the digital world. In: Technology-Based Assessments for 21st Century Skills, pp. 13–53 (2012)
10. Arieli-Attali, M., Ward, S., Thomas, J., Deonovic, B., von Davier, A.A.: The expanded evidence-centered design (e-ECD) for learning and assessment systems: a framework for incorporating learning goals and processes within assessment design. Front. Psychol. **10**, 1–17 (2019). https://doi.org/10.3389/fpsyg.2019.00853
11. Smith, G., Shute, V., Muenzenberger, A.: Designing and validating a stealth assessment for calculus competencies. J. Appl. Test. Technol. **20**, 52–59 (2019)
12. Min, W., et al.: DeepStealth: game-based learning stealth assessment with deep neural networks. IEEE Trans. Learn. Technol. **13**, 312–325 (2020). https://doi.org/10.1109/TLT.2019.2922356
13. Kim, Y.J., Almond, R.G., Shute, V.J.: Applying evidence-centered design for the development of game-based assessments in physics playground. Int. J. Test. **16**, 142–163 (2016). https://doi.org/10.1080/15305058.2015.1108322
14. Westera, W.: Why and how serious games can become far more effective: accommodating productive learning experiences, learner motivation and the monitoring of learning gains. Educ. Technol. Soc. **22**, 59–69 (2019)
15. Westera, W., et al.: Artificial intelligence moving serious gaming: presenting reusable game AI components. Educ. Inf. Technol. **25**, 351–380 (2020). https://doi.org/10.1007/s10639-019-09968-2
16. Ali, L.: The design of curriculum, assessment and evaluation in higher education with constructive alignment. J. Educ. e-Learning Res. **5**, 72–78 (2018). https://doi.org/10.20448/journal.509.2018.51.72.78
17. Biggs, J., Tang, C.: Applying constructive alignment to outcomes-based teaching and learning. In: Training Material for "Quality Teaching for Learning in Higher Education" Workshop for Master Trainers, pp. 23–25. Ministry of Higher Education, Kuala Lumpur (2010)

18. Biggs, J., Collis, K.F.: Evaluating the Quality of Learning: The SOLO Taxonomy. Academic Press, New York (1982)
19. Anderson, L.: A Taxonomy for Learning, Teaching and Assesing: A Revision of Bloom's Taxonomy. Pearson, New York (2013)
20. Dawson, P.: Assessment rubrics: towards clearer and more replicable design, research and practice. Assess. Eval. High. Educ. **42**, 347–360 (2017). https://doi.org/10.1080/02602938.2015.1111294
21. Jonsson, A., Svingby, G.: The use of scoring rubrics: reliability, validity and educational consequences. Educ. Res. Rev. **2**, 130–144 (2007). https://doi.org/10.1016/j.edurev.2007.05.002
22. Udeozor, C., Russo Abegão, F., Glassey, J.: Measuring learning in digital games: applying a game-based assessment framework. Br. J. Educ. Technol. (2023)
23. Domínguez Alfaro, J.L., et al.: Mobile augmented reality laboratory for learning acid-base titration. J. Chem. Educ. **99**, 531–537 (2022). https://doi.org/10.1021/acs.jchemed.1c00894
24. Shute, V., Ventura, M.: Stealth Assessment: Measuring and Supporting Learning in Video Games. MIT Press, London (2013)
25. Shute, V.J., Rahimi, S.: Stealth assessment of creativity in a physics video game. Comput. Human Behav. **116**, 106647 (2021). https://doi.org/10.1016/j.chb.2020.106647

A Platform for Analyzing Students' Behavior in Virtual Spaces on Mozilla Hubs

Kojiro Yano[✉]

Osaka Institute of Technology, Hirakata, Osaka, Japan
kojiro.yano@oit.ac.jp

Abstract. Social Virtual Reality (VR) or "Metaverse" platforms provide teachers with the opportunity to use educational virtual spaces for both distance learning and face-to-face teaching, to take advantage of its unique learning affordances. However, designing virtual spaces and incorporating them into teaching presents a challenge. Since teachers are typically not around when students use virtual spaces, it is difficult for them to ascertain how the spaces are being used during the classes. This article outlines a project to develop a data-logging and visualization tool for teachers making use of Mozilla Hubs. The tool tracks student behavior and presents the data in 3D as raw data points or heatmaps and only requires a standardized set-up with no need for client or server-side programming, thus allowing teachers with limited programming experience to use it. This framework will be further developed to include more visualization and analytical tools, such as trajectories and clustering, and will be made publicly available upon completion of the development.

Keywords: Virtual reality · Mozilla hubs · Virtual Spaces · Learning analytics

1 Introduction

As the demand for distance learning has increased due to COVID-19-related school closures, virtual spaces have become increasingly prevalent in education. The ease of authoring and publishing virtual spaces, thanks to social VR or so-called "Metaverse" platforms such as VRChat, Spatial, and Mozilla Hubs, enabled users to access a wide variety of virtual spaces. These virtual spaces offer realistic presence, object interactions, and communications not possible with other learning media, making them ideal for social and collaborative learning, situated learning, and experiential learning [18]. As a result, virtual spaces are now being used for a variety of educational purposes, such as language learning [5], health [13], and STEM [14].

However, designing virtual spaces for learning is a complex process that requires unique know-how distinct from that which is required to design other

This work was supported by JSPS KAKENHI Grant Number JP 22K02875.

M.-L. Bourguet et al. (Eds.): iLRN 2023, CCIS 1904, pp. 209–219, 2024.
https://doi.org/10.1007/978-3-031-47328-9_16

learning media, such as videos or websites. It is necessary to adapt room layouts to different learning activities and styles so that students can feel comfortable when learning [11,25]. For instance, a large space with a virtual screen may be suitable for lectures, while a collection of small spaces may be more appropriate for group activities in order to promote a sense of closeness among students. If activities involve interactive objects, clear instructions should also be provided so that students, who are not necessarily familiar with the platforms, understand which objects are interactable, how to use them, and what the learning objectives are [7]. If the space has a number of 3D objects, it will be helpful to provide sufficient space to enable students to inspect objects from different angles. Additionally, various visual cues should be utilized to help students navigate a space and direct their attention naturally so as to reduce the cognitive load of using the space [17].

Even though careful planning of virtual spaces may be undertaken, there is no assurance that they will be used as intended during classes. Consequently, it is crucial to assess how students use these spaces and what impact they have on their learning in order to be able to feed this information back into the planning of virtual spaces and associated teaching plans for the next iteration. To this end, summative evaluations [10] can be conducted by gathering data from students, such as assessments based on what they should have learned in virtual spaces and student feedback forms. These evaluations are inexpensive, easy to implement, and beneficial to gain an understanding of their subjective feelings regarding motivation, emotion, and learning success during their experience in virtual spaces. However, it is challenging to link the gathered data from the summative evaluations to the specific design of the virtual spaces. It is also difficult to record data repeatedly or in real-time during lectures. Therefore, it is vital to embed the capability of directly and continuously monitoring how students behave in virtual spaces.

The use of monitoring methods for users in virtual spaces has been a subject of considerable interest, particularly in the gaming industry [9], where various gameplay metrics [23] are employed to track a player's in-game time, location, the number of actions they take, and the number of in-game items they have collected. Furthermore, more sophisticated tracking methods may be adopted, such as eye [24] and body tracking [16], to collect detailed data on a player's movements, including the speed and direction of their movements, as well as their eye movements and what they are looking at. These data can be used to gain insights into players' preferences, behavior, and skill level, as well as to improve the overall gaming experience by making play elements more intuitive and personalized.

In addition to collecting the data on users' behaviors in virtual spaces, it is important to analyze data effectively. It is often the case that a large quantity of data is collected, but no meaningful insights are obtained from it when the analysis is not done correctly [4]. Therefore, it is crucial to focus on the right metrics that will help identify patterns, trends, and correlations in the data. The most common way of analyzing user behavior data in virtual space is visualization. For spatial data, density fields such as heatmap [20] and trajectories [2] are commonly used for this purpose. Heatmaps can be used to show the location of data points in relation to each other, as well as the relative density of points in a given area, while trajectories can be used to illustrate the journeys taken by a user within a virtual space, as well as the patterns of movement that emerge from a population of users. Both heatmaps and trajectories can provide valuable insights into user behavior and help inform the decision-making of the creators of virtual spaces.

This paper presents a project to develop a data-logging and visualization tool for teachers using virtual spaces in their teaching practices. The goal of this project is to provide teachers with a simple framework that enables user tracking analysis for commonly-used metaverse platforms Mozilla Hubs without requiring either client or server-side programming. By combining a tracking system with an open web analytics platform for data storage and a Unity-based standalone app for data visualization, teachers should be able to generate 3D heatmaps of students' movement and looked-at areas. I believe that this framework will facilitate the understanding of students' behavior in virtual spaces and help improve the design of the spaces for better learning outcomes.

2   Related Research

Tracking and visualization of users' spatial patterns in virtual spaces have been studied for understanding users' behaviors [1,15]. Drachen [8] presented case studies of tracking player positions and analysis of spatial patterns of death in a scenario-based first-person shooter game. They showed how the design of a map in a scenario-based could affect the behavior of its players and how that information can be used to fine-tune the game levels. Arya [3] used Web. Alive tool to record user positions and social interactions (e.g., encounters and conversations) of students during lectures. Based on visualization of histograms and 2D heatmaps, they identified popular areas for students and conversation influence on active duration. Similarly, Williamson [26] used a custom build of Mozilla Hubs to observe and analyze interactions during an academic workshop in virtual environments. Based on the analysis of the distance distribution between participants and 2D heatmaps of their positions, they revealed the effects of space size on group formation, shared attention, and personal space.

While many of the studies on users in virtual spaces used 2D heatmaps to visualize the locations of users, they are not convenient when you want to take users' visual attention into account. So, Chittaro [6] used interactive 3D heatmaps that combined heatmaps for users' movements and looked-at areas to identify navigation strategies, patterns, and coverage of specific areas in terms of movement and look-at behaviors. Among the options for visualizing look-at areas as heatmaps [22], Chittaro [6] adapted surface-based attentional map because it operates on pixels rather than vertices of 3D objects, and therefore the result will not be affected by the number of vertices used to model the object, and it can exclude objects occluded from users' view.

Although the usefulness and technologies for tracking and analyzing users' behaviors in virtual spaces are well-established, there have been very few off-the-shelf analytical tools available on major Metaverse platforms. Therefore a variety of tools and plug-ins have been developed by researchers to assist creators in analyzing users in their virtual spaces with minimal client or server-side programming efforts. Al-Kouz [1] introduced Smart Tempo-Spatial Hot-spots Finder for Second Life which detects spatiotemporal characteristics of user locations to identify and visualize hotspots that avatars tend to gather in as heatmaps and predict where future hotspots will be. Müller [19] developed a collection of plug-ins for recording gameplay data for Minecraft. They tested their framework over two weeks and successfully visualized players' positions using 2D heatmaps to recognize different kinds of activity on the map. More recently, Steed [21] developed Ubiq-Exp, a distributed logging system that supports local and remote logging, and is integrated into Ubiq [12], a toolkit built on the Unity platform for the construction of social virtual reality systems. While this system is intended for running remote experiments, it should be possible to use this monitoring remote classrooms considering the ability of Ubiq as a remote teaching platform. For more common metaverse platforms, Williamson [26] made their fork of Mozilla Hubs for tracking users available on GitHub (https://github.com/ayman/hubs/tree/hubs-cloud). And there is a Unity library for VRChat called YAIBA (https://github.com/ScienceAssembly/YAIBA-VRC) with position and rotation logging and questionnaire features, though only local logging is possible.

3   Setting up the Environment

This project uses Hubs Cloud Personal, a self-hosted version of Mozilla Hubs (https://hubs.mozilla.com/), to develop and host virtual spaces. It is hosted on Amazon Web Services (AWS), and step-by-step instructions to set up a Hubs instance are available from Mozilla's website (https://hubs.mozilla.com/cloud). I added a short script to Hubs Cloud's server to send user's positions and rotations to Plausible (https://plausible.io/), an open-source project for web analytics, as custom events using their API. Data is accumulated every 5 s and is sent to the Plausible server every 30 s to minimize the costs.

The events' log data are downloaded to a Unity-based visualization app using Plausible's Stats API. The app imports a project file (.spoke) from Spoke, the scene editor for Mozilla Hubs, processes its JSON data to download 3D model files and 2D image files from the Hubs server and displays the virtual space. In Mozilla Hubs' terminology, a "scene" means a template of a virtual space, and a "room" is created from a "scene" for each user. In this app, users' logs may be displayed for a specific room, practically a single session, or for all the rooms created from the same scene during a specific period. Their heads' positions and rotations are shown as arrowheads (Fig. 1). The size of the arrowheads can be adjusted for the best visibility. The scene camera for the virtual space is first-person and can be rotated by a mouse or can be moved by arrow keys, which should help viewers to inspect the scene and the data from different angles.

In order to have better ideas of what users were looking at, a 3D heatmap can also be used. To display the heatmap, another texture with a jet colormap shader is overlayed onto the virtual space. In "look-at" or *attention* heatmap, cylinder

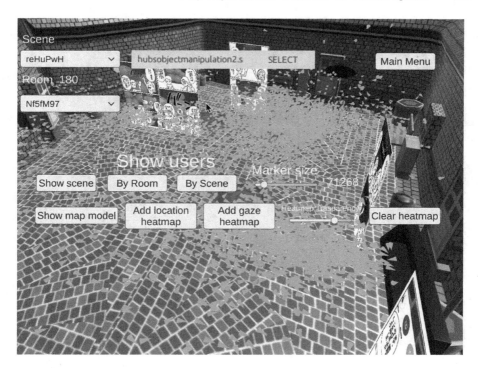

Fig. 1. Scene view of the virtual space with the arrowheads on the visualization app

raycasts are sent from all the data points (or randomly selected data points when the number of points is very large) in the recorded directions from the recorded positions and projected onto the heatmap texture. The cylinder, instead of a point, raycast was chosen to reflect the field of views of the users. The projected intensity is accumulated across the data points and displayed with red color as high intensity without smoothing. *Location* heatmap can also be displayed by projecting raycasts downwards from the users' recorded head positions.

A pilot study was carried out in a lecture for mostly first-year college students (n = 142) majoring in information science at the author's institution. The lecture was the inaugural lecture of a Biology course and was intended as a general introduction to the course and tutorial for navigations and object manipulations in Mozilla Hubs. The play time varied among students but typically did not exceed 20 min.

4   Results and Discussion

Figure 2 shows a virtual space used in this study for a tutorial on object manipulations on Mozilla Hubs. The tutorial scene had four points of interest (POIs) (Fig. 3) and three tasks: 1) A manga instruction on object manipulation, 2)

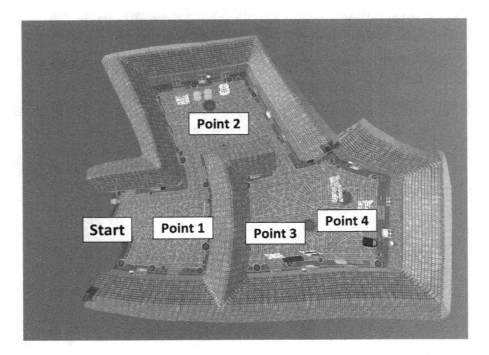

Fig. 2. Virtual space on Mozilla Hubs used in this study

Fig. 3. Four points of interest in the virtual space

The first task. Find which of the balls is movable and move it into the basket. Accompanied by a page of manga for the direction of the task. 3) *The second task.* Instantiate a text tag (done by typing on Mozilla Hubs' chat window) and place it on a nameplate. Accompanied by two pages of manga with instruction of text tag instantiation on the right and the direction for the task on the left, 4) *The final task.* Move and rotate the key and insert it into the lock. The manga on the near left is a general instruction for object deletion and rotation, and the one in the middle is the direction for the task.

Students were asked to complete these tasks during a lecture. A URL for the tutorial scene was given, and they created their own rooms to explore on PC. After finishing the last task, they were asked to take screenshots of the keys in the locks and submit them on Google Classroom. In total, data from 180 rooms were recorded during the lecture. This number is larger than the number of students registered for the lecture, but since students' IDs were not recorded in the virtual spaces, it was not possible to determine who used multiple rooms.

The records of students' positions in virtual spaces are shown in Fig. 4. The arrowhead plot shows students' positions and rotations. It shows that the students gather around the four points of interest. The crowds seem to be largest for the second and the fourth points. The task assigned to the students at the second point required them to grab the ball and move closer to the basket, thus resulting in the arrowhead plot being dispersed across the area of the second point. The situation was similar at the fourth spot, but the task was more difficult and required more movements, which is reflected in the greater number of arrows covering a larger area around the point, indicating the students' struggles.

The spatial pattern of student locations can also be seen using the location heatmap, and the impression is significantly different from the arrowhead view. The third point of interest has denser spots than the second point, indicating that students spent a significant amount of time doing the second task. It is consistent with the author's observation that students struggled with this task more than the first object transfer task. This difficulty was likely due to the requirement of using a chat window along with the main screen, as well as the requirement to press a special button to spawn texts, which some students did not follow correctly. As the use of the chat window does not require movement, the area covered by the spots was relatively small.

Moreover, there are prominent red spots in the second, third and fourth points of interest. They are from the users who stayed in the same position for quite a long time. This would not be noticed from the arrowhead view because all the arrows will be seen as one if the user stays in the same position. Students often leave the instance running and start doing something else, and in such case, a hotspot will appear even though they are not actually engaged in any tasks on these spots.

Arrow-head plot   Location heatmap

Fig. 4. Arrowhead plot and location heatmap of students' positions and rotations

Figure 5 shows the attention heatmap of four points of interest. At the first point, the signal on the right panel is stronger than the left, which is expected since Japanese manga is read from right to left. At the second point, the balls on the right had stronger signals than those on the left, which was because students had to test which one was movable, and they started testing from the right-hand side. At the third point, the nameplate had the strongest signal, as expected, and the right manga panel had a significantly wider signal pattern than the left. That was because the right panel had an instruction on how to use a button in the Chat window to instantiate the text tag, and many students needed to read it more thoroughly to complete the task. At the fourth point, there are two manga panels on the left, but the one on the right-hand side had a much stronger signal than the other. The area with the strong signal had instruction on how to use the context menu, and because this information was necessary to perform the final task, quite a few students looked at it for a prolonged period. The key and the lock the students used for the third task also have strong signals, as expected.

The current form of this framework is found to have some limitations. First of all, since the heatmap is painted onto the textures of 3D models, all the models have to be fully textured with clean UV. This means that no overlapping area or texture tiling in UV maps is allowed, and vertex colors will not work. It is also important to have enough margins between islands in UV maps. In the trial shown above, there have been some instances of bleeding, causing false high signal artifacts in heatmaps (see the small high signal in the top left area in Point 1 of Fig. 5).

While these issues can be easily fixed using 3D modeling tools like Blender, it would be more desirable if they could be fixed in the app. Another issue is the over-representation of users who left the room running even when they were

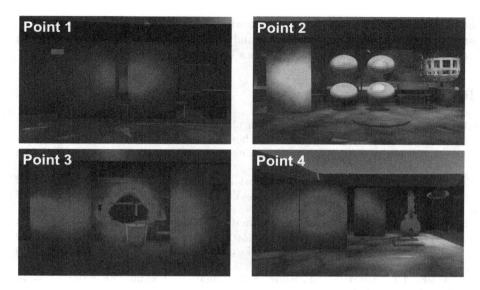

Fig. 5. Attention heatmaps of students from the four POIs

not engaged in activities. Although the lecturer instructed students to close the rooms as soon as they finished tasks, not all students followed it. Those dormant players are still tracked, sometimes for longer than an hour, by the system, and it can yield "false" hot spots. Therefore, an algorithm to remove such outliers will need to be developed.

5 Conclusion

In conclusion, this article presented a framework for tracking and visualizing users' locations and look-at areas on Mozilla Hubs, with the aim of enhancing the understanding of student behavior in virtual spaces and improving the overall learning experience by optimizing the design of the spaces. The framework has shown promising results in identifying points of interest and areas where students struggle, providing valuable insights for educators and content creators. Despite its potential, the current framework has some limitations, including the requirement for fully textured 3D models with clean UV maps and the overrepresentation of inactive users. Addressing these issues and refining the visualization techniques will be crucial for the framework's future development. The author plans to add more features to the framework, such as trajectory visualization, clustering, and live data display. These enhancements will allow teachers to obtain a more comprehensive understanding of student behavior in virtual spaces and to make informed decisions about the design and implementation of virtual spaces for learning. Once the existing issues are resolved and the planned features are integrated, the framework will undergo alpha testing and eventually be made available to the public. By offering this tool to a wider audience, the author hopes to contribute to the virtual education communities and help the development of better learning outcomes in virtual spaces.

References

1. Al-Kouz, A., Luca, E.W.D., Clausen, J., Albayrak, S.: The smart-TSH-finder: crawling and analyzing tempo-spatial hotspots in second life. In: LWA 2010 - Lernen, Wissen und Adaptivitat - Learning, Knowledge, and Adaptivity, Workshop Proceedings (2010)
2. Andrienko, N., Andrienko, G.: Visual analytics of movement: an overview of methods, tools and procedures. Inf. Vis. **12** (2013). https://doi.org/10.1177/1473871612457601
3. Arya, A., Nowlan, N., Sauriol, N.: Data-driven framework for an online 3D immersive environment for educational applications. In: Proceedings of the International Conference on Education and New Learning Technologies (EDULEARN 2010) (2010)
4. Avella, J.T., Kebritchi, M., Nunn, S.G., Kanai, T.: Learning analytics methods, benefits, and challenges in higher education: a systematic literature review. J. Asynchronous Learn. Netw. **20** (2016). https://doi.org/10.24059/olj.v20i2.790
5. Chen, B., Wang, Y., Wang, L.: The effects of virtual reality-assisted language learning: a meta-analysis. Sustainability (Switzerland) **14** (2022). https://doi.org/10.3390/su14063147
6. Chittaro, L., Serafini, M.: Visualization of user's behavior in indoor virtual environments through interactive heatmaps. In: Ardito, C., et al. (eds.) INTERACT 2021. LNCS, vol. 12934, pp. 600–609. Springer, Cham (2021). https://doi.org/10.1007/978-3-030-85613-7_38
7. DePape, A.M., Barnes, M., Petryschuk, J.: Students' experiences in higher education with virtual and augmented reality: a qualitative systematic review. Innov. Pract. High. Educ. **3** (2019)
8. Drachen, A., Canossa, A.: Towards gameplay analysis via gameplay metrics (2009). https://doi.org/10.1145/1621841.1621878
9. Drachen, A., Schubert, M.: Spatial game analytics and visualization. In: IEEE Conference on Computational Intelligence and Games, CIG (2013). https://doi.org/10.1109/CIG.2013.6633629
10. Draper, S.W.: Prospects for summative evaluation of CAL in higher education. Res. Learn. Technol. **5** (2011). https://doi.org/10.3402/rlt.v5i1.10549
11. Ford, A.: Planning classroom design and layout to increase pedagogical options for secondary teachers. Educ. Plan. **23** (2016)
12. Friston, S., et al.: Ubiq: a system to build flexible social virtual reality experiences. In: Proceedings of the ACM Symposium on Virtual Reality Software and Technology, VRST (2021). https://doi.org/10.1145/3489849.3489871
13. Gerup, J., Soerensen, C.B., Dieckmann, P.: Augmented reality and mixed reality for healthcare education beyond surgery: an integrative review. Int. J. Med. Educ. **11**, 1 (2020)
14. Johnson-Glenberg, M.C.: The *necessary nine*: design principles for embodied VR and active stem education. In: Díaz, P., Ioannou, A., Bhagat, K.K., Spector, J.M. (eds.) Learning in a Digital World. SCI, pp. 83–112. Springer, Singapore (2019). https://doi.org/10.1007/978-981-13-8265-9_5

15. Kappe, F., Zaka, B., Steurer, M.: Automatically detecting points of interest and social networks from tracking positions of avatars in a virtual world. In: Proceedings of the 2009 International Conference on Advances in Social Network Analysis and Mining, ASONAM 2009 (2009). https://doi.org/10.1109/ASONAM.2009.66

16. Kröger, J.L., Raschke, P., Campbell, J.P., Ullrich, S.: Surveilling the gamers: privacy impacts of the video game industry. SSRN Electron. J. (2021). https://doi.org/10.2139/ssrn.3881279

17. Lidwell, W., Holden, K., Butler, J.: Universal Principles of Design: 125 ways to enhance usability, influence perception, increase appeal, make better design decisions, and teach through design. Rockport (2010)

18. Liu, R., Wang, L., Lei, J., Wang, Q., Ren, Y.: Effects of an immersive virtual reality-based classroom on students' learning performance in science lessons. Br. J. Educ. Technol. 51 (2020). https://doi.org/10.1111/bjet.13028

19. Müller, S., et al.: Statistical analysis of player behavior in Minecraft. In: Proceedings of the 10th International Conference on the Foundations of Digital Games. Foundations of Digital Games (FDG 2015) (2015)

20. Pokojski, W., Panecki, T., Słomska-Przech, K.: Cartographic visualization of density: exploring the opportunities and constraints of heat maps. Polish Cartographical Rev. 53 (2021). https://doi.org/10.2478/pcr-2021-0003

21. Steed, A., et al.: Ubiq-exp: a toolkit to build and run remote and distributed mixed reality experiments. Front. Virtual Reality 3 (2022). https://doi.org/10.3389/frvir.2022.912078. https://www.frontiersin.org/articles/10.3389/frvir.2022.912078

22. Stellmach, S., Nacke, L., Dachselt, R.: 3D attentional maps - aggregated gaze visualizations in three-dimensional virtual environments. In: Proceedings of the Workshop on Advanced Visual Interfaces AVI (2010). https://doi.org/10.1145/1842993.1843058

23. Su, Y., Backlund, P., Engström, H.: Comprehensive review and classification of game analytics. Serv. Oriented Comput. Appl. 15 (2021). https://doi.org/10.1007/s11761-020-00303-z

24. Sundstedt, V., Garro, V.: A systematic review of visualization techniques and analysis tools for eye-tracking in 3D environments. Front. Neuroergonomics 3 (2022)

25. Talbert, R., Mor-Avi, A.: A space for learning: an analysis of research on active learning spaces. Heliyon 5 (2019). https://doi.org/10.1016/j.heliyon.2019.e02967

26. Williamson, J., Li, J., Vinayagamoorthy, V., Shamma, D.A., Cesar, P.: Proxemics and social interactions in an instrumented virtual reality workshop. In: Proceedings of the 2021 CHI Conference on Human Factors in Computing Systems, pp. 1–13 (2021)

Galleries, Libraries, Archives and Museums (GLAM)

A Serious Game Based on Hidden Objects for Art History in Fully Immersive Virtual Reality

Hubert Cecotti$^{(\boxtimes)}$

Department of Computer Science, California State University, Fresno, CA, USA
hcecotti@csufresno.edu

Abstract. Fully immersive virtual reality has been recently used for the creation of virtual museums, art galleries, and other applications related to cultural heritage. While the content of these applications typically has an educational value, it remains difficult to engage users into art and the humanities by only presenting the artworks and their descriptions through an immersive experience. We propose in this paper to better engage users in the analysis of paintings through a serious game based on the principle of wimmelbooks and hidden picture books, e.g., "Where is Waldo". This serious game provides the user with different art galleries in which the player is asked to search for a piece of painting inside a collection of paintings, engaging the players in the visual analysis of paintings. The pieces of paintings are selected manually, and we also assess the extent to which machine learning may help in defining regions of interest such as faces as potential targets. The evaluation of the approach is a practical example of how serious games can be used for better engaging users into art history in immersive learning.

Keywords: Virtual reality · Art · Serious game · Education

1 Introduction

Immersive learning systems use new technologies, such as fully immersive virtual reality (VR) for creating immersive learning environment that can better engage users, and students in particular [13, 25]. Thanks to consumer-grade VR headsets, the VR technology offers an excellent approach for creating applications that put the users close to the learning material, using its true size, and allowing learners to have different vantage points. With VR, it is possible to bring famous paintings to under-represented minority (URO) students and communities who would not otherwise appreciate these paintings and connect with cultural landmarks from our society. It is however necessary to go beyond the simple presentation and manipulation of 3D objects to engage and retain users in the application. It is critical that activities happen within immersive learning environments, going beyond a walking simulator with multimedia content that can be accessed in various locations. Museums educate people. Specifically, cultural history museums educate people about people, about how people of the past reacted to their

© The Author(s), under exclusive license to Springer Nature Switzerland AG 2024
M.-L. Bourguet et al. (Eds.): iLRN 2023, CCIS 1904, pp. 223–238, 2024.
https://doi.org/10.1007/978-3-031-47328-9_17

environment and the effects of those reactions to our past, present, and future. History museums have a unique opportunity to engage students in many different areas of interest. As nearly 30% of museums in the United States remained closed due to the global Covid pandemic, VR based museums provide a unique opportunity to give students a faithful representation of artworks.

In the case of applications related to cultural heritage, most of them can be assimilated to walking simulators, with limited interactions with the content [5]. It is in fact closer to an interactive book than to a video game with rich gameplay. Virtual museums and art galleries do not include gaming component or activities that directly engage the users, beyond the assessment of the users with questions [4].

In this paper, we propose a serious game based on the principle of wimmelbooks or hidden picture book, where the user has access to different art galleries of paintings. In each gallery, the player must search for a particular target. The target is not limited to a specific type of element (e.g., a person), it is a piece of painting that invites the user to better analyze the paintings. The goal of this serious game is to invite users to search and analyze artworks at a deeper level than just skimming through a series of images. Being able to analyze an artwork is in fact an essential skill for better understanding the artwork's content, but also for improving as an artist and to better appreciate the creation of the artists. The formal analysis of an artwork includes four steps: 1) the description of the artwork, it is the raw description of the content without any value judgements; 2) the analysis of the artwork, it is about determining the characteristics of the artwork and why the artist has used these characteristics; 3) the interpretation of the artwork, it is about determining the cultural and historical context and reasons about the creation of the artwork; 4) the judgement of the artwork, it deals with the selection of criteria for judging the artwork and showing evidence in relation to these chosen criteria [1]. The first step is about what the user sees. A formal analysis is more than just a description of a painting. It corresponds to an argument that is based on the personal visual evidence of the user, creating a meaningful discussion in relation the formal elements of the work. A painting is an expressive object, which is made by an artist, and that, unlike any regular object, is always about something. Therefore, paintings call for interpretations that require time. It is needed to provide means that increase the time that is spent on the analysis of artworks.

The goal of this project is to create a serious game in virtual reality using famous paintings. To reach this goal, we propose to research machine learning and computer vision algorithms to automatically label and extract salient parts of images that are needed to create the serious game. This task is difficult because contrary to photography, the objects and people vary across paintings in relation to different painting styles. The task of classifying pieces of fine art is extremely complex. When examining a painting, an art expert can usually determine its style, its genre, the artist, and the period to which it belongs. Art historians often go further by looking for the influences and connections between artists.

Besides the realistic representation of the artwork, it is necessary to automatically extract information from these paintings. It includes the objects and elements that are contained in the scene. This step can be performed manually or automatically using artificial intelligence techniques. The automatic annotation of paintings has multiple purposes: 1) to help research in the digital humanities to organize and query paintings, 2) to provide information that can be used for describing the painting's content automatically, 3) to determine potential targets for searches, as proposed in this serious game.

The paper is organized as follows: First, we describe in Sect. 2 the rationale of the serious game, with related works in VR, and the Hidden Object Search concept in images. Then, we present the gameplay of the serious game in Sect. 3. In Sect. 4, we provide an analysis of how face detection may be used with paintings for the creation of targets in a Hidden Object Game. The experiment and the results corresponding to the evaluation of the serious game are presented in Sect. 5. Finally, the results of the proposed serious game are discussed in Sect. 7.

2   Related Works

2.1   Rationale

The proposed serious game is an additional feature of an existing virtual museum developed for VR that allows players to browse among more than 1000 famous paintings presented in art galleries. The problem with collection of arts is that it can be challenging to engage the audience, to connect the audience with the different artworks. A large collection of paintings in a museum does not necessarily imply that the museum will be better. It is the curator's duty to select and organize the paintings so they can be fully appreciated by the visitors. In a virtual museum, there are no constraints of space: rooms can be enlarged as needed, the number of rooms can be determined in relation to the size of the collection. The main problem is how to keep users engaged over time with the overabundance of content. If users skim through art galleries, then the impact of the paintings and art galleries is significantly reduced. Unless a person is really interested in art and/or art history with the will to investigate the painting's content, it is challenging to invite people to spend time on looking at artworks. Art and games are often connected but it can be challenging to bring games into a serious field such as art history, where paintings can represent important cultural and historical landmarks.

2.2   VR Art Galleries

Multiple art galleries and virtual museums exist in fully immersive virtual reality. However, none of them provide gaming components that directly engage the users. The VR Museum of Fine Art by Finn Sinclair has high-fidelity sculptures and some famous paintings [10]. The Kremer Collection VR Museum has paintings by Rembrandt, Aelbert Cuyp, Frans Hals and other Old Masters from the Dutch Golden Age [19]. The Infinite Art Museum also has a large collection [20]. Mocove Arts VR has more than 1000 paintings [18]. The Smithsonian American

Art Museum is another realistic museum for VR [26]. Great Paintings VR has more than 1000 famous paintings, from the early Renaissance to the beginning of the twentieth century [3]. The Museum of ThroughView showcases 2D to 3D conversions of famous paintings and old photographs [29], adding values to the paintings. The OmniGallery is another VR museum with ancient paintings presented in different locations [9]. Art Plunge is a VR experience containing an art gallery with multiple paintings [27]. The Finnish Virtual Art Gallery is a VR museum focusing on 9 Finnish painters [21]. Most of the VR museums can be found on the Steam platform. Other applications are for the Oculus types of headsets: Boulevard is for Rift, Rift S VR headsets [30], Virtual Museum De Fornaris is a VR art gallery for Rift, Rift S VR headsets showing 70 masterpieces from the De Fornaris collection [14]. VR Museum: Art Through Time is another VR museum for Rift, Rift S VR headsets with 60 paintings from the 1500 s to 1800 s [7]. Finally, Städel Time Machine is for Gear VR and Oculus Go [28].

2.3 Wimmelbooks and Hidden Object Search

Wimmelbooks can be defined as a type of wordless picturebooks that display a series of panoramas that are filled with a large number of elements, i.e., with many characters and/or objects [23]. The images are full of various elements that make visual search and target detection tasks difficult. The high amount of content within the images can be related to horror vacui, which is about filling the complete area of the image with detail. The word "wimmelbook" is an English adaptation of the German Wimmelbuch. It corresponds to wordless picturebooks that do not contain any direction about what to do.

Wimmelbooks can be used as games where the goal is to find a particular target within the image, or to count the number of objects belonging to a particular category. Because images contain a high number of details with different objects, it is necessary for the players to know exactly what the target is, e.g., to search a particular animal in a scene containing multiple animals require the player to be able to make a distinction between the different types of animals and to search only for the requested animal. Such a game can stimulate children's visual literacy by identifying specific targets and establishing connections between words and their corresponding visual presentations. Wimmelbooks are different than search books because they rely on the readers to establish a narrative through the rich content of the images. It suggests to readers to establish a connection between the different elements that are present in the scene.

Wimmelbooks can be formally defined by a list of properties. First, they are large books to allow rich detailed illustrations. These books have a large-format, often characterized by full-spread drawings depicting scenes richly detailed with objects, humans, animals, and plants. Here, VR can bring large images to the user without the need to scroll up and down as it would happen in a computer screen. In VR, the user can also move closer to the image as it would happen with a book. Second, wimmelbooks do not contain verbal texts. Third, images are rich with many details. Fourth, situations should be familiar to the audience for a better connection with the users. Fifth, wimmelbooks should engage readers of different ages [6]. However, many books have been classified as wimmelbooks while some of the criteria are not completely respected, such as the addition of text such as for the suggestion of targets to search in the images. It includes "Where is Wally" [11] and "What do people do all day" [24]. "Where is Wally (UK)/Waldo (USA)" has been ported as video games in different consoles. For instance, "The Great Waldo Search" was developed for the Super NES [22]. These games were developed at a time for the resolution of TVs and computer screens could not allow the representation of images swarming with details. The main characteristic is the presence of images swarming of various persons and objects that are all connected, stressing the holistic view of the images, i.e., the images cannot be broken down into small images that isolate small scenes. The words that can be present are there to guide the reader and typically have an optional role.

3   Gameplay

Serious Games have proved to have potential for immersive learning. Their use increases in an educational context for better engaging students, from primary school to higher education. Formal approaches and methodologies are fundamental in the implementation of educational games. It is to find the right balance between meeting learning outcomes to be conveyed, fulfilling game objectives, and the gameplay. This serious game is based on the Learning Mechanics-Game Mechanics (LM-GM) framework. The approach is to engage the audience to explore and analyze the details of paintings through a visual search. The core gameplay of the serious game for enhancing the connection between a wide audience and the humanities is based on the search of a particular element (e.g., the face of a person) in a set of paintings. The player has a piece of a painting containing the face to search, and the player has to search this element within the paintings. After the successful completion of the search, the player has the possibility to go back to the main menu, or to go into another level, i.e., a scene containing different paintings and a new piece of painting to find. We associate learning outcomes based on the formal analysis of paintings, i.e., their description, with the search task in the game.

The gameplay of the proposed serious game is based on the wimmelbook principle. We consider art galleries with paintings corresponding to artistic movement or from a single artist. Instead of considering a single image, the task is to search through the whole gallery. This choice is based on the lack of details that can happen in many paintings (e.g., portrait), where an isolated painting does not offer enough details to be used for searching for hidden objects.

An example of the user interface depicting the target and the task is presented in Fig. 2. It includes the pieces of the image to search. In addition, the target is displayed next to both hands, so the user can see the target at any moment. A magnifying glass is also provided in the VR environment, so the user does not need to be too close to the paintings. We also provide the possibility to enable a hint that changes the color of the laser pointer based on the distance between the user and the target (dark blue for being close to the target, yellow for being far away from the target); the user can then scan the art gallery with the laser pointer to determine the location of the target. Selecting the target gives a penalty of 60 s on the total number of times for finding the target. Visual and auditory feedback are provided after the correct selection of a target (see Fig. 1).

Fig. 1. Left: target next to the hand; **Middle**: painting containing the target; **Right**: selected target in the painting.

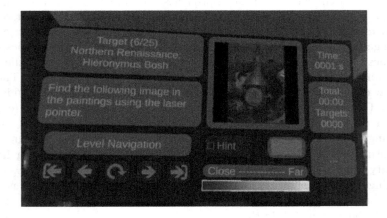

Fig. 2. Representative example of a painting with labelled targets for the game.

The paintings have been manually labelled with bounding boxes representing potentially relevant targets to be searched for with the paintings. The task was performed with the Image Labeler tool of Matlab. Depending on the size of the painting, the level of details, we have considered different potential targets that may appear in the background or foreground of the scene.

In the case of large portraits, we have isolated different parts of the face. For instance, the target represents the eyes of the person only, or not the nose and mouth of the person, or the hands, what the person is holding. It allows the users to better search and compare the different portraits that exist in a scene. Two levels of the game illustrate this approach. First, a series or self-portrait from Rembrandt is in a gallery and the goal is to search for a target corresponding to the gaze of one of the self-portraits. Another example is the gallery that contains Christ and the Apostles by El Greco (Apostolados). In this gallery, targets include the faces and hands of the characters present in the scene. Depending on the painting and the style, relevant and meaningful targets must be selected. A good target is a piece of the painting that is salient and unique in the painting and in the set of selected paintings in the art gallery. Hence, textures or faces that look very similar to other faces cannot be selected. Contextual information can often be needed to make sure that the target is unique. Figure 3 provides an example of targets that have been considered.

The serious game includes 620 paintings grouped into 34 art galleries from the Northern Renaissance to the post-impressionist period. It includes Early Netherlandish paintings and the Dutch and Flemish Renaissance paintings with artists such as Pieter Brueghel the Elder and Hieronymus Bosch who have created rich paintings that can be used as part as wimmelbooks. Paintings such as *The Garden of Earthly Delights* by Bosh and *Children's Games* by Brueghel are key examples of rich paintings that can be used in a wimmelbook. The average number of paintings per art gallery is 18.23 ± 7.25, there is a total of 4514 targets in the game, with 7.28 ± 6.27 targets per painting.

Fig. 3. Example of a painting with its regions of interests/targets for the game.

3.1   Controls

The serious game was implemented with Unity 2019.4.8f1 with the SteamVR plugin. The controls are identical for both left and right hands, they are limited to the trigger to activate buttons in the VR environment through the laser pointers, and the joystick for teleportation and quick turns. The buttons in the controllers for different headsets are depicted in Fig. 4.

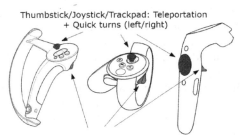

Fig. 4. Controls with different VR headsets (Valve Index, Oculus Touch, and HTC Vive).

4   Automatic Face Detection as Targets

While it is possible to consider predefined targets that have been labeled manually, we have also explored the extent to which it would be possible to determine targets automatically, by focusing on the detection of faces in paintings. Faces represent salient elements in paintings and the detection of people can bring be used for the game but also as a means to segment the images and determine who is who in the paintings.

Recent advances in machine learning and computer vision, coupled with the growing availability of large digitized visual art collections, have opened new opportunities for researchers to assist the art community with automatic tools to analyze and further understand visual arts. Among other benefits, a deeper understanding of visual arts has the potential to make them more accessible to a wider population, ultimately supporting the spread of culture. Machine learning and computer vision techniques can leverage the creation of serious games with automatic content generation for better engaging students with visual arts.

4.1   Data

We have considered a dataset of 372 paintings containing large faces (mainly portraits), representing a total of 494 faces (1.32 ± 0.89 faces per painting). We have applied a state-of-the-art method for the detection of faces to determine if it is possible to reliably detect faces as potential targets for a game. The face detection is based on the Multi-Task Cascaded Convolutional Neural Networks (MTCNN) approach. It is a deep learning neural network that detects faces and facial landmarks on images [31]. It is based on different convolutional neural networks (P-Net, R-Net, and O-Net) that predict face and landmark location.

4.2 Performance Evaluation

For assessing the performance of face detection, we consider the Intersection-Over-Union (Jaccard Index) and the Dice Coefficient (F1 Score). The Jaccard index is a statistic that is used for determining the similarity and diversity of sample sets. The Jaccard coefficient measures similarity between finite sample sets:

$$J(A, B) = \frac{|A \cap B|}{|A \cup B|} = \frac{|A \cap B|}{|A| + |B| - |A \cap B|}.$$ (1)

We consider two images, A and B, corresponding to the ground truth of the paintings. The Jaccard coefficient is used to assess the overlap that A and B share with their attributes. Each attribute of A and B can either be 0 (a pixel not belonging to a face) or 1 (a pixel belonging to a face). M_{11} represents the total number of pixels where A and B both have a value of 1. M_{01} represents the total number of pixels where the attribute of A is 0 and the attribute of B is 1. M_{10} represents the total number of pixels where the attribute of A is 1 and the attribute of B is 0. M_{00} represents the total number of pixels where A and B both have a value of 0. Hence, we have: $M_{11} + M_{01} + M_{10} + M_{00} = N_x \times N_y$. where N_x and N_y are the width and height of the image, respectively. The Jaccard similarity coefficient (J) is then defined by:

$$J = \frac{M_{11}}{M_{01} + M_{10} + M_{11}}$$ (2)

The performance of face detection in the paintings is presented i Fig. 5, it provides the distribution of the Dice Coefficient and the Jaccard Index across the faces present in the 372 different paintings. The average Dice Coefficient and Jaccard Score across paintings are 0.74 ± 0.30 and 0.65 ± 0.28, respectively.

While a large number of faces are well detected, a large number of faces are not detected suggesting that the automatic detection of faces in paintings is a difficult problem, in particular in relation to presence of various art movements and painting styles.

5 Experiments

Fifteen adult participants (age: 24.33 ± 5.35, 2 females) took part to an experiment to assess the workload, usability, flow, virtual reality sickness symptoms, and the game engagement. Prior to the experimental task, participants were

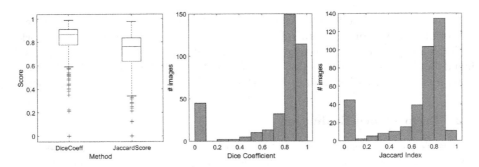

Fig. 5. Performance evaluation for face detection in paintings.

informed about the rules and goals of the game. No financial aid was given to the participants for their participation or performance in the game. The experiments with human participants follow the Helsinki Declaration of 2000. Participants had to play the game for about 20 min and then answer different questionnaires for assessing the performance. The goal was to find targets, with the possibility to use the hint option.

5.1   Performance Evaluation

We have used the following questionnaires to assess the performance of the game. The NASA Task Load Index (TLX) assesses mental workload [12], using six scales. The System Usability Scale (SUS) is a questionnaire for measuring usability based on 10 questions with Likert answers (from Strongly agree to Strongly disagree) [2]. We have also considered a Virtual Reality Sickness questionnaire with 9 items [17]. For each potential symptom, participants provide a value ranging from 0 to 3: 0 for no effect, 1 for slight effect, 2 for moderate effect, to 3 for severe effect. We have measured the flow with the 9 FSS scales of the 36-item instrument representing the dimensions of flow, and each scale is measured by 4 items [8,15,16]. The Cronbach's Alpha value (α) is used to measure the internal consistency of a questionnaire.

6   Results

The workload (NASA-TLX) and the System Usability Test results are presented in Tables 1 and 2. The workload performance across participants is 23.57 ± 10.82 (maximum being 100) ($\alpha = 0.66$), and the system usability score is 83.50 ± 10.04 ($\alpha = 0.70$), indicating a low workload and a high overall usability. The VRSQ was used for potential symptoms related to the use of VR, with locomotion, with the need to teleport in different places in the art galleries. The results from the

VRSQ indicate minimum effects (see Table 3) ($\alpha = 0.70$). The highest value is obtained with the criterion "difficulty focusing", while there was an absence of vertigo across all the participants. The results of the Flow questionnaire are given in Table 4, ($\alpha = 0.67$). The evaluation of the flow shows a high performance, with values greater than 4 or close to 4 for all the criteria, except for the last one "I am completely lost in though" with only an average of 1.87. The results obtained with the game engagement questionnaire vary substantially across participants and across questions. The GEQ results are presented in Table 5. They suggest that there is no disconnection between the users and the outside world while performing the experiment (questions 6 and 10); the highest score is obtained with question 16 "Playing makes me feel calm". The Cronbach's Alpha value $\alpha = 0.79$ indicates a good internal consistency.

Table 1. Workload assessment with the NASA-TLX test (1–20 scale).

	Criteria - Questions	values: 1–20
1	Mental Demand: How mentally demanding was the task?	6.93 ± 4.33
2	Physical Demand: How physically demanding was the task?	3.33 ± 2.41
3	Temporal Demand: How hurried or rushed was the pace of the task?	5.33 ± 2.53
4	Performance: How successful were you in accomplishing what you were asked to do?	4.60 ± 2.69
5	Effort: How hard did you have to work to accomplish your level of performance?	9.40 ± 4.53
6	Frustration: How insecure, discouraged, irritated, stressed, and annoyed were you?	3.27 ± 3.22
All	Total (0–100)	23.57 ± 10.82

Table 2. System Usability Scale assessment (Likert scale).

	Statements	values: 1–5
1	I think that I would like to use this feature frequently.	4.00 ± 0.93
2	I found the feature unnecessarily complex.	1.60 ± 0.91
3	I thought the feature was easy to use.	4.47 ± 0.74
4	I think that I would need the support of a technical person to be able to use this feature.	1.67 ± 0.72
5	I found the various functions in this feature were well integrated.	4.07 ± 0.88
6	I thought there was too much inconsistency in this feature.	1.40 ± 0.51
7	I would imagine that most people would learn to use this feature very quickly.	4.27 ± 0.59
8	I found the feature very cumbersome to use.	1.53 ± 0.64
9	I felt very confident using the feature.	4.60 ± 0.63
10	I needed to learn a lot of things before I could get going with this feature.	1.80 ± 1.01
All	Total (0–100)	83.50 ± 10.04

Table 3. Virtual Reality Sickness Questionnaire.

	Symptoms	values: 0–3
1	General discomfort	0.27 ± 0.46
2	Fatigue	0.13 ± 0.35
3	Eyestrain	0.27 ± 0.59
4	Difficulty focusing	0.53 ± 0.74
5	Headache	0.13 ± 0.35
6	Fullness of head	0.27 ± 0.59
7	Blurred Vision	0.27 ± 0.46
8	Dizzy (eyes closed)	0.20 ± 0.41
9	Vertigo	0.00 ± 0.00

Table 4. Evaluation of the flow (Likert scale).

	Criteria	values: 1–5
1	I feel just the right amount of challenge	4.07 ± 0.96
2	My thoughts/activities run fluidly and smoothly	4.27 ± 0.70
3	I do not notice time passing	3.93 ± 1.03
4	I have no difficulty concentrating	4.27 ± 1.03
5	My mind is completely clear	4.33 ± 0.90
6	I am totally absorbed in what I am doing	4.40 ± 0.63
7	The right thoughts occur of their own accord	4.13 ± 0.99
8	I know what I have to do each step of the way	4.60 ± 0.74
9	I feel that I have everything under control	4.20 ± 0.77
10	I am completely lost in thought	1.87 ± 0.83

Table 5. Game Engagement Questionnaire (Likert scale).

	Criteria	values: 1–5
1	I lose track of time	3.60 ± 1.18
2	Things seem to happen automatically	3.13 ± 1.41
3	I feel different	2.67 ± 1.23
4	I feel scared	1.07 ± 0.26
5	The game feels real	3.33 ± 1.29
6	If someone talks to me, I don't hear them	1.53 ± 0.74
7	I get wound up	1.93 ± 1.28
8	Time seems to kind of stand still or stop	2.53 ± 1.36
9	I feel spaced out	2.80 ± 1.47
10	I don't answer when someone talks to me	1.53 ± 1.06
11	I can't tell that I'm getting tired	2.33 ± 0.98
12	Playing seems automatic	3.47 ± 1.19
13	My thoughts go fast	3.00 ± 1.36
14	I lose track of where I am	3.13 ± 1.36
15	I play without thinking about how to play	3.13 ± 1.41
16	Playing makes me feel calm	4.00 ± 0.65
17	I play longer than I meant to	3.20 ± 1.01
18	I really get into the game	4.33 ± 0.72
19	I feel like I just can't stop playing	3.07 ± 1.10

7 Discussion and Conclusion

Immersive environments in VR are not sufficient for learning; they can provide an additional value and enhance learning. The immersion does not guarantee that learning will take place when interacting with its content. It is necessary to embed learning activities within immersive environments to convey learning outcomes to the learners.

Serious games based on VR technology can significantly change the way users, including students, can process visual information. Presenting large images corresponding to scientific content or paintings in a virtual environment allows users to access information and interact with the images in a more natural way. However, the presentation of the learning materials should provide ways so it is not just skimmed, and users can dedicate a substantial amount of time on them.

In this paper, we have proposed an adaptation of the famous game "Where is Wally/Waldo?", which is a search game using elements of the wimmelbooks. We have transposed the space of pages in a book into an immersive room in which players have to search for a target, the same way that readers have to search Wally in pages. We have also investigated how targets corresponding to faces could be extracted using machine learning algorithms. This task is difficult and highlights the limitations of current computer vision techniques when applied on non-realistic images, with different art styles and different scales. The problem of identifying potential targets that are suitable to a search game can be tackled from different perspectives: 1) a bottom-up approach where salient parts of the image are detected, or 2) a top-down approach where the type of targets (i.e., animals, faces, ...) are selected and recognized within the image.

The gameplay is currently limited to the search of pieces of paintings. It provides one step towards the formal analysis of paintings but the targets lack cultural and historical context that could be exploited for educational purposes in art history courses. For instance, the task could be to search for a particular historical figure, or to find more complex targets that require a deeper understanding of the paintings. However, such a gameplay may prevent players who have no knowledge of art history to fully appreciate the game. Being limited to a pure visual analysis of the paintings increases the accessibility of the application: it can be used by a wide audience, including children. The process of painting labelling is also easier when it does not require specific knowledge of art history.

Future work will deal with the evaluation of the serious game using students in art history or art, and to assess how they get better engaged in the classroom. Some regions of interest could be labelled to include the name of the person who is portrayed. Additional investigations should be carried out in algorithms that can automatically create unique targets so instructors would be able to import images into the application, which would deal with the detection of the most relevant objects in paintings.

Acknowledgements. The study was partially supported by the Claude Laval Jr. Award for Innovative Technology and Research.

References

1. Barrett, T.: Criticizing Art. Mayfield, Mountain View (1994)
2. Brooke, J.: SUS: a "quick and dirty" usability scale. In: Jordan, P.W., Thomas, B., Weerdmeester, B.A., McClelland, A.L. (eds.) Usability Evaluation in Industry. Taylor and Francis, London (1986)
3. Cecotti, H.: Great paintings VR. https://store.steampowered.com/app/1511090/Great_Paintings_VR/. Accessed 14 Jan 2021
4. Cecotti, H., Day-Scott, Z., Huisinga, L., Gordo-Pelaez, L.: Virtual reality for immersive learning in art history. In: Proceedings of the 6th International Conference of the Immersive Learning Research Network, pp. 1–7 (2020)
5. Cecotti, H.: Cultural heritage in fully immersive virtual reality. Virtual Worlds **1**(1), 82–102 (2022). https://doi.org/10.3390/virtualworlds1010006. https://www.mdpi.com/2813-2084/1/1/6
6. Dolan, E.: How Wimmelbooks work: a snail's guide. Sequentials **1**(1) (2017)
7. Dracan Works, LLC: VR museum: Art through time. https://www.dracanworks.com/. Accessed 06 Aug 2020
8. Engeser, S., Rheinberg, F.: Flow, performance and moderators of challenge-skill balance. Motiv. Emot. **32**, 158–172 (2008)
9. Eternal Echoes VR: The omnigallery. https://store.steampowered.com/app/1587200/The_OmniGallery/. Accessed 30 Apr 2021
10. Finn Sinclair: The VR museum of fine art. https://store.steampowered.com/app/515020/The_VR_Museum_of_Fine_Art/. Accessed 20 Aug 2016
11. Handford, M.: Where's Wally. Walker Books, London (1987)
12. Hart, S.G., Staveland, L.E.: Development of NASA-TLX (task load index): results of empirical and theoretical research. In: Hancock, P. Meshkati, N. (eds.) Human Mental Workload, pp. 139–183. Elsevier Science, Amsterdam (1988)
13. Hawes, D., Arya, A.: VR-based context priming to increase student engagement and academic performance. In: 2022 8th International Conference of the Immersive Learning Research Network (iLRN), pp. 1–8 (2022). https://doi.org/10.23919/iLRN55037.2022.9815929
14. Infinity REPLY: Virtual museum de Fornaris. http://www.fondazionedefornaris.org/. Accessed 07 Jan 2021
15. Jackson, S.A., Eklund, R.C.: Assessing flow in physical activity: the flow state scale-2 and dispositional flow scale-2. J. Sport Exercise Psychol. **24**(2), 133–150 (2002)
16. Jackson, S.A., Marsh, H.: Development and validation of a scale to measure optimal experience: the flow state scale. J. Sport Exercise Psychol. **18**(1), 17–35 (1996)
17. Kim, H.K., Park, J., Choi, Y., Choe, M.: Virtual reality sickness questionnaire (VRSQ): motion sickness measurement index in a virtual reality environment. Appl. Ergon. **69**, 66–73 (2018). https://doi.org/10.1016/j.apergo.2017.12.016. https://www.sciencedirect.com/science/article/pii/S000368701730282X
18. Mocove Studio: Mocove arts VR. https://store.steampowered.com/app/652540/Mocove_Arts_VR/. Accessed 21 June 2017
19. Moyosa Media BV: The Kremer collection VR museum. https://store.steampowered.com/app/774231/The_Kremer_Collection_VR_Museum/. Accessed 08 June 2018
20. Nigel Fogden: Infinite art museum. https://store.steampowered.com/app/1011000/Infinite_Art_Museum/. Accessed 06 Jan 2020

21. Polvinen, T.: The Finnish virtual art gallery. https://store.steampowered.com/app/745450/The_Finnish_Virtual_Art_Gallery/. Accessed 31 Oct 2018
22. Radiance: The great waldo search (1992)
23. Rémi, C.: Reading as playing: the cognitive challenge of the Wimmelbook. In: Emergent Literacy: Children's Books from 0 to 3, pp. 115–139. John Benjamins, Amsterdam (2010)
24. Scarry, R.: What Do People Do All Day? Random House Books for Young Readers, New-York (1968)
25. Shah, M., Gouveia, C., Babcock, B.: Undergraduate nursing students' experiences and perceptions of self-efficacy in virtual reality simulations. In: 2022 8th International Conference of the Immersive Learning Research Network (iLRN), pp. 1–7 (2022). https://doi.org/10.23919/iLRN55037.2022.9815933
26. Smithsonian American Art Museum: Smithsonian American art museum "beyond the walls". https://store.steampowered.com/app/1087320/Smithsonian_American_Art_Museum_Beyond_The_Walls/. Accessed 06 Jan 2020
27. Space Plunge: Art plunge. https://store.steampowered.com/app/570900/Art_Plunge/. Accessed 11 Sept 2019
28. Städel Museum: Städel time machine. http://zeitreise.staedelmuseum.de/. Accessed 24 Aug 2016
29. Wolf, E.: The museum of throughview. https://store.steampowered.com/app/689210/The_Museum_of_ThroughView/. Accessed 17 Aug 2017
30. WoofbertVR: Boulevard. https://www.blvrd.com/. Accessed 12 May 2016
31. Zhang, K., Zhang, Z., Li, Z., Qiao, Y.: Joint face detection and alignment using multitask cascaded convolutional networks. IEEE Signal Process. Lett. **23**(10), 1499–1503 (2016). https://doi.org/10.1109/LSP.2016.2603342

STEAM Project Exhibition in the Metaverse for Deaf High School Students' Affective Empowerment: The Power of Student Museum Exhibitions in Social Virtual Reality

Stylianos Mystakidis[1](✉) ⓘ, Peny Theologi-Gouti[1], and Ioannis Iliopoulos[1,2] ⓘ

[1] Science and Technology Museum, University of Patras, 26504 Rion, Greece
smyst@upatras.gr
[2] Department of Geology, University of Patras, 26504 Rion, Greece

Abstract. The Metaverse is the three-dimensional iteration of the Internet, a perpetual open web of persistent, networked environments merging physical reality with digital virtuality. Science Technology Engineering Art Mathematics (STEAM) education bridges two knowledge domains often perceived as disjointed: science and technology with art, humanities and social studies. This paper presents the design and development of a multi-school transdisciplinary STEAM project orchestrated by the University of Patras Science and Technology Museum. The deliverables of the project were analog and digital artifacts produced by K-12 primary and secondary school students on digital literacy and future citizenship. These were presented in an innovative virtual reality exhibition that was open and accessible in a web-based 3D online environment. The study employs an exploratory case study design involving deaf high school students and teachers. Data was collected from observation and semi-structured interviews. Results showed that the exhibition of deaf student creations in a multiuser platform in the Metaverse produced a series of social ripple effects around the students themselves, school peers, with and without hearing difficulties as well as educators. Its main contribution is the practical demonstration of the social affordances of the Metaverse in educational projects for children and adolescents with hearing disabilities.

Keywords: Metaverse · Virtual Reality · Social Virtual Reality · STEAM Education · Museum Education · K-12 Education · Informal Learning · Webxr · Disability · Special Needs · Special Educational Needs · Deafness · Special Education

1 Introduction

Students with hearing impairments face a multitude of challenges in secondary education around communication and self-efficacy that influence subsequently academic performance [1]. Consequently, there is a persistent disparity in the employment between hearing and deaf people [2]. A study of outstandingly successful deaf high school students stresses the importance of skills development, social skills practice and realistic goals pursuit [3]. Collaborative synthetic projects can address these issues and enhance essential self-efficacy and self-determination skills [4]. Currently, there is a scarcity of transdisciplinary projects in special education as teachers require continuous support for complex projects' implementation [5]. At the same time, innovative educational projects combining science with art can help children with hearing disabilities achieve spectacular results [6]. Museums of science and technology besides accommodating tours and visits can design, implement and provide informal learning experiences [7]. These programs, structured or unstructured, can be arranged around active learning approaches such as creation, play and experimentation towards deep meaningful and transformative learning [8]. Play is a fundamental human practice that can spark curiosity and facilitate skill acquisition and behavioral change with the help of educational technology [9, 10]. The current study presents the design and development of a transdisciplinary STEAM project orchestrated by the University of Patras' Science and Technology Museum (UP-STM) and the social ripple effects that were observed when integrating open social virtual reality in the Metaverse as an exhibition space of student deliverables.

2 Theoretical Background

2.1 STEAM Education

Science Technology Engineering Art Mathematics (STEAM) education is an approach that merges natural sciences with art and social studies [11]. It bridges two wide knowledge domains often perceived as disjointed: science and technology on the one hand and art with humanities on the other [12]. STEAM education has been associated with the development of creativity and innovation through problem-solving, critical competences for the 21st century [12]. As a result, a STEAM educators' competence framework is under development to facilitate the cross disciplinary professional development of teachers [11]. STEAM applications in mixed, augmented and virtual reality 3D immersive environments empower learners by providing opportunities for cognitive engagement, ill-defined problem solving and critical reflection [13]. Virtual field trips using immersive virtual reality (VR) head-mounted displays are increasing self-efficacy and sparking interest in science [14].

2.2 Digital Museum Exhibitions and Virtual Reality

A museum exhibition is an action of mass communication with a meaning making purpose [15]. Digital exhibitions in online environments are offering learning opportunities to wider audiences [15]. As there is a move toward phygital models of education and learning that combine simultaneously physical and digital components, it has been suggested that museums should explore methods to encourage active participation, social interaction and cooperation [16].

Thanks to immersive technologies such as virtual reality (VR) and the Metaverse, the concept of a virtual museum, a museum without walls [17], has been extended to travel back in time, visit remote, exotic places such as the ocean floor and experience artworks as living spaces [18]. Notable studies in the history and heritage fields include the Picts & Pixels exhibition [19] and an immersive experience around the Antikythera mechanism, the first analog computer of the world [20]. VR can be instrumental in visualizing objects and structures of historical significance that do no longer exist in the physical environment [21]. However, as VR efforts in museums were based on stand-alone immersive VR systems with single user experiences, the lack of social interaction was identified as the primary limitation and challenge [18]. This gap can be addressed with virtual museum exhibitions in the Metaverse, an open and persistent multiuser environment merging physical reality with digital virtuality [22].

2.3 Special Education in the Metaverse

The Metaverse is the three-dimensional iteration of the Internet, a perpetual open web of networked environments merging physical reality with digital virtuality [23]. Its underlying technologies are VR and augmented reality. It is comprised of the virtual Metaverse and the augmented or mixed Metaverse. The virtual Metaverse relies on social, multiuser VR platforms [24]. Avatars reside, create, communicate in multiuser spaces forming communities of practice [25].

Social VR environments can be advantageous for people with disabilities and autism spectrum disorder [24]. 3D virtual worlds have supported the formation of vibrant, international communities of people with disabilities where they were able to have rich, empowering experiences [26]. The documentary film Our Digital Selves: My Avatar Is Me provides ethnographic insights into the value proposition of these communities [27].

Extended reality technologies such as Microsoft Kinect and Leap Motion controllers have been used to accommodate the learning needs of people with hearing disability [28, 29]. A serious fantasy game was developed in VR to facilitate the development and practice of British sign language communication skills [29]. Lessons from previous studies stress the importance of participatory co-design with neurodiverse students such as inclusive VR STEM games [30].

3 Thematic Network STEM/STEAM Projects

The Science and Technology Museum of the University of Patras (UP-STM) aspires to be a catalyst of change towards an educated society building bridges between the academic community, research and the local society. This vision is realized through various actions such as transdisciplinary projects in cooperation with K-12 schools. One capstone project type is called "thematic museum-school network". These thematic networks are 9-month STEM/STEAM projects around topics such as environment and sustainability, diversity, inequality and social justice, science (e.g. the human brain), technology (e.g. internet safety) and culture.

These projects are organized in collaboration with local and regional primary and secondary education authorities, associations and non-governmental organizations on science and culture. Network projects are based on the innovative school-museum co-creation model and constitute a medium of inspiration and creation [31]. They constitute opportunities to experience academic discourse and practices through seminars, workshops and educational activities as well as UP-STM's exhibitions and collections. Using interdisciplinary and experiential approach, networks give the opportunity to school student and university student groups to work creatively, autonomously or by interacting together and with the museum to produce new educational material. It is worth noting that these thematic network projects have been organized voluntarily from the museum staff and collaborators free of charge for all participating schools and without any external funding or sponsorship.

From September 2020 to May 2021, two thematic networks were organized in tandem "Understanding diversity through a book – making the book go alive in the Museum" and "Digital literacy: Inspiring and educating the citizen of the future through the museum". Seven local schools participated, two elementary schools and five high schools. The structure of the project is illustrated in Fig. 1.

During the first months of the project regular teacher webinars were organized around the topics of interest. Simultaneously, schools visited the museum and participated in educational programs from the UP-STM's portfolio of playful and gamified informal learning actions custom-made for each age grade [32]. Then self-formed school teams of five to ten K-12 primary and secondary school students planned and implemented collaboratively their projects. Their outputs were analog and digital artifacts that were presented in the final event through presentations and videos. All project activities were implemented based on the existing protocols and protective measures to prevent the spread of the COVID-19 pandemic.

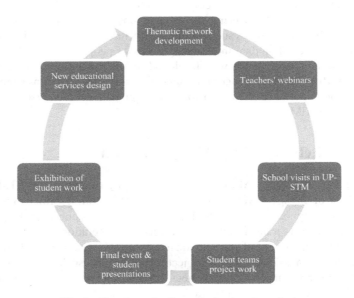

Fig. 1. Structure of a thematical network project.

Instead of displaying the works in a temporary museum exhibition space, a digital exhibition was developed to alleviate the lack of physical activities and display pupils' work publicly in the Metaverse. The rationale behind this decision was to create one exhibition in a 3D virtual simulated hall in the Metaverse that can be explored in manners that resemble social experiences in physical museum spaces.

Fig. 2. Members of the project team from classes for the deaf in the 18th High School of Patras (left and center), and the poster of their project "1821-2021: From the heroes of the past to the heroes of today" (right).

4   Methods

Would the decision to exhibit student work in a social VR platform have any impact on the students? Hence, the leading research question of this study is "What are the effects of exhibiting deaf students STEAM project work in the Metaverse? The rationale to focus the research solely on students with special needs was based on the persistent appeal of virtual worlds to people with all form of disability [26, 27]. Therefore, it is useful to investigate if the final deliverable of this project, the virtual exhibition would make any difference to the students' perceptions and beliefs.

The present study employs an exploratory case study design. Case studies provide grounds for deeper exploration of specific aspects of educational interventions. An evaluative case study produces accounts, narratives, explanations and interpretations [33]. The participants were seven deaf high school students aged seventeen to twenty years old and two of their teachers. The fact that adult students are among the study's participants is not surprising as deaf pupils attend high school at a later age. Data was collected from student behavior observation as well as semi-structured interviews with students and teachers during online meetings. It is important to note here that the use of a Metaverse of multiuser networked nature was decided late in the project and this aspect was unknown to them. Therefore, it was possible to record their thoughts and reactions upon learning about the exhibition and visiting it.

Observation was based on three sources: students' behavior and communication during (i) their visit in UP-STM, (ii) the presentation of their deliverables at the final event and (iii) teachers' feedback. Semi-structured interviews took place online after the end of the project. The semi-structured interview protocol included the following questions:

1. How long did your visit last at the virtual exhibition in the Metaverse?
2. What device did you use?
3. How was it conducted?
4. What were your impressions from the virtual exhibition? What did you like or dislike?
5. Did you face any difficulties of technical or other nature?
6. What did you feel or think when visiting the virtual exhibition?
7. Can you recall any memorable event from your visit?

Based on transcribed interview notes, data was analyzed manually by two researchers examining interpretively the context and premise of responses in order to identify common, emerging themes in relation to the investigated areas. Eventual discrepancies were resolved through discussion. After an initial set of codes was generated based on the participants' responses, more comprehensive and thorough themes were refined by merging and summarizing topics [34].

5   The Case of the 18^(th) Junior High School of Patras

The 18th Junior High School of Patras operates grades for deaf students. In the academic year 2020–21, the 12th grade of students with hearing difficulties was one of the participants in the thematic network project on digital literacy and future citizenship. Students decided to focus their project on the topic "1821-2021: From the heroes of the past to the heroes of today". The year 2021 marked the 200th anniversary of the start of the Greek War of Independence (also called Greek revolution) against the Ottoman occupation that led to the declaration and recognition of Greece as an independent state. Students illustrated portraits of heroes of the war and drew parallels to heroes of modern peaceful times emphasizing the challenges of the global COVID-19 pandemic age.

After planning the project's scope, deliverables and milestones, students formed sub-groups based on their talents and interests, they searched for information from multiple online sources, they practiced with new communication and technological tools to capture and present their findings. More specifically, they started with the concepts of heroism and duty, local heroes of the Greek revolution, modern heroes: doctors and medical personnel, volunteers and solidarity groups. Subgroups dealt with the artistic, literary and technological aspects of the project. For instance, the cover poster of the team's work depicted a medical staff member in uniform whose shadow has the figure of a freedom fighter bearing the Greek flag (Fig. 2).

6   Results

6.1   Virtual Exhibition Development

The digital exhibition was implemented in the social VR platform Mozilla Hubs. Mozilla Hubs is an opensource Metaverse software that allows the easy and flexible creation of 3D environments for multiple purposes such as remote group meetings, class lessons, conferences and collaboration spaces. Mozilla Hubs operate on the WebXR device group of standards that render the platform functional across the full spectrum of compatible XR devices and conventional computers and mobile devices. The exhibition was visitable from a simple url address without the need to create any account or to install any software. It was hosted in an elegant 3D space that can accommodate up to 40 concurrent users. The hall had a minimalist design with realistic features such as windows and light shadows along with a few fantasy decorative elements. Student project outputs were exhibited on all side walls. Visitors are visible in the exhibition hall as digital agents, called avatars (Fig. 3). Avatars can move freely in the space and can communicate with each other through voice and chat messages. Clicking on each work allows zooming in on each frame.

Fig. 3. Visitors appearing as avatars in the sharted virtual student-generated STEAM museum exhibition space in the Metaverse.

6.2   Ripple Effects of the Use of a Virtual Reality Museum Exhibition

Results from the semi-structured interviews showed that the exhibition of deaf student creations in a multiuser virtual space in the Metaverse produced a series of social ripple effects that can be organized around the students themselves, their school peers, both with and without hearing difficulties, as well as educators in wider school community. First, all students loved the freedom to explore and discover topics of interest in the relevant topic, select and use media or platforms of their choice and produce cooperatively a deliverable they liked. Regarding the VR exhibition, students reported high levels of satisfaction with the usability and user-friendliness of the technological medium. The VR exhibition was very easy to access and navigate. Additionally, three main themes emerged from the interviews' qualitative data analysis:

Enhanced Self-confidence and Sense of Pride. The main experienced emotion of deaf students was surprise and pride. They were accustomed to working with two-dimensional platforms and digital tools. Roaming and exploring the VR exhibition they perceived that their work achieved the status of a featured work in a real museum space. Moreover, its equal inclusion deemed it worthy to be displayed in a permanent space that was publicly available. The fact that their work was presented next to works of hearing students granted them unequivocal recognition. This enhanced their self-confidence and the self-efficacy due to the fact that they were able to help and push each other to improve their skills. It is worth mentioning here that the students had no technical difficulties whatsoever to visit and use the exhibition in the Mozilla Hubs. Intuitively they discovered all functions and were able to modify and use their avatars and have fun in the process.

Indicative student quotes: "I explored the work of groups from schools and thought that our work was on par or better. This increased my confidence that I can do a good job." (Student B). "I enjoyed the integration of technology and multimedia with history. More similar projects should be organized in other subjects." (Student C). Moreover, student E reported notably that his experience in the project was instrumental in deciding his professional career path. His ability to solve technical problems for the team, cooperate with peers and provide solutions to authentic tasks and challenges confirmed this inclination and encouraged him to select a career towards STEM fields and computer science.

Viral Motivation for Active Participation. The existence of the VR exhibition motivated and energized the deaf students to share their experiences in novel and direct ways with their peers. They demonstrated their work and the outputs of the overall project to other deaf students of younger age on multiple occasions in their schools by providing a guided tour of the virtual exhibition. These younger deaf students in turn were first impressed, but then became quite agitated: they demanded from their teachers to know why they were excluded from such an exciting work. They asked formally to enter similar actions and have the opportunity to participate themselves in similar projects. The transdisciplinary nature of the STEAM project was particularly appealing to them as it went beyond conventional teaching methods, it integrated technological tools with exciting topics and research that allowed them to assume an active role and agency in the planning and production of educational material.

Peer Recognition in the Wider School Community. After the creation of the VR exhibition, the participation of the deaf students was publicized on the school website. As a result, this work became wider known in the school community. As the supervising teachers reported, their peer computer science teachers took the initiative and presented the work of the deaf students in their classes of hearing students. Moreover, they congratulated the teachers of the deaf students and formulated proposals together to implement a new joint transdisciplinary project between classes of hearing and deaf students. "One computer science teacher who had visited the Metaverse exhibition congratulated us for a fantastic work and asked for more details to organize a similar exercise for his class" (Teacher B).

Another reaction of the deaf students was to share the link of the VR with peers in other schools in other regions of the country. Hence the participation of the deaf students went viral in the wider community and generated very positive comments. "My first impulse after visiting the exhibition was to share the link with my friends on social

media to show them our work. They were impressed and asked us how we did it."
(Student A).

7 Discussion and Conclusions

This study explored the impact of a virtual exhibition of deaf high school students work
in the framework of a STEAM project in the Metaverse. Although the produced artifacts
were not created with the knowledge of exhibition in the Metaverse, the innovative nature
of simulated museum 3D spaces elevated the recognition of student-generated materials
to new heights for the students themselves, their school peers and schoolteachers. This
enhanced the confidence and self-esteem of the students. They were activated and shared
their work with their peers within and outside the school. This extraordinary achievement
motivated in turn more deaf students and teachers to initiate new cooperative actions in
this direction of STEAM education. This observation is of great importance in an era
where the active engagement of students is a persistent challenge.

The current study has several limitations that prevent findings from being considered generalizable, mainly due to the limited size of the studied sample, which therefore
cannot be assumed representative of the entire population. Moreover, as demonstrated
by student's E comment on his career choice, some of the beneficial effects could be
attributed to the practical nature of the project involving authentic creative, technical
and communication tasks. However, the results obtained so far seem promising and can
further trigger the agile involvement of museums to experiment "metaversing" their collections and educational activities, engaging excluded social groups. Additional studies
employing quantitative and mixed research methods will be useful to elucidate this topic
from different perspectives. Indicatively, a future study could investigate if the a priori
knowledge of an exhibition of their works in a 3D virtual space in the Metaverse would
influence students' motivation and output quality.

This work has several implications for practice. Its main contribution is the practical
demonstration of the social affordances of the Metaverse in educational projects for
children and adolescents with hearing disabilities. STEAM education can be appealing
to many museums to combine science and technology with arts and social sciences
in creative and experiential projects. On the strategic level, this study demonstrates a
concrete method to engage new, diverse and remote audiences in the Metaverse. Virtual
exhibitions in the Metaverse can be an extremely useful tool for museums to provide
added value to a multitude of stakeholders and attract especially younger demographics
through exploration and entertainment [35]. Digital exhibitions can become archives of
educational materials and evidence of activity that can be reused and repurposed for
educational activities. As Metaverse exhibitions are universally openly and accessible,
educators can use them as open educational resources and integrate them into their lesson
plans. Moreover, virtual exhibitions increase the reach of the museum. A museum is no
longer confined to focus on audiences that are in their geographical proximity. Schools
from remote, rural regions or from abroad can have equal access to the digital Metaverse
environments, connect, communicate and interact with institutions and peers that are
located in urban areas. Hence, the Metaverse has the potential to become an equalizing
factor in education that increases significantly the range of a museum's activity as long

as the museum has developed the capacity to provide valuable, meaningful services to schools, educators and the society.

References

1. Perkins-Dock, R.E., Battle, T.R., Edgerton, J.M., McNeill, J.N.: A survey of barriers to employment for individuals who are deaf. JADARA. **49** (2015)
2. Garberoglio, C.L., Palmer, J.L., Cawthon, S.W., Sales, A.: Deaf people and employment in the United States (2019)
3. Charlson, E.S., Bird, R.L., Strong, M.: Resilience and success among deaf high school students: three case studies. Am. Ann. Deaf **144**, 226–235 (1999). https://doi.org/10.1353/aad.2012.0186
4. Luckner, J.L., Muir, S.: Successful students who are deaf in general education settings. Am. Ann. Deaf **146**, 435–446 (2001)
5. Gess, A., Kuo, N.-C.: An investigation of special education preservice teachers' perspectives and practices of STEAM education. J. Am. Acad. Spec. Educ. Prof. **41**, 63 (2019)
6. Gacharna, T.A.N., et al..: Implementation of the STEAM method to motivate and inspire primary and secondary school students in Colombia to pursue space science research, NASA Human Exploration Rover Challenge (HERC) 2020, 2021, 2022 Project Case study. In: 2022 IEEE Global Humanitarian Technology Conference (GHTC), pp. 393–396. IEEE (2022)
7. Chen, G., Xin, Y., Chen, N.-S.: Informal learning in science museum: development and evaluation of a mobile exhibit label system with iBeacon technology. Educ. Tech. Res. Dev. **65**(3), 719–741 (2017). https://doi.org/10.1007/s11423-016-9506-x
8. Dede, C., Grotzer, T.A., Kamarainen, A., Metcalf, S.: EcoXPT: designing for deeper learning through experimentation in an immersive virtual ecosystem. J Educ Techno Soc. **20**, 166–178 (2017)
9. Montag, C., Panksepp, J.: Primary emotional systems and personality: an evolutionary perspective. Front Psychol. **8** (2017). https://doi.org/10.3389/fpsyg.2017.00464
10. Mystakidis, S., Filippousis, G., Tolis, D., Tseregkouni, E.: Playful metaphors for narrative-driven e-learning. Appl. Sci. **11**, 11682 (2021). https://doi.org/10.3390/app112411682
11. Spyropoulou, N.D., Kameas, A.D.: Investigating the role of STE(A)M educators: a case study in Greece. In: 2020 11th International Conference on Information, Intelligence, Systems and Applications (IISA), pp. 1–6. IEEE (2020)
12. Perignat, E., Katz-Buonincontro, J.: STEAM in practice and research: an integrative literature review. Think Skills Creat. **31**, 31–43 (2019). https://doi.org/10.1016/j.tsc.2018.10.002
13. Birt, J., Cowling, M.: Toward future "mixed reality" learning spaces for STEAM education. Int. J. Innov. Sci. Math. Educ. **25** (2017)
14. Andersen, M.S., Klingenberg, S., Petersen, G.B., Creed, P.A., Makransky, G.: Fostering science interests through head-mounted displays. J. Comput. Assist. Learn. **39**, 369–379 (2022). https://doi.org/10.1111/jcal.12749
15. Lester, P.: Is the virtual exhibition the natural successor to the physical? J. Soc. Arch. **27**, 85–101 (2006). https://doi.org/10.1080/00039810600691304
16. Nofal, E., Reffat, M., vande Moere, A.: Phygital heritage: an approach for heritage communication. In: Immersive Learning Research Network Conference. pp. 220–229. Verlag der Technischen Universität Graz, Graz (2017)
17. Schweibenz, W.: The virtual museum: an overview of its origins, concepts, and terminology. Mus. Rev. **4**, 1–29 (2019)
18. Shehade, M., Stylianou-Lambert, T.: Virtual reality in museums: exploring the experiences of museum professionals. Appl. Sci. **10**, 4031 (2020). https://doi.org/10.3390/app10114031

19. Cassidy, C.A., Fabola, A., Rhodes, E., Miller, A.: The making and evaluation of picts and pixels: mixed exhibiting in the real and the unreal. In: Beck, D., et al. (eds.) Immersive Learning Research Network, pp. 97–112. Springer, Cham (2018). https://doi.org/10.1007/978-3-319-93596-6_7

20. Chrysanthakopoulou, A., Kalatzis, K., Moustakas, K.: Immersive virtual reality experience of historical events using haptics and locomotion simulation. Appl. Sci. **11**, 11613 (2021). https://doi.org/10.3390/app112411613

21. Morsman, A., et al.: Work-in-progress—using virtual reality in museums to assist historical learning. In: 2022 8th International Conference of the Immersive Learning Research Network (iLRN), pp. 1–3 (2022)

22. Mystakidis, S., Lympouridis, V.: Immersive Learning. Encyclopedia. **3**, 396–405 (2023). https://doi.org/10.3390/encyclopedia3020026

23. Mystakidis, S.: Metaverse. Encyclopedia **2**, 486–497 (2022). https://doi.org/10.3390/encyclopedia2010031

24. Hutson, J.: Social virtual reality: neurodivergence and inclusivity in the metaverse. Societies **12**, 102 (2022). https://doi.org/10.3390/soc12040102

25. Mystakidis, S.: Motivation enhancement methods for community building in extended reality. In: Fisher, J.A. (ed.) Augmented and Mixed Reality for Communities, pp. 265–282. CRC Press, Boca Raton (2021)

26. Forman, A.E., Baker, P.M.A., Pater, J., Smith, K.: Beautiful to me: identity, disability, and gender in virtual environments. Int. J. E-Polit. **2**, 1–17 (2011). https://doi.org/10.4018/jep.2011040101

27. Boellstorff, T.: Paraethnographic film: virtual enactment and collaboration in *our digital selves*. Vis. Anthropol. Rev. **37**, 8–30 (2021). https://doi.org/10.1111/var.12225

28. Zafrulla, Z., Brashear, H., Starner, T., Hamilton, H., Presti, P.: American sign language recognition with the kinect. In: Proceedings of the 13th International Conference on Multimodal Interfaces - ICMI '11, p. 279. ACM Press, New York (2011)

29. Economou, D., Russi, M., Doumanis, I., Mentzelopoulos, M., Bouki, V., Ferguson, J.: Using serious games for learning British sign language combining video, enhanced interactivity, and VR technology. JUCS – J. Univ. Comput. Sci. **26**, 996–1016 (2020). https://doi.org/10.3897/jucs.2020.053

30. Dahlstrom-Hakki, I., et al.: Inclusive VR through inclusive co-design with neurodiverse learners. In: 2021 7th International Conference of the Immersive Learning Research Network (iLRN), pp. 1–5. IEEE (2021)

31. Theologi-Gouti, P., Iliopoulos, I., Mystakidis, S.: Harnessing the power of local museum-school cultural, environmental and health education networks. Univ. Mus. Collect. J. **14**, 131 (2022)

32. Koufou, A., Theologi-Gouti, P.: Science and technology museum of Patras university and department of cultural education in primary education, Prefecture of Achaia, Greece. An example of cooperation and knowledge dissemination. In: Rivera, R.D.R., Fernández, I.G. (eds.) Congreso Internacional Museos Universitarios: Tradición y Futuro, pp. 367–371. Universidad Complutense de Madrid, Madrid (2015)

33. Merriam, S.B.: Qualitative Research: A Guide to Design and Implementation. Wiley, Hoboken (2009)

34. Braun, V., Clarke, V.: Using thematic analysis in psychology. Qual. Res. Psychol. **3**, 77–101 (2006). https://doi.org/10.1191/1478088706qp063oa

35. Lee, H.-K., Park, S., Lee, Y.: A proposal of virtual museum metaverse content for the MZ generation. Digit. Creat. **33**, 79–95 (2022). https://doi.org/10.1080/14626268.2022.2063903

Designing an AR-Based Materials Library for Higher Education: Offering a Four-Know Learning Structure for Design and Engineering Students

Yuanyuan Xu[1], Mengjie Huang[1(✉)], Wenxin Sun[1,2], Rui Yang[3], Massimo Imparato[1], and Hai-Ning Liang[3]

[1] Design School, Xi'an Jiaotong-Liverpool University, Suzhou, China
mengjie.huang@xjtlu.edu.cn
[2] School of Engineering, University of Liverpool, Liverpool, UK
[3] School of Advanced Technology, Xi'an Jiaotong-Liverpool University, Suzhou, China

Abstract. The development of immersive technologies can offer broader possibilities to future-oriented materials education in Design and Engineering. Augmented reality (AR) is an immersive technology that delivers a variety of information superimposed on top of the physical world via see-through glasses. Incorporating sensorial experiences provided by the physical materials library and the informative benefits of AR technology, an AR materials library comprising the Four-Know framework is proposed. Aside from material information retrieval, this library supplements sensory experience by overlapping the virtual model with specific materials in the real world. After the development of the user interface and AR functionalities, students with design and engineering backgrounds participated in a user test. The results indicated that the proposed design provided positive outcomes. In the future, this AR-based materials library is expected to serve as a design guide for the materials learning community and can be extended to other disciplines in higher education.

Keywords: Augmented Reality · Materials Library · Design and Engineering Education · Material Learning Framework · Disciplinary Communication

1 Introduction

One of the challenging topics that academia is facing to address the UN goals for sustainable development is that of Education for Sustainable Development (ESD). The UNESCO proposes a holistic and interdisciplinary approach to education that develops the knowledge and skills for a sustainable future is necessary [1]. As a central determinant of manufacturing, the correct use of materials like metals for mass production of products affects society significantly [2]. Materials education has been deployed and delivered in various forms; in the mid-1970s, Materials libraries for design education were established first at the Royal College of Art. Later in the 21st century, University

College London also started to explore materials-oriented design education. Physical libraries perform an important role in materials education as they allow intuitive sensory experiences to facilitate dialogue with the materials [2, 3]. However, physical materials libraries face challenges in terms of funding, sustainability and more than anything else update [3]. Overall, education in materials today demands more from educators. The incorporation of more futuristic and sustainable materials needs to be considered, while education requires innovation to keep up with the times. As augmented reality (AR) is considered to be future-oriented, leading to significant changes in education, it can help foster materials education [4]. AR, as an emerging technology, complements the physical environment or objects in the real world with computer-generated visuals that are mixed with the physical environment [5].

In this study, an AR-based materials library is introduced, and a relevant learning structure for materials education is explored. This paper will begin with a literature review, including the significance of materials education for design and engineering students, as well as its sustainability and the application of AR technology in education. Following this, design details of the AR Materials Library and the results of user testing will be presented. In the end, the design of the materials library will be discussed and summarized.

2 Related Works

2.1 Materials Learning

How a product is manufactured, how it functions and is experienced are affected by its designers' choice of materials [6, 7]. It is essential for design and engineering educators to understand how to engage and empower students to make informed and independent choices about appropriate materials [8, 9]. Currently, some universities allow direct access to material samples by creating physical collections of materials, thereby enhancing students' learning experience [2, 3]. These physical materials libraries facilitate interdisciplinary exchange, provoke dialogue with the materials, and enable more in-depth research [10, 11]. However, there have been many difficulties in establishing a physical materials library. Aside from the high cost of investment and the space required, updating the content of the materials library is also considerable. Accordingly, universities and organizations have ventured into the development of virtual online materials libraries. Cambridge Engineering Selector (CES), for example, opens up materials information and news for the public [8, 12]. In addition, sustainability in education also has focused its attention on this aspect, as reflected in the experimentation with materials learning and the research on new materials carried out by different institutions. The Glasgow School of Art launched its "Materials Futures" in recent years, investigating sustainable and environmentally friendly textile designs [13]. Materials engineering research has been carried out to generate open access knowledge on materials created with leftovers from industrial productions or single use products [14]. Opensource platforms have been established to gather research on regenerative material solutions [15]. New materials are continually evolving as designers and engineers need to advance their knowledge of materials to create the ideal user experience for their products. This requires information updating, and some platforms, such as Material ConneXion, are delivering the latest information on materials to provide their users with value [6, 16]. Keeping the information up to date in material education by contacting multiple parties has been explored [17]. Overall, materials education today demands more consideration to keep up to date with the growing needs.

2.2 AR-Assisted Education

Developments in information technology (IT) have enabled people to benefit from various dimensions. Not only is it facilitating educational transformation, but IT also helps to promote knowledge sharing [4]. AR, as an emerging technology in the information age, allows for a deeper sensory experience by overlaying virtual information with physical reality [4, 18]. Studies demonstrated that integrating digital elements into real-life educational activities through AR technology can boost student engagement, interest, and motivation [19–22]. Currently, several fields utilize generic interactive knowledge of the physical world to interact with educational content. By enabling students to change their perspective, shift the scale, move objects and other activities, AR can enhance their sensory experience in a spatial way and heighten learning motivation [23, 24]. An example is the visualisation of the crystal's molecular structure through AR, through which students can experience the molecular structure in the real world using their mobile devices [25]. Layering knowledge over the physical environment in a digital way delivers a novel experience, which could be thought of the guidance for material education. Interactive experiences such as touching and smelling will influence students' perception of the materials, but understanding the details and context of the materials is also vital to the selection of materials [7]. This work attempts to explore the benefits of AR to complement the information experience in materials learning and thus promote sustainable education about materials.

3 System Design

The above literature review provides support for developing an AR-based materials library, along with a design framework requiring investigation. Current materials education consists of two approaches: one based on science from microstructure to macro application, and another based on design from macro requirements to special microstructure of a particular material [26]. A study suggests that less quantifiable mechanisms are recommended, considering that sensory perception and practical application would be preferable to assist those with a design background in choosing materials [27]. In addition, some scholars have incorporated different disciplinary methodologies into material learning, the so-called Four-Know framework, which is Know-What, Know-Who, Know-How, and Know-Why [28]. Taking sustainability and information upgrading into consideration, the system proposed in this study will also introduce new materials.

3.1 Four-Know Structure as the Learning Basis

Overall, the core information of the system is presented based on the Four-Know framework shown in Fig. 1 from macro to microstructure. Know-What offers users a general introduction to the material and sensory perception information. Know-Who associates with the end-user of the materials, in particular the application area and examples of the materials. Know-How provides guidance on usage, including advantages, disadvantages, and sustainability of materials. Know-Why is related to micro information, containing specific data on the properties of materials.

Fig. 1. Framework of Four-Know structure in the system.

3.2 System Design

As Fig. 2 shows, this system consists of two main functions: information retrieval and AR showcase. Firstly, the materials database is collated from sources like publications and official institutions. The present information of each material is based on the Four-Know structure mentioned above. Detailed information on various materials is provided, as well as opening the news of new materials, including those not yet developed in bulk. Another aspect is that this system also features visual interaction using AR for material application examples so that students can expand their sensory experience.

Fig. 2. Information architecture of the system.

3.3 Implementation

The application is implemented to give users access to an AR-based materials library for educational purposes. This application is developed using the Unity engine along with

C#. Unity is a tool for accomplishing various tasks related to the development process of an application, and it is efficient at supporting the development of AR programs and interactive simulations. Besides, Vuforia Engine, a software development kit, is also used to support AR features, enabling applications to recognize images (e.g., QR codes) and configure them for real-time interaction. This application is intended to allow users to view different materials through the application on mobile devices, such as smartphones and tablets.

Fig. 3. User interfaces of the application - Home & Materials Library page.

User interface implementation. The current interface developed is displayed in Fig. 3, which mainly includes the home, the materials library, and the material content page. The home page contains two main parts: the materials information rotation banner and the new materials section. The rotation banner shows different categories of materials like plastic, wood, and so on. The new materials section provides newly updated materials information derived from officially published resources, such as materials researched and developed in academic environments. When users click on an article from the home page, the content is displayed, with the source of the article cited at the end. Materials Library page mainly focuses on the retrieval function. Users can enter the material's name to search and filter to find materials based on Category and Industry where it is employed. Material Content page displays different levels of information according to the Four-Know structure mentioned before, as shown in Fig. 4. The first part is Introduction (Know-What), which pictures a brief background of the material and provides sensorial information like color and texture. The second is Application (Know-Who), providing industries for material usage and examples. In addition, users can click the examples to experience the AR view. The third is Design guide (Know-How), which illustrates the pros and cons related to the use of the material, together with the environmental performance information such as energy used and recycled ratio. Last is Technical reference

(Know-Why) that introduces the physical properties of the material; comparisons with other materials are visualised in figures in this part to improve the user experience with the material data.

Fig. 4. User interfaces of the application - Material Content page.

Scan function implementation. Both Home page and Materials Library page contain an AR QR code scanning icon at the bottom, which is considered to interact with possible physical materials libraries (although not mandatory). When users experience a physical sample, a QR code is provided for it. User can scan the code directly and the system will automatically jump to the corresponding Material Content page, so that the user no longer needs to manually enter the name for searching the material. At the same time, students can also click the icon in the bottom to scan the QR code for the same functions. Such a function opens the possibility for the integration of online and offline material libraries.

AR function implementation. As shown in Fig. 5, users can click the case study part on Material Content page to view the example models in AR environment. The application then displays a new page for scanning QR codes and automatically enables the camera on the mobile device. For users to view a 3D model with one specific material on the screen, they must place the QR code within the range of the camera. Different perspectives are available for viewing the 3D model and its materials.

Fig. 5. AR demonstration in the case study.

4   User Test and Discussion

4.1   Data Collection

Fourteen students from design and engineering majors were invited to the user test. They all experienced materials education and were invited to view demonstrations of the features, from the home page to the material content page and the AR showcase. In the end, they were asked to complete questionnaires consisting of usability (SUS) and Kano model [29, 30]. The System Usability Scale (SUS) is a Likert scale questionnaire consisting of 10 items that helps to assess usability in a statistical format [29]. The Kano model is an analytical tool that assists in understanding the way in which users' emotional responses to a product or function [30].

4.2   Data Analysis

Some data on the current design and implementation scores were collected and analyzed. The overall usability (SUS) score is 72.68 at a good ([70; 80]) level. As shown in Fig. 6, the Kano model indicates that the AR showcase and new materials section are attractive, while the material content is perceived as a must. In addition, the material search on the Materials Library page is indifferent to them. Overall, the user test assists in evaluating this system in a statistical way. The general usability is positive for the current system, and participants show their interest towards the AR showcase used in the materials case study and new materials part.

Overall, participants showed their positive attitude towards the system, potentially grounded on the logical framework of learning combined with the novel experience offered by AR technology. Specially, AR showcase and new materials deliver a differentiated experience that allows users to explore the material learning journey actively. Moreover, as an accessible technology, AR allows users to anticipate its achievability and therefore believe in the availability of the product in a short timeframe.

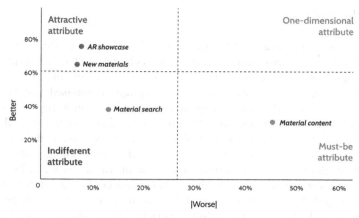

Fig. 6. Kano model for positioning functions.

4.3 Future Work

Future advances for this system will mainly focus on the material data collection and collation and refining the implementation of AR. The database for the materials library is derived from published books and official materials institutions and organizations. Considering the AR is the most attractive function, as evidenced in the user test, the exploration of AR will continue to be developed as a priority. Currently, the AR functionality is still in development, and more functionalities will be included in the future. For example, one function is allowing students to render their own models in real-time by selecting suitable materials from the materials library. In addition, collaboration with more organisations to supplement new materials will be explored in the future. Work on system evaluation will continue, and as fuller functionality is developed a controlled trial based on different learning methods will be set up for further user research.

4.4 Contribution

In general, the contribution of this paper focuses on promoting sustainable materials education by leveraging the advantages of technology. Firstly, the content of the materials library allows for multidisciplinary integration, as knowledge is fused together to trigger dialogues between multiple parties. Secondly, AR technology is applied to broaden students' sensory experience and supplement the perceptual information in the physical materials library. Thirdly, this system introduces a new section on materials that promotes the information update and offers new insights to the students. Moreover, the application developed for this system provides information and sensory supplements for students and promotes sustainable development of materials. The requirements of a physical materials library will be lowered when linked to the system, somewhat reducing the problems of high cost and large space requirements. Lastly, this system provides guidance for material learning with the Four-Know framework application, which can also be expanded in other disciplines.

5 Conclusion

This study aims to propose an AR-based materials library to facilitate the materials education for design and engineering students, and is based on literature review of materials learning and AR-assisted education. The advantages of current physical materials libraries and online platforms developed for learning are summarised, and their integration is also considered. The practical application of AR in education is also explored for generating system design concepts. Then further research into the materials learning framework is conducted, and the Four-Know structure is decided as the core methodological approach to design the system. Next comes the implementation to describe the application development including information and interaction content. Fourteen participants were invited to the user test. The overall results confirm the importance of AR applications together with the positive usability and user experience assessment. These insights provide valuable guidance for future work for further development of the system to promote sustainable development of materials education through the integration of AR technology.

Acknowledgments. This work is supported by the Teaching Development Fund of Xi'an Jiaotong-Liverpool University (TDF21/22-R23–164).

References

1. Unesco. https://www.unesco.org/en/education/sustainable-development. Accessed 04 Feb 2023
2. Wilkes, S.E.: Materials libraries as vehicles for knowledge transfer. Anthropol. Matters **13**(1) (2011)
3. Akın, F., Pedgley, O.: Sample libraries to expedite materials experience for design: a survey of global provision. Mater. Des. **90**, 1207–1217 (2016)
4. Voogt, J., Fisser, P.: Computer-assisted instruction. Int. Encycl. Soc. Behav. Sci. **4**, 493–497 (2015)
5. Pathania, M., Mantri, A., Kaur, D., Singh, C., Sharma, B.: A chronological literature review of different augmented reality approaches in education. Technol. Knowl. Learn. **28**, 329–346 (2021)
6. Haug, A.: Acquiring materials knowledge in design education. Int. J. Technol. Des. Educ. **29**(2), 405–420 (2019)
7. Pedgley, O., Rognoli, V., Karana E.: Materials experience as a foundation for materials and design education. Int. J. Technol. Des. Educ. **26**(4), 613–630 (2016)
8. Zuo, H.: The selection of materials to match human sensory adaptation and aesthetic expectation in industrial design. METU J. Fac. Archit. **27**(2), 301–319 (2010)
9. Zhou, Z., Rognoli, V.: Material education in design: from literature review to rethinking. In: Fifth International Conference for Design Education Researchers, pp. 111–119 (2019)
10. Hornbuckle, R.: Mobilizing materials knowledge: exploring the role of samples for supporting multidisciplinary collaborative design for materials development, In: Des. J. **24**(2), 277–297 (2020)
11. Wilkes, S.E., Miodownik, M.A.: Materials library collections as tools for interdisciplinary research. Interdisc. Sci. Rev. **43**(1), 3–23 (2018)

12. Cambridge Engineering Selector. http://www-g.eng.cam.ac.uk/125/now/ces.html. Accessed 04 Feb 2023
13. McHattie, L.-S., Ballie, J.: Material futures: design-led approaches to crafting conversations in the circular economy. J. Text. Des. Res. Pract. **6**(2), 184–200 (2018)
14. Upcycling Material Database. https://materialdb.miniwiz.com/. Accessed 04 Feb 2023
15. Materiom. https://materiom.org/. Accessed 04 Feb 2023
16. Azuma, R.T.: A survey of augmented reality. Presence: Teleoperators Virtual Environ. **6**(4), 355–385 (1997)
17. Material ConneXion. https://materialconnexion.com/. Accessed 04 Feb 2023
18. Xu, Y., Huang, M., Imparato, M., Yang, R., Liang, H.-N.: Work-in-progress—towards an AR materials library for design and engineering education. In: 2022 8th International Conference of the Immersive Learning Research Network (iLRN) (2022)
19. Milgram, P., Takemura, H., Utsumi, A., Kishino, F.: Augmented reality: a class of displays on the reality-virtuality continuum. In: Telemanipulator Telepresence Technologies, vol. 2351, pp. 282–292 (1995)
20. Bower, M., Howe, C., McCredie, N., Robinson, A., Grover, D.: Augmented reality in education - cases, places and potentials. Educ. Media Int. **51**(1), 1–15 (2014)
21. Burbules, N.C., Fan, G., Repp, P.: Five trends of education and technology in a sustainable future. Geogr. Sustain. **1**(2), 93–97 (2020)
22. Chiang, F., Shang, X., Qiao, L.: Augmented reality in vocational training: a systematic review of research and applications. Comput. Hum. Behav. **129**, 107125 (2022)
23. Bujak, K.R., Radu, I., Catrambone, R., MacIntyre, B., Zheng, R., Golubski, G.: A psychological perspective on augmented reality in the mathematics classroom. Comput. Educ. **68**, 536–544 (2013)
24. Karuppathal, R.: Impact of augmented reality education on students interactivity. Int. J. Pharm. Res. **13**(2), 1–9 (2021)
25. Eriksen, K., Nielsen, B., Pittelkow, M.: Visualizing 3D molecular structures using an augmented reality app. J. Chem. Educ. **97**(5), 1487–1490 (2020)
26. Ashby, M., Shercliff, H., Cebon, D.: Materials: Engineering, Science, Processing and Design. Kidlington, Oxford, United Kingdom (2019)
27. Laughlin, Z.: Beyond the swatch: how can the science of materials be represented by the materials themselves in a materials library? University of London (2010)
28. Lundvall, B.Å., Johnson. B.: The learning economy. J. Ind. Stud. **1**(2), 23–42 (1994)
29. Brooke, J.: SUS: a 'quick and dirty' usability scale. In: Usability Evaluation In Industry, pp. 207–212 (1996)
30. Rashid, M.M.: A review of state-of-art on Kano model for research direction. Int. J. Eng. Sci. Technol. **2**(12), 7481–7490 (2010)

Development of a 3D Modelling Gallery Based on Virtual Reality

Zhaoyu Xu[1], Mengjie Huang[2(✉)], Rui Yang[1], Liu Wang[2,3], and Yixin Liu[2,3]

[1] School of Advanced Technology, Xi'an Jiaotong-Liverpool University, Suzhou, China
[2] Design School, Xi'an Jiaotong-Liverpool University, Suzhou, China
`mengjie.huang@xjtlu.edu.cn`
[3] School of Engineering, University of Liverpool, Liverpool, UK

Abstract. Virtual reality (VR) technology has been widely applied in various fields, including entertainment, healthcare and education. In design and engineering education, VR technology shows the potential to improve traditional education practices by enhancing creativity and motivation through immersive learning experiences. With the interactive features and high-quality scenes provided by VR, the students' learning of 3D modelling in design and engineering disciplines may be highly motivating. This paper aims to develop a 3D modelling gallery based on VR to assist design and engineering students in learning 3D modelling. The system offers two main features, a virtual campus scene and a practice showcase, which allow students to explore and understand the modelling process of 3D models in a virtual environment. The integration of the 3D Modelling Gallery into the curriculum can help deepen students' understanding of 3D modelling, break the limitations of traditional teaching, and increase students' learning interest in 3D modelling.

Keywords: Virtual Reality · 3D Modelling · Design and Engineering Education · Virtual Campus

1 Introduction

Three-dimensional (3D) modelling is a fundamental process for industrial manufacturing and is an essential skill for designers and engineers engaging in design activities. Therefore, 3D modelling is integral in the modular structure of some design and engineering disciplines in higher education, such as industrial design and mechanical engineering. The traditional course of 3D modelling is usually delivered through briefing lectures and computer practices. The lecturer delivers knowledge of 3D modelling and demonstrates the modelling process of examples in software (e.g., Creo and Rhino) mainly by projector slide shows or real-time demonstrations. Students follow the demonstrations and practice the modelling skills. However, this teaching approach does not fundamentally change the limitations of traditional teaching or maximise students' initiative to learn 3D modelling.

M.-L. Bourguet et al. (Eds.): iLRN 2023, CCIS 1904, pp. 260–270, 2024.
https://doi.org/10.1007/978-3-031-47328-9_20

Virtual reality (VR) is a technology that generates a simulated environment in which users can immerse themselves and interact. With the rapid advancement of VR technology, it has grown beyond its early limited applications and has been applied to various areas of relevance. In recent years, the combination of VR technology with education has also gained recognition and popularity. VR show promises to benefit 3D modelling courses with irreplaceable advantages. For example, learning modelling in VR breaks the limitations of time and space, allowing students to enter virtual scenes to experience 3D modelling. The students' learning process can also be accelerated by feeling the scale and depth of 3D models intuitively and experiencing the modelling concepts and methods in an immersive learning environment [1]. With the immersive, interactive, and imaginative features of VR, students' learning interest in 3D modelling can be enhanced by the hands-on experiences and spatial and depth perceptions [2].

This study aims to create a VR 3D Modelling Gallery that can be integrated into the learning of 3D modelling for design and engineering students. The gallery presents two main features, a virtual campus scene that allows students to explore the 3D modelling through the models of campus buildings and a practice showcase including the 3D models from the computer practices of the course to study modelling skills. The proposed system will enable students explore the 3D Modelling Gallery and study the creation methods and skills of 3D models in an interactive and immersive learning environment.

2   Related Works

Immersive technology, such as virtual and augmented reality, is currently a very promising tool and is increasingly used in a variety of fields, such as healthcare, entertainment, and education [3–7]. VR technology enables users to interact with virtual objects in virtual scenes immersively through controllers and high-quality screens in VR glasses [8], featuring traditional education practices to be more engaging and motivating. The application of VR technology in the industrial design education field shows the potential to assist industrial designers through immersive education and enhanced experiences that foster their creativity in design processes [9].

One of the most significant advantages of VR is that it enables intuitive and natural interactions [10]. For 3D modelling education, VR breaks through the two-dimensional space of the traditional computer screen and brings students to a new dimension of experience and interaction and a higher level of engagement [11]. Most industrial design students still learn 3D modelling using the traditional learning method, which means lectures demonstrating modelling processes and modelling operations through slides. Students spend most of their time learning about 3D modelling on boring slides or static images rather than actually perceiving and touching the models. The communication of design thinking may be lacking when studying in this way. Huang et al. [12] argued that the conventional, lecture-style seating arrangement used in 3D modelling education can result in inflexible learning, as the singular and unchanging teaching method can limit students' ability to experiment and develop their own ideas. In the current learning of 3D modelling, students have rarely had the opportunity to access new technologies [13]. The combination of VR and modelling education can help students have more access to 3D models and may motivate their learning.

Previous researchers suggested that VR has the potential to greatly enhance traditional learning methods, as it combines interactivity with a simulated learning environment that can replicate real-world objects [14]. The integration of VR technology into education has been explored by researchers in recent years. For instance, Gomes et al. [15] utilised VR technology in the studying of music history, enabling users to take a virtual tour of music museum. The study found that incorporating music games and other interactive elements into the VR experience greatly improved both the students' learning outcomes and their engagement in the learning process. Southgate et al. [16] utilised VR technology to build 3D plant models, which allowed the students to deepen their understanding of plant respiration and photosynthesis. Their results showed that VR could improve learners' awareness of spatial concepts. Students involved in this study reported that being fully immersed in the virtual world helped them eliminate distractions, improved their focus and enhance their learning experience. Cheng et al. [17] have integrated VR technology into the study of language and culture, giving learners the opportunity to immerse themselves in Japanese culture through a virtual environment. Participants learned the proper timing and technique for bowing by using the VR program, which enhanced a higher level of involvement with Japanese culture. The outcomes indicated that VR technology offers a unique platform for cultural engagement and boosts motivation for language education.

The studies discussed above demonstrate the widespread application of VR technology in education and learning. For design education, an immersive design environment allows designers to improve spatial awareness, creativity, and aesthetics [18]. The integration of VR technology into students' learning of 3D modelling is expected to be very promising and bring many benefits to the field of industrial design. Therefore, the development of a 3D Modelling Gallery platform based on VR technology may assist the 3D modelling learning of design and engineering students.

3 System Design

The system of the 3D Modelling Gallery in this study was mainly developed by Unity (2021.3.6f1c1), a real-time development platform for building 3D applications. PTC Creo Parametric and Blender, 3D modelling software, were also used for the system design to assist with preparing the 3D models of the virtual campus and the practice examples. The VR device applied in this study is Oculus Quest 2 headset with its two hand controllers shown in Fig. 1 in order to facilitate the virtual environment of the 3D Modelling Gallery system. The VR headset has a dual eye resolution of 3664×1920 and a maximum refresh rate of 120 Hz. A physical tracking area of $2 \times 2 \times 2$ m is required for users sitting and standing while using the system.

The first main feature of the 3D Modelling Gallery is a virtual campus scene that allows students to explore the 3D modelling through the virtual models of their campus buildings shown in Fig. 2 and Fig. 3. In order to provide students with an immersive learning experience and improve students' motivation for learning 3D modelling, the virtual campus scene in the gallery was built with reference to the authors' campus. By scaling the real scenes to an appropriate scale as virtual scenes and reconstructing each of the building models, the students can feel the novelty of 3D modelling and be inspired to learn this skill.

Fig. 1. VR device used in the gallery system.

Fig. 2. Virtual campus scene (part one).

Fig. 3. Virtual campus scene (part two).

The proposed system provides two movement options in the virtual campus, including joystick and teleportation. Students can walk freely around the scenes in the virtual environment and navigate the vibrant virtual Campus. When touring the virtual campus, students can switch between joystick movement, which is more precise but slower, and teleportation, which has larger steps and is suitable for longer distances, as shown in Fig. 4.

The other main feature of the gallery is the practice showcase, displaying the 3D models from the computer practices in the corresponding module (e.g., IND112 Computer-aided Design and Modelling). This module is delivered through briefing lectures and computer practices, and the lecturer uses examples to demonstrate the modelling process in class. With this practice showcase in the established gallery, students can interact with the 3D models from the module and learn about their creation process in the immersive environment. Besides displaying the 3D models, the practice showcase also provides functions such as demonstration of the modelling process and modelling tips, and implementation of auditory and vibration feedback to enhance the interaction experience.

The practice showcase of the 3D Modelling Gallery is located at the "The Gate of Wisdom", one landmark in the centre of the south campus of the authors' university. The practice showcase displays the 3D models from the module (IND112 Computer-aided Design and Modelling). Students can interact with the 3D model by using the VR controllers, which will appear as virtual hands in the scene. When the virtual hand meets the 3D model, the controller provides vibration feedback to indicate that it is ready for grabbing. After grabbing the model, the user can freely manipulate it by rotating it in any perspective or moving it either closer or farther to observe all the modelling details as presented in Fig. 5.

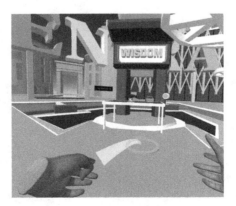

Fig. 4. Teleportation movement.

Fig. 5. Interaction with the 3D model.

Fig. 6. Demonstration of the modelling process.

Fig. 7. Modelling tips for the modelling stage.

When students want to see the process of modelling of a 3D model, they can use the right controller to point at the model and pull the trigger, the model will change to its initial state in the modelling history. As the user controls, the model will change sequentially to demonstrate different stages in the modelling process. When the user aims the right-hand controller at the model, a ray will appear in front of the right-hand controller indicating that the modelling process demonstration is ready to start. The user can then trigger the model to switch to its initial modelling state by pulling the trigger on the right-hand controller. Subsequently, each time the user aims at the model and pulls the trigger, the model will switch in the order of the modelling process until it reaches its final state.

Figure 6 shows the state ready for demonstrate the modelling process. If the user gets confused about any of the modelling stages, he or she can use the virtual hand to press the Tips button in the scene. When the button is pressed, the operation performed at that step appears on the model and the part that changes due to the operation is highlighted in yellow colour on the 3D model, providing the user with visual and accurate tips shown as Fig. 7. When the virtual hand leaves the Tips button, the button will automatically pop up and the modelling tips will be hidden at the same time. Sound feedback will be provided when the button is pressed or popped up to inform the user whether the operation is successful or not, in order to enhance the interaction experience of the user when displaying or hiding the modelling tips.

4   User Test

A user test was conducted through experiments to investigate the effectiveness of using the 3D Modelling Gallery system as a tool to enhance students' learning of 3D modelling.

4.1 Participants

Twelve participants (8 males and 4 females) between the ages of 18 and 30 were recruited for this study. All participants had no prior experience in 3D modelling and had not received any prior instruction in the subject. Before the study began, each participant signed a written informed consent form outlining the purpose of the study, their rights as participants, and the procedures involved. Participants were assured that their data would remain confidential and anonymous throughout the study.

4.2 Procedure

The experiment of the user study consisted of two phases, with the first phase based on the learning of 3D modelling through traditional instruction methods and the second phase focusing on the implementation of 3D Modelling Gallery into the learning process.

In the first phase, participants learned how to model using traditional instruction methods. Participants were given a slide deck which outlined the 3D modelling process for a specific object and a video tutorial in which an instructor demonstrated the modelling process in the Creo software. Participants were instructed to follow along with the slide and video tutorial, attempting to model the object themselves in Creo. After this session, participants were asked to complete a survey in which they provided feedback on their learning experience.

In the second phase, participants used the 3D Modelling Gallery developed in this study in a VR environment for the learning of 3D modelling. Using the VR headset and hand controllers provided, participants were able to interact with the model in the VR environment. By using the practice showcase in the 3D Modelling Gallery, participants received prompts and guidance on the modelling process of the specific object, which helped them to attempt to model the object themselves in Creo. Participants were also instructed to take a virtual tour inside the virtual campus which was built by 3D modelling techniques according to participants' campus. After this session, participants were again asked to provide feedback on their experience through a survey.

4.3 Survey

Participants were asked to complete a survey that contained four questions about their learning experience after completing each phase of the experiment. These questions aimed to evaluate the effectiveness and experiences of the learning method based on the following aspects: 1) ease of understanding the 3D model; 2) efficiency of the learning process; 3) confidence in completing modeling tasks; 4) improvement in interest in 3D modelling. In the survey conducted after the second experiment phase, an additional question was included regarding whether the virtual campus scene could increase participants' interest in modelling. Each question was answered on a 5-point Likert scale, with options ranging from strongly disagree (-2) to strongly agree (2). The survey responses were then analysed to compare the learning experiences between the two phases of the experiment.

4.4 Results and Discussion

As shown in Fig. 8, the experiment results showed that in three aspects, ease of understanding the model, confidence in completing the modelling exercises and interest in modelling (Q1, Q3 and Q4), the combination of 3D Modelling Gallery and the traditional learning demonstrated a significant advantage over the traditional learning method alone ($p < 0.05$). Moreover, in terms of the efficiency of the learning process (Q2), the feedback from the participants indicated a significant advantage of combining 3D Modelling Gallery with the traditional learning ($p < 0.01$). According to the additional question result regarding the virtual campus in the gallery, the data ($M = 1.5, SD = 0.52$) showed that the majority of participants believed that the virtual campus environment could enhance their interest in 3D modelling.

Based on the experiment results, it can be concluded that the use of 3D Modelling Gallery in VR environment has shown significant improvement in terms of model comprehension, participants' confidence in completing modelling exercises, and their interest in modelling. The feedback from participants also suggests that the use of 3D Modelling Gallery in VR environment is significantly more effective in terms of learning efficiency. The results have demonstrated the benefits of using VR technology for education. The immersive nature of VR can enhance the learning experience by providing

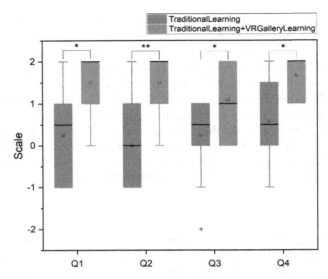

Fig. 8. Results of questions on the experiences of learning modelling for two different methods (* p < 0.05; ** p < 0.01).

a more engaging and interactive environment. The use of VR in this study allowed participants to interact with the model in a more natural and intuitive way, which could have contributed to the observed improvements in learning outcomes. One limitation of the current study is the small sample size, which may limit the generalizability of the findings. Future studies with a larger sample size could provide more robust evidence of the benefits of using VR technology for modelling education.

Overall, the results of this study suggest that the use of 3D Modelling Gallery in VR environment has the potential to enhance the effectiveness and efficiency of the learning of 3D modelling in design and engineering education. This technology could be particularly valuable for students without any prior modelling experience, as it provides an immersive and engaging learning environment that can facilitate the acquisition of new skills.

5   Conclusion

In conclusion, this study developed a VR system for educational purposes to assist the learning of 3D modelling for design and engineering students. The whole system is based on a virtual campus which allows users to move freely through scenes of the campus wearing a VR headset and touring the campus. Each architectural model in the virtual campus can motivate and inspire students to learn 3D modelling. The practice showcase in the developed system is designed for students to freely select the model from the module practices they want to view and manipulate, better understand the construction of the model, and obtain modelling guidance. It is anticipated that this innovative approach to education will serve as a reference for future learning methods in design and engineering courses of 3D modelling, providing students with an engaging and effective learning experience.

For future work, one focus will be the research of further integration of the gallery system into the learning of 3D modelling in practice. Another feature to be added into the gallery in the future is a practice for the lighting in the rendering of 3D model, which allows students to freely move the position of the lights and set different light intensities in the VR environment to learn about the lighting in rendering.

Acknowledgements. This work is supported by the Teaching Development Fund of Xi'an Jiaotong-Liverpool University (TDF21/22-R23-164) and the Summer Undergraduate Research Fellowship of Xi'an Jiaotong-Liverpool University (SURF2022116).

References

1. Freina, L., Ott, M.: A literature review on immersive virtual reality in education: state of the art and perspectives. In: The International Scientific Conference E-learning and Software for Education (2015)
2. Soliman, M., Pesyridis, A., Dalaymani-Zad, D., Gronfula, M., Kourmpetis, M.: The application of virtual reality in engineering education. Appl. Sci. **11**(6), 2879 (2021)
3. Huang, H., Lee, C.F.: Factors affecting usability of 3D model learning in a virtual reality environment. Interact. Learn. Environ. **30**(5), 848–861 (2019)
4. Wang, L., Huang, M., Yang, R., Liang, H.-N., Han, J., Sun, Y.: Survey of movement reproduction in immersive virtual rehabilitation. IEEE Trans. Visual. Comput. Graph. **29**(4), 2184–2202 (2023)
5. Wang, L., et al.: Movement modulation in virtual rehabilitation: its influence on agency and motor performance. In: 9th International Conference on Serious Games and Applications for Health, pp. 1–8 (2021)
6. Sun, W., Huang, M., Wu, C., Yang, R.: Exploring virtual object translation in head-mounted augmented reality for upper limb motor rehabilitation with motor performance and eye movement characteristics. In: Adjunct Proceedings of the 35th Annual ACM Symposium on User Interface Software and Technology, pp. 1–3 (2022)
7. Xu, Y., Huang, M., Imparato, M., Yang, R., Liang, H.-N.: Work-in-progress—towards an AR materials library for design and engineering education. In: 8th International Conference of the Immersive Learning Research Network (iLRN), pp. 1–3 (2022)
8. Guo, Z., Zhou, D., Chen, J., Geng, J., Lv, C., Zeng, S.: Using virtual reality to support the product's maintainability design: immersive maintainability verification and evaluation system. Comput. Ind. **101**, 41–50 (2018)
9. Raptis, G.E., Fidas, C., Avouris, N.: Effects of mixed-reality on players' behaviour and immersion in a cultural tourism game: a cognitive processing perspective. Int. J. Hum. Comput. Stud. **114**, 69–79 (2018)
10. Lawson, G., Salanitri, D., Waterfield, B.: Future directions for the development of virtual reality within an automotive manufacture. Appl. Ergon. **53**, 323–330 (2016)
11. Radianti, J., Majchrzak, T.A., Fromm, J., Wohlgenannt, I.: A systematic review of immersive virtual reality applications for higher education: design elements, lessons learned, and research agenda. Comput. Educ. **147**, 103778 (2020)
12. Huang, H., Lin, C., Cai, D.: Enhancing the learning effect of virtual reality 3D modeling: a new model of learner's design collaboration and a comparison of its field system usability. Univ. Access Inf. Soc. **20**, 429–440 (2021)

13. Marks, B., Thomas, J.: Adoption of virtual reality technology in higher education: an evaluation of five teaching semesters in a purpose-designed laboratory. Educ. Inf. Technol. **27**, 1287–1305 (2022)
14. Zhou, Y., Jia, S., Xu, T., Wang, Z.: Promoting knowledge construction: a model for using virtual reality interaction to enhance learning. Procedia Comput. Sci. **130**, 239–246 (2018)
15. Gomes, J., Figueiredo, M., Amante, L.: Musical journey: a virtual world gamification experience for music learning. Int. J. Adv. Educ. Res. **1**(1), 1–21 (2014)
16. Southgate, E., et al.: Embedding immersive virtual reality in classrooms: ethical, organisational and educational lessons in bridging research and practice. Int. J. Child-Comput. Int. **19**, 19–29 (2019)
17. Cheng, A., Yang, L., Andersen, E.: Teaching language and culture with a virtual reality game. In: Proceedings of the 2017 CHI Conference on Human Factors in Computing Systems (2017)
18. Rieuf, V., Bouchard, C., Meyrueis, V., Omhover, J.F.: Emotional activity in early immersive design: sketches and moodboards in virtual reality. Des. Stud. **48**, 43–75 (2017)

Inclusion, Diversity, Equity, Access, and Social Justice (IDEAS)

Access to Escape - An Immersive Game-Based Learning Experience for Accessibility Education in Virtual Reality

Paula Wiesemüller[✉], Saba Mateen, Andreas Dengel, and Sarah Voß-Nakkour

Goethe University, studiumdigitale, Frankfurt am Main, Germany
{wiesemueller,mateen,voss}@studiumdigitale.uni-frankfurt.de,
dengel@uni-frankfurt.de
https://www.studiumdigitale.uni-frankfurt.de/

Abstract. The accessibility of digital systems determines the participation of a large number of people in everyday life. Therefore, it is important to teach this topic to future developers of the said systems. As accessibility can be hard to grasp due to one's inability to experience the problematic barriers people with disabilities face, Virtual Reality (VR) comes into play. VR technology offers the opportunity to simulate situations encountered by persons with disabilities and enables the possibility of new experiences. To further analyze the suitability of a VR application to teach accessibility, we developed Access to Escape, an Immersive Game-Based Learning Experience for Accessibility Education in Virtual Reality. A first evaluation with 11 participants could show that the VR Escape Room helped to develop a different perspective through the simulated limitation of their senses and sensitize them to the issue of accessibility. The participants reported that they have discovered new connections concerning accessibility. Furthermore, the use of VR was perceived as very enjoyable, especially due to the increase of motivation and the simplification of the topic. Besides that, the results of the User Experience Questionnaire (UEQ) could show that the participants perceived the VR Escape Room as attractive, stimulating and novel. The evaluation demonstrates that a Game-Based Learning Experience in a virtual environment might lead to cognitive as well as affective learning outcomes. The use of the VR Escape Room in education has the potential to improve learning, especially to raise awareness of accessibility.

Keywords: Immersive learning · Accessibility education ·
Game-based learning · Virtual escape room · Immersive escape room

1 Introduction

To ensure equal access to digital resources for everyone, these resources must be accessible as required by laws such as Section 508[1]. Recommendations like

---

[1] https://www.section508.gov/.

the Web Content Accessibility Guidelines 2.2[2] (WCAG) offer assistance for the proper development of accessible web resources by stating 78 success criteria where each describes an accessibility need. However, many websites and online applications do not fully meet accessibility criteria [6]. Simultaneously accessibility does not receive the required attention in education. Even in Computer Science Education, the topic of accessibility is not always part of the basic courses. Although the content can be learned in elective modules, it is not mandatory, which can lead future developers of digital systems to have no knowledge of accessibility [1,3,20]. Because of that, there is a need to sensitize and educate future computer scientists about accessibility. As mentioned, accessibility courses are often optional, which is why this need should be fulfilled by a learning resource that has a low threshold and can motivate students. Another challenge the learning resource would need to counteract is the lack of opportunities to fully grasp the consequences of barriers. This counteraction could be achieved artificially, for example, with the use of VR technology. VR makes it possible to virtually restrict selected senses and thereby, the users can experience simulated situations that are otherwise encountered by people with disabilities.

This paper presents a possible approach to the mentioned challenges. We developed the VR Escape Room *Access to Escape* which aims to sensitize and educate computer science students about the importance of accessible content and the problems that arise when accessibility is not provided. Facing different barriers in the VR Escape Room, such as missing alternative texts, the students are supposed to learn how to eliminate those. To evaluate the VR Escape Room *Access to Escape*, we formulate the following research question:

1. *What aspects of user experience in a VR Escape Room can contribute to raising awareness and fostering learning about accessibility in Higher Education?*

2   Accessibility Education in Virtual Environments

Accessibility Education has gained importance in Computer Science Education in recent years as more and more multimedia content is consumed by people with various impairments. The growing challenges, but also possibilities to make such content accessible have strengthened pedagogic research efforts within this fields.

Lewthwaite and Slaon [10] argue that to understand the pedagogic challenges related to Accessibility Education, the extent of knowledge and skills required by accessibility and thus the best-suited pedagogic approaches to teaching the subject need to be considered. As a combination of theoretical understanding, procedural knowledge, and technical skills competence regarding accessibility topics, Accessibility Education covers a variety of topics related to the complexity of accessibility as a sociotechnical challenge, as well as the knowledge and skills needed to create accessible digital resources [10].

---

[2] https://www.w3.org/TR/WCAG22/.

Such general pedagogic approaches for Accessibility Education are mostly referred to the use of lectures, courses, or lab settings. For example, Shi et al. [16] created five Accessibility Learning Labs (ALL) where an experiential learning structure was used to teach foundational concepts of computing accessibility while also demonstrating the necessity to create accessible software. These labs provide complete educational experiences, containing materials such as lecture slides, activities, and quizzes. Shi et al. could show that such labs are an effective way to teach participants about accessible digital resources and that experiential learning approaches show potential benefits in motivating participants to learn about the importance of creating accessible software. Another finding showed that the used empathy material increased learning retention.

In the READi project (Research and Education in Accessibility, Design, and Innovation) from Kang et al. [7], students get an interdisciplinary accessibility training comprising a graduate course on accessibility and inclusive design, a team project, a retreat, workshops, and a symposium. In a first program assessment, Kang et al. [7] analyzed students' self-reported learning outcomes, future endeavors, and possible program improvements.

Regarding digital approaches to teaching about web accessibility, Benavídez et al. [2] present the use of digital tools for web accessibility education: In the *Contramano* project, students work on a website designed to fail every accessibility checkpoint. The fictitious website offers information for left-handed people, along with games, curiosities, and a shop. Its subpages contain numerous bad practices, such as having an animation as a start page, non-accessible videos, screen flickering, bad color contrasts, and time-dependent interaction. The website exemplifies such bad practices and can be used for short exercises focused on specific checkpoints.

Several approaches broaden the use of digital media for Accessibility Education and awareness by using game-based approaches: In *Lola's first semester* the player is a first-semester student who does not yet know her way around the university. The game aims to raise awareness of players for the problems of students with impairments in everyday university life. Therefore, the game offers five integrated mini-games where each game takes the perspective towards a different barrier faced by people with visual impairment. For example, during the 'Lecture' game, players need to make buy-sell decisions during a stock market simulation. The signals are given by red and green arrows that are not distinguishable for people with red-green color blindness [14].

Kletenik and Adler [8] report on the performance and results of the survey of three games that simulate disabilities such as visual impairment (color blindness), audio impairment (deafness), and physical/motor impairment (jitteriness). The games have red, green, and yellow balls moving across the screen. Players are told to click on one of the red or green balls (color chosen randomly) to get a point. If they choose the wrong color, the computer 'opponent' wins a point, and the player loses one. Afterward, another color is chosen and the game continues until the time limit of 30 s is reached. All games were presented in different modes: a game mode (no simulated disability), a simulation mode (simulated disability), a game+accessibility mode (no simulated disability but the game is accessible) and a simulation + accessibility mode (simulated disability and the game is accessible). Their results of a study with 113 students showed that playing the games induced student empathy towards people with disabilities and motivated them towards learning about accessible design.

According to Gay [5], one challenge in teaching accessibility is getting learners (i.e. web developers and web content creators) to apply what they learn in the future. One reason may be the lack of own experience with barriers that might otherwise trigger memories of lessons learned about accessibility. *Accessibility Maze* is created to teach learners the basics of web accessibility by experiential learning. The three main goals of the game are to create an effective introduction to the basics of accessibility and activities that confront players with barriers on the Internet, giving them experiences that they associate with frustration and emotion. It is also meant to be a challenging game that can be played with a screen reader. This allows players to have their own, perhaps frustrating, experience with a screen reader.

Games like these show learners that making web content accessible does not have to make websites "boring" (a common *web accessibility myth* among learners, as Ellcessor [4] argues in her analysis of web references from 1997 to 2012). Instead, these games are examples of how web accessibility cannot just foster cognitive learning outcomes about accessible web design, but also empathy and awareness.

In our efforts to build on these existing approaches, we combined the ideas of using learning labs, digital tools, and game-based approaches. In *Lola's first semester*, in Kletenik and Adler's impairment simulation game, and also in *Accessibility Maze*, the focus is on the playful experience of digital barriers combined with a content transfer on the topic of accessibility. The players are supposed to empathize with a person who, for example, cannot operate a website independently. The immersion might create an even stronger connection with the people, fostering empathy with and awareness of the topic. As a result, we built the immersive experience *Access to Escape*, which we present in the next section.

3 Access to Escape

We developed the VR Escape Room *Access to Escape* to provide a low-threshold introduction to the topic of accessibility through a supervised Game-Based Learning format. The development process has been accompanied by design-based research iterations through accessibility experts to constantly monitor the quality of the resulting game [11]. The learning outcomes primarily relate to affective objectives, as we want to create awareness of the problem of digital barriers. In addition, the learning outcomes also relate to cognitive objectives, as the Escape Room conveys knowledge related to the design and development of accessible digital resources. The Escape Room is implemented in a virtual environment to achieve an immersive experience. We used Unreal Engine provided by Epic Games and the Valve Index VR Headset, including controllers for the development process. The player interacts within the virtual environment through real movements and also by using two controllers that enable teleportation and the ability to change viewing angles.

The narrative of the game begins with the supervisors introducing the player to the story: they are a student experiencing their first day at university who needs to find the way to a certain lecture hall by using an elevator. After becoming familiar with the VR technology, the player uses the elevator to find the lecture hall. Instead of moving to the right floor, the elevator crashes and moves to the basement. The elevator display reveals that there is supposed to be a learning center on this floor. As the game progresses, it will turn out that this center has not been used for a long time. The player must solve all five puzzles to get the elevator back to working properly. Each puzzle is intended to draw attention to a certain barrier that people with disabilities face when using digital resources.

Puzzle 1. The first puzzle starts after the elevator crashed. While the player is still in the elevator, a security box opens and displays the four digits '0000'. Further, there are three slots and above them are three symbols representing different languages: French, English, and German. Initially, there is a card in the slot that represents the French language. The player has to discover the correct code to solve this puzzle. After pushing the elevator's emergency button, a French sounding announcement can be heard. When the card is exchanged from the French slot to the German slot, the assumed German player is able to understand the audio in German and acquires information about the needed code. As soon as the code is entered, the elevator doors open. The learning outcome of this puzzle is based on *WCAG-guideline 3.1.1 Language of Page*. This guideline demands the possibility to obtain information about the language within the program. Therefore, the first puzzle should sensitize the player to the barrier that occurs when a language is not set properly. This barrier arises in everyday life for people using a screen reader whenever the digital resource is provided without or with an unsuitable language tag. In this case, the audio is read out in a sound image of another language, making the audio incomprehensible.

Puzzle 2. After the player exits the elevator, they are in the foyer of the former computer science learning center. In addition to various items, there is an access card that can be used to open the room for the second puzzle. There are several blocks in this room that are labeled with different letters. Sitting on one block, the Guiding Character can be found. Also, a blurred image can be seen, which is projected onto the wall. On another wall, there is a hint saying *bei uns können Alle Leute Teilnehmen* (engl. everyone can participate with us). With the help of the Guiding Character, the player discovers that the capital letters correspond to the solution of the puzzle. When the correct blocks (A, L, T) are placed on the designated shelves, an alternative text appears on the monitor (see Fig. 1) and, in addition, the blurred image becomes clear. Both the alternative text on the monitor and the projector image provide information about the code required to open a door lock at the back of the room. After entering the code, which consists of three pictures of robotic animals, a cabinet opens that contains another access card. The idea of this puzzle is that the player experiences the barrier that arises when there is no alternative textual access for non-textual content. This need for alternative access is described in *WCAG-guideline 1.1.1 Non-text Content*. For instance, if an image does not have an alternative text specified, not everyone can absorb the information that the image conveys.

Fig. 1. The arrangement of the blocks is symbolic of the alternative text needed to make non-text information accessible.

Puzzle 3. Using the access card from the cabinet in Puzzle 2, the player can open the room of the third puzzle. This puzzle is intended to simulate a color vision deficiency (deuteranopia) through the usage of a color filter in the virtual environment. This causes the player to only see shades of blue and yellow colors, even though the room was previously colorful (see Fig. 3). There is a shelf that is designed to accommodate five blocks, where each shelf option is labeled with the name of a color. However, as mentioned, the player cannot see all colors. Coincidentally, each shelf option is labeled with a different pattern. Now, the player's task is to find a so-called color scanner to add a pattern to each desired block. As soon as these blocks are scanned with the color scanner, which can be attained from a coin-dozer-like machine, patterns appear on the initially blank blocks (see Fig. 2). The blocks can now be sorted appropriately according to the patterns. The learning outcome of this puzzle is to understand the content of the *WCAG-guideline 1.4.1 Use of Color*. This guideline states that color should not be the only way to convey important information as people with impairment of color perception cannot perceive this information. Here, a possible solution is to add patterns that represent the information.

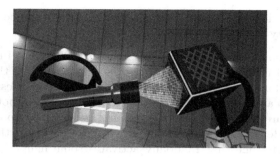

Fig. 2. The 'color scanner' enables patterns on the blocks so that relevant information is not only conveyed through color.

Fig. 3. In this puzzle, a color filter allows the player to experience the perception of a person with a color vision deficiency (left image: with color filter; right image: without color filter).

Puzzle 4. By solving Puzzle 3, the door opens to the room of the fourth puzzle. The player faces a giant chasm that must be crossed to reach the other end of the room. The Guiding Character communicates that it is 'fine to fly but poor to fall'. After getting the hint, the player moves to a magic carpet where they can choose between three buttons with the labels 'h3', 'h4', and 'h1'. Taking the hint into account, the correct button should be selected. If the player selects the wrong button, e.g. 'h4', the carpet flies forward a bit, then four levels down, and afterward back to the previous position. By choosing the right button, the carpet flies to the corresponding level and three new buttons appear. In this manner, the other end of the room can be reached. Alternatively, this puzzle can be solved in a game mode that does not involve changes in height dimension to avoid simulator sickness. After crossing the chasm using one of the described game modes, the player can find a portable truth table. Since a similar table is located in the foyer, the player should recognize it. The learning outcome of this puzzle is to deal with the content of *WCAG-guideline 1.3.1 Info and Relationships*. This guideline requires that the structure of digital content must be detectable within the used system. The correct order of heading hierarchies should be explained to the player. Only a properly ordered heading hierarchy allows screen reader users to navigate through a digital resource. Otherwise, the comprehensibility of the digital content is restricted.

Puzzle 5. As soon as the player touches the truth table from Puzzle 4, another door opens, and they can return to the foyer. In addition to the existing one, there is a space for the second truth table. This insertion creates an equation on the wall: A logical conjunction is created from the digits of both truth tables. Six lights that are next to the equation should be switched on or off according to the results. Below each light, there is one button to turn the light on, one to turn it off, and one that randomly activates some lights. The challenge is that the desired ON-button is tiny and, therefore, difficult to reach without inevitably touching the other two. However, the ability to switch the lights is blocked after a few failed attempts. The player must turn a switch in a security box that modifies the size of the ON-button. Now the puzzle can be easily solved according to the truth tables. After solving the puzzle, a button turns from red to green accompanied by an acoustic signal and textual information. Simultaneously, the elevator doors open and the player can finally go to the lecture hall. Based on the *WCAG-guideline 2.5.5 Target Size* the importance of appropriate sizes for interactive elements should be understood. It is necessary to comply with minimum sizes to ensure that people with motor disabilities can easily interact with the elements.

After the Escape Room is solved, the supervisors explain the connections between each puzzle and the real barriers. To provide basic knowledge of the topic of accessibility to a large number of people, it would be beneficial to embed the VR Escape Room in a programming course, for instance at a university. Thereby, many future developers and designers can be taught to create accessible digital resources.

4   Method

4.1   Sample

A sample of 11 people, 6 male and 5 female, evaluated the VR Escape Room by playing the single-player game. Only 2 of them had prior experience using VR. The participants were contacted through multiple (university) platforms. All participants have or had contact with programming in their studies, which included Computer Science, Business Administration, Mathematics, Bioinformatics, Biology, and Cognitive Science. The VR Escape Room was evaluated by 6 bachelor students ranging from studying in the third to eleventh semester, 2 masters students in their fifth semester, 2 persons having their master's degree, and 1 having their bachelor's degree. Due to the COVID-19 restrictions it was not appropriate to evaluate the VR Escape Room by a large number of participants. However, as a study of Virzi [21] shows, even a small number of about five participants is often sufficient to find 80% of the problems regarding the usability of an application.

4.2   Instruments

The evaluation of the implemented VR Escape Room was based on three instruments. First, the method of observation was used, which is a common data gathering practice in the field of social sciences. The following forms of observation were used in this evaluation study [9]: **Partially structured observation:** The observation did not follow a predefined structure, but rather focused on actions that seemed relevant. The observers recorded subjectively significant situations. However, a constantly controlled component is the time that was recorded for all participants per puzzle. **Active participatory observation:** The observers interacted with the participants during the observation process (e.g. by giving warnings about the real-life surroundings) and thus influenced their further actions. **Open observation:** The participants were aware of being observed while playing. **Unmediated observation:** The observers perceived information unmediated and recorded observations immediately. **Laboratory observation:** The observation took place in a controlled and artificial environment which was specially prepared for conducting the evaluation. The observation was conducted by two computer science students in their Master's program with teaching experience in Accessibility Education. Immediately after each VR session, the two independent and subjective observations were discussed and combined to form a more balanced view.

Second, the User Experience Questionnaire (UEQ) [15] was used which is a standardized questionnaire that was developed by usability experts and aims on measuring the quality of an interactive application. The UEQ allows the comparison of the quality of the own to other applications to gain insight into the average usability of the developed application. The rating of the UEQ is based upon the following 6 scales: 'Attractiveness', 'Perspicuity', 'Efficiency', 'Dependability', 'Stimulation', and 'Novelty'. These scales contain 26 items in total, each describing a criterion that the users can rate between -3 and 3.

Lastly, the Course Evaluation Questionnaire (CEQ) of the Goethe University was deployed, which is a tool that is already known by the participants. It is divided into three sections: 'General', 'Educational claim', and 'Learning format'. 15 of the 17 items are measured by using a 6-point Likert scale ranging from 1 (strongly agree) to 6 (strongly disagree). The two remaining items represent open-ended questions. The UEQ and the CEQ were created with the help of the survey and testing software EvaSys[3] which is used at the Goethe University for quality management, among other things [18].

4.3   Procedure

At the beginning of the learning session, the supervisors explain how to use the VR controllers. Following that, the rules such as the need to stand still during the upcoming elevator ride, are explained; the topic of the Escape Room and digital accessibility, is communicated; and open questions on the part of the learner are

---

[3] https://evasys.de/.

discussed. After the participant puts on the VR headset, they are introduced to the game by an introductory text and have the opportunity to get to know how the VR technology works in a training room. From this point on, the supervisors noted relevant observations. When the player is ready, they can start the actual game. At any time during the playing process, the player has the opportunity to ask the attendants for hints and feedback. Once the Escape Room is completed, the learner will be debriefed by the supervisors about the content of the course. In this dialogue, the experiences from the Escape Room are compared with the theoretical teaching content. Afterward, participants were asked to participate in an online survey on-site.

4.4   Results

Through the first instrument, the method of observation, some bugs but also some successful implementations could be determined. In the first puzzle, participants exhibited expected behaviors and responses. Inadvertently, two of the participants entered the correct code which is needed to solve the puzzle. After the participants entered another room, the Guiding Character occurs and utters an acoustic hint. This created irritation to some participants as the Guiding Character had no mouth movement. The second puzzle required three letters to be solved which were the capitalized letters in a hint. The first letter of the sentence was capitalized, too. Therefore, many participants mistakenly focused on this letter. The players responded well to the missing colors in the third puzzle: they realized that they needed another way to perceive the information. Especially in the fourth puzzle, the participants asked for more concrete hints. Due to multi-sensory feedback, the participants solved the fifth puzzle as expected. Based on the participants' statements, they lost their sense of time.

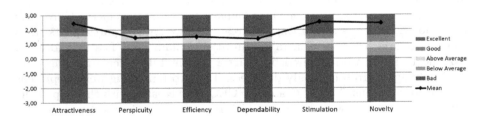

Fig. 4. UEQ Scale results of the VR Escape Room.

After the Escape Room was completed by the participants, they were asked to fill in the UEQ (Fig. 4). The first scale *Attractiveness* (M = 2.44; SD = 0.26) measures the overall impression concerning the Escape Room. Although all reviews were above average, it is noticeable that the items *attractive or unattractive*, as well as *pleasant or unpleasant*, got a slightly lower rating. One of the five puzzles includes a journey on a magic carpet where the height dimension is relevant.

In this scenario, as well as during the elevator ride, some participants reported an increase in negative sensations. The items of the second scale *Perspicuity* (M = 1.46; SD = 0.49) can be used to assess if it is easy to learn the initial usage of the Escape Room and to get familiar with it. This scale performed slightly worse, although still above average.

The scale *Efficiency* (M = 1.5; SD = 0.76) evaluates whether the users had to invest avoidable effort to complete their tasks. Compared to other scales that evaluated Escape Room, this scale was also rated slightly worse. There were different opinions with respect to the item *fast or slow* as well as the item *impractical or practical*. The focus of the scale *Dependability* (M = 1.36; SD = 0.84) is on whether participants feel in control of the interaction. This scale contains the worst-rated item of all items measured: *unpredictable or predictable*.

The scale *Stimulation* (M = 2.52; SD = 0.49) deals with the rating of positive tension and motivation caused by the application and represents the best-rated scale of the Escape Room.

The scale *Novelty* (M = 2.43; SD = 0.62) measures if the product is perceived as innovative and creative and if it arouses interest. The items on this scale received only positive reviews.

Table 1. CEQ: Mean values (1: strongly agree - 6: strongly disagree).

Category	Mean	Example (translated from German)
General	1.45	The completion of the Escape Room leads to a an increase in knowledge. (M = 1.5)
Educational Claim	1.5	The learning experience makes me see things differently and makes me recognize new connections. (M = 1.5)
Learning Format	1.32	I would be excited if such formats were be used more frequently in education. (M = 1.2)

The second questionnaire CEQ evaluates the suitability of the game for education (see Table 1). The first category *general* assesses the viewpoint of the participants regarding the learning experience. For example, they reported that the completion of the Escape Rooms leads to an increase in knowledge. Further, the participants reported that they received helpful feedback while playing the Escape Room and perceived an appreciative atmosphere. In the category *educational claim* the potential of stimulating internal processes like developing an own position through the learning experience is measured. Students reported discovering new connections and perspectives regarding accessibility. The last category *learning format* explores whether the implemented learning format is appropriate and convenient for education. Regarding that, the participants reported that they would be excited if similar learning formats were used more frequently in education. The VR technology but also the format of an Escape Room were perceived positively and activating. However, not all participants fully committed that the relevance of the treated topics became clear.

As mentioned, in the last two items of the CEQ, the participants could rate strengths and improvements regarding the Escape Room by answering open-ended questions.

Table 2. Evaluation of the open questions using the Qualitative Content Analysis according to Mayring [12].

Category (# mentions)	Examples (translated from German)
Sensitization (5)	'The format is innovative and creates attention for a topic that otherwise often seems out of reach for the uninvolved. The feeling of having a disadvantage in everyday life becomes practical'
Benefits of learning through gamification (5)	'The visualization supports learning. Game-based learning motivates and stimulates learning'
Novelty (5)	'Change from the usual learning format'
Simplified learning (3)	'One is encouraged to reflect, making it easier to learn new things (information about digital accessibility), the brain is receptive'
Appealing aesthetics (3)	'Pleasant visualization', 'visually appealing'
More sound (2)	'more soundeffects (the silence made it a tiny bit boring)'
More hints (2)	'A few more hints for playing because sometimes you can be a bit overwhelmed'
Single mentions	'The explanation received after the game should be integrated into the game', 'easy control', 'interactive',

A Qualitative Content Analysis by Mayring [12] was used to analyze the feedback of the open-ended CEQ items (see Table 2). Each written reply has been shortened to just content-bearing text modules. Subsequently, these modules were compared and categorized to filter out significant feedback. Table 2 shows an overview of the resulting categories. For example, these include 'Simplified learning'. That category describes the feedback regarding the aspects, that simplified the learning process. Mentions of this category included reports of encouragement and a more receptive brain. Another example is the category 'Novelty' where participants reported that they perceived the VR Escape Room as a learning experience that distinguishes itself from other learning formats.

5 Discussion and Limitations

Based on the initial evaluation, necessary improvements, as well as advantages of the learning format, could be identified. The results of the UEQ could show that the participants perceived the Escape Room as pleasant. Reported excitement and interest towards the game and the activation through the game are indicators for a positive attitude toward the presented learning format. This increase in motivation is underlined by the results of the CEQ, which show that the participants were motivated to try learning formats, including Escape Rooms and VR. Accordingly, the implemented learning format might have the potential to motivate learners in advance and further motivate them during the learning process. As the first category *general* of the CEQ suggests, the Escape Room also has the potential to communicate the learning content clearly and understandable. Based on the participants' statements gathered using the observation method, some participants lost their sense of time, which leads to the conclusion that they had an immersive experience. However, a positive learning experience does not necessarily correlate with a consistent learning outcome. Due to limited time resources, it was not possible to measure a long-term learning effect. Also, measuring the learning outcome would have required a prior assessment of the learners' knowledge, which could affect the learning effect as a test, at least implicitly, conveys knowledge. For instance, asking whether the participants know about a minimum button size already provides knowledge about this barrier.

Although the examination of prior knowledge and (long-term) learning outcomes clearly was a limitation, a different kind of learning outcome could be identified: the potential to invoke sensitization. The responses of the CEQ indicate that the participants might have gained a new awareness of barriers. In particular, the possibility to grasp otherwise unreachable experiences was mentioned. By that, a new perspective could be developed to be more sensitized to the challenges regarding (digital) accessibility. These kinds of experiences were possible through VR, as one of its advantages is the creation of immersive experiences. In future developments of *Access to Escape*, it could be interesting to add an avatar for the player to induce a sense of embodiment that might strengthen this potential for sensitization even more (i.e. through implicit learning, see [17]). To not disturb that immersive experience, the virtual game was separated from the following debriefing of the learning content. The positively received debriefing is necessary to connect experiences within the VR Escape Room to theoretical learning content, which makes it an essential part of the learning format. It should be considered to combine the playing and debriefing, e.g. by debriefing the player within the game by the Guiding Character. But even without the one-on-one debriefing, human supervisors would be needed as they are in charge of giving hints. Although this challenge could be overcome through good planning, e.g. by giving hints under certain conditions or on request, it should be noted that, as in a conventional escape room, players need individual hints. It is necessary to use nuances of expressions in order not to give away too much nor too little. Subsequently, a rather negatively rated item of the UEQ is 'unpragmatic or pragmatic'. Although the learning format tended to be assessed as 'pragmatic', in comparison to other items the assessment was negative. This scoring could be due to the use of VR. The majority of the players stated that they had no previous experience with VR. This makes the use of VR applications unfamiliar and thus more complex and unpragmatic. Also, VR in general could have been regarded as unpragmatic due to the complex hardware required. The item 'unpleasant or pleasant' has another comparatively negative rating. This can be traced back to the so-called simulator sickness which can occur with a VR experience and can lead to an unpleasant feeling. Even though this may not be completely avoidable, triggers can be decreased. Those triggers appear particularly in the journey on the magic carpet and during the elevator ride where the height dimension is relevant. An alternative way to solve the puzzle was already offered in the first implementation. However, not all triggers can be eliminated, as this would require a complete overhaul of the game story. But there are also easily implementable improvements such as time-independent hints, bug fixes, or more multisensory elements. Further, unlike justified negative ratings, there are also items of the UEQ that are rated negatively but do not necessarily need to be considered as negative. Examples are the items 'unpredictable or predictable' and 'complicated or easy'. As an Escape Room is based on certain difficulty and even confusion, a level of complexity and unpredictability is desired. Here, it is difficult to separate general user frustration from intended frustration which should support the sensitization.

11 people participated in this evaluation study, which was enough to get an insight into the advantages and disadvantages of the implemented learning format. But to gain a deeper understanding of the potential of a VR Escape Room as a teaching tool, including the measurement and comparison of learning outcomes, more participants would be required.

Summarizing, the learning format of *Access To Escape* has the potential to motivate learners and get their attention. It can communicate information in an interactive way that can awaken or even restrict the senses of the players. Like that, otherwise impossible experiences are made possible, which, for example, can be useful for raising awareness. But to have more input on the actual gain for education, actions like measuring learning outcomes and a broad evaluation with a focus on the use of VR should be conducted.

6   Conclusion

Our goal was to explore which aspects of user experience in a VR Escape Room could contribute to raising awareness and fostering learning about accessibility in Higher Education. The results of the evaluation study indicate that the implemented learning format has the potential to motivate the learners and sensitize them by offering a new perspective. However, the evaluation pointed out some necessary improvements: the development of a suitable method to measure the (long-term) learning outcome; the specification of future uses in education; and the revision of the implementation, for example, the minimization of simulator sickness triggers within the VR Escape Room.

This first proof-of-concept gives several implications for the successful learning process using immersive experiences for Accessibility Education in VR:

- *learning:* The qualitative evaluation of *Access to Escape* could provide first indicators that such immersive experiences might lead to learning outcomes not only in the cognitive but also in the affective domain. This compares well with the reported findings of similar studies targeting Accessibility Education through sensitization [8,14].

- *design:* The assessment via the UEQ gave insights into possible design patterns that can be used for Game-Based Learning settings in Accessibility Education. Similar to Thiel and Steed [19] who developed an accessibility metric for VR games consisting of Impulsiveness, Energy, Directness, Jerkiness, and Expansiveness, we observed differences in the players' experiences.
- *use:* The findings show that the game is not only attractive to users but also triggers positive stimulation and a novelty effect, presumably contributing to a positive perception of the learning context [13]. Doing so, these factors are of interest for learning in Higher Education. Especially, qualitative feedback indicated the benefits of the active use of immersive experiences for Accessibility Education in the classroom, such as simplification of the topic and possible gamification of a rather dry subject.

The findings of this paper and these implications are not surprising and align with existing research on non-immersive experiences, such as Kletenik and Adler's report on fostering not just motivation on learning about web accessibility through their game, but also inducing awareness among players [8]. We could provide first evidence that game-based immersive experiences are accepted as a tool for learning about accessibility in Higher Education settings.

For future iterations of this study, we plan to evaluate the implications gathered from the qualitative feedback in more depth. After the game is revised, a future study will investigate how existing sensitization, novelty, simplification, and aesthetics in the virtual environment contribute to the intended affective and cognitive learning outcomes.

References

1. Beach, C.S.U.L.: Program: Computer science, b.s. (2022). http://catalog.csulb.edu/preview_program.php?catoid=5&poid=1863. Accessed 23 Nov 2022
2. Benavídez, C., Fuertes, J.L., Gutiérrez, E., Martínez, L.: Teaching web accessibility with "Contramano" and Hera. In: Miesenberger, K., Klaus, J., Zagler, W.L., Karshmer, A.I. (eds.) ICCHP 2006. LNCS, vol. 4061, pp. 341–348. Springer, Heidelberg (2006). https://doi.org/10.1007/11788713_51
3. Berkley, U.: Computer science (2022). https://guide.berkeley.edu/undergraduate/degree-programs/computer-science/#planofstudybatext. Accessed 23 Nov 2022
4. Ellcessor, E.: <ALT="textbooks">: web accessibility myths as negotiated industrial lore. Crit. Stud. Media Commun. **31**(5), 448–463 (2014)
5. Gay, G.: Teaching accessibility awareness with games. In: Proceedings of the 18th International Web for All Conference, W4A 2021. Association for Computing Machinery, New York (2021)
6. Harper, K.A., DeWaters, J.: A quest for website accessibility in higher education institutions. Internet High. Educ. **11**(3–4), 160–164 (2008)
7. Kang, J., Chan, A.D.C., Trudel, C.M.J., Vukovic, B., Girouard, A.: Diversifying accessibility education: presenting and evaluating an interdisciplinary accessibility

training program. In: 21st Koli Calling International Conference on Computing Education Research. Association for Computing Machinery, New York (2021)

8. Kletenik, D., Adler, R.F.: Let's play: increasing accessibility awareness and empathy through games. In: Proceedings of the 53rd ACM Technical Symposium on Computer Science Education, SIGCSE 2022, vol. 1, pp. 182–188. Association for Computing Machinery, New York (2022)

9. Kochinka, A.: Beobachtung. In: Mey, G., Mruck, K. (eds.) Handbuch Qualitative Forschung in der Psychologie, pp. 449–461. Springer, Cham (2010). https://doi.org/10.1007/978-3-531-92052-8_32

10. Lewthwaite, S., Sloan, D.: Exploring pedagogical culture for accessibility education in computing science. In: Proceedings of the 13th International Web for All Conference, pp. 1–4 (2016)

11. Mateen, S., Wiesemüller, P., Voß-Nakkour, S.: Design of an Accessible VR-Escape Room for Accessibility Education. Smart Accessibility (2023, in press)

12. Mayring, P.: Qualitative Inhaltsanalyse, vol. 14, chap. 4. UVK Univ.-Verl. Konstanz (1994)

13. Price, L.: Modelling factors for predicting student learning outcomes in higher education. In: Learning Patterns in Higher Education, pp. 72–93. Routledge (2013)

14. Rustemeier, L., Voß-Nakkour, S., Mateen, S., Hossain, I.: Creation and future development process of a serious game: raising awareness of (visual) impairments. In: Fletcher, B., Ma, M., Göbel, S., Baalsrud Hauge, J., Marsh, T. (eds.) JCSG 2021. LNCS, vol. 12945, pp. 131–137. Springer, Cham (2021). https://doi.org/10.1007/978-3-030-88272-3_10

15. Schrepp, M.: User experience questionnaire handbook. All you need to know to apply the UEQ successfully in your project (2015)

16. Shi, W., Khan, S., El-Glaly, Y., Malachowsky, S., Yu, Q., Krutz, D.E.: Experiential learning in computing accessibility education. In: Proceedings of the ACM/IEEE 42nd International Conference on Software Engineering: Companion Proceeding, ICSE 2020, pp. 250–251. Association for Computing Machinery, New York (2020)

17. Slater, M.: Implicit learning through embodiment in immersive virtual reality. In: Liu, D., Dede, C., Huang, R., Richards, J. (eds.) Virtual, Augmented, and Mixed Realities in Education. SCI, pp. 19–33. Springer, Singapore (2017). https://doi.org/10.1007/978-981-10-5490-7_2

18. studiumdigitale: Qualitätsentwicklung durch Evaluation (2022). https://www.studiumdigitale.uni-frankfurt.de/58533111/Evaluation. Accessed 23 Nov 2022

19. Thiel, F.J., Steed, A.: Developing an accessibility metric for VR games based on motion data captured under game conditions. Front. Virtual Reality 3 (2022)

20. University, C.S.: Computer science, b.s. (2022). Accessed 23 Nov 2022

21. Virzi, R.A.: Refining the test phase of usability evaluation: how many subjects is enough? Hum. Factors 34(4), 457–468 (1992)

Introducing a New Technology Quality Indicator for Intervention Design in Special Education

Georgia Iatraki$^{(\boxtimes)}$ ⓘD and Tassos A. Mikropoulos ⓘD

University of Ioannina, 45110 Ioannina, Greece
g.iatraki@uoi.gr

Abstract. There's significant value in following a systematic methodology in educational research, not only to gain valid and reliable empirical data, but also to determine which interventions meet quality indicators and consistently generate expected results. Looking at Special Education, and in line with the necessity for methodological rigor, specific quality indicators to ensure evidence in educational empirical study designs have been developed. In this sense, digital technologies, and recently, immersive technologies are increasingly being used in educational interventions due to the positive learning outcomes seen in cognitive, affective, and psychomotor domains. Nevertheless, the affordances of the technology used in such interventions are hardly considered indicating a research gap worth investigating further. Single subject design seems to support effective instructional interventions because of the unique characteristics of every student with a specific disability. This work introduces Augmented Reality, among other quality indicators, to measure the extent of which the structure of matter is understood by students with Intellectual Disabilities. The empirical study set forth in this paper satisfactorily met all existing quality indicators, in addition to the newly introduced AR technology indicator. Findings showed that the research design of the enriched set of quality indicators increased student motivation and their understanding of abstract Physics concepts. The students with ID acquired targeted physics concepts, as well as inquiry skills thanks to their involvement in a vivid experience. These results point to the contribution of AR technology through its affordances as a new quality indicator among the existing set.

Keywords: Augmented Reality · Intellectual Disabilities · Single Subject Design · Evidence-based Practices · Structure of Matter

1 Introduction

A foundational concept in educational research is the design and methodology applied to empirical studies in both general and special education. However, when Seidel and colleagues [1] set out to measure teaching effectiveness, as evaluated in studies published from 1995 to 2004, they identified several methodological issues. More specifically, the research team looked at specific learning activities delivered according to several research designs, as well as validation and reliability measures of instructional characteristics (components of teaching and their effects on learning). The researchers' meta-analytic

M.-L. Bourguet et al. (Eds.): iLRN 2023, CCIS 1904, pp. 289–299, 2024.
https://doi.org/10.1007/978-3-031-47328-9_22

findings associated teaching components with the largest effect sizes encountered in experimental designs.

In the last 20 years, research in special education has focused on designs that ensure rigor in methodology and practice. One such prominent research design used in special education is the single subject design (single-case or n = 1), i.e., an experimental design identified as rigorous in evidence-based practice [2, 3]. In turn, an evidence-based practice teaches a targeted skill shown to be effective following high-quality research designs [4]. To this end, the single subject design uses a methodology that supports effective instructional practices by using a small number of participants, systematic observation, the manipulation of variables, repeated measurements, and data analysis [2]. The aim of the single subject design is to assess causal relations between one or more independent variables that are systematically manipulated under the experimenter's control and one or more dependent variables that measure performance at many different timepoints comparing changes over time [2]. Its main advantage is the rigorous objective experimental assessment of the effectiveness of a one-to-one intervention that focuses on the individual (i.e., student) [2, 3].

Overall seeking evidence-based practices reflects a necessity for the conceptualization of scientific research in special education and recommended standards exist that define high quality research [4–6]. Consequently, a group of experts of the Council for Exceptional Children's Division for Research developed targeted standards/guidelines to categorize the complexity of conducting research in special education. These standards are relevant to different research questions using different research methodologies to evaluate the effect of an operationally defined intervention on students' outcomes [6]. The standards for each research design (i.e., group, case study, and single subject) comprise a detailed and comprehensive description of participants and settings, dependent and independent variables, baseline, experimental control/internal validity, external validity, and social validity [7–10]. Moreover, more current scientific reviews seek to include high-quality studies that account for the heterogeneity per disability, special education settings, different types of research designs, and the context of professionals or nonprofessionals involved [11]. To determine methodological soundness, Knight and colleagues [12] conducted a visual analysis of 15 studies published between 2009 and 2018 on teaching science to students with Intellectual Disabilities (ID). The authors then went one step further and identified the evidence on teaching science practices that also contribute to positive learning outcomes. Supplementary teaching techniques (i.e., multiple exemplar training, task analysis and time delay) were shown as effective in teaching academic skills through single subject designs. Such adaptations in instructional procedures help students with ID meet their individualized needs and overcome certain limitations in mental processes and better perform on grade-aligned content.

Another factor that further strengthens a high-quality study is digital technology as it enables the predictors of positive learning outcomes in the cognitive, affective, and psychomotor domains of students with ID [13–17]. The integration of digital technology in science education in particular helps students with ID enhance understanding and gain science literacy, as well as remain highly engaged during the teaching process [18]. More recently, immersive technologies, such as Augmented Reality (AR), provide learning environments that grant further promise for the equitable access of students with ID to advanced educational opportunities through engagement, enthusiasm, motivation, and positive outcomes in science teaching [19].

Nevertheless, and despite the use of robust methodologies in special education research, the appropriate use of technological affordances, is hardly considered. In other words, there appears to be a research gap in documenting the role of technology in empirical educational studies and teaching interventions. Gersten and Edyburn [20] introduced a set of 30 quality indicators when incorporating digital technology to establish evidence of instructional design in special education.

A recent review by Carreon and colleagues [21] indicated the necessity of affordances in Virtual Reality (VR) interventions in an academic setting for students with disabilities. Considering AR technology, the review of Köse and colleagues [22] investigated the "properties" of AR on the development of immersive environments in 19 studies published between 2013 and 2019. The sense of immediacy, presence, and deepening were included among technological affordances which supported the design of efficient educational environments and provided elements of user-medium interaction.

Mikropoulos and Iatraki [23] conducted a review that included 21 empirical studies between 2013 and 2021 and highlighted increased student motivation when using digital technology in special education science teaching. The researchers listed the affordances of each technological implementation, but with an emphasis on AR technology, as an additional quality indicator for evidence-based practice in special education. Specifically, AR's affordances, namely immersion/contextuality, real time interaction, first order experiences, spatial size, reification, and presence serve as a strong argument to establish AR as a recognized quality indicator.

Moreover, to support the design of evidence-based interventions for students with ID, Delimitros and colleagues [24] combined the technological and learning affordances of immersive technologies together with the Universal Design for Learning principles. The analysis of the above dimensions resulted in the construction of the Model for the design of Immersive Learning Enactments for Students with Intellectual Disabilities (MILES-ID). The MILES-ID was then applied to a systematic review between 2013 and 2021 and highlighted the positive impact of immersive educational interventions on the performance of students with ID.

The purpose of this work is to provide a basic understanding of applied guidelines which improve evidence-based teaching practices in science by adding the quality indicator of digital technology to the existing quality indicators of Horner and colleagues [2]. The axes of this research work consist of: a) the summary of standards of rigor and the recommended quality indicators for best evidence practices regarding designing, conducting, and communicating high quality single subject research and b) the description of a step-by-step single subject study that integrates AR technology in an inquiry-based physics intervention administered to three students with ID. The structure of matter was chosen as the subject area to seek evidence on the effectiveness of this research design and methodology.

2   Method

A single subject design (AB quasi-experimental), which involves repeated measurements of intervention condition data, was used for the purpose of this study. Phase A includes the baseline conditions where the intervention is absent, while phase B introduces the intervention to investigate any changes to the intervention condition data. The following sections describe the application of existing and new quality indicators based on Horner's and colleagues [2] recommendations for providing quality science instruction to students with ID. The research question this study attempts to answer is two-fold:

- How does this empirical study of an AR inquiry-based physics intervention measure the seven quality indicators?
- How do we define the AR quality indicator of technology?

  Subsequent paragraphs, however, are indented.

2.1   Description of Participants and Settings

The first quality indicator includes the detailed description of the participants, setting, and selection process that would allow other researchers to replicate the process in a step-by-step fashion [2].

According to our AR-based single subject design, the inclusion criteria of the participants were as follows: three students with mild ID (a) attending a special vocational high school, (b) with a diagnosis of ID, (c) no physical disability that could affect the performance of the activity, (d) adequate visual and auditory discrimination skills, (e) could respond verbally, and (f) demonstrate basic reading and writing skills. The three students (two males and one female, age range: 15–17 years old), for whom parental permission was obtained (pseudonyms were used), experienced reading comprehension difficulties. Their demographic data which included students' individualized characteristics in academic (barriers in concentration, memory deficits, problem solving difficulties), communicative, and social (limited communication with peers) aptitude, as well as in practical domains, could be listed in detail.

Regarding the study's context, Horner et al. [2] recommend a detailed description of the probes used to allow other researchers to replicate its conditions. Our study was conducted in two different rooms located within the grounds of the participants' school. The first room hosted the baseline intervention and included two student desks, one teacher desk, a large whiteboard, and a table with wheels. The main intervention, maintenance and generalization study phases were conducted in a separate room. The students received one-to-one instruction based on standard special education practices. Additionally, two observers (i.e., members of the school's interdisciplinary team) helped the students become acquainted with the procedure and collected reliability and validity data across conditions.

2.2 Dependent Variable

The second quality indicator is operational precision as well as quantification, to generate valid measurements and ensure their replication over time. Regarding the reliability of data collection, Interobserver Agreement (IOA) through a second person was necessary [2].

Specifically, this study measured the number of correct responses on the physics probe as well as the inquiry skills students may have developed. There were seven questions per session on the microscopic level of water states. The students followed verbal guidelines, completed the activity while wearing a pair of AR glasses and answered the application questions. Their responses were recorded on data sheets during the probe sessions. Correct responses given in the probe session assessment were plotted on a graph (Fig. 3).

In addition, IOA data were collected across all conditions (five sessions at T baseline and three sessions during the intervention) by a second observer. Agreement was established when both the researcher and the observer recorded the same response. Moreover, the two parties coded and evaluated students' responses. IOA was determined by dividing the consensus count by the total number of the consensus plus non-consensus count and multiplying by 100. The IOA was 100% for all students.

2.3 Independent Variable

The third quality indicator concerns the independent variable that must be described with replicable precision and systematically manipulated under the control of the experimenter [2]. In our study, the independent variable was an AR inquiry-based intervention. The students with ID wore AR glasses and observed the water molecules in a glass beaker per state.

The description of the process and duration of each session depended on the individualized profile of each student. The main instruction included the phases of an inquiry approach, and supplemental techniques, such as task analysis (breaking down the task into steps), prompting (verbal praise) and time delay (simplified vocabulary and repetition of the physics terms), based on students' individualized needs. The structured inquiry approach included the phases of orientation, conceptualization, investigation, conclusion, and discussion – applying new knowledge and skills which were described sufficiently to allow future researchers to replicate the process [25, 26]. To facilitate students in inquiry skills training, such as making observations, asking questions, searching, evaluating information and communicating conclusions, the researchers made certain adaptations to the procedures [26]. The learning outcomes of students were plotted on individualized graphs that presented the variable's changes over time (Fig. 3).

2.4 Baseline

The fourth quality indicator is the baseline phase of the intervention. The baseline provides repeated measurements of a dependent variable and establishes a pattern of responding that can be used to predict the pattern of future performance, assuming the introduction or manipulation of the independent variable had not occurred. Baseline conditions are described with replicable precision to allow others to follow specific steps to acquire these outcomes [2]. Our study provided descriptions of the 13 sessions, divided and delivered in five sets. Two sessions presented daily materials to students to engage them at a macroscopic level. Three sets of sessions followed (one per microscopic water state) which consisted of three sub-sessions each (description of the molecules, position, and velocity). All sets used a Digital Learning Object (Fig. 1). The final two sessions included a comparison assessment of the three states. Each session lasted 10–15 min depending on the student's profile.

Fig. 1. A screenshot of the baseline conditions.

2.5   Experimental Control/Internal Validity

The fifth quality indicator involves the design which should provide at least three demonstrations of the experimental effect at three different points in time [27]. The results document a pattern that demonstrates experimental control. We designed the baseline phase to provide 13 demonstrations of experimental effect at 13 different points in time (Fig. 3) to increase confidence that there is evidence of a functional relationship between the intervention and the outcome [3, 10].

2.6   External Validity

Experimental effects replicated across participants, settings, or materials establish this next quality indicator; external validity [2]. The activity lasted 8–10 min, where each student could see a real glass beaker through the AR glasses that contained virtual molecules moving in different positions (Fig. 2). The participants could move freely around the augmented world and observe the virtual or real objects.

Fig. 2. A participant during the AR-based intervention.

2.7 Social Validity

Four criteria identify social validity. Social importance relates to the dependent variable and the magnitude of change in the specific variable that results from the intervention. Social validity is enhanced as the independent variable is implemented over extended time periods, by common intervention agents, in common physical and social contexts [2].

To collect feedback on students' experience, a 3-point Likert-type scale questionnaire devised based on the Learning Object Evaluation Survey for Students (LOES-S) tool [28] was administered, with learning, quality, engagement, and presence as key factors. Moreover, the questions were verbally adapted by the researcher to facilitate students' understanding and reduce barriers in the reading process.

2.8 Technology

Our empirical study used the AR technological affordances of immersion/contextuality, real time interaction, first order experiences, spatial size, reification, and presence. These affordances emerged from the macroscopic consideration of the real world augmented by the microcosmic consideration of the digital world, experienced through the Magic Leap OneTM device. The students with ID had this experience in the real world, rather than in an all-digital virtual environment.

Via the see-through AR glasses, each student had a first-person point of view and lived relevant experiences of the real world (the classroom and its real objects), augmented with the virtual objects (virtual water molecules in three states). The students in turn immerse themselves into the microcosm and feel present among the water molecules. The affordances of intuitive and real time interaction were met too, as each student tried to touch the molecules or remove the cap of the beaker in a gas state all the while observing the molecules being released. The affordances of size in space and time, transduction and reification were equally applied through the visualization of the molecules. During the experiment each student with ID could see the virtual molecules in the glass beaker and remain on task with regards to the microscopic structure of matter. These elements contribute to minimizing discrimination difficulties regarding the shape, size, and color of the virtual molecules. In addition, the students could enhance their autonomy and navigation skills using the AR device.

3   Results and Discussion

The results of the AR intervention are presented in line with the quality indicators of the single subject design. The learning outcomes of the dependent variable of the intervention were analyzed visually (Table 1) and graphed (Fig. 3).

a. The three students saw their number of correct responses on the physics probe trials increase from baseline to intervention and a functional relation between dependent and independent variables proved to be robust. The features evaluated through outcome changes following the AB design were level, trend, variability, overlap, immediacy of effect, and consistency of data patterns across similar conditions [2, 3, 10]. b. Overall, students' performance during the intervention was higher than at baseline, indicating changes in performance and stability after the intervention was introduced (Table 1). Each participant's performance is described with sufficient detail - and more generally, as low (baseline) and high or stable (intervention). c. In addition, the range of correct responses at the baseline and intervention sessions is reported, as well as the mean and standard deviation (SD). d. The immediacy of effect when the intervention was introduced, and the correct responses increased abruptly by changing level. During the intervention, the three students experienced an immediacy of effect and showed an important increase in correct responses. e. To determine the effectiveness of each student's academic performance between the baseline and intervention phases we calculated effect size of the Percentage of Nonoverlapping Data (PND), which was 100% for this study [29, 30].

Table 1. Effectiveness Data.

Student	Baseline			
	Mean ± SD	Range	Visual Analysis	
John	3.3 ± 0.8	2–5	low level, stable trend, slight variability	
Manos	2.4 ± 1.4	0–4	low level, variable, unstable trend	
Helen	2.2 ± 1.1	1–4	low level, variable, unstable trend	
	Intervention			
	Mean ± SD	Range	Visual Analysis	PND
John	6.8 ± 0.4	6–7	immediate change, stable trend	100
Manos	6.2 ± 0.7	5–7	immediate change, stable trend	100
Helen	6.8 ± 0.4	6–7	immediate change, stable trend	100

The six sessions of the AR intervention (sessions 14–20) met the criterion of the experimental control as the design documented at least three demonstrations of the experimental effect at three different points in time with a single participant [2]. The changes (and/or variability) were immediate, readily discernible, and maintained (sessions between 16–24) over time (Fig. 3). The three students acquired four or five inquiry skills in the generalization probes (sessions 22, 23). Acquired skills included "asking questions", "planning and carrying out investigations", "analyzing and interpreting data", "constructing explanations" and "obtaining, evaluating and communicating information".

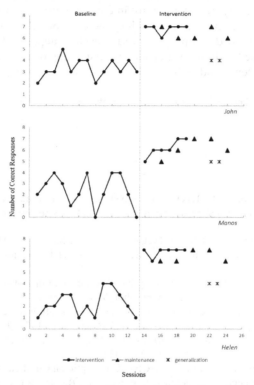

Fig. 3. Number of correct responses for the students. Baseline: 0–13, intervention: 14–20, maintenance: 16–24, generalization: 22–23.

The outcomes for social validity, as per it four criteria, are described in the methods section. The three students strongly agreed that they enjoyed the AR experience and reported that the glasses were easy to use and helped them engage and learn. In addition, they reported that the molecules were located at the same place, highlighting a high sense of presence. They also felt satisfaction in learning physics with the glasses and they reported wanting to use them in other subjects.

The use of AR technology helped the students with ID to remain on task indicating increased interest and motivation [31]. The dynamic three-dimensional representations in the AR application helped the students observe and describe the abstract concepts of water molecules reducing their discrimination barriers.

4 Conclusions

This study suggests an extended set of quality indicators to researchers and professionals when designing evidence-based experiments in special education. All existing quality indicators (a. description of participants and setting, b. dependent variable, c. independent variable, d. baseline, e. experimental control/internal validity, f. external validity, g. social validity) together with the proposed technology indicator of AR and its affordances were met in this work therefore developing a powerful teaching approach for students with ID. The students enhanced their motivation and understanding of abstract physics concepts acquiring new knowledge and skills.

Acknowledgements. The authors would like to thank the students for their participation in the study.

References

1. Seidel, T., Shavelson, R.J.: Teaching effectiveness research in the past decade: the role of theory and research design in disentangling meta-analysis results. Rev. Educ. Res. **77**(4), 454–499 (2007)
2. Horner, R.H., Carr, E.G., Halle, J., McGee, G., Odom, S., Wolery, M.: The use of single-subject research to identify evidence-based practice in special education. Except. Child. **71**(2), 165–179 (2005)
3. Kratochwill, T.R., Levin, J.R.: Enhancing the scientific credibility of single-case intervention research: randomization to the rescue. Psychol. Methods **15**(2), 124–144 (2010)
4. Cook, B.G., Cook, L.: Research designs and special education research: different designs address different questions. Learn. Disabil. Res. Pract. **31**(4), 190–198 (2016)
5. Cook, B.G., Love, H.R., Cook, L.: Mixed-methods approaches in special education research. Learn. Disabil. Res. Pract. **37**(4), 314–323 (2022)
6. Council for Exceptional Children. TEACHING Exceptional Children **46**(6), 206–212 (2014)
7. Brantlinger, E., Jimenez, R., Klingner, J., Pugach, M., Richardson, V.: Qualitative studies in special education. Except. Child. **71**(2), 195–207 (2005)
8. Gersten, R., Fuchs, L.S., Compton, D., Coyne, M., Greenwood, C., Innocenti, M.S.: Quality indicators for group experimental and quasi-experimental research in special education. Except. Child. **71**(2), 149–164 (2005)
9. Odom, S.L., Brantlinger, E., Gersten, R., Horner, R.H., Thompson, B., Harris, K.R.: Research in special education: scientific methods and evidence-based practices. Except. Child. **71**(2), 137–148 (2005)
10. Kratochwill, T.R., et al.: Single-case intervention research design standards. Remed. Spec. Educ. **34**(1), 26–38 (2012)
11. Talbott, E., Maggin, D.M., Van Acker, E.Y., Kumm, S.: Quality indicators for reviews of research in special education. Exceptionality **26**(4), 245–265 (2017)
12. Knight, V.F., Wood, L., McKissick, B.R., Kuntz, E.M.: Teaching science content and practices to students with intellectual disability and autism. Remed. Spec. Educa. **41**(6), 327–340 (2019)
13. Baragash, R.S., Al-Samarraie, H., Alzahrani, A.I., Alfarraj, O.: Augmented reality in special education: a meta-analysis of single-subject design studies. Eur. J. Spec. Needs Educ. **35**(3), 382–397 (2019)

14. Fernández-Batanero, J.M., Montenegro-Rueda, M., Fernández-Cerero, J.: Use of augmented reality for students with educational needs: a systematic review (2016–2021). Societies **12**(2), 36 (2022)

15. Kang, Y.S., Chang, Y.J.: Using an augmented reality game to teach three junior high school students with intellectual disabilities to improve ATM use. J. Appl. Res. Intellect. Disabil. **33**(3), 409–419 (2019)

16. Montoya-Rodríguez, M.M., et al.: Virtual reality and augmented reality as strategies for teaching social skills to individuals with intellectual disability: a systematic review. J. Intellect. Disabil. (2022)

17. Yenioglu, B.Y., Ergulec, F., Yenioglu, S.: Augmented reality for learning in special education: a systematic literature review. Interact. Learn. Environ. 1–17 (2021)

18. Mallidis-Malessas, P., Iatraki, G., Mikropoulos, T.A.: Teaching physics to students with intellectual disabilities using digital learning objects. J. Spec. Educ. Technol. **37**(4), 510–522 (2021)

19. McMahon, D.D., Cihak, D.F., Wright, R.E., Bell, S.M.: Augmented reality for teaching science vocabulary to postsecondary education students with intellectual disabilities and autism. J. Res. Technol. Educ. **48**(1), 38–56 (2015)

20. Gersten, R., Edyburn, D.: Defining quality indicators for special education technology research. J. Spec. Educ. Technol. **22**(3), 3–18 (2005)

21. Carreon, A., Smith, S.J., Mosher, M., Rao, K., Rowland, A.: A review of virtual reality intervention research for students with disabilities in K–12 settings. J. Spec. Educ. Technol. **37**(1), 82–99 (2020)

22. Köse, H., Güner-Yildiz, N.: Augmented reality (AR) as a learning material in special needs education. Educ. Inf. Technol. **26**, 1921–1936 (2021)

23. Mikropoulos, T.A., Iatraki, G.: Digital technology supports science education for students with disabilities: a systematic review. Educ. Inf. Technol. **28**, 3911–3935 (2022)

24. Delimitros, M., Stergiouli, A., Iatraki, G., Koutromanos, G., Mikropoulos, T.A.: A model for the design of immersive learning enactments for students with intellectual disabilities. In: Conference on Software Development and Technologies for Enhancing Accessibility and Fighting Info-Exclusion. ACM (2022)

25. McDermott, L.C., Shaffer, P.S., Constantinou, C.P.: Preparing teachers to teach physics and physical science by inquiry. Phys. Educ. **35**(6), 411–416 (2000)

26. Pedaste, M., et al.: Phases of inquiry-based learning: definitions and the inquiry cycle. Educ. Res. Rev. **14**, 47–61 (2015)

27. Horner, R.H., Swaminathan, H., Sugai, G., Smolkowski, K.: Considerations for the systematic analysis and use of single-case research. Educ. Treat. Child. **35**(2), 269–290 (2012)

28. Kay, R., Knaack, L.: Developing learning objects for secondary school students: a multi-component model. Interdisc. J. e-Skills Lifelong Learn. **1**, 229–254 (2005)

29. Scruggs, T.E., Mastropieri, M.A., Casto, G.: The Quantitative synthesis of single-subject research: methodology and validation. Rase **8**(2), 24–33 (1987)

30. Scruggs, T.E., Mastropieri, M.A.: How to summarize single-participant research: ideas and applications. Exceptionality **9**, 227–244 (2001)

31. Cheng, S.-C., Lai, C.-L.: Facilitating learning for students with special needs: a review of technology-supported special education studies. J. Comput. Educ. **7**(2), 131–153 (2019)

A Multimodal Document Viewer in Fully Immersive Virtual Reality

Rogelio Romero⬥ and Hubert Cecotti$^{(\boxtimes)}$⬥

Dept. of Computer Science, California State University, Fresno, CA, USA
hcecotti@csufresno.edu

Abstract. Immersive learning using fully immersive virtual reality (VR) is typically utilized to present 3D objects that cannot be represented easily on a computer screen. In the last few decades, the use of e-books to visualize documents has become prevalent. However, transferring an original document designed to be printed requires extraction of the document's logical structure. The document must be broken down into fragments of text and images with the extraction of its logical structure. The fragments are then recomposed together to be presented as an e-book. In this paper, we propose a novel paradigm where documents can be presented in their original form without the need to be physically restructured, thanks to VR. With a VR headset, the proposed document visualizer allows users to access, display, and annotate documents. Such a system is particularly relevant for students and scholars in the humanities who investigate ancient documents where the distinct elements composing the document are intertwined. Furthermore, VR technology enhances the accessibility and equity of learning by offering various input modalities.

Keywords: Virtual reality · Document reader · Immersive learning

1 Introduction

It is critical that learning and teaching are as inclusive and accessible as possible [13]. On the one hand, virtual reality (VR) technology brings some obstacles in relation to its cost and the required facilities to be used in the classroom. On the other hand, VR can substantially enhance the accessibility of learning materials and provide ease of use in the classroom. An argument can be made that students cannot physically see and manipulate learning materials presented as 3D objects. Through VR, the same learning materials can now be available to people with disabilities. Immersive learning can enhance electronic learning technology and promote the inclusion of students with various disabilities in education [1].

VR has a clear impact on the improvement of education, as it has been shown that VR classrooms can bring better learning motivation, learning outcomes, and positive impacts on students' achievement scores [10]. Immersive learning can happen in fully immersive virtual reality environments at different educational

M.-L. Bourguet et al. (Eds.): iLRN 2023, CCIS 1904, pp. 300–310, 2024.
https://doi.org/10.1007/978-3-031-47328-9_23

levels. For example, undergraduate classes in various areas of study (e.g., kinesiology, dance, literature, and art history) [5] can utilize VR to improve the learning process.

Immersive learning in VR provides several advantages over traditional learning approaches. Immersive learning can increase student engagement with the material by creating an interactive 3D environment. VR for learning can enhance comprehension, helping students to better understand complex concepts and ideas. Through visual aids and interactive exercises, immersive learning results in students gaining a more nuanced understanding of the subject matter. VR can also increase the student motivation to learn by providing a more engaging and enjoyable experience. According to Krokos et al. [8], using a VR head-mounted display (HMD) can lead to a statistically significant improvement in recall accuracy compared to a desktop. Immersive learning can increase activity in the parietal cortex of the brain [14], the area of the brain responsible for spatial processing.

Consumer-grade VR technology advancements have made the technology more accessible and affordable for students to use for learning purposes. Students can now access various learning activities in a VR environment, requiring students to interact with learning materials. Virtual representations of classrooms can be presented as 3D objects in VR as they would be presented in the real world. However, it is also crucial to present more basic learning content in the VR world, such as books and documents. Indeed, documents are the most used learning materials. While electronic documents are now prevalent, books use bookbinding, which creates books as 3D objects. Thanks to VR, artifacts can be presented in their actual size and shape, enhancing connections with the real world.

In the past decades, ancient documents have been digitized using optical character recognition and document analysis techniques so that such documents can be displayed on different devices of various sizes (computer screens, tablets, ...) and provide additional abilities (index, search, ...) [12]. Ancient documents often merge textual content with images, where the entire document page can be considered artwork. They include information extracted from the page, such as the text, the style associated with the text, and the surrounding images. Documents such as maps that are usually large and cannot be fully displayed on a computer screen strongly benefit from a presentation in a VR environment.

Document Analysis and Recognition (DAR) aims to extract information presented on paper, initially addressed for human comprehension, automatically. The desired output of DAR systems is usually in a suitable symbolic representation that can subsequently be processed by computers [11]. An abstract document model mediates between the message of a text and its physical presentation. Nevertheless, it is possible for the logical and physical structures to be linked. For scholars in the humanities, this step may destroy important information about documents of historical and contextual significance. As a result, researchers in both the humanities and DAR often need domain expertise to assess the performance of algorithms that segment a document properly. VR helps to circumvent DAR issues, as the document can be presented in its original form, without the need to separate the text from the physical structure of the page. In particular, documents with complex structures, such as maps and manuscripts, benefit from VR, as the presentation in VR can remain faithful to the document's original presentation.

The use of e-book readers has become widely popular among college students [4]. Typically, an original document is converted into an electronic format to be presented on such devices. However, such a process often involves changing particular design and formatting elements, resulting in a reduction or even suppression of some of the characteristics of the original document, which was designed as a combination of textual and graphical elements to be presented in a particular format. It is vital for scholars in the humanities who want to study documents in their earlier editions to have access to a system that can accurately recreate real-world representations of the documents. Many historical documents have been converted to a digital format through collections of images (.jpg, .png). While books could be displayed using a traditional document reader in this format, it does not accurately portray the document's physical characteristics. It can be the case for ancient documents such as the Bible, that differences in versions can carry historical and theological significance. Many versions of the Bible exist, translated into various languages at different eras in time. Some versions of the Bible, such as the Gutenberg Bible, contain certain aesthetic elements such as illuminated manuscripts, intricate calligraphy, and unique formatting. These elements cannot be fully represented in a static image format. These elements can be displayed in VR through post-processing effects. The size of the Gutenberg bible is also of importance, as the size of the paper that it was printed on provides insight into fifteenth-century printing practices. By presenting such documents in their original form, a greater understanding of the historical context of the cultural, social, and political landscape of the historical period can be gained.

In this paper, we propose a VR-based system that includes an interface for presenting and browsing documents with multiple pages, such as books, by presenting documents in their original size. A key feature of the system is the multimodal input aspect, where it is possible to access different commands through different types of inputs [15]. As learning must be fully inclusive, VR not only adds immersive components to a system by looking at objects as if they are real with a VR headset but also brings novel ways to interact with the environment with the VR controllers. VR technology transcends beyond visual features. Instead of using a keyboard and a mouse with a laptop or desktop or touch controls with a tablet or phone, VR technology brings hand controllers that can be used in different ways. Both the hands and the head can be used as means to point at objects in a virtual world through laser pointers. Selecting an element can be accomplished via a trigger, a button press, or a dwell time, as is the case with eye-trackers. These types of controls are the current ways to interact within a VR environment. They are more inclusive, as people with severe disabilities can utilize the head pointer, i.e., anybody that can move their neck. Multimodal interaction provides many benefits over classical unimodal approaches such as WIMP (Windows, Icons, Menus, Point and Click) interfaces [6]. The remainder of the paper is organized as follows: The Multimodal VR Document Viewer is described in Sect. 2. Then, the system's impact is discussed in Sect. 3. The main contributions are summarized in Sect. 4.

2   System Overview

2.1   System Specifications

The multi-modal document viewer was implemented using version 2021.3.9f1 of the Unity game engine. For VR support, the Valve OpenVR XR plugin was utilized. The Valve OpenVR XR plugin uses SteamVR to allow compatibility with widely available VR Head-mounted Displays (HMDs) without explicitly defining actions for every specific headset. The book model is composed of various 3D objects overlapping to form visual components. There are 3D objects for the front cover of the book, the back cover of the book, the left and right pages of the book, and a hidden page to animate the turning of pages. Each element of the book has two 3D objects associated with it, corresponding to the front and back sides of the object. The universal render pipeline was used to render and apply the various textures, shaders, and lighting incorporated into the project. Textures for the 3D objects are loaded through image files and mapped to the corresponding object dimensions. The universal render pipeline provides a more efficient and flexible render path than the default render pipeline used by Unity to modify textures. It allows basic image processing functions to be performed to change contrast and brightness.

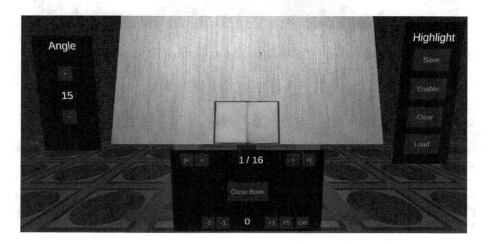

Fig. 1. VR User Interface.

2.2   Functionalities

The user interface of the document viewer, shown in Fig. 1, offers several functionalities to be activated through the laser pointer (from the head or from the hands). The interface allows the user to flip through the pages of the book one by one or to flip to the beginning and end of the book. A navigation feature exists that allows users to select a specific page to turn to. This is done by incrementing or decrementing a counter by one or five, then selecting the go button to turn to the specified page. By default, the book is placed on a table angled at 90°. Using the UI, the user can adjust the angle of the table, with a max angle of 45°. A system for annotation of the book pages was implemented. The user can activate the highlighting feature through the user interface. This allows the user to highlight sections of the pages of the book using the laser pointer. The annotations can then be saved and loaded from an image file, as well as cleared if an undesired portion was highlighted. The interface includes a magnifying glass to enable the user to look closely at the details of the document. The magnifying glass is important for viewing the document as the documents are presented in their original size, and many small details may not be well visible (see Fig. 2). An option exists to enable certain post-processing effects with shader maps.

Fig. 2. Magnifying glass on pages of ancient documents.

2.3   Accessibility

Immersive learning technologies must be fully inclusive and able to be used by as many people as possible, including people with severe disabilities. In addition, such technology may be the only way for some people to access documents autonomously. This facilitates the way these users can browse among a collection of documents and navigate across the pages of these documents. For accessing the different buttons in the interface, we consider the use of:

– A laser pointer coming from the hands of the VR controllers to point at the buttons and select using the trigger button of the controllers. In this condition, a beam of light comes from the hands.

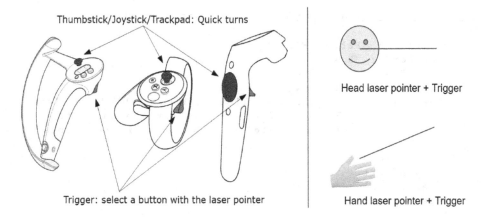

Fig. 3. Controls for the laser pointer and trigger with different VR headsets (**left**: Valve Index, **middle**: Oculus Touch, **right**: HTC Vive).

– A laser pointer coming from the head so the user can point at the buttons using only head motion, with the selection happening with the trigger button of a controller. The trigger button can be easily replaced by another button that can be accessed through the mouth (mouth switch), the side of the head, or any other modality. In this condition, only a black disk is shown, instead of a beam of light, to represent the point the user can select.

Not only is the laser pointer suitable for people with disabilities who cannot use their hands, but anyone can use it as well. The different controls are presented in Fig. 3.

2.4   Physical Structure of Documents

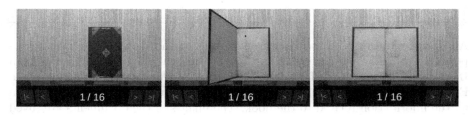

Fig. 4. Presentation of the Hebrew Bible: (**left**: Front cover, **middle**: Book Opening, **right**: Open Book.

Data 1.1. Example of the structure of a book.

```
{
    "title" : "Hebrew Bible",
    "author" : "N/A",
    "year" : "1491",
    "language" : "Hebrew",
    "description" : "The so-called 'Holkham Bible'. 23 leaves
        missing. First leaf blank. Without the index to
        Haftarot (Italian rite) that appears in some copies",
    "coverheight" : 324,
    "coverwidth" : 241.412,
    "pageheight" : 309,
    "pagewidth" : 230.235,
    "pages" : [
        {
            "filename" : "HebrewBible/HebrewBible1.png",
            "pageDirection" : "Right",
            "pageNumber" : 1,
            "pageOrientation" : "Portrait",
            "notes" : "HebrewBiblepage1Annotation"
        },
        {
            "filename" : "HebrewBible/HebrewBible2.png",
            "pageDirection" : "Left",
            "pageNumber" : 2,
            "pageOrientation" : "Portrait",
            "notes" : "HebrewBiblepage2Annotation"
        }
    ],
    "currentpage" : 1,
    "frontcover" : "HebrewBible/BackCover.png",
    "backcover" : "HebrewBible/FrontCover.png",
    "innerfrontcover" : "HebrewBible/InnerBackCover.png",
    "innerbackcover" : "HebrewBible/InnerFrontCover.png"
}
```

All documents can be presented through the system following the format proposed in the example corresponding to the Hebrew Bible from the Bodleian Libraries, University of Oxford, UK (see Data 1.1) with corresponding images in Fig. 5. A structured document using JSON data format was created to contain all the information related to the book. The images of the documents are saved in a specific folder with the JSON data representing physical information about the cover and the pages (height and width in mm). This data is combined with metadata corresponding to the title, the author, the language, the year, and a brief description of the book. For each page, we define the side of the page (left or right), the page number, the orientation of the page, and the corresponding filename with the texture of the page. Furthermore, notes can be included for

Front Cover   Inner Front Cover   Page   Page

Inner Back Cover   Back Cover

Fig. 5. Example of the Hebrew Bible with representative pages.

each page. This data format is simple, and anyone can edit it. Therefore, any user can easily add new books or documents for use with the system (Fig. 4).

3 Discussion

Preliminary testing was conducted with three participants. Participants were tasked with reading the first two pages from the prologue of The Canterbury Tales by Geoffrey Chaucer, sourced from the Bodleian Libraries, University of Oxford, UK., through both an e-book reader on a computer screen and the proposed VR document viewer. Participants took a 3-question quiz shortly after reading the passage. The preliminary testing results were similar for both the e-book reader and the VR document viewer, with participants scoring an average of 55 percent on the quiz, regardless of the medium. When asked about the usability of the system, 2 out of 3 users preferred interacting with the document via the VR system over the e-book reader. Improvements to the proposed document reader depend on the advancement of the technology. Participants commented that while the ease of use of the VR system was overall positive, the resolution of the screen was not high enough to clearly display the fine details of the calligraphy in the book.

The proposed document viewer represents one step towards displaying documents in their original size to users, including learners and scholars, who can benefit from of a faithful representation of documents that mix text and drawings in ways that make their logical structure extraction difficult. Many libraries provide extensive collections of ancient documents that are scanned and available through web portals. In most cases, these documents are rendered on a 2D screen, preventing users from grasping the original perspective. In addition, some documents are not designed to be presented in conventional formats. For instance, the Dead Sea Scrolls in Jerusalem's Shrine of the Book are displayed on a circular surface in their real-world presentation. This allows visitors to view the document from multiple angles and analyze its text easier. Certain documents are formatted right-to-left (RTL). It is imperative to represent such documents accurately in a virtual world to ensure that they reflect cultural norms and provide a natural reading experience.

The proposed VR system will differ from a traditional e-book reader in how the user interacts with the medium. A user typically interacts with an e-book in a 2D format, using their mouse or touchscreen to navigate through the pages of the book and perform certain actions, such as zooming in and out and annotating the pages of the document. However, the 2D e-book does not recreate the real-world experience of reading a physical book. A 3D object in VR can immerse the user by representing the real-world characteristics and interactions of a book. With the proposed VR document reader, when the user navigates through the book, the pages will physically turn. The VR system can also display full pages of the book, allowing the user to zoom in by physically moving closer to the 3D object, or through the magnifying glass feature. Other aspects of a real-world book, such as the texture and the weight, can be simulated in VR, adding to the immersion the user feels, which may enhance the user's engagement with the material.

We distinguish three directions in which the proposed system can be applied. First, in education, using the proposed VR document viewer, students can assess historical documents the same way they would in a museum. For example, instead of reading about them in a textbook or through images, students could view the documents from different angles. This would give them a better understanding of the historical context in which the document was produced. Second, people with physical disabilities would greatly benefit from the application. The option to select an alternative, user-friendly modality from the interface makes it easier for users to interact with documents, regardless of physical limitations. This can be particularly useful for individuals with physical disabilities that may have difficulty using eye-tracking technology, as they can navigate digital documents through alternative means. Third, the application can benefit scholars in digital humanities and cultural heritage, such as art history [3]. By representing documents the way they were originally produced, the publisher's intended vantage point can be preserved. This allows scholars to study and analyze the historical and cultural significance of the document. For example, art historians could utilize the proposed system to study documents that contain elements, such as unique calligraphy. This allows them to better understand the context in which the document was produced.

Virtual reality becomes a means of displaying such documents, as it would not be possible to display such a document on a computer screen. Most VR headsets do not include eye-tracking technology, so cursor control in the VR environment can only be achieved by moving the VR headset, i.e., by moving the neck and orienting the center of the VR headset towards the desired location for button selection. Eye-tracking technology could improve the user experience substantially, so the button selection is performed through gaze control.

Different modalities for visualizing documents, including books, can be considered for learning purposes. It is essential to consider the various audiences that will use the system and the extent to which it can impact the quality of reading when developing a document visualizer tool. When comparing e-book reading versus paper-based reading, it has been suggested that it may not be the medium of reading, but how students engage with each medium can affect their comprehension of text [9]. Cavalli et al. [2] suggests that reading from an e-book hinders some aspects of reading comprehension for adults with dyslexia. They show that by reading a printed book without time pressure, college students with dyslexia performed at the same level or better than non-impaired readers [2].

In the same way that old generations of e-book reading mediums did not provide a high resolution and screen quality good enough to be used for reading as it would induce visual fatigue, it is now completely acceptable/common to use an e-book to browse and annotate documents. While it was difficult to read a text with the first generations of VR headsets, it is fair to expect the same progress as e-readers with VR headsets [16]. The first HTC Vive headset contains 2 OLED display panels with a resolution of 1080×1200 per eye (2016); the HTC Vive Pro 2 has a resolution of $2,448 \times 2,448$ per eye (2021). Hence, such a resolution allows comfortable text reading. According to Steve Jobs, 300 pixels per inch is enough for a normal person if the display is viewed from a distance of 10"-12" from the eye. This translates to 57 pixels per degree. It has been shown that reading on paper is better than reading on screen in terms of understanding and comprehension. However, reading on paper is not significantly different from reading on screen in terms of reading speed [7]. The use of VR technology should be investigated in more detail for reading speed and reading comprehension.

4 Conclusion

Applications such as virtual desktops and virtual environments for accessing multimedia content such as movies happening in virtual movie theaters or for streaming services like Netflix being presented through VR headsets with the Oculus Quest 2 provide an alternative to the traditional way to access content. In this paper, we propose a system for displaying documents in their original size and easily navigating across their pages. The contributions are multifold: 1) students can access documents that are typically presented in libraries or museums, 2) documents can be manipulated without damaging the original documents, and 3) the system increases document access for people with severe disabilities through its multimodal interface. The system presented highlights the potential of VR technology to provide a more accessible and inclusive learning environment. We explore the different types of input modalities in VR to make a case for the implementation of VR learning systems in educational environments.

References

1. Bjekić, D., Obradović, S., Vučetić, M., Bojović, M.: E-teacher in inclusive e-education for students with specific learning disabilities. Procedia - Soc. Behav. Sci. **128**, 128–133 (2014)
2. Cavalli, E., Colé, P., Brèthes, H., Lefevre, E., Lascombe, S., Velay, J.L.: E-book reading hinders aspects of long-text comprehension for adults with dyslexia. Ann. Dyslexia **69**(2), 243–259 (2019)
3. Cecotti, H.: Cultural heritage in fully immersive virtual reality. Virtual Worlds **1**(1), 82–102 (2022)
4. Foasberg, N.M.: Adoption of e-book readers among college students: a survey. Inf. Technol. Libr. **30**(3) (2011)
5. Hurrell, C., Baker, J.: Immersive learning: applications of virtual reality for undergraduate education. Coll. Undergraduate Libr. **27**(2–4), 197–209 (2021)
6. Jacob, R.J., et al.: Reality-based interaction: a framework for post-wimp interfaces. In: Proceedings of the SIGCHI conference on Human factors in computing systems, pp. 201–210 (2008)
7. Kong, Y., Seo, Y.S., Zhai, L.: Comparison of reading performance on screen and on paper: a meta-analysis. Comput. Educ. **123**, 138–149 (2018)
8. Krokos, E., Plaisant, C., Varshney, A.: Virtual memory palaces: immersion aids recall. Virtual Reality **23**(1), 1–15 (2019). https://doi.org/10.1007/s10055-018-0346-3
9. Lim, J., Whitehead, G.E., Choi, Y.: Interactive e-book reading vs. paper-based reading: Comparing the effects of different mediums on middle school students' reading comprehension. System **97**, 102434 (2021)
10. Liou, W.K., Chang, C.Y.: Virtual reality classroom applied to science education. In: 2018 23rd International Scientific-Professional Conference on Information Technology (IT), pp. 1–4 (2018). https://doi.org/10.1109/SPIT.2018.8350861
11. Marinai, S.: Introduction to document analysis and recognition. In: Marinai, S., Fujisawa, H. (eds.) Machine Learning in Document Analysis and Recognition. Studies in Computational Intelligence, vol. 90, pp. 1–20. Springer, Heidelberg (2008). https://doi.org/10.1007/978-3-540-76280-5_1
12. Milic-Frayling, N., Sommerer, R.: SmartView: enhanced document viewer for mobile devices. Technical report MSR-TR-2002-114 (2002). https://www.microsoft.com/en-us/research/publication/smartview-enhanced-document-viewer-for-mobile-devices/
13. Moriña, A.: Inclusive education in higher education: challenges and opportunities. Eur. J. Spec. Needs Educ. **32**(1), 3–17 (2017)
14. Sjölie, D., Bodin, K., Elgh, E., Eriksson, J., Janlert, L.E., Lars, N.: Effects of interactivity and 3D-motion on mental rotation brain activity in an immersive virtual environment, vol. 2 (2010). https://doi.org/10.1145/1753326.1753454
15. Turk, M.: Multimodal interaction: a review. Pattern Recogn. Lett. **36**, 189–195 (2014)
16. Zhan, T., Yin, K., Xiong, J., He, Z., Wu, S.T.: Augmented reality and virtual reality displays: perspectives and challenges. iScience **23**(8), 101397 (2020)

STEM Education (STEM)

Novel Behaviors of Youth in a Virtual Reality Chemistry Lab

Elliot Hu-Au[1]($\boxtimes$) (ID), Pooja Addla[1] (ID), Janani Harinarayanan[1], Zhanlan Wei[1] (ID), Chuhe Wu[2], Zoey Yichen Liu[1] (ID), and Mara Danoff[1] (ID)

[1] Teachers College, Columbia University, New York, NY 10027, USA
emh2223@tc.columbia.edu
[2] Barnard College, Columbia University, New York, NY 10027, USA

Abstract. Virtual reality's (VR) unique affordances of enabling risk-free and exploratory behaviors [1] pose an unknown variable in its use as a learning environment for science education. In VR science laboratory simulations, do students follow typical safety and behavior norms or do they engage largely in "non-lesson related" behaviors [2]? In addition, VR is touted for increasing student interest and motivation in subjects but how exactly does this happen in these environments? We observed seventy-six 11–18 yr.-olds (N = 76) conduct a chemistry experiment in a VR lab simulation. Observations focused on lab safety behaviors and behaviors typically not exhibited in real-life situations (novel). Results showed that > 75% of students still follow basic safety rules but only 49% conducted cleaning behaviors in VR. Novel behaviors were observed in 51% of the participants. Behaviors most observed were moving around the room with no obvious intent, throwing objects or breaking glassware, and playing with lab equipment. We argue that the existence of these behaviors can be viewed as students expressing their curiosities, an important step in encouraging STEM pursuits. The freedom to engage in this behavior is a clue to the motivational affordances VR can provide. Positive responses were confirmed through individual debrief interviews with the participants.

Keywords: Virtual Reality · Immersive Learning Environments · Science Education · Student Behaviors

1 Introduction

Virtual reality (VR) continues to grow in importance in education and can be utilized in many situations across multiple subjects. Language learning can benefit from the contextual learning and constructivist affordances of VR [3]. VR can also help students develop better problem-solving skills by lessening their cognitive load and allowing them to use their cognitive resources more effectively [4]. Science, technology, engineering, and math (STEM) subjects can particularly benefit from its use. In a chemical engineering context, a study showed that VR provided a high level of immersion for learners, visualizing abstract ideas that are unattainable with 2D tools [5]. In STEM

© The Author(s), under exclusive license to Springer Nature Switzerland AG 2024
M.-L. Bourguet et al. (Eds.): iLRN 2023, CCIS 1904, pp. 313–329, 2024.
https://doi.org/10.1007/978-3-031-47328-9_24

subjects, VR games have been seen to provide a more authentic environment and tangible interactions to support learners in developing better spatial awareness and a deeper understanding of the interrelationships across multiple objects. Also, an increase in students' collaboration skills, effective teamwork, the development of interdependence, information sharing, and resource distribution have all been observed in student interactions these VR games [6]. Across many subjects, VR holds great potential for offering learners novel and motivating experiences to interact with academic content.

1.1 VR Behaviors and Science Laboratory Education

Virtual reality science laboratory simulations and programs are growing in their coverage of STEM topics. This is beneficial because these subject areas generally have large amounts of abstract concepts that make it difficult for learners to visualize the underlying foundations [7]. They also allow students to easily learn from their mistakes in environments where serious consequences do not exist [8]. Similar to virtual labs, VR labs can also provide easy repetition of exercises [9] and focus attention more directly on the targeted phenomena [10]. There are a few VR laboratory experiences commercially available and this study uses *The VR Chemistry Lab* for Oculus Quest [11].

Unfortunately, research is thin on analyzing the variety of behaviors exhibited by students in immersive VR science laboratory environments. Hu-Au and Okita [10] observed only the lab safety and cleaning behaviors of graduate students and found cleaning behaviors to be less frequent in VR. In a study on VR training for safe fire behavior, it was observed that participants initially would act in risky ways, coming closer to fires or even standing in fire [12]. Apart from these examples, most research has focused on the learning outcomes or students' experiences of presence, immersion, etc. (e.g. [13, 14]). Student behaviors in these VR environments represent an overlooked area of research that can give great insight into their learning results and application designs.

Studying student behaviors is a valuable tool because it can give insight into a student's motivations and postures for learning. In the setting of the science laboratory, research on student behaviors is typically observed for signs of showing knowledge, verbal discussions, manipulations of lab equipment, etc. [15]. Other valuable behaviors that are observed are often categorized as "non-lesson related" behaviors [2]. These non-lesson related behaviors take on a new meaning when it is a VR environment. Due to students perceiving VR environments as similar to video games [16], it is likely they will behave differently during VR simulations. In the case of VR simulations of science laboratories this can be more positive than negative. Behaviors that students are free to exhibit in VR environments can act as practice for real-life situations or they can be explorations of normally impermissible actions. It is these actions that are the focus of this study.

1.2 Using VR to Stimulate Curiosity

The science laboratory is a setting where student behaviors are often highly restricted. Although many situations in the lab will pique a student's interest to explore, there are many dangers present to its participants. Traditionally, the laboratory exercise focused on safety and control, where the "cookbook" style rigidly led students through procedures to attain an expected outcome [17]. Unfortunately, this style often leads to lower amounts of interest as well as students only performing "low level practical skills" [2]. The physical laboratory environment also naturally restrains (or encourages) students from acting out on curious or risky behaviors because of the very real threat of physical harm. These limitations, while paramount for the safety of students and teachers, often restrict students from indulging in their scientific curiosities.

Limited opportunities to explore can be costly to students as curiosity can be considered the seed for a lifetime of learning [18]. Encouraging a student to become a curious individual can promote positive wellbeing, openness to experience, and persistence in learning [19]. One of the methods to encourage growth in curiosity is to allow students to encounter moments of "cognitive incongruity", where they are confronted with unexpected information (p. 2474) [18]. These kinds of encounters are prolific in VR learning simulations, where many of the restrictive norms in formal environments are absent. This allows students to discover their own surprises, answer their own curiosities, and explore their desired knowledge paths. Exploratory behaviors follow these "epistemic emotions" of curiosity and surprise and often lead to greater knowledge generation (p. 2474) [18]. Thus, when instances of these epistemic emotions manifest in the learner, in what we call "novel behaviors", they potentially signify moments of increase in learning, motivation, and interest.

1.3 Research Questions

Our research study is designed to answer the following questions:

RQ1. What types of behavior do middle and high school students engage in when in a virtual reality science lab simulation?
RQ2. How do students participating in a virtual reality science lab simulation perceive the experience?

1.4 Hypotheses

Regarding RQ1, we believe students will engage in exploratory behaviors they would not normally engage in when in a real-life laboratory. This includes actions such as: touching extraneous equipment, breaking glassware, playing with safety equipment, and starting fires. As a result, responses will be positive but motivation for studying science may not increase. From the results of a similar study [10], behaviors regarding safety rules will most likely be followed by students in VR. However, cleaning behaviors will be less frequent. For RQ2, students will probably enjoy the simulation but may feel like it is more of a game rather than an educational experience. This may lead to feelings of having fun but perhaps not as much learning.

2 Methodology

2.1 Sample Population

This study was designed to explore the behaviors of middle and high school-aged students when conducting an experiment in a VR science lab simulation. The target population was from a large, diverse city in the United States and involved urban youth attending public and charter schools. Seventy-six (n = 76) youth, ages 11–18 yrs.-old, participated in the study during local after-school programs and summer camps. 97% of the students identified as African American, Latino, or a mix of both ethnicities. Gender balance was almost equally males (n = 37) and females (n = 39). 57 of the participants were in middle school (grades 6th–8th) and 19 were in high school (grades 9th–12th).

2.2   Study Design

The study design included an initial demographic questionnaire, a 5-min lab safety video, the VR chemistry lab simulation, and then a semi-structured debrief interview (Fig. 1). In total, a single session for each participant required approximately 40 min. Each student participated in the study individually without any other students involved.

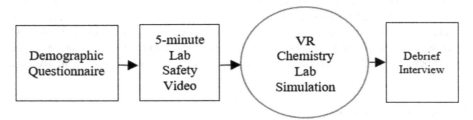

Fig. 1. Study flowchart.

Demographic Questionnaire. Students completed a demographic questionnaire that surveyed their age, ethnicity, and previous experience with VR. The questionnaire was adapted from the demographic section of the STEM-Career Interest Survey [20].

Lab Safety Video. The lab safety video was designed to prepare students with a baseline understanding of proper safety behaviors for the typical school laboratory environment. The video was a combination of example clips from the VR lab exercise and a safety video from the American Chemistry Society [21]. The importance of the selected behaviors was also verified by referencing the Laboratory Exercise Behavior List [22]. The following safety behaviors were directly referenced in the video that students were shown: wear gloves, wear eye goggles, wear lab apron, read the entire instructions first, set thermometer away from the edge of table in a safe place, waft technique for smelling, dispose of excess chemicals in trash, and wash equipment at lab conclusion.

The Design of the VR Chemistry Lab Simulation. The *VR Chemistry Lab* is a 3-dimensional immersive simulation of a traditional American school science laboratory. It was created using Unity3D, implemented on a Meta Quest 2 VR headset, and an example scene is shown in Fig. 2. As per recommendations by the American Chemistry Society [23] for physical laboratory spaces, the virtual classroom contains a demonstration table with a sink as well as extra tables to support student workstations. Safety equipment such as eye goggles, gloves, and an apron are interactable and can be worn by the player. Safety stations, such as a shower, eye wash station, and fire extinguisher, are all functional 3D models. Glassware such as beakers, Erlenmeyer flasks, thermometers, and test tubes are accurately modeled and will realistically break if dropped to the floor.

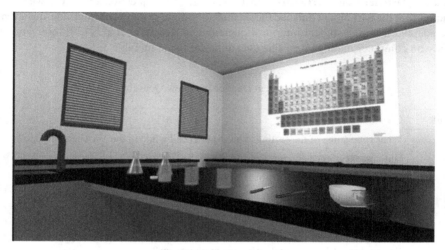

Fig. 2. The digital environment of the VR Chemistry Lab simulation.

The intent behind the design of the virtual environment is founded upon situated learning theory. According to Lave and Wenger, "learning, thinking, and knowing are relations among people engaged in activity in, with, and arising from the socially and culturally structured world" [24, p. 67]. The socio-cultural emphasis of this learning theory is important in the design of the virtual environment, not because of the social interactions (of which there are none currently), but because of the implied learning atmosphere due to the cultural cues of the room. The simulation of a traditional laboratory classroom is achieved with spartan black countertops, wood frames, white boards on plain walls, and a large wall-mounted periodic table poster. The intent is to mimic the learning atmosphere of traditional lab classrooms, one of "conversation, collaboration, and discovery" [24, p. 67].

The Design of the VR Chemistry Laboratory Exercise. The VR chemistry laboratory exercise is centered on the Next Generation Science Standard MS-PS1-2: Matter and its Interactions [25]. It states that students who demonstrate an understanding can "Analyze and interpret data on the properties of substances before and after the substances interact to determine if a chemical reaction has occurred" [25, p. 56].

The laboratory experiment involves mixing anhydrous copper (II) chloride with water then introducing a piece of aluminum metal to the aqueous solution (shown in Fig. 3). This particular lab exercise is recommended for middle to high school (ages 11–18 years) chemistry students by the American Association of Chemistry Teachers [26]. It is of the "cookbook" style of laboratory design where procedural steps are detailed and meant to be followed closely. While research has shown that inquiry-based labs may promote a more active and meaningful learning process [27], the cookbook method was chosen for two reasons: it is still a frequently used classroom pedagogy [28] and it is currently easier to develop a digital learning environment with a more rigid procedure.

Student Debrief Semi-structured Interview. A seven-question interview was conducted after the participant finished the second attitudinal survey. The interview questions are adapted from the student interview questions in Kebritchi et al.'s [29] motivational study on computer math games. The questions are listed in Table 1.

Table 1. Student Debrief Interview Questions.

Qn#	Question Text
1	What were some of the feelings you experienced while in the VR chemistry lab?
2	Did you experience any problems while in the VR lab?
3	Did you experience any surprises while in the VR Chemistry Lab?
4	Is there anything in particular about the VR Chemistry Lab that you enjoyed?
5	Is there anything about the VR Chemistry Lab that you disliked?
6	If you could, how would you improve the VR Chemistry Lab?
7	Do you have any additional questions or comments?

2.3 Data Analysis and Synthesis

Video Behavior Analysis. Observations of lab safety actions focused on those presented in the video. The novel behaviors were determined through careful analysis of all videos to identify the most obvious and frequently seen behaviors. As most of the lab safety behaviors only required action once and at particular moments, a participant was marked as a "success" based on if they were observed at the correct instance in the experiment (e.g., wearing safety gloves before touching any chemicals, taring the scale with only the weigh boat). The percent of successful participants was calculated for each behavior. A breakdown by gender, school level, and past VR experience was also conducted and significant differences between these categories were checked using a Mann-Whitney U test. Analysis of age groups were separated by whether the participant was in middle school (grades 6–8) or high school (grades 9–12). Experience with VR was a self-reported value on a five-level Likert scale.

Novel behaviors from observations of the participant videos were observed by first analyzing the video recordings for any non-lesson related behaviors. Not all participants exhibited novel behaviors. For those that did, the amount of time in seconds would be recorded for the duration of their behavior. Multiple instances of a behavior would be summed together and the total time then reported.

Lab safety and novel behavior analysis was conducted by six reviewers who trained in video observations to maintain consistency in behavior reporting. Inter-rater reliability (IRR) was conducted by first training as a group on positive matches for a specific behavior category. Then reviewers individually rated the same video and all ratings were compared and Krippendorff's alpha was calculated [30]. This measure of IRR was used due to its ability to ignore missing data, handle various sample sizes, accept multiple raters, and apply to any measurement level. The standard value of $\alpha_K > .8$ was used for an acceptable level for the video behavior analysis.

Student Debrief Semi-structured Interview. The semi-structured interviews were transcribed and coded for similar themes between participants. A similar process to the one for video behavior analysis was used to ensure IRR for coding interviews. Six reviewers were employed and they did not separately analyze an interview until $\alpha_K > .8$ was achieved when calculating for the Krippendorff alpha.

3 Results

3.1 Novel Behaviors

Behavior analysis of novel behaviors revealed that students engaged in many different "non-lesson" related behaviors. Thirty-seven (37) students, slightly below half the total tested adhered to the lab procedure and did not deviate significantly. However, for the other 39 students, the novel behaviors, in order of highest percentage of students to exhibit them, were: moving around the room or teleporting excessively (38%), throwing objects and breaking glassware (27%), pretending or playing with lab equipment (22%), looking at the periodic table wall poster (16%), playing with or lighting the Bunsen burner (16%), using the fire extinguisher (13%), using the shower and eyewash station (11%), mixing chemicals together unnecessarily (7%), spilling chemicals on purpose (7%), throwing equipment in the garbage can (4%), and pretending to eat chemicals (1%).

Of the students who demonstrated these novel behaviors, we also calculated the average amount of time they spent engaging in them. A few of note are that the 16% of students who played with the Bunsen burner would do so for an average of 54.1 s, usually attempting to figure out how to light it. The 13% of students who played with the fire extinguisher averaged 31.7 s each, the 16% of students who looked at the periodic table wall poster did so for an average of 8.57 s, and the 27% of students who threw objects or broke glass engaged in this activity for 35.8 s. The rest of the totals can be found in Table 2.

Pearson correlation tests were computed among demographic categories and the novel behaviors. The results suggest that most demographic categories did not correlate with novel behaviors and are shown in Table 3. However, there were a few findings of statistically significant correlation between a student's level of familiarity or previous experience with VR and their tendency to play with the Bunsen burner, $r(76) = .299$, $p < .05$, and to play with the fire extinguisher, $r(76) = .422$, $p < .05$. In general, the results suggest that age and gender do not significantly impact novel behaviors while familiarity with VR does.

Table 2. Novel Behaviors.

Novel Behaviors	#[a]	Min[b]	Max[b]	Mean[c]	SE	SD
Moving/Teleporting Excessively	28	12	85	38.4	5.3	22.0
Throwing Objects/ Breaking Glass	20	3	112	35.8	10.6	36.6
Playing with lab equipment	16	4	105	32.1	9.53	30.5
Periodic Table	11	3	19	8.57	2.37	6.27
Bunsen Burner	11	4	157	54.1	20.4	53.9
Fire Extinguisher	9	7	69	31.7	9.75	23.9
Shower/EyeWash	8	9	51	26.6	7.31	16.3
Mixing Chemicals	5	7	40	23.3	9.53	16.5
Spilling Chemicals	3	11	19	15.0	4.00	5.66
Throw Away Equipment	3	3	32	17.5	14.5	20.5
Eating Chemicals	2	8	10	9.00	1.00	1.41

[a] Number of students who demonstrated this behavior
[b] Minimum or maximum time in seconds a student demonstrated this behavior
[c] Mean time (secs) engaged in this behavior based only on students who demonstrated behavior

Table 3. Correlation for Demographics and Novel Behaviors.

Novel Behaviors	Age (N = 76)		Gender (M/F) (N = 76)		VR Familiarity (N = 76)	
	r	p	r	p	r	p
Moving/Teleporting Excessively	.093	.533	.063	.674	.126	.400
Throwing Objects/ Breaking Glass	−.131	.380	−.149	.316	.285	.053
Playing with lab equipment	−.102	.496	−.112	.455	.237	.109
Periodic Table	.079	.596	.028	.851	−.016	.914
Bunsen Burner	−.041	.786	−.149	.318	.299	.041[*]
Fire Extinguisher	−.200	.177	−.009	.950	.422	.003[*]
Shower/ EyeWash	.091	.543	−.044	.771	.226	.127
Mixing Chemicals	−.199	.179	.215	.146	.246	.095
Spilling Chemicals	−.190	.201	.022	.881	.142	.342
Throw Away Equipment	.161	.280	−.138	.353	−.163	.274
Eating Chemicals	−.141	.344	−.127	.395	.237	.108

[*] Correlation is significant at the 0.05 level (2-tailed)

3.2 Safety Behaviors

Lab safety behaviors were observed at varying rates for the participants. Total participants were N = 76. For some categories (e.g., Attempted Clean Up of Mess, Dispose of Excess Chemicals), the participant did not have an opportunity to conduct the behavior because there was no situation where it was necessary. In these cases, these participants were excluded from the statistics for these categories.

Participants adhered to some lab safety behaviors frequently, but others were much less consistent (see Table 4). Safety gloves were worn on average 92% of the time (SE = .031, SD = .270), eye goggles 86% of the time (SE = .040, SD = .352), and a safety apron 75% of the time (SE = .049, SD = .434). Other safety measures such as placing the glass thermometer on a safe surface (M = 49%, SE = .057, SD = .503), using a wafting motion to smell (M = 5%, SE = .025, SD = .223), and reading all the instructions prior to beginning the experiment (M = 37%, SE = .057, SD = .486) were conducted by a minority of the participants. Finally, cleaning actions were also relatively low in the VR lab: cleaning up a mess during the exercise (M = 53%, (M = 42%, SE = .062, SD = .497) and cleaning up at the end of the exercise (M = 53%, SE = .057, SD = .502).

Table 4. Lab Safety Behaviors

Lab Safety Category	Successfully Completed by Participant (N = 76)			
	Count	*Mean*	*SE*	*SD*
Wear Safety Gloves	71	.92	.031	.270
Wear Eye Goggles	66	.86	.040	.352
Wear Safety Apron	58	.75	.049	.434
Use Weigh Boat	26	.34	.054	.476
Safe Thermometer Placement on Table	38	.49	.057	.503
Wafting (smelling)	4	.05	.025	.223
Clean Up Mess During Exercise[a]	37	.53	.060	.503
Dispose of Excess Chemicals Properly[b]	27	.42	.062	.497
Read All Instructions	27	.37	.057	.486
Clean Up at the End	41	.53	.057	.502

[a]Excludes 7 participants who did not need to do this
[b]Excludes 12 participants who did not need to do this

Pearson correlation tests were computed among the demographics categories and the lab safety behaviors. The results shown in Table 5 suggest that the age of the participant does not correlate with following lab safety rules. Gender does correlate in the category of Safety Apron, where females statistically tended to wear safety aprons more than males, r (76) = .233, p < .05. The level of familiarity with VR correlates significantly with the wearing of safety gloves, r (76) = .263, p < .05. In general, participant age does not statistically affect their adherence to lab safety behaviors, while gender and familiarity with VR have minor effects.

To further explore the lab safety behavior results, a Mann-Whitney U test was performed to find significant differences between males and females (Table 6). Significant differences were found where females (M = 85%) wore safety aprons significantly more than males (M = 65%) (Z = 1.974, p = .048) and females cleaned up messes (M = 67%) during the exercise more than males (M = 42%) (Z = 2.065, p = .039).

Table 5. Correlations for Demographics and Lab Safety Behaviors

Lab Safety Behaviors	Age (N = 76)		Gender (M/F) (N = 76)		VR Familiarity (N = 76)	
	r	p	r	p	r	p
Wear Safety Gloves	−.214	.061	.108	.348	.263	.021*
Wear Eye Goggles	−.064	.578	.127	.270	.082	.478
Wear Safety Apron	−.126	.275	.233	.041*	.203	.076
Use Weigh Boat	.036	.754	.137	.235	.149	.197
Safe Thermometer Placement	−.203	.076	.169	.141	.086	.457
Wafting (smelling)	−.100	.389	.108	.350	.025	.832
Clean Up Mess During Exercise	−.232	.053	.231	.055	.091	.455
Dispose of Excess Chemicals Properly	−.154	.219	.195	.119	.174	.167
Read All Instructions	−.229	.051	.131	.268	.111	.349
Clean Up at the End	−.047	.687	.141	.222	−.011	.926

* Correlation is significant at the 0.05 level (2-tailed)

Table 6. Mann-Whitney U: Gender and Lab Safety Behaviors

Lab Safety Behaviors	Males			Females			Mann-Whitney U Test[a]	
	Mean	*SE*	*SD*	*Mean*	*SE*	*SD*	*Z*	*p*
Wear Safety Gloves	.89	.052	.315	.95	.036	.223	−.912	.362
Wear Eye Goggles	.81	.065	.397	.90	.049	.307	−1.066	.287
Wear Safety Apron	.65	.080	.484	.85	.059	.366	−1.974	.048*
Use Weigh Boat	.27	.074	.450	.38	.079	.493	−1.053	.292
Safe Thermometer Placement on Table	.41	.082	.498	.56	.080	.502	−1.374	.169
Wafting motion (smelling)	.03	.027	.164	.08	.044	.273	−.994	.320
Clean Up Mess During Exercise	.42	.083	.500	.67	.083	.479	−2.065	.039*
Dispose of Excess Chemicals Properly	.32	.081	.475	.53	.093	.507	−1.683	.092
Read All Instructions	.31	.078	.467	.42	.083	.500	−.975	.330
Clean Up at the End	.46	.083	.505	.59	.080	.498	−1.129	.259

[a] Comparing mean difference from males to females
* significant difference at p < .05

3.3 Self-reported Learning in VR

Participants were also asked to answer the question: "On a scale from 1 (very little) to 10 (a lot), how much do you think you learned in the VR experience?". The responses had a mean average of $M_{mean} = 7.61$ and a median average of $M_{median} = 8.00$.

3.4 Student Debrief Interviews

Student responses to the debrief interviews had many common themes. 95% of participants expressed positive feelings, some saying they "liked it", it was "cool", and they were "impressed". Many also experienced a great sense of immersion where they felt like they were "really in a lab". Unsurprisingly, some students also expressed feelings of confusion when first in the VR experience.

"I'm a little confused, but then after I got it, I learned how to grab and then after that I started doing the experience."

Getting acquainted with the controls and locomotion in the VR experience proved to be a difficult experience as well.

"It's very hard to, like, move stuff around."

"It took a little bit of getting used to the controls and then it got easier."

"I couldn't grasp onto certain things and it was kind of difficult, like, trying to mix the solution."

Some students felt like they especially embodied the scientific atmosphere of the scene itself.

"I felt like a real scientist."

"I was surprised about how everything like was so life-like, and I was able to grab stuff, but everything seemed like a real, like, laboratory."

Interactions with objects were commented on frequently.

"I enjoyed mixing the chemicals together."

"Yeah, I liked mixing the stuff."

An awareness of the liminal nature of VR was also described.

"It was a lot of work…It seemed real though, actually seemed like you're working in a lab, but like at the same time you're not. But it's also kind of fun."

Finally, students articulated their improved preparation for real-life science experiences.

"So I feel like it gave me future knowledge on the specific topics we were doing. I feel like I'll be able to know what to do when it comes to working in a lab."

4   Discussion

4.1   Behaviors in VR Lab Simulations

This study aimed to provide a clearer picture of the behaviors of adolescent students when engaged in a VR chemistry lab simulation. RQ1 directed observations towards lab safety behaviors like wearing safety goggles, gloves, and aprons, which were still followed by the majority of students. Though there is no physical danger or need for these articles of clothing, the majority of students still adhered to these rules of laboratories. An argument could be made that the level of immersion of the VR simulation is so high that students behave similarly to how they would in a real-life laboratory [10]. However, an alternate argument might be that students followed these rules simply because they are following the procedural instructions as well as the accepted behavior of safety in a lab environment. Research supports this observation of engaging in rule-following behavior when there is no consistent contact with consequences from doing the contrary [32]. In this case, most students did not experience any situations out of the norm and so they followed the expected safety rules.

Comparing lab safety behavior tendencies across gender led to some interesting findings. Only one correlation was observed, and it was positive among females and "wearing the safety apron" behavior. Demonstration of wearing the safety apron and "cleaning up messes during exercise" were both found to be significantly greater in female students than male students. In general, female students tended to demonstrate lab safety behaviors at a higher rate since they had higher averages than males in every category. Research in gender differences in personality traits supports this result, as conscientiousness, a trait associated with rule-following and orderliness, is scored higher on by females, on average, than males [33]. Thus, when women frequently defer to men on handling equipment in school laboratories [34] we now have potential evidence that the opposite should occur.

However, general issues of cleanliness arose for both genders during the intervention. A little more than half of the students would clean up during the exercise. When spilling chemicals, most seemed to understand that there was no real harm in just leaving the chemicals out. They also generally did not adhere to protocols designed to lower the risk of sample contamination as only a small minority used the weigh boat or disposed of excess chemicals properly. This confirms what was observed in a similar study with adult students [10]. This is somewhat alarming as it appears to lead to conclusions that contradict that VR training has been found to be highly effective [34]. So are we training students to become less attentive to cleanliness in science laboratories? It is possible but there is no evidence currently to suggest this. Also, while most research demonstrating success in behavior change in immersive environments focuses on targeted behaviors [35], this study did not intentionally aim to teach proper safety behaviors. The students were not explicitly told they needed to practice cleaning (although it was stated in the procedure and safety video), so they most likely focused their attention on more interesting things in the simulation.

"Novel behaviors" is our term for behaviors exhibited in the VR simulation that are typically not seen in real-life situations. The reasons for this are that the behaviors are usually not socially acceptable or could cause physical harm. The student population split almost equally between those that engaged in novel behaviors (51%) and those that didn't (49%). Usually, students would exhibit a few novel behaviors (i.e., throw objects and break glassware, play with the fire extinguisher) but not every category of novel behavior.

We believe the existence of these novel behaviors demonstrates the freedom students' felt to explore areas of their own curiosity. By allowing students to perform normally taboo actions or play with traditionally "off-limits" equipment, the VR simulation enables them to explore and engage in more information-seeking behaviors. This continues the cycle of curiosity, conducting information-seeking behaviors, and forming new questions and curiosities. Crucially for STEM subjects, this cycle of curiosity and its attendant behaviors are essential for scientific thinking and instilling a desire for future scientific learning in children [36].

This curiosity-novel behavior dynamic is consistent with the Cognitive Affective Model of Immersive Learning (CAMIL) framework, which primarily explains how presence and the sense of agency influence interest and intrinsic motivation [37]. This framework identifies the novel behaviors as effects of intrinsic motivation in the learning environment. Since the students have the agency to pursue these motivations within the VR environment, they are reinforcing their own "self-determination" in their learning [38, p. 68]. Thus, the novel behaviors are indicators that situational interest has been triggered and that participants are likely to pursue long-term knowledge-seeking behaviors [37].

One encouraging result demonstrating the promise of using VR simulations to promote this cycle of curiosity was a positive correlation between familiarity with VR and the novel behaviors playing with *Bunsen burner* and *Fire Extinguisher*. This showed that the greater amount of time a student had been using VR, the more likely they were to act on their curiosities about using Bunsen burners and fire extinguishers. Engaging in these behaviors would often lead to other curiosities forming for students, continuing the cycle and leading to more opportunities for knowledge formation.

4.2   Student Perceptions of the VR Science Lab Simulation

As seen in the results from the debrief interviews, students had very positive learning experiences in the VR intervention. Many had feelings of surprise and fun and wished that there were more science lab exercises to do. Many students also enjoyed the level of immersion that VR provides, some even forgetting that virtual tables could not be rested upon. The most promising responses involved the fact that the VR simulation provided the students with an opportunity to do something that was unavailable at their school. By using the VR lab simulation, they could have a hands-on chemistry experience that was not available to them under normal circumstances. Similar reasons have been identified in other studies on virtual labs [39], where safety, ability to individually conduct experiments, and ease and quickness of exercise repetition bolster the case for greater VR lab adoption.

Regarding RQ2, students seemed to perceive the VR experience as a fun, educational experience. They self-reported it as a strong learning experience and interview responses were very positive. Identification with the scientist role emerged as a theme from the interviews and provides evidence for the perspective-taking promise that VR affords [40]. The results also concur with many other studies that find VR to be a highly motivation and interest-building tool for educational topics [41]. One other important aspect of this intervention is that it occurred outside of normal school hours. Before the study, it was surmised that having students participate in such a focused, school-like experience in an after-school program could have a negative effect, as if we were forcing them to "do more school". However, this fear seemed unwarranted as the majority of students expressed positive feelings toward the experience. Even though some initially had fears and confusion about VR, the interactivity of the experience seemed to enable them to persevere.

5 Conclusion

This study illuminates some of the most common behaviors students engage in when in a VR science lab simulation. Specific lab safety behaviors are followed as in real-life, but many cleaning behaviors are eschewed. Novel behaviors that are either too risky or typically not allowed in real-life were engaged in by about half of the students. Students had some negative experiences but mostly reported the VR science lab simulation as educational and fun. Experiences like these can be significant for children, motivating them to continue pursuing their interests in STEM. This study provides evidence for why students find VR experiences motivating and can hopefully inform future educational VR experiences.

References

1. Gay, E., Greschler, D.: Is virtual reality a good teaching tool? Virtual Reality Spec. Rep. 1(4), 51–59 (1994). https://doi.org/10.1089/vir.1994.1.51
2. Okebukola, P.: Science laboratory behavior strategies of students relative to performance in and attitude to laboratory work. J. Res. Sci. Teach. 22(3), 221–232 (1985). https://doi.org/10.1002/tea.3660220306
3. Alizadeh, M.: Virtual reality in the language classroom: theory and practice. Comput. Assist. Lang. Learn. Electron. J. 20, 21–30 (2019). https://doi.org/10.4995/call2019.10706
4. Araiza-Alba, P., Keane, T., Chen, W., Kaufman, J.: Immersive virtual reality as a tool to learn problem-solving skills. Comput. Educ. 164, 104–121 (2021). https://doi.org/10.1016/j.compedu.2020.104010
5. Bell, J.T.,Fogler, H.S.: The investigation and application of virtual reality as an educational tool. In: American Society for Engineering Education 1995 Annual Conference, Anaheim, CA (1995)
6. Thompson, M.M., Wang, A., Roy, D., Klopfer, E.: Authenticity, interactivity, and collaboration in VR learning games. Front. Robot. AI 2, 734083 (2018). https://doi.org/10.3389/frvir.2021.734083
7. Johnstone, A.H.: Science education: we know the answers, let's look at the problems. In: Proceedings of the 5th Greek Conference "Science Education and New Technologies in Education" (2007)
8. Standen, P.J., Brown, D.J.: Virtual reality and its role in removing the barriers that turn cognitive impairments into intellectual disability. Virtual Reality 10(3), 241–252 (2006). https://doi.org/10.1007/s10055-006-0036-9
9. Olympiou, G., Zacharia, Z.C.: Blending physical and virtual manipulatives: an effort to improve students' conceptual understanding through science laboratory experimentation. Sci. Educ. 96(1), 21–47 (2012). Gay, E., Greschler, D.: Is virtual reality a good teaching tool? Virtual Reality Spec. Rep. 1(4), 51–59 (1994)
10. Hu-Au, E., Okita, S.: Exploring differences in student learning and behavior between real-life and virtual reality chemistry laboratories. J. Sci. Educ. Technol. 30, 862–876 (2021)
11. Meta: The VR Chemistry Lab on Oculus Quest 2. In: Oculus.com. https://www.oculus.com/experiences/quest/3919613214752680/ (2021). Accessed 1 Nov 2022
12. Çakiroğlu, Ü., Gökoğlu, S.: Development of fire safety behavioral skills via virtual reality. Comput. Educ. 133, 56–68 (2019)
13. Hernandez-de-Menendez, M., Vallejo Guevara, A., Morales-Menendez, R.: Virtual reality laboratories: a review of experiences. Int. J. Interact. Des. Manuf. 13, 947–966 (2019)

14. Makransky, G., Terkildsen, T.S., Mayer, R.E.: Adding immersive virtual reality to a science lab simulation causes more presence but less learning. Learn. Instr. **60**, 225–236 (2019)

15. Kyle, W.C., Others, A.: Assessing and analyzing behavior strategies of instructors in college science laboratories. J. Res. Sci. Teach. **17**(2), 131–137 (1980)

16. Rubio-Tamayo, J.L., Barrio, M.G., Garcia, F.G.: Immersive environments and virtual reality: systematic review and advances in communication, interaction and simulation. Multimodal Technol. Interact. **1**(4), 21 (2017)

17. Hofstein, A., Lunetta, V.N.: The laboratory in science education: foundations for the twenty-first century. Sci. Educ. **88**(1), 28–54 (2004)

18. Vogl, E., Pekrun, R., Murayama, K., Loderer, K., Schubert, S.: Surprise, curiosity, and confusion promote knowledge exploration: evidence for robust effects of epistemic emotions. Front. Psychol. **10**, :2474 (2019)

19. Peterson, E.: Supporting curiosity in schools and classrooms. Curr. Opin. Behav. Sci. **35**, 7–13 (2020)

20. Kier, M.W., Blanchard, M.R., Osborne, J.W., Albert, J.L.: The development of the STEM career interest survey (STEM-CIS). Res. Sci. Educ. **44**(3), 461–481 (2014)

21. American Chemical Society: Safety Video. https://www.youtube.com/watch?v=9o77QE eM-68 (1991). Last accessed 27 Nov 2022

22. ACS Institute: Student Laboratory Code of Conduct, https://institute.acs.org/lab-safety/educat ion-and-training/high-school-labs/student-lab-code-of-conduct.html. Last accessed 27 Nov 2022

23. American Chemical Society: The Laboratory, https://www.acs.org/education/policies/mid dle-and-high-school-chemistry/laboratory.html. Last accessed 27 Nov 2022

24. Lave, J., Wenger, E.: Situated Learning: Legitimate Peripheral Participation. Cambridge University Press, New York, NY (1991)

25. National Research Council: Next Generation Science Standards: For States, By States (2013)

26. American Association of Chemistry Teachers: Classroom Resources | Observing a Chemical Reaction. https://teachchemistry.org/classroom-resources/observing-a-chemical-reaction. Last accessed 27 Nov 2022

27. Zacharia, Z.C., et al.: Identifying potential types of guidance for supporting student inquiry when using virtual and remote labs: a literature review. Education Tech. Research Dev. **63**(2), 257–302 (2015)

28. Akuma, F.V., Callaghan, R.: Teaching practices linked to the implementation of inquiry-based practical work in certain science classrooms. J. Res. Sci. Teach. **56**(1), 64–90 (2019)

29. Kebritchi, M., Hirumi, A., Bai, H.: The effects of modern mathematics computer games on mathematics achievement and class motivation. Comput. Educ. **55**(2), 427–443 (2010)

30. Hayes, A.F., Krippendorff, K.: Answering the call for a standard reliability measure for coding data. Commun. Methods Meas. **1**(1), 77–89 (2007)

31. Mugivhisa, L.L., Baloyi, K., Olowoyo, J.O.: Adherence to safety practices and risks associated with toxic chemicals in the research and postgraduate laboratories at Sefako Makgatho Health Sciences University, Pretoria, South Africa. Afr. J. Sci. Technol. Innov. Dev. **13**(6), 747–756 (2021)

32. de Almeida, J.H., Cortez, M.D., de Rose, J.C.: The effects of monitoring on children's rule-following in a computerized procedure. Anal. Verbal Behav. **36**(2), 295–307 (2020)

33. Quinn, K.N., Kelley, M.M., McGill, K.L., Smith, E.M., Whipps, Z., Holmes, N.G.: Group roles in unstructured labs show inequitable gender divide. Phys. Rev. Phys. Educ. Res. **16**(1), 010129 (2020)

34. Jensen, L., Konradsen, F.: A review of the use of virtual reality head-mounted displays in education and training. Educ. Inf. Technol. **23**(4), 1515–1529 (2018)

35. Dirksen, J., Ditommaso, D., Plunkett, C.: Augmented and Virtual Reality for Behavior Change. The eLearning Guild, Santa Rosa, CA (2019)

36. Jirout, J.J.: Supporting early scientific thinking through curiosity. Front. Psychol. **11**, 1717 (2020)
37. Makransky, G., Petersen, G.B.: The cognitive affective model of immersive learning (CAMIL): a theoretical research-based model of learning in immersive virtual reality. Educ. Psychol. Rev. **33**(3), 937–958 (2021)
38. Deci, E.L., Ryan, R.M.: Self-Determination Theory. In International Encyclopedia of the Social & Behavioral Sciences, 2nd edn, pp. 486–491. Oxford, Elsevier (2015)
39. Tatli, Z., Ayas, A.: Effect of a virtual chemistry laboratory on students' achievement. J. Educ. Technol. Soc. **16**(1), 159–170 (2013)
40. Bailenson, J.N., Yee, N., Blascovich, J., Beall, A.C., Lundblad, N., Jin, M.: The use of immersive virtual reality in the learning sciences: digital transformations of teachers, students, and social context. J. Learn. Sci. **17**(1), 102–141 (2008)
41. Maas, M.J., Hughes, J.M.: Virtual, augmented and mixed reality in K–12 education: a review of the literature. Technol. Pedagog. Educ. **29**(2), 231–249 (2020)

Shifts in Student Attitudes and Beliefs About Science Through Extended Play in an Immersive Science Game

Shari J. Metcalf[1]([✉]) [iD], David Gagnon[2] [iD], and Stefan Slater[3]

[1] Graduate School of Education, Harvard University, Cambridge, MA 02138, USA
`shari_metcalf@gse.harvard.edu`
[2] School of Education, University of Wisconsin-Madison, Madison, USA
[3] Graduate School of Education, University of Pennsylvania, Philadelphia, USA

Abstract. This research considers the impact of a digital science game that provides immersive experiences in which participants take on the role of a scientist and learn through active engagement with simulated science environments and tools. *Wake: Tales from the Aqualab* is an immersive web-based middle school science game designed to teach science practices of experimentation, modeling, and argumentation in aquatic ecosystems. This paper describes findings from a study of approximately 250 middle school students who used a beta version of the game over two weeks. A pre-post survey of affective measures found significant gains in student science identity, self-efficacy, and interest. Classroom observations and interviews with students and teachers supported these findings, suggesting that the immersive qualities of the game helped students think of themselves as scientists and engage in authentic science practices, contributing to shifts in students' attitudes and beliefs about science.

Keywords: Game · Ecosystem · Science · Identity · Self-Efficacy

1 Introduction

Immersive environments allow participants to feel like they are participating in an experience. They are actively engaged in a virtual representation of a different reality. This work looks at impacts on learners of actional immersion, defined as "empowering the participant in an experience to initiate actions impossible in the real world that have novel, intriguing consequences." [1]. Actional immersion can be experienced through headset virtual reality, desktop virtual environments and videogames - the essential element is that the user has agency to participate and engage in meaningful activities with virtual elements. For game-based learning, participants experience actional immersion when they feel like they are "in" the game, taking on a role.

This paper focuses on the use of an immersive serious game for learning science. Immersive environments for science allow students to learn science by doing science. This approach has been demonstrated to be valuable for learning. Immersive environments can provide a rich inquiry-based context for engaging in science exploration,

M.-L. Bourguet et al. (Eds.): iLRN 2023, CCIS 1904, pp. 330–342, 2024.
https://doi.org/10.1007/978-3-031-47328-9_25

discovery, and developing mastery of science concepts and practices [2]. Specifically, this paper presents outcomes from pilot testing of Wake: Tales from the Aqualab, an immersive web-based middle school science game designed to teach science practices of experimentation, modeling, and argumentation in aquatic ecosystems. Immersive elements of the game helped students think of themselves as scientists and engage in authentic science practices. Findings from classroom research of 250 middle school students using the game over two weeks demonstrated positive shifts in students' attitudes and beliefs about science.

2 Literature Review

Immersive environments for science learning are powerful opportunities to provide authentic, situated, and constructivist learning experiences for students. Constructivism is the idea that learning is an active process gained through experience and interactions in the world [3]. The constructivist approach includes a focus on meaningful engagement and authentic practice. Students are put in situations "where they have to do the really interesting work" [3]. Students are challenged to take on a problem, to choose an approach, to evaluation solutions, etc. Digital simulations and games have been really powerful in enabling these authentic scenarios, providing situated learning in knowledge-rich virtual contexts and simulating environments and experiences otherwise impossible in school settings [4–6].

Important features of immersive environments for situated science learning include role-play, using the tools of the practice, encountering the challenges faced by practitioners, and self-directed learning. *Role-play* in immersive environments involves students taking on a virtual identity. In general, roleplaying can enhance feelings of immersion. For example, [7] looked at a roleplaying VR called The Next Fairy Tale, describing design principles to help players to experience a sense of transformation into the fictional character in a story. In science, taking on the virtual role of a scientist may help the student feel more like a scientist, contributing to a sense of science identity [8]. *Identity* is an affordance of virtual environments that promotes engagement and motivation, drawing learners into a new experience [9]. Serious games and virtual environments that provide role-play opportunities to be a scientist can influence students' identity as a scientist, even inspiring thoughts of future STEM careers [10, 11]. Virtual learning environments can encourage student science identity exploration through role-play, meaningful practice, student-led inquiry, and opportunities for self-reflection [12].

One of the most powerful features of immersive environments is the ability to provide virtual representations of authentic experiences for learners [13, 14]. In an immersive science learning experience, authentic practice includes *using the tools of the practice*, and *encountering the challenges faced by practitioners*. As simulated experiences, these tools and challenges may be scaffolded to support learners at their level of understanding, but fundamentally, such environments allow students to virtually become a scientist, by collecting data, running experiments, analyzing results, and using findings as evidence to support hypotheses. For example, EcoMUVE is a desktop multi-user virtual environment in which students visit a virtual pond and conduct scientific inquiry to determine why all the large fish in the pond died. They use a virtual avatar to explore the pond and surrounding area, talk to non-player characters to get information, and engage in authentic science practices including observation, collecting and analyzing data [15]. By providing meaningful, realistic tools and challenges, students are able to both learn the science itself and also to learn what scientists do, impacting both learning and emotional engagement [3, 16].

Research on immersive games and environments for science learning has shown potential for supporting growth in affective measures such as self-efficacy, interest in science, and science identity (e.g.,[8, 17–20]). Self-efficacy, belief in one's ability to succeed, is strongly influenced through experiencing success in one's own past experiences. This resonates well with ways that many games are designed, adapting to players over time with transitions from easier to more challenging levels, e.g., games in which enemies get more formidable as the player gets more powerful weapons [21]. Gee [22] describes this idea as "cycles of expertise," where the game increases the complexity of the tasks once the player has demonstrated mastery over the current challenges. Games and other immersive environments with these opportunities for iterative success over time are helpful in building self-efficacy [16].

Through self-directed learning, having the freedom to work at their own rate, and having more choice about what they are doing, middle school students in science class have been found to show more motivation and interest, leading to greater achievement [23]. Immersive environments for learning can be designed with expansive agency and control, which is associated with positive affect and intrinsic motivation. Intrinsic motivation is linked to autonomy (a sense of initiative and ownership of one's actions), competence, and belonging [24]. STEM games and virtual environments provide opportunities for design that support students in exploring and having agency about their learning. For example, in a study of EcoMUVE, researchers found that an important factor in students' sustained motivation to engage with a two-week long virtual ecosystem curriculum was the opportunity for self-directed learning within the environment [25]. Other examples of self-directed exploration in STEM immersive environments include Quest Atlantis [2], River City [26], and the Radix Endeavor [27].

3   Methods

3.1   Description of the Intervention

Wake is an immersive learning game for middle school science, iteratively designed by Field Day Lab, at the Wisconsin Center for Education Research at the UW–Madison School of Education, as part of an NSF grant-funded research project in collaboration with Harvard University and the University of Pennsylvania. The game was developed over a three-year period. During pre-production concepting, weekly interviews with an aquatic ecologist explored the contemporary practices, questions, challenges and tools of the domain. Prototypes explored potential interaction structures with the core mechanics of the game, namely experimentation, modeling and arguing from evidence. The content team which developed the scientific content and different challenges for the game worked iteratively with the art team to conduct studies for the different species and ecosystems, exploring art and animation styles that would serve both the learning goals as well as encourage immersion from the players.

Version (6.5) of the game was utilized for this study, which had fully developed art and simulation code for 60 species and fourteen environments (Figs. 1 and 2), but only placeholder art for most species' animations, scientific tools, and navigation elements as they were still under active development (Figs. 3 and 4). This version also contained only rudimentary story elements, such as a guide character, Kevin, who could be asked for help, and a main directive to "earn money to pay off your ship."

Fig. 1. Immersive Environment Art for Coral Reef Edge.

To facilitate self-directed learning, *Wake* is designed as an open world sandbox game, where the player has the freedom to explore a total of four distinct ecosystem types (coral reefs, the bayou dead zone, kelp forests, and arctic) embodied across fourteen research "sites." The game is structured through a total of 35 "jobs" that the player chooses to take, each requiring scientific or engineering practices to be conducted to answer an ecological question of interest to the researchers in that area. To answer these questions, the player travels to a research site, where they might need to scan the species that live there, estimate populations, conduct experiments, and/or build models. Each job concludes with the player making a claim using evidence derived from their efforts.

In *Wake*, players role-play as a young scientist, October, who is traveling to different research stations to do science and engineering work for hire. Despite the narrative still being in active development and quite minimal, the writing and dialog were designed to mimic the kinds of questions and challenges faced by scientists at each of these ecosystems. For example, players are asked to visit an ecosystem overrun by purple urchins and use their experimentation and modeling tools to determine what caused this condition and simulate different management approaches. Jobs are presented through simulated conversations with a virtual scientist; for example, one early job at the Coral

Fig. 2. Warm Kelp Forest.

Fig. 3. Prototype Navigation.

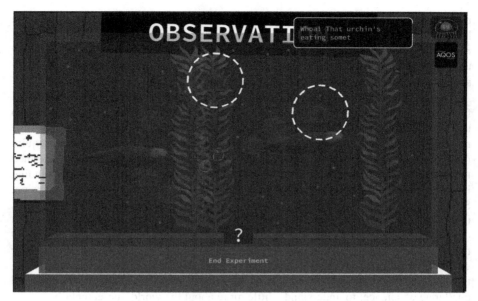

Fig. 4. Prototype Science Tool (Experiment tank).

Reef has "Professor Cempaka," saying "We need help monitoring the populations of turtles at the reef edge. Can you help us get the current population?" Once the student successfully scans and counts the turtle population at that site, and returns to the office to report their findings, the Professor says "That looks great! It looks like you are getting good at studying populations with your sub." A badge appears showing the job completed and the money earned.

The game's mechanics are aligned with the **tools** of scientific practice. *Wake* opens with the player standing in the helm of a research ship and then taking their submersible down into a kelp forest to make observations. They are given a tablet computer that records everything they've discovered about each species and ecosystem, a system called AQOS. Shortly after, they unlock the experimentation lab on the ship where they are able to study the interactions between species in a controlled environment. By the end of the initial onboarding sequence, intended to take no more than 20 min, the player has all the tools required to demonstrate the fundamental enterprise of science: making observations, conducting experiments, and making models of the world that form evidence-based claims about how the world works. Dialog with the scientist at the kelp forest encourages the student to keep going and reinforces their success: the kelp scientist says "You're doing some excellent work for us! I have some colleagues in other parts of the ocean that would love some help." A world map is unlocked, allowing access to other research stations.

Following this initial sequence, the tools expand through the introduction of a shop where the player can spend the funds they earn from completing jobs on upgrades to their submersible and their ship. Ship upgrades, such as a measurement tank and numerical modeling, allow the player to conduct new kinds of experiments or make new kinds of models. Submersible upgrades, which include items such as a prop guard, high-pressure hull, and ice breaker, allow the player to navigate to areas that were previously out of reach. Together, these upgrades allow the player to have significant choice over how their experience unfolds, while offering opportunities for the gradual scaffolding of new scientific practices and content, to avoid overwhelming them.

The creative direction for the game makes a fundamental assumption: that the reward for doing science should be found in discovery itself. As such, the game is designed so that the fundamental challenge is always about needing to access or to understand some natural phenomena. Some areas require new equipment to visit. Some questions require new forms of experiments or models to understand. In all cases, the game is designed to reflect another fundamental value of the science community, that our understanding is never perfect or complete, but is always developing and always open to revision. Structurally, this is reflected in the fact that the game has a fundamental collection of facts, the rules that govern the simulation. The player's job is to use the tools they are provided (and choose) to attempt to discover these facts. At many times they are able to understand the world well enough to meet the requirements of a job and progress, but only later encounter the limitations of their understanding and need to build a better understanding to pass some new challenge. In this regard, the game attempts to capture the fundamental challenge of science: to understand a little more about the world, incrementally.

3.2 Game Mechanics

The game is designed around the three science practices of experimentation, modeling, and argumentation. Different jobs will require different levels of engagement with each of these practices; for some jobs students might just collect data, such as the approximate count of sea turtles in an ecosystem, while other jobs require different combinations of experimenting and model building. All jobs conclude with an argument.

There are three types of experiments in the game, represented as different tanks in the Experiment Lab on the ship. *Observation* experiments involve adding up to four different organisms to a tank, and identifying eating relationships between them. *Stress* tank experiments determine a species' tolerance to different ranges of environmental variables through exposure to variations in temperature, light, and pH. *Measurement* experiments are used to measure rates: the rate at which one organism eats another, the rate that an organism reproduces, and the rate at which an organism interacts with the environment (e.g., uses oxygen). By choosing the environment in which to measure rates, students may obtain these measurements for both stressed and unstressed conditions.

The Modeling Lab of the ship supports students building four types of models of ecosystems. A *visual* model represents the food web in an ecosystem, based on the eating relationships identified by observation experiments. A *descriptive* model generates a graph of change over time, which allows the model to be tested by setting initial values of model parameters and seeing how well the model output aligns with historical data. A *predictive* model allows students to make predictions with the model, by running simulations of future changes. An *intervention* model lets students change the model by adding or removing organisms or changing populations, and running the model to predict the effect of a change.

Argumentation in the game is a conversation with a virtual scientist in which students are asked to support a claim with evidence from their experiments and models. Argumentation is the opportunity for students to demonstrate what they have learned. Arguments become more complex as students are asked to bring multiple types of data together in support of a claim, or to choose between claims by deciding which claim is best supported by evidence.

3.3 Study Design and Data Collection

Data presented here are derived from an implementation of a beta version of Wake at one middle school with four teachers and 16 7th grade classes in a high-SES suburban school district, and one teacher with three 8th grade classes in a medium-SES rural school district, both in the northeastern United States, for a total of approximately 250 middle school students. The first four teachers used Wake with their students for approximately 6–8 class periods, or about 4 h. The fifth teacher used the game during three 80-min blocks or about 2–3 h. The study was conducted with IRB approval and parent and student consent to collect research data. Researchers were present in all four of the teacher classrooms in the first district throughout the implementation, observing and collecting classroom video in at least one class of each teacher each day.

The research question for this study looks at how the game impacts three affective measures: student self-efficacy, science identity, and interest in science. A pre-post survey was used to explore students' attitudes and interests in science. The survey was a validated instrument [20] that contained three constructs, self-efficacy, science identity, and interest, each consisting of multiple Likert scale questions. For questions pertaining to self-efficacy, students were asked to respond on a scale of 1 to 6, for example, "How confident are you that you can investigate what causes change in an environment." Questions about science interest and identity similarly used a scale of 1–6, in which students were asked, "Click the button that best describes how true or false each statement is for you," followed by statements such as "I consider myself a science person" (identity) and "I am interested in learning about ecosystems" (interest).

Qualitative data from students consisted of brief informal interviews with students across the five classes during or following their completion of the curriculum. Students were identified by teachers based on their prior consent and parental permission, as well as their willingness to be interviewed. Questions asked of students included opinions about the game, what they liked or didn't like, what they learned, whether they'd ever used a game like this in science class before, how they thought learning with a game was different than other science classes, and any suggestions for making the game better. Teachers were asked to complete a post-survey after their use of the curriculum, and teachers also shared feedback through brief, video-recorded conversations during implementation.

4 Findings

4.1 Quantitative Findings

Because of student absences, missing parental permission, or other factors, some students were unable to contribute data for either the pretest or posttest. Our final dataset (n = 208) consisted of students who had successfully completed both halves of data collection, as well as provided appropriate consent and assent for their data to be used. Individual survey questions were combined into scales measuring self-efficacy, science identity, and interest. Cronbach's alpha for each scale suggested high internal reliability for our survey measures. Our lowest construct was the measure of pretest interest, with a Cronbach's alpha of 0.872. All other reliability measures for scales were at or above 90%.

To examine the effects of playing the game on these constructs, three paired-samples t-tests were conducted. Significant differences were found from pre to post for each construct. Students' average self-reported self-efficacy in science increased from 3.98 (of a possible 6) in the pretest, to 4.50 in the posttest, $t(207) = 5.87$, $p < 0.001$. Students' average self-reported science identity increased from 3.12 (of a possible 6) in the pretest to 3.44 in the posttest, $t(207) = 4.18$, $p < 0.001$. Finally, students' average self-reported interest in science increased from 3.71 (of a possible 6) in the pretest, to 3.97 in the posttest, $t(207) = 2.93$, $p = 0.004$.

Finally, an ANOVA was constructed to examine the potential influence of mediating factors, such as students' gender or videogame experience, on these changes. The ANOVA was used so that we could measure the effects of multiple between-subjects factors at the same time. The analysis found no significant effects of students' science ability, frequency of videogame play, classroom teacher, or interactions between these measures, on observed differences from pretest to posttest.

4.2 Qualitative Findings

Interviews with students at the end of the implementation found that students generally enjoyed playing the game, and found it fun as well as helpful for learning science content and practices. Students enjoyed getting to "do the missions," one noting that "other games just do it all for us; in this game we do the work." One student said that "I liked how it talked to you, as if you were a professional scientist and not just a kid in a classroom who's playing a game." Students also provided feedback on software glitches and UI issues, and described points in the game that were confusing or repetitive.

A representational sample of five students in one class were asked an open-ended question about what they liked about the game, and three of the five specifically noted that they appreciated the way the game supported self-directed learning:

- "I liked that I could play at my own pace, and do jobs as I'm ready."
- "In this you get to… go around and do missions, instead of the teacher saying 'read from this, and write how the thing is, blah blah blah.' It was more independent and free thinking, which is good."
- [Compared to other games in science class] "you had more freedom than other games, so you could choose whatever job you wanted at a time."

Another student described a predictive modeling task about an urchin barren that he thought was "one of the best parts of the game. You really had free control and you had to look at how the ecosystem interacted and then try to figure it out from all your options." Other things that students specifically noted as enjoyable parts of the game centered on the tools and challenges, including that "the best part was getting to go to different areas," that it was "fun to drive the submarine and see all the new species and scan things," and that they liked "reporting back to the professors and discussing what I learned overall with them." Students also noted that certain jobs could be confusing, but overall they felt that it was better than traditional science lessons, and as one student said, "this really made me understand it more and it was a fun way to do it, not just talking about it. 'Cause it grabs people's attention more and makes it stay with them."

We've since interviewed other students who have been playtesting the game during class the next fall. One 8th grade student specifically called out the role-playing nature of the game, saying, "When you're playing the game, it's more of you interacting, doing stuff that a marine biologist would usually do." Asked if she felt like she was "being a marine biologist," she agreed that she did, and that the game maybe helped her think that this was something she could see herself doing. Another student echoed constructivist theories of learning by explaining that, "this is interesting because it's subtly showing you things to learn rather than teaching you things," adding "I learned more about the ways that scientists figure things out – there's the problem and then you go and find, figure out what do you need to solve, and then you go and find things like population of something and then you can go and experiment with it, and then yeah, you can make a claim out of it."

Finally, one middle school teacher who tested the game with her students was asked about its possible impact on science identity, and she said that taking on the role of a scientist "was the biggest thing for my kids, because they were like, 'I really feel like a scientist. I can't believe this is what scientists do, because I'm doing it. And I'm figuring it out on my own.'" She added that a few of her students were even concerned enough to ask – "in the game we get paid and use the money to buy tools to put on our ship, shouldn't we get more money to live on? Does that happen to real scientists?".

5 Discussion and Future Directions

This study used a beta version of *Wake: Tales from the Aqualab* in formal classroom contexts to study the game's overall feasibility and usability with a focus on self-efficacy, science identity, and science interest. Findings demonstrated that by leveraging design elements of role-play, tools and challenges of the practice, and self-directed learning, the game produced significant increases in all three measures of self-efficacy, science identity, and science interest. These findings contribute evidence for the validity of these design theories for immersive games for STEM learning. Practically, this game and findings contribute an example of how these approaches can be actualized through design.

This study is faced with several limitations. The study looks only at student experiences as a whole, without a means to consider specific design elements individually. The interfaces for the primary navigation and scientific tools were prototypes, and likely led to some usability issues. And as an incomplete version of the game, the story elements were almost non-existent, so role-play was only partially explored. In future work, the team will be researching the final version of the game in similar classroom contexts. Now that the core mechanics and content of the game have been established, the full story and navigation are under development. Over a dozen characters have been developed, and a storyline has been designed that places the player character within a family of multilingual scientists immediately following the traumatic loss of their daughter. The game's overarching narrative involves the player coming to terms with their own relationship with the dangerous and inspiring world of aquatic research. Full-fidelity interfaces have been implemented for all the game's mechanics. New infrastructure, currently in development, will allow questionnaires to be embedded directly within game play.

Within this context, individual elements of the art, story and progression are planned to be tested using rapid randomized control trials, commonly known as A/B tests, with large public audiences. This approach was piloted in previous work by the authors to explore the role of humor in educational game script writing [28]. These tests, driven from analytic data, will allow the researchers to investigate the effects of individual design elements such as versions of the script, representations of non-player characters, and structures for unlocking the different tools and environments within the game. Another interesting future area of study would be to look more deeply at the types of immersion that students experience during game play, using instruments that measure immersion e.g., the Temple Presence Inventory (TPI), a set of questionnaire items that can be used to measure dimensions of presence [29]. This work hopes to contribute to the field of immersive learning research by providing insight on design elements that support actional immersion, and research findings on gains in affective science measures during student use of a multi-hour science game in which they take on the role of a scientist and engage in meaningful scientific activities.

Acknowledgments. This material is based upon work supported by the National Science Foundation under grants DRL-1907384, DRL-1907398, and DRL-1907437. Any opinions, findings and conclusions or recommendations expressed in this material are those of the authors and do not necessarily reflect the views of the National Science Foundation.

References

1. Dede, C.: Immersive interfaces for engagement and learning. Science **323**(5910), 66–69 (2009). https://doi.org/10.1126/science.1167311
2. Barab, S., Dede, C.: Games and immersive participatory simulations for science education: an emerging type of curricula. J. Sci. Educ. Technol. **16**, 1–3 (2007)
3. Wilson, B.G.: Constructivism in practical and historical context. Trends Issues Instruct. Des. Technol. **3**, 45–52 (2012)
4. Dede, C., Grotzer, T., Kamarainen, A., Metcalf, S., Feldman, R.: Designing immersive authentic simulations that enhance motivation and learning: EcoLearn. Learning science: Theory, research, practice, pp. 229–259 (2019)
5. Di Natale, A.F., Repetto, C., Riva, G., Villani, D.: Immersive virtual reality in K-12 and higher education: a 10-year systematic review of empirical research. Br. J. Edu. Technol. **51**, 2006–2033 (2020)

6. Bodzin, A., Junior, R.A., Hammond, T., Anastasio, D.: An immersive virtual reality game designed to promote learning engagement and flow. In: 2020 6th International Conference of the Immersive Learning Research Network (iLRN), pp. 193–198. IEEE (2020)
7. Gupta, S., Tanenbaum, T.J., Muralikumar, M.D., Marathe, A.S.: Investigating roleplaying and identity transformation in a virtual reality narrative experience. In: Proceedings of the 2020 CHI Conference on Human Factors in Computing Systems, pp. 1–13 (2020)
8. Trujillo, G., Tanner, K.D.: Considering the role of affect in learning: monitoring students' self-efficacy, sense of belonging, and science identity. CBE—Life Sci. Educ. 13(1), 6–15 (2014). https://doi.org/10.1187/cbe.13-12-0241
9. Kolodner, J.L., Said, T., Wright, K., Pallant, A.: Drawn into science through authentic virtual practice. In: Proceedings of the 2017 Conference on Interaction Design and Children, pp. 385–391 (2017)
10. Beier, M.E., Miller, L.M., Wang, S.: Science games and the development of scientific possible selves. Cult. Sci. Edu. 7, 963–978 (2012)
11. Foster, A., et al.: Virtual learning environments for promoting self transformation: iterative design and implementation of Philadelphia land science. In: Beck, D., et al. (eds.) iLRN 2018. CCIS, vol. 840, pp. 3–22. Springer, Cham (2018). https://doi.org/10.1007/978-3-319-93596-6_1
12. Barany, A., Foster, A., Shah, M.: Design-based research iterations of a virtual learning environment for identity exploration. In: 2020 6th International Conference of the Immersive Learning Research Network (iLRN), pp. 101–108. IEEE (2020)
13. Hu-Au, E., Lee, J.J.: Virtual reality in education: a tool for learning in the experience age. Int. J. Innov. Educ. 4, 215–226 (2017)
14. Dalgarno, B., Lee, M.J.: What are the learning affordances of 3-D virtual environments? Br. J. Edu. Technol. 41, 10–32 (2010)
15. Metcalf, S.J., Kamarainen, A.M., Torres, E., Grotzer, T.A., Dede, C.: EcoMUVE: a case study on the affordances of MUVEs in ecosystem science education. In: Qian, Y. (ed.) Integrating Multi-User Virtual Environments in Modern Classrooms:, pp. 1–25. IGI Global (2018). https://doi.org/10.4018/978-1-5225-3719-9.ch001
16. Chen, J.A., Dede, C.: Youth STEM Motivation: Immersive Technologies to Engage and Empower Underrepresented Students (2011)
17. Chen, J.A., Metcalf, S.J., Tutwiler, M.S.: Motivation and beliefs about the nature of scientific knowledge within an immersive virtual ecosystems environment. Contemp. Educ. Psychol. 39, 112–123 (2014)
18. Portnoy, L., Schrier, K.: Using games to support STEM curiosity, identity, and self-efficacy. J. Games Self Soc. 1, 66–96 (2019)
19. Lu, Y.-L., Lien, C.-J.: Are they learning or playing? Students' perception traits and their learning self-efficacy in a game-based learning environment. J. Educ. Comput. Res. 57, 1879–1909 (2020)
20. Reilly, J.M., McGivney, E., Dede, C., Grotzer, T.: Assessing science identity exploration in immersive virtual environments: a mixed methods approach. J. Exp. Educ. 89, 468–489 (2021)
21. Raph, K.: A theory of fun for game design (2005)
22. Gee, J.P.: What Video Games Have to Teach Us about Learning and Literacy: Revised and Updated Edition. Palgrave Macmillan (2007)
23. Roth, W.-M.: STEM and affect in adolescence: A cultural-historical approach. In: Jorgensen, R., Larkin, K. (eds.) STEM Education in the Junior Secondary, pp. 15–36. Springer Singapore, Singapore (2018). https://doi.org/10.1007/978-981-10-5448-8_3
24. Ryan, R.M., Deci, E.L.: Intrinsic and extrinsic motivations: classic definitions and new directions. Contemp. Educ. Psychol. 25, 54–67 (2000)

25. Metcalf, S.J., et al.: Transitions in student motivation during a MUVE-based ecosystem science curriculum: an evaluation of the novelty effect. In: Becnel, K. (ed.) Emerging Technologies in Virtual Learning Environments:, pp. 96–115. IGI Global (2019). https://doi.org/10.4018/978-1-5225-7987-8.ch005
26. Ketelhut, D.J., Clarke, J., Nelson, B.C.: The development of River City, a multi-user virtual environment-based scientific inquiry curriculum: historical and design evolutions. In: Jacobson, M.J., Reimann, P. (eds.) Designs for Learning Environments of the Future, pp. 89–110. Springer US, Boston, MA (2010). https://doi.org/10.1007/978-0-387-88279-6_4
27. Rosenheck, L.: Designing for Collaborative Play: Why Games Need MUVEs and MUVEs Need Games. In: Qian, Y. (ed.) Integrating Multi-User Virtual Environments in Modern Classrooms, pp. 26–49. IGI Global (2018). https://doi.org/10.4018/978-1-5225-3719-9.ch002
28. Gagnon, D.J., et al.: Exploring players' experience of humor and snark in a grade 3–6 history practices game. arXiv preprint arXiv:2210.09906 (2022)
29. Lombard, M., Bolmarcich, T., Weinstein, L.: Measuring Presence: The Temple Presence Inventory (2009)

Superfrog: Comparing Learning Outcomes and Potentials of a Worksheet, Smartphone, and Tangible AR Learning Environment

Sebastian Oberdörfer[1]([⊠]) [iD], Anne Elsässer[1], Silke Grafe[2] [iD],
and Marc Erich Latoschik[1] [iD]

[1] Human-Computer Interaction, University of Würzburg, Würzburg, Germany
{sebastian.oberdoerfer,anne.elsaesser,marc.latoschi}@uni-wuerzburg.de
[2] School Pedagogy, University of Würzburg, Würzburg, Germany
silke.grafe@uni-wuerzburg.de

Abstract. The widespread availability of smartphones facilitates the integration of digital, augmented reality (AR), and tangible augmented reality (TAR) learning environments into the classroom. A haptic aspect can enhance the user's overall experience during a learning process. To investigate further benefits of using TAR for educational purposes, we compare a TAR and a smartphone learning environment with a traditional worksheet counterpart in terms of learning effectiveness, emotions, motivation, and cognitive load. 64 sixth-grade students from a German high school used one of the three conditions to learn about frog anatomy. We found no significant differences in learning effectiveness and cognitive load. The TAR condition elicited significantly higher positive emotions than the worksheet, but not the smartphone condition. Both digital learning environments elicited significantly higher motivation, in contrast to the worksheet. Thus, our results suggest that smartphone and TAR learning environments are equally beneficial for enhancing learning.

Keywords: Augmented reality · Education · Serious games · Gamification · Tangible user interfaces

1 Introduction

The widespread availability of smartphones allows teachers to develop technology-based teaching concepts [20]. Using smartphones not only provides access to digital learning environments, but also enables an integration of Augmented Reality (AR) in teaching concepts [56]. Following an approach of media didactics, a learning environment provides a simulation of a given subject that enables learners to interact as well as experiment with and to observe the results of their actions [53]. Thus, a learning environment requires self-directed learning and, depending on the desired structure of the learning, finding a solution to a

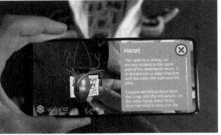

Fig. 1. When detecting the markers with a smartphone, *Horst-TAR* displays 3D models of the organs. Touching the organ reveals biological information.

problem, design of a product, and evaluation of a situation. Using AR for teaching and learning can result in higher learning gains, motivation, and experiential gains through direct application of learning content [4].

AR-based learning environments can also be extended by a tangible user interface (TUI), thus giving the learning process a physical aspect [8]. Combining physical objects with so-called fiducial markers achieves *Tangible AR (TAR)* [8]. TAR allows learners to inspect augmented objects from all angles by manipulating them directly in six degrees of freedom [5]. This intensifies the direct application of learning content and enables spatial learning.

TAR results in a higher complexity of the learning environment. Besides the requirement of a smartphone, a teacher also must provide enough physical markers for the entire class. This becomes even more challenging when learners should continue to learn at home. In addition, teachers must acquire technological pedagogical content knowledge to successfully integrate AR learning environments in classroom teaching [28,39]. Hence, the educational benefits of using TAR should outweigh the preparation complexity to justify a classroom integration. Therefore, it is of high importance to investigate the potential advantages of TAR for educational purposes to derive guidelines as well as recommendations for developers and educators.

2   Contribution

The present study investigates the learning effectiveness of a TAR learning environment in comparison to a smartphone and traditional worksheet counterpart at a local high school. We use the TAR and smartphone version of the gamified learning environment *Horst – The Teaching Frog* [41]. To enable a baseline measurement, we designed a worksheet providing the same declarative information about a frog's organs. The learning environments target the learning of the anatomy of frogs as shown in Fig. 1.

While the digital versions simulate dissection, the worksheet approach conveys the information with illustrations and text only. The three versions of the learning environment differ only in the way knowledge is presented, i.e., smartphone, TAR, and worksheet. In our user study, we found no significant difference between the conditions in terms of learning effectiveness and cognitive load. However, the TAR version elicited significantly higher positive emotion than the worksheet, but not the smartphone version. In addition, the TAR and smartphone versions elicited significantly higher motivation compared to the worksheet. Thus, our results suggest that smartphone and TAR learning environments are equally beneficial for enhancing learning, with TAR even eliciting slightly higher positive emotion.

3   Theoretical Background

AR three-dimensionally integrates virtual elements into the real-world that are interactive in real time [2]. Users can experience AR using headworn, handheld, and projected displays [27]. Handheld AR commonly is achieved using smartphones and tablets that are turned into a "Magic Lens" [6] revealing the augmentations. However, headworn and projected displays provide a greater freedom to users by keeping their hands free. Smartphone AR benefits from the widespread availability and familiarization of the users with these devices [32]. This makes smartphone AR especially useful for educational use cases [56].

Besides interacting with virtual elements on the device, they can also be manipulated using a TUI [19]. A TUI uses real world objects as input and output devices, thus connecting digital information with real world objects [23]. A TAR interface similarly links virtual information to physical objects. This allows for an augmentation of physical objects and an interaction with the AR system by manipulating the respective objects [8]. TAR not only suits the visualization of 3D models [5], but also yields a very intuitive experience [8].

3.1   Benefits of AR for Learning

Using AR for educational purposes can facilitate the learning and knowledge acquisition [10]. This potentially can lead to an overall positive attitude towards the learning content and hence to higher academic success [24]. AR learning environments further assist the learning of complex constructs by providing spatial and direct visualization of learning content [15]. For instance, *Mathland* demonstrates the mathematics behind Newtonian physics and allows users to modify and hence explore the physical laws [26]. However, AR can also be beneficial for vocabulary learning leading to better short-term retention in contrast to a non-AR counterpart [54]. Finally, as AR allows for a direct interaction with real-world objects, AR learning environments can further support the requirements of special needs education [49]. Similarly, a TAR learning environment can evoke a higher degree of joy and motivation in comparison to Graphical User Interfaces (GUIs) [22] as well as reduce the cognitive load [12]. Using TAR in an educational context can intensify work on learning material, improve usability, and support mental skills as well as collaboration [1]. Overall, TAR learning environments address three core aspect particularly relevant for learning according to the theories of self-determination [47] and cognitive load [51]: positive emotions, higher motivation, and lower cognitive load. These are also key attributes of learning using extended reality [13].

Different emotions can have different effects on the mediators memory processes, regulation of learning, cognitive load, and motivation [45]. Thus, it is assumed that learning performance is positively influenced by positive emotions like joy and negatively influenced by emotions with negative valence, such as anxiety [33]. Zuckerman and Gal-Oz [58] showed a higher preference and a higher rating with respect to stimulation and entertainment of TUIs in comparison to GUIs. Oberdörfer et al. [40] found first indications that TAR learning environments are more stimulating, attractive, and novel as well as yield a higher preference in comparison to AR and smartphone counterparts.

Intrinsic motivation or internalized forms of extrinsic motivation lead to higher learning performance than externally regulated forms of motivation [46]. AR demonstrated to evoke such a higher degree of motivation in comparison to other learning media [18]. For example, students experienced high motivation in learning about georeferenced information when using an AR tool to visualize relief [11]. This effect could be due to the perceived autonomy in using the technology and the multisensory experience that allows learners to interact in a natural way [18].

The goal of successful instructional design is to make optimal use of the capacity of working memory. To achieve this, multimedia principles can be implemented to reduce extraneous cognitive load, manage intrinsic cognitive load, and promote germane cognitive load [35]. Digital learning environments can present and allow for a direct interaction with three-dimensional information. In contrast to printed textbooks, this reduces the cognitive load of mentally rotating objects to analyze and understand them. For instance, learners reported lower extraneous and intrinsic cognitive load when completing chemistry exercises [25] or learning anatomy [29] in AR.

3.2   Playful Learning Experiences

The overall learning process can be embedded in a gamified approach [38]. Gamified learning environments can either be *serious games* [17] or non-gaming learning applications enhanced by *gamification* [48]. Following such an approach, the learning can become an engaging, vivid, and inspiring experience [36]. Serious games map the learning contents to central game mechanics or core interactions, thus achieving their application and demonstration [42]. Gamification refers to the integration of game elements in non-gaming environments [14]. Gamification enhances the motivation of pupils [34] leading to more repetitive learning and development of sustainable knowledge. This general effect of gamification also applies to AR learning environments, yielding a higher joy, interest, and engagement [31].

4   Horst – The Teaching Frog

To investigate the effects of TAR technology on learning, we selected the gamified TAR learning environment *Horst – The Teaching Frog* [41]. *Horst – The Teaching*

Frog simulates a dissection of a frog, thus enabling the learning about a frog's anatomy. Digital simulations can yield a more effective learning in comparison to real dissections [57]. The learning environment is designed as a supplementary material for sixth grade biology lessons dealing with anatomy of amphibians [7]. During the simulation, learners can either acquire and deepen the encoded knowledge in a virtual dissection or assess their learning progress in a quiz. The learning content presented is based on two textbooks on amphibians [21, 50] and defined in collaboration with educators. Besides the TAR version (*Horst-TAR*), a smartphone (*Horst-S*) and AR-only version (*Horst-AR*) were developed that encode the same learning content, provide the same functions, but differ in the technology used [40]. A study revealed that all versions of Horst are comparable with respect to intuitive use, but differ regarding user experience [40]. User experience was highest for *Horst-TAR* followed by *Horst-AR*. Thus, this study paved the way for our experiment by ruling out potential confounds on our learning effectiveness measurements caused by differences in the usability.

To compare the TAR learning environment to the de-facto standard of digital learning environments, i.e., smartphones, we also included *Horst-S* in our study. We further designed an additional worksheet version (*Horst-WS*) to compare *Horst-TAR* to a traditional learning method and to generate a baseline measurement. *Horst-WS* presents the same learning content as the digital versions and follows the structure of common textbooks. This ensures that measured differences in the learning outcome are caused by the technology and not differences in the learning contents. However, we decided against including *Horst-AR* in our experiment. Similar to TAR, AR would cause a higher preparation complexity as additional markers must be provided besides AR devices.

Horst – The Teaching Frog is available for download at our lab's website[1].

4.1 Digital Learning Environments

The digital versions of *Horst* provide two dissection modes, i.e., assisted and free dissection, a quiz to self-assess the individual learning progress, and an achievement as well as highscore system. The assisted mode guides a user through the process of dissecting a frog, thus scaffolding the learning process. By explaining each step in detail, this mode provides additional information about the anatomy of a frog. After reading the description of a step provided by the pedagogical agent Horst, learners must find the relevant organ, extract it, and display as well as read the organ's biological information as displayed in Fig. 1. Subsequently, the learning environment displays the next task. Learners cannot skip a step during the assisted dissection. In contrast, the free dissection provides no guidance, but allows for a free examination of the frog's organs. The learning environment currently includes seven organs that are sequenced in the following order during the assisted mode: heart, liver, lungs, stomach, gut, kidney, and bladder.

Horst-TAR is based on a large, but realistic soft toy of a frog. A pouch featuring a zipper was added to the belly of the plush frog, thus allowing for its

---

[1] https://hci.uni-wuerzburg.de/projects/horst-the-teaching-frog/.

Fig. 2. *Horst-S* allows for a frog dissection on smartphones, thus presenting the de-facto standard for mobile learning.

dissection as shown in Fig. 1. Inside this pouch, extractable *tangible* paper-card-based markers are attached to the frog using a piece of velcro. Each tangible object represents an individual organ and features two 2D images of the respective organ as image targets. The front side shows an image of the organ's outer side and the back side an image the organ's inner side as seen from the belly. The *Horst-TAR* application displays a 3D model of each organ above the relevant markers when detecting them with the smartphone's camera. This visualizes the anatomy of a frog. By physically extracting a marker, learners can inspect the 3D organ model from all angles up close. While scanning the front side, learners can inspect the outer side of the organ. Vice-versa, scanning the back side allows for an inspection of the organ's inner side. *Horst-TAR* displays biological information about an organ when touching it on the smartphone display. In contrast, *Horst-S* displays a 3D model of a frog and its individual organs as shown in Fig. 2. A user merely needs to touch an organ to display the relevant biological information and to inspect it up close using drag gestures.

The quiz contains 16 multiple-choice questions that test learners' knowledge of frog anatomy and functions of their organs. Learners receive an immediate audiovisual feedback about the correctness of their selections. While correct answers are marked in green and rewarded with a quack sound, wrong answers are marked in red and emphasized with the sound of a buzzer. The learning environment removes a correctly answered question from the list but returns a wrongly answered question to it. In this way, learners get an additional chance to reflect about the exercise and hence to deepen their knowledge.

Finally, the learning environment motivates the learning process and repetition of the provided learning opportunities with an achievement and highscore system. Achievements present clear tasks like completing five dissections, thus giving learners an incentive to repeat the process. The highscore system rewards the completion of an assisted dissection as well as a good performance in the quiz.

Fig. 3. We designed a worksheet version for the learning content presented in the digital versions.

4.2   Worksheet

Horst-WS consists of a short instruction, a picture of the 3D-model used in *Horst-S* supplemented by the labeling of the individual organs, and information texts on the individual organs in dissection order as displayed in Fig. 3. For the purpose of contextualization, we added an adapted version of the introductory text of the chapter "The water frog – a life in water and on land" from the biology textbook Natura 1 [3] to the worksheet and illustrated it with two photos of a frog. The introductory text is also used in the digital versions, but narrated by the agent Horst from the first-person perspective. Thus, the three versions of *Horst – The Teaching Frog* only differ with respect to the presentation technology used.

5   Study Design

The overall goal of our research is to investigate the effects of using TAR in comparison to smartphones and traditional worksheets for educational purposes. In particular, we targeted the acquisition of declarative knowledge about the organs and their functions. We defined the following learning goal: *After the learning phase, the participants can name and explain the seven included organs.*

To ensure for such an acquisition of declarative knowledge and hence a comparability of our results, we limited the functions of *Horst-TAR* and *Horst-S* to the assisted dissection, only. Also, we disabled the quiz as well as highscore feature and reduced the achievement system to a minimum. Participants receive four achievements throughout the entire learning process. The first one is unlocked when starting the tutorial, the second one when finishing the tutorial, the third one after having inspected the first half of the organs, and the last one upon completion of the dissection. In this way, the three conditions focused the memorization and understanding of facts.

We assume the following hypotheses based on the analysis of the theoretical work in Sect. 3 and the design of *Horst – The Teaching Frog* in Sect. 4.

H1 The learning effectiveness is higher with *Horst-TAR* than *Horst-S* and *Horst-S* than *Horst-WS*.

H2 A learner's emotions are more positive after using *Horst-TAR* than *Horst-S* and *Horst-S* than *Horst-WS*.

H3 A learner's motivation is higher when learning with *Horst-TAR* than *Horst-S* and *Horst-S* than *Horst-WS*.

H4 A learner's cognitive load is lower when learning with *Horst-TAR* than *Horst-S* and *Horst-S* than *Horst-WS*.

To compare the three versions and to answer the four hypotheses, we conducted a user study following a between-groups design. Participants were randomly assigned to either one of the three learning environments and completed an assisted dissection. Before and after the learning phase, participants answered various questionnaires. In addition, we conducted a semi-structured interview with teachers to gain additional insights into the feasibility of integrating TAR learning environments in classroom teaching.

The institutional review board of Human-Computer Media at the University of Würzburg approved our ethics proposal for this study.

5.1 Measures

We used the following measures to compare the conditions.

Learning Effectiveness. To measure learning effectiveness and to factor out a potential influence of prior knowledge, we assessed the participants' knowledge with a written exam before and after learning. Both exams tested our defined learning goal, i.e., knowing and comprehending the seven included organs, and contained the same 10 exercises. We presented the exercises in randomized order except for the first task, i.e., labeling the organs. The remaining exercises required the participants to either name the organ that fulfills a specific purpose or to describe functions of a particular organ. The formulation of the exercises was based on official guidelines and reviewed by biology teachers. The maximum achievable score is 22.

The exam consisted of the following exercises:

1. Labeling of the individual organs depicted in a screenshot of the 3D model used in *Horst-S*.
2. Name the scientific term for the intestinal tract of frogs.
3. Name the scientific term for the mixture of oxygenated and deoxygenated blood.
4. Name the two organs that are part of the digestive tract.
5. Name the organ that pumps blood through the frog's body.

6. Name the breathing type of frogs in which they take in oxygen through their skin.
7. Name the two functions of the liver.
8. Name the parts into which the heart is divided. Use scientific terms.
9. Describe how oral cavity breathing works in frogs.
10. Name the two functions of the kidney.

Emotion. We assessed the current affect using a short version of the *Positive and Negative Affect Schedule for Children (PANAS-C)* [16]. The short version of the PANAS-C contains 10 items, which can be equally divided into the dimensions Positive Affect (PA) and Negative Affect (NA). We sequenced the items according to the original version of the PANAS-C [30]. We directly translated each item to German, e.g., "sad" to "traurig" and "joyful" to "fröhlich", and used the validated German translation of the Likert scale labels [9]. The instructions were also based on the validated German version of the *PANAS* [9], but adjusted in their wording to facilitate understanding for the children.

Motivation. To measure motivation, we used the *Short Scale of Intrinsic Motivation (KIM)* [55]. The scale is based on the *Intrinsic Motivation Inventory (IMI)* [47] and was developed for high school students. It contains 3 items each for the factors interest/enjoyment (short: enjoyment), perceived competence (short: competence), perceived choice (short: choice), and pressure/tension (short: pressure), and thus a total of 12 items. In the original, the 5-point Likert scale ranges from 0 "do not agree at all" to 4 "agree completely". We changed the numbering to 1 "do not agree at all" to 5 "agree completely" for the purpose of uniform interpretation.

Cognitive Load. We used the 9-point *Paas* subjective rating scale [43, 44] ranging from 1 "very, very little mental effort" to 9 "very, very high mental effort" to assess the experienced cognitive load. Although the scale does not differentiate between extraneous and intrinsic of cognitive load, the scale has been shown to be a valid measurement tool for cognitive load in general and requires little time to complete [52]. We translated the scale to German and reworded it for improving comprehensibility by directly naming the learning content: "In learning the organs of the frog, I invested ..." / "Beim Lernen der Organe des Frosches habe ich mich ... angestrengt".

Feedback. We posed three closed questions to obtain subjective feedback from the participants on their version of the learning environment and respective learning process. Participants could agree to statements about the willingness to repeat learning with their learning environment and desire to learn with the respective technology in other subjects. We used the same 5-point Likert scale as in the KIM. In addition, we asked the participants to rate their learning environment with school grades ranging from 1 "very good" to 6 "unsatisfactory".

Teacher Interview. To gain preliminary feedback on the potential integration of *Horst – The Teaching Frog* in teaching concepts, we gauged the teachers' perspectives on the different learning environments. We conducted an oral semi-structured interview with three teachers of whom two were pre-service teachers. At the end of a study day, the teachers and experimenter came together to inspect the learning environments. Before allowing the teachers to use the learning environments, we gave them a quick overview and explained all possible interactions. Subsequently, we conducted the interview. In favor of the flow of speech, we did not pay attention to a consistent wording of the questions. The teacher interview took place in parallel to our user study. The question pool included the following items:

1. Which of the three learning environments do you prefer and why?
2. How would you use your favorite in a classroom scenario?
3. What effect do you hope your favorite will have?

Fig. 4. The left image provides an overview of the high school's library. The right image shows the setup of the study prior to the start of an experimental trial.

5.2 Procedure

We conducted the study in the library of a German high school as displayed in Fig. 4. There were always 2–3 students participating in the study at the same time. After welcoming the participants, we briefly explained the experiment. The students randomly chose one of the three conditions by drawing a labeled card. They were then assigned to workstations where they were first to read the student participant information. Once all students completed this step, they completed the pre-trial phase consisting of the demography questionnaire, PANAS-C, and pre-trail exam. Subsequently, they started the learning phase with the respective version of Horst. To ensure that each student knew how to use their learning environment, we provided a separate learning instruction for each condition.

The learning time was limited. All students in the *Horst-WS* condition had 15 min and all students in the *Horst-S* and *Horst-TAR* condition had 14 min. We shortened the learning time for the two digital versions as their tutorials already explain the first organ and hence the participants start the learning phase while familiarizing them with the learning environment. After the learning phase, the experimenters collected the learning materials and handed out the post-trial materials. These materials consisted of Paas scale, PANAS-C, KIM, post-trial exam, and feedback questions. The sequence of the materials ensured a direct assessment of the cognitive load, current affect and motivation, while reducing the chance for a recency effect when completing the exam.

5.3 Participants

The sample was recruited from the pupils attending the sixth-grade at a German highschool. All parents received an information sheet in advance describing the purpose and procedure of the study, COVID-19 infection control measures, voluntariness and anonymity, data protection and handling of the anonymized data. Based on this, they were able to make a decision as to whether they agreed to their child's participation in the study. Only children who had a signed parental consent form and voluntarily wished to partake in the study participated.

A total of $N = 68$ high school students participated in the study. However, the data sets of 4 students had to be excluded from the analysis because of missing information and conspicuous answers in the quantitative and qualitative data. In the end, the data of $N = 64$ students were evaluated. Of these, 27 subjects were male (42.86%), 36 subjects were female (56.25%), and 1 subject was diverse (1.56%). The average age was 11.98 years ($SD = 0.42$). The majority of students (56; 87.50%) reported speaking German at home. No student showed comprehension problems during the study. The majority of students had quite a bit or a lot (27 each; 42.19%) of experience with smartphone apps at the time of the survey, while a small proportion had little (9; 14.06%) or no experience (1; 1.56%) with them. In terms of experience with AR apps, the ratio was reversed. Thus, the majority had no (17; 26.56%) or little (24; 37.50%) experience with AR apps and a minority had quite a bit (16; 25.00%) or a lot (7; 10.94%) of experience. Interest in biology was in the middle range on the scale of 1 "Not at all" to 4 "Very much" ($M = 2.45$; $SD = 0.66$).

6   Results

We tested the reliability of the scales by computing Cronbach's α if applicable. To compare the different learning environments, we calculated one-factor analyses of variance (ANOVA) for the results of the PANAS-C, Paas scale, KIM, and score on the post exam. As a measure of effect size, we computed the partial eta squared η_p^2. Homoscedasticity was checked using Levene's test before each ANOVA. Alternatively, if there was no homogeneity of variances, a Welch

Table 1. Descriptive statistics; $N = 64$. Values are $M(SD)$.

Scale	Horst-WS ($n = 22$)	Horst-S ($n = 22$)	Horst-TAR ($n = 20$)
Exam			
Pre	2.55 (2.13)	2.91 (2.27)	3.10 (2.40)
Post	12.32 (4.08)	11.98 (5.07)	10.25 (5.28)
PANAS-C			
PA_{pre} ($\alpha = .75$)	3.15 (0.92)	3.14 (0.65)	3.23 (0.61)
PA_{post} ($\alpha = .90$)	2.62 (1.08)	2.99 (0.91)	3.15 (0.69)
NA_{pre} ($\alpha = .58$)	1.31 (0.29)	1.28 (0.38)	1.36 (0.50)
NA_{post} ($\alpha = .47$)	1.25 (0.28)	1.14 (0.19)	1.24 (0.35)
KIM			
Enjoyment ($\alpha = .91$)	2.86 (1.25)	3.95 (1.00)	3.82 (0.95)
Competence ($\alpha = .81$)	3.15 (0.91)	3.68 (0.83)	3.60 (0.58)
Choice ($\alpha = .85$)	3.84 (1.19)	3.86 (0.97)	4.00 (0.99)
Pressure ($\alpha = .71$)	2.83 (1.08)	2.08 (0.70)	2.23 (0.91)
Paas			
Total score	5.55 (1.68)	4.59 (1.68)	5.25 (1.68)
Feedback			
Repetition of learning	3.32 (1.55)	4.05 (1.05)	3.25 (1.37)
Technology for other subjects	2.50 (1.44)	4.32 (0.95)	3.65 (1.18)
Grade	2.86 (1.24)	1.91 (1.15)	1.93 (0.65)

ANOVA was calculated. Since ANOVA is robust to violation of the normal distribution, no corrective action was taken in case of violation. Some analyses of variance, including PA_{post}, NA_{post}, and post exam, required consideration of one or more covariates (ANCOVA). In this case, an additional ANOVA was computed to ensure the independence of the covariates and the learning environments. If an omnibus test produced a significant difference, we calculated Tukey-Kramer comparisons for unequal sample sizes or Games-Howell tests for unequal variances and unequal sample sizes. The descriptive statistics are displayed in Table 1.

6.1   Learning Effectiveness

We analyzed the knowledge gain of the participants by computing two-sided repeated measures t-tests. All learning environments caused a significant knowledge gain with a strong effect size, *Horst-WS* $t(21) = 9.86$, $p < .001$, $d = 2.10$; *Horst-S* $t(21) = 9.94$, $p < .001$, $d = 2.12$; *Horst-TAR* $t(19) = 7.51$, $p < .001$, $d = 1.68$.

Computing an ANCOVA revealed that the $exam_{pre}$ score was significantly related to the $exam_{post}$ score, $F(1, 60) = 12.27$, $p < .001$, $\eta_p^2 = .17$. However, the exam$_{post}$ score did not differ significantly between conditions, $F(2, 60) = 1.84$, $p = .17$, $\eta_p^2 = .06$.

6.2   Emotion

Computing an ANCOVA of PA$_{post}$ with PA$_{pre}$ as a covariate showed that PA$_{pre}$ was significantly related to PA$_{post}$, $F(1, 60) = 76.16$, $p < .001$, $\eta_p^2 = .56$. Moreover, PA$_{post}$ differed significantly between the conditions with a medium effect size controlling for PA$_{pre}$, $F(2, 60) = 3.60$, $p = .03$, $\eta_p^2 = 0.11$. Post-hoc Tukey-Kramer comparisons substantiated that *PA* was significantly higher after using *Horst-TAR* than after using *Horst-WS*, $t(60) = 2.46$, $p = .04$. The differences of *Horst-WS* and *Horst-S*, $t(60) = 2.14$, $p = .09$, and *Horst-S* and *Horst-TAR*, $t(60) = .37$, $p = .97$, were not significant.

Computing an ANCOVA of NA$_{post}$ with NA$_{pre}$ as a covariate showed a significant relationship of NA$_{post}$ and NA$_{pre}$, $F(1, 60) = 48.83$, $p < .001$, $\eta_p^2 = .45$. We found no significant differences between the learning environments with respect to *NA* controlling for NA$_{pre}$, $F(2, 60) = 1.26$, $p = .29$, $\eta_p^2 = .04$.

6.3   Motivation

The analyses of the subscales *choice*, $F(2, 61) = .14$, $p = .87$, $\eta_p^2 = .01$, and *competence*, $F(2, 61) = 2.82$, $p = .07$, $\eta_p^2 = .09$, did not reveal any statistically significant differences. In contrast, significant effects with a medium effect size were detected for the *pressure* scale, $F(2, 61) = 4.21$, $p = .02$, $\eta_p^2 = .12$. Subsequent Tukey-Kramer comparisons showed that subjects in the *Horst-S* condition felt significantly less pressure than subjects in the *Horst-WS* condition, $t(61) = -2.76$, $p = .02$. *Horst-TAR* and *Horst-WS*, $t(61) = -2.13$, $p = .09$, and *Horst-S* and *Horst-TAR*, $t(61) = .56$, $p = .84$, did not differ significantly. Also, we found a significant difference with a strong effect size for the *enjoyment* subscale, $F(2, 61) = 6.57$, $p = .003$, $\eta_p^2 = .18$. Post-hoc comparisons revealed that *Horst-S*, $t(61) = 3.34$, $p = .004$, and *Horst-TAR*, $t(61) = 2.86$, $p = .02$, caused higher learner interest and enjoyment than *Horst-WS*. *Horst-S* and *Horst-TAR* were not significantly different, $t(61) = -.39$, $p = .92$.

These effects remained stable when controlling for the possible covariates *experience with AR* and *interest* by testing with an ANCOVA, independence of covariates given, $p > .05$; $F(2, 59) = 7.10$, $p = .002$, $\eta_p^2 = .19$.

6.4   Cognitive Load

A one-factor ANOVA revealed no significant differences between the conditions with respect to the *Paas* total score, $F(2, 61) = 1.85$, $p = .17$, $\eta_p^2 = .06$.

6.5   Feedback

We found no significant differences with regard to the willingness to repeat learning with the previously tested learning environment, $F(2, 61) = 2.34$, $p = .11$, $\eta_p^2 = .07$.

Calculating a Welch ANOVA, we found significant differences with a strong effect size between the conditions for the *desire to use the same technology for learning different subjects*, $F(2,39) = 12.13$, $p < .001$, $\eta_p^2 = .38$. Subsequent Games-Howell tests showed that the desire was significantly higher for *Horst-S*, $t(36.3) = 4.95$, $p < .001$, and *Horst-TAR*, $t(39.6) = 2.84$, $p = .02$ than for *Horst-WS*. We did not find a significant difference between *Horst-S* and *Horst-TAR*, $t(36.4) = 2.01$, $p = .12$.

Computing an ANOVA revealed a significant difference with a strong effect size for the *grades of the learning environments*, $F(2,61) = 5.80$, $p = .005$, $\eta_p^2 = .16$. Post-hoc Tukey-Kramer comparisons showed that *Horst-S*, $t(61) = -3.00$, $p = .01$, and *Horst-TAR*, $t(61) = -2.88$, $p = .02$, were graded significantly better than *Horst-WS*. We did not find a significant difference between *Horst-S* and *Horst-TAR*, $t(61) = .05$, $p = .99$.

6.6   Teacher Interview

Two teachers preferred *Horst-S*, while one teacher preferred *Horst-TAR*. They justified the preference for *Horst-S* with the self-explanatory and intuitive design as well as the faster completion time compared to *Horst-TAR*. With respect to *Horst-TAR*, the teachers stated that the technology is novel and represents a compromise between digital teaching via app and classical biology teaching with props.

Different approaches were listed for the possible integration of the learning environments into classroom teaching. *Horst-S* could be used to repeat the most recently acquired knowledge at the beginning of a lesson. For instance, students could use the free dissection mode to look up information on individual organs. Furthermore, *Horst-S* and *Horst-TAR* could be used to enhance a lesson. Using this approach, small groups of up to four students could complete the assisted dissection. However, it would be important to contextualize the learning content beforehand and, if necessary, to provide an introduction to the respective learning environment. For example, the teachers mentioned the body structure of the frog in comparison to other vertebrates, such as dogs, cats, pigs, and horses, as a possible context. They also emphasized that students should be taught additional information about the usual process of dissection in contrast to digital dissection. It would be of great importance for students to recognize that a real dissection involves the death of an animal and is distinctly different olfactory, visually, and tactilely. Finally, it is also necessary to discuss and consolidate the knowledge acquired after finishing the simulation.

The teachers expected a gain of knowledge and the development of digital competencies among students when using *Horst-S*. By using smartphones in classroom, students should no longer regard them only as a means of entertainment, but also as an easy access to knowledge. For *Horst-TAR*, a greater interest, sustainability and transfer of the acquired knowledge was assumed. The teachers expected using this learning environment to be fun for students.

7   Discussion

The present study investigated the effects of TAR technology on effectiveness, emotion, motivation, and cognitive load in an educational context.

7.1   Learning Effectiveness

All learning environments successfully led to a significant knowledge gain of the participants over the course of the learning period. As learning is a multidimensional concept that has proven challenging to measure in previous studies [37] and rarely resulted in statistical differences in comparative media studies [53], the lack of a statistical difference is not surprising. As displayed in Table 1, the participants started with a very low knowledge level before the experiment and yielded a significant improvement in their exam score after the learning phase. Although we did not find a significant difference between the conditions, this result is promising. It supports that digital learning environment are comparable in their learning effectiveness to established approaches, but cause a stronger motivation and higher enjoyment during the learning process [38]. Overall, this validates the approach of technology-based learning and can be a notable insight for teachers searching for new learning methods. Despite these promising results, we need to reject **H1**.

7.2   Emotion

The analysis of the NA scales show that NA_{post} did not differ significantly between the conditions. The negative affect declined over the learning phase and generally was at a low level. This indicates that no condition evoked negative emotions in the participants during the learning phase. PA_{post} also declined over the learning period, but remained in the middle range. In direct comparison, participants of the *Horst-TAR* condition reported a significantly higher PA_{post} than the participants of the *Horst-WS* condition. This suggests that the interactions and higher user experience of the TAR learning environment evoked more positive emotions in the participants. Although not significantly different, *Horst-S* also yielded a higher PA_{post} score than the traditional worksheet approach. Thus, we need to reject **H2**. Although not fully supporting our hypothesis, our results support the benefits of using digital and gamified learning environments over traditional learning methods for achieving an emotionally positive learning process.

7.3   Motivation

The analysis of the KIM subscales revealed no significant differences for *choice* and *competence*. However, we found significant differences in the results of the *pressure* subscale. Participants felt moderately tense while learning with *Horst-WS*, whereas participants were more relaxed during the learning phase with

Horst-S and *Horst-TAR*. Surprisingly, *Horst-S* yielded the lowest score on the pressure subscale. This effect could be explained by the different interactions with the two learning environments. The smartphone version only requires touch interactions, whereas the TAR version requires users to extract and manipulate physical objects in addition to holding the smartphone. Similarly, the participants reported a significantly higher *enjoyment and interest* after using *Horst-S* and *Horst-TAR* than *Horst-WS*. This result supports our PANAS-C measurements indicating a higher positive effect. Our measurements provide further evidence of the benefits of using smartphones and gamification for educational purposes [34].

Taken together, we can assume that the two digital learning environments cause a higher motivation during learning which leads to a better learning experience. However, we need to reject **H3** as TAR did not evoke a higher motivation than the smartphone-only version.

7.4 Cognitive Load

We did not find any significant differences in the Paas measurements between the three conditions. Assessing the cognitive load of the overall learning process, this result is still of high importance. It indicates that the two digital learning environments invoked no cognitive overload in the participants compared to the traditional method. Our results support that high user experience and the application of multimedia principles [35], such as coherence, signaling, segmentation, personalization, embodiment, and spatial and temporal proximity principles, prove to be reliable methods to avoid overloading cognitive resources. This suggests that smartphone and TAR learning environments following these design principles can safely be integrated in classroom teaching without risking to cause negative side effects. However, we need to reject **H4**.

7.5 Feedback

The willingness to repeat the learning with *Horst-WS* and *Horst-TAR* was in the middle range. *Horst-S* yielded an above average score. While not significantly different, the scores support the positive results of the measurements of emotion and motivation. The digital learning environments led to an overall better learning experience. This outcome is supported by the significant differences in the desire to use the same technology for learning different subjects. In particular, *Horst-S* and *Horst-TAR* evoked a significantly higher desire compared to *Horst-WS*. The participants saw benefits in using technology-based learning. Finally, the participants graded *Horst-S* and *Horst-TAR* significantly better than *Horst-WS*. This feedback supports the overall results of our study.

7.6 Implications

We found no significant difference between *Horst-TAR* and *Horst-S* for any of the measured qualities. Our measurements suggest a higher positive emotion when

Table 2. Comparison of worksheet, smartphone, and TAR learning environments.

	Worksheet	Smartphone	TAR
Material	Highest accessibility	Moderate accessibility	Lowest accessibility
	Paper	Smartphone	Smartphone & tangible markers
Features	Lowest time expenditure	Moderate time expenditure	Highest time expenditure
	No operation instruction needed	Operation instruction required	Operation instruction required
	Cannot display 3D	Can display 3D & animations	Can display 3D & animations in a natural way
Positive aspects	Efficient & effective, medium cognitive load	Effective, better affect, less pressure, higher enjoyment, medium cognitive load, high appreciation	Effective, higher enjoyment, medium cognitive load, high appreciation

using *Horst-TAR* than *Horst-WS*. In contrast, *Horst-S* outperformed the traditional learning method with respect to perceived pressure. Both digital learning environments evoked a higher enjoyment during the learning process. Thus, our study suggests that both tested technologies are equally beneficial for learning compared to the traditional worksheet method. Gamified smartphone and TAR learning environments indicate to evoke a better learning experience while yielding a similar learning effectiveness to traditional approaches. A different study already showed a significantly higher stimulation and attractiveness of *Horst-TAR* compared to its AR and smartphone counterparts [40]. In combination with our insights, TAR indicates the potential to cause a better overall learning experience. This, however, comes at the price of a higher preparation complexity for classroom integration.

Based on the assessment of three teachers, it is important to contextualize the learning environments when embedding them in a lesson and to reflect on the learning content after the learning phase. As using TAR learning environments also requires teachers to provide augmented objects for each learner, this positive aspect should ideally be used for the introduction of very complex learning content to add an additional stimulating aspect to the learning process. For all other subjects, smartphone learning environments might provide the best alternative to traditional worksheet approaches. They can be self-explanatory, intuitive, and easy to use. Additionally, using smartphones enables students to develop important digital competencies. Table 2 provides a direct comparison of the positive effects of using a worksheet, smartphone, and TAR learning environments.

7.7   Limitations

Our results could have been influenced by a novelty effect. Only 23 participants reported a high experience with AR apps. In addition, the integration of smartphones is not common praxis, yet. This could have resulted in a higher motivation and general more positive feedback when a digital learning environment was used. However, our statistical analysis revealed no effect of previous experience with AR on the reported motivation.

In contrast to *Horst-WS*, both digital versions included gamification. This might have confounded the evaluation of the experienced emotions and motivation. However, this influence is only true for direct comparisons to *Horst-WS*. Both digital versions used the same gamification elements and hence the comparison of emotions and motivation should not be confounded in a direct comparison between them.

Finally, the subjective feedback of the participants on their condition could have been influenced by an effect of social desirability. This might have confounded the results of the feedback questions.

8   Conclusion

In the present study, we investigated the effects of different technologies on the learning effectiveness, emotion, motivation, and cognitive load of a biology learning environment. Our user study at a local high school found no significant difference between conditions in learning effectiveness and cognitive load. However, the TAR version yielded a significantly higher positive emotion in comparison to the worksheet conditions while not being significantly different to the smartphone version. The two digital learning environments evoked a significantly higher motivation in comparison to the traditional worksheet approach. These findings can be of high importance for teachers and developers. While TAR can cause higher positive emotions, it is also more complex with respect to the required materials. Thus, TAR potentially is more suited for the introduction of new and very challenging learning content to benefit from the positive emotions, whereas smartphone learning environments are generally more practical for a very motivated learning process. Future work shall investigate whether our results are affected by a novelty effect. Also, a long-term study shall investigate whether the tested technologies improve the retention of learning content. Finally, research shall evaluate whether true three-dimensional targets, such as 3D-printed organ markers, can improve the learning process even further.

Acknowledgements. We would like to thank principal Wolfgang Naumann and the teachers of LuO Darmstadt Gymnasium for their support of our study.
This research was performed within the *"Die Zukunft des MINT-Lernens"* project, supported by the Deutsche Telekom Stiftung.

References

1. Antle, A., Wise, A.: Getting down to details: using learning theory to inform tangibles research and design for children. Interact. Comput. **25**, 1–20 (2013). https://doi.org/10.1093/iwc/iws007
2. Azuma, R.T.: A survey of augmented reality. Presence: Teleoperators Virtual Environ. **6**(4), 355–385 (1997)
3. Baack, K., Göbel, R., Maier, A., Marx, U., Remé, R., Seitz, H.J.: Natura 1. Biologie für Gymnasien, Klett (2013)
4. Bacca, J., Baldiris, S., Fabregat, S., Graf, S., Kinishuk: Augmented reality trends in education: a systematic review of research and applications. Educ. Technol. Soc. **17**(4), 133–149 (2014)
5. Bach, B., Sicat, R., Beyer, J., Cordeil, M., Pfister, H.: The hologram in my hand: how effective is interactive exploration of 3D visualizations in immersive tangible augmented reality? IEEE Trans. Visual Comput. Graphics **24**(1), 457–467 (2018)
6. Bier, E.A., Stone, M.C., Pier, K., Buxton, W., DeRose, T.D.: Toolglass and magic lenses: the see-through interface. In: Proceedings of the 20th Annual Conference on Computer Graphics and Interactive Techniques, pp. 73–80. SIGGRAPH 1993, Association for Computing Machinery, New York, NY, USA (1993). https://doi.org/10.1145/166117.166126
7. für Schulqualität und Bildungsforschung München, S.: Lehrplanplus (2020). https://www.lehrplanplus.bayern.de/
8. Billinghurst, M., Kato, H., Poupyrev, I.: Tangible augmented reality. In: ACM SIGGRAPH ASIA 2008 Courses (2008). https://doi.org/10.1145/1508044.1508051
9. Breyer, B., Bluemke, M.: Deutsche version der positive and negative affect schedule PANAS (GESIS panel) (2016). https://doi.org/10.6102/zis242
10. Cabero-Almenara, J., Roig-Vila, R.: The motivation of technological scenarios in augmented reality (AR): results of different experiments. Appl. Sci. **9**(14), 2907 (2019). https://doi.org/10.3390/app9142907
11. Carrera, C.C., Perez, J.L.S., de la Torre Cantero, J.: Teaching with AR as a tool for relief visualization: usability and motivation study. Int. Res. Geog. Environ. Educ. **27**(1), 69–84 (2018). https://doi.org/10.1080/10382046.2017.1285135
12. Chandrasekera, T., Yoon, S.: The effect of tangible user interfaces on cognitive load in the creative design process. In: 2015 IEEE International Symposium on Mixed and Augmented Reality - Media, Art, Social Science, Humanities and Design, pp. 6–8 (2015). https://doi.org/10.1109/ISMAR-MASHD.2015.18
13. Dengel, A., Mägdefrau, J.: Immersive learning explored: subjective and objective factors influencing learning outcomes in immersive educational virtual environments. In: 2018 IEEE International Conference on Teaching, Assessment, and Learning for Engineering (TALE), pp. 608–615 (2018). https://doi.org/10.1109/TALE.2018.8615281
14. Deterding, S., Dixon, D., Khaled, R., Nacke, L.: From game design elements to gamefulness: defining gamification. In: Proceedings of the 15th International Academic MindTrek Conference: Envisioning Future Media Environments (MindTrek 2011), pp. 9–15. ACM, Tampere, Finland (2011). https://doi.org/10.1145/2181037.2181040
15. Diegmann, P., Schmidt-Kraepelin, M., Van den Eynden, S., Basten, D.: Benefits of augmented reality in educational environments - a systematic literature review. In: Proceedings of the 12th International Conference on Wirtschaftsinformatik, pp. 1542–1556. Osnabrück, Germany (2015)

16. Ebesutani, C., Regan, J., Smith, A., Reise, S., Higa-McMillan, C., Chorpita, B.:
    The 10-item positive and negative affect schedule for children, child and parent
    shortened versions: application of item response theory for more efficient assess-
    ment. J. Psychopathol. Behav. Assess. **34**, 191–203 (2012). https://doi.org/10.
    1007/s10862-011-9273-2
17. de Freitas, S., Liarokapis, F.: Serious games: a new paradigm for education? In:
    Ma, M., Oikonomou, A., Jain, L.C. (eds.) Serious Games and Edutainment Appli-
    cations, pp. 9–23. Springer, London (2011). https://doi.org/10.1007/978-1-4471-
    2161-9_2
18. Garzón, J., Pavón, J., Baldiris, S.: Systematic review and meta-analysis of aug-
    mented reality in educational settings. Virtual Reality **23**, 447–459 (2019). https://
    doi.org/10.1007/s10055-019-00379-9
19. Gervautz, M., Schmalstieg, D.: Anywhere interfaces using handheld augmented
    reality. Computer **45**(7), 26–31 (2012). https://doi.org/10.1109/MC.2012.72
20. Gikas, J., Grant, M.M.: Mobile computing devices in higher education: student
    perspectives on learning with cellphones, smartphones & social media. Internet
    High. Educ. **19**, 18–26 (2013). https://doi.org/10.1016/j.iheduc.2013.06.002
21. Glandt, D.: Amphibien und Reptilien. Springer, Heidelberg (2016). https://doi.
    org/10.1007/978-3-662-49727-2
22. Gutiérrez Posada, J.E., Hayashi, E.C.S., Baranauskas, M.C.C.: On feelings of com-
    fort, motivation and joy that GUI and TUI evoke. In: Marcus, A. (ed.) DUXU
    2014. LNCS, vol. 8520, pp. 273–284. Springer, Cham (2014). https://doi.org/10.
    1007/978-3-319-07638-6_27
23. Ishii, H., Ullmer, B.: Tangible bits: towards seamless interfaces between people,
    bits and atoms. In: Proceedings of the 1997 CHI Conference on Human Factors in
    Computing Systems (CHI 1997), pp. 234–241. Atlanta, USA (1997). https://doi.
    org/10.1145/258549.258715
24. Kalemkuş, J., Kalemkuş, F.: Effect of the use of augmented reality applications
    on academic achievement of student in science education: meta analysis review.
    Interact. Learn. Environ. (2022). https://doi.org/10.1080/10494820.2022.2027458
25. Keller, S., Rumann, S., Habig, S.: Cognitive load implications for augmented reality
    supported chemistry learning. Information **12**(3), 96–115 (2021). https://doi.org/
    10.3390/info12030096
26. Khan, M., Trujano, F., Choudhury, A., Maes, P.: Mathland: playful mathematical
    learning in mixed reality. In: CHI 2018 Extended Abstracts. Montréal, Canada
    (2018)
27. Kim, K., Billinghurst, M., Bruder, G., Duh, H.B., Welch, G.F.: Revisiting trends
    in augmented reality research: a review of the 2nd decade of ISMAR (2008–2017).
    IEEE Trans. Visual Comput. Graph. **24**(11), 2947–2962 (2018). https://doi.org/
    10.1109/TVCG.2018.2868591
28. Koehler, M., Mishra, P.: What happens when teachers design educational tech-
    nology? the development of technological pedagogical content knowledge. J. Educ.
    Comput. Res. **32**(2), 131–152 (2005)
29. Küçük, S., Kapakin, S., Göktaş, Y.: Learning anatomy via mobile augmented real-
    ity: effects on achievement and cognitive load. Anat. Sci. Educ. **9**(5), 411–421
    (2016). https://doi.org/10.1002/ase.1603
30. Laurent, J., et al.: A measure of positive and negative affect for children: scale
    development and preliminary validation. Psychol. Assess. **11**, 326–338 (1999)
31. Li, J., Van der Spek, E.D., Feijs, L., Wang, F., Hu, J.: Augmented reality games for
    learning: a literature review. In: International Conference on Distributed, Ambient,
    and Pervasive Interactions (2017). https://doi.org/10.1007/978-3-319-58697-7_46

32. Liu, L., Wagner, C., Suh, A.: Understanding the success of Pokémon go: impact of immersion on players' continuance intention. In: Schmorrow, D.D., Fidopiastis, C.M. (eds.) AC 2017. LNCS (LNAI), vol. 10285, pp. 514–523. Springer, Cham (2017). https://doi.org/10.1007/978-3-319-58625-0_37

33. Loderer, K., Pekrun, R., Lester, J.C.: Beyond cold technology: a systematic review and meta-analysis on emotions in technology-based learning environments. Learn. Instr. **70**, 101162 (2018)

34. Majuri, J., Koivisto, J., Hamari, J.: Gamification of education and learning: a review of empirical literature. In: Proceedings of the 2nd International GamiFIN Conference (GamiFIN 2018), pp. 11–19 (2018)

35. Mayer, R.E.: Cognitive theory of multimedia learning. In: Mayer, R.E. (ed.) The Cambridge Handbook of Multimedia Learning, pp. 43–71. Cambridge University Press (2014). https://doi.org/10.1017/CBO9781139547369.005

36. McGonigal, J.: Reality is Broken: Why Games Make Us Better and How They Can Change the World, 1st edn. Penguin Press, New York (2011)

37. Ni, A.Y.: Comparing the effectiveness of classroom and online learning: Teaching research methods. J. Public Affairs Educ. **19**, 199–215 (2013). https://doi.org/10.1080/15236803.2013.12001730

38. Oberdörfer, S.: Better Learning with gaming: knowledge encoding and knowledge learning using gamification. Ph.D. thesis, University of Würzburg (2021). https://doi.org/10.25972/OPUS-21970

39. Oberdörfer, S., Birnstiel, S., Latoschik, M.E., Grafe, S.: Mutual benefits: interdisciplinary education of pre-service teachers and HCI students in VR/AR learning environment design. Front. Educ. **6**, 233 (2021). https://doi.org/10.3389/feduc.2021.693012

40. Oberdörfer, S., Elsässer, A., Grafe, S., Latoschik, M.E.: Grab the frog: comparing intuitive use and user experience of a smartphone-only, AR-only, and tangible AR learning environment. In: Proceedings of the 23rd International Conference on Mobile Human-Computer Interaction (MobileHCI 2021). Toulouse & Virtual, France (2021). https://doi.org/10.1145/3447526.3472016

41. Oberdörfer, S., Elsässer, A., Schraudt, D., Grafe, S., Latoschik, M.E.: Horst - the teaching frog: Learning the anatomy of a frog using tangible AR. In: Proceedings of the 2020 Mensch und Computer Conference (MuC 2020), pp. 303–307. Magdeburg, Germany (2020). https://doi.org/10.1145/3404983.3410007

42. Oberdörfer, S., Latoschik, M.E.: Gamified knowledge encoding: knowledge training using game mechanics. In: Proceedings of the 10th International Conference on Virtual Worlds and Games for Serious Applications (VS Games 2018). 2018 IEEE. Reprinted, with permission., Würzburg, Germany (2018). https://doi.org/10.1109/VS-Games.2018.8493425

43. Paas, F.G.W.C.: Training strategies for attaining transfer of problem-solving skill in statistics: a cognitive-load approach. J. Educ. Psychol. **84**(4), 429–434 (1992)

44. Paas, F.G.W.C., Ayres, P., Pachman, M.: Assessment of cognitive load in multimedia learning - theory, methods and applications. In: Robinson, D.H., Schraw, G. (eds.) Recent Innovations in Educational Technology that Facilitate Student Learning, pp. 11–35. Information Age Publishing Inc. (2008)

45. Pekrun, R.: The control-value theory of achievement emotions: assumptions, corollaries, and implications for educational research and practice. Educ. Psychol. Rev. **18**, 315–341 (2006). https://doi.org/10.1007/s10648-006-9029-9

46. Ryan, R.M., Deci, E.L.: Intrinsic and extrinsic motivation from a self-determination theory perspective: Definitions, theory, practices, and future directions. Contemp. Educ. Psychol. **61**, 101860 (2020). https://doi.org/10.1016/j.cedpsych.2020.101860

47. Ryan, R., Deci, E.: Self-determination theory and the facilitation of intrinsic motivation, social development, and well-being. Am. Psychol. **55**, 68–78 (2000). https://doi.org/10.1037/0003-066X.55.1.68

48. Seaborn, K., Fels, D.I.: Gamification in theory and action: a survey. Int. J. Hum Comput Stud. **74**, 14–31 (2015). https://doi.org/10.1016/j.ijhcs.2014.09.006

49. Steinhaeusser, S.C., Riedmann, A., Haller, M., Oberdörfer, S., Bucher, K., Latoschik, M.E.: Fancy fruits - an augmented reality application for special needs education. In: Proceedings of the 11th International Conference on Virtual Worlds and Games for Serious Applications (VS Games 2019). IEEE, Vienna, Austria (2019)

50. Storch, V., Welsch, U.: Amphibia, Lurche. In: Kükenthal Zoologisches Praktikum, pp. 372–392. Springer, Heidelberg (2014). https://doi.org/10.1007/978-3-642-41937-9_13

51. Sweller, J.: Cognitive load during problem solving: effects on learning. Cogn. Sci. **12**(2), 257–285 (1988)

52. Sweller, J.: Measuring cognitive load. Perspect. Med. Educ. **7**(1), 1–2 (2018)

53. Tulodziecki, G., Herzig, B., Grafe, S.: Medienbildung in Schule und Unterricht. 3. vollst. akt. u. überarb. Auflage. Klinkhardt, Bad Heilbrunn (2021)

54. Weerasinghe, M., et al.: Vocabulary: learning vocabulary in AR supported by keyword visualisations. arXiv, 2207.00896, cs.HC (2022). https://doi.org/10.48550/ARXIV.2207.00896

55. Wilde, M., Bätz, K., Kovaleva, A., Urhahne, D.: Überprüfung einer kurzskala intrinsischer motivation (KIM) (2009)

56. Yin, X., Li, G., Deng, X., Luo, H.: Enhancing k-16 science education with augmented reality: a systematic review of literature from 2001 to 2020. In: 2022 8th International Conference of the Immersive Learning Research Network (iLRN), pp. 215–219 (2022). https://doi.org/10.23919/iLRN55037.2022.9815958

57. Youngblut, C.: Use of multimedia technology to provide solutions to existing curriculum problems: virtual frog dissection. Ph.D. thesis, George Mason University, United States (2001)

58. Zuckerman, O., Gal-Oz, A.: To TUI or not to TUI: evaluating performance and preference in tangible vs. graphical user interfaces. Int. J. Hum.-Comput. Stud. **71**(7–8), 803–820 (2013). https://doi.org/10.1016/j.ijhcs.2013.04.003

An Immersive Laboratory Environment for a Customized Learning Experience

Michael Holly$^{(\boxtimes)}$ (iD), Sandra Brettschuh, and Johanna Pirker (iD)

Graz University of Technology, Graz, Austria
{michael.holly,johanna.pirker}@tugraz.at, brettschuh@student.tugraz.at

Abstract. Science, technology, engineering, and mathematics (STEM) are important drivers of innovation, yet students are often unmotivated and do not understand why they need to learn these subjects. Virtual reality (VR) and virtual environments are useful tools for conceptual understanding with a high degree of immersion. They enable the creation of engaging and inspiring learning experiences. Additionally, personalization and customization can promote motivated usage and high user acceptability. A customized experience that takes into account the unique characteristics of the player can thus be an essential factor in learning. In this paper, we explore the potential of a customized learning environment to increase students' motivation in learning physics. We present an AB study with 95 students to evaluate their motivation and experience during the learning process. The results indicate that the learning experience slightly increases when the learning process takes place in a customizable experimental environment.

Keywords: STEM education · Virtual reality · Customized learning

1 Introduction

Teaching and learning science, technology, engineering, and mathematics (STEM) are often challenging and time-consuming. Getting people engaged in science across STEM disciplines is essential for national success, as it can lead to a better and more competent workforce able to address the requirements of the 21st-century economy [17]. For many students, STEM fields are uninteresting, complex and hard to learn. Traditional learning methods describe complex phenomena often as a collection of formulas that results in high failure rates. Instead of reading or listening, the new generation prefers learning through activities and in a more personalized way. Immersive and interactive technologies such as virtual reality (VR) provide new ways to create engaging and motivating learning experiences [15]. The interaction with the virtual environment allows the user to become more fully immersed and engaged. Using it in combination with virtual laboratories, they must react realistically to the experimental conditions. To create an even more engaging and inspiring learning experience, personalization and customization features can be used to promote motivated usage and high

M.-L. Bourguet et al. (Eds.): iLRN 2023, CCIS 1904, pp. 365–375, 2024.
https://doi.org/10.1007/978-3-031-47328-9_27

user adoption. Learning can benefit from a personalized experience of this kind that takes the characteristics of the user into account [13].

In this paper, we present an immersive laboratory environment for a customized learning experience. The main research objectives are defined as:

- Exploring the motivation and learning experience of users in a customizable VR experiment room.
- Identifying how customization features affect the VR experience.

Contribution. In this paper, we present an AB study with 95 students, discussing a customizable learning experience in an immersive VR laboratory for STEM education. The research focus is on the student's motivation and experience during the learning process and on identifying and discussing the benefits and challenges of customization features in a learning environment.

2   Background and Related Work

Digital learning experiences that promote interactive learning and engage students are becoming increasingly relevant [9]. Specific concepts can be visualized using interactive simulations to support students in understanding the underlying phenomena, especially in STEM education [19]. However, developing educational tools is increasingly challenging. Bonde et al. [4] demonstrated that a gamified digital learning laboratory can increase the student's motivation and their learning outcomes significantly when compared to traditional teaching methods. Another interactive and engaging learning environment was described by Pirker et al. [20]. They developed a virtual environment for physics classes where students can collaborate together and discuss simulations. One way to create a more immersive and engaging learning experience is through the usage of VR technologies [6]. Recent studies have demonstrated that interactive VR simulations have a positive effect on motivation, enjoyment, and concentration [16,18,24]. To create an even more engaging and inspiring learning experience, individualization elements can be integrated into a virtual learning application. Two strategies for achieving individualization are personalization and customization. While customization offers flexibility, allowing users to change the content presentation, format layouts, and navigation features, personalization includes the automatic adjustment of information, structure, and presentation to each individual user [23]. According to Lin et al. [14], personalized learning paths can enhance students' creativity. Combining game-based learning with personalized learning could lead to higher levels of engagement and learning outcomes. The usage of personalized content recommendations in learning systems can also increase the learning time and improve motivation as well as performance [7]. Customization can help in fulfilling user needs by taking their preferences into account. This gives users the ability to adapt their virtual representation, which leads to an enhanced user experience and an increased feeling of presence and enjoyment [2,3]. Adding additional customization features can further reduce the failure rate, increase user acceptance and lead users to work more efficiently [5,11]. Kleinsmith and Gillies [12] applied such a customization approach to a sport-game where the players were able to customize the behavior of their characters using their own movements while playing. As a result, users felt more engaged with the game and the design process, due to the sense of personal ownership of the movement.

3   Learning Application

We used an existing virtual laboratory environment with multiple interactive and engaging learning methods for developing the learning application. The lab environment is implemented in Unity supporting web, desktop, and VR applications with different immersion levels. The laboratory consists of a main lab hall which represents a 3D menu from where users can choose an experiment by navigating to the experiment station. After selecting an experiment, the user is placed into a distinct experiment room where the experiment content is presented [22].

3.1   Experiment Setup

To evaluate customization features in a VR learning experience, we integrated customization features into a wave simulation named the Huygens principle. The experiment demonstrates the physical model of diffraction. In the experiment room, a basin filled with water is placed in the center of the room where the user can observe the wave propagation. To demonstrate diffraction, an adjustable slit plate is put into the basin. In this scenario setting, users can observe the experiment outcome when changing different experiment parameters. The users can change the wave amplitude, the wavelength, the wave frequency, and the propagation mode to influence the experiment. Figure 1 illustrates the drawer object for the different adjustments. Here, the drawer object acts as a control unit where the users can change the experiment parameters, the system language, and the customization features. Furthermore, the user can arrange the position and the height of the drawer object to have a perfect view of the experiment outcome when changing parameters. To customize the laboratory environment, the user can change the floor and wall material, add decorative elements and plants, and choose between different wall pictures and hand models. Additionally, for the wave simulation, the color of the waves, basin, and plate can be changed using a color picker device. A quest manager provides the instructions that must be followed and the tasks that must be performed by the user in the course of the experiment. Experiment information is displayed on a whiteboard via images. Teleportation markers located in front of the controls highlight at which position users can move. Figure 2 shows the initial room setting and a customized version of the experiment room.

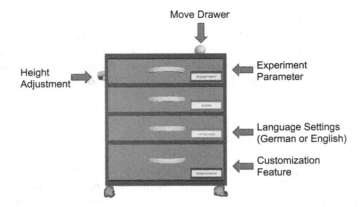

Fig. 1. Drawer object to change the experiment settings.

(a) Initial experiment room.　　　　(b) Customized experiment room.

Fig. 2. Experiment room with customization features.

4　Evaluation

The goal of this study was to investigate the effects of customization features within a VR learning environment to determine how students' motivation and learning experience change. The evaluation was conducted as an AB study with 95 students to compare two different versions of the VR learning application. While participants in group A were able to use the customization features, participants in group B were unable to unlock the customization drawer. The research focus was on the learning experience and motivation of the users and the customization features. Motivation refers to the self-determination theory of Deci and Ryan [8], with intrinsic motivation as a subcategory of autonomous motivation.

4.1   Material and Setup

We used two portable setups for the evaluation. The setup includes a gaming notebook, an HTC Vive HMD with two controllers, and two lighthouses. The two setups were placed in a single classroom side by side where each participant had a play area of at least 2 m × 2 m. In that way, two participants could perform the study at the same time, while the other students had the opportunity to observe the active participants. In addition, we ensured that all participants who were in the room belonged to the same group. We did not use the option of utilizing headphones with the HTC Vive, as this allowed the communication with the participants while they conducted the experiment.

4.2   Method and Procedure

In order to conduct the study, we recruited 95 students from different local educational institutions. After assigning them to one group, we asked the participants to fill out a pre-questionnaire that included personal information about their age, gender, and previous experiences with various technologies such as VR and gaming. Afterward, they were given a brief introduction to VR and how to use the controls to interact with the virtual environment. Additionally, participants were able to ask questions at any time during the experiment if controls or tasks were unclear. During the virtual simulation, participants were asked to complete the following tasks:

1. Look around and familiarize yourself with the controls
2. Start the experiment by pressing the play button.
3. Move in front of the drawer object and try to change the experiment parameters.
4. Try to customize the experiment room according to your preferences (only for group A).

After completing the tasks, we asked the participants to fill out a post-questionnaire where they had to rate their player and learning experience as well as their motivation. The learning experience and motivation questionnaire was based on [10,21] evaluated on a Likert scale between 1 (strongly disagree) and 7 (strongly agree). For the player experience, we used the Player Experience Inventory (PXI) questionnaire [1] with scores between −3 (strongly disagree) and 3 (strongly agree). Participants of group A were also asked open-ended questions about the customization elements to get feedback about the distraction effect and the overall system acceptance. For group B, we were also interested in whether they think that such features could enhance their learning experience. Finally, we asked all participants some general feedback questions for improvements.

4.3   Participants

For recruiting participants, we asked students from local educational institutions. In total, 95 students (50 female, 45 male) aged between 9 and 31 (AVG = 13.0,

SD = 5.3) participated in the study and were divided into two groups (57 students in group A, 38 in group B). 30% of the participants reported having a visual impairment such as glasses. However, all the participants managed to use the VR setup and were thus able to participate. They were also asked to rate their experience with computers, video games, and VR on a Likert scale between 1 (no expert at all) and 5 (expert). Most users felt experienced with video games (AVG = 3.26, SD = 1.50), followed by computers (AVG = 2.87, SD = 1.21) and VR (AVG = 2.17, SD = 1.28). 12% reported that they have already used a Google cardboard and the Oculus Quest, 11% the Samsung Gear VR, and only 8% used an HTC Vive before. There were only 14 participants who reported cybersickness in their previous VR usage.

5   Results

The following sections present the results with a focus on motivation, the user experience, and the impact of customization features on learning in VR.

5.1   Learning Experience and Motivation

To rate the learning experience and motivation, we asked the participants 16 questions on a Likert scale between 1 (fully disagree) and 5 (fully agree) about how they assessed the experiment. Both groups reported that the experience was engaging and fun. They found that the VR experiment made the learning content more interesting and easier to understand. Although there was no significant difference between the two groups, it was noticed that the participants with the customization features rated their experience slightly higher than the users from the control group (see Table 1). To measure the payer experience during the experiment, we used the PXI questionnaire. It consists of several categories with three sub-statements rated on a scale from −3 (strongly disagree) to 3 (strongly agree). For the evaluation, we used the average of the three sub-statements to obtain an indicator for the corresponding category. Furthermore, we performed a Wilcoxon Rank Sum test to identify significant differences. Table 2 shows the summarized categories for the different user groups with the p-value from the test. The results show a significant difference in the clarity of goals. It suggests that users without built-in customization features have a clearer goal, which indicates that goal clarity is disrupted by adding customization features to the learning experience. In addition, both groups had good challenge and immersion levels. It was also observed that participants in the customization group rated their sense of mastery slightly lower than participants in group B (A: AVG = 1.98, SD = 1.00; B: AVG = 2.28, SD = 0.97). However, group A rated their level of autonomy higher (A: AVG = 2.33, SD = 0.85; B: AVG = 2.23, SD = 0.85).

5.2   Impact of Customization Features

To evaluate the customization feature acceptance in the learning environment, we asked the participants to rate their acceptance level on a Likert scale between

Table 1. Learning experience rated on a scale from. *1 (strongly disagree)* to *7 (strongly agree)*

	Group A		Group B	
	AVG	SD	AVG	SD
I would like to learn with it	6.23	1.16	5.87	1.71
It is a good idea to use it for learning	5.98	1.42	5.70	1.73
It is a good supplement to regular learning	6.16	1.18	5.58	1.69
I learned something	6.00	1.45	5.82	1.87
It makes the content more interesting	6.37	1.05	6.14	1.40
It makes the content easier to understand	5.82	1.25	5.50	1.35
It makes learning more engaging	6.61	0.91	6.37	1.30
It makes learning more fun	6.72	0.77	6.29	1.45
It makes learning more interesting	6.44	0.96	6.16	1.37
I would like to learn with it at home	6.19	1.34	5.87	1.74
I would like to learn with it in class	6.39	1.07	5.84	1.76
The experience inspired me to learn more about Huygens's Principle	5.16	1.84	5.16	1.74
Learning was more motivating than with ordinary exercises	6.26	1.13	6.16	1.33
I would prefer to learn physics with VR than with traditional methods	5.60	1.61	5.13	1.86
I find regular physics classes boring	3.90	2.10	4.47	1.93
Seeing the Huygens simulation in VR was engaging	5.95	1.45	5.30	2.00

Table 2. PXI rating on a scale from *-3 (strongly disagree)* to *3 (strongly agree)*.

	Group A		Group B		p-value
	AVG	SD	AVG	SD	
Clarity of goals	**1.04**	**0.64**	**1.34**	**0.62**	**0.02**
Challenge	1.82	1.12	1.81	1.10	0.89
Progress feedback	1.24	1.32	1.41	1.36	0.43
Audiovisual feedback	1.98	1.04	2.17	1.17	0.26
Meaning	2.01	1.00	1.95	1.44	0.53
Curiosity	2.15	0.99	2.17	1.07	0.84
Mastery	1.98	1.00	2.28	0.97	0.08
Immersion	1.85	1.08	2.00	0.97	0.44
Autonomy	2.33	0.85	2.23	0.85	0.59

1 (not at all) and 5 (a lot). Except for one participant in group A, all the users used the integrated customization features. Participants who used the customization features reported that they like the implemented customization features very much (AVG = 4.46, SD = 0.91). Furthermore, the users disagreed with the statement that the customization feature distracted from the actual experiment (AVG = 2.75, SD = 1.41). In additional open-ended questions, group A users mentioned that they felt more welcome, comfortable, and motivated. Furthermore, they reported that these features improved their experience by making it more fun and varied. Around 66% of the users without the ability to

customize their environment thought that such features would have improved their experience.

5.3   General Comments

Finally, we asked the participants to share their likes and dislikes as well as suggestions for improvement. Most of the collected feedback was positive. Users stated that they liked the customization features and the interactable elements in the experiment. However, some of the users wished for more customization features and experiment tasks within the virtual environment.

6   Discussion

In this study, we attempted to explore user motivation and the learning experience in a customized virtual environment. The positive results from the learning experience and the PXI questionnaire match the reported positive feedback from the open-ended question and motivation we observed directly during the experiment evaluation. Comparing it with previous studies [blinded Ref], we can conclude that customization features in an immersive learning environment can enhance the learning experience and motivation. These results are in line with the observations of Zhao et al. [24], Makransky et al. [16] and Petersen et al. [18] showing that VR simulations have a positive impact on the motivation and enjoyment of users. Although the results of both groups indicate a high motivational factor due to the VR experiment without significant differences in motivation. The results of the learning experience suggest that the additional customization features can slightly enhance users' motivation. This observation can be aligned with the study by Burkolter et al. [5], which showed that a customized user interface increases user acceptance and that users rated usefulness significantly higher than users without a customized user interface. Ku et al. [13] also showed that customization features increased learning performance and perceptions. This shows a high potential for customized VR experiences for learning. In addition, the results of the PXI questionnaire indicate that both versions of the learning environment are equally challenging. However, the group without customization features rated their level of mastery and progress feedback slightly higher. The significant difference in goal clarity implies that users without built-in customization features have a clearer goal. An enhanced agency to customize the VR environment can lead to the distracting of the learners from their learning goals. The results indicate that providing customization features for the learning process disrupts goal clarity. However, users mentioned that they do not feel disrupted by the customization features. Furthermore, users in the customization group rated their autonomy higher, indicating that adding customization features helps improve autonomy and motivation. Game achievements could increase the focus on the experiment itself before customization features are unlocked as an additional reward. This could motivate the users to spend more time with the experiment and explore different scenarios and variables. In comparison to traditional teaching methods, Bonde et al.

[4] have already shown that a gamified digital learning laboratory can increase the student's motivation and their learning outcomes significantly. As noted in the general feedback, the customization features left a lasting impression on users, as many of them mentioned the positive impact of these features and that they liked certain customization features. Moreover, many users emphasized that these features helped them feel more comfortable and motivated in the virtual environment. In addition, the majority of the participants without customization features expressed the wish that they would have liked to use features of this kind and they believed that these features improved their experience.

6.1 Limitations

The study was designed as a first exploration of the user motivation in a customizable VR experiment room. We recruited participants from different local educational institutions, leading to a wide age range from 9 to 31 (pupils and students). A smaller age range and participants with the same background knowledge would lead to more meaningful conclusions. Furthermore, the study only considered participants' self-assessments and did not include any type of learning outcome or knowledge assessment. It would also be interesting to include long-term effects to obtain more detailed results. Although the setup was consistently put together in the same way, the study was, however, still conducted in different locations, a factor which could have an influence on the results.

7   Conclusion

In conclusion, we observed that the motivation of the users and their learning experience increased slightly when they were provided with customization features. However, the results suggest that these features had a small distraction effect from the main learning experiment, even though the participants themselves indicated that they did not feel this way. Users also stated that they would require more customization features and experiment tasks within the virtual environment. Improving the goal clarity for customization users would be essential to create a more effective learning experience. A combination of a quest system and game achievements could also be useful to improve goal clarity. Additional personalized features and game-based learning strategies could further improve user engagement and learning outcomes, as well as the learning time. Game achievements could increase the focus on the experiment itself before customization features are unlocked as an additional reward to motivate the users to spend more time with the experiment. A further study could investigate the impact of such achievements on user engagement as well as the correlation between motivation, learning, and exploring the experiment.

References

1. Abeele, V.V., Spiel, K., Nacke, L., Johnson, D., Gerling, K.: Development and validation of the player experience inventory: a scale to measure player experiences at the level of functional and psychosocial consequences. Int. J. Hum Comput Stud. **135**, 102370 (2020). https://doi.org/10.1016/j.ijhcs.2019.102370
2. Bailey, R., Wise, K., Bolls, P.: How avatar customizability affects children's arousal and subjective presence during junk food-sponsored online video games. CyberPsychol. Behav. **12**(3), 277–283 (2009)
3. Barr, P., Biddle, R., Brown, J.: Changing the virtual self: avatar transformations in popular games. In: Proceedings of the 3rd Australasian Conference on Interactive Entertainment, pp. 83–90 (2006)
4. Bonde, M.T., et al.: Improving biotech education through gamified laboratory simulations. Nat. Biotechnol. **32**(7), 694–697 (2014)
5. Burkolter, D., Weyers, B., Kluge, A., Luther, W.: Customization of user interfaces to reduce errors and enhance user acceptance. Appl. Ergon. **45**(2), 346–353 (2014)
6. Checa, D., Bustillo, A.: A review of immersive virtual reality serious games to enhance learning and training. Multimedia Tools Appl. **79**(9), 5501–5527 (2020)
7. Chiu, P.H., Kao, G.Y.M., Lo, C.C.: Personalized blog content recommender system for mobile phone users. Int. J. Hum Comput Stud. **68**(8), 496–507 (2010)
8. Deci, E.L., Ryan, R.M.: Self-determination theory: a macrotheory of human motivation, development, and health. Can. Psychol. **49**(3), 182 (2008)
9. Freeman, S., et al.: Active learning increases student performance in science, engineering, and mathematics. Proc. Natl. Acad. Sci. **111**(23), 8410–8415 (2014)
10. Holly, M., Pirker, J., Resch, S., Brettschuh, S., Gütl, C.: Designing VR experiences-expectations for teaching and learning in VR. Educ. Technol. Soc. **24**(2), 107–119 (2021)
11. Jorritsma, W., Cnossen, F., van Ooijen, P.M.: Adaptive support for user interface customization: a study in radiology. Int. J. Hum Comput Stud. **77**, 1–9 (2015)
12. Kleinsmith, A., Gillies, M.: Customizing by doing for responsive video game characters. Int. J. Hum Comput Stud. **71**(7–8), 775–784 (2013)
13. Ku, O., Hou, C.C., Chen, S.Y.: Incorporating customization and personalization into game-based learning: a cognitive style perspective. Comput. Hum. Behav. **65**, 359–368 (2016)
14. Lin, C.F., Yeh, Y.C., Hung, Y.H., Chang, R.I.: Data mining for providing a personalized learning path in creativity: an application of decision trees. Comput. Educ. **68**, 199–210 (2013)
15. Liou, W.K., Chang, C.Y.: Virtual reality classroom applied to science education. In: 2018 23rd International Scientific-Professional Conference on Information Technology (IT), pp. 1–4. IEEE (2018)
16. Makransky, G., Andreasen, N.K., Baceviciute, S., Mayer, R.E.: Immersive virtual reality increases liking but not learning with a science simulation and generative learning strategies promote learning in immersive virtual reality. J. Educ. Psychol. **113**(4), 719–735 (2021). https://doi.org/10.1037/edu0000473
17. Olson, S., Riordan, D.G.: Engage to excel: Producing one million additional college graduates with degrees in science, technology, engineering, and mathematics. report to the president. Executive Office of the President (2012)
18. Petersen, G.B., Petkakis, G., Makransky, G.: A study of how immersion and interactivity drive VR learning. Comput. Educ. **179**, 104429 (2022). https://doi.org/10.1016/j.compedu.2021.104429

19. Pirker, J., Gütl, C.: Educational gamified science simulations. In: Reiners, T., Wood, L.C. (eds.) Gamification in Education and Business, pp. 253–275. Springer, Cham (2015). https://doi.org/10.1007/978-3-319-10208-5_13
20. Pirker, J., Gütl, C., Belcher, J.W., Bailey, P.H.: Design and evaluation of a learner-centric immersive virtual learning environment for physics education. In: Holzinger, A., Ziefle, M., Hitz, M., Debevc, M. (eds.) SouthCHI 2013. LNCS, vol. 7946, pp. 551–561. Springer, Heidelberg (2013). https://doi.org/10.1007/978-3-642-39062-3_34
21. Pirker, J., Holly, M., Gütl, C.: Room scale virtual reality physics education: use cases for the classroom. In: 2020 6th International Conference of the Immersive Learning Research Network (iLRN), pp. 242–246. IEEE (2020)
22. Pirker, J., Holly, M., Lesjak, I., Kopf, J., Gütl, C.: MaroonVR—an interactive and immersive virtual reality physics laboratory. In: Díaz, P., Ioannou, A., Bhagat, K.K., Spector, J.M. (eds.) Learning in a Digital World. SCI, pp. 213–238. Springer, Singapore (2019). https://doi.org/10.1007/978-981-13-8265-9_11
23. Treiblmaier, H., Madlberger, M., Knotzer, N., Pollach, I.: Evaluating personalization and customization from an ethical point of view: an empirical study. In: Proceedings of the 37th Annual Hawaii International Conference on System Sciences, 2004, p. 10. IEEE (2004)
24. Zhao, J., Lin, L., Sun, J., Liao, Y.: Using the summarizing strategy to engage learners: empirical evidence in an immersive virtual reality environment. Asia Pac. Educ. Res. 29(5), 473–482 (2020). https://doi.org/10.1007/s40299-020-00499-w

Language, Culture and Heritage (LCH)

Work, Trade, Learn: Developing an Immersive Serious Game for History Education

David Fernes[1]([✉])[ID], Sebastian Oberdörfer[2][ID], and Marc Erich Latoschik[2][ID]

[1] Goethe University Frankfurt, Frankfurt, Germany
`fernes@em.uni-frankfurt.de`
[2] University of Würzburg, Würzburg, Germany
`sebastian.oberdoerfer@uni-wuerzburg.de`

Abstract. History education often struggles with a lack of interest from students. Serious games can help make learning about history more engaging. Students can directly experience situations of the past as well as interact and communicate with agents representing people of the respective era. This allows for situated learning. Besides using computer screens, the gameplay can also be experienced using immersive Virtual Reality (VR). VR adds an additional spatial level and can further increase the engagement as well as vividness. To investigate the benefits of using VR for serious games targeting the learning of history, we developed a serious game for desktop-3D and VR. Our serious game puts a player into the role of a medieval miller's apprentice. Following a situated learning approach, the learner operates a mill and interacts with several other characters. These agents discuss relevant facts of the medieval life, thus enabling the construction of knowledge about the life in medieval towns. An evaluation showed that the game in general was successful in increasing the user's knowledge about the covered topics as well as their topic interest in history. Whether the immersive VR or the simple desktop version of the application was used did not have any influence on these results. Additional feedback was gathered to improve the game further in the future.

Keywords: Serious game · Immersive learning · History education · Situated learning · Interest

1 Introduction

"Those that fail to learn from history are doomed to repeat it."

- Winston Churchill

While maybe not in quite the dramatic way that Churchill meant most history teachers would agree that learning about history is very important. However, history education suffers from the issue that past times can neither be demonstrated

M.-L. Bourguet et al. (Eds.): iLRN 2023, CCIS 1904, pp. 379–396, 2024.
https://doi.org/10.1007/978-3-031-47328-9_28

nor experienced directly. While museums might allow for the development of a certain understanding especially when populated with actors, they still cannot entirely recreate the past. Other teaching materials might be even less vivid and often purely consist of texts. Hence, history lessons are often seen as very boring, dry, and not very interesting by students.

In contrast to textbooks, video games do have the potential to present nearly any subject in an engaging and vivid way. The mechanics of video games can be used to encode the knowledge of history lessons to create what is commonly known as a serious game [31]. Serious games utilize the entertaining aspects of video games for educational purposes by turning learning content into the central game element. Besides using regular computer screens, the gameplay can also be presented in immersive Virtual Reality (VR). In the case of history subjects, VR allows users to spatially explore and directly interact with situations of the past, thus nearly realizing time travel. This can allow learners to observe past situations, get in social exchange with agents, and construct knowledge about past eras.

To investigate the potential of immersive serious games for history education, we developed a game putting the learner into the role of a medieval miller's apprentice. This enables situational learning about life in the Middle Ages. In an evaluation, we compared the game's desktop-3D to its VR version to find out to what extend the degree of immersion influences learning and what lessons can be learned for the development of these kinds of applications.

Fig. 1. Picture of the interior of the real mill in the franconian open-air museum in Bad Windsheim on which part of the game was based.

2   Related Work

Serious games are not only developed for entertainment, but also serve the purpose of teaching players about the game's topics [31]. This can be achieved by encoding the knowledge within game mechanics [23]. This means that the information that players are supposed to learn is packaged in a gameplay element where this knowledge is applied [4]. This approach has already been used for educational games for several topics, like transformations in 3D spaces [23]. Some commercial games also implement characteristics of serious games like for example Kerbal Space Program [32] which lets users build rockets using real physics to calculate their flight.

2.1   Learning and Interest

Serious games and VR both allow users to feel like they are present in a virtual environment and situations. This can be helpful for situated learning which indicates that learning is always situated in a specific environment, including a specific social context [17]. This means that both the physical situation as well as the social context in which knowledge is obtained is important. This concept is based on the theory of constructivism which says that "Knowledge is constructed in the mind of the learner" [8]. This means that a learner's knowledge is constructed by themselves through their own experiences.

The theories of constructivism and situated learning indicate that new information is best learned in its natural context where learners can make their own experiences with the learning content. This is especially difficult in history education since it is very difficult to experience history in its natural context, as time travel, is sadly not possible or at least not feasible for educational settings.

As previously mentioned history education can suffer from a lack of interest from students. Interest can be defined as a "psychological state characterized by focused attention, increased cognitive and affective functioning, and persistent effort" [2]. Different types of interest can be differentiated like individual, situational or topic interest. Situational Interest is "interest, which is evoked by certain features or characteristics of stimuli" [14]. Situational interest can be helpful when teaching about topics that students do not have much individual interest in [7]. Topic interest describes the interest in a certain topic. It can be shaped by both the learner's individual interest as well as the situational interest for the learning situation [1]. Interest in general was shown to have a positive effect on learning outcomes [26]. Therefore, the application should present the learning content in an engaging and vivid way, thus evoking a higher interest in the learners. While serious games in general can present learning content in an engaging and vivid way [20], providing a higher immersion can further improve these qualities [30].

2.2   Immersive Technology and Learning

Immersion according to Slater and Wilbur is "the extent to which the computer displays are capable of delivering an inclusive, extensive, surrounding and vivid illusion of reality to the senses of a human participant" [29]. It can also be defined as "the boundaries within which [presence] can occur" [28].

Presence is defined by Skarbez et al. [27] as the feeling of "being there" in a virtual environment. There are many different definitions of presence but for simplicity's sake, this paper will focus on the provided definition [19].

According to Steuer [30] immersion can be further broken down into the components vividness and interactivity. Vividness describes the representational richness of the environment. Interactivity describes the extent to which users are able to modify the content and shape of a virtual reality in real-time.

A wide variety of different immersive learning applications has already been developed for a variety of topics. Although most immersive learning applications are designed for computer science and engineering topics and have university students as their target audience [13].

There has also been some research into which factors can influence learning in VR or serious games. Dengel and Mägdefrau [9] presented a framework, that describes presence as the central factor influencing learning, which is in turn influenced by immersion and personal factors of the user. Jensen and Konradsen [16] investigated several studies and found that immersive technologies can improve learning outcomes, especially when conveying visual or spatial information. But higher immersion can also lead to lower learning outcomes because users can be distracted by the virtual environment or get motion sickness if implemented badly. They also found that the quality of the investigated studies in general was below average, so it is not sure how reliable these results are. Ritterfeld et al. [25] have shown that more interactivity can improve the learning outcomes in the context of serious games.

This research shows that interactivity can enhance the success of serious games, while the influence of immersion still needs further research. However, since both serious games and higher immersion can improve the engagement and vividness, the influence of both concepts must be tested individually.

2.3 History Education with Serious Games and Immersive Learning

Different serious games have already been developed to teach about history [3]. One example is the Roma Nova project which recreates ancient Rome and enables players to explore the city and interact with different people there [24]. One commercial game which also has a similar topic is "The Forgotten City" [21], in which players can learn about life in ancient Rome and mythology, by also talking to different characters and hearing about their life.

Although most VR applications are designed for other topics there have also been some immersive learning applications for history education. But many of these applications are not fully immersive and are only for desktop computers. A large portion of these applications are also simple reconstructions or virtual museums which do not offer much interactivity [6]. Dong et al. [10] for example developed an immersive VR application where users could experience a medieval tannery which was highly immersive but it did not offer any way to interact with the virtual environment. Ijaz et al. [15] on the other hand developed a game where players could explore the ancient city of Ur and interact with many different people. While this application offered a high level of interactivity it did not use immersive VR and was instead playable on a desktop PC. Overall it can be said that there is still a lack of immersive VR applications for history education that offer meaningful ways to interact with the virtual environment.

3 Design

Fig. 2. A screenshot of the VR version of the game showing the mill scene. The teleportation interaction and the highlighting of objects can be seen.

Based on this analysis of previous work, providing a serious game in immersive VR should improve the learning of historical facts. By allowing learners to immerse themselves in the current situation of a person in the past, they can construct knowledge about this era. Also, by providing agents as conversational partners, a substitute for a social interaction becomes possible. This fulfills the core requirements for situated learning. Finally, using an immersive VR serious game should provide the learning content in an engaging and vivid way, thus potentially increasing the overall interest in history.

To test these assumptions an immersive serious game was developed, by expanding a previously developed learning environment [12]. The game is designed for history lessons in 7th grade secondary school education in Germany and its contents were modeled after the official school curriculum.

In order to fit into the lesson plan of these history lessons the following five topics should be covered in the final application:

1. Life in medieval towns
2. Work of a medieval miller
3. Religion and Protestantism
4. Invention of the printing press
5. Medieval cures for the plague

For this purpose, 10 questions were designed with two questions per topic. The learning goal was that students should be able to answer those questions after playing the game. Since the developer of the application was a student from a computer science background a pre-service history teacher helped designing these questions.

3.1 Game Mechanics

Since interactivity can improve learning outcomes and increase interest by making learning more engaging different game mechanics for interacting with the virtual environment were developed (Fig. 2).

Players can pick up different objects, like a bag of flour or a loaf of bread, and carry them around to use them later. Other objects are static and can only be interacted with, like a lever for starting the mill. These game mechanics can be used to operate the virtual mill and learn about its core mechanics. Simultaneously, the game mechanics recreate and hence demonstrate the work of a miller in the Middle Ages.

Since the social context is also important for situated learning the player can also talk to different characters embodied by virtual agents. They can initiate conversations with them by approaching them and can make choices about what to say to the characters at different points in the conversation. These interactions are used to make the player solve different tasks, like trading flour for bread at the market and learning about the life of different people in the Middle Ages.

Finally, we used the game mechanics to encode learning content that the game should teach. Which of these game mechanics is used to encode which information can be seen in Table 1.

Table 1. Table showing in which part of the serious game each topic is encoded.

Topic	Encoding
Life in medieval towns	Dialogue with baker
Work of a miller	Task in mill scene
Religion	Dialogue with priest
Printing press	Dialogue with priest
Cures for the plague	Dialogue with priest

3.2 Narrative

The game follows a short narrative where the player takes on the role of a medieval miller's apprentice and experiences a shortened version of a typical

Fig. 3. A screenshot of the Desktop version of the game showing the mill scene. The miller character gives instructions to the player.

day in their life. When the game starts the player hears the call of a rooster and has the choice to stay sleeping or wake up. Depending on their choice the miller is either angry at them or proud of them. Independent of his mood he tells the apprentice that a farmer brought over some grain to be turned into flour. He then instructs the player step by step on how to turn it into flour and explains how the mill works (Fig. 3).

Afterwards he sends the apprentice to the market with a small bag of flour in order to trade it for bread. The player then goes to the market in the town square where the baker tells him about life in the city. After giving the baker the flour, he has to wait until the bread is ready and hears a priest talking about cures for the plague. When approached the priest talks about the plague, the invention of the printing press and how Martin Luther's followers split from the catholic church until the baker calls the apprentice back over. He then takes the bread and returns to the mill where the miller sends him back to sleep after eating dinner.

3.3   Scenes

The locations that the player visits during the game are represented by four different scenes. The Mill scene consists of the main mill room, the apprentice's bedroom which also functions as a storage room and the entry hall. The doors to all other rooms of the mill are closed so the player cannot get lost. The mill is filled with several flour sacks and there are flour stains on the floor. Through a small door in the main room an outside area can be entered overlooking the mill wheel. The mill is modeled after a real mill which is currently located the

Franconian Opn-Air Museum in Bad Windsheim (Fig. 1). The virtual mill was largely modeled after the state of the real mill except where the current state did not reflect the time period presented in the game.

The second scene consists of a market in a town square in a small town (Fig. 4). In contrast to the mill this town square is not based on a particular town but rather the general layout of a town square in the Middle Ages. It contains multiple market stalls with different objects for sale. The square is surrounded by houses and filled with different characters, including some of which can be interacted with, like a baker and a priest.

The third scene is largely identical to the first mill scene, but the time of day is evening and there are fewer objects that can be interacted with. The last scene is a small tutorial scene to learn all interactions. It consists of an empty room with a small platform and two objects that can be interacted with.

Fig. 4. A screenshot of the Desktop version of the game showing the market scene.

4   Implementation

Based on this design the final game was developed. How this was done is described in the following.

4.1   Tools

All objects used in the game were modeled in Blender or taken from free asset packs from the Unity asset store. Out of these objects the different scenes were then constructed in the Unity game engine version 2020.3.14f1. The SteamVR framework was used for implementing the interaction in VR. Two versions of the application were developed: One using immersive VR with an HTC Vive Head Mounted Display (HMD) and one to be used on a simple Desktop PC with a keyboard and mouse.

4.2 Agents

Since the interaction with the people of the Middle Ages is an important part of this game virtual agents to represent the people in the virtual world had to be added. These agents were created from two modular asset packs bought form the Unity asset store. These agents include characters that can talk to the player like a miller, a baker, and a priest as well as multiple different background characters in the market scene that can not be interacted with.

All talking characters' dialogue was fully voiced by friends and colleagues. Using authentic medieval accents was considered but in the end modern German was used in order to make the dialogue more understandable for players. In addition to the spoken dialogue clips, speech bubbles were displayed over the characters' heads so players can also read the dialogue. These speech bubbles were visible even through walls and always rotated towards the player to improve legibility. The crowd in the market scene had no recorded dialogue but a crowd noise audio sample was used to simulate them talking to each other.

4.3 Interaction

Two different interaction systems were developed, one for each version of the game.

In the VR version players can interact with the application using the HTC Vive controllers. They can move around by physically moving inside the tracking space or teleport by clicking the controllers' touchpad and pointing to where they want to teleport to (Fig. 2). Players can grab objects by touching them with the controller and pressing down the trigger. Dialogue choices can be selected by touching speech bubbles with the controllers. Smaller objects can be put into the bag around the avatar's waist by pulling them into it and pulled out again by grabbing them out of the bag. Possible actions are always shown next to the controllers.

In the Desktop version players can interact with a keyboard and mouse. They can move around by using the WASD or arrow keys. They can look around by moving the mouse. They can interact with and pick up objects by left clicking on them. Picked up objects can be dropped again by right clicking. Dialogue choices are selected by left clicking on speech bubbles (Fig. 5). Smaller objects can be put into the bag by left clicking on it while carrying an object and retrieved again by left clicking on the bag again. Interaction possibilities are shown next to the crosshair. Which objects should be interacted with to progress the story are highlighted in green in both conditions.

Fig. 5. A screenshot of the dialogue system in the Desktop version of the game.

5   Evaluation

The game was then evaluated in a study to see if it was successful in conveying the learning content to the participants and increasing their interest in history. Additionally the VR and Desktop versions were compared in order to see if the level of immersion influenced these results. The study was conducted in a between-subjects design where each participant used only one version of the game, either VR or Desktop. We randomly assigned the participants to one of the conditions.

5.1   Participants

Participants were recruited from students who received course credit for participation. 38 people took part in the evaluation, with 19 participants per condition. The mean age of participants was 22.61 (SD = 2.57) years. 29 participants identified as female, 8 as male and 1 as neither. 36 participants spoke German as their native language while the 2 remaining were business fluent. Only 4 participants used VR weekly or daily. 30 had only experienced VR in studies or never at all. 12 participants played computer games weekly or daily, while 11 had only experienced computer games in studies or never at all. All participants used computers daily or weekly.

5.2   Measurements

The participants' knowledge of history was measured with a knowledge test that was designed with the learning goals of the application in mind. The test consisted of 10 questions with 2 questions per covered topic. Participants took this test before and after playing the game. The pre-test featured 5 questions (1 per topic), with the post-test containing the remaining 5. Which questions appeared in which test was randomized for each participant in case some questions were easier than others.

The knowledge test was repeated 2 weeks after the study in an online questionnaire. Which questions appeared in this questionnaire was randomized independently of the first two tests.

The topic interest was measured with a questionnaire from Ferdinand [11] in the version adapted by Baumgartner [5] for the topic of history before and after playing the game. The situational interest was measured with a questionnaire from the same source only after playing the game. At the end of the questionnaire participants were also asked two open questions about what they liked about the game and what they would like to improve.

All questionnaires were presented digitally on a laptop via Limesurvey [18].

5.3 Hypotheses

Playing the game should increase the participants' knowledge about the covered topics as well as their interest in the topic. A higher level of immersion should further improve engagement and vividness, thus leading to higher situational and topic interest as well as learning outcomes. Therefore the hypotheses are as follows:

- H1: The participants answer more questions in the history test correctly after playing the game.
- H2: The participants' improvement in the history test is higher in the VR condition than in the Desktop condition.
- H3: The topic interest for history is higher after playing the game.
- H4: The increase in topic interest for history is higher in the VR condition than in the desktop condition.
- H5: The situational interest is higher in the VR condition than in the Desktop condition.
- H6: The participants answer more questions in the history test correctly two weeks after playing the game than before playing the game.
- H7: The participants' improvement in the history test after two weeks is higher in the VR condition.

5.4 Procedure

For the study a laptop was used both to fill out the questionnaires as well as run the application. For the VR condition an HTC Vive HMD was used. For the Desktop condition the laptop was used with a keyboard and mouse and a pair of headphones.

At first participants were greeted by the experimenter and sat at a desk where they could read the study information and sign a consent form on paper. Afterward they moved to a laptop where they filled out all pre-questionnaires.

After finishing the questionnaire, they played the game. The exact procedure varied between conditions. In the Desktop condition they stayed at the laptop and only put on headphones. In the VR condition they had to stand in the middle of the room and put on the VR headset and were handed the VR controllers. Before starting the full application, they played a short tutorial. In the tutorial all controls and possible interactions were explained to them by the experimenter and they could try them out. When they indicated that they understood all controls the game was started. When they finished the game's story it closed by itself and they then continued with the post questionnaires on the laptop. Once they finished it, they were thanked for their participation and their e-mail address was collected in order to send them an additional online survey at a later date. After the participant had left all used hardware was disinfected and the room was aired out for 15 min, due to the study being conducted during the corona pandemic.

2 weeks after participating in the study each participant received a link to an online questionnaire with an additional knowledge test to check for differences in the retention of the learned knowledge. Of the 38 participants that participated in the main part of the study 34 also filled out this additional knowledge test.

6   Results

The results of this study were evaluated with R in R-Studio.

6.1   Knowledge Test

To analyze if the game increased the participants' knowledge of history the results of the knowledge test of the pre- and post-tests were compared to each other. Since a Shapiro-Wilk test did not show any signs of non-normality ($W = 0.96, p = 0.16$) a t-test for paired samples was calculated. The knowledge test results in the post-test ($M = 3.39, SD = 1.27$) were significantly higher than in the pre-test ($M = 1.66, SD = 1.08$) ($t(37) = 6.113, p < 0.001$) (Fig. 6).

To compare the test results between the conditions the difference between post- and pre-test was calculated for each participant. This difference in knowledge test results was then compared between conditions. A Shapiro-Wilk test did not show any signs of non-normality for the Desktop ($W = 0.92, p = 0.11$) or VR condition ($W = 0.96, p = 0.63$). Since a Levene test did not indicate unequal variances ($F = 2.95, p = 0.09$) as well an independent samples t-test was calculated. The increase in knowledge scores did not differ significantly between the Desktop ($M = 1.95, SD = 1.28$) and the VR ($M = 1.53, SD = 1.76$) condition ($t(36) = 0.82, p = 0.42$).

6.2   Knowledge After 2 Weeks

To investigate if the knowledge test scores are still higher after 2 weeks the scores before using the application are compared to those two weeks after the study.

A Shapiro-Wilk test indicated non-normality ($W = 0.91, p < 0.01$). Based on this a Wilcoxon signed rank test was calculated. The results in the test after 2 weeks ($M = 3.00, SD = 1.11$) were significantly higher than in the pre-test ($M = 1.74, SD = 1.09$) ($Z = 6.5, p < 0.001$).

The scores directly after playing the game were also compared to the scores after 2 weeks. A Shapiro-Wilk test indicated non-normality ($W = 0.93, p < 0.05$). Based on this a Wilcoxon signed rank test was calculated. The results in the test after 2 weeks ($M = 3.00, SD = 1.11$) were not significantly different from the scores in the post-test ($M = 3.32, SD = 1.30$) ($Z = 217, p = 0.13$).

To compare the results after 2 weeks between conditions the difference between test scores before the application and 2 weeks after using the application is calculated. These differences are then compared between conditions. A Shapiro-Wilk test indicated non-normality for the Desktop ($W = 0.87, p < 0.05$) but not for the VR condition ($W = 0.92, p = 0.17$). Therefore, a Mann-Whitney U test was calculated. The increase in scores did not differ significantly between the Desktop ($M = 1.32, SD = 0.98$) and the VR ($M = 1.2, SD = 0.98$) condition ($U = 149.5, p = 0.81$).

6.3   Topic Interest

The topic interest scores for history of the pre- and post-tests were compared to each other. Since a Shapiro-Wilk test did not show any signs of non-normality ($W = 0.96, p = 0.23$) a t-test for paired samples was calculated. The topic interest scores in the post-test ($M = 20.8, SD = 5.54$) were significantly higher than in the pre-test ($M = 19.58, SD = 6.03$) ($t(37) = 2.58, p < 0.05$).

To compare the topic interest in history between conditions the difference between the post- and pre-test results was calculated and those were compared between conditions. A Shapiro-Wilk test did not show any signs of non-normality for the Desktop ($W = 0.96, p = 0.62$) or VR condition ($W = 0.92, p = 0.12$). A Levene test did not indicate unequal variances ($F = 0.05, p = 0.82$). Therefore, an independent-samples t-test was calculated. The difference in pre- and post-questionnaire scores did not differ significantly between the Desktop ($M = 1.47, SD = 2.66$) and the VR ($M = 1.05, SD = 3.25$) conditions ($t(36) = 0.43, p = 0.67$)

6.4   Situational Interest

The situational interest scores were compared between the two conditions. A Shapiro-Wilk test did not show any signs of non-normality for the Desktop ($W = 0.93, p = 0.18$) or VR condition ($W = 0.96, p = 0.62$). A Levene test did also not indicate unequal variances ($F = 0.18, p = 0.67$). Therefore, an independent-samples t-test was calculated. The situational interest did not differ significantly between the Desktop ($M = 31.58, SD = 5.30$) and the VR ($M = 29.11, SD = 5.60$) condition ($t(36) = -0.88, p = 0.38$).

6.5   Negative Feedback

The most commonly mentioned aspect that participants would like to see improved was the application's graphics, which were mentioned by 11 participants. 5 participants wanted more interactive elements and 4 wanted more content in general. 3 people criticized the controls of the application, independent of which condition they used.

6.6   Positive Feedback

The most commonly mentioned aspect that participants liked about the application was the controls, which 10 people in total mentioned. These mentions were evenly split between the two conditions. The tasks in general, the virtual environment as well as the characters and their dialogues were mentioned by 8 participants each as a positive point. 4 people mentioned that they liked the highlighting of objects that can and should be interacted with.

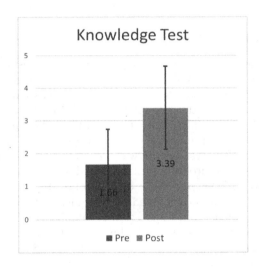

Fig. 6. Results of the knowledge test before and after using the application. Error bars indicate standard deviation.

7   Discussion

7.1   General Effectiveness

The results show that the serious game was successful in increasing the knowledge and interest in the topic of history (see Fig. 6). Hypotheses H1 and H3 can therefore be accepted. Since there is no significant difference between test scores directly after playing the game and 2 weeks later the increase in knowledge seems to persist even some time after playing the game. H6 can therefore also be accepted. Our results thus indicate that the application achieved its goals of teaching users about life in the Middle Ages and increasing their general interest in history.

Although there was a general increase in the participants' knowledge the results of the post test could still be better since only 3.39 out of 5 questions were answered correctly. In order to determine what the reasons for this were a closer look was taken at the percentage of correct answers for each individual question. It could be seen that the questions to which the answer was not clearly stated in the dialogue and instead only implied were the ones with the lowest amount of correct answers. This means that in order to learn important information through this kind of dialogue based mechanics the knowledge should be presented as clearly as possible.

7.2   Influence of Immersion

Which condition was used did not seem to make any difference on the results of the knowledge test as well as topic and situational interest scores. The remaining hypotheses (H2, H4, H5, H7) therefore have to be rejected. It can therefore be assumed that the level of immersion does not have any influence on these learning factors, at least in the context of this specific game. This is not very surprising since learning is very challenging to measure with many factors influencing it and often did not show any significant differences in other studies comparing different kinds of media [22,33].

Immersion having no effect on the results may not be what was hypothesized but that is not necessarily a bad thing. Considering the rather rare availability of HMDs at most schools, our results indicate that our serious game can still safely be integrated in teaching concepts by only using the Desktop-3D version without risking to lose positive aspects of a higher immersion. Yet, it cannot be guaranteed that there are no other learning benefits of the VR version that were not covered by this evaluation, like general motivation or the players' emotions.

7.3   Limitations

The main target audience for this game are 7th grade students in a German secondary school. Since an evaluation with school students was difficult to organize during the covid pandemic the study was instead conducted with university students. The results may therefore not be fully generalizable for the target audience, because university students might have more previous knowledge about history. Since most students came from technology centered courses of study the general attitude towards using technology for learning may also be different. To make sure that these results are also applicable for the actual target audience the study should be replicated with 7th grade students in the future.

One possibility to help players better remember the knowledge would be to give them the ability to choose what they want to talk about with the characters instead if just having them talk about everything in a predefined order. This would also enable them to repeat the important dialogue so it can be listened to more than once. Additionally this would add more interactivity to the dialogue mechanics which was something participants of the study wished for.

7.4   Further Development

Feedback indicates that players liked interacting with the agents and the interaction with the environment in general. This means that using virtual agents for interaction is generally a good idea for this kind of serious game. This should be kept in mind when expanding the game or when developing similar applications.

Since participants wanted more interactive elements and more content in general the game could be expanded further in future versions. But when adding additional content the context of a school lesson has to be kept in mind. If too much content is added the game may not fit into the timeframe of a single school lesson anymore, especially since some time for the introduction of the topic and the technology is needed. But these problems could be fixed if players had the choice of just experiencing parts of the application or continuing where they left off last time.

8   Conclusion

In this paper an immersive serious game for learning about life in the Middle Ages was presented. This game is designed for use in history lessons in school or as an exhibit in a museum. A first evaluation showed that the game was successful in conveying the learning content and increasing topic interest of the users. The level of immersion on the other hand did not seem to have any influence on the players' knowledge or interest.

Feedback showed that people especially liked the interaction with the other virtual characters. Most users wanted even more interaction and wished for more content in general. From the results and feedback some general guidelines for developing serious games for this context could be gathered:

- Important information should be presented as clearly as possible
- Players should have the option to repeat important dialogues

In the future this game may be improved even further based on the gathered feedback and developed guidelines, and more features might be added for future versions. An improved version of this game can be used in history lessons in schools or as an exhibit in a museum.

References

1. Ainley, M., Hidi, S., Berndorff, D.: Situational and individual interest in cognitive and affective aspects of learning. In: American Educational Research Association Meetings, Montreal, Quebec, Canada (1999)

2. Ainley, M., Hidi, S., Berndorff, D.: Interest, learning, and the psychological processes that mediate their relationship. J. Educ. Psychol. **94**(3), 545 (2002)
3. Anderson, E.F., McLoughlin, L., Liarokapis, F., Peters, C., Petridis, C., de Freitas, S.: Serious games in cultural heritage (2009)
4. Arnab, S., et al.: Mapping learning and game mechanics for serious games analysis. Br. J. Edu. Technol. **46**(2), 391–411 (2015)
5. Baumgartner, I.: Einfluss von fachinteresse auf situationales interesse bei der bearbeitung von aufgaben im fach geschichte. eine treatment-studie mit variation der aufgabeninteressantheit am beispiel" deutscher widerstand im nationalsozialismus". PAradigma: Beiträge aus Forschung und Lehre aus dem Zentrum für Lehrerbildung und Fachdidaktik 7, 107–118 (2014)
6. Bekele, M.K., Pierdicca, R., Frontoni, E., Malinverni, E.S., Gain, J.: A survey of augmented, virtual, and mixed reality for cultural heritage. J. Comput. Cul. Heritage (JOCCH) **11**(2), 1–36 (2018)
7. Bergin, D.A.: Influences on classroom interest. Educ. Psychol. **34**(2), 87–98 (1999)
8. Bodner, G.M.: Constructivism: a theory of knowledge. J. Chem. Educ. **63**(10), 873 (1986)
9. Dengel, A., Mägdefrau, J.: Immersive learning explored: subjective and objective factors influencing learning outcomes in immersive educational virtual environments. In: 2018 IEEE International Conference on Teaching, Assessment, and Learning for Engineering (TALE), pp. 608–615. IEEE (2018)
10. Dong, Y., Webb, M., Harvey, C., Debattista, K., Chalmers, A.: Multisensory virtual experience of tanning in medieval coventry. In: GCH, pp. 93–97 (2017)
11. Ferdinand, H.: Entwicklung von Fachinteresse: Längsschnittstudie zu Interessenverläufen und Determinanten positiver Entwicklung in der Schule, vol. 89. Waxmann Verlag (2013)
12. Fernes, D., Oberdörfer, S., Latoschik, M.E.: Recreating a medieval mill as a virtual learning environment. In: Proceedings of the 27th ACM Symposium on Virtual Reality Software and Technology, pp. 1–3 (2021)
13. Freina, L., Ott, M.: A literature review on immersive virtual reality in education: state of the art and perspectives. In: The International Scientific Conference Elearning and Software for Education, vol. 1, pp. 10–1007 (2015)
14. Hidi, S.: Interest and its contribution as a mental resource for learning. Rev. Educ. Res. **60**(4), 549–571 (1990)
15. Ijaz, K., Bogdanovych, A., Trescak, T.: Virtual worlds vs books and videos in history education. Interact. Learn. Environ. **25**(7), 904–929 (2017)
16. Jensen, L., Konradsen, F.: A review of the use of virtual reality head-mounted displays in education and training. Educ. Inf. Technol. **23**(4), 1515–1529 (2018)
17. Lave, J., Wenger, E.: Situated Learning: Legitimate Peripheral Participation. Cambridge University Press, Cambridge (1991)
18. LimeSurvey GmbH: LimeSurvey (2022). https://www.limesurvey.org/de/
19. Lombard, M., Jones, M.T.: Defining presence. In: Lombard, M., Biocca, F., Freeman, J., IJsselsteijn, W., Schaevitz, R.J. (eds.) Immersed in Media, pp. 13–34. Springer, Cham (2015). https://doi.org/10.1007/978-3-319-10190-3_2
20. McGonigal, J.: Reality is Broken: Why Games Make us Better and How they can Change the World. Penguin, New York (2011)
21. Modern Storyteller Pty Ltd.: The forgotten city (2021). https://forgottencitygame.com/
22. Ni, A.Y.: Comparing the effectiveness of classroom and online learning: teaching research methods. J. Public Aff. Educ. **19**, 199–215 (2013). https://doi.org/10.1080/15236803.2013.12001730

23. Oberdörfer, S., Latoschik, M.E.: Knowledge encoding in game mechanics: Transfer-oriented knowledge learning in desktop-3D and VR. Int. J. Comput. Games Technol. **2019** (2019). https://doi.org/10.1155/2019/7626349

24. Panzoli, D., et al.: A level of interaction framework for exploratory learning with characters in virtual environments. In: Plemenos, D., Miaoulis, G. (eds.) Intelligent Computer Graphics 2010. Studies in Computational Intelligence, vol. 321, pp. 123–143. Springer, Heidelberg (2010). https://doi.org/10.1007/978-3-642-15690-8_7

25. Ritterfeld, U., Shen, C., Wang, H., Nocera, L., Wong, W.L.: Multimodality and interactivity: connecting properties of serious games with educational outcomes. Cyberpsychol. Behav. **12**(6), 691–697 (2009)

26. Schiefele, U.: Interest, learning, and motivation. Educ. Psychol. **26**(3–4), 299–323 (1991)

27. Skarbez, R., Brooks, F.P., Jr., Whitton, M.C.: A survey of presence and related concepts. ACM Comput. Surv. (CSUR) **50**(6), 1–39 (2017)

28. Slater, M.: Place illusion and plausibility can lead to realistic behaviour in immersive virtual environments. Philos. Trans. R. Soc. B: Biol. Sci. **364**(1535), 3549–3557 (2009)

29. Slater, M., Wilbur, S.: A framework for immersive virtual environments (five): speculations on the role of presence in virtual environments. Presence: C Virtual Environ. **6**(6), 603–616 (1997)

30. Steuer, J.: Defining virtual reality: dimensions determining telepresence. J. Commun. **42**(4), 73–93 (1992)

31. Susi, T., Johannesson, M., Backlund, P.: Serious games: an overview (2007)

32. Take-Two Interactive: Kerbal space program (2015). https://www.kerbalspaceprogram.com/

33. Tulodziecki, G., Herzig, B., Grafe, S.: Medienbildung in Schule und Unterricht. 3. vollst. akt. u. überarb. Auflage. Klinkhardt, Bad Heilbrunn (2021)

Digitising the Cultural Landscape of North Uist

Sharon Pisani[1]([✉])[ID], Alan Miller[1][ID], and Màiri Morrison[2]

[1] School of Computer Science, University of St Andrews, St Andrews, UK
{sp259,alan.miller}@st-andrews.ac.uk
[2] Comann Eachdraidh Uibhist a Tuath (CEUT), North Uist Historical Society,
Western Isles, UK
https://ceut.northernheritage.org/

Abstract. North Uist lies in the Western Isles, at the heart of the vernacular Gaelic community. The area is rich in heritage, with unique archaeological sites accompanied by artefacts, stories, poems, and songs about local legends or contemporary accounts of past events. Many are available in English, but are at their most expressive and authentic in the original Gaelic. Currently, there is a crisis in the vernacular community; decade-on-decade reductions in the numbers of people using Gaelic in their day-to-day lives presents an urgent problem for the community. The recent revolution in the way that digital technologies are being used offers innovative opportunities to preserve the 'Cultural Landscape', to make it more widely available, and indeed to contribute to its development. Capturing this requires the representation of the landscape that provides the setting for North Uist's heritage. Emergent immersive and mobile technologies offer the possibility of integrating digital representations of these elements into the Gaelic medium, with the goal of capturing vernacular interpretation of Uist heritage, ensuring that Gaelic expression is part of emergent media and that the transmission of heritage and language is authentic.

Keywords: Cultural landscapes · Gaelic · Virtual reality · Cultural heritage · Wellbeing · Immersive learning

1 Introduction

The cultural landscape of North Uist is enriched by powerful interactions between the Gaelic language, archaeology, and tangible and intangible heritage. In recent years digital innovations in immersive and mobile technologies have created opportunities to represent cultural and natural heritage in new ways. Through community co-creation, developing digital heritage resources together can enhance engagement with heritage using the linguistic and cultural strengths of the vernacular community.

Our collaborative digitisation work is focused on capturing the essence of North Uist's 'Cultural Landscape'. By 'Cultural Landscape' we refer to

© The Author(s), under exclusive license to Springer Nature Switzerland AG 2024
M.-L. Bourguet et al. (Eds.): iLRN 2023, CCIS 1904, pp. 397–407, 2024.
https://doi.org/10.1007/978-3-031-47328-9_29

UNESCO's definition as works of nature and humankind which 'express a long and intimate relationship between peoples and their natural environment' [21]. Features of note for North Uist include the land and seascape, numerous archaeological sites and monuments [1], collections of artefacts held by Taigh Chearsbhagh Museum and Comann Eachdraidh Uibhist a Tuath (CEUT - North Uist Historical Society) as well as in many people's homes, and the body of Gaelic poetry, music, and song, all closely mapped with the North Uist environment.

This paper presents a case study which implements and evaluates a set of digital tools that aim to capture the Gaelic language and culture, and which can be used to foster innovative Gaelic heritage learning. This is part of an ongoing community co-creation project developing digital resources and investigating their importance to community wellbeing. This project serves two purposes: to create an archive of regional cultural heritage and to evaluate how far representation of cultural heritage may support people's wellbeing in informal learning settings. The digital content of this study encompasses 360° virtual cultural walks, archaeological reconstructions, 3D artefacts accompanied by oral histories, and a music and performance digital collection, built on previous work done in collaboration with CEUT and Taigh Chearsabhagh Museum.

The aim of this case study is to promote digital engagement with heritage, thereby strengthening the vernacular community and positively impacting wellbeing. We investigate how the digitisation of cultural heritage can preserve and make heritage available for use through various digitisation activities. The results are obtained from the evaluation of visitors who experienced a series of Gaelic virtual walks and contributed to an archive of historical and social artefacts. It looks to see how these digital tools, including immersive reproductions of virtual reality walks, best contribute to social inclusion, social cohesion, prosperity, and wellbeing.

The next section discusses related work which shaped the approach taken throughout the project. The design aspects of the collaborative digitisation practices implemented are discussed in Sect. 3. These were evaluated during a Digital Fèis, a festival at the local school showcasing the digital products. The results are discussed in Sect. 4, followed by recommendations and future work that is evolving from this case study.

2   Related Work

The importance of heritage spaces to a community's wellbeing is an area of research attracting more importance. There is evidence pointing to the therapeutic health advantages that people can gain from taking part in locally-based heritage conservation. Work such as [20] indicates that community-based heritage conservation can result in members experiencing a range of positive effects, such as passion and curiosity, which in turn contribute to a wider experience of belonging, engagement, and social wellbeing, all tied to the location in which the community practice is taking place [20]. Local heritage activities can supplement wellbeing with a range of health benefits, due in part to visiting and walking between local places. Additionally, there is a sense of empowerment when a community has control over and is directly involved in the creation of its cultural heritage.

The discourse enabling co-creation between researchers and community members can lurch between imperatives couched in the seemingly impenetrable registers of academic research and the community's perceptions as to which aspects of these, expressed in lexis that is easily understood, are likely to be practically helpful to their needs. Digital tools may make it easier and more inclusive for people from the community to feel comfortable that they can contribute valuable insights, be respected, and work together. In this way, they can feel they are 'doing with' rather than 'being done to'. An example of this would be the use of a wiki to record intangible heritage [12]. However, this work notes that there can be an issue of privacy. Small communities, like the ones found on Scottish islands, tend to be private in their written word; they are more comfortable sharing aspects of their life on the island in face-to-face interactions. In our study, we have facilitated this by preferring conversational recordings.

Community-based work in the Western Isles is not a new concept. Island Voices/Guthan nan Eilean is a community-based online language capture project which seeks to record the life and stories of the islands [13]. Bilingual recordings in Gaelic and English with short videos introducing authentic speech interviews with community members give viewers a closer, more personal insight into the subject at hand. Not only does this project capture the heritage of the islands, but it also preserves the Gaelic language and its unique linguistic features, such as North Uist dialectal nuance, intonation, register and idiom within the storytelling and descriptive genres of the language. The project has been extended to include 'Other Tongues', with the videos also dubbed in other languages, ensuring that content in endangered languages, such as Gaelic, can be enjoyed by people who do not know the language.

The work of this project draws on the collaborative history of working with immersive technologies in the community of North Uist [15]. This included a North Uist 360° exhibition at Taigh Chearsabhagh museum, which featured music composed by local musicians, 360° images and drone footage of archaeological sites, together with stories relevant to the sites interpreted by school students of the primary schools on the island. Digital resources representing the North Uist island of St Kilda include a digital reconstruction, creative interpretation by school students, and representations of legends connected to the island [15, 17]. With increasing coastal erosion, Community Rescue Archaeology can play an important role in the communication of heritage of endangered places [8].

The application of gaming technologies enables widespread digital literacy to be used in exploring heritage [11]. Mixed reality exhibits can bring together physical and virtual representations of heritage enriching both [2]. Digital reconstructions help us visualise archaeology and appreciate the value of archaeological sites [14]. These can connect with social histories like the Highland Clearances and the crofting movement [18]. Museums without walls hold the prospect of digital heritage being deployed more accessibly and widely in museums, the home and the landscape [7, 9, 16].

The potential of digitisation of heritage artefacts to make digital exhibits in community museums is explored in [3], whilst [19] discusses synthesising 3D modelling and digitisation to produce digital models that represent artefacts as they were in the past. Digital reconstruction of the past is explored in [10] and [11]. In this case study, digital reconstructions are used to give visitors an informative virtual walk experience that recreates a site in the past.

The work outlined here presents a scene that places immersive digital tools in the centre of community cultural practices. Cultural participation and co-creation have been shown to increase wellbeing and community cohesion. In this work, this concept is integrated with digitisation and gaming technologies to provide informal immersive learning opportunities for the Gaelic community in North Uist.

3 Methodology

Ensuring North Uist's cultural landscape is extended into the digital world requires the digitisation, archiving, and availability of these elements. The digitisation and archiving activities of this project include:

1. The creation of 'Virtual Walks' based on real walks organised by members around archaeological sites.
2. Digital reconstructions of historic places and exhibits developed using game technology.
3. Digitisation of artefacts and their histories.
4. Recording of poems, music, and stories associated with the island and the wider Gaelic culture.

These were chosen based on the literature and other projects highlighted above. An element of community-based heritage was crucial to the core of the project, and thus the community was involved in the creation of these digital assets. Previous work with 360° photos and audio/video material as used in [15] was integrated into the virtual multimedia walks. Building on the work of [2] and others, digital reconstructions were created to allow exploration of the heritage sites. The digitisation of 3D artefacts—typically an expert activity—was designed to allow community members to take part by recording the stories behind the objects. This was done in both Gaelic and English to address the Gaelic language issues and ensure bilingual digital content creation. The design of these activities is outlined below.

3.1 Virtual Walks: Heritage, Place, and Language

Three walks were organised around Trinity Temple, Barpa Langais, and Dun an Sticir, each a site of cultural significance. The walks were advertised in advance and a guided tour in Gaelic was provided. The first walk attracted 20 people whilst the others suffered from the weather.

Fig. 1. The remains of the Broch as seen in the virtual walk tour.

We then developed a virtual walk of the Dun an Sticir walk and trialled it at the Digital Fèis. The Virtual Walk application consists of an introductory video providing a flyover of the site with music inspired by the site; and an interactive map with a menu system providing access to further content and hotspots that open a spherical image which links to other images of the location. The map provides location context to the 360° tours. The menu was the entry point for the following content:

Gaelic Information. A sequence of 360° images of the ruins, each accompanied by Gaelic interpretation. This sequence represents a virtual walk along the route marked on the map with Gaelic commentary (Fig. 1).

Video Library. This contains three videos representing stories associated with the island. One has commentators providing snippets of archaeological evidence. The others relate the story of the Lord of the Broch at Dun an Sticir with a series of posed scenes narrated in Gaelic and in English by local children.

Reconstruction Video. A video of a digital reconstruction of the Broch. The reconstruction places the Broch in its landscape in the centre of the island and shows how it might have been in 500 BC. It is accompanied by an animation showing how a Broch would have been built.

Virtual Historical Walk. A tour around the recreated virtual environment, which provides interactive engagement with the Broch as it looked in 500 BC. Essentially, this provides another layer to the virtual tour, allowing the visitor to experience a walk around the location, both as it stands now and as it would have looked in the past (Fig. 2).

This application integrates the community involvement aspects with Gaelic digital content creation, providing a tool for immersive learning of these historical sites. It was replicated across four platforms. A web version links to the CEUT website and provides online access [6]. A local version running on a NUC connected with a touch screen provides an exhibit which is not reliant on internet access. An iOS and Android app provides touchscreen interaction on phones and tablets. An Oculus version provides an immersive virtual reality experience with a stand-alone headset, enabling visitors to virtually walk around the site, putting them in control of the locations they visit.

Fig. 2. The reconstructed Broch in the Virtual Reality app.

3.2   3D Digitisation: Artefacts and Stories

In advertising the Fèis, a call was put out for community members to bring artefacts from their homes for digitisation into 3D and story recording. The goal was to create a digital archive that represented artefacts of significance to the community and collecting stories about the objects in the owners' words. The objects brought varied from family heirlooms to crofting and other working tools. They were scanned using the Artec Spider laser scanner. This scanner was chosen because it facilitated quick scanning of objects with real-time editing, so the community could be present during the entire process. The recording of the stories was done in both video and audio, allowing the member of the community to explain the history and importance of the artefact, thus creating an interactive digital North Uist community museum.

The addition of community objects that do not form part of a museum collection, means that these heritage items are now available to the public. Moreover, the owners of these objects had an active role in documenting the artefact's history and metadata, including Gaelic traditional names, providing valuable information that goes beyond a name on a label.

This archive contains over 15 new 3D objects and over 20 associated stories and photographs and continues to expand as it includes other artefacts from North Uist. It is available online on a project platform built using open-source components including Omeka, Open Street maps and the International Image Interoperability Framework for digital galleries. It can be accessed in [5].

3.3   Music and Song

The final activity revolved around capturing Gaelic auditory culture, by working with the local Fèis committee and recording performances of school students. These included solos and group performances on a variety of traditional instruments: accordion, chanter, and bagpipes. Traditional Gaelic singing was also recorded.

This digitisation work was an effort to include the young members of the community as commonly, local community heritage work mainly attracted an older audience. The recording of Gaelic music builds upon another project, Ceòl Uibhist a Tuath (Music of North Uist), which identifies and preserves the music of North Uist across the ages [4]. The database now contains over 170 tracks capturing music and song associated with the culture of North Uist.

4   Results and Findings

During the Digital Fèis, visitors contributed through the digitisation (3.2) and music (3.3) activities, and experienced the virtual reality walks (3.1. Visitors were free to walk around the space and spend as much time as they wanted with any or each activity. They were invited to complete a survey about the virtual walk experience to evaluate specifically how the immersive activity could benefit the community. There were 14 respondents: 45–54 years (1), 55–64 years (3), 65–74 years (7), and 75 years or older (3). When asked about their experience using digital tools, 3 had a lot, 7 had some experience, 1 had a little, and 3 had none.

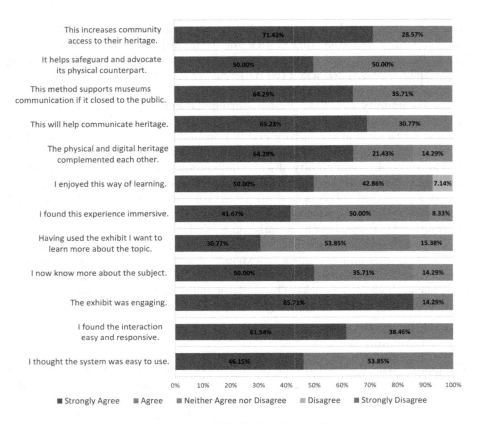

Fig. 3. Virtual Walk Exhibit results.

Figure 3 shows the response to a series of statements. The questions were chosen to find out whether the community felt that these digital tools preserved their heritage, whether they make heritage more available, and whether they found this experience enjoyable and engaging. Five themes were analysed: Societal impact (Questions 1–2), Value for promotion and preservation of heritage (Questions 3–5), Learning benefit (Questions 6–7), Suitability of digital tools for the community (Questions 8–10), and Usability (Questions 11–12).

It stands out that the responses were very positive, overwhelmingly strongly agreeing or agreeing with the statements. This also reflects our observation that people liked and engaged with the exhibits, particularly the Virtual Tour element with the Gaelic commentary, which provided an opportunity for some people to hear Gaelic outside their normal home environment, and for others to practice it or hear it for the first time.

The strongest positive answers were for questions 1, 4, 10, and 11, suggesting a good response across the categories. This indicates that the immersive experience was suitable for the task of communicating the heritage at hand. These responses also indicate that with the increased access to engaging heritage content, community members can feel part of their society, and can further heighten social inclusion through co-creating digital materials.

The least, but still relatively positive, responses came from questions 8 and 9. These questions deal with the community's knowledge of the heritage: the ability to learn using this technology, and the desire to learn more after being exposed to this technology. This highlights an important consideration that has to be taken when developing immersive cultural landscape activities: that they should guide the user on an informative journey which focuses on certain elements of the landscape in order to provide information that can be retained after the user removes the headset. In addition, the immersive experience should sit as part of other resources which the user can turn to for additional learning if desired. These could be other forms of media or the co-creation activities that were offered on the day.

The positive response to the digitised virtual walk means we will use it as a model for further Gaelic heritage walks, in fact an additional virtual walk for Trinity Temple has already been added. The technology and the variety of devices it can be accessed through suggest that cultural heritage is increasingly available to everyone.

5   Discussion and Future Work

This case study has shown that combining digitisation techniques can aid in the production and archiving of digital content. Moreover, the role of the community in creating these materials is not to be disregarded. Whilst the feedback was taken on a relatively small sample, this is representative of the small communities in remote areas of Scotland. It is worth noting that these respondents were attracted by the premise of the community digital festival, wanting to see community heritage in action.

The digitisation activities can be replicated for audiences in similar small communities and tried on larger communities as a next step. The live digitisation of community artefacts works particularly well in archiving pieces of history that do not form part of museum collections. A further use of these digital tools is in formal education, where students have an opportunity to interact with their heritage in different forms.

The next activities include a more comprehensive survey on the wellbeing of the community. The results of this survey are currently being reviewed, after receiving almost 100 responses. This survey seeks to find which sectors contribute to the wellbeing of the community, with the available digital heritage tools created in this study forming one of the sectors. A second digital festival is in the works, providing an opportunity for more people to be part of this project and experience their heritage virtually.

As a result of these tools and the digital fèis, regular 'cupans', or coffee mornings, are being held in the school, calling for community members to meet and look at the photos, videos, and songs collected in a relaxed environment. This is providing an additional source of information, with people often recognising unnamed faces in photos, or giving additional information about long-forgotten Gaelic place names of the heritage sites. The recorded music performed by the youth group was broadcasted during an online ceilidh, bringing people together and strengthening the community during the winter.

6   Conclusion

This paper has shown how elements of immersive learning can be applied to cultural heritage to aid in the wellbeing of vernacular communities by increasing their sense of social inclusion. This was achieved through the co-creation of digital content, such as 3D digitising of community artefacts accompanied by bilingual audio/video recordings, and contribution to a virtual walk which is experienced in VR. The immersive nature of the virtual walks aids in learning about the cultural heritage present in this region and makes the hard-to-reach locations available for community members who are not able to visit these locations, whether due to mobility and health issues or because they do not live close to these remote places. Moreover, these digital activities give an idea of how vernacular Cultural Landscapes can be preserved.

References

1. Beveridge, E.: North Uist: Its Archaeology and Topography, with Notes Upon the Early History of the Outer Hebrides ... Brown (1911). https://books.google.co.uk/books?id=bDbM112QcFcC
2. Cassidy, C., et al.: Digital pathways in community museums. Museum Int. **70**(1–2), 126–139 (2018). https://doi.org/10.1111/muse.12198
3. Cassidy, C.A., Fabola, A., Rhodes, E., Miller, A.: The making and evaluation of Picts and Pixels: mixed exhibiting in the real and the unreal. In: Beck, D., et al. (eds.) iLRN 2018. CCIS, vol. 840, pp. 97–112. Springer, Cham (2018). https://doi.org/10.1007/978-3-319-93596-6_7
4. CEUT: Ceól Uibhist a Tuath. https://ceol.scot/
5. CEUT: North Uist historical artefacts (2022). https://ceut.northernheritage.org/galleries/gallerycontents.php?id=12
6. CEUT: North Uist virtual walks (2022). https://ceut.northernheritage.org/virtual-walks/
7. Davies, C., Miller, A., Allison, C.: A view from the hill: where cross reality meets virtual worlds. In: Proceedings of the 20th ACM Symposium on Virtual Reality Software and Technology, pp. 213–213. ACM, United States (2014). https://doi.org/10.1145/2671015.2671138
8. Dawson, T., Oliver, I., Miller, A., Vermehren, A., Kennedy, S.: Digitally enhanced community rescue archaeology. In: Digital Heritage International Congress (DigitalHeritage), 2013, vol. 2, pp. 29–36. IEEE (2013). https://doi.org/10.1109/DigitalHeritage.2013.6744726
9. Fabola, A., Miller, A., Fawcett, R.: Exploring the past with google cardboard. In: Guidi, G., (eds.) et al Proceedings of the 2015 Digital Heritage International Congress, vol. 1, pp. 277–284. IEEE (2015). https://doi.org/10.1109/DigitalHeritage.2015.7413882

10. Getchell, K., Miller, A., Allison, C., Hardy, R., Sweetman, R., Crook, V.: The lava project: a service based approach to supporting exploratory learning. In: IADIS International Conference WWW/Internet (2006)

11. Getchell, K., Miller, A., Nicoll, J., Sweetman, R., Allison, C.: Games methodologies and immersive environments for virtual fieldwork. IEEE Trans. Learn. Technol. **3**(4), 281–293 (2010). https://doi.org/10.1109/TLT.2010.25

12. Giglitto, D.: Community empowerment through the management of intangible cultural heritage in the isle of Jura, Scotland. Imperial J. Interdisc. Res. **3**, 567–578 (2017). https://ssrn.com/abstract=3000953

13. IslandVoices: Guthan nan Eilean: About (2012). https://guthan.wordpress.com/about/

14. Kennedy, S., et al.: Exploring canons and cathedrals with Open Virtual Worlds: The recreation of St Andrews cathedral, St Andrews day, 1318. In: Digital Heritage International Congress (DigitalHeritage) 2013, vol. 2, pp. 273–280. IEEE (2013). https://doi.org/10.1109/DigitalHeritage.2013.6744764

15. Kennedy, S., Oliver, I., Rhodes, E., Miller, A.: St Kilda 1880: digital reconstruction of St Kilda set in 1880 (2020, online). https://www.openvirtualworlds.org/st-kilda/

16. McCaffery, J., Miller, A., Vermehren, A., Fabola, A.: The virtual museums of caen: a case study on modes of representation of digital historical content. In: Guidi, G., Scopigno, R., Torres, J., Graf, H. (eds.) Proceedings of the 2015 Digital Heritage International Congress, vol. 2, pp. 541–548. IEEE (2015). https://doi.org/10.1109/DigitalHeritage.2015.7419571

17. McCaffery, J., Kennedy, S., Miller, A., Oliver, I., Watterson, A., Allison, C.: Immersive installation: "a virtual St Kilda". In: Ebner, M., Erenli, K., Malaka, R., Pirker, J., Walsh, A.E. (eds.) EiED 2014. CCIS, vol. 486, pp. 101–113. Springer, Cham (2015). https://doi.org/10.1007/978-3-319-22017-8_9

18. McCaffery, J., et al.: Exploring heritage through time and space: supporting community reflection on the highland clearances. In: Digital Heritage International Congress (DigitalHeritage) 2013, vol. 1, pp. 371–378. IEEE (2013). https://doi.org/10.1109/DigitalHeritage.2013.6743762

19. Pisani, S., Miller, A., Hall, M.: Digitally restoring artefacts using 3D modelling techniques for immersive learning opportunities. In: Dengel, A., (eds.) et al Proceedings of the 2022 8th international conference of the Immersive Learning Research Network (iLRN), pp. 149–156. iLRN (2022). https://doi.org/10.23919/iLRN55037.2022.9815895

20. Power, A., Smyth, K.: Heritage, health and place: the legacies of local community-based heritage conservation on social wellbeing. Health Place **39**, 160–167 (2016). https://doi.org/10.1016/j.healthplace.2016.04.005

21. UNESCO: Cultural landscapes. Online (2022). https://whc.unesco.org/en/culturallandscape/

Nature & Environmental Sciences (NES)

Evaluating the Efficacy of a Desktop Virtual Reality Field Trip for Public Outreach

Alec Bodzin[1]([⊠]), Robson Araujo-Junior[1], Thomas Hammond[1], David Anastasio[1], and Chad Schwartz[2]

[1] Lehigh University, Bethlehem, PA 18015, USA
amb4@lehigh.edu
[2] Lehigh Gap Nature Center, Slatington, PA 18080, USA

Abstract. This evaluation study examines the implementation of a desktop virtual reality field trip (dVFT) for public outreach. After experiencing the dVFT, 139 participants completed a survey to examine their immersion, presence, engagement, perceived learning about the local environment, VR design features, and affective learning. The majority of participants reported favorable outcomes regarding all the variables above. No significant differences were found between male and female learners for each of the six constructs. No significant differences were found between adults' and youths' perceptions of immersion, presence, and attitudes. Adults ages 19 and older had statistically significant higher mean engagement levels, mean perceptions of learning about the local environment, and VR design features than youth. Our findings support that learning about one's local environment with a dVFT can have a positive impact on engagement and learning, particularly in public outreach settings.

Keywords: Desktop Virtual Reality · VR Field Trip · Public Outreach

1 Introduction

Learning about one's local environment with a desktop VR field trip (dVFT) holds much potential to have a positive impact on engagement and learning for public outreach. A VR field trip presents several characteristics of great appeal to learners and can be an enhancement to a STEM education center's outreach programs or for informal home learning. Features such as active control of the user experience and realistic representation of real-world situations may increase engagement and learning. A VR field trip experience can also provide a sense of authentic immersion and presence of being physically at specific geographic locations that are either inaccessible (in time or space) or problematic (dangerous) [1]. In a dVFT environment, authentic imagery, content, animations, video, and narration can be incorporated to provide learners with a highly immersive learning experience. Since VR technology allows for such supports in an immersive environment, it can be designed to provide improved access to STEM-related content for those who are physically unable to visit an outdoor location due to mobility disabilities or transportation issues. In addition, Leung et al. [2] found that virtual immersion in the natural world was sufficient to enhance a sense of connection to nature, including for individuals with a low affinity to nature.

© The Author(s), under exclusive license to Springer Nature Switzerland AG 2024
M.-L. Bourguet et al. (Eds.): iLRN 2023, CCIS 1904, pp. 411–425, 2024.
https://doi.org/10.1007/978-3-031-47328-9_30

Web-based VR tours can offer a sense of agency through the ability of changing one's perspective of the environment in any direction within the 360° media with little physical effort [3]. Some dVFTs are highly structured and include multimodal media to describe specific features across a sequence of locations. Other dVFTs may be more exploratory, including only a few locations or points of interest to attract learners' attention where one has the freedom to observe their surroundings by panning and zooming at their own pace [4].

The majority of published studies pertaining to VR field trips have occurred in formal learning, including university settings (e.g., [3]), middle and high school classrooms (e.g., [5]), and elementary school settings (e.g., [6]). Many of these studies used headset VR during implementation. Zhao et al. [4] found that both desktop VR and headset VR field trips had more positive learning effects than a traditional field trip, and although students reported higher motivation and being more present in the headset VR group, they did not learn more compared to those in the desktop VR group.

VR experiences have been effective for promoting learning in public outreach settings. Markowitz et al. [7] conducted a headset VR study at a film festival in which participants had an underwater experience to learn about ocean acidification. They reported that total physical movement was a predictor of inquisitiveness. Bibic et al. [8] developed a VR game that engaged the public with learning about biochemistry and shifted perceptions about spider venoms. Kersting et al. [9] reported that VR facilitated the visualization of abstract astronomy concepts among participants at a science festival.

While headset VR experiences likely provide a more immersive user experience than a desktop VR experience, most STEM centers, public libraries, and homes do not have headset VR equipment. Hence, dVFTs can provide more accessibility to learners of all ages for public outreach learning. Thus, this evaluation study investigated the implementation of a dVFT developed in partnership with an environmental education center for public outreach. Specifically, we examined levels of immersion, presence, engagement, perceptions of learning about the local environment, and affective learning. In addition, we were interested in users' perceptions of the dVFT's narrative and guidance as design features. Since public outreach activities involve a wide range of audiences, we were also interested in differences between adults and youth, as well as female and male learners.

2 Background and Theoretical Framework

Our project draws primarily from two theoretical frameworks: Science Learning Activation Theory [10] and Malone's theory of intrinsically motivating instruction [11]. These theories of engagement and motivation form the basis for designing a dVFT to promote user engagement and learning.

Engagement can be defined as one's focus, participation, and persistence within a task, and therefore related to adaptive or self-regulated learning [10, 12]. Engagement is what happens during a task, a result of the interaction between the learner and the characteristics of both the task itself and the supporting environment. Dorph et al. [10] discussed three dimensions of engagement: (1) behavioral engagement that focuses on what a person involved in a learning activity would look like or be doing (e.g., actively participating in a learning task or doing off-task behaviors); (2) cognitive engagement that focuses on thought processes or attention directed at processing and understanding the content in a learning task; and (3) affective engagement that includes one's emotions that are experienced during a science activity. Research suggests that a combination of these three aspects of engagement supports students to learn [12], and all can be enhanced by VR. In addition, agentic engagement, a more recent aspect of learner engagement, refers to one's constructive contribution and proactive behaviors into the flow of instruction they receive [13]. When thoughtfully designed, a VR field trip experience can provide learners with autonomous control to intentionally select a pathway to achieve a task and thus personalize their learning through this interaction.

Malone's theory of intrinsically motivating instruction [11] argues that intrinsic motivation is created by three qualities: challenge, fantasy, and curiosity. Challenge depends upon activities that involve uncertain outcomes due to variable levels, hidden information, or randomness. Goals should be meaningful to the learner, and learners need some form of performance feedback to tell whether they are achieving their goal. For an environment to be challenging, the outcome must be uncertain. Fantasy should depend upon skills required for the instruction. Curiosity can be aroused when learners believe their knowledge structures are incomplete. According to Malone's theory, intrinsically motivating activities provide learners with a broad range of challenge, concrete feedback, and clear-cut criteria for performance. Thus, to promote learners' curiosity and engagement, feedback should be surprising and constructive.

Much VR literature has focused on the design elements for developing immersion and a sense of presence [14] in a VR environment. Immersion is the level of sensory fidelity that a VR system provides and can also describe one's experience of using VR [15]. This technology works by exchanging sensory input from reality with digitally generated sensory input, such as images and sounds [16]. Spatial immersion is a term used in VR and occurs when a player feels that the simulated world is perceptually convincing; it looks "authentic" and "real," and players feel that they actually are "there" [1]. Presence is a user's subjective psychological response to a VR system where the user responds to the VR environment as if it were real [17].

3   The Desktop VR Field Trip

The Lehigh Gap Story (the dVFT) was designed to help learners understand the environmental changes that occurred in the Lehigh River watershed in Pennsylvania during the past two centuries as a result of a zinc smelting plant operation at the Lehigh Gap. A green mountain ridge became a barren "moonscape" as a result of zinc smelting activities that began in the 1890 s. The smelting plant emitted approximately 3,450 lb of sulfur dioxide per hour from 1918 to 1970, along with heavy metals, into the atmosphere [18]. Smelter emissions produced acid rain, which spread over the surrounding landscape. Five years after the smelting plants ceased operations, a comprehensive and laborious revegetation project was initiated by the U.S. Environmental Protection Agency (EPA) and a local community group. The Lehigh Gap is revitalized today through a mixture of warm-season grasses that have trapped the heavy metals in the soil. Today, the site includes a 756-acre wildlife refuge and the Lehigh Gap Nature Center (LGNC), which is used for education, research, and outdoor recreation. The dVFT tells this story through an interactive experience. Both local geographic factors and industrial smelting led to the locus of pollution and environmental degradation at LGNC.

The Lehigh Gap Story Starts by loading a main menu screen containing two distinct experiences to select from: Story Mode and Exploration Mode (Fig. 1). In Exploration Mode, a trail pathway map (Fig. 2) allows an independent tour of the area by choosing photospheres (i.e., 360° photos) enriched with ambient audio, 2D media, and 3D assets. In Story Mode, the avatar bird, Brownie, guides the user through a sequence of seven photospheres using audio narration, subtitles, and related historic photos. The first photosphere has a short play-through tutorial sequence for users to familiarize with the dVFT interactivity and locate the interface elements (UI). As soon as the tutorial is completed, the bird avatar prompts users to "talk to Brownie" by pressing the "T" on the keyboard or using the cursor to click Brownie, on screen, to start narration of the story of the Lehigh Gap area (Fig. 3). The dVFT features collapsible (i.e., non-persistent) UI on each corner of the screen for on-demand support, including the game controls panel,

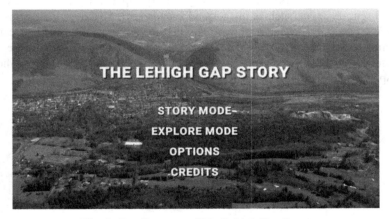

Fig. 1. Landing page of The Lehigh Gap Story.

help cards, and a progression checklist. The checklist must be completed (in any order) before Brownie invites the users to proceed to the next photosphere by interacting with a green arrow (Fig. 4).

Fig. 2. The trail map in Exploration mode. Placing a cursor over a location site displays the site's main content.

Fig. 3. Image of the first photosphere. The checklist is displayed in the upper right hand corner of the screen.

Fig. 4. Image of Brownie prompting the user to move to the next photosphere.

Each photosphere focuses on a specific topic. In the second photosphere, the geology of the area is highlighted, and users are able to manipulate virtual rock pieces of anthracite, quartzite, sphalerite, and coal that are relevant the Lehigh Gap story (Fig. 5). Users also learn about the importance of zinc for making products such as batteries. The third and fourth photospheres focus on the historical canal and railway transportation routes for bringing coal and zinc through the Lehigh Gap and also for transporting coal to areas further south in the watershed for other manufacturing processes (Fig. 6). The fifth and sixth photospheres focus on the New Jersey Zinc Company and the establishment of the company-town of Palmerton, PA. Users learn about the zinc smelting process to produce zinc ingots and other zinc-based products (Fig. 7). Next, learners view an acid

Fig. 5. Brownie prompting the user to examine the rocks.

rain animation to learn how the smelting process from the plant denuded the mountain (Fig. 8). The final photosphere focuses on the specification of the area as an EPA Superfund site, the testing of mixtures of warm-season grasses to restore the ecological health of the mountain, and the success of establishing diverse habitats that can be observed today (Fig. 9). For additional details on the design and development of the dVFT, see Bodzin et al. [19].

Fig. 6. Image of Brownie talking about the development of a railway bridge at the Lehigh Gap.

Fig. 7. Brownie discussing the zinc smelting process at the New Jersey Zinc Company west plant.

Fig. 8. Image from the acid rain animation.

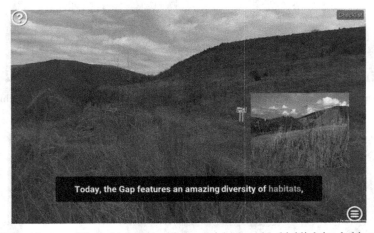

Fig. 9. Current image of the Lehigh Gap with Brownie's narration highlighting habitat diversity.

4 Methodology

This evaluation study was implemented in the context of public outreach settings. In August 2022, the dVFT was placed on a public website and linked through the Lehigh Gap Nature Center's (LGNC) website. The website included passive consent materials to participate in the study. That is, users of the dVFT could opt in to complete a Qualtrics Web survey that was linked to the green arrow at the end of the last photosphere in Story Mode. Information about the dVFT was shared by the dissemination channels of the LGNC and our college. Data collection was open for three months. Additional data was collected from 37 participants who attended a seasonal festival at the LGNC and 35 students and 9 college-age tutors from an after-school middle school homework club.

In total, the resulting data collection included 150 responses. Eleven responses were removed from the data set due to zigzag patterns and straight lines responses, or missing survey data. Responses that omitted demographic items were kept in the data set. The final data set resulted in 139 valid responses. The sample included 76 (54.68%) women, 56 (40.29%) men, 2 (1.43%) who self-identified as non-binary, and 5 (3.59%) who preferred not to answer or respond to the gender demographic item. Ethnicity responses included 86 White or Caucasian, 27 Hispanic or Latino, 13 Asian, 8 Black or African American, 5 Middle Eastern or North African, 2 some other race, ethnicity, or origin, and 8 who preferred not to answer this question. Participants were able to select multiple ethnicities for this demographic item. Age range responses included 27 (19.42%) under 13 years old, 31 (22.30%) 13–18 years old, 25 (17.99%) 19–24 years old, 18 (13.04%) 25–40 years old, 17 (12.95%) 41–55 years old, 14 (10.07%) 55–70 years old, 6 (4.32%) over 70 years old, and 1 (0.72%) who did not respond to this item.

The survey included 24 Likert scale items (see Appendix) that were scored with a five-point scale of 1 (Strongly Disagree) to 5 (Strongly Agree). The data was analyzed in IBM SPSS version 29. The survey subscales included Engagement (7 items), Presence (3 items), Immersion (3 items), VR design features (2 items), Learning local environment (5 items), and Affective learning (4 items). The Engagement subscale items measure a respondent's self-reported cognitive, behavioral, and affective engagement during a science learning opportunity and were modified from Chung et al. [20]. The original measure was designed specifically for science learning activities in informal science centers. Presence, Immersion, and Affective learning subscale items were modified from the Perceptions of Learning with VR Games survey [21] and were modified for the desktop VR field trip context. Subscale reliabilities (Cronbach's alpha) from this study were Engagement = 0.815, Presence = 0.812, Immersion = 0.842, VR design features = 0.773, Learning local environment = 0.832, and Affective learning = 0.767.

Means, standard deviations, and frequencies of each survey item were calculated. Subscale totals were generated for each of the six constructs, including their score range, means, and standard deviations. Independent t-tests were conducted for each subscale to compare differences between adults and youth, as well as women and men. Levene's test for equality was used to check for homogeneity of variance for each t-test. Given the multiple hypothesis testing, the alpha level for each test was set at 0.01 to control for familywise Type I error.

5 Results

Table 1 displays the score range, means and standard deviations for the six subscales. We viewed favorable responses for each item to have a mean of 4.0. Overall, participants reported favorable perceptions of the VR design features and affective learning, and high perceptions of learning about the local environment. In general, the participants enjoyed the dVFT storyline ($\overline{x} = 4.33$, $SD = 0.73$), as well as receiving guidance and feedback during the VR field trip ($\overline{x} = 4.22$, $SD = 0.81$). The majority of participants (88.49%) found the dVFT to be a worthwhile experience ($\overline{x} = 4.33$, $SD = 0.69$) and a rewarding experience ($\overline{x} = 4.31$, $SD = 0.67$). Many participants (80.58%) found the dVFT to be very interesting ($\overline{x} = 4.17$, $SD = 0.86$). Only seven participants (5.04%) responded that the dVFT did not hold their attention.

The results indicated participants' favorable perceptions of learning about their local environment ($\bar{x}$ = 4.49, SD = 0.60), local history ($\bar{x}$ = 4.54, SD = 0.54), and local environmental issues ($\bar{x}$ = 4.50, SD = 0.58). The majority of participants (88.49%) found that the "real-life" context of the dVFT made learning about the local environment interesting ($\bar{x}$ = 4.35, SD = 0.72). However, only 56.1% of the sample found the things that they learned in the dVFT to be relevant to their daily lives ($\bar{x}$ = 3.63, SD = 0.98).

The mean difference between adults ages 19 and older (n = 80; $\bar{x}$ = 22.04, SD = 2.50) and youth (n = 59; $\bar{x}$ = 20.78, SD = 2.88) perceptions of learning about the local environment were statistically significant (t = -2.748, p = 0.007). The mean difference between adult (n = 80, $\bar{x}$ = 8.82, SD = 1.25) and youth (n = 59, $\bar{x}$ = 8.19, SD = 1.50) were statistically significantly different for their perceptions of the VR design features (t = -2.730, p = 0.007). The mean difference between adult (n = 80) and youth (n = 59) were not statistically significantly different for affective learning (t = -2.550, p = 0.012). No significant differences were found between women (n = 76) and men (n = 56) for VR design features (t = -2.069, p = 0.041), perceptions of learning about the local environment (t = -2.225, p = 0.028), and affective learning (t = -0.964, p = 0.337).

Table 1. Subscales total scores descriptive statistics

Survey Subscale	Score Range	Mean	Standard Deviation
Engagement	7–35	28.90	4.29
Presence	3–15	12.12	2.27
Immersion	3–15	12.73	2.00
VR design features	2–10	8.55	1.39
Learning local environment	5–25	21.50	2.73
Affective learning	4–20	16.94	2.41

Note. N = 139

Overall, the study participants in the sample reported high levels of engagement, presence, and immersion while using the dVFT. The mean difference between adult (n = 80; $\bar{x}$ = 29.95, SD = 3.99) and youth (n = 59; $\bar{x}$ = 27.47, SD = 4.30) engagement were statistically significant (t = -2.748, p = 0.007). While most participants were engaged with the dVFT, 15 participants (10.79%) responded that their mind was elsewhere when they used the VR field trip, 9 participants (6.48%) responded that they were not focused most of the time, 16 participants (11.51%) felt bored when they used the VR field trip. Moreover, 16 participants (11.51%) responded that time did not go by quickly when they used the VR field trip. The mean difference between adults and youth for presence (t = -1.380, p = 0.170) and immersion (t = -0.538, p = 0.591) were not significantly different. There were no significant mean differences for female and male learners for engagement (t = -1.140, p = 0.257), immersion (t = -2.203, p = 0.029), and presence (t = -1.852, p = 0.066).

6   Discussion

An important goal of public outreach is to develop learning experiences that are engaging for a wide range of audiences. This is a prominent design challenge for VR field trip developers who seek to develop learning activities for a wide age range of people that would include adolescents and senior citizens. Throughout our iterative design and development process, we engaged a wide range of age groups to use the prototype and pilot-test versions of The Lehigh Gap Story. Early in the development process, participants reported that interactivity was important, since they enjoyed having tasks to complete in each photosphere. In each photosphere, participants would need to complete a series of tasks before moving on to the next photosphere. The user had the autonomy to select the order in which they wished to complete these tasks. We believe that this autonomy likely contributed to the participants' engagement of the dVFT experience.

The narrative storyline also likely contributed to the participants' engagement. One hundred twenty-one participants (87.05%) responded that they enjoyed the storyline. The Lehigh Gap Story was narrated by Brownie, a bird avatar who shares an emotional storyline about her ancestors' habitat destruction. Emotionally appealing storylines can serve to motivate and engage a person and lead to increased learning [22]. It is likely that Brownie's story hooked the users' attention at the beginning of the dVFT experience. The storyline may also have served to activate other design characteristics of the dVFT experience such as curiosity, interactivity, autonomous control, and feedback.

Careful attention during the iterative design and development of the dVFT was placed on ensuring that the narrative story and the interactive elements in the experience did not demand a high cognitive load on the user. Too much interactivity may affect users' cognitive load during the experience and impact learning. In previous implementation studies with middle school and college students using learning games in formal learning environments, the combination of storylines and interactivity was found to either decrease or have no effect on learning and have mixed effects on motivation and engagement [23]. Our findings may have differed from these past studies due our public outreach context. Learners in formal school environments may often focus on extrinsic motivation for task completions compared to public outreach settings in which people seek intrinsically rewarding experiences. That said, not all participants were completely engaged throughout the entire dVFT experience. The type of interactivity in the dVFT might account for the lower levels of engagement with youth. Compared to dynamic video games that youth tend to play, the interactivity features in the dVFT are not as dynamic. The most dynamic feature was the ability to manipulate the rocks on the trail by rotating and zooming. While the historical signs within the photospheres had images and text that could be magnified, users had to read the text on these signs. There was not an option for this text to be read aloud to the users. This may have affected the engagement of some of the participants, especially those who may be reluctant readers.

When designing VR field trips for public outreach, a challenge is to optimally design interactive experiences that focus on learning without cognitively overwhelming the user with other elements that may distract learners from a learning focus. Given the favorable levels of engagement and perceived learning that the participants experienced, a combination of the design features, local contexts, and the VR features of immersion and presence may have led to users' engagement. We conducted a post-hoc correlation analysis and found that each of the subscales statistically correlated with each other. In our next study, we intend to conduct a path analysis to explore the relationships of each construct.

The local context was likely an important component of the dVFT that led to the perceived learning and engagement of the participants. Local and regional learning can support learners' agency in public outreach learning contexts by providing experiences regarding authentic environmental issues. VR field trip designers can incorporate features such as avatars and storylines to achieve an emotional connection between users and place [24]. In addition, The Lehigh Gap Story included high-fidelity, photo-realistic imagery and realistic ambient sound, coupled with navigational agency for the users to freely explore the virtual environment at their own pace. These visual and auditory components likely contributed to the high levels of immersion and presence that the users experienced and may have contributed to keeping the users engaged and on task, which may have led to their perceived learning. However, only 56.1% of the sample found the things that they learned in the dVFT to be relevant to their daily lives. It is likely that some of the study participants have not actually visited the LGNC to hike on the trails on the revegetated mountain and thus did not have a personal connection to this area. In addition, some participants may have lived in geographical areas that are distant from the LGNC.

There are other factors that may have contributed to our evaluation study findings. First, this study only included three types of public outreach settings. There are many different types of public outreach events that STEM and environmental education centers conduct. Future studies may examine differences among these settings. Second, it is possible that many participants had a favorable bias towards engaging with the dVFT. Those who attended the seasonal festival at the LGNC may have been intrinsically motivated to learn more about an environmental site that they were visiting for a public outreach event. Third, the dVFT itself may have provided a novelty effect for the participants due to the dVR technology experience.

7   Conclusion

This evaluation study examined immersion, presence, engagement, perceived learning about the local environment, VR design features, and affective learning with a dVFT in public outreach settings. We found that immersion, presence, engagement, learning about local environment, VR design features, and affective learning were perceived favorably by the majority of the study's participants. No significant differences were found between the gender groups for each of the six constructs that were measured. No significant differences were found between adults' and youths' perceptions of immersion, presence, and affective learning. Adults had statistically significant higher mean engagement levels, perceptions of learning about the local environment, and design features than youth. Our findings support that learning about one's local environment with a dVFT can have a positive impact on engagement and learning, particularly in public outreach learning environments. Since most STEM and environmental education centers do not have headset VR equipment, dVFTs placed on a public website can provide access to engaging learning experiences for outreach experiences, thus providing equity for novel VR learning experiences.

Acknowledgments. We thank Sarah Kiel, Tyler Hogue, Austin Lordi, Brad DeMassa, Challen Adu, Kanaruj Chanthongdee, Yolanda Liu, Max Louissaint, Anthony Blakely, and Brantley Balsamo for their development work with us on the dVFT.

Appendix. Survey Measure Items

Engagement subscale items:

I felt excited when I used the VR field trip.
My mind was elsewhere when I used the VR field trip. (reverse code).
I was focused on the VR field trip most of the time.
I felt bored when I used the VR field trip. (reverse code).
Time went by quickly when I used the VR field trip.
I was doing other things when I used the VR field trip. (reverse code).
When I used the VR field trip, I talked to others about things not related to the VR field trip. (reverse code).

Presence subscale items:

I had a sense of "being there" when using the VR field trip.
I was able to concentrate easily when using the VR field trip.
I felt present in the VR field trip.

Immersion subscale items:

The VR field trip had a realistic-looking environment.
My seeing and hearing senses were fully used during the VR field trip.
I felt immersed when using the VR field trip.

VR design features subscale items:

I enjoyed the storyline of the VR field trip.
I enjoyed receiving guidance and feedback during the VR field trip.

Perceptions of learning about one's local environment subscale items:

I learned about my local environment with the VR field trip.
I learned about local history while using the VR field trip.
I learned about local environmental issues when using the VR field trip.
The "real-life" context of the VR field trip made learning about the local environment interesting.
The things I learned while using the VR field trip were relevant to my daily life.

Affective learning subscale items:

Using this VR field trip was a rewarding experience.
Using this VR field trip was a worthwhile experience.
This VR field trip did not hold my attention. (reverse code).
I would describe this VR field trip as very interesting.

References

1. Jennett, C., et al.: Measuring and defining the experience of immersion in games. Int. J. Hum-Comp. Stu. **66**(9), 641–661 (2008)
2. Leung, G.Y.S., Hazan, H., Chan, C.S.: Exposure to nature in immersive virtual reality increases connectedness to nature among people with low nature affinity. J. Env. Psyc. **83**, 101863 (2022)
3. Klippel, A., et al.: The value of being there: toward a science of immersive virtual field trips. Virt. Real. **24**(4), 753–770 (2020). https://doi.org/10.1007/s10055-019-00418-5
4. Zhao, J.Y., LaFemina, P., Carr, J., Sajjadi, P., Wallgrun, J.O., Klippel, A.: Learning in the field: Comparison of desktop, immersive virtual reality, and actual field trips for place-based STEM education. In: 2020 IEEE Conference on Virtual Reality and 3D User Interfaces (VR), pp. 893–902 (2020). https://doi.org/10.1109/VR46266.2020.00012
5. Petersen, G.B., Klingenberg, S., Mayer, R.E., Makransky, G.: The virtual field trip: investigating how to optimize immersive virtual learning in climate change education. Brit. J. Educ. Tech. **51**(6), 2099–2115 (2020). https://doi.org/10.1111/bjet.12991
6. Han, I.: Immersive virtual field trips in education: a mixed-methods study on elementary students' presence and perceived learning. Brit. J. Edu. Tech. **51**(2), 420–435 (2020). https://doi.org/10.1111/bjet.12842
7. Markowitz, D.M., Laha, R., Perone, B.P., Pea, R.D., Bailenson, J.N.: Immersive virtual reality field trips facilitate learning about climate change. Fron. Psyc. **9**, 2365 (2018). https://doi.org/10.3389/fpsyg.2018.02364
8. Bibic, L., Druskis, J., Walpole, S., Angulo, J., Stokes, L.: Bug off pain: an educational virtual reality game on spider venoms and chronic pain. J. Chem. Educ. **96**, 1486–1490 (2019)
9. Kersting, M., Steier, R., Venville, G.: Exploring participant engagement during an astrophysics virtual reality experience at a science festival. Int. J. Sci. Edu. Part B. **11**(2), 17–34 (2021)
10. Dorph, R., Cannady, M.A., Schunn, C.D.: How science learning activation enables success for youth in science learning experiences. Elec. J. Sci. Edu. **20**(8), 49–83 (2016)
11. Malone, T.W.: Toward a theory of intrinsically motivating instruction. Cog. Sci. **5**(4), 333–369 (1981)
12. Fredricks, J., McColskey, W., Meli, J., Mordica, J., Montrosse, B., Mooney, K.: School engagement: potential of the concept, state of the evidence. Rev. Edu. Res. **74**(1), 59–109 (2004)
13. Reeve, J., Tseng, C.-M.: Agency as a fourth aspect of students' engagement during learning activities. Con. Edu. Psy. **36**(4), 257–267 (2011). https://doi.org/10.1016/j.cedpsych.2011.05.002
14. Jensen, L., Konradsen, F.: A review of the use of virtual reality head-mounted displays in education and training. Edu. Inf. Tech. **23**(4), 1515–1529 (2018)
15. Slater, M.: A note on presence terminology. Pres Co. **3**(3), 1–5 (2003)
16. Freina, L., Ott, M.: A literature review on immersive virtual reality in education: state of the art and perspectives. In: The 11th International Scientific Conference ELearning and Software for Education, pp. 133–141 (2015)
17. Sanchez-Vives, M.V., Slater, M.: From presence to consciousness through virtual reality. Nat. Rev. Neuro. **6**, 332–339 (2005)
18. Bleiwas, D.I., DiFrancesco, C.: Historical zinc smelting in New Jersey, Pennsylvania, Virginia, West Virginia, and Washington, D.C., with estimates of atmospheric zinc emissions and other materials. (U.S. Geological Survey Open File Report 2010-1131). U.S. Department of the Interior (2010). https://pubs.usgs.gov/of/2010/1131/pdf/OF10-1131.pdf
19. Bodzin, A., Araujo Junior, R., Schwartz, C., Anastasio, D., Hammond, T., Birchak, B.: Learning about environmental issues with a desktop virtual reality field trip. Inn. Sci. Tea Edu. **7**(1) (2022). https://innovations.theaste.org/learning-about-environmental-issues-with-a-desktop-virtual-reality-field-trip/

20. Chung, J., Cannady, M.A., Schunn, C., Dorph, R., Bathgate, M.: Measures technical brief: Engagement in science learning activities, 1–8 (2016). http://www.activationlab.org/wp-con tent/uploads/2016/02/Engagement-Report-3.1-20160331.pdf
21. Bodzin, A., Araujo Junior, R., Hammond, T., Anastasio, D.: Investigating engagement and flow with a placed-based immersive virtual reality game. J. Sci. Educ. Technol. **30**(3), 347–360 (2020). https://doi.org/10.1007/s10956-020-09870-4
22. Habgood, M.P.J., Ainsworth, S.E., Benford, S.: Endogenous fantasy and learning in digital games. Sim. Gam. **36**(4), 483–498 (2005)
23. Novak, E.: A critical review of digital storyline-enhanced learning. Educ. Tech. Res. Dev. **63**(3), 431–453 (2015). https://doi.org/10.1007/s11423-015-9372-y
24. Jenkins, H.: Game design as narrative architecture. In: Harrington, P., Frup-Waldrop, N. (eds.) First Person. MIT Press (2002)

Flood Adventures: Evaluation Study of Final Prototype

Robson Araujo-Junior[1]([✉]) [ID], Zilong Pan[1], Alec Bodzin[1], Kathryn Semmens[2],
Thomas Hammond[1], David Anastasio[1], Sarah Sechrist[1], Nathan Lerro[1], Evan Rubin[1],
and Jessica Vogel[1]

[1] Lehigh University, Bethlehem, PA 18015, USA
junior@lehigh.edu
[2] Nurture Nature Center, Easton, PA 18042, USA

Abstract. It is vital that individuals of all ages know what preparations to make prior to a flooding event and what actions to take during an actual flood event. To address this, we have designed and developed a fully functional prototype of a digital game-based learning experience in desktop VR called Flood Adventures to be used in non-formal and informal learning environments. We describe and illustrate the game final prototype as well as the gameful elements designed to promote increased motivation, engagement, and learning during gameplay. This paper presents the results of a usability study conducted with fifteen adults. The responses obtained in the sixteen-item survey were positive. The findings suggest that participants gained knowledge of flooding through gameplay. Feedback collected with four open-ended questions is discussed and players' recommendations will improve the last iteration of the game.

Keywords: Flood Preparedness · Digital Game-based Learning · Desktop VR · Usability Study

1 Introduction

Flooding has become a major global concern due to an intensified hydrologic cycle caused by climate change [1]. Flooding events produce a high risk to people's safety and cause severe damage to property and infrastructure [2]. Understanding how to prepare for flooding events in one's community is an important educational need that can reduce one's risk during a flood event. It is vital that individuals of all ages know what preparations to make prior to a flooding event and what actions to take during an actual flood event. To address this, we have designed and developed, in partnership with the Nurture Nature Center, a fully functional prototype of a digital game-based virtual reality (VR) learning experience called Flood Adventures, designed for non-formal and informal learning environments. The main aim of Flood Adventures is to help individuals learn about best practices for flood preparation at their home by using a desktop VR (dVR) simulation game.

© The Author(s), under exclusive license to Springer Nature Switzerland AG 2024
M.-L. Bourguet et al. (Eds.): iLRN 2023, CCIS 1904, pp. 426–435, 2024.
https://doi.org/10.1007/978-3-031-47328-9_31

Digital game-based learning can have a positive impact on engagement since learners are engaged by interactive experiences [3]. VR learning games can include features such as active control of the user experience, naturalistic, yet safe environments, and realistic representation of real-world situations that are interactive and promote learner engagement [4]. The goal of Flood Adventures is to improve people's understanding of flood preparation, so they know how to take appropriate action if a flooding event occurs in their community.

Our project builds on Malone's theory of intrinsically motivating instruction [5], and the Science Learning Activation Theory [6], which supports our design of engaging VR game-based activities for learning. Intrinsic motivation is created by three qualities: challenge, fantasy, and curiosity [5]. A learner can have emotional and cognitive attachment with science topics and experiences that serve as an intrinsic motivator towards various forms of participation, since the activated science learner is fascinated by natural and physical phenomenon [6].

2 Study Context

This was a usability study conducted during an institutional expo presentation. We developed 16 survey items to focus on participants' feedback about four aspects: the efficacy of the tutorial (e.g., "The tutorial helped me learn how to play the game"), the instructional media (e.g., "The images and captions were interesting"), player input (e.g., "I could move around the house without any problems"), and players' perceptions of learning (e.g., "I liked using this game for learning about flood preparedness"). We also had open-ended questions ("Did you encounter any bugs/glitches during your gameplay?", "What suggestions do you have to improve the game?", "What did you like most/least about the game?") that allowed participants to provide overall or more in-depth feedback on their experience.

This paper starts with a design and development update about the work done based on the usability feedback from the initial Flood Adventures prototype house and its functionalities (i.e., movement and ability to pick up objects) [7]. It continues with a description of the gameful elements introduced in this iteration: an inventory system, a weight system, and a feedback system that includes metacognitive prompts. Then, we summarize the results of the usability study with 15 adults who played, from start to finish, the complete final prototype of the Flood Adventures game in dVR.

3 Flood Adventure: The Experience

This paper describes the completed version of Flood Adventures, which focuses on flood preparedness. The game unfolds in three phases designed to take 5–10 min each to complete. This section narrates the gameplay experience while the next section describes the design of each gameful element.

3.1 The Intro Phase (i.e., just a dream...)

A 20-s cutscene shows the rainy weather and the player's house located by a creek (Fig. 1). Once inside the house, a 90-s TV broadcast informs players of how climate change increases the risk of localized flooding, which can threaten one's life and property. The game begins with a playthrough tutorial that introduces players to the environment (e.g., rooms, items), the controls (e.g., movement, interactivity), the user interface (UI), the gameful elements (e.g., time, feedback), and is followed by a 3-min gameplay practice to grab their belongings and leave their house during a flash flood. Players receive feedback on their initial performance.

Fig. 1. Screenshots from the initial cutscene that introduces the location where *Flood Adventures* takes place. The zoomed cutout shows the player's house and its proximity to the creek.

3.2 The Preparation Phase (i.e., assembling the emergency supplies kit)

The game continues with a cutscene showing the player waking up from a nightmare and moving towards the living room. A one-minute TV broadcast presents how we can prepare for a flood emergency and what we can do to learn more about it (Fig. 2). After experiencing the hardships of a flash flood in the dream, the player decides to assemble their emergency supply kit during a gameplay sequence with an itemized checklist organized by rooms. This time, however, without the pressure of a countdown timer. Glowing particles appear on top of the next item to be gathered from the list should a player feel lost or not know what to do next (Fig. 3).

Fig. 2. News broadcast video explaining how to prepare for a flooding emergency.

Fig. 3. Assistive UI elements. A checklist to guide the preparation of the emergency kit (left). A tooltip showing the name and weight of the selected item, as well as the guiding glowing particles (center).

3.3 The Flood Phase (i.e., run for your life!)

Upon the completion of their emergency kit, players are prompted to return to the living room, where a flash flood alert starts blaring on the TV (Fig. 4). A metacognitive prompt (i.e., thought balloon), in the dialogue box, reminds players that everything they need should be in their flood kit (Fig. 4). After three minutes, a cutscene plays in the background showing the player driving out of their house and the flooding area while the 5-star summary feedback UI is presented in the foreground (Fig. 5).

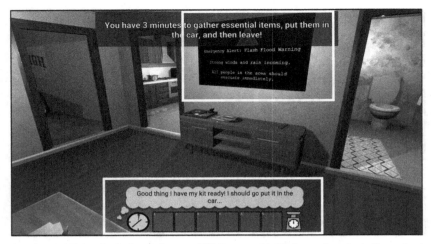

Fig. 4. Top highlight: flash flood alert on TV. Bottom highlight: a thought balloon (top), the expanded inventory slots when using the backpack (bottom), the countdown clock (left), and the weight scale (right).

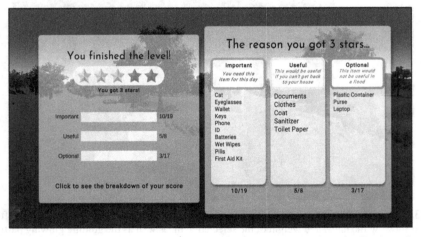

Fig. 5. UI interface that summarizes player's performance and provides feedback on how to improve the star rating received.

4   Gameful Elements

Some real-life constraints that mimic one's capabilities were designed to make Flood Adventures challenging, in addition to the widespread gaming mechanic of playing against the clock. As meaningful learning also derives from life experiences [8], different types of feedback and metacognitive prompts were included as gameful elements designed to support gameplay. Most UI elements are located at the bottom of the screen, except the game tutorial or narrative prompts (Fig. 4).

4.1 Inventory

Inspired by Minecraft, it was designed to illustrate the number of objects being carried by the player (i.e., four item slots). It can expand by two slots if players wear a backpack, found on the bedroom floor. Players can drop objects by pressing a keyboard number of the item's corresponding position.

4.2 Weight System

Each object's weight is shown in a tooltip upon selection. The more one carries, the slower they will be able to move. A scale on the right side of the inventory displays how much weight players are carrying. If all inventory slots are used and players try to grab anything else, the metacognitive prompt *"My hands are full! I should go to the garage and place the items in the kit..."* is triggered. As weight increases, besides a pointer moving clockwise, the scale changes color from blue to yellow to red. Once its limit is reached or surpassed, players cannot move anymore. Then, the UI displays reminders with the self-reflection message *"It's too heavy to carry all of this! I should drop something..."* while the scale color flashes yellow and red.

4.3 Metacognitive Dialogue Box

Supportive and instructional guidance in the form of advice, feedback, prompts, and scaffolding can promote deeper learning [9]. Thus, self-reflective prompts were designed to appear whenever players make choices or to support the storyline progression (Fig. 4).

4.4 Contextual Feedback

Flood Adventures has guided exploration (e.g., task checklist) and metacognition (e.g., thought balloons) to assist players, since they can enhance learning for transfer [10]. During the game, players' interactions prompt contextual feedback: a tooltip when selecting (Fig. 3) and a thought balloon (Fig. 4) when grabbing objects.

4.5 Ongoing Support

The game provides different forms of feedback *before* (gameplay practice), *during* (responsive UI), as well as *after* the intro and flood phases by displaying the 5-star score system and feedback on one's performance (Fig. 5).

5 Results and Discussion

The results of the usability study were generally positive (see Table 1). Among the four items regarding the game tutorial (#4, #8, #12, #13), 87% of the participants (n = 13) responded that the tutorial helped them to understand what the game was asking them to do for advancing. In addition, 67% of the participants (n = 10) strongly agreed that the tutorial helped them understand the inventory system, the game interface, and how to play the game. In average, 90% of participants positively perceived the tutorials as effective in scaffolding their gameplay. As noted by a user: "The tutorial was extremely helpful. I learned a lot."

Table1. Usability Testing Results from the Final Prototype of Flood Adventures.

Statement	M	SD	Frequency				
			SA	A	N	D	SD
1. The text in the game was easy to understand	4.73	0.59	12	2	1	0	0
2. The images and captions were interesting	4.67	0.62	11	3	1	0	0
3. The narrative was clear and made sense	5.00	0.00	15	0	0	0	0
4. The tutorial helped me learn how to play the game	4.53	0.74	10	3	2	0	0
5. I felt overwhelmed by the amount of information presented on the screen. (R)	2.13	0.92	0	2	1	9	3
6. I learned things about flood prepareness that I did not know	4.20	0.77	5	9	0	1	0
7. I liked using this game for learning about flood preparedness	4.60	0.63	10	4	1	0	0
8. I understood how to use the inventory system to get objects into the car	4.60	0.63	10	4	1	0	0
9. I could move around the house without any problems	4.20	1.08	8	4	1	2	0
10. I found the game easy to use	4.20	0.77	6	6	3	0	0
11. The game was responsive to my actions	4.40	0.63	7	7	1	0	0
12. I understood what the game asked me to do	4.47	1.06	11	2	0	2	0
13. Learning to use the game interface was easy	4.60	0.63	10	4	1	0	0
14. I found the feedback system to be helpful	4.40	0.91	9	4	1	1	0
15. The graphic quality of the game was good	4.80	0.41	12	3	0	0	0
16. I liked the sounds that were used in the game	4.60	0.63	10	4	1	0	0

Notes. $N = 15$. (R) = Reverse scored items. Strongly Agree (SA) = 5; Strongly Disagree (SD) = 1

Six items (#1, #2, #3, #5, #15, #16) surveyed the instructional media aspect of *Flood Adventures* in the usability testing. All participants ($n = 15$) strongly agreed that the narrative was clear and made sense. Most respondents (80%, $n = 12$) strongly agreed that the overall graphic quality was high, and the texts were easy to understand. Similarly, 80% ($n = 12$) of the participants reported not feeling overwhelmed by the amount of information displayed on the screen. Moreover, several players reported that they enjoyed the graphics and liked the "text display to indicate category of the item." Most participants (93%, $n = 14$) agreed that images, captions, and the moving cat provided interesting gameplay experiences. Although one respondent expressed their desire to limit the meowing sound effects from the cat, 67% ($n = 10$) and 27% ($n = 4$) of respondents strongly agreed or agreed that they liked the sound effects in the game. Finally, 13 out of 15 respondents chose instructional media as their favorite aspect of the game.

In the three items (#9, #10, #11) related to player input, 80% ($n = 12$) of players found the game easy to use, while 20% ($n = 3$) were neutral. When asked about whether participants felt the game was responsive to their actions, both strong agreement and agreement rates were 47% ($n = 7$). For example, a participant mentioned that "the hit/click detection was sometimes a little off." Furthermore, most participants (80%, $n = 12$) reported they could move around the house without any problems. Differing perceptions (20%, $n = 3$) might be due to the fact that some participants were "not used to playing 3D games," especially *Flood Adventures*, which required using the WASD or arrow keys on a keyboard for directional movement.

Responses to the three items about players' perceptions of learning (#6, #7, #14) are mostly positive. Specifically, 67% ($n = 10$) and 27% ($n = 4$) of the participants strongly agreed and agreed, respectively, that they enjoyed using this game to learn about flood preparedness. The results are in line with participants reporting that they "learned a lot" and liked the "educational aspect" of the game. Moreover, 87% ($n = 13$) of the participants agreed that the feedback system was helpful. Furthermore, 93% ($n = 14$) of the participants either strongly agreed or agreed that they learned new information about flood preparedness that they did not know before. Thus, participants gained knowledge of flooding through gameplay.

6 Conclusions and Next Steps

We conducted a usability study on the final prototype of the *Flood Adventures* game. Fifteen adult participants played the dVR version. Gameplay was designed to take between 20–45 min, depending on participants' gaming skills. After the participants completed the task, we asked them to complete a usability survey with 16 items that focused on the efficacy of the tutorial, the quality of the instructional media, player input, and players' perceptions of learning about flood preparedness. Furthermore, four open-ended items elicited players' feedback to enhance the game and whether they enjoyed playing it.

Flood Adventures players reported that they appreciated the "beautifully designed" graphics and the interactivity while "exploring and finding things to pick up". Some participants also commented that they liked the "educational value" while others appreciated the gameful elements of "playing against the time" and "the feedback system".

Players also enjoyed two gameful elements designed to support cognitive resources management during gameplay: the "glowing object during tutorial" and "how items were illuminated to draw attention to them and also the checklist." These findings show that the instructional and gameful design developed in this iteration of the game provided the players with enjoyable and informative gameplay that was well facilitated by the tutorial system.

Recommendations for improving the game were provided as well. For instance, a player suggested "enhancing the ending scene visually" and another suggested gameplay improvements such as an "option for pausing the game." Two other players requested skip options, as in "a skip button for scenes, maybe a scene selector would be useful for players resuming" or being able to skip "the intro video if it's the returning play." This feedback provided researchers with practical implications for updating the dVR version and, principally, paved a way for the future headset VR (hVR) version. Three players reported being excited about playing the upcoming hVR version, one of whom felt that the "headset would make it more intuitive for all."

After this last round of feedback is applied to the dVR version, we will convert the game for Meta Quest VR headsets, followed by usability testing of the working prototype. Data from the hVR prototype tests will inform revisions to the first complete iteration of the game in hVR. The revised *Flood Adventures* hVR version will undergo usability testing at two non-formal environmental education centers and will be hosted on our university's server for general public access.

Acknowledgements. We would like to thank Ben Zalatan, Kenneth Straw, and Surui Huang for the initial design and development work. We are very grateful to Daphne Mayer (Delaware & Lehigh National Canal Museum), Rob Neitz (Jacobsburg Environmental Education Center), and Chad Schwartz (Lehigh Gap Nature Center) for their feedback during the design and development of *Flood Adventures*.

References

1. Yu, L., Josey, S., Bingham, F., Lee, T.: Intensification of the global water cycle and evidence from ocean salinity: a synthesis review. Ann N.Y. Acad. Sci., 1472(1), 76–94 (2020). https://doi.org/10.1111/nyas.14354
2. IPCC Homepage, "Global Warming of 1.5°C", Intergovernmental Panel on Climate Change," https://www.ipcc.ch/sr15, last accessed 2022/02/01
3. National Research Council: Learning Science in Informal Environments: People, Places, and Pursuits. The National Academies Press, Washington, DC, USA (2009). https://doi.org/10.17226/12190
4. Bodzin, A., Araujo-Junior, R., Hammond, T., Anastasio, D.: Investigating engagement and flow with a placed-based immersive virtual reality game. J Sci Educ Tech. **30**(3), 347–360 (2021). https://doi.org/10.1007/s10956-020-09870-4
5. Malone, T.: Toward a theory of intrinsically motivating instruction. Cog Sci **5**(4), 333–369 (1981)
6. Dorph, R., Cannady, M., Schunn, C.: How Science Learning Activation Enables Success for Youth in Science Learning Experiences. Elec J Sci Edu. **20**(8), 49–83 (2016)

7. Bodzin, A., Araujo-Junior, R., Straw, K., Huang, S., Zalatan, B., Semmens, K., Anastasio, D., Hammond, T.: Flood Adventures: A Flood Preparedness Simulation Game. In: 8th International Conference of the Immersive Learning Research Network (iLRN), pp. 1–5. IEEE, Vienna, Austria, (2022). https://doi.org/10.23919/iLRN55037.2022.9815906
8. Carneiro, R.: Living by learning, learning by living: The quest for meaning. Int. Rev. Educ. **59**(3), 353–372 (2013). https://doi.org/10.1007/s11159-013-9355-3
9. Azevedo, R., Aleven, V. (eds.): International Handbook of Metacognition and Learning Technologies. Springer Science+Business Media, New York, USA (2013). https://doi.org/10.1007/978-1-4419-5546-3
10. National Research Council: Learning science through computer games and simulations. The National Academies Press, Washington, DC, USA (2011). https://doi.org/10.17226/13078

Workforce Development and Industry Training (WDIT)

Opening the "Black Box" of VR for Workforce Development: Investigating Learners' Device, Usage, and Identities

Eileen McGivney[⊠] [iD], Tessa Forshaw[iD], Rodrigo Medeiros, Mingyue Sun, and Tina Grotzer[iD]

Harvard Graduate School of Education, Cambridge, MA 02138, USA
`eileen_mcgivney@g.harvard.edu`

Abstract. Virtual reality (VR) technologies are increasingly used in workforce development and training, and studies show they can be effective tools to increase learning of procedural skills, content knowledge, and affective outcomes like confidence. Most studies of VR in education and training, however, have focused on the hardware by comparing learning with VR to other devices in controlled lab experiments. This "black box" approach does not attend to variation beyond the device, such as how learners use an application and the influence of their identity and context on their learning with VR. This study addressed the need for more research on learning with VR in authentic workforce development contexts to better understand how diverse participants use these programs and to what extent their individual characteristics impact their experience. Using data from 1,154 users of a VR-enabled job interview training for individuals affected by the criminal justice system, we assessed variation in how participants used the program and their reported changes in confidence, and estimated associations with device, usage, and learners' characteristics. We find learners' experience and context is a stronger predictor of increased confidence level than device or usage activities, particularly whether participants are currently or formerly incarcerated. Further, we demonstrate how cluster analysis on log-file data can distinguish learners' use patterns, a promising method for personalizing feedback and training.

Keywords: Workforce Development · Virtual Reality · Affective Learning Outcomes · Justice-Involved Individuals

1 Introduction

Virtual reality (VR) technologies are increasingly used in workforce development and training, promising to make programs more efficient and effective by giving people "hands-on" practice in low-stakes environments [1]. Research on the effectiveness of learning with VR has primarily focused on comparing learners' change in content knowledge retention or procedural skills with a VR headset compared to a different device [2]. While such studies ask whether VR is an effective tool, the focus on hardware leads to a "black box" approach that does not attend to questions of how people learn in these

M.-L. Bourguet et al. (Eds.): iLRN 2023, CCIS 1904, pp. 439–452, 2024.
https://doi.org/10.1007/978-3-031-47328-9_32

immersive environments, or the importance of what they do while using them on their learning. Further, research has been primarily conducted in controlled experiments with small samples [3] and has not typically included some of the most vulnerable populations that workforce development programs aim to serve. Research on VR highlights the importance of people's identities and prior experiences in how they will experience such immersive environments [4], but work on how race, gender, and experience affect learning with VR in authentic workforce development contexts remains nascent. This exploratory study used data from a workforce development VR application to ask how participants varied in their use and self-reported outcomes, whether their use and ratings varied based on device or their individual characteristics and identities, and what their variation in activity within the simulation reveals about different patterns of usage. The findings shed light on the importance of how learners use VR, their characteristics, and their contexts to open the "black box" of learning with VR beyond the device. The study also demonstrates the need for more research on VR in authentic workforce development contexts that account for the scale and diversity of learners these technology-enabled programs aim to reach.

2   Related Work and Research Questions

Workforce development and corporate training programs are increasingly looking at the affordances of VR to improve instruction and learning outcomes [1]. Reviews of VR in education and training find it is more effective than other media at increasing participants' procedural and spatial skills, but is mixed in increasing other learning outcomes like knowledge acquisition [2, 5–7]. Because it engages participants in practice that feels real, studies also find that VR enhances affective dimensions of learning, including increasing learners' motivation and confidence [2, 5] This affordance may be particularly beneficial for vulnerable jobseekers, including for incarcerated individuals, as simulated interviews provide practice that increase their skills and beliefs [8].

Much research on VR in education and workforce development has been "hardware focused," comparing the technology to other devices, but there is a need to understand not only if VR should be used, but how and for what [9], echoing calls to understand for whom and under what conditions educational technology is effective beyond whether the technology "works" [10]. Recent work on learning in immersive environments has suggested the way the experiences are designed and facilitated influences how learners use them and what they learn from them—for example interactivity, reflection, and activities outside of VR [11–13]. There is also increasing understanding of individual variation and the ways people's identities affect their experience in immersive environments [4].

This study addressed the need to open the "black box" of learning with VR by looking beyond a comparison of devices in a laboratory experiment to understand how people use an immersive application in an authentic workforce development program, and how their use and outcomes vary based on their experience with the justice system and identities. We asked how participants in a VR-enabled training program used the application in terms of completing different activities, their reported confidence changes, and in their patterns of responses. We also asked whether those variations were associated with the device, their program use, and their experiences and identities.

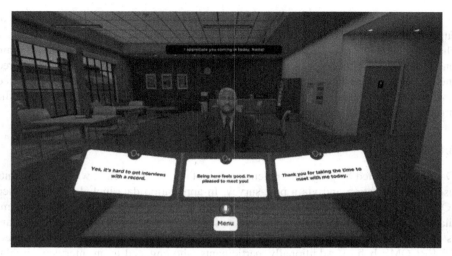

Fig. 1. Project OVERCOME screenshot.

3   Methods

This study employs secondary data analysis using data collected in 2022 during the pilot implementation of Project OVERCOME, a VR application from Accenture designed to allow jobseekers who have been impacted by the criminal justice system (i.e., justice-involved individuals or JII) to practice interview skills. The program was piloted by 11 Goodwill Industry International sites as part of their reentry training programs that support JII gain employment to reenter society. A limited number of non-JII were also allowed to participate in the program during the pilot phase. The program has two main components: 1) Journeys, in which users hear stories from other JII who navigated the job search and 2) Interview simulation, in which participants participate in a mock interview with a hiring manager. In the simulation the user role plays as Nadia, who was formerly incarcerated and is interviewing for a position at an industrial laundry facility. It follows a branched narrative model, in which each response a participant selects determines the subsequent question from the interviewer: there are hundreds of potential pathways through the interview. Participants select an answer by reading it out loud. The narrative of the interview, including the questions asked and answer options provided were developed by interviewing justice-involved individuals about their job-seeking experience, including the types of jobs they interviewed for and where they struggled in the interviews. Additionally, they worked with Goodwill's employer partners who frequently hire JII through reentry programs on the types of questions they ask in interviews and what good performance looks like in this context.

Based on how they answer the interview questions, the hiring manager may ask them if they want to talk about their past and give them an opportunity to practice what is called the "elevator speech," a brief description of their past justice involvement and how they are moving on. The interviewer does not know about Nadia's prior justice involvement.

See Fig. 1 for a depiction of the interview simulation. The VR program aims to support JII to increase their confidence in interviewing and discussing their past, a challenge these jobseekers face in gaining employment [14]. All sites offered the program on a Quest 2 VR headset or on a PC. Typically, sites used the VR headset and offered the PC version to participants uncomfortable using VR. Each participant was instructed how to use the program by a facilitator, who met with them one-on-one to set up the program and debrief with them after.

3.1 Data

Data was collected by program implementers, not the research team, while participants used the application and via a post-survey. In-application data included: device used (Quest VR headset or a PC), whether the participant used the journeys, interview simulation, and if they engaged in the elevator speech, as well as whether the participant is JII, participating in a reentry program, had used VR before, and had used Project OVERCOME before. Additionally, participants who engaged in an interview simulation had each response recorded in log-file data. The post-survey asked their gender and racial/ethnic identity, type of justice-involvement (currently or formerly incarcerated or diversion), age, and whether they felt more, equally, or less confident about interviewing after using Project OVERCOME.

3.2 Participants

1,154 participants used the application, 537 completed the post-survey. Therefore, questions about application use could be assessed using all 1,154 participants, while questions about participant demographics and their reported confidence levels could only be assessed on the 537 participants who completed the post-survey with those items. Some participants were given an anonymous ID to link the data collected while they used the application to their post-survey data. There were 303 such participants, which we termed the linked dataset connecting the two sources of data.

Of the total participants, 75% of all participants were JII, 81% were reentry program participants, 21% had used VR before. Of the participants who completed the post-survey, 42% were currently incarcerated, 38% were formerly incarcerated, 11% diversion, and 9% none. 66% identified as female, 41% as Black or African American, 47% as White, 7% Hispanic or Latino, and 5% other. The mean age was 37.9. No personally identifying information was collected. This study was approved by the Harvard University Institutional Review Board.

3.3 Analysis

We used regression analyses to estimate the associations between device and individual characteristics with program use (interview simulation completion, elevator speech use, and journeys use), and participants' confidence ratings. Logistic regression was used for binary program component usage variables and ordinal logistic regression for confidence ratings. For example, (1) illustrates the model for predicting interview completion for participant i:

$$logit(Interview_i = 1) = \beta_0 + \beta_1 Device_i + \beta_2 ProgramParticipant_i$$
$$+\beta_3 JusticeInvolved_i + \beta_4 UsedVR_i + \beta_5 MultipleUse_i + \epsilon_i \quad (1)$$

This model was repeated to predict likelihood of engaging in the elevator speech (for those who used the interview simulation) and journeys. An ordinal logistic regression model predicted likelihood of reporting feeling more confident controlling for racial/ethnic identity, gender identity, type of justice involvement, age, and for those whose data could be linked, device and usage of the application. We report the results of the analyses in odds ratios in Tables 1 and 2, but also report predicted probabilities of significant predictors for ease of interpretation. These predicted probabilities hold control variables at the mean, unless otherwise noted.

Additionally, we used cluster analysis of the log-file data to identify patterns in the way participants answered the questions in the interview simulation. We used k-modes clustering, a machine learning method that assesses the similarity of observations based on their responses to categorical variables. It is an extension of the k-means algorithm, but rather than using the centroids of mean values, it assesses mismatches between categorical responses to determine the distance between observations [15], as illustrated in (2):

$$d_1(X, Y) = \sum_{j=1}^{m} \delta(x_j, y_j) \text{ where} : \delta(x_j, y_j) = \begin{cases} 0(x_j = y_j) \\ 1(x_j \neq y_j) \end{cases} \quad (2)$$

where X and Y are two categorical objects defined by m categorical attributes. The smaller the number of mismatches, the more similar the two objects are. In our dataset, the objects are participants using the interview simulation, and the categorical attributes are the questions to which they responded in order of their response.

We identified prototypical participants by looking at descriptors of the data including which questions led to which other questions, how many questions participants answered, and where were common points to reach the elevator speech or the conclusion. We identified seven prototypical users and used these as the modes in the k-modes clustering algorithm, reducing the number of clusters until they had balanced numbers and were interpretable as distinct use patterns. These seven prototypical users were identified by looking at the most and least commonly answered questions in the interview simulation, whether they engaged in the elevator speech, and how many questions varied participants tended to answer. Our focus was on identifying important characteristics we hypothesized would change a user's pattern of usage including whether they had completed the simulation multiple times. In this sense, we identified users as what we called common trajectories that we could see across all the 1,154 participants and that we could identify as qualitatively important differences in how participants answered the questions.

4 Results

4.1 Regression Analyses

Of the total 1,154 participants, 67% ($N = 770$) used the application on a VR headset. Figure 2 shows how participants varied in their use of the VR application, as nearly two-thirds completed an interview simulation ($N = 749$), but only 25% reached the elevator speech practice portion ($N = 294$) and just 10% used the journeys ($N = 119$).

Of the 537 participants who completed the post-survey, 50% ($N = 273$) said they felt more confident in their interview skills after using the simulation, 48% ($N = 264$) felt equally confident, and 2% ($N = 10$) felt less confident.

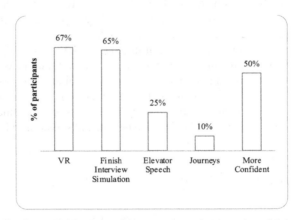

Fig. 2. Participant use of the program and reported confidence.

Logistic regression analysis revealed that the device was predictive of participants' completion of the interview simulation and engaging in the elevator speech practice, but not in a consistent way: VR users were more likely to complete an interview but less likely to engage in the elevator speech. However, being a participant in a reentry services program was a stronger predictor of completing an interview simulation. Figure 3 visualizes the predicted probability for participants to complete the interview simulation based on the device they use and whether they are a reentry program participant. For example, the likelihood a reentry program participant using VR will complete the interview simulation is 82% compared to 26% for a non-reentry program participant using a PC.

Using data from the participants who completed the post-survey, logistic regression results indicate that participants' type of justice involvement and racial/ethnic identity are both associated with their confidence ratings. Gender is not a significant predictor.

Participants who were currently incarcerated were less likely to report feeling more confident after using the VR simulation than those who were formerly incarcerated or diversion. The predicted probabilities illustrated in Fig. 4 show substantive importance of these associations, highlighting how a currently incarcerated individual would be 28–46% likely to feel more confident, while a formerly incarcerated individual would be

Table 1. Predictors of program component use, odds ratio.

	Dependent variable		
	Interview completion	Elevator speech	Used journeys
Device: PC	0.26***	1.52*	1.25
Reentry program participant	3.22***	0.83	0.56*
Justice-Involved	1.43	1.21	0.68
Used VR	1.14	1.29	1.61*
Multiple Uses of Application	0.52**	0.60	0.70
Intercept	*0.96*	*0.51**	*0.20***
N	1151	747	1151
R^2 Tjur	0.20	0.01	0.02
*$p < .05$ **$p < .01$ ***$p < .001$*			

Note: Odds ratios greater than 1 indicate greater likelihood for participants in that category, less than 1 indicates a lesser likelihood

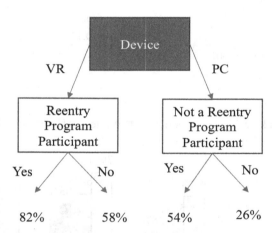

Fig. 3. Predicted probabilities of completing the interview simulation.

48–67% likely. Further, the graph illustrates that those who identify as Black or African American are predicted to report feeling more confident than White and Hispanic or Latino participants across all justice-involvement groups.

Using the data that could be linked between participants' program use and their survey responses, Table 3 shows how the device used, racial/ethnic identity, and gender are not predictive in reporting feeling more confident, but justice involvement type has a significant association. This model also controls for participants' usage of the application in terms of engaging in the elevator speech and journeys but does not find a significant association between these activities and participants reporting feeling more confident. The association between justice involvement type and reporting feeling more confident is

446   E. McGivney et al.

Table 2. Predictors of reporting more confident, odds ratios (post-survey data).

Justice involvement (Reference: Currently incarcerated)	
Formerly incarcerated	2.42***
Diversion	4.35***
None	2.19*
Racial/ethnic identity (Reference: Black or African American)	
White	0.57**
Hispanic or Latino	0.46*
Other	0.77
Age	0.99
Gender: Male	0.85
*Intercept - less	equally*	*0.01****
*Intercept - equally	more*	*0.96*
N	537
R^{2}Tjur	0.15

*p < .05 **p < .01 ***p < .001

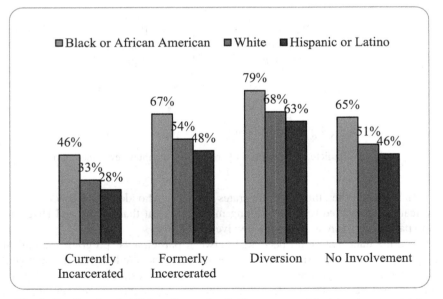

Fig. 4. Predicted probabilities of reporting feeling more confident (post-survey data).

substantial. For a woman of average age who identifies as Black or African American, we would predict she is 82% likely to report feeling more confident after using the program if she is formerly incarcerated, and only 33% likely if she is currently incarcerated.

Table 3. Predictors of reporting more confident, odds ratios (linked dataset).

Device: PC	0.71
Justice involvement (Reference: Currently incarcerated)	
Formerly incarcerated	9.47***
Diversion/none	9.79***
Gender: Male	0.83
Racial/ethnic identity (Reference: Black or African American)	
White	0.94
Hispanic or Latino	0.64
Other	1.03
Age	1
Used VR	1.13
Journey	0.51
Elevator	1.68
*Intercept - less	equally*	*0.03***
*Intercept - equally	more*	*2.93*
N	303
R^2Tjur	0.291

4.2 Cluster Analysis

While the regression analyses describe the ways participants varied in their activities within the simulation and those associations with their confidence ratings, the cluster analysis provided another way to explore variation in participants' activity in the branched narrative interview simulation. Based on prototypical responses to the interview questions in each cluster, we characterize the four clusters in Table 4. These clusters revealed there were patterns in how participants answered the interview questions not only in terms of the number they answered, but how likely they were to be asked a question that leads them into the elevator speech, and additionally if they answered in a way that allowed them to practice that speech.

This method illustrates how log file data can be valuable in understanding the differences between users in VR programs. Participants in clusters 1, 2, and 3 were all likely to complete the interview simulation, but those in clusters 1 and 2 were more likely to be asked questions that would provide an opportunity for the elevator speech. Users in cluster 1 were more likely to respond in a way that allowed them to actually practice the elevator speech, whereas those in cluster 2 were more likely to say they did not want to get into the details. Users in cluster 4 represent those who were in many ways least successful in using the program, meaning they either did not finish the interview or did not answer in an optimal way. This cluster may account for noise in the data, including users who were testing the program but not using it as a participant, as fewer of these users identified as JII.

The distinctions between cluster 1, 2, and 3 may provide a different way of identifying participants who need practice on different skills. For example, users in clusters 1 and 2 may need coaching on responding to questions about their past in ways that indicate they are open to discussing their history and how they want to move on. Users in cluster 3 may need training on the other interview questions to ensure the interviewer stays interested and allows them more opportunities to discuss their past. This can be a valuable way of connecting the way participants use a branched narrative program to ways they can improve that go beyond just whether they completed the simulation.

Table 4. Cluster results

Cluster number & description		Pattern of usage	Int	Qs	Elev	N	VR	JII
1	Most likely to practice the elevator speech	Highly likely to complete the simulation, and most likely to engage in the elevator speech. Answered questions in a way that prompted the interviewer to ask if they want to talk about their mistakes: prototypical user answered "it is time to be open and honest."	95%	10.3	47%	390	75%	84%
2	Most likely to miss an opportunity to practice the elevator speech	Highly likely to complete the simulation, and answered similar questions to cluster 1, and prompted interviewer to ask if they want to open up about their mistakes: prototypical user answered "I don't want to get into the details right now."	97%	10.8	17%	141	77%	85%

(*continued*)

Table 4. (*continued*)

Cluster number & description		Pattern of usage	Int	Qs	Elev	N	VR	JII
3	Likely to complete the interview in a short time	Highly likely to complete the program, but in fewer questions than clusters 1 and 2. The prototypical user did not answer questions in a way that prompted the interviewer to ask about their past mistakes	95%	8.7	21%	149	84%	79%
4	Least likely to complete the program	Less likely to complete the simulation. Many of the users in this cluster either stopped using the program without finishing or answered the first few questions in a way that prompted the interviewer to cut it short	46%	4	22%	246	53%	59%

Column labels: Int = Interview completed, Qs = Mean interview questions answered, Elev = Elevator speech, N = Number of participants, VR = Device used was VR, JII = Justice-involved individuals

5 Discussion

Our findings reveal important considerations for learning with VR beyond the device and begin to open the "black box" by looking at learners' identities and how they use immersive applications. Regression analysis showed how the device can be a factor in participants' use of the program, for example predicting whether they completed an interview simulation, but that the device is relatively less predictive than other character-istics of the participants. Being in a reentry program was more predictive of completing the interview simulation, indicating that a user's purpose and context is important, as these participants are more likely committed to training that will help them in their job search.

Further, participants' identities and experience were more predictive of whether they reported feeling more confident in their interview skills after using the application than the device or usage characteristics. In terms of identity, in some analyses participants' racial/ethnic identity predicted reporting feeling more confident: those who identified as black or African American were more likely than other groups to report feeling more confident. This may be due to the race of the interviewer in the simulation, or because those participants had lower levels of confidence to begin with. As this is a correlational study, we cannot identify the reason for this association. Interestingly, however, gender was not a predictor of confidence in the regression analysis, even though the participant was in the shoes of Nadia, a woman.

Across the varied models and subsets of data we found that participants who were currently incarcerated were less likely than other participants to report feeling more confident. This association was strong even after controlling for the device used, which aspects of the program they used, and other characteristics like racial, ethnic, and gender identity. The association between reported confidence and justice involvement type raises questions about targeting the use of VR in workforce development for specific populations or contexts. On one hand, there may have been systematic differences in how currently incarcerated participants used the application or the way it was facilitated that made VR less impactful on their reported feelings of confidence. Alternatively, the variation may be due to the simulation's scenario in which participants role play as Nadia, a formerly incarcerated individual, whose story may be less relatable or less relevant for currently incarcerated people. Our analysis suggests that these issues go beyond which aspects of the program or device the participants used and raises important questions about the target population and context in which VR-enabled workforce development programs are implemented.

We also find that using a cluster analysis on participants' log file data reveals patterns of usage based on the way different participants navigated the program. This data-driven method is a promising way of distinguishing user profiles that may identify the types of training the participants need. For example, users in clusters 1 and 2 may need support in how to answer questions from an interviewer about their past mistakes in a way that allows them to construct an elevator speech about their past, while users in cluster 3 may need feedback on how to answer the interview questions to keep the interviewer interested and have them ask about their past. Such profiles reveal subtle differences in usage of the program beyond whether they completed an interview or engaged in specific parts of the program and may be useful in workforce development programs to help identify targeted interventions for learners. Such interventions like receiving feedback and additional practice opportunities could be integrated into a VR program itself or could be part of the larger training program tailored to the needs of the individual based on their pattern of activity in the simulation.

This study also highlights the need for more research to be conducted on VR-enabled programs in authentic workforce development contexts, rather than only in controlled lab experiments. While our findings are correlational due to using secondary data analysis on data collected during a pilot rather than in an experiment, the sample we worked with is larger, more diverse, and represents actual participants workforce development programs aim to support. In this sense the noisiness of the data represents the complexity of implementing VR in workforce development programs that we would expect to see in other contexts. Our results highlight the importance of participants' experience, racial and ethnic identity, and varied usage of the program that may not have surfaced in a smaller and more controlled study. Future research should continue to investigate issues of participants' identities, purpose, context, and experience along with their within-VR activity in both controlled and authentic environments. Such studies will provide the field of workforce development a better understanding of the potential and limitations for immersive technologies to enhance learning opportunities for vulnerable jobseekers.

Acknowledgment. We are grateful for the assistance of Anna Kornick, Tony Worlds, and Charles Fatunbi from Accenture, and Jennifer Lynch and Kristin Pratt from Goodwill Industries International for making this study possible. This work was developed with funding from Goodwill Industries International in connection with the Next Level Lab at the Harvard Graduate School of Education, which is funded by Accenture Corporate Giving. The opinions here are those of the authors and do not necessarily reflect the views of the funder.

References

1. Xie, B., et al.: A review on virtual reality skill training applications. Fron. Virtual Reality **2** (2021). https://doi.org/10.3389/frvir.2021.645153
2. Abich, J., Parker, J., Murphy, J.S., Eudy, M.: A review of the evidence for training effectiveness with virtual reality technology. Virtual Reality **25**, 919–933 (2021). https://doi.org/10.1007/s10055-020-00498-8
3. Jun, H., Miller, M.R., Herrera, F., Reeves, B., Bailenson, J.N.: Stimulus sampling with 360-videos: examining head movements, arousal, presence, simulator sickness, and preference on a large sample of participants and videos. IEEE Trans. Affect. Comput. **13**, 1416–1425 (2022). https://doi.org/10.1109/TAFFC.2020.3004617
4. Nakamura, L.: Feeling good about feeling bad: virtuous virtual reality and the automation of racial empathy. J. Vis. Cult. **19**, 47–64 (2020). https://doi.org/10.1177/1470412920906259
5. Hamilton, D., McKechnie, J., Edgerton, E., Wilson, C.: Immersive virtual reality as a pedagogical tool in education: a systematic literature review of quantitative learning outcomes and experimental design. J. Comput. Educ. **8**, 1–32 (2021). https://doi.org/10.1007/s40692-020-00169-2
6. Radianti, J., Majchrzak, T.A., Fromm, J., Wohlgenannt, I.: A systematic review of immersive virtual reality applications for higher education: design elements, lessons learned, and research agenda. Comput. Educ. **147** (2020)
7. Wu, B., Yu, X., Gu, X.: Effectiveness of immersive virtual reality using head-mounted displays on learning performance: a meta-analysis. Br. J. Edu. Technol. **51**, 1991–2005 (2020). https://doi.org/10.1111/bjet.13023
8. Smith, M.J., et al.: Virtual reality job interview training for adults receiving prison-based employment services: a randomized controlled feasibility and initial effectiveness trial. Crim. Justice Behav. **50**, 272–293 (2023). https://doi.org/10.1177/00938548221081447
9. Jensen, L., Konradsen, F.: A review of the use of virtual reality head-mounted displays in education and training. Educ. Inf. Technol. **23**, 1515–1529 (2018). https://doi.org/10.1007/s10639-017-9676-0
10. Fishman, B., Dede, C.: Teaching and technology: new tools for new times. In: Gitomer, D.H., Bell, C.A. (eds.) Handbook of Research on Teaching, pp. 1269–1334. American Educational Research Association (2016). https://doi.org/10.3102/978-0-935302-48-6_21
11. Johnson-Glenberg, M.C., Bartolomea, H., Kalina, E.: Platform is not destiny: embodied learning effects comparing 2D desktop to 3D virtual reality STEM experiences. J. Comput. Assist. Learn. **37**, 1263–1284 (2021). https://doi.org/10.1111/jcal.12567
12. Parong, J., Mayer, R.: Learning science in immersive virtual reality. J. Educ. Psychol. **110** (2018). https://doi.org/10.1037/edu0000241
13. Georgiou, Y., Tsivitanidou, O., Ioannou, A.: Learning experience design with immersive virtual reality in physics education. Educ. Technol. Res. Dev. **69**, 3051–3080 (2021). https://doi.org/10.1007/s11423-021-10055-y

14. Park, N., Tietjen, G.: "It's not a conversation starter." Or is it?: stigma management strategies of the formerly incarcerated in personal and occupational settings. J. Qualita. Crimi. Just. Criminol. (2021). https://doi.org/10.21428/88de04a1.df4b4cc7

15. Huang, Z.: Extensions to the k-means algorithm for clustering large data sets with categorical values. Data Min. Knowl. Disc. **2**, 283–304 (1998). https://doi.org/10.1023/A:100976970 7641

Role of Adaptation Phase in Educational Results of Virtual Reality Communication Training for Managers

Dmitriy Vinitskiy[1]([✉]) [iD], Lidia Yatluk[2] [iD], Sergey Goryushko[1], Evgeny Blagov[3] [iD], Sergey Lukashkin[3] [iD], Evgeniya Tribunskaya[3], and Rostislav K. Speransky[2] [iD]

[1] Research and development department, Knowledge Lab LLC, Moscow, Russia
vinitskiy_da@mail.ru
[2] Research and development department, Modum Lab LLC, Saint Petersburg, Russia
[3] Graduate School of Management, Saint Petersburg Center of Digital Education Technologies, Saint Petersburg State University, Saint Petersburg, Russia

Abstract. Adaptation to new devices and interfaces is actively studied by user experience and human-computer interaction specialists but is typically neglected by organizers and researchers of corporate training with virtual reality. The study tests how the adaptation phase to technology affects the educational outcome and cognitive load. For the study, 102 people (35.3 ± 11.2 years old), including students and working managers, were trained to give feedback to a colleague. They were divided into three groups: general adaptation, specialized adaptation for communication training, and no adaptation. EEG was used to measure cognitive load score. As a result, it was found that both groups with pre-adaptation showed higher educational outcomes and experienced less cognitive load during the main training. No difference was found between the types of adaptation.

Keywords: VR Adaptation · Communication Training · EEG · Cognitive Load · Multimedia Education

1 Introduction

The new generation of Virtual reality (VR) appeared as a new hope for corporate training to enhance skills transfer. Virtual environments allow us to recreate authentic environments and equipment, support collaborative learning, and practice different situations. Specifically, VR has been used to teach communication skills: teaching doctors problematic conversations with patients about vaccinations [1], developing negotiation skills in bank employees [2], and developing social skills in children with autism spectrum disorders [3].

But recent meta-analysis shows that the results of VR usage in learning remain ambiguous: educational effects are recorded to be as good as alternative solutions [4]. Positive results according to subjective evaluations are related to the technological novelty attractiveness, while usefulness is based on fewer risks in training organization

M.-L. Bourguet et al. (Eds.): iLRN 2023, CCIS 1904, pp. 453–465, 2024.
https://doi.org/10.1007/978-3-031-47328-9_33

and implementation. Another meta-analysis shows that multiple training sessions are required for VR to be more effective than alternative formats [5]. In this case, the specificity of VR can be demonstrated.

Two common reasons can be identified for the weak effects of VR in education. First, the technology is often applied naively, without taking into account existing advances in pedagogical design theories, educational psychology, and multimedia practices. As Hamilton, McKechnie, Edgerton, and Wilson show in their meta-analysis, of the 29 papers reviewed, 24 mentioned learning theories only in the introduction section and did not rely on them to create learning environments [5]. Developers rely on the sufficiency of immersiveness and presence effects in VR to obtain results.

Another reason is the lack of considered adaptation to the technology. Like any other novel device or interface, VR requires preparations and adjustment. The topic of technology adoption and diffusion is actively developing in the fields of manufacturing, e-commerce, banking, web services, and other areas [6]. In the VR technology research field, the question has most often been asked about technology penetration statistics and common drivers [7, 8]. Issues of individual adaptation in VR have been addressed much less frequently.

Researchers show that learners often experience high cognitive load due to difficulties with the equipment [9, 10]. A similar situation occurs with learning new types of interfaces. For example, participants who do not encounter computer games in everyday life spend a lot of time mastering the controls in the game during the study [11].

We consider cognitive load within the following frameworks: Mayer's model of multimedia learning [12] and Sweller's cognitive load theory [13]. According to the first, a person has several information acquisition channels, limited in their capacity. According to the second, learning material creates cognitive load, which can be divided into internal and external. Internal is the cognitive load associated with the studied material elements, which cannot be reduced without loss of content, while external refers to additional elements that are not directly related to the studied material but rather to the educational format peculiarities. For example, attractive pictures or fun examples could act like elements that cause external cognitive load.

VR involves many external cognitive load factors that cannot be removed - new devices, new control tools, new sensations in the virtual environment, and new interfaces. Thus, learning with new technology without training can lead to excessive cognitive load and a decrease in the quality of education.

The problems with adapting to VR and the need to remove the cognitive load of mastering navigation are shown in a meta-study of using VR as a pedagogical tool [5]. Also, they showed that poor familiarity with the technology could cause anxiety and decrease educational outcomes.

Several researchers have made similar interpretations of findings on individual preferences and educational outcomes. For example, Madden and colleagues [14] suggest that students rated the experience of exploring the Moon on a computer compared to VR higher due to the more familiar and comfortable controls, as evidenced by responses to open-ended questions. It is hypothesized that educational outcomes in different formats may change once the technology is more common among students.

Virvou and Katsionis [11] took the most significant step in their research on adapting to VR learning. However, their study focused on a non-immersive version of the popular "EngageVR" educational platform. They showed that unresolved difficulties and the length of time that informants could not move around due to navigational problems were significantly higher for novices. At the same time, newcomers seemed to be more motivated to use the platform.

By applying cognitive load theory [13] and a multimedia learning model [12], we intend to understand whether prior adaptation to virtual reality affects educational outcomes, whether generic adaptation to the technology is sufficient, or whether preparation for specific interfaces and interactions is required.

We focused our research on the following hypotheses:

H1: The success of mastering a communication skill for VR-naïve users increases when there is an adaptation phase for VR.

H2: The success of mastering a communication skill for VR-naïve users increases when there is an adaptation phase for VR and the adaptation and training user interface is the same.

H3: Learners without prior adaptation to VR experience a higher cognitive load during VR training.

To test these hypotheses, we divided the participants into 3 experimental groups: generic adaptation (the simulation for adaptation was different from the training simulation), specialized adaptation (the simulation for adaptation was similar to the training simulation), and a control group without adaptation. We used EEG indicator scores to measure cognitive load during VR training. Both the generic and specialized adaptation groups showed higher training scores and lower cognitive load scores than the control group. We found no difference between the two adaptation groups.

2 Methods

2.1 Participants

The study included 102 participants, 56 women and 46 men. Mean age of participants was 35.3 ± 11.2 years old. The main inclusion criterion was that participants had no prior experience of interaction with VR technologies. Participants included 90 managers and 12 students of Management majors (in year 3 or 4 of a bachelor's or master's programme). Participants had no psychophysiological contraindications to the use of VR technologies, reported to have no psychiatric disorders or drug use, and had not participated in focus groups, in-depth interviews or usability tests or had participated more than six months ago. All participants signed paper informed consent.

Participants were divided into three groups, depending on the type of adaptation to the VR technology: generic adaptation (35), specialized adaptation (34), and control group with no adaptation (33).

2.2 Experimental Setup

The material used during the experiments included:

- Computer to show the theoretical part of the training,
- Head-mounted display (HMD) – Oculus 2 for generic adaptation,
- HMD – Pico G2 4K for dialogue simulation,
- Muse headband (2016 model) was used to collect EEG data [15].

Participants wore headbands during all stages. Frontal electrodes were placed as AF7 and AF8 in the international 10–20 system.

2.3   VR Training Simulation

The simulation is based on an algorithm utilized in the routine management practices of a large processing corporation. These practices named "regular management" and provide guidance for day-to-day management activities. They were developed based on scientific management principles and a thorough investigation of existing methods. The core set of practices included: 'Feedback', 'Conducting Meetings', 'Line Walking', 'Visual Management', 'Performance Discussion', 'Development Dialogue' and 'Behavioral Safety Audit'. Feedback was chosen as the main focus of the simulation because it is the most easily transferable practice to other enterprises.

The simulation consists of three parts: theory, learning, and training. To reduce the time spent in virtual reality for novice users, the theory was converted into a computer format. The simulation employs a problem-based learning approach with the task of giving corrective feedback to an employee. The trainee learns the algorithm and deconstructs it in a learning dialogue with each of the elements, such as responding constructively to employee anger or summarizing agreements. At each stage, a comment is given on which decision was correct and why. In training mode, the trainee gathers the necessary elements to solve the problem and receives a detailed analysis of the conversation, along with recommendations for improvement at the end of the exercise.

The overall format of interaction in the simulation is structured as follows. The trainee chooses the characteristics of the meeting (time, place, and presence of other staff in the room) and then the dialogue begins. The bot and the trainee exchange replicas. During the person's response period, he/she is offered several lines of response - the response has to be formulated by himself/herself. Depending on the chosen response direction, the bot reacts differently to the statement. In the final analysis of the conversation, politeness and respectfulness of the speech are also taken into account. The overview of the experimental setup and a screenshot of the training simulation are shown in Fig. 1.

During the process of training the user can use auxiliary materials on the laptop: in learning mode, it is the algorithm and the description of the situation, in training mode only the description of the situation is left. In other practice simulations a list of meeting participants, previously submitted reports, and so on can be available.

The simulation is developed using Unity with the integration of speech-to-text recognition services and categorization of lines by meaning for scenario management and analytics.

Fig. 1. Dialogue simulation: left – setup, right – interface of the simulation.

2.4   Experimental Task

Participants were trained to give corrective oral feedback to a colleague using a dialog simulation in VR. Corrective feedback is made to change undesirable behavior patterns in employees, such as the use of harsh language or corporate process violations.

The experiment consisted of the following steps (Fig. 2): signing informed consent, instruction, dialog test before VR training, VR adaptation (generic or specialized adaptation – 6–8 min - or no adaptation based on an experimental group type), watching theory about the feedback algorithm on a computer (4 min), VR training in dialog simulation (approximately 7–14 min), dialog test after VR training, and a feedback questionnaire.

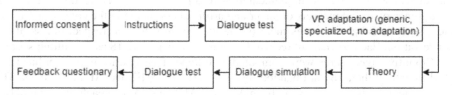

Fig. 2. Participant's journey.

Dialog tests before and after training were phone conversations with the actor, where subjects were given the role of a manager aiming to give corrective feedback to the employee, who has violated corporate ethics according to the legend. The professional actor used the same detailed dialogue script to communicate with all the informants and did not know who belonged to which group. Telephone conversation instead of the classical face-to-face format was chosen to reduce the influence of prejudice towards the character being played based on the actor's appearance and to bring the testing situation closer to the training format. Similar dialog tests were conducted before and after the VR training to measure the educational effect.

During adaptation stage different groups experienced different simulations (Fig. 3). Generic adaptation group used the Oculus "First steps" simulation. Specialized adaptation group used a custom simulation for sales assistants, which was similar in design and assets to the simulation used for VR training. The control group skipped the adaptation step.

Fig. 3. Participant's Adaptation forms: left – generic, right – specialized.

The final questionnaire assessed the subjective educational effect and feeling of comfort in the learning process, where the degree of agreement with the statements from 1 to 9 was required, as well as several open-response questions.

2.5 Data Pre-processing

The dialogues were evaluated by the instructional designer using a checklist. The instructional designer did not know which participants were in which group when assessing the dialog. In difficult cases, the evaluation was additionally checked with another expert. The checklist included the implementation of all elements of the feedback exercise, the absence of verbal markers of anger and artificial confusion in the conversation, and the assessor's subjective assessment of the level of anxiety and respectfulness of the conversation. Each participant received a score between 0 and 18 as a resulting score.

Cognitive load scores were computed as follows. Fast Fourier transform has been used to extract theta rhythm bandpower (4–7 Gz) from AF7 and AF8 electrodes. The sum of theta rhythm band powers from AF7 and AF8 was taken at each time point [16]. Then that sum within each participant was converted to Z-scores. Outlier data points different from the average by more than three standard deviations were removed from the analysis. The following statistical analysis used average cognitive load scores during the VR training stage per participant.

3   Results

Educational outcome was estimated with mixed-design repeated measures ANOVA with the difference between test scores before and after VR training. It was used as a within-subjects factor, and experimental conditions were used as a between-subjects factor. Homogeneity was checked with Levene's test, which was insignificant, meaning that the homogeneity assumption was met (before VR training $F(2,99) = 0.35$, $p = 0.71$, after VR training $F(2,99) = 0.55$, $p = 0.58$). Before VR training participants showed the following dialogue test results: the training group with generic adaptation $M = 8.94$, $SD = 3.29$, the group with specialized adaptation $M = 9.53$, $SD = 2.63$, and the control group $M = 9.88$, $SD = 3.05$. After VR training, the following results were demonstrated:

the generic adaptation group M = 12.43, SD = 2.36, the specialized adaptation group M = 12.32, SD = 2.09, the control group M = 11.33, SD = 2.75 (Fig. 4).

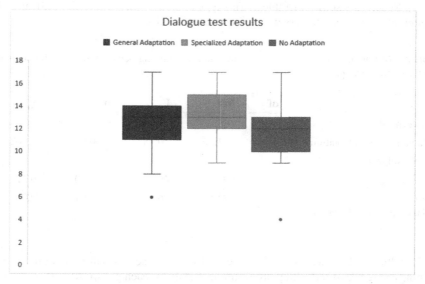

Fig. 4. Dialogue test results.

Results of repeated measures ANOVA are shown in Table 1. Difference in the between-subjects factor was not significant. The within-subjects factor of VR training was significant with a large effect size. Interaction between factors was on the verge of statistical significance with a small effect size.

Table 1. Repeated measures ANOVA before and after training between groups

Source	df	MS	F	p	η_p^2
Between subjects					
Experimental groups	2	1.877	0.19	0.82	0.004
Within subjects					
VR training	1	338.79	65.99	< 0.001	0.4
VR training * Experimental groups	2	9.69	3.51	0.03	0.07

Groups with generic adaptation and specialized adaptation were not significantly different in their educational results. This could explain the weak statistical difference in the interaction between factors in our analysis. Another repeated measure ANOVA was calculated by combining different adaptation groups in one. The differences were measured between the groups with adaptation (N = 69) and the control group (N = 33). Homogeneity assumption was met (Levene's test for measures before training is $F(1,100) = 0.003$, p = 0.958, and for measures after training $F(1,100) = 0.991$, p = 0.322). Results are shown in Table 2. This type of analysis has shown a significant effect of interaction between factors with a medium effect size.

Table 2. Repeated measures ANOVA before and after training between groups with adaptation and the control group.

Source	df	MS	F	p	η_p^2
Between subjects					
Adaptation / no adaptation	1	1.76	0.18	0.67	0.002
Within subjects					
VR training	1	236.13	46.09	< 0.001	0.32
VR training * Adaptation / no adaptation	1	31.89	6.23	0.01	0.06

Results of VR education (differences between test scores before and after the VR training) were measured with paired-sample T-tests for each group. All test scores were normally distributed (Shapiro-Wilk test for generic adaptation group W = 0.954, p = 0.154, for specialized adaptation group W = 0.96, p = 0.24, and for the control group, W = 0.9785, p = 0.924; for both adaptation groups combined W = 0.98, p = 0.352) as shown in Table 3.

Table 3. Statistical difference in test scores before and after learning for all three groups.

Groups	df	Statistic (paired-sample t-test)[a]	Significance	Effect size estimation, Coen's d
Generic adaptation	34	$t = -5.35$	$p < 0.001$	$d = -0.906$
Specialized adaptation	33	$t = -7.81$	$p < 0.001$	$d = -1.34$
No adaptation (control group)	32	$t = -2.46$	$p = 0.02$	$d = -0.43$
Generic and specialized adaptation	68	$t = -8.42$	$p < 0.001$	$d = -1.01$

Subjective estimates of educational effectiveness failed to show any difference between experimental groups. Mean subjective differences were as follows: generic adaptation group 7.55 ± 1.24, specialized adaptation group 7.86 ± 0.71, control group 7.94 ± 0.99 out of 9 points possible.

To test the hypothesis about the role of cognitive load, the cognitive load score during training in VR was measured, and then group differences were compared with ANOVA.

The cognitive load score was standardized into z-score across the whole experiment duration (all steps of the experiment). During VR training standardized cognitive load score for the generic adaptation group was $M = -0.304$, $SD = 0.41$, group with specialized adaptation $M = -0.29$, $SD = 0.51$, and control group $M = -0.06$, $SD = 0.40$. Homogeneity assumption was met with Levene's $F(2,99) = 0.98$, $p = 0.38$. Overall, ANOVA results are significant, as shown in Table 4, but the post hoc test failed to show significant differences between groups.

Table 4. Repeated measures ANOVA before and after training between groups with adaptation and control group.

Source	df	MS	F	p	η^2
Adaptation / no adaptation	2	0.63	3.16	0.05	0.06

Post hoc test for the three-way ANOVA failed to meet statistical significance after multiple comparisons correction (see Table 5). Overall, between-group differences in cognitive load scores mimic the between-group differences in test scores. Differences between groups with different types of adaptation were not significant, while differences between the control group with no adaptation and groups with different adaptation types were significant before the correction for multiple comparisons, but lost statistical significance after the correction.

Table 5. Statistical difference in cognitive load score between experimental groups.

Groups	df	Statistic (paired-sample t-test)	p Tukey-corrected	Effect size estimation, Coen's d
Generic adaptation and specialized adaptation	65	$t = -0.11$	0.99	$d = -0.03$
Generic adaptation and no adaptation	64	$t = -2.245$	0.07	$d = -0.6$
Specialized adaptation and no adaptation	63	$t = -2.12$	0.09	$d = -0.53$

Combining the two adaptation groups, on the other hand, provides a much more powerful effect of differences in mean cognitive load score between subjects with and without adaptation to VR technology. Assumption about equality of variances was met (Levene's $F(1,100) = 0.471$, $p = 0.49$). Differences between generic and specialized adaptation groups combined and the control group were significant, $t(100) = -2.52$, $p = 0.013$, Cohen's $d = -0.53$. Average cognitive load score was significantly higher during VR training in the control group with no adaptation. It confirms our hypothesis about the role of excessive cognitive load on training in VR.

Additionally, we measured the differences between students and managers. The main difference was that students were better learners. Mean score difference before and after learning for students is 4, and for managers it is 2.4. But it is important to note that student sample is substantially smaller (12 students to 90 managers), so this result should be treated with caution.

4 Discussion

Our findings suggest that a lack of VR experience could be detrimental to educational outcomes of communication VR training. Often, VR is proposed for corporate learning where learners may have little to no experience with the technology. This may explain the modest results of such training programs. We found that adding short VR activities before the VR training can improve the effectiveness of acquiring a new skill in VR. We also found that the content of such adaptational activities is largely irrelevant. No differences were found between different types of adaptation on the educational result.

The results of the study confirmed H1 and H3, but hypothesis H2 was not confirmed. Thus, in line with the model of multimedia learning [12], preliminary adaptation to VR in any format leads to educational effect improvement due to the reduction of cognitive load during training.

For someone who has no previous experience with VR it could be challenging to understand the rules for interacting with the environment. For example, you should use head movements to navigate the space, which is very different from a traditional desktop setting. And hand controls are very different from mouse and keyboard, or even a conventional gamepad. Suddenly, hand position is a part of the input, and you can't look at your fingers and button layout. Input in general relies heavily on tactile sensitivity and movement. This causes tremendous confusion in VR-naïve users, leading to a significant increase in external cognitive load [9].

The positive effect of pretraining on learning in VR was shown in another study based on the model of multimedia learning [17]. Participants learned about the structure of the biological cell in VR or with a video, with or without pretraining. Pretraining improved educational results for VR format, but for video format. VR condition was implemented with the Samsung smartphone attached to the Samsung Gear VR HMD. The authors argued that while the complexity of the learning material is not enough to cause cognitive overload in the video condition, cognitive overload occurs when the complexity of the learning material is combined with the cognitive load caused by the VR itself. Thus, reducing the cognitive load of the learning material with the pretraining helped to avoid cognitive overload in the VR condition.

In contrast to the discussed study, we reduced the cognitive load from the VR rather than from the learning material. Theoretically, cognitive load is additive [12], which means that both cognitive load from learning material and cognitive load from the learning format could be the targets of the intervention. Indeed, our study shows that the adaptation phase can reduce the cognitive load of VR to improve the educational outcome. Other important differences are that we used fully immersive dialog simulation rather than immersive video, and our participants learned communicative skills rather than declarative knowledge.

We used a dialog simulation with fairly simple controls. However, simulations involving movement in space or interaction with other people in the form of avatars may require different skills and a higher level of training.

An alternative explanation could be given. Participants who had an adaptation phase studied for a longer period of time, so the difference in cognitive load could be due to the time spent while studying rather than the effects of adaptation. A number of studies have found that students who study for longer periods of time have better educational outcomes [18]. Learning during the adaptation phase was not related to the communicative skill of giving the corrective feedback, meaning that adaptation was irrelevant to the measured educational outcome. Another consideration is that prolonged exposure to VR could lead to simulation sickness [19]. From this point of view, adding an adaptation phase shortens the amount of time that could be spent on learning the skill in question. In our study, the adaptation phase was relatively short, between 6 and 8 min. If the training simulation is about 20 min or less, an adaptation period of this length should not be detrimental.

For longer training simulations, it could be argued that the adaptation phase is unnecessary. It should happen naturally over the duration of the training. We believe that possible negative effects should still be addressed. There is a risk that material, given at the beginning of simulation, will not be learned properly. This issue could be addressed either by having a separate adaptation phase or by including it at the beginning of the training with material that is not critical or very simple.

Some VR training programs may span multiple sessions. In this case, adaptation may only be required during the first training session. Our study is limited in that we only did not measure multiple sessions. It is not known how stable the effect of adaptation is over time. It is possible that additional stages of adaptation may be required if the training sessions are far apart.

The adaptation simulation type had no significant effect on the educational outcome. The practical implication is that almost any available simulation or VR game could be used for this purpose. Probably, some types of adaptation, for example those, that force the use of a wide range of controls and explore more possibilities in VR, could be more cost effective. Generic adaptation formats themselves can be differentiated for people who differ by various parameters, e.g., gender, age, psychological traits (e.g., different values of cognitive styles such as equivalence rate width, field independence or impulsivity/reflexivity [20]). Further studies are needed to answer which properties of the simulation are important for this task.

Simple EEG correlates of higher order concepts such as cognitive load should be treated with caution. We used theta rhythm as a widely accepted indicator. However, other EEG correlates of cognitive load have been proposed in the literature [21, 22]. Our EEG acquisition was also limited to only two frontal channels, provided by Muse headband as temporal channels were considered to be too noisy when participants wore Muse and VR headset at the same time. Despite it, we found that our cognitive load score difference was similar to educational result.

We investigated the effects of the adaptation phase on cognitive load in VR training. The adaptation phase can affect subsequent training through other psychological mechanisms, such as attention or emotion. Possible other psychological mechanisms and corresponding psychophysiological correlates should be investigated in future studies. It is also important to know whether this effect would differ in different social or economic groups. VR is used to train various skills to a wide demographic range. It is possible, that adaptation phase should have different characteristics depending on the type of training.

Acknowledgments. We would like to thank the St. Petersburg State University Graduate School of Management for providing the space for the study, the Modum Lab LLC for the development of the dialog simulation and technical support of the project, and the Knowledge Lab LLC for neural signal processing software.

References

1. Kleinsmith, A., Rivera-Gutierrez, D., Finney, G., Cendan, J., Lok, B.: Understanding empathy training with virtual patients. Comput. Hum. Behav. **52**, 151–158 (2015). https://doi.org/10.1016/j.chb.2015.05.033
2. Kickmeier-Rust, M.D., Leitner, M., Hann, P.: Virtual reality in professional training: an example from the field of bank counselling. In: 2020 6th International Conference of the Immersive Learning Research Network (ILRN), pp. 210–214. IEEE, San Luis Obispo, CA, USA (2020). https://doi.org/10.23919/iLRN47897.2020.9155083
3. Yuan, S.N.V., Ip, H.H.S.: Using virtual reality to train emotional and social skills in children with autism spectrum disorder. London Journal of Primary Care **10**(4), 110–112 (2018). https://doi.org/10.1080/17571472.2018.1483000
4. Angel-Urdinola, D.F., Castillo-Castro, C., Hoyos, A.: Meta-Analysis Assessing the Effects of Virtual Reality Training on Student Learning and Skills Development. The World Bank (2021). https://doi.org/10.1596/1813-9450-9587
5. Hamilton, D., McKechnie, J., Edgerton, E., Wilson, C.: Immersive virtual reality as a pedagogical tool in education: a systematic literature review of quantitative learning outcomes and experimental design. J. Comput. Educ. **8**(1), 1–32 (2021). https://doi.org/10.1007/s40692-020-00169-2
6. Williams, M.D., Dwivedi, Y.K., Lal, B., Schwarz, A.: Contemporary trends and issues in it adoption and diffusion research. J. Inf. Technol. **24**(1), 1 (2009). https://doi.org/10.1057/jit.2008.30
7. Syed-Abdul, S., et al.: Virtual reality among the elderly: a usefulness and acceptance study from Taiwan. BMC Geriatr. **19**(1), 223 (2019). https://doi.org/10.1186/s12877-019-1218-8
8. Sagnier, C., Loup-Escande, E., Lourdeaux, D., Thouvenin, I., Valléry, G.: User acceptance of virtual reality: an extended technology acceptance model. Int. J. Hum.-Comp. Intera. **36**(11), 993–1007 (2020). https://doi.org/10.1080/10447318.2019.1708612
9. Makransky, G., Terkildsen, T.S., Mayer, R.E.: Adding immersive virtual reality to a science lab simulation causes more presence but less learning. Learn. Instr. **60**, 225–236 (2019). https://doi.org/10.1016/j.learninstruc.2017.12.007
10. McFaul, H., FitzGerald, E.: A realist evaluation of student use of a virtual reality smartphone application in undergraduate legal education. Br. J. Educ. Technol. **51**(2), 572–589 (2020). https://doi.org/10.1111/bjet.12850
11. Virvou, M., Katsionis, G.: On the usability and likeability of virtual reality games for education: the case of VR-ENGAGE. Comput. Educ. **50**(1), 154–178 (2008). https://doi.org/10.1016/j.compedu.2006.04.004

12. Mayer, R.E., (ed.): The Cambridge Handbook of Multimedia Learning, 2nd ed. Cambridge University Press (2014). https://doi.org/10.1017/CBO9781139547369
13. Sweller, J., Ayres, P., Kalyuga, S.: Cognitive Load Theory. Springer New York, New York, NY (2011). https://doi.org/10.1007/978-1-4419-8126-4
14. Madden, J., Pandita, S., Schuldt, J.P., Kim, B., Won, A.S., Holmes, N.G.: Ready student one: exploring the predictors of student learning in virtual reality. PLoS ONE 15(3), e0229788 (2020). https://doi.org/10.1371/journal.pone.0229788
15. Krigolson, O.E., Williams, C.C., Norton, A., Hassall, C.D., Colino, F.L.: Choosing MUSE: Validation of a Low-Cost, Portable EEG System for ERP Research. Front. Neurosci. 11 (2017). https://doi.org/10.3389/fnins.2017.00109
16. Trejo, L.J., Kubitz, K., Rosipal, R., Kochavi, R.L., Montgomery, L.D.: EEG-based estimation and classification of mental fatigue. PSYCH 06(05), 572–589 (2015). https://doi.org/10.4236/psych.2015.65055
17. Meyer, O.A., Omdahl, M.K., Makransky, G.: Investigating the effect of pre-training when learning through immersive virtual reality and video: a media and methods experiment. Comput. Educ. 140, 103603 (2019). https://doi.org/10.1016/j.compedu.2019.103603
18. Everaert, P., Opdecam, E., Maussen, S.: The relationship between motivation, learning approaches, academic performance and time spent. Acc. Educ. 26(1), 78–107 (2017). https://doi.org/10.1080/09639284.2016.1274911
19. Balk, S.A., Bertola, M.A., Inman, V.W.: In: Proceedings of the 7th International Driving Symposium on Human Factors in Driver Assessment, Training, and Vehicle Design: Driving Assessment 2013, pp. 257–263. University of Iowa, Bolton Landing, New York, USA (2013). https://doi.org/10.17077/drivingassessment.1498
20. Blagov, E., Eroshkin, D.: Platform solution for building project teams on the cognitive styles synergy basis. In: ECKM 2021- Proceedings of the 22nd European Conference on Knowledge Management, 975–978. Academic Conferences limited, Coventry, UK (2021)
21. Yoshida, K., Hirai, F., Miyaji, I.: Learning system using simple electroencephalograph feedback effect during memory work. Procedia Computer Science 35, 1596–1604 (2014). https://doi.org/10.1016/j.procs.2014.08.243
22. Mazher, M., Abd Aziz, A., Malik, A.S., Ullah Amin, H.: An EEG-based cognitive load assessment in multimedia learning using feature extraction and partial directed coherence. IEEE Access 5, 14819–14829 (2017). https://doi.org/10.1109/ACCESS.2017.2731784

Self and Co-regulated Learning
with Immersive Learning Environments
(SCILE)

Immersive Educational Recycling Assistant (ERA): Learning Waste Sorting in Augmented Reality

Qiming Sun[1], I-Han Hsiao[1]([⊠]), and Shih-Yi Chien[2]

[1] Santa Clara University, Santa Clara, CA 95053, USA
{qsun4,ihsiao}@scu.edu
[2] National Chengchi University, Taipei, Taiwan
sychien@mail2.nccu.tw

Abstract. For a sustainable living, it is everyone's responsibility to do our best at recycling. However, waste classification can be complex. The existing resources may not have sufficient information or dynamic feedback to resolve our everyday garbage disposal. In this work, we design an interactive mobile Augmented Reality (AR) application, Educational Recycling Assistant (ERA), to educate people in doing sound day-to-day waste management. ERA utilizes dynamic object detection and provides in-situ guidance for proper garbage disposal. A user study was designed and conducted to investigate the effects and the user experiences. We found that the users achieved significantly higher garbage binning accuracy with the ERA app. The participants also improved their recycling and garbage disposal knowledge after using the app, particularly in complex items.

Keywords: Augmented reality · Educational technology · Object detection · Smart recycling

1 Introduction

Recycling is the foundation for a sustainable living environment. Although the mission is easy to understand, it is sometimes very hard to carry out consistently. In reality, our daily trash is often messy. It consists of a combination of recyclable and non-recyclable materials. Moreover, the body of waste knowledge and the complexity of waste classification can also be very confusing (i.e., Not all plastic is recyclable; recycling regulations may vary by the county in the United States, etc.) To educate and facilitate day-to-day garbage disposal, we often see signs, slogans or infographics on the trash cans or pamphlets to remind and to exercise proper waste categorization (Fig. 1). However, those graphics of items for trash or recycle categories may not always be comprehensive or exhaustive. The signs and infographics are not interactive. There is no feedback or guidance to promptly resolve the confusion or uncertainty when people are throwing out their waste. In addition, the cleanliness of the disposal items or the location of the local

© The Author(s), under exclusive license to Springer Nature Switzerland AG 2024
M.-L. Bourguet et al. (Eds.): iLRN 2023, CCIS 1904, pp. 469–483, 2024.
https://doi.org/10.1007/978-3-031-47328-9_34

recycling regulation can drastically increase the complexity at the moment of throwing it out. Therefore, to address the aforementioned issues, our research team aims to leverage modern technologies to tackle the challenges in performing everyday recycling.

Fig. 1. Garbage bins with Landfill, Recycle and Compost classification example infographics on the bins.

We have seen a few image classification projects attempt to address the waste classification issue [21,24,39], but none of them focused on providing feedback to the users with educational resources at the point of disposal. Thus, we propose an interactive mobile Augmented Reality (AR) application to engage and to educate people in doing sound day-to-day waste management. The homegrown immersive application is called Educational Recycling Assistant (ERA). The application utilizes dynamic object detection and provides in-situ guidance and feedback for proper garbage disposal. The nature of the mobile application permits the ubiquitous use of garbage disposal. The immersive AR experience is specifically engineered to reinforce positive behavior and to promote active learning. We hypothesize that the use of ERA will foster conscious recycling behavior and adaptively troubleshoot during garbage disposal. To investigate further, we formulate the following research questions and design a user study to evaluate the ERA effects and the user experiences. Research questions: (1) What are the impacts of Augmented Reality on garbage disposal experience and process? (2) How does waste management pre-knowledge affect garbage disposal behavior? (3) What are the learning outcomes after using ERA? The rest of the paper is organized with a section of relevant work in AI in waste management, informal learning and immersive learning with AR. We elaborate on the design and architecture of ERA, as well as the user study in the methodology section. Finally, we present the evaluation results and summarize the work with a discussion and future work.

2   Literature Review

2.1   Artificial Intelligence in Waste Management

AI techniques in waste management have been rising drastically in recent years. As waste management often involves various ill-defined problems regarding waste characterization, collection, and separation, the AI-based applications are capable of solving uncertain datasets and handling incomplete data, which is well-suited for improving waste management processes [32]. A number of AI models have been applied to offer an alternative to developing sustainable waste management systems. For instance, artificial neural networks (ANNs), genetic algorithm (GA), linear regression analysis (LR), support vector machines (SVM), and decision trees (DT) are the most frequently used AI approaches in the waste management field [3]. ANNs rank first among these models, which have been successfully utilized in predicting waste generation and classification. Although ANNs are effective in analyzing cause-effect relationships as well as retrieving nonlinear relationships in complex contexts, ANNs cannot identify the relative importance among the variables and may inevitably lead to overfitting issues.

Several datasets have been established exclusively for building waste detection models. TACO is an open image dataset that collects 1,500 images of waste in the wild with over 4,700 annotations [26]. The project is still accepting community contributions and the size of its database is still growing. TrashCan is another dataset that provides 7,212 annotated images for undersea wastes [14]. Kraft's team also released a set of trash images taken from an unmanned aerial vehicle as a part of their research [19]. Other similar datasets include TrashICRA19 [13], MJU-Waste [38], and TrashNet [2], which are all open-source datasets with specific waste categories.

With the development of AI technologies, especially the evolution of convolutional neural networks (CNN) and transform learning frameworks, multiple methods are adopted to train a waste detection model. Researchers have utilized EfficientDet [33] to detect waste in urban and natural environments [1], perform plastic waste sorting [25], and identify COVID-19 waste [8]. YOLO algorithms are also widely used in the field, such as helping separate non-biodegradable waste [4] or recyclables [36], multi-label waste classification [41], and sorting components from waste printed circuit boards [22]. Other schemas, such as DenseNet, ResNet, and MobileNet also have their appearances in waste classification [23,27,28]. These methods generally use a pre-defined model and then perform transform learning on specific waste datasets. For example, Hanxiang's team developed a mobile application, integrated with a CNN model, to classify bulky wastes in real life [37]. A few studies therefore combine different AI models (i.e., a hybrid model approach) to compensate for the shortcoming resulting from the non-hybrid approach. For example, Soni et al. [31] compare a number of AI-based models to evaluate their capability in forecasting the amount of waste generation, where the hybrid model of GA-ANN achieves the highest accuracy rate and outperforms the other six AI models. Hybrid models generally perform better than non-hybrid models; however, most of the proposed hybrid models are evaluated in a specific context (i.e., a limited number of datasets or a small number of experimental validations) rather than a comprehensive examination [3].

AI-based waste management applications consist of various complex algorithms that, in spite of the best design efforts, do not work perfectly under a variety of real-world conditions, i.e. YOLO-Green [21]. As a result, providing perfectly reliable automated systems is extremely challenging in reality. It is therefore essential to examine how human operators collaborate with AI-assisted aids in various situations along with different types of AI assistance. With regard to improving waste management processes, there is very limited work focused on utilizing AI in facilitating the learning and practices in waste management. This work will directly contribute to this pipeline.

2.2 Informal Learning

There has been a national effort to improve informal STEM education, which the goal is to create environments that increase curiosity among learners about the world around them. The National Research Council suggests that these experiences should generate "excitement, interest, and motivation to learn about phenomena in the natural and physical world" [10]. Best practices in informal STEM education are to provide learning opportunities that people can connect to their own experiences, provide interactive learning environments, and provide a framework for people to understand scientific processes [6]. In educational practices, several learning theories and principles encourage hands-on activities (including constructivism theory [35], situated learning [7,29] and experiential learning theory [18]). The underlying concept in all of these approaches is to allow learners to directly manipulate and engage with the materials and reflect on their experiences. In this project, we aim to provide a technological solution to cultivate recycling knowledge from daily garbage disposal experiences.

2.3 Learning in Augmented Reality

There are three important properties defining an AR system [5]: (1) it combines real and virtual objects in a real environment; (2) AR runs interactively, and in real-time; and (3) AR registers (aligns) real and virtual objects with each other. These properties afford AR to provide opportunities for creating engaging user interfaces, which has been largely exploited in the areas of marketing, architecture, entertainment, etc. Over the past decade, many empirical studies have shown that even lesser-degrees of immersion in terms of embodied learning [16] can still enhance the learning experience when designed properly [11,15]. In the context of learning, recent work has identified several ways that AR can reach the great potential in education [40], for instance:

1. Visualization: AR can be used in objects modeling, which allows learners to envision how a given item would look in different settings. The visualization affords individuals to contextualize (to visualize) an abstract concept in the real world and brings out otherwise inaccessible representations [17];

2. Interactivity: AR offers a unique opportunity for making learning highly interactive, permits students to simulate (to interact) and to perform low-cost and low-risk experiments [9,17], as well as to allow physical practice for learning of tacit knowledge [34];

3. Discovery-based learning support: AR can provide information in the most educationally-relevant context [12], which offers the opportunities for discovery-based learning. For example, historic sites may use AR to convey virtual and audio information when visitors are walking; Field trips can be turned into"scavenger hunts" with specific information provided in AR systems. In our case of applying workbench tools to solve problems, one can easily take the advantage of the AR technology to assist one's school projects, and extend the usage and learning to any home improvement projects.

3   Methodology

3.1   ERA AR Application

Our proposed application integrates real-time object detection into an augmented reality environment. When a user opens the ERA application, a step-by-step tutorial will be shown on the homepage (Fig. 2a). To detect which category of trash or recycle the garbage belongs to, one has to activate the waste scanner and place the garbage in front of the camera to obtain the suggested label on the screen. Lastly, if the user places the garbage in between the camera and the trash bins, the suggested disposal bins will be highlighted. The use case is presented in Fig. 2b and Fig. 3.

The ERA waste scanner function can be accessed by clicking the 'Scan Waste' button on the bottom right corner. The object detection will then be activated, and our model can identify the categories of wastes presented in the camera stream and label them in real-time (Fig. 2b). Each piece of the detected waste will be annotated in a dashed rectangle and the suggested category will be given in the label. The color is aligned with the recycling theme: recyclable garbage will be shown in blue, landfill ones are black, and composts are green. All of the detected objects with their categories are also listed in the detection history panel for further references. In the meantime, if ERA is used nearby the trash bins, the application can also detect and track the suggested disposal bins' labels, such as Recycle, Landfill, and Compost; a 'green check' sign will be overlaid in the AR view on the suggested bins; in addition, 'red crosses' will be displayed on the other bins to indicate the inappropriateness of discarding items to those bins (Fig. 3). In this way, the user would have more intuitive information on which bin they should put the trash into.

3.2   System Architecture

The overall structure of the system is demonstrated in Fig. 4. Several datasets are adopted to train the object detection model, including TrashNet[1], Open Image Dataset (OIDv6, for straw & plastic bags) [20], TACO [26], and our self-built dataset (for paper and plastic objects). Additional cleaning and processing were implemented to unify the format of annotations, which resulted in 4,835 distinct

---

[1] https://github.com/garythung/trashnet.

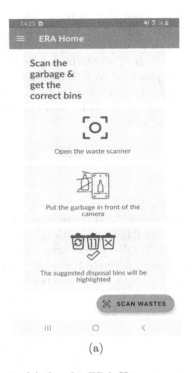 

(a)   (b)

Fig. 2. (a) On the ERA Homepage, a graphical step-by-step introductory tutorial is presented. (b) ERA's Waste Scanner function activates object detection at the center of the camera focusing area. The object label and the suggested bin will be presented in the AR view. They are color-coded and aligned with the universal garbage recycling theme: landfill is black, recycling is blue, and compost is green. All the detected objects will be listed under the Detection History panel. (Color figure online)

Fig. 3. The suggested bins to throw will be highlighted when ERA's used in front of the bins. In this case, we see a plastic bag is detected and a recycling bin is highlighted.

images with corresponding labels. We also randomly selected some of the images for augmentation and generated 8,596 samples in our dataset. The model was trained under the EfficientDet [33] and then converted to a tflite model for real-time object detection in the mobile platform. Based on our test involving the daily objects shown in Table 2, the final model has a mean average precision (mAP) of 0.794 (at intersection of union = 0.5). During the object detection process, identified items with a confidence of 0.5 or more will be labeled and presented to the user.

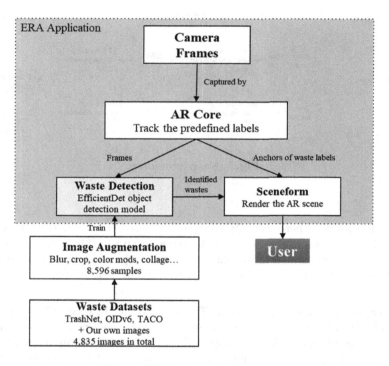

Fig. 4. ERA system architecture.

The prototype is developed for Android using ARCore[2]. It is designed to be compatible with Android 8.1 (Oreo) platform or the later version of the OS and has been tested on a Samsung Galaxy S9+ (Android 10), a Redmi K20 Pro (Android 11), and a Galaxy S10 (Android 12). For every frame captured by the camera, the object detector annotates the categories of possible wastes. Given the position of the trash bin labels in the background and the suggested bins to be thrown into, an AR scene will be rendered by Sceneform[3], which creates 'cross' and 'check' marks in front of the bins.

---

[2] https://developers.google.com/ar.

[3] https://github.com/google-ar/sceneform-android-sdk.

3.3 Study Design

A mixed-method usability study was designed. Participants were randomly assigned to experience the ERA and to perform tasks. Before and after performing tasks, the participants were surveyed on the garbage disposal knowledge. Upon the completion of the survey, they were also briefly interviewed on the general experience in waste management, as well as the ERA feedback. The study procedure is presented in Fig. 5.

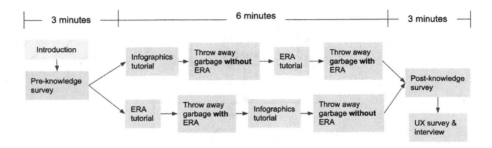

Fig. 5. Study procedure.

1. Participants. There were 28 subjects recruited from a web usability class offered by the computer science engineering program. The participants were invited to join the user study as part of the course participation to experience a bona fide user-based testing. They are junior/senior year college students.

2. Instruments and Measures. To examine the learning effects with the ERA educational technology treatment, we asked the pre and post recycling knowledge questions, including single item and multiple items disposal among landfill, recycle and compost bins. There were a total of 5 questions in pre-test and the same 5 questions in the post-test. Items include paper, napkin, straw and cup, hot coffee cup, plastic bag and receipt.

3. Tasks. There were a total of four tasks performed per user. Each task consisted of an actual item or a set of items physically presented in front of the user. Items range from a piece of paper, a clean napkin, a clean boba tea plastic straw and plastic cup, a clean Starbucks hot coffee cup without coffee, and a grocery plastic bag and a piece of receipt. In each task, the user would simulate casting the item away to the bins of their choices. There were two tasks in which the users were asked to use the ERA app and make a final decision on the disposal bins; in two other tasks they would just cast the items away without the ERA support. The order of the tasks was randomized. Four items were randomly selected.

4. Exit Survey and Interview. Two five-point Likert style questions were designed to survey the users' confidence in using ERA and whether they would recommend the application to people. Three short-answer questions were created to solicit opinions and feedback in understanding the pain point in waste management. *"What are your general concerns in disposing? What challenges do you face during disposal? What items do you find the most challenging to throw away?"*

4 Evaluation

4.1 ERA Effects

The user study results demonstrated that with the ERA app support, the users achieved significantly higher garbage binning accuracy than no app support, ($t_{27} = -8.49$, $p < 0.01$) (Table 1 and Fig. 6). In addition, disregarding the garbage complexity (a simple item or complex items), users were able to consistently achieve high accurate performances while using ERA app (100% for single item and 92.9% for multiple items disposal, Table 1). On the contrary, without the app support, users were seemingly achieving medium (64.3% in Table 1) garbage binning accuracy in single item disposal, but the accuracy significantly dropped when throwing away multiple items (42.9% in Table 1), ($t_{27} = 2.112$, $p < 0.01$). Such an outcome not only highlights the ERA app's positive impact on correct waste management, but also discloses the challenges of discarding daily trash in general, especially when the daily trash becomes complex. In fact, if we only look at the performance without the app support condition, the average accuracy is about 0.5, which means it is just as good as a guess. Moreover, the users exhibited a larger variance when throwing away a single item, compared to throwing away multiple garbage items (Table 1 standard deviation statistics). The variances among the group could be attributed to their recycling pre-knowledge in general. To verify the assumption of users' pre-knowledge on garbage binning accuracy, we performed a correlational analysis. We found that there is a weak to medium correlation between pre-knowledge and throwing a single item ($r = 0.243$) and multiple items ($r = 0.352$), but no such correlations between pre-knowledge and garbage binning when using ERA. It confirms our interpretation of the statistics, when people throw away simple things, they tend to rely on what they have already known. When one knows more about waste management, s/he tends to make sound decisions, and vice versa. However, pre-knowledge can only serve as far. When garbage becomes complex, which is acknowledged as a norm, although people will still rely on pre-knowledge to help make judgments on throwing away trash and recycling, the precision in correctly recycling is worse than a coin toss (42.9% in Table 1). Thus, the problem accentuates the need for a smart tool like ERA, assisting proper waste binning when you need it.

4.2 Learning Outcome

To investigate further on ERA's learning impact, we analyzed the pre and post waste disposal knowledge. The results revealed that students gained significantly

Table 1. Waste disposal accuracy by complexity with and without ERA app

	Single	Multiple
No app	0.643 ± 0.488	0.429 ± 0.224
ERA app	1.000 ± 0	0.929 ± 0.131

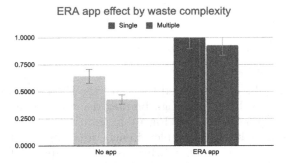

Fig. 6. Users achieved significantly higher waste disposal accuracy with ERA support versus no support.

higher post-knowledge after the user study ($t_{27} = -3.471$, $p < 0.01$). The effect was particularly pronounced in complex objects disposal, such as Straw & Cup, Coffee cup, and Plastic bag & Receipt (C3–C5 in Table 2). If we only look at what users had known in disposing of the complex trash (Straw & Cup, Coffee Cup, Plastic bags & Receipts) before they learned from ERA, the understanding was way subpar (below 50%) (Fig. 7). The result indicated the odds that a user threw away complex items accurately without support was basically worse than a coin toss. However, with the support of ERA, it educated users on the spot with the waste detection and the associated disposal bin labels. It successfully increased 20% knowledge on average in discarding complex trash (average C3–C5 in Table 2). Such an increase is not trivial. It paints a very promising picture for our daily sustainable life, where everyone can contribute at the front line of proper waste binning. Nevertheless, although the knowledge gain is smaller in simpler waste disposal (C1 & C2), it is still a positive improvement and can serve as a knowledge-refresher, to brush up the potential outdated information about recycling that one might previously have had.

4.3   Self-reported Usability Results

Based on the exit survey with the user study participants, we found that ERA app was highly praised and recommended (4.39 ± 0.49). Users also expressed high confidence in operating the ERA app (4.43 ± 0.68). This positive feedback indicates the desirability and the practicality of such a tool.

Table 2. Waste disposal accuracy by complexity with and without ERA app

	C1	C2	C3	C4	C5
	Paper	Napkin	Straw & Cup	Coffee Cup	Plastic Bag & Receipt
Pre	0.8571	0.5893	0.4857	0.3036	0.4821
Post	0.9286	0.7500	0.6964	0.5179	0.6429

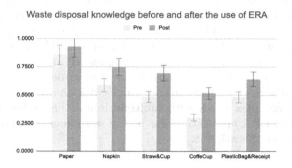

Fig. 7. Users gained knowledge after using ERA, the effects were more pronounced in complex items disposal.

In addition to the short survey to gauge users' feelings on ERA, we also interviewed them to understand the general challenges and concerns in discarding trash in their daily lives. The users unanimously mentioned the confusion in binning items as the number one challenge. This outcome aligned with the underlying assumption that given the existing support of infographics or solid pre-knowledge, it is still extremely confusing at the moment of garbage disposal or recycling. An agile interactive feedback is demanded to support users as needed. Another common challenge that users identified was the uncertainty in separating recycling and compost items, which emphasized the confusion in pre-knowledge and/or the inability to make sound decisions during disposal with the existing setup. Hence, an app like ERA can be introduced to resolve the doubts and confusions.

Moreover, the users were asked to freely express their general concerns in waste management. They shared a common feeling of uneasiness particularly after discarding items. They worried they threw items to the wrong bins or contaminated the items in the current bins. It again highlighted the difficulty in garbage disposal and recycling. The users also explicitly conveyed their concerns about the waste complexity, which once more validated the need for a tool like ERA, to alleviate the challenges during disposal and to educate users bona fide waste management knowledge. Finally, when the users were asked what was the most challenging thing they had encountered to discard away, the following list of items was recorded: *items with food, cups, dirty items, electronics, complex items.*

5   Discussions

5.1   Summary

This paper presented an educational recycling assistant that is designed to help people learn proper recycling in an augmented reality application (ERA app). An object detection model was trained from multiple waste datasets and integrated into the application to recognize wastes from the video stream in real-time. The suggested garbage bins will also be highlighted in the AR environment.

We also presented a usability study with 28 student participants and investigated the impacts of ERA and the learning effects. The results showed that with the assistance of the ERA, the users significantly increased the accuracy of putting the garbage in the correct bins. In the meantime, we also found that the users gained garbage classification knowledge after the use of ERA, especially in the cases of complex trash with multiple items. The subjective evaluation also revealed that ERA application was highly recommended and the users were highly confident in operating it.

5.2   Limitations

There are a few limitations that were discovered during the development and the user study. First of all, garbage is naturally messy and highly diversified in the real world. The size of the dataset we used to train the model was only limited to identifying finite common categories, such as paper and plastic materials. To represent a more realistic garbage disposal scenario, the waste detection model is required to improve the training data set to incorporate wider diversities of waste materials and categories. Secondly, based on the user feedback, there are several design aspects of the ERA that could be improved. For instance, a search feature to substitute object detection; an animated tutorial; a more obvious detected object label, etc.

5.3   Future Work

To move forward with the goal of sustainable living, we have identified sets of short and long term objectives. Our immediate next step is to further improve the app, including introducing a larger training set containing diverse and various kinds of garbage to enhance the waste detection model. Additionally, we would also like to upgrade the implementation with more interactive features, such as a better tutorial, visual and voice feedback when a user throws garbage correctly. For a longer term agenda, we aim to address the recycling mission with our ERA solution to adapt to a broader audience and align with government policy and regulations. For instance, due to the fact that garbage classification regulations may vary across different states and countries, the app could capitalize the mobile nature and enable the geolocation feature in order to provide recycling suggestions accordingly. Furthermore, we also envision a citizen science approach [30] to collectively enlarge and contribute to the waste detection model training data and the prediction accuracy.

References

1. Deep learning-based waste detection in natural and urban environments. Waste Management 138, 274–284 (2022)
2. trashnet (2022). https://github.com/garythung/trashnet. Accessed 27 Sept 2022
3. Abdallah, M., Talib, M.A., Feroz, S., Nasir, Q., Abdalla, H., Mahfood, B.: Artificial intelligence applications in solid waste management: a systematic research review. Waste Manage. **109**, 231–246 (2020)
4. Aishwarya, A., Wadhwa, P., Owais, O., Vashisht, V.: A waste management technique to detect and separate non-biodegradable waste using machine learning and YOLO algorithm. In: 2021 11th International Conference on Cloud Computing, Data Science & Engineering (Confluence). IEEE (2021)
5. Azuma, R., Baillot, Y., Behringer, R., Feiner, S., Julier, S., MacIntyre, B.: Recent advances in augmented reality. IEEE Comput. Graphics Appl. **21**(6), 34–47 (2001)
6. Bell, J., et al.: Informal stem education: resources for outreach, engagement and broader impacts. Sci. Educ. (CAISE), 1–28 (2016)
7. Boud, D., Garrick, J., Greenfield, K.: Understanding learning at work (2000)
8. Buragohain, A., Mali, B., Saha, S., Singh, P.K.: A deep transfer learning based approach to detect COVID-19 waste. Internet Technol. Lett. **5**(3), e327 (2022)
9. Chung, C.Y., Awad, N., Hsiao, I.H.: Collaborative programming problem-solving in augmented reality: multimodal analysis of effectiveness and group collaboration. Australas. J. Educ. Technol. **37**(5), 17–31 (2021)
10. Council, N.R., et al.: Learning Science in Informal Environments: People, Places, and Pursuits. National Academies Press, Washington (2009)
11. Dede, C.: Immersive interfaces for engagement and learning. Science **323**(5910), 66–69 (2009)
12. Dunleavy, M., Dede, C.: Augmented reality teaching and learning. In: Spector, J.M., Merrill, M.D., Elen, J., Bishop, M.J. (eds.) Handbook of Research on Educational Communications and Technology, pp. 735–745. Springer, New York (2014). https://doi.org/10.1007/978-1-4614-3185-5_59
13. Fulton, M.S., Hong, J., Sattar, J.: Trash-ICRA19: a bounding box labeled dataset of underwater trash (2020)
14. Hong, J., Fulton, M., Sattar, J.: Trashcan: a semantically-segmented dataset towards visual detection of marine debris. arXiv preprint arXiv:2007.08097 (2020)
15. Ibáñez, M.B., Delgado-Kloos, C.: Augmented reality for stem learning: a systematic review. Comput. Educ. **123**, 109–123 (2018)
16. Johnson-Glenberg, M.C., Megowan-Romanowicz, C.: Embodied science and mixed reality: how gesture and motion capture affect physics education. Cogn. Research: Principles Implications **2**(1), 1–28 (2017)
17. Kaufmann, H., Dünser, A.: Summary of usability evaluations of an educational augmented reality application. In: Shumaker, R. (ed.) ICVR 2007. LNCS, vol. 4563, pp. 660–669. Springer, Heidelberg (2007). https://doi.org/10.1007/978-3-540-73335-5_71
18. Kolb, D.A.: Experiential Learning: Experience as the Source of Learning and Development. FT press, Upper Saddle River (2014)
19. Kraft, M., Piechocki, M., Ptak, B., Walas, K.: Autonomous, onboard vision-based trash and litter detection in low altitude aerial images collected by an unmanned aerial vehicle. Remote Sens. **13**(5), 965 (2021)
20. Kuznetsova, A., et al.: The open images dataset v4. Int. J. Comput. Vision **128**(7), 1956–1981 (2020)

21. Lin, W.: YOLO-green: a real-time classification and object detection model optimized for waste management. In: 2021 IEEE International Conference on Big Data (Big Data), pp. 51–57. IEEE (2021)
22. Lu, Y., Yang, B., Gao, Y., Xu, Z.: An automatic sorting system for electronic components detached from waste printed circuit boards. Waste Manag. **137**, 1–8 (2022)
23. Mao, W.L., Chen, W.C., Wang, C.T., Lin, Y.H.: Recycling waste classification using optimized convolutional neural network. Resour. Conserv. Recycl. **164**(105132), 105132 (2021)
24. Narayan, Y.: Deepwaste: applying deep learning to waste classification for a sustainable planet. arXiv preprint arXiv:2101.05960 (2021)
25. Padalkar, A.S.: An Object Detection and Scaling Model for Plastic Waste Sorting (Doctoral dissertation). Ph.D. thesis, Dublin, National College of Ireland (2021)
26. Proença, P.F., Simões, P.: Taco: trash annotations in context for litter detection. arXiv preprint arXiv:2003.06975 (2020)
27. Rabano, S.L., Cabatuan, M.K., Sybingco, E., Dadios, E.P., Calilung, E.J.: Common garbage classification using MobileNet. In: 2018 IEEE 10th International Conference on Humanoid, Nanotechnology, Information Technology, Communication and Control, Environment and Management (HNICEM). IEEE (2018)
28. Ruiz, V., Sánchez, Á., Vélez, J.F., Raducanu, B.: Automatic image-based waste classification. In: Ferrández Vicente, J.M., Álvarez-Sánchez, J.R., de la Paz López, F., Toledo Moreo, J., Adeli, H. (eds.) IWINAC 2019. LNCS, vol. 11487, pp. 422–431. Springer, Cham (2019). https://doi.org/10.1007/978-3-030-19651-6_41
29. Sefton-Green, J.: Literature review in informal learning with technology outside school. A NESTA Futurelab Series (2004)
30. Silvertown, J.: A new dawn for citizen science. Trends in Ecol. Evol. **24**(9), 467–471 (2009)
31. Soni, U., Roy, A., Verma, A., Jain, V.: Forecasting municipal solid waste generation using artificial intelligence models–a case study in India. SN Appl. Sci. **1**(2), 1–10 (2019)
32. de Souza Melaré, A.V., González, S.M., Faceli, K., Casadei, V.: Technologies and decision support systems to aid solid-waste management: a systematic review. Waste Manage. **59**, 567–584 (2017)
33. Tan, M., Pang, R., Le, Q.V.: Efficientdet: Scalable and efficient object detection. In: Proceedings of the IEEE/CVF Conference on Computer Vision and Pattern Recognition, pp. 10781–10790 (2020)
34. Tang, A., Owen, C., Biocca, F., Mou, W.: Comparative effectiveness of augmented reality in object assembly. In: Proceedings of the SIGCHI Conference on Human Factors in Computing Systems, pp. 73–80 (2003)
35. Vygotsky, L.: Interaction between learning and development. Read. Dev. Child. **23**(3), 34–41 (1978)
36. Wahyutama, A.B., Hwang, M.: YOLO-based object detection for separate collection of recyclables and capacity monitoring of trash bins. Electron. (Basel) **11**(9), 1323 (2022)
37. Wang, H., Li, Y., Dang, L.M., Ko, J., Han, D., Moon, H.: Smartphone-based bulky waste classification using convolutional neural networks. Multimed. Tools Appl. **79**(39–40), 29411–29431 (2020)
38. Wang, T., Cai, Y., Liang, L., Ye, D.: A multi-level approach to waste object segmentation. Sensors **20**(14), 3816 (2020)
39. Yang, M., Thung, G.: Classification of trash for recyclability status. CS229 Proj. Rep. **2016**(1), 3 (2016)

40. Yuen, S.C.Y., Yaoyuneyong, G., Johnson, E.: Augmented reality: an overview and five directions for AR in education. J. Educ. Technol. Dev. Exch. (JETDE) **4**(1), 11 (2011)
41. Zhang, Q., et al.: A multi-label waste detection model based on transfer learning. Resour. Conserv. Recycl. **181**(106235), 106235 (2022)

IVE: An Immersive Virtual Environment for Automotive Security Exploration

Richard Owoputi$^{(\boxtimes)}$ ⬭, Md Rafiul Kabir ⬭, and Sandip Ray ⬭

Department of Electrical and Computer Engineering, University of Florida,
Gainesville, FL32611, USA
{rowoputi,kabirm}@ufl.edu, sandip@ece.ufl.edu

Abstract. With the increasing integration of electronics, software, and
sensors, autonomous vehicles are becoming highly complex, distributed
cyber-physical systems. Consequently, these systems are also getting
increasingly vulnerable to various cyber-attacks. Nevertheless, – and
despite its great need, – cybersecurity of automotive systems needs to be
better understood, even by critical stakeholders. This paper addresses
this problem through an immersive virtual environment for exploring
security vulnerabilities in automotive systems. Our approach enables the
use of VR technologies to provide a comprehensive environment for non-
experts to perform hands-on exploration of security attacks and understand the implications of these attacks. We demonstrate our platform in
exploring and training users in attacks on automotive ranging sensors.

Keywords: Immersive learning · Automotive security ·
Cyberattacks · Exploration

1 Introduction

The automotive industry has witnessed a fast-paced transformation in which
many mechanical components are substituted by electrical components, sensors,
and software. A modern automobile includes hundreds of Electronic Control
Units (ECUs) connected to various sensors and actuators, several in-vehicle networks, interfaces, and wireless protocols for interfacing with several external
entities, and several hundred megabytes of software. A key focus of this prolifer-
ating electrification is *automation*, i.e., supplementing and sometimes replacing
the operation of the human driver. Automation holds the promise of drastically
increasing the safety and efficiency of transportation by reducing and eliminat-
ing human errors and utilizing the transportation infrastructure better than a
human operator. However, an obvious upshot of autonomy is the increased sus-
ceptibility of these systems to cyber-attacks. Recent research has shown that it
is feasible,—and surprisingly easy at times,—for a malicious entity to subvert
a vehicular system, causing catastrophic accidents and possibly bringing down
the transportation infrastructure [3,6,12,13]. The proliferation, or even adoption of autonomy in transportation, crucially depends on our ability to conceive,
develop, and deploy cyber-resiliency in vehicular systems.

M.-L. Bourguet et al. (Eds.): iLRN 2023, CCIS 1904, pp. 484–496, 2024.
https://doi.org/10.1007/978-3-031-47328-9_35

Despite its critical need, awareness of the role of security in vehicular systems remains limited across the spectrum of stakeholders, including designers, parts suppliers, platform integrators, policy enforcement authorities, and even the broader cybersecurity community. While several high-profile papers have been published in the past decade demonstrating compromises to vehicular systems and transportation infrastructure, these works remain perceived as niche topics. A critical bottleneck for the community to comprehend cybersecurity challenges in automotive systems is the need for a platform that enables hands-on exploration of automotive security vulnerabilities. Note that hands-on exploration is particularly relevant to security exploration: appreciation of security challenges and solutions can be effectively attained by learning to hack a system. On the other hand, the demonstrations of celebrated hacks have been performed by experts with a deep understanding of automotive systems and security. While they provide compelling evidence of the vulnerability of these systems, a novice user observing a successful attack performed by an expert would see it as "magic": this would not provide the relevant intuition on the system's vulnerabilities and how they can be exploited.

This paper addresses this problem by developing an immersive exploration platform that enables users to comprehend attacks on autonomous automotive systems. We focus specifically on attacks on ranging sensors. These sensors are used by an autonomous vehicle to develop an internal perception model of the environment. An adversary who provides the vehicle with incorrect or misleading sensor values can coerce it into unsafe or inefficient driving maneuvers. Our platform, IVE (for "Immersive Virtual Environment"), uses VR infrastructure to enable users to play with various automobile security breaches while simulating the operational process in the real world. To our knowledge, IVE represents the first exploration platform that exploits VR infrastructure for automotive security training and education. We discuss some of the challenges in building such a platform. We also provide extensive usability evaluation to demonstrate the effectiveness of IVE.

The remainder of the paper is organized as follows. Section 2 discusses related research in immersive learning techniques for automotive security. We present the research challenges addressed by the platform's development in Sect. 3, and the architectural design of the platform was discussed in Sect. 4. We evaluated the usability of our platform in Sect. 5, and the evaluation result was described in Sect. 5. We conclude in Sect. 6.

2   Background and Related Work

2.1   Cybersecurity of Automotive Ranging Sensors

Ranging sensors enable a vehicle to perceive objects in its environment (e.g., signs, obstacles, pedestrians, etc.) and collect the data required for safe driving. These include radars, LIDARs, and various ultrasonic sensors, among others [15]. Different categories of sensors operate through different physical principles. For instance, ultrasonic sensors are used for parking and navigating through bumper-to-bumper traffic: they emit high-frequency sound pulses and determine the distance from an obstacle from the time elapsed between the transmission and the echo. Data from sensors is processed and evaluated through in-vehicle computation to transmit the relevant commands to the car's actuation controls, such as steering, acceleration, and braking. There are two common attacks on ultrasonic sensors: jamming and spoofing. A jamming attack occurs when the adversary introduces noise signals that cause interference with the sensor signals. A spoofing attack entails an adversary creating a fake signal so that the victim vehicle "thinks" it is an actual signal. For instance, in the case of ultrasonic sensors, a spoofed signal from the adversary may be mistakenly assumed by the victim vehicle to be the echo of its transmitted pulse. This can cause the victim to make wrong inferences regarding the presence or location of an obstacle [18].

Autonomous vehicles rely heavily on their ranging sensors to navigate safely and efficiently. However, these sensors are vulnerable to jamming attacks, which can disrupt their accuracy and cause significant safety risks. There have been numerous studies on this topic, including research conducted by Wenyuan et al. [20], who described a jamming attack against ultra-sonic sensors in moving vehicles, including a Tesla Model S vehicle. This study demonstrated the real-world impact of such attacks on autonomous vehicles. Another study by Lim et al. [8] highlighted various vulnerabilities of ranging sensors, such as the commonly used ultrasonic sensors. These researchers emphasized the need for improved security measures to protect autonomous vehicles against jamming attacks. In addition, Various researches also described jamming attacks against liDAR sensors [2,16].

As autonomous vehicles become more prevalent on the roads, the security of ranging sensors has become a crucial area of concern. While considerable research has been conducted on this topic, Yang et al. [21] proposed a robust sensor fusion algorithm that employs multiple sensors to detect attacks and provide a reliable estimate of correct sensor information. Other studies, such as those conducted by Zhang et al. [22] and Van Wyk et al. [19], have also explored additional security measures against ranging sensor attacks. Ensuring the safety of autonomous vehicles hinges on securing ranging sensors, making it a critical focus for researchers and industry professionals in the years ahead.

2.2   Related Work

VR technologies have been recently used as a means to help individuals learn models, systems, or scenarios by mimicking "real-world" experiences but in a safer environment. Immersive virtual reality (I-VR) has been used as a pedagogical tool in education, while high-fidelity graphics and immersive content delivered via head-mounted displays (HMD) have allowed students to learn in ways that traditional teaching methods cannot [5]. Merchant et al. [10] discussed a meta-analysis of three virtual reality technology i.e., games, simulations, and virtual worlds for educational settings. The VR games provide the user with complete freedom to explore the connected virtual world and achieve desired goals through complete immersion in those settings [14]. Bhattacharjee et al. [1] proposed an educational model using VR on mobile platforms for personalized learning paths

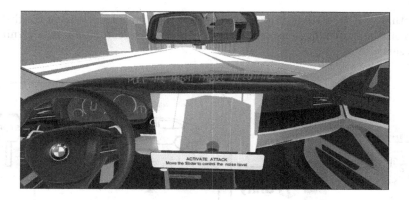

Fig. 1. The Dashboard and Windshield View with IVE

for individual users. Markowitz et al. [9] showed the usage of HMD for learning the effect of climate change on underwater environments.

In the area of automotive systems, Liang et al. [7] presented a fully structural interactive platform that provides graphical stereoscopic views of scenarios in 3D that is developed based on the technologies of CAD, database, distributed VR, and computing networking. Milella et al. [11] described how an automotive system could benefit from the use of VR when it is evaluated in the framework of the Product Emergence Process (PEP). A pilot study [17] showed the use of VR for students to learn the basics of assembling a motor block. The students were randomly assigned to three different learning conditions: the VR condition, a 360° movie condition, and a traditional movie condition. The experienced immersion results implied that students felt more engaged with the VR approach.

3 Research Challenges and IVE Approach

The goal of IVE is to provide an immersive environment where users can explore attacks on automotive sensors. Developing such a platform requires addressing a variety of challenges in design and implementation. *First*, an immersive environment must enable a natural setting where a user can explore attacks on a vehicle and its impact. More precisely, the user must be able to play the role of both the attacker (to explore various attack parameters) and the victim (since they need to "feel" the attack's impact). *Second*, the environment must faithfully simulate real-world scenarios in the VR setting. Recall from above that attacks on sensors use *physical* phenomena (e.g., signal interference). For the platform to be effective, the user must get an intuitive sense of how to control these parameters and play with them to create a successful attack. *Finally*, the environment must incorporate the uncertainties experienced by a hacker when performing the same security subversion in an imperfect physical world environment (e.g., for an actual vehicle, a slight imperfection in the instrument measuring the distance between the attacking sensor and the victim vehicle can result in a significant divergence in impact).

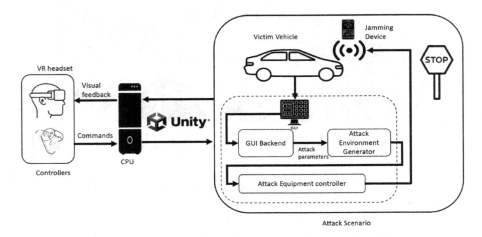

Fig. 2. IVE System Architecture

IVE addresses these challenges through a carefully designed scenario selection and system design. The immersive environment designed for attack exploration situates the user in the role of an attacker as a passenger in the autonomous vehicle. This enables the user to both perform the attack and experience the impact of the attack on the vehicle. A more interesting aspect is to provide a natural setup to show the "perception" of an object by the vehicle during an attack vis-a-vis ground truth. Recall that an attack on a ranging sensor would result in inaccurate computation of the location or presence of an obstacle. To reconcile this difference while still providing an immersive, natural environment for exploring security attacks, our VR environment defines two views: a *dashboard view* and a *windshield view*, as shown in Fig. 1. The dashboard view defines the perception of the vehicle. The windshield view mimics the effect of the user looking through the windshield and observing the ground truth. If an attack confuses the vehicle into thinking there is an object when there is not, the dashboard view would indicate the object's presence while the windshield view would not. To enable the user to play with attacks, the dashboard includes (virtual) controls that the user can use to tweak various attack parameters. Finally, the scenarios are crafted carefully to ensure that the behavior experienced in the VR environment corresponds to the effect of the same attack on the real vehicle. Note that this is non-trivial and cannot be culled from the information available from successful attacks by experts. In particular, the user of IVE can explore various parameter values, even those that may not be relevant to the attack being performed, e.g., a ranging sensor frequency setting for the attacking sensor that is drastically different from the setting of the victim sensor. This would not result in a successful attack. However, IVE must faithfully implement the impact of this attacking frequency on the victim vehicle, which may not have been defined. This can be addressed through a secondary hardware platform with actual hardware sensors to comprehend the effect of such "uncharacteristic" parameter values on the victim vehicle, which is then exported to the virtual environment of IVE.

4   IVE Design

4.1   System Architecture

Figure 2 shows the high-level architecture of IVE which is primarily designed to provide users with a virtual environment to simulate and experiment with various attack scenarios. The main interface of the system is an Oculus headset, which is used by the user to interact with the virtual environment.

The virtual environment consists of a graphical user interface (GUI) panel mounted on the dashboard of the victim vehicle, which the user can control. The system is implemented through Unity, a popular game engine that allows for the creation of realistic and interactive 3D environments.

The system design consists of three main components

- **GUI Backend:** The GUI Backend is responsible for allowing users to design and engage with unique attack scenarios through a graphical user interface. The user can select attack parameters through the GUI, which are then sent to the attack environment generator. The GUI Backend also triggers the type of scenario based on the user's attack parameter selection.
- **Environment Generator:** This component is responsible for generating multiple attack scenarios based on the attack parameters chosen by the user. The attack environment is developed using Unity 3D software and consists of multiple paths and triggers that are activated based on the parameters sent from the GUI backend.
- **Attack Equipment Controller:** This includes a virtual jamming device that simulates the noise produced by a jamming device in real life. The noise produced by the virtual jamming device varies based on the attack parameters selected by the user.

Hardware and Software. In order to develop a fully immersive 3D VR application, we needed a development platform that could create a near-realistic experience. After researching several options, we chose Unity3D for its large user community and free student version that provides all implementation features. Unity3D also supports Oculus Integration, which was essential for the project. For exploring the immersive simulator, we selected the Oculus Quest 2 due to its low latency, accurate positional tracking, and extensive user community for FAQ. This allowed us to create an immersive experience that closely mimicked real-life situations. To implement the platform, we needed several software packages, including the Oculus SDK, various 3D models, and the Unity3D software

[4]. We obtained the various 3D models from the Unity asset store and open-sourced projects on the internet. The Unity software functionalities were written using the C$^\sharp$ programming language, which is commonly used for game development. Finally, the platform was designed using the Nvidia GeForce RTX 3060Ti graphics card to handle the high graphical demands of the project. The RTX 3060Ti is a high-performance graphics card that offers real-time ray tracing, which was essential for creating realistic lighting and shadows in the immersive simulator (Fig. 3).

4.2 User Interaction Model

Fig. 3. User interacting with IVE.

The success of IVE as a hands-on exploration platform for automotive security attacks hinges on its front end. A novice user must be able to intuitively understand and operate the system's various knobs and sliders used to adjust the noise level in the attack infrastructure. In Fig. 4, we see the system's front end, which provides users with a tactile sense of these controls.

Users can explore and experiment with different attack scenarios by simply tweaking the parameters through the intuitive interface panel. Unlike other systems that require sensor technology expertise, our platform guides users through the process and provides feedback on the attack's progress. For example, if the noise level is too low, the user is notified that the attack is unlikely to succeed. On the other hand, when the noise level is sufficient to implement the attack, the user receives a notification.

The system provides users with a controlled environment to explore different attack scenarios. Using the controllers, users can interact both virtually and physically with the environment, which helps to develop soft skills and operational knowledge. The hands-on experience allows users to gain a deeper understanding of the attack scenarios and the necessary countermeasures.

Fig. 4. IVE Front End. (a) Unsuccessful attack: Vehicle stopping at the stop sign. (b) Successful attack: Vehicle crashing with an incoming vehicle.

5   Usability Evaluation

We conducted a user evaluation to determine the effectiveness of IVE as a platform for novice users to comprehend challenges and approaches to automotive security. In this section, we briefly summarize the evaluation process.

Evaluation Procedure Summary. The evaluation of IVE involved eight participants who were college students with an average age of 28.3, ranging between 25 and 30 years old. The participants came from diverse academic backgrounds, including electrical engineering, computer science, and the arts, among others. The male-to-female ratio was 7 : 1, and none of the participants had prior automotive security training.

Each participant experienced the setup individually with the first author present, who provided initial instructions on using the VR equipment and explained the motivation for the evaluation. The participants were not informed of the other participants in the evaluation to ensure unbiased feedback.

After the evaluation, the participants provided post-evaluation feedback via an anonymous survey conducted using Google Forms as seen in Fig. 5 and Fig. 6. The survey did not request any personally identifying information from the participants to maintain anonymity. The survey questions focused on various aspects of the system, including ease of use, realism, and effectiveness in simulating automotive security attacks.

The data collected from the survey was analyzed to evaluate the effectiveness of IVE in providing a hands-on exploration platform for automotive security attacks

Procedure Details. The evaluation included the following sequence of operations.

1. The experimental confidentially guidelines were conveyed.
2. The participants were made aware of the overall experimental purpose.
3. They were asked to fill a pre-evaluation survey.
4. They were instructed on how to utilize the Oculus VR equipment.
5. They were provided a pre-training session that lasted about 5 min (participants could ask for more or less training time if they felt more or less comfortable IVE).
6. They were then allotted a regular session of 10 minutes to play with security attacks themselves.
7. After the session we sent the participants a link containing the evaluation survey. The survey questions could be filled offline. We estimate that the survey questions took about 20 minutes to complete for each participant.

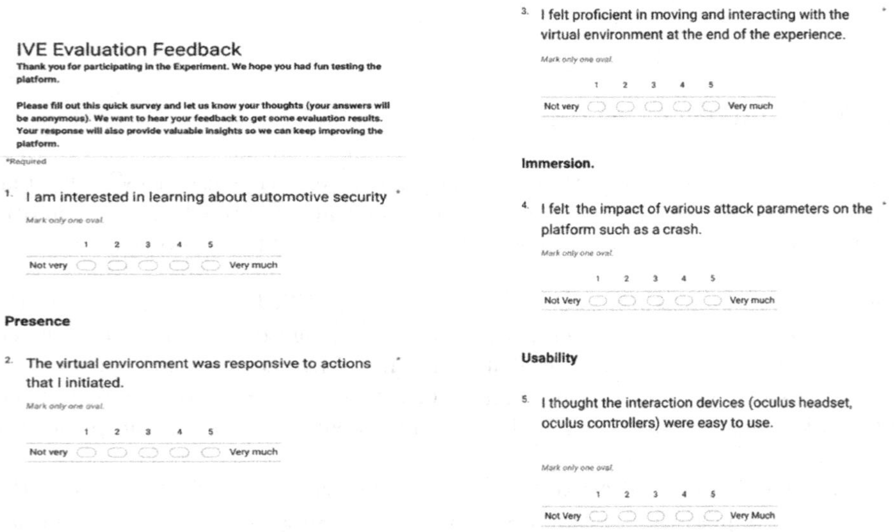

IVE Evaluation Feedback
Thank you for participating in the Experiment. We hope you had fun testing the platform.

Please fill out this quick survey and let us know your thoughts (your answers will be anonymous). We want to hear your feedback to get some evaluation results. Your response will also provide valuable insights so we can keep improving the platform.

*Required

1. I am interested in learning about automotive security *
Mark only one oval.
1 2 3 4 5
Not very ○ ○ ○ ○ ○ Very much

Presence

2. The virtual environment was responsive to actions that I initiated.
Mark only one oval.
1 2 3 4 5
Not very ○ ○ ○ ○ ○ Very much

3. I felt proficient in moving and interacting with the virtual environment at the end of the experience.
Mark only one oval.
1 2 3 4 5
Not very ○ ○ ○ ○ ○ Very much

Immersion.

4. I felt the impact of various attack parameters on the platform such as a crash.
Mark only one oval.
1 2 3 4 5
Not Very ○ ○ ○ ○ ○ Very much

Usability

5. I thought the interaction devices (oculus headset, oculus controllers) were easy to use.
Mark only one oval.
1 2 3 4 5
Not Very ○ ○ ○ ○ ○ Very Much

Fig. 5. User Evaluation Survey for IVE: Page 1

Pre-training. Pre-training entailed a quick warm-up to acquaint participants with the use of VR controllers to reduce the negative bias of user research results caused by their possible unfamiliarity with VR controllers. The objective of the training was to give a user practice with two fundamental tasks: choosing an attack type and intensity and controlling navigation. No performance assessments were taken during pre-training. The experiments shown comprised two scenarios:

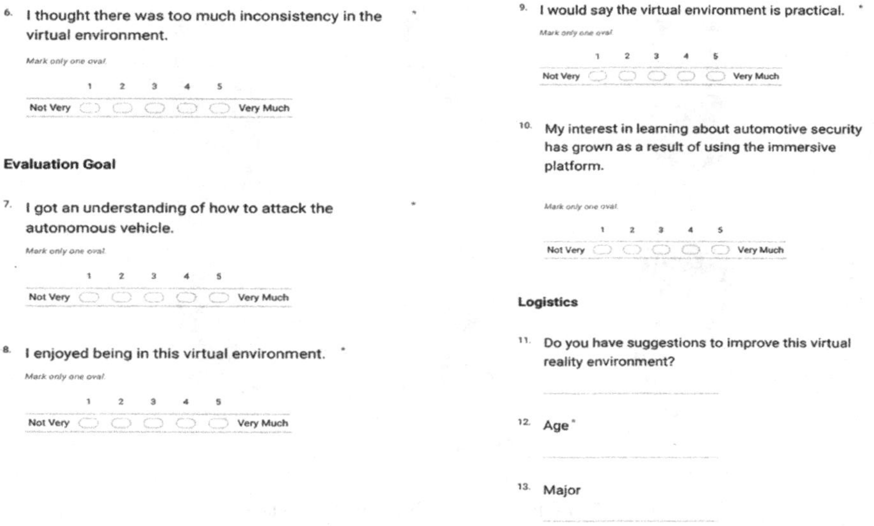

6. I thought there was too much inconsistency in the virtual environment.

Mark only one oval.

   1   2   3   4   5

Not Very ⬭ ⬭ ⬭ ⬭ ⬭ Very Much

9. I would say the virtual environment is practical.

Mark only one oval.

   1   2   3   4   5

Not Very ⬭ ⬭ ⬭ ⬭ ⬭ Very Much

10. My interest in learning about automotive security has grown as a result of using the immersive platform.

Mark only one oval.

   1   2   3   4   5

Not Very ⬭ ⬭ ⬭ ⬭ ⬭ Very Much

Evaluation Goal

7. I got an understanding of how to attack the autonomous vehicle.

Mark only one oval.

   1   2   3   4   5

Not Very ⬭ ⬭ ⬭ ⬭ ⬭ Very Much

Logistics

11. Do you have suggestions to improve this virtual reality environment?

_____

8. I enjoyed being in this virtual environment.

Mark only one oval.

   1   2   3   4   5

Not Very ⬭ ⬭ ⬭ ⬭ ⬭ Very Much

12. Age*

_____

13. Major

_____

Fig. 6. User Evaluation Survey for IVE: Page 2.

- **Benign Scenario:** In this scenario, the participant feels the environment through the VR headset and correlates the windshield and dashboard views. No attack is initiated during this step. The participant observes the vehicle as it stops at a stop sign and avoids the oncoming vehicle.
- **Malicious Scenario:** In this scenario, the user chooses the attack type from a drag menu and selects the attack intensity using a slider button. The participant observes the effect of the attack, e.g., the vehicle ignoring the stop sign and colliding with the incoming vehicle as explained in Sect. 4.2.

For each scenario, we walk the participants through the possibilities and interaction techniques that are provided in the immersive environment. Then they had time to try the attack technique as long as they liked. On average, participants spent about 5 min exploring the attack action (Fig. 7).

Result and Discussion. The evaluation of the IVE prototyping platform was conducted to measure its effectiveness in enhancing the learning experience of automotive security issues. The evaluation process involved 20 participants who were asked to interact with the platform and provide feedback on their experience. The evaluation results showed high scores in the presence and immersion categories, indicating that the platform was successful in creating a realistic and engaging environment for the participants.

The usability rating was also high, with 75% of the participants providing a high rating for usability questions. This indicates that the platform was user-friendly and easy to navigate, even for those who had to learn quickly. Additionally, 75% of the participants reported that the platform increased their interest

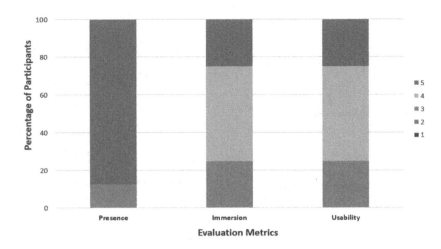

Fig. 7. IVE User Evaluation Statistics

in learning about automotive security, which is an essential factor in enhancing the learning experience.

Moreover, the participants reported that the environment was practical, with 75% of the participants agreeing, while the remaining 25% were indifferent. This suggests that the platform was effective in simulating real-world scenarios and provided a practical experience for the users. All participants enjoyed playing with the immersive platform, indicating that it was successful in creating an engaging and entertaining experience.

The open-ended feedback provided valuable insights into the areas for improvement of the platform. Participants requested more control and suggested including sensations like vibration to improve immersion. These suggestions will be considered in future developments of the platform.

The evaluation of the IVE prototyping platform demonstrated its effectiveness in assisting users in comprehending automotive security issues. The high scores in the presence, immersion, and usability categories indicate that the platform was successful in creating a realistic, engaging, and user-friendly environment for the participants. The results of the evaluation highlight the potential of the platform in enhancing the learning experience of automotive security and its applications in related fields.

6   Conclusion and Future Work

Security is critical to the adoption and proliferation of autonomous vehicles but is unfortunately not well understood even among the cybersecurity communities. In this paper, we developed an exploration platform IVE to address this problem. IVE permits users to comprehend ranging sensor attacks by playing with different attack parameters and experiencing their impact in an immersive VR environment. Our user evaluation suggests that IVE can improve the understanding of various automotive security concepts irrespective of the user's level of expertise.

In future work, we propose to extend IVE for exploration of more complex sensor attacks and to add certain augmented reality features. We also aim to broaden the scope of our evaluation and expand our user sample, as the current study was limited by a relatively small number of participants.

Acknowledgements. This project has been partially supported by the National Science Foundation under Grants CNS-1908549 and SATC-2221900.

References

1. Bhattacharjee, D., Paul, A., Kim, J.H., Karthigaikumar, P.: An immersive learning model using evolutionary learning. Comput. Electr. Eng. **65**, 236–249 (2018)
2. Cao, Y., et al.: Adversarial sensor attack on lidar-based perception in autonomous driving. In: Proceedings of the 2019 ACM SIGSAC Conference on Computer and Communications Security, pp. 2267–2281 (2019)
3. Checkoway, S., et al.: Comprehensive experimental analyses of automotive attack surfaces. In: 20th USENIX Security Symposium (USENIX Security 11) (2011)
4. Haas, J.K.: A history of the unity game engine (2014)
5. Hamilton, D., McKechnie, J., Edgerton, E., Wilson, C.: Immersive virtual reality as a pedagogical tool in education: a systematic literature review of quantitative learning outcomes and experimental design. J. Comput. Educ. **8**(1), 1–32 (2021)
6. Koscher, K., et al.: Experimental security analysis of a modern automobile. In: 2010 IEEE Symposium on Security and Privacy, pp. 447–462. IEEE (2010)
7. Liang, J.S.: Modeling an immersive VR driving learning platform in a web-based collaborative design environment. Comput. Appl. Eng. Educ. **20**(3), 553–567 (2012)
8. Lim, B.S., Keoh, S.L., Thing, V.L.L.: Autonomous vehicle ultrasonic sensor vulnerability and impact assessment. In: 2018 IEEE 4th World Forum on Internet of Things (WF-IoT), pp. 231–236 (2018). https://doi.org/10.1109/WF-IoT.2018.8355132
9. Markowitz, D.M., Laha, R., Perone, B.P., Pea, R.D., Bailenson, J.N.: Immersive virtual reality field trips facilitate learning about climate change. Front. Psychol. **9**, 2364 (2018)
10. Merchant, Z., Goetz, E.T., Cifuentes, L., Keeney-Kennicutt, W., Davis, T.J.: Effectiveness of virtual reality-based instruction on students' learning outcomes in k-12 and higher education: a meta-analysis. Comput. Educ. **70**, 29–40 (2014)
11. Milella, F.: Problem-solving by immersive virtual reality: towards a more efficient product emergence process in automotive. J. Multidisc. Eng. Sci. Technol. (JMEST) **2**(4), 860–867 (2015)
12. Miller, C., Valasek, C.: A survey of remote automotive attack surfaces. black hat USA 2014, 94 (2014)
13. Miller, C., Valasek, C.: Remote exploitation of an unaltered passenger vehicle. Black Hat USA 2015(S 91) (2015)
14. Peppler, K., Kafai, Y.: What videogame making can teach us about literacy and learning: Alternative pathways into participatory culture (2007)

15. de Ponte Müller, F.: Survey on ranging sensors and cooperative techniques for relative positioning of vehicles. Sensors **17**(2), 271 (2017)
16. Stottelaar, B.G.: Practical cyber-attacks on autonomous vehicles. Master's thesis, University of Twente (2015)
17. Struyf, D., Willems, S.: A pilot study on the use of immersive technologies in the teaching of automotive technology students. In: BAPS 2019, Date: 2019/05/13-2019/05/14, Location: Liège, pp. 64–64 (2019)
18. Sun, J.S., Cao, Y.C., Chen, Q.A., Mao, Z.M.: Towards robust lidar-based perception in autonomous driving: General black-box adversarial sensor attack and countermeasures. In: USENIX Security Symposium (Usenix Security'20) (2020)
19. Van Wyk, F., Wang, Y., Khojandi, A., Masoud, N.: Real-time sensor anomaly detection and identification in automated vehicles. IEEE Trans. Intell. Transp. Syst. **21**(3), 1264–1276 (2019)
20. Xu, W., Yan, C., Jia, W., Ji, X., Liu, J.: Analyzing and enhancing the security of ultrasonic sensors for autonomous vehicles. IEEE Internet Things J. **5**(6), 5015–5029 (2018). https://doi.org/10.1109/JIOT.2018.2867917
21. Yang, T., Lv, C.: A secure sensor fusion framework for connected and automated vehicles under sensor attacks. IEEE Internet Things J. **9**(22), 22357–22365 (2021)
22. Zhang, J., et al.: Detecting and identifying optical signal attacks on autonomous driving systems. IEEE Internet Things J. **8**(2), 1140–1153 (2020)

Immersive Learning Environments for Self-regulation of Learning: A Literature Review

Daniela Pedrosa[1,2](✉) [ID], Leonel Morgado[3,4] [ID], and Dennis Beck[5] [ID]

[1] Research Centre On Didactics and Technology in the Education of Trainers (CIDTFF),
Universidade de Aveiro, Aveiro, Portugal
daniela.pedrosa@ese.ipsantarem.pt
[2] Polytechnic Institute of Santarém, Santarém, Portugal
[3] Universidade Aberta, Coimbra & Lisbon, Portugal
leonel.morgado@uab.pt
[4] INESC TEC, Porto, Portugal
[5] University of Arkansas, Fayetteville, AR, USA
debeck@uark.edu

Abstract. Self-regulation of learning (SRL) plays a decisive role in learning success but characterizing learning environments that facilitate development of SRL skills constitutes a great challenge. Given the growing interest in Immersive Learning Environments (ILE), we sought to understand how ILE are built with attention to SRL, via a literature review of pedagogical uses, practices and strategies with ILE that have an explicit focus on SRL. From a final corpus of 25 papers, we collected 134 extracts attesting use of ILE for SRL. We classified and mapped them using the Beck, Morgado & O'Shea framework and its three dimensions of the immersion phenomenon: system, narrative and challenge. There is a predominance of uses of ILE for SRL aligned with Challenge-based immersion: Skill Training, Collaboration, Engagement, and Interactive Manipulation and Exploration. In contrast, uses aligned with System-based immersion (Emphasis, Accessibility, Seeing the Invisible) were not identified. There were few cases of use of Narrative-based immersion. Uses combining the three dimensions of immersive had residual prevalence. We concluded that there is greater tendency in studies of SRL in ILE to enact active roles (aligned with the Challenge dimension of immersion). The low prevalence of Narrative immersion and System immersion evidence gaps in the diversity of pedagogical uses of ILE to develop SRL, which indicate opportunities for research and creation of innovative educational practices.

Keywords: Immersion · Self-regulated Learning · Educational Uses · Educational Practices · Educational Strategies

1 Introduction

Self-Regulated Learning (SRL) skills are a key element for successful learning [1], enabling learners to be independent, caring about what and how to learn [2]. Developing SRL skills requires learning environments that help students align their actions towards their learning process and goals [3].

© The Author(s), under exclusive license to Springer Nature Switzerland AG 2024
M.-L. Bourguet et al. (Eds.): iLRN 2023, CCIS 1904, pp. 497–511, 2024.
https://doi.org/10.1007/978-3-031-47328-9_36

There are opportunities and challenges for educators to support development of SRL skills using Immersive Learning Environments (ILE), since they are characterized by being highly engaging [4, 5]. However, their pedagogical integration requires instructional design suited to educational goals and results [6]. Thus, research is needed on how to combine ILE with SRL [7]: ILE involve high cognitive agency, which can adversely affect SRL, if immersive classes do not offer an opportunity for reflection [4].

Environments that present high levels of interaction can affect the student's ability to monitor and adapt their metacognitive, cognitive, motivational, and affective processes, an effect that can be minimized if the instructional design is well structured [8, 9]. The instructional designer can facilitate SRL by considering challenges and reflection activities that enable learners to activate their metacognitive processes.

To support instructional design that employs ILE in developing SRL skills, we conducted a systematic literature review, which identified actual accounts of educational use, practices, and strategies with ILE to develop SRL skills. We classified and mapped these per in thematic analysis, using the Beck et al. framework [10]. The outcome provides an understanding of how ILE are being used to support SRL, in the conceptual space of immersion theory. It also enabled the identification of gaps of low or null application of ILE use methods towards SRL skills development in that conceptual space, identifying areas for future research and development of innovative practices.

2   Related Work

2.1   Immersion and Immersive Learning Environments

Immersive learning has been an area of increasing interest [4]. Recent research explores immersive learning as processes [11] from three perspectives [12]: a) educational outcomes; b) internal processes of active construction and ability to adapt cognitive, affective, and psychomotor models; and c) educational methods for ILE as learning tools.

The core concept of ILE is Immersion. It is a phenomenon reflecting a psychological deep state of mental involvement affecting cognitive and sensory processes [10, 11, 13], used as a lens for analyzing, interpreting, and adjusting the learning context [10]. Immersion contributes to learning by removing peripheral aspects, controlling variables, and providing student feedback [14] and emerges from three dimensions, which can be affected by technologies or other mediating elements, such as human intervention [10, 13]:

1) Challenge, immersion from agency, occurring when one experiences and actively engages in tasks and initiatives involving cognitive and physical processes, and application of competences. This dimension is the one that most requires the subject to exert agency, being active and interacting.

2) Narrative, immersion from intensely focusing on a story, on meanings, or on interpretations of elements such as characters, spatiotemporal contexts, objects, sounds, etc. (and interactions between these elements). It most involves identifying meaning and context from the experience.

3) System, immersion from feeling subjectively surrounded or present within an environment. Commonly associated with technology (e.g., virtual reality, pervasive technology), but also with the physical environment that envelops us and other surrounding systems: organizational, political, economic, and sociocultural aspects.

In immersive environments, the phenomenon is experienced, arising from one or more of these dimensions. ILE are such immersive environments where the learning phenomenon is manifested [15]. They can be simulated/augmented environments built using digital technologies (e.g., head-mounted monitors, tactile devices, mobile devices) [16–20], but also entirely physical environments [15] or atopical environments, independent of location [21].

2.2 Self-regulation of Learning

SRL is a complex process that depends on several factors, and enables the construction of meanings, objectives, and strategies from the information available in the physical and psychological environment [22]. Is considered as a meta-process [23] that requires active participation of students in the control and regulation of their metacognitive, cognitive, behavioral, emotional, and motivational and environmental processes. It requires skills for selection and use of strategies for personal learning processes, with the purpose of achieving the outlined goals and stimulate self-knowledge, self-awareness and self-efficacy [23–25].

3   Methodology

3.1   Planning: Purpose, Goals, and Research Question

This systematic literature review focus on providing an overview of studies that use ILEs for development of SRL skills, identifying and mapping their educational uses, practices, and strategies. We understand these as: 1) a 'use' is when the educational action is clear but without an explicit pedagogical rationale; 2) a 'practice' is when the educational action is clear and provided with an explicit pedagogic rationale; 3) a 'strategy' is either an overarching goal (or inspiring philosophy) for an educational approach, or an explicit pragmatic pattern guiding decision-making and practices towards pedagogic goals [26].

The specific goals are: 1) Identify studies in which ILE are used for SRL providing an overview in terms of year, field, and educational context; 2) Provide a mapping on how ILE are used for SRL; 3) Identify areas for research development in this topic.

Given that the phenomenon of immersion can emerge from three conceptual dimensions [13], our research question to fulfil these goals is "What is the panorama of educational approaches for developing SRL with ILE in the conceptual space of immersion?".

3.2   Work Process

This review searched for papers that focus on ILEs for promoting SRL, regardless of technology use, and explicitly contain the terms "self-regulation of learning" and "immersion". The work process along five phases [27]: Literature Search; Screen for inclusion; Extraction; Analysis; Systematization and final discussion (Fig. 1).

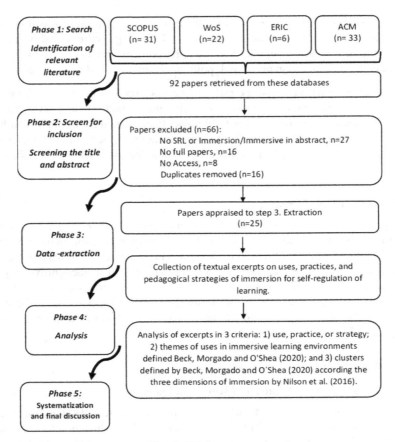

Fig. 1. Work process.

In phase 1, we searched for relevant literature on bibliographic databases: SCOPUS, WoS, ACM, and ERIC. From the research goals and question, we defined the search string: ("Self-Regulated learning" OR "Self-Regulation of Learning") AND ("Immersion" OR "Immersive"), without delimiting publication date and only considering peer-reviewed papers in these languages: English, Portuguese, or Spanish. In this phase, 92 papers were identified as potentially relevant (SCOPUS, n = 31; WoS, n = 22; ERIC, n = 6; ACM, n = 33).

In phase 2, we screened papers for inclusion, beginning by analyzing their titles and abstracts. We followed these inclusion criteria: a) written in English, Portuguese, or Spanish languages; b) explicitly including in the abstract: "self-regulated learning" or "self-regulation learning", and "immersion" or "immersive" to make the study more focused. We considered all educational contexts and research designs. We eliminated papers to which we did not have access or were found to be duplicated. This excluded 66 papers: a) 27 without both terms in their abstracts; b) 16 papers without full text; c) 8 papers we could not access, and d) 16 duplicates. After this process, 25 papers constituted the corpus (see Table 1). Also, we provide the list of papers as an open dataset companion [28].

Table 1. Dataset of final papers.

ID	Authors	Year	Title
P1	Zheng et al	2009	Nurture Motivated, Confident, and Strategic Learners in Engineering through Cognitive and Psychological Instructions for an Entry-Level Course
P2	Shih et al	2010	Integrating Self-Regulated Learning Instruction in a Digital Logic Course
P3	Rahayu & Jacobson	2012	Speaking self-efficacy and English as a foreign language: learning processes in a multi-user
P4	Mikroyannidis et al	2016	Applying a methodology for the design, delivery and evaluation of learning resources for remote experimentation
P5	Cho et al	2017	Medical student changes in self-regulated learning during the transition to the clinical environment
P6	Pellerin	2018	Affordances of New Mobile Technologies: Promoting Learner Agency, Autonomy, and Self-regulated Learning
P7	Cárdenas-Robledo & Peña-Ayala	2019	A holistic self-regulated learning model: A proposal and application in ubiquitous learning
P8	Nurieva	2019	E-learning as Part of Self-Regulated Foreign Languages Acquisition (A Case Study of Bauman Moscow State Technical University)
P9	Sakdavong et al	2019	Virtual Reality in Self-regulated Learning: Example in Art Domain
P10	Chen & Hsu	2020	Self-regulated mobile game-based English learning in a virtual reality environment
P11	Wan et al	2021	Self-regulatory school climate, group regulation and individual regulatory ability: towards a model integrating three domains of self-regulated learning
P12	Talamantes	2021	A Critical Classroom Study of Language Oppression: Manuel and Malena's Testimonios, "Sentía como que yo no valía nada… Se reían de mí
P13	Nachtigall et al	2022	Fostering cognitive strategies for learning with 360° videos in history education contexts
P14	del Moral Pérez et al	2022	Producción de narraciones orales con una app en educación infantil: análisis del engagement y la competencia narrativa
P15	Spiliotopoulos et al	2019	A Mixed-reality Interaction-driven Game-based Learning Framework
P16	Boomgaard et al	2022	A Novel Immersive Anatomy Education System (Anat_Hub): Redefining Blended Learning for the Musculoskeletal System
P17	Hayashida et al	2020	Virtually Alone- How Facilitated Aloneness Affect Self-Study in IVE -
P18	Wan et al	2021	Examining Flow Antecedents in Game-Based Learning to promote Self-Regulated Learning and Acceptance

(continued)

Table 1. (*continued*)

ID	Authors	Year	Title
P19	Li	2017	Design of Multimedia Teaching Platform for Chinese Folk Art Performance Based on Virtual Reality Technology
P20	Heaysman & Kramarski	2021	Supporting Teachers' SRL Beliefs and Practices with Immersive Learning Environments: Evidence from a Unique Simulations-Based Program
P21	Nietfeld et al	2014	Self-Regulation and Gender Within a Game-Based Learning Environment
P22	Cheng & Tsai	2020	Students' motivational beliefs and strategies, perceived immersion and attitudes towards science learning with immersive virtual reality: A partial least squares analysis
P23	Pedrosa et al	2016	Self-regulated Learning in Computer Programming: Strategies Students Adopted During an Assignment
P24	Berthold et al	2012	An Initial Evaluation of Metacognitive Scaffolding for Experiential Training Simulators
P25	Perera & Allison	2015	Self-Regulated Learning in Virtual Worlds – An Exploratory Study in OpenSim

In phase 3, text excerpts were collected from these 25 papers, for the following aspects: 1) Field, and Pedagogical context towards the first research goal; 2) Accounts of uses, practices or pedagogical strategies for SRL in ILE, towards the second and third goals. The text excerpts were collected by a researcher (first author) through a complete reading of the papers, collecting the original texts excerpts and put them into a database in excel format, according to the protocol (aspects) defined by the research team (authors these paper). A total of 134 accounts were extracted.

In phase 4, we conducted descriptive statistical analysis of the studies (goal 1). For the 134 accounts extracts (goals 2 and 3) we performed thematic content analysis [29]. Firstly, we labelled accounts as uses, practices, or strategies [26]. Then we analyzed and classified them under themes according to the Beck et al. framework of uses of ILE [10, 28]. Then descriptive statistical analysis was conducted to identify their prevalence in SRL studies. Finally, the themes were situated in the "immersion cube" conceptual space [13] to identify opportunities for research development and practice innovation. In this phase, the reliability of the researchers was guaranteed through inter-rating voting.

In phase 5, for systematization and final discussion of results, we present the results in the next section where we discuss and reflect on the status and research opportunities for employing ILE for developing SRL skills.

4 Results

4.1 Overview of Studies about ILE for SRL

Studies on ILE for SRL emerged recently: the first paper is from 13 years ago (2009). The last 4 years saw sudden growth in publications, revealing it is a current topic of interest. Regarding subject areas there are account across a large variety of disciplines, 'general' (unspecific) and 'languages' being the most common, followed by engineering, health, art, and technology (Fig. 2).

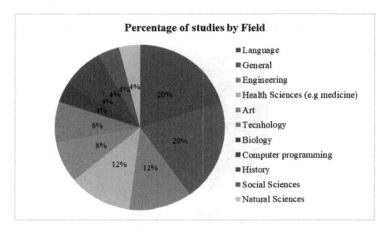

Fig. 2. Percentages of studies by field.

Regarding educational contexts, higher education is predominant, with preschool education being the least common (Fig. 3).

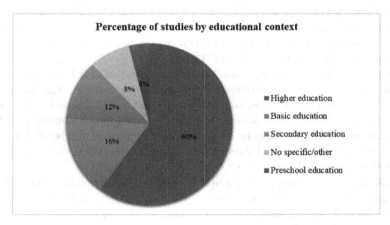

Fig. 3. Percentages of studies by educational context.

Regarding educational uses, practices, and strategies, roughly half of the 134 extracts (54%) were uses, with practices (24%) and strategies (22%) having similar prevalence (Fig. 4). This indicates that most accounts of ILE use for SRL do not provide an explicit pedagogic rationale.

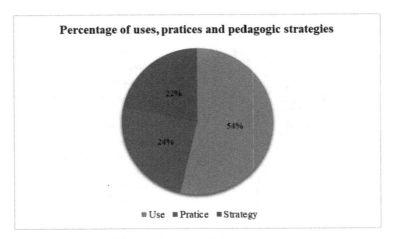

Fig. 4. Percentages of uses, practices and pedagogic strategies.

4.2 Themes of Uses, Practices, and Strategies of ILE for SRL

Table 2 presents how the 134 accounts (uses, practices, and strategies) were associated with the 18 themes of ILE for SRL. These include 13 of the 16 themes from Beck et al.'s framework, and 2 new themes. 3 of the framework themes have no matching accounts using ILE for SRL. The two new themes, which were not present in the interpretative framework, are: "Mobile Learning" and "LMS".

The theme "Mobile learning" involved activities labelled as ILE but lacking further description beyond the mere use of mobile devices. Sample extracts: "(…) learners were asked to use an iPod to make a video recording of their co-construction of knowledge." P6; "the digital content [was] delivered by the U–LMS through ubiquitous devices." P7. The theme "LMS" similarly involved activities labelled as ILE but lacking further description beyond the use of a Learning Management System. Example: "(…) Moodle LMS as the on-line environment." P23.

The theme with highest prevalence in ILE for SRL is "Skill training" (31%), found in most papers (68%). E.g.: "SRL training that fostered students' acquisition of cognitive strategies for processing history-related 360° videos" P13 (Practice).

Themes "Collaboration", "Engagement", and "Interactive manipulation and exploration" follow in prevalence (10%–12%) and are commonly found in the papers (36%–44%). These are all themes sharing high levels of Challenge-based (agency) immersion, indicating activities that imply an active role of the learner for developing knowledge and its personal, motivational, and social skills. E.g.: "Immersion architecture is designed for mixed reality and smart learning environments, which will afford interaction with content and among learners as well as self-regulated learning". P15 (practice – interactive manipulation and exploration).

Table 2. Themes of ILE for SRL.

Immersion Themes	No. of accounts	Prevalence accounts (n = 134)	No. of papers	Prevalence papers (n = 25)
Skill training	42	31,3%	17	68%
Collaboration	16	11,9%	11	44%
Engagement	14	10,4%	10	40%
Interactive manipulation and exploration	13	9,7%	9	36%
Complement/Combine contexts, media or items	8	6%	8	32%
(new) Mobile Learning	8	6%	5	20%
Logistics	8	6%	5	20%
Changing human behavior	6	5%	5	20%
Simulate the physical world	5	3,7%	3	12%
Augmented context	4	3%	3	12%
Multimodal interaction	3	2,2%	3	12%
(new) LMS	2	1,5%	2	8%
Data collection	2	1,5%	2	8%
Perspective switching	2	1,5%	2	8%
Emotional and cultural experiences	1	0,7%	1	4%
Emphasis	0	0%	0	0%
Accessibility	0	0%	0	0%
Seeing the invisible	0	0%	0	0%

With lower prevalence, we then found the themes "Complement/Combine contexts, media or items", "Mobile Learning" (new theme), "Logistics", and "Changing human behavior" (5%–6%), but still somewhat common in papers (20%–32%). E.g.: "Metacognitive Scaffolding Service (MSS), which has been integrated into an already existing and mature medical training simulator." P24 (use – complement/combine).

With less prevalence, we found the themes "Simulate the physical world"; "Augmented context"; "Multimodal interaction", "LMS" (new theme), "Data collection"; "Perspective switching" and "Emotional and cultural experiences" which are uncommonly found in the papers (4%–12%). E.g.: "(…) displayed text changed automatically after every pre-determined time slot (…) short breaks at any point between task (…) reading each English text" P17, (use – Multimodal interaction). These are themes with a variety of immersion characteristics, mostly with Mid/High narrative immersion or Mid/High system immersion.

The themes "Emphasis", "Accessibility", "Seeing the invisible" (0%) were not identified. Their immersion characteristics share Mid/High system immersion.

5 Discussion

5.1 Overview of Studies about ILE for SRL Themes of ILE for SRL per Immersion Dimensions

In Fig. 5, we see the panorama of ILE uses for SRL. The position of each bubble and their clustering (1 to 6) was given by the reference framework, but we sized them according to their prevalence in this survey. To place the bubble for the two new themes, we interpreted them as system-based immersion only, given the lack of information on narrative or challenges: Mobile learning: System 50%, Narrative 0%, Challenge 0%; LMS: System 25%, Narrative 0%, Challenge 0%. These two themes partly hit what the framework called "Voids" 0 and 1, with Low/Mid system, Low narrative, and Low challenge. Thus, we deemed them to form their own cluster, henceforth Cluster 7 (new cluster). The prevalence of ILE for SRL themes within each cluster, we get, most to least:

Cluster 4 (red bubbles): High Challenge, Low-Mid Narrative, Low System. Themes: Skill training (31,3%), Collaboration (11,9%), Engagement (10,4%). Total prevalence (TP): 53,6%
Cluster 3 (dark blue bubbles): Mid-High Challenge, Low Narrative, High System. Themes: Data collection (1,5%), Interactive exploration and manipulation (9,7%). TP: 11,2%

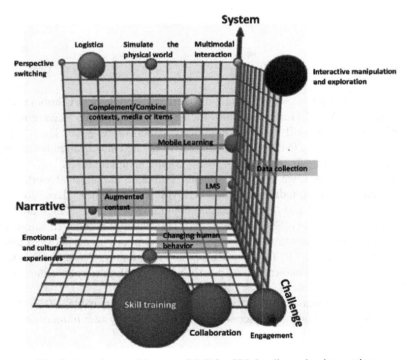

Fig. 5. Prevalence of themes of ILE for SRL by dimension immersion.

Cluster 2 (green bubbles): Mid-High Challenge, Mid-High Narrative, High System. Themes: Simulate the physical world (3,7%), Logistics (6%). TP: 9,7%

Cluster 5 (brown bubbles): Mid Challenge, Mid-High Narrative, Low System. Themes: Augmented context (3%), Emotional and cultural experiences (0,7%), Changing human behavior (5%). TP: 8,7%.

Cluster 1 (yellow bubbles): Low Challenge, Low Narrative, High System. Themes: Complement/Combine (6%), Emphasis (0%), Multimodal Interaction (2.2%). TP: 8.2%

Cluster 7 (new) (orange bubbles): Low Challenge, Mid-Low System, Low Narrative. Themes: LMS (1,5%), Mobile Learning (6%). TP: 7.5%.

Cluster 6 (light blue bubbles): Low Challenge, High Narrative, Mid-High System. Themes: Perspective switching (1,5%), Accessibility (0%), Seeing the invisible (0%). TP:1,5%.

This enables us to interpret the current existence and absence of research within the immersion cube for SRL (Fig. 6).

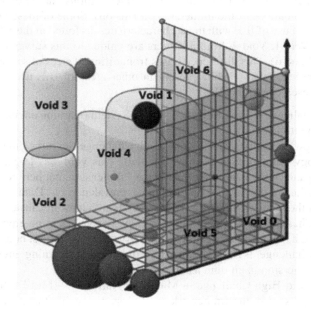

Fig. 6. Voids in research ILE for SRL.

The use of ILE studies for SRL has quite distinct prevalence differences regarding the overall use of immersive learning environments in general, provided by the reference framework (whose highest prevalence was in the clusters 5, 4, 2, & 1). In our data, focused on SRL there is greater prevalence of themes with High or Mid-High challenge-based immersion (clusters 2, 3 and 4), with a combined prevalence of 74,5%. Thus, unlike use of immersive learning environments in general, ILE use for SRL is strongly correlated with challenge-based immersion.

The remaining dimensions (system/narrative) do not exhibit a clear relationship. We find Low/Mid/High system-based immersion clusters in the most, middle, and least prevalent clusters, and similarly for narrative-based immersion.

6 Conclusions

We conclude that studies on ILE for SRL have increased recently, particularly in Higher Education and in general fields or languages. This highlights an opportunity to explore other educational contexts. Regarding approaches that combine the three immersion dimensions (Cluster 2), its combined prevalence is only 9,7% of all accounts, pointing towards the need for more research and practice reports combining the three dimensions of immersion when using ILE for SRL.

We considered the empty spaces of the representation of Fig. 2 to infer gaps in research contributions ("voids"). These can help researchers and pedagogical practitioners identify areas where innovative design interventions can be explored, tailored to different combinations of the immersion dimensions. Some of these voids reflect an overall absence of use of ILE with those characteristics, as found in the reference framework: Void 0, Void 1, Void 2, Void 3. Others are unique to this survey of ILE uses for SRL (Void 4, 5 and 6). This difference arises from different sizes of several use themes, reflecting approaches that – while present in other areas of ILE use – are not being exploited nor researched for SRL.

Void 0: Low Challenge + Low Narrative + Low System (learning environments that do not contemplate immersion).

Void 1: Mid-Low Narrative, Mid System, High Challenge (learning environments with some technology but significant learner agency). This void was larger in the framework, covering the entire span of the "challenge" dimension, but here restricted to only the "High" challenge dimension, due to higher prevalence of "Data collection" (mid challenge) and the new low challenge but mid-system themes in Cluster 7.

Void 2: High Challenge + High Narrative + Low System (learning environments with low tech, but high meaning and agency, such as role-playing games, board games, etc.).

Void 3: High Challenge + High Narrative + High System (learning environments that contemplate immersion in all dimensions).

Void 4 (new): Mid-High Challenge + Mid-High Narrative + Mid-High System. This void was also present in the framework but is less noticeable there due to their high prevalence of "Augmented context" accounts, unlike in our results. It suggests the need for more augmented context uses of ILE for SRL.

Void 5 (new): Mid Challenge + Low Narrative + Low System (learning environments with a moderate amount of challenge-based immersion, such as traditional learning activities, possibly this represents the lack of details in the descriptions of the themes "LMS" or "Mobile learning").

Void 6 (new): Low Challenge + Mid Narrative + entire span of System (this void is a consequence of the small dimension of themes in clusters 1, 2, 5 & 6, hence points the need for more research in their themes).

7 Final Thoughts

This work offers facets of how ILE have been employed for development of SRL skills. These environments have predominantly exploited approaches highly based in the Challenge dimension of immersion, where the learner takes an active role in the development of personal, social and motivational skills: "Skill training", "Collaboration", "Engagement" and "Interactive manipulation and exploration".

The opportunities for research and to innovate educational practices, partly stem from lack of accounts on ILE use in general, but partly originate in lack of accounts specifically for ILEs application to SRL (Emphasis, Accessibility, Seeing the Invisible) all highlighting potential pathways.

The paper presents as a limitation, restricted focus, in Phase 2, looking for both terms in the title and in the abstract, which may have excluded other potential works.

As future work we intend to carry out a comprehensive systematic review of the literature, considering various aspects of self-regulated learning (SRL) beyond the term itself, such as time management, planning, organization and much more. We plan to use additional search terms such as "SRL", "ILE" and others to ensure a complete search.

Acknowledgment. This work is financially supported by National Funds through FCT – Fundação para a Ciência e a Tecnologia, I.P., under the project UIDB/00194/2020. D. Pedrosa wishes to thank FCT and CIDTFF – Universidade de Aveiro, Portugal, for Stimulus of Scientific Employment – CEECIND/00986/2017 Individual Support 2017.

References

1. Pedrosa, D., Cravino, J., Morgado, L., Barreira, C.: Self-regulated learning in computer programming: strategies students adopted during an assignment. In: Allison, C., Morgado, L., Pirker, J., Beck, D., Richter, J., Gütl, C. (eds.) Immersive Learning Research Network, pp. 87–101. Springer International Publishing, Cham (2016)
2. Kramarski, B., Heaysman, O.: A conceptual framework and a professional development model for supporting teachers' "triple SRL–SRT processes" and promoting students' academic outcomes. Educ. Psychol. **56**, 298–311 (2021). https://doi.org/10.1080/00461520.2021.1985502
3. Panadero, E.: A review of self-regulated learning: six models and four directions for research. Front. Psychol. **8**, 422 (2017). https://doi.org/10.3389/fpsyg.2017.00422
4. Makransky, G., Petersen, G.B.: The cognitive affective model of immersive learning (CAMIL): a theoretical research-based model of learning in immersive virtual reality. Educ. Psychol. Rev. **33**, 937–958 (2021). https://doi.org/10.1007/s10648-020-09586-2
5. Makransky, G., Wismer, P., Mayer, R.E.: A gender matching effect in learning with pedagogical agents in an immersive virtual reality science simulation. J. Comput. Assist. Learn. **35**, 349–358 (2019). https://doi.org/10.1111/jcal.12335
6. Wagner, C., Liu, L.: Creating immersive learning experiences: a pedagogical design perspective. In: Hui, A., Wagner, C. (eds.) Creative and Collaborative Learning through Immersion, pp. 71–87. Springer International Publishing, Cham (2021)
7. Jiang, Y., Clarke-Midura, J., Baker, R.S., Paquette, L., Keller, B.: How immersive virtual environments foster self-regulated learning. In: Digital Technologies and Instructional Design

for Personalized Learning, pp. 28–54. IGI Global (2018). https://www.igi-global.com/cha pter/how-immersive-virtual-environments-foster-self-regulated-learning/www.igi-global. com/chapter/how-immersive-virtual-environments-foster-self-regulated-learning/199531

8. Makransky, G., Andreasen, N.K., Baceviciute, S., Mayer, R.E.: Immersive virtual reality increases liking but not learning with a science simulation and generative learning strategies promote learning in immersive virtual reality. J. Educ. Psychol. **113**, 719–735 (2021). https:// doi.org/10.1037/edu0000473

9. Meyer, O.A., Omdahl, M.K., Makransky, G.: Investigating the effect of pre-training when learning through immersive virtual reality and video: a media and methods experiment. Comput. Educ. **140**, 103603 (2019). https://doi.org/10.1016/j.compedu.2019.103603

10. Beck, D., Morgado, L., O'Shea, P.: Finding the gaps about uses of immersive learning environments: a survey of surveys. J. Univers. Comput. Sci. **26**(8), 1043–1073 (2020)

11. Agrawal, S., Simon, A., Bech, S., Bærentsen, K., Forchhammer, S.: Defining immersion: literature review and implications for research on audiovisual experiences. J. Audio Eng. Soc. **68**, 404–417 (2020). https://doi.org/10.17743/jaes.2020.0039

12. Dengel, A.: What is immersive learning? In: 2022 8th International Conference of the Immersive Learning Research Network (iLRN), pp. 1–5 (2022)

13. Nilsson, N.C., Nordahl, R., Serafin, S.: Immersion revisited: a review of existing definitions of immersion and their relation to different theories of presence. Hum. Technol. **12**, 108–134 (2016). https://doi.org/10.17011/ht/urn.201611174652

14. Fernandes, L., Morgado, L., Paredes, H., Coelho, A., Richter, J.: Immersive learning experiences for understanding complex systems. In: ILRN 2019 London – Workshop Long Short Paper Poster Demos SSRiP Proceedings of the Fifth Immersive Learning Research Network Conference, pp. 107–113 (2019). https://doi.org/10.3217/978-3-85125-657-4-11

15. Heaysman, O., Kramarski, B.: Supporting teachers' SRL beliefs and practices with immersive learning environments: evidence from a unique simulations-based program. In: 2021 7th International Conference of the Immersive Learning Research Network (iLRN), pp. 1–5. IEEE, Eureka, CA, USA (2021)

16. Hayes, D., Symonds, J.E., Harwell, T.A.: Preventing pollution: a scoping review of immersive learning environments and gamified systems for children and young people. J. Res. Technol. Educ. 1–19 (2022). https://doi.org/10.1080/15391523.2022.2107589

17. Pirker, J., Lesjak, I., Kopf, J., Kainz, A., Dini, A.: Immersive learning in real VR. In: Magnor, M., Sorkine-Hornung, A. (eds.) Real VR – Immersive Digital Reality, pp. 321–336. Springer International Publishing, Cham (2020)

18. Naul, E., Liu, M.: Why story matters: a review of narrative in serious games. J. Educ. Comput. Res. **58**, 687–707 (2020). https://doi.org/10.1177/0735633119859904

19. Abadia, R., Calvert, J., Tauseef, S.M.: Salient features of an effective immersive non-collaborative virtual reality learning environment. In: Proceedings of the 10th International Conference on Education Technology and Computers, pp. 268–278. Association for Computing Machinery, New York, NY, USA (2018)

20. Philippe, S., et al.: Multimodal teaching, learning and training in virtual reality: a review and case study. Virtual Real. Intell. Hardw. **2**, 421–442 (2020). https://doi.org/10.1016/j.vrih. 2020.07.008

21. Schlemmer, E.: Digital culture and qualitative methodologies in education. In: Schlemmer, E. (ed.) Oxford Research Encyclopedia of Education. Oxford University Press (2019). https:// doi.org/10.1093/acrefore/9780190264093.013.508

22. Pintrich, P.R.: A conceptual framework for assessing motivation and self-regulated learning in college students. Educ. Psychol. Rev. **16**, 385–407 (2004). https://doi.org/10.1007/s10648-004-0006-x

23. Zimmerman, B.J.: From cognitive modeling to self-regulation: a social cognitive career path. Educ. Psychol. **48**, 135–147 (2013). https://doi.org/10.1080/00461520.2013.794676

24. Panadero, E., Alonso-Tapia, J.: ¿Cómo autorregulan nuestros alumnos? Modelo de Zimmerman sobre estrategias de aprendizaje. An. Psicol. Ann. Psychol. **30**, 450–462 (2014). https://doi.org/10.6018/analesps.30.2.167221

25. Pedrosa, D., Cravino, J., Morgado, L., Barreira, C.: Self-regulated learning in higher education: strategies adopted by computer programming students when supported by the SimProgramming approach. Production **27**, e20162255 (2017). https://doi.org/10.1590/0103-6513.225516

26. Beck, D., Morgado, L., O'Shea, P.: Educational Practices and Strategies with Immersive Learning Environments: a Meta-analysis of Reviews for using the Metaverse (in press)

27. Kitchenham, B.A., Budgen, D., Brereton, P.: Evidence-Based Software Engineering and Systematic Reviews. Chapman and Hall/CRC (2015)

28. Pedrosa, D., Morgado, L., Beck, D.: Companion dataset for paper "Immersive Learning Environments for Self-Regulation of Learning: A Literature Review," https://zenodo.org/record/7568158 (2023)

29. Braun, V., Clarke, V.: Thematic analysis. In: Cooper, H., Camic, P.M., Long, D.L., Panter, A.T., Rindskopf, D., Sher, K.J. (eds.) APA Handbook of Research Methods in Psychology, vol 2: Research Designs: Quantitative, Qualitative, Neuropsychological, and Biological, pp. 57–71. American Psychological Association, Washington (2012)

Special Track: Immersive learning across Latin America: State of Research, Use Cases and Projects

Digital Twins, Metaverse, and Learning. Review and Proposal of Conceptual Framework

Gustavo Alberto Moreno López[✉] , Hernando Recaman Chaux ,
and Paula Andrea Molina Parra

Politécnico Colombiano Jaime Isaza Cadavid, Medellín, Colombia
{gamoreno,hrecaman,pamolina}@elpoli.edu.co

Abstract. Digital twins (DT) technology has advanced and is gaining momentum of applicability in different contexts. The metaverse enables immersive experiences that integrate the real world with the digital. Given the importance of DT in the metaverse, this article seeks to review the literature (between 2018–2022) on the articulation of DT, metaverse, and learning, and propose a conceptual framework towards Education 5.0. The review indicates few works in this regard and specifically in Latin American countries the research and application in educational contexts is insufficient. There is an interest in defining frameworks and articulating with other extended reality technologies. The possibilities offered by DT and the metaverse are wide, and that is why it is necessary to reduce the gap in this regard, with more research, projects, dissemination, and agreements. This study contributes to the investigation and projection of the DT, metaverse in learning scenarios, as well as to continue delving into frameworks or models under the Industry/Society 5.0 approach.

Keywords: Digital Twin · Metaverse · Learning · Framework · Education 5.0

1 Introduction

A DT refers to a virtual representation or copy of any entity, object or system (physical twin), and these are interconnected through real-time data exchange. In theory, a DT mimics the state of its physical twin in real time and vice versa. The DT can use simulation and Artificial Intelligence (AI) techniques to aid in decision-making. This is indicated by authors such as Yin et al. [1], that DT should be composed of three fundamental components: physical element, digital representation, and interconnections.

The concept of DT technology first appeared between 1991–1993, in David Gelernter's book Mirror World [2], imagining that software models mimic reality from the input of information from the physical world. Michael Grieves also introduced the concept in 2003 in the Product Lifecycle Management course at the University of Michigan, talking about a virtual product as a digital replica of the physical product and its connections, and already in 2011, he extends the term "Digital Twin" [3, 4]. In the preliminary version of NASA's technology roadmap in 2010 [5], the name "Digital Twin" (DT) appears for the first time.

© The Author(s), under exclusive license to Springer Nature Switzerland AG 2024
M.-L. Bourguet et al. (Eds.): iLRN 2023, CCIS 1904, pp. 515–532, 2024.
https://doi.org/10.1007/978-3-031-47328-9_37

DT can be applied in design, planning, real-time tracking or monitoring, optimization, predictive maintenance, asset management, remote access, security, among others. This makes it very useful in training and learning scenarios.

Growth in DT implementation is expected, a market worth $73.5 billion by 2027, according to MarketsandMarkets [6]. These advances in DT technologies allow reshaping the physical world into a virtual digital space and provide technical support to build the Metaverse [7]. The Metaverse is a digital immersive environment in which people interact using immersive technologies and is shaping a new way of interacting and socializing [8]. DTs are intimately related to the Metaverse and present diverse forms of expression. As reiterated by [9], DTs can play an important role in the metaverse, where the hypothetical scenario can be successfully executed by providing real data to the components of the metauniverse.

The objective of this article is to review the articulation of DT in the Metaverse and its uses in learning. In addition, areas of application are identified, and a conceptual framework towards Society/Education 5.0 is proposed. This will allow further exploration of possibilities for the future, whether in application in educational contexts, research, or development of extension projects.

To address this, a literature review process is carried out. Subsequently, the illustrative framework framed in the era of the Metaverse and Industry/Society 5.0 is proposed.

The article continues to be organized as follows: Sect. 2 presents the review, starting with concepts of DT, metaverse, the literature review process, and the results of the literature review. Section 3 expands on DT and articulation with the metaverse, the evolutionary path, areas of application of DT in education, challenges, and future lines of research. Section 4 proposes a conceptual framework, and finally the conclusions.

2 Review

2.1 Digital Twins (DT) Concept

Several concepts related to digital twins are found in the literature. In [10], DTs attempt to build a "complete and independent mirror" of the physical world in the digital world through digital means.

DTs are used to create agents similar to real objects in the virtual world and predict outcomes through simulations of situations that could occur in real life. It is used to maintain properties and states throughout the life cycle of a digital twin and predict what will happen in the future. With that, the physical world can be optimized and used in industrial, social, and manufacturing issues to improve operational performance and business processes significantly [11]. In the Metaverse, the avatar is an important element and has a similar meaning to the digital twin and the digital self in the virtual world. Conceptually, the digital twin is different in that it objectively interprets the real self, while the digital self interprets it subjectively [11].

Authors such as Zhang et al. [12], indicate that DT is a technology that integrates multiphysics, multiscale and multidisciplinary properties. At the same time, it has the characteristics of real-time synchronization, faithful mapping, and high fidelity. It can realize the interaction and integration of the physical world and the information world.

According to Digital Twin Consortium [13], it is defined as a virtual representation of real-world entities and processes, synchronized at a specific frequency and fidelity. And it contemplates:

- DT systems transform business by accelerating holistic understanding, optimal decision making, and effective action.
- DTs use historical and real-time data to represent the past and present and simulate predicted futures.
- DTs are results-driven, tailored to use cases, integration-driven, data-driven, guided by domain knowledge, and implemented in IT/OT (information technology and operational technology) systems.

2.2 Metaverse Concept

Authors such as Yang et al. [10], indicate that the Metaverse connects the real and virtual worlds and is the carrier of human digital survival and migration.

The Metaverse represents an idea of a hypothetical "parallel virtual world" that represents ways of living and working in virtual cities as an alternative to the smart cities of the future [14]. The Metaverse or post-reality universe is a perpetual and persistent multi-user environment that combines physical reality and digital virtuality [15]. Dr. Yu Yuan, cited by [16] refers to the Metaverse as a type of experience in which the external world is perceived by users as a universe built on digital technologies as a different universe ("Virtual Reality"), a digital extension of our current universe ("Augmented Reality" or "Mixed Reality"), or a digital counterpart of our current universe ("Digital Twin"). Named after the universe, a metaverse must be persistent and must be massive, complete, immersive, and self-consistent. Described as "meta", a metaverse must be ultra-realistic, accessible, ubiquitous, and can be decentralized.

2.3 Literature Review Process

The intention of the literature review was to identify works that integrate DT, metaverses, and their application in learning. In addition, within this exploration, to identify proposals or authors at the Latin American level. The following criteria were considered for the search: date range between 2018–2022 (last five years), databases (IEEE, Scopus, Web of Science and Science Direct), journal publications, English language, words (digital twins AND metaverse AND (learning OR education)), and then an exhaustive review of DT, metaverse, applied in an educational context and the detail of the contribution (model, framework, concept, etc.).

In the search process, 116 articles were initially obtained. One of the main thematic areas of classification of the articles is computer science and engineering, and among the countries of the greatest origin of articles is China. In Latin American countries, see Table 1, there are articles from Colombia, Ecuador, and Mexico.

Other articles with the search criteria (digital twin AND education), Latin American authors such as Martinez et al. [23], from Mexico, who detail the automation pyramid as a builder of a complete digital twin, through a case study (didactic manufacturing system). Another work proposed in [24], with authors from Chile and Mexico, contemplates a

Table 1. Articles from Latin America.

Author	Affiliation / country	Area of Application / Contribution
[17]	Universidad Politécnica Estatal del Carchi / Ecuador, Cooperative University of Colombia, Universidad Autónoma de Nariño / Pasto (Colombia)	Smart factory / Framework for a VR system as a proposal for the creation of online multi-user 3D virtual environment projects There is a relationship with learning. University students participate in prototype testing
[18]	International Iberoamerican University / Mexico **But** the author is from India	Energy / Description of digital technologies such different stages of energy. Also, digital as IoT, artificial intelligence (AI), edge computing, blockchain, big data, and their implementation in the twins in smart grid modeling, and virtual power plants with Metaverse. There is no relationship with learning
[19]	European Institutions / One author is of Italian and Argentine nationality One author is Colombian	Energy sciences / Immersive games to learn about energy There is a relationship with learning
[20]	University of Medellín / A Colombian author	Health-medicine / A benchmark for the realization of a holistic DT model of human health and well-being for real-world medical applications. There is no relationship with learning
[21]	Instituto Tecnológico de Tijuana / México	Freight transportation / An integrated decision-making model is proposed to prioritize alternatives for measuring freight fluidity. There is no relationship with learning. Does not include DT
[22]	University of North Carolina at Charlotte / **But** there is an author of Brazilian origin	Production and supply chain system / A framework integrating production and logistics processes that employs a machine learning-enabled digital twin to ensure adaptive production scheduling and resilient supply chain operations. There is no relationship with learning

study to identify the factors that explain the acceptance of Industry 4.0 technologies by technical students in rural areas.

Continuing with the review protocol, of the 116 articles, 31 were discarded because the title, abstract or keywords did not refer to Metaverse, DT and learning. This left 85 articles, which were subsequently discarded 2 that were not from journals, 4 duplicates and 70 after a more detailed review. Finally, only 9 articles that raise something related to DT, metaverse, and applied in learning context, are left for a more detailed analysis. This procedure is explained in Fig. 1 below.

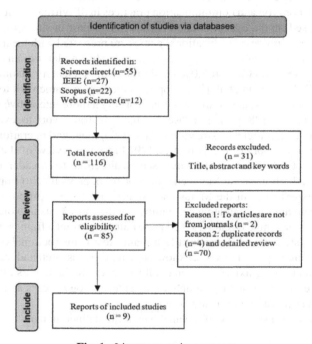

Fig. 1. Literature review process.

2.4 Results of the Review of Defined Articles

As a result of the analysis of the defined articles, it is indicated that there are few works in Latin America that articulate DT, metaverses with learning, or in educational contexts. Of the 9 articles analyzed, there are two works of Latin American participation [17, 19], 5 are frameworks, 4 works are prototypes, 3 proposals are for general purposes in education, and others for specific educational contexts (medicine, nature, energy, Smart factoring, aviation, and control engineering). It is appreciated that there is an interest in defining frameworks and articulating with other extended reality technologies. It is also found in the literature review that there is still little articulation of proposals with industry 5.0 or citizenship 5.0, where user-centered solutions are focused.

In [25], students' perception of metaverse application in the United Arab Emirates (UAE) for medical-educational purposes is assessed. The study finds user satisfaction as an essential determinant of users' intention to use the metaverse. In [26], the potential demand for digital forest recreation in the metaverse was analyzed from the perspective of university students who are potential users. The findings of the study revealed their preferences for outdoor adventure and a digital twin nature in the metaverse. These findings suggested that this digital forest recreation could influence users and their interactions with nature in the future by providing a new opportunity for people to learn about nature and experience a DT of the existing nature in the metaverse. In [17] the objective is to improve collaboration and communication practices in 3D virtual worlds with VR and metaverse focused on the educational and productive sector in smart factories. In [19] two interactive and immersive educational games are presented with the aim of popularizing the field of energy storage: a multi-user multi-scale simulator of an electricity grid in Mixed Reality, Smart Grid MR 2.0 and a digital twin of a battery manufacturing pilot line, SIMUBAT 4.0. Dahan et al. [27], propose a metaverse framework to be applied in e-Learning environments, and to make online learning a more interactive and enjoyable process. Alsalehr et al. [28] propose a "ReImagine Lab" framework to leverage DTs and extended reality technologies to streamline the development and operation of hands-on, virtual, and remote laboratories. Tlili et al. [29] Present a review of the Metaverse in education, projecting a roadmap of future research directions to consider and investigate to enhance the adoption of the Metaverse in education, as well as to improve learning and teaching experiences in the Metaverse. Siyaev and Jo [30] proposed a metaverse for education and aircraft maintenance training for Boeing 737 using voice interactions with virtual objects in mixed reality. In [31], the authors present a framework of the Edu-Metaverse ecosystem, which consists of four main axes: 1) instructional design (ID) and performance technology (PT) axis; 2) knowledge axis; 3) research and technology axis; and 4) talent and training axis. Common to all four axes are the factors of: 1) infrastructure, commerce, industry, and communication; 2) technology access and equity; and 3) user rights, data security and privacy policy.

Table 2 presents a summary of the analysis of the defined items.

Table 2. Summary analysis of defined studies.

Author	Area of application	Form of DT integration with Metaverse	Contribution
[31]	In General,	Metavirsity (Meta-University)- higher education university that has been recreated as a digital twin using XR technologies	Generalities, framework for the Edu-Metaverse ecosystem
[25]	Medical education University students participate	Users in the metaverse will develop content in the DTs	Conceptual framework for investigating intention to use the metaverse. Study of perception of metaverse use

(continued)

Table 2. (*continued*)

Author	Area of application	Form of DT integration with Metaverse	Contribution
[26]	Nature-forest University students participate	Digital twin of nature	Study of the demand for digital forest recreation in the metaverse. Contributed empirically to identify opportunities and challenges for user-centered development in the metaverse
[17]	Smart factory	The real environment can be replicated in a virtual world through DT	Framework for a VR system for the creation of online multi-user 3D virtual environment projects Contemplates prototyping and application testing with users
[19]	Energy Sciences / Master students of Universite de Picardie Jules Verne (Amiens, France)	Digital twin of a pilot lithium-ion battery manufacturing line	Immersive games to learn about energy. Prototypes
[27]	In General,	Digital twin to simulate, duplicate and visualize augmented and virtual reality to get the benefit of all layers and capabilities of the metaverse	Framework for virtual learning environments
[28]	Control engineering	Remote and virtual laboratories are DT XR is used to allow a higher level of interaction and visualization than the DT representation offers	DT and XR laboratory framework Prototype and usability study of the system
[29]	In General,	DTs are virtual replicas of physical environments that are used synchronously	A bibliometric analysis of the metaverse in education
[30]	Aviation	Digital twin aircraft to interact with MR	Prototyping with testing of the aircraft maintenance metaverse, creating a mixed reality digital venue for Boeing 737 maintenance education enhanced with a voice interaction module on Microsoft HoloLens 2 smart glasses

3   Digital Twins and Metaverse

With the improvements in DT and extended reality, the concept of metaverse is becoming a very popular topic. The following are some considerations indicated in the literature on the importance and articulated work of DT with the metaverse.

Cyber-physical systems (CPS) will be the foundations of the Metaverse in the future, particularly in Industry 4.0 and 5.0. On the other hand, DTs play a similar role in both CPSs and Metaverse platforms [32].

DT technologies and the Metaverse continue to emerge as key technologies and important tools for improving efficiency, effectively playing their roles in model design, data collection, analysis, prediction, and simulation. They help to promote digital industrialization, industrial digitization, and the integration and development of digital and real economies [10]. The authors Yang et al. [10], state that DTs and Metaverse can perform real-time modeling, monitoring, analysis, prediction, control adjustment and some degree of transformation on physical objects by combining machine learning, IoT, 5G, and other emerging technologies. DT can assist in the development of industry knowledge, analysis and prediction of general industry trends, and the generation of forward-looking recommendations. It has the potential to significantly improve complex problems in manufacturing, such as industrial chain coordination and comprehensive urban governance, as well as change the operational mode of various industries.

With DT and other emerging innovative technologies, such as Artificial Intelligence, Big Data and IoT, the Metaverse has the potential to redefine city design activities and service delivery to increase urban efficiency, accountabilities, and quality performance by providing rich data sets and advanced computational understanding of human behavior [14]. This is reiterated by authors such as Stacchio et al. [33], indicating that thanks to advances in artificial intelligence, Big Data analysis and the Internet of Things paved the way for the use of DTs as technologies to "twin" (the pair or twin) the life of a physical entity in different fields, ranging from industry to healthcare. At the same time, the advent of Extended Reality (XR) in industrial and consumer electronics has provided novel paradigms that can be leveraged to visualize and interact with DTs. XR technologies can support person-to-person interactions for remote training and assistance and could transform DTs into collaborative intelligence tools. For example, in [30], moving towards metaverses in aircraft maintenance, it is indicated that mixed reality (MR) creates enormous opportunities for interaction with virtual aircraft (digital twins) that provide a near-real experience.

With DT technology, it supports simulation and management optimization, but also establishes an independent virtual world where a more imaginative, creative realm such as the metaverse might be emerging [34]. Lv et al. [35], indicate that the metaverse, which is parallel to the physical world, needs a mature and secure DT technology in addition to parallel intelligence to enable it to evolve autonomously. Blockchain is required to secure the digital mapping process, VR to visualize and interact with the virtual world and DT, it is necessary to synchronize data such as the state and attributes of physical entities in real time through the Internet of Things and make predictions using artificial intelligence. In Dwivedi et al. [36], indicate that the digital twin, a replica of real operations in virtual form, helps organizations to minimize costs, accidents, optimize planning and resource allocation. The metaverse also incorporates DT and other interface functions. Academics can analyze the complementary requirements of the digital twin and other organizational requirements that need to be integrated into the metaverse platform for seamless operation and superior customer experience. The DT is one of the fundamental building blocks of the metaverse. As reiterated by Huynh-The et al. [37], DTs function as the gateway for users to enter and enjoy services in the virtual world by creating exact replicas of reality, including structure and functionality. For example, technicians can handle 3D representations of complex systems in multilevel sophistications (i.e., descriptive, informative, predictive, comprehensive, and autonomous) for a wide range of purposes, such as technical training and commercial customization. In Lv et al. [7], it is indicated that the construction of the metaverse using DT can be at different scales (from micro to macro), states (solid, liquid, gaseous, plasma and other uncertain states) and interpersonal (friends, partners, and family) and social (ethics, morals, and law) relationships. Figure 2 below illustrates the projection of DT at different scales.

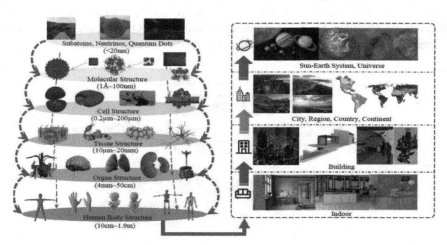

Fig. 2. DT projection at different scales [7]. The figure is posted with permission of the author (e-mail April 12, 2023).

The DT and the metaverse are enablers of Industry 5.0. Industry 5.0 in addition to the cyber-physical system, it has a human-centric systems approach. In Industry 5.0, DT technologies provide a powerful online emulation tool to support the (re)design, (re)configuration, commissioning (or decommissioning) and optimized operation of human-centered manufacturing systems [16]. Authors such as Yao et al. [38], indicate the potential of DT as analysis and evaluation, predictive diagnostics, and performance optimization. The emergence of DT offers exciting possibilities for real-time simulation of the entire product life cycle. Through interaction and collaboration of the virtual model and the physical object, the virtual model can be synchronized and optimized with the physical object, and the physical object can be dynamically adjusted according to direct instructions from the virtual model.

3.1 Evolutionary Path of the DTs and the Metaverse

Metaverse is a much more complex concept than DT, and it is generally stated that DT is a subset or one of the enabling technologies for Metaverse. DT was originated in the industrialization of complex product development and is moving towards socialization and globalization, while Metaverse originated in the gaming and entertainment industry and is expanding from globalization to socialization and industrialization. Although both Metaverse and DT are concerned with the connection and interaction between the real world and the virtual world, the essential difference between the two is that they have completely different starting points. Metaverse is directly oriented towards humans, while DT is technology (things) oriented first. However, both complement each other [38]. Other authors such as Lu et al. [39] indicate that the scientific theory behind metaverses and DTs is parallel intelligence. This parallel intelligence is based on parallel system theory, which is a scientific research paradigm for modeling, analysis, management, and control of complex systems. Parallel system theory consists of three main parts: artificial systems, computational experiments, and parallel execution. Figure 3 illustrates the Qingdao Academy of Intelligent Industries (QAII) operation framework scheme for a parallel factory in the metaverse.

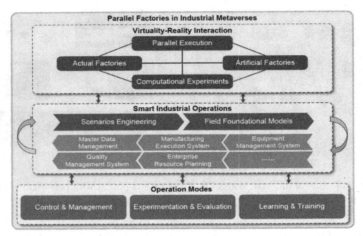

Fig. 3. Framework for a parallel factory in the metaverse [39]. The figure is posted with permission of the author (e-mail April 12, 2023).

3.2 Examples of Application Areas

Table 3 below presents a summary of DT and metaverse use cases, which can be projected to have an impact in educational contexts, either as a complement or to facilitate learning, to favor or initiate the acquisition of skills, among others.

Other application areas, such as: Agriculture, Smart city management, Real estate industry, Transportation systems (aerospace, maritime, land), Defense, Agriculture, Food, Infrastructure in general (architecture, engineering, construction & operation), Natural resources, Use cases in finance, Process and asset management in companies/industries, Telecommunications/networks – smart environments, among others. In the field of telecommunications, there are scenarios involving different networks, applications of the Internet of Things (smart farms, smart homes or buildings, smart city, among others). For example, in the application of internal telecommunications regulations in homes. The network provides a solid basis for building the world of "digital twins". At the same time, in the face of increasing business types, scale and complexity,

Table 3. Examples of use cases.

Area of application	Authors
Health. Medicine, body care, mental health	[40, 41]
Culture. History	[42]
Nature-forest	[26]
Energy systems	[19, 43]
Supply chain management	[44]
Geotechnics	[45]
Smart factory	[39]
Aircraft maintenance	[30]
Wisdom manufacturing as industrial metaverse for industry/society 5.0	[38]
Marketing	[46]
Fintech	[47]
Music, concerts	[48]

the network also needs to use DT technology to look beyond the physical network for solutions.

3.3 Implications on Learning

There are several positions put forward by authors on the implications of using DT and metaverses for learning, such as, for example:

- The Metaverse offers enhanced immersive experiences and a more interactive learning experience for students in educational and learning environments [25].
- Metaverse applied in virtual learning environments, will make it more interactive and enjoyable process [27].
- Incorporating extended reality into digital representation allows for more interaction with the object while allowing students and instructors to collaborate with each other [28].
- According to various authors and studies, they show that the implementation of the Metaverse can expand educational opportunities to explore environments that have historically been inaccessible due to space, time, and cost barriers, thus solving real-world problems in virtual worlds [29].
- Training supported in the metaverse has the potential to aid in the transfer of skills in a risk-free environment. In addition, to enable multi-site learning and collaborative work [19].
- The metaverse provides an enormous potential to bring the physical world to life in the classroom using DT and a new style of immersive teaching [36].
- DT technology has significantly positive influences on the effect of ubiquitous learning. The authors Zhang et al. [49], state that there are important references to build

a personalized learning space of DT, facilitate the construction of digital campuses, accelerate the deep integration of intelligent technologies in education reform, and promote personalized learning for students.

- DT technology can increase motivation to study and enhance learning when properly implemented [50].

3.4 Challenges and Future Research Directions

Facing the development and projection of the digital twins and in general of the metaverse, several challenges are contemplated, such as:

- Interoperability between solutions, devices, applications, among others. It is necessary to advance in the respective standardization of the entire metaverse ecosystem.
- Ease of development or configurations. To achieve a wide massification and appropriation of these technologies, it is required that the platforms for application development be low-code or no-code.
- Integrity of the solutions. Aspects related to security, protection, privacy, availability, and resilience must be maintained at a certain level. In terms of privacy, for example, how to regulate data in immersive environments.
- Product or solution costs. Possibly as the market evolves, prices will become more affordable for people in general.
- Strengthening digital competences. It is a permanent issue in acquiring the knowledge, skills, and attitudes to use technologies properly, safely and with appropriation in various contexts, business, education, among others.
- Availability of applications or solutions. Making the metaverse persistent, with guaranteed availability, backup options and how to access them.
- Governance of the metaverse. Who and how the metaverse will be controlled.
- Economy in the metaverse: What economy will govern, who controls them, types and exchange of currencies.
- Other challenges in the metaverse such as addiction, keeping people from getting sick, and ethical issues.
- With digital twins, there is an urgent need for intelligent fault diagnosis technologies that integrate signal analysis, modeling, and knowledge processing.
- Extensive information about the product, service, or process under study (life cycle, design specifications, performance details, etc.) needs to be collected, so that the simulation model can deliver more complex predictions.
- Achieve that the virtual representation of real-world entities and processes are synchronized at a specific frequency and fidelity. Based for example on IoT data, and implemented digital models, and so on.
- To have digital models with a certain degree of accuracy and reliability, so as to guarantee the success of the implementations (mainly to complete physical twins in the real world). To this end, the use of AI has been projected to support the creation of DT systems and in predictive models for analysis and simulation.
- DTs require them to be adaptive and flexible, as for example products in real life can be affected by various factors such as temperature, force, etc.
- In the educational context, in addition to the technological challenges, there are the pedagogical ones.

Future lines of research include the following:

- Articulation of VR, AR, MR, and lifelogging scenarios with digital twins.
- The articulation of digital twin standards initiatives with those of metaverse.
- The integration of supporting technologies such as blockchain, AI, telecom networks such as 5G/6G, cloud and edge computing.
- Use of machine learning methods to create DTs and predictive and simulation models.
- Extending immersive experiences with haptic technologies and more intuitive interactions.
- Analyze and apply instructional design approaches or others for proper application in teaching/learning processes.
- Analyze the efficacy and regulatory impacts of immersive technologies and the metaverse in educational environments [51]. Topics for continuing to expand on the metaverse and the future of education such as computing and communications technologies, platforms, pedagogies, theoretical frameworks, ecological structure, design principles, evaluation, and various challenges and barriers (access, ethics, privacy, and data management).
- Deepen the application of lifelogging in Metaverse education [29].
- Development of inclusive metaverse solutions (e.g., for people with different needs) and analysis of their impact.
- Metaverse architectures.
- Others proposed by Chang et al. [52], such as Perceptual Realization, Code of Ethics, Balance Between Virtual and Reality, Limited Hardware – energy consumption.
- Ali et al. [53], also pose subject as Energy-Efficient and Green Metaverse, Digital Twin Edge Network, Communications and Protocol Design, security, Intelligent Blockchain.

4 Proposal for a Conceptual Framework towards Industry/Society/Education 5.0

The metaverse and DTs, in conjunction with the advance of various technologies, will have a greater impact on Industry/Society 5.0. In the vision of Industry 5.0, in addition to efficiency and productivity as the sole objectives, the role and contribution of industry to society are strengthened and enable smart, resilient, sustainable, and human-centered solutions [38]. Society 5.0 envisions revolutionizing not only industry through IT integration, but also human living spaces and habits. The Society 5.0 vision is characterized by four parallel concepts, namely "a human-centered society", "merging cyberspace with physical space", "a knowledge-intensive society" and "a data-driven society" [16]. The transformation of industry can impact society, and vice versa, and these in turn can impact education and students, that is why in this proposal we also talk about Education/student 5.0. This 5.0 education is characterized by being: student-centered, intelligent learning, involved with reality, life wellbeing and social problem solving, empowered by technology and high immersive experiences.

The conceptual framework is proposed as an ecosystem focused on industry, society, and education 5.0, Fig. 4. In this education 5.0 route, the central axis is humans (in this case the student) and there is a high interaction of the real world with the digital world, enabling extensive experiences (immersive, communicative, collaborative, creative, among others) to support the teaching/learning process. The real world is part of a universe or several universes, from our planet earth (with all its living elements, physical products, environments, etc.), to the moon or other planets. The digital world involves different metaverse scenarios (mirror world, VR, MR, AR, lifelogging) and other supporting technologies (IoT, NFT, data analytics and visualization, blockchain, AI, virtual learning environments, among others). With digital twins, a virtual representation of the real world is made, IoT technologies allow to collect data, AI will support in the construction of the digital model, analysis, and predictions, and XR technologies, for example, will allow to be able to interact or visualize. In this scenario of education 5.0, intelligent solutions are designed with students as the central axis, which with the support of these technologies that converge the real world with the virtual world, will help them in their training process, with a vision of sustainability and resilience. The data provided by the context, the users, the use of products or applications, will support the respective feedback or to evaluate the impact. The framework is presented in this way to emphasize that we are part of a universe, that there is an interaction between the real and virtual worlds, where students are at the center of the solutions, and we are moving towards an era of the metaverse and Industry/Society 5.0, with options to build parallel universes. Various aspects of the educational context, such as pedagogical and other aspects, will have to consider this evolution towards Industry/Society/Education 5.0.

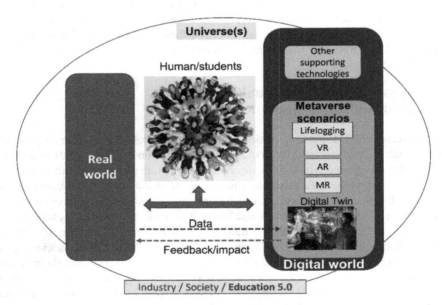

Fig. 4. Illustrative Framework on the 5.0 education route.

5 Conclusions

Given the technological progress and importance of DT and how it contributes to the construction of the metaverse, and the implications for learning, this article presents a review of contributions according to the literature. This was done with the purpose of continuing with the exploration and projection of applications. In addition, a framework was provided under the approach of the evolution to Industry/Society 5.0, and the concept of education 5.0 is added, which allows on the one hand the design of user-centered experiences, i.e., the student, and continue with the research and creation of models in this regard. The University must be attentive and project itself into the era of the Metaverse and Industry/Society 5.0.

Digital twins are important in the construction of the metaverse, bringing the real world to life. XR technologies will enable interaction and visualization with the digital twins. In this scenario, a broader convergence of the real and virtual worlds can be provided, for enriching experiences, more interaction or intelligent and relevant solutions that seek to have a holistic view, optimize processes, or strengthen the acquisition of knowledge or skills, simulate possible scenarios, and make the respective feedbacks in industrial, societal, and educational contexts,

There is undoubtedly much research, development, and application work to be done on the topic of digital twins and the metaverse, and specifically in the educational context. Advance in the exploration of use cases and evaluation of the impact on learning supported with digital twins and metaverse technologies. Review on the various platforms, devices, instructional design approaches, pedagogies, theories, evaluation, among others. In the case of accessibility and for it to be of massive use, it will be required that the platforms to develop metaverse solutions for education be very simple or without code. In future work, it is expected to review and deepen in tools and platforms for the construction of DT and Metaverse. Investigate in depth the application in different areas (such as telecommunications, and administration, among others). Realize a metaverse prototype that integrates DT with extended reality (XR) technologies. Review, deepen or improve the proposed framework.

References

1. Yin, Y., Zheng, P., Li, C., Wang, L.: A state-of-the-art survey on augmented reality-assisted digital twin for futuristic human-centric industry transformation. Robot. Comput.-Integr. Manuf. **81**, 102515 (2023). https://doi.org/10.1016/j.rcim.2022.102515
2. Gelernter, D.H.: Mirror Worlds: or the Day Software Puts the Universe in a Shoebox...How It Will Happen and What It Will Mean. Oxford University Press, New York (1993)
3. Grieves, M.: Virtually Perfect: Driving Innovative and Lean Products through Product Lifecycle Management. Space Coast Press, Cocoa Beach, Florida (2011)
4. Grieves, M.: Digital twin: manufacturing excellence through virtual factory replication. White Paper **1**, 7 (2014)
5. National Aeronautics and Space Administration (NASA): DRAFT Modeling, Simulation, Information Technology and Processing. Technology Area 11 input. https://www.nasa.gov/pdf/501321main_TA11-MSITP-DRAFT-Nov2010-A1.pdf (2010)
6. MarketsandMarketsate: Digital Twin Market (2023)

7. Lv, Z., Xie, S., Li, Y., Shamim Hossain, M., El Saddik, A.: Building the metaverse by digital twins at all scales, state, relation. Virtual Reality Intell. Hardware. **4**, 459–470 (2022). https://doi.org/10.1016/j.vrih.2022.06.005

8. Zallio, M., Clarkson, P.J.: Designing the metaverse: a study on inclusion, diversity, equity, accessibility and safety for digital immersive environments. Telematics Inform. **75**, 101909 (2022). https://doi.org/10.1016/j.tele.2022.101909

9. Lv, Z., Shang, W.-L., Guizani, M.: Impact of digital twins and metaverse on cities: history, current situation, and application perspectives. Appl. Sci. **12**, 12820 (2022). https://doi.org/10.3390/app122412820

10. Yang, B., Yang, S., Lv, Z., Wang, F., Olofsson, T.: Application of digital twins and metaverse in the field of fluid machinery pumps and fans: a review. Sensors. **22**, 9294 (2022). https://doi.org/10.3390/s22239294

11. Park, S.-M., Kim, Y.-G.: A Metaverse: taxonomy, components, applications, and open challenges. IEEE Access. **10**, 4209–4251 (2022). https://doi.org/10.1109/ACCESS.2021.3140175

12. Zhang, R., Wang, F., Cai, J., Wang, Y., Guo, H., Zheng, J.: Digital twin and its applications: a survey. Int. J. Adv. Manuf. Technol. **123**, 4123–4136 (2022). https://doi.org/10.1007/s00170-022-10445-3

13. Digital Twin Consortium: Digital Twin: https://www.digitaltwinconsortium.org/ (2023)

14. Allam, Z., Sharifi, A., Bibri, S.E., Jones, D.S., Krogstie, J.: The metaverse as a virtual form of smart cities: opportunities and challenges for environmental, economic, and social sustainability in urban futures. Smart Cities. **5**, 771–801 (2022). https://doi.org/10.3390/smartcities5030040

15. Mourtzis, D., Panopoulos, N., Angelopoulos, J., Wang, B., Wang, L.: Human centric platforms for personalized value creation in metaverse. J. Manuf. Syst. **65**, 653–659 (2022). https://doi.org/10.1016/j.jmsy.2022.11.004

16. Leng, J., et al.: Industry 5.0: prospect and retrospect. J. Manuf. Syst. **65**, 279–295 (2022). https://doi.org/10.1016/j.jmsy.2022.09.017

17. Alpala, L.O., Quiroga-Parra, D.J., Torres, J.C., Peluffo-Ordóñez, D.H.: Smart factory using virtual reality and online multi-user: towards a metaverse for experimental frameworks. Appl. Sci. **12**, 6258 (2022). https://doi.org/10.3390/app12126258

18. Singh, R., Akram, S.V., Gehlot, A., Buddhi, D., Priyadarshi, N., Twala, B.: Energy system 4.0: digitalization of the energy sector with inclination towards sustainability. Sensors **22**, 6619 (2022). https://doi.org/10.3390/s22176619

19. Franco, A.A., et al.: From battery manufacturing to smart grids: towards a metaverse for the energy sciences**. Batteries Supercaps. **6**, e202200369 (2023). https://doi.org/10.1002/batt.202200369

20. Al-Zyoud, I., Laamarti, F., Ma, X., Tobón, D., El Saddik, A.: Towards a machine learning-based digital twin for non-invasive human bio-signal fusion. Sensors **22**, 9747 (2022). https://doi.org/10.3390/s22249747

21. Deveci, M., Gokasar, I., Castillo, O., Daim, T.: Evaluation of Metaverse integration of freight fluidity measurement alternatives using fuzzy Dombi EDAS model. Comput. Ind. Eng. **174**, 108773 (2022). https://doi.org/10.1016/j.cie.2022.108773

22. Greis, N.P., Nogueira, M.L., Rohde, W.: Towards learning-enabled digital twin with augmented reality for resilient production scheduling. IFAC-PapersOnLine. **55**, 1912–1917 (2022). https://doi.org/10.1016/j.ifacol.2022.09.678

23. Martinez, E.M., Ponce, P., Macias, I., Molina, A.: Automation pyramid as constructor for a complete digital twin, case study: a didactic manufacturing system. Sensors **21**, 4656 (2021). https://doi.org/10.3390/s21144656

24. Castillo-Vergara, M., Álvarez-Marín, A., Villavicencio Pinto, E., Valdez-Juárez, L.E.: Technological acceptance of industry 4.0 by students from rural areas. Electronics. **11**, 2109 (2022). https://doi.org/10.3390/electronics11142109

25. Almarzouqi, A., Aburayya, A., Salloum, S.A.: Prediction of user's intention to use metaverse system in medical education: a hybrid sem-ml learning approach. IEEE Access **10**, 43421–43434 (2022). https://doi.org/10.1109/ACCESS.2022.3169285

26. Jaung, W.: Digital forest recreation in the metaverse: opportunities and challenges. Technol. Forecast. Soc. Chang. **185**, 122090 (2022). https://doi.org/10.1016/j.techfore.2022.122090

27. Dahan, N.A., Al-Razgan, M., Al-Laith, A., Alsoufi, M.A., Al-Asaly, M.S., Alfakih, T.: Metaverse framework: a case study on e-learning environment (ELEM). Electronics **11**, 1616 (2022). https://doi.org/10.3390/electronics11101616

28. Alsaleh, S., Tepljakov, A., Kose, A., Belikov, J., Petlenkov, E.: ReImagine lab: bridging the gap between hands-on, virtual and remote control engineering laboratories using digital twins and extended reality. IEEE Access **10**, 89924–89943 (2022). https://doi.org/10.1109/ACCESS.2022.3199371

29. Tlili, A., et al.: Is Metaverse in education a blessing or a curse: a combined content and bibliometric analysis. Smart Learn. Environ. **9**, 24 (2022). https://doi.org/10.1186/s40561-022-00205-x

30. Siyaev, A., Jo, G.-S.: Towards aircraft maintenance metaverse using speech interactions with virtual objects in mixed reality. Sensors **21**, 2066 (2021). https://doi.org/10.3390/s21062066

31. Wang, M., Yu, H., Bell, Z., Chu, X.: Constructing an edu-metaverse ecosystem: a new and innovative framework. IEEE Trans. Learn. Technol. **15**, 685–696 (2022). https://doi.org/10.1109/TLT.2022.3210828

32. Khalaj, O., et al.: Metaverse and AI digital twinning of 42SiCr steel alloys. Mathematics **11**, 4 (2022). https://doi.org/10.3390/math11010004

33. Stacchio, L., Angeli, A., Marfia, G.: Empowering digital twins with extended reality collaborations. Virtual Reality Intell. Hardware **4**, 487–505 (2022). https://doi.org/10.1016/j.vrih.2022.06.004

34. Shi, Y., Gao, Y., Luo, Y., Hu, J.: Fusions of industrialisation and digitalisation (FID) in the digital economy: industrial system digitalisation, digital technology industrialisation, and beyond. J. Dig. Econ. **1**, 73–88 (2022). https://doi.org/10.1016/j.jdec.2022.08.005

35. Lv, Z., Qiao, L., Li, Y., Yuan, Y., Wang, F.-Y.: BlockNet: beyond reliable spatial digital twins to parallel metaverse. Patterns **3**, 100468 (2022). https://doi.org/10.1016/j.patter.2022.100468

36. Dwivedi, Y.K., et al.: Metaverse beyond the hype: multidisciplinary perspectives on emerging challenges, opportunities, and agenda for research, practice and policy. Int. J. Inf. Manage. **66**, 102542 (2022). https://doi.org/10.1016/j.ijinfomgt.2022.102542

37. Huynh-The, T., Pham, Q.-V., Pham, X.-Q., Nguyen, T.T., Han, Z., Kim, D.-S.: Artificial intelligence for the metaverse: a survey. Eng. Appl. Artif. Intell. **117**, 105581 (2023). https://doi.org/10.1016/j.engappai.2022.105581

38. Yao, X., Ma, N., Zhang, J., Wang, K., Yang, E., Faccio, M.: Enhancing wisdom manufacturing as industrial metaverse for industry and society 5.0. J. Intell. Manuf. (2022). https://doi.org/10.1007/s10845-022-02027-7

39. Lu, J., Wang, X., Cheng, X., Yang, J., Kwan, O., Wang, X.: Parallel factories for smart industrial operations: from big AI models to field foundational models and scenarios engineering. IEEE/CAA J. Autom. Sinica. **9**, 2079–2086 (2022). https://doi.org/10.1109/JAS.2022.106094

40. Yang, D., et al.: Expert consensus on the metaverse in medicine. Clin. eHealth. **5**, 1–9 (2022). https://doi.org/10.1016/j.ceh.2022.02.001

41. Yang, D., Zhou, J., Song, Y., Sun, M., Bai, C.: Metaverse in medicine. Clin. eHealth **5**, 39–43 (2022). https://doi.org/10.1016/j.ceh.2022.04.002

42. Zhang, X., et al.: Metaverse for cultural heritages. Electronics **11**, 3730 (2022). https://doi.org/10.3390/electronics11223730

43. He, Q., Wu, M., Liu, C., Jin, D., Zhao, M.: Management and real-time monitoring of inter-connected energy hubs using digital twin: machine learning based approach. Sol. Energy **250**, 173–181 (2023). https://doi.org/10.1016/j.solener.2022.12.041

44. Tsang, Y.P., Yang, T., Chen, Z.S., Wu, C.H., Tan, K.H.: How is extended reality bridging human and cyber-physical systems in the IoT-empowered logistics and supply chain management? Internet Things **20**, 100623 (2022). https://doi.org/10.1016/j.iot.2022.100623

45. Phoon, K.-K., Ching, J., Cao, Z.: Unpacking data-centric geotechnics. Underground Space **7**, 967–989 (2022). https://doi.org/10.1016/j.undsp.2022.04.001

46. Kevin, G.B., Shah, D.: Marketing in the Metaverse: conceptual understanding, framework, and research agenda. J. Bus. Res. **155**, 113420 (2023). https://doi.org/10.1016/j.jbusres.2022.113420

47. Bhat, J.R., AlQahtani, S.A., Nekovee, M.: FinTech enablers, use cases, and role of future internet of things. J. King Saud Univ. – Comput. Inform. Sci. **35**, 87–101 (2023). https://doi.org/10.1016/j.jksuci.2022.08.033

48. Jin, C., Wu, F., Wang, J., Liu, Y., Guan, Z., Han, Z.: MetaMGC: a music generation framework for concerts in metaverse. J. Audio Speech Music Proc. **2022**, 31 (2022). https://doi.org/10.1186/s13636-022-00261-8

49. Zhang, Y., Pang, L., Wang, D., Liu, S.: Influences of digital twin technology on learning effect. J. Eng. Sci. Technol. Rev. **15**, 140–145 (2022). https://doi.org/10.25103/jestr.154.20

50. Liljaniemi, A., Paavilainen, H.: Using digital twin technology in engineering education – course concept to explore benefits and barriers. Open Eng. **10**, 377–385 (2020). https://doi.org/10.1515/eng-2020-0040

51. Wang, M.: Editorial preface: new leadership new era. IEEE Trans. Learning Technol. **15**, 434–438 (2022). https://doi.org/10.1109/TLT.2022.3197345

52. Chang, L., et al.: 6G-enabled edge ai for metaverse: challenges, methods, and future research directions. J. Commun. Inf. Netw. **7**, 107–121 (2022). https://doi.org/10.23919/JCIN.2022.9815195

53. Ali, M., Naeem, F., Kaddoum, G., Hossain, E.: Metaverse Communications, Networking, Security, and Applications: Research Issues, State-of-the-Art, and Future Directions

Emotional and Cognitive Empathy, Enjoyment and Ease of Use of a Virtual Reality Environment about Migration in Colombia

Jorge Bacca-Acosta(✉) ⓘ, Myriam Sierra-Puentes ⓘ, Cecilia Avila-Garzon ⓘ,
Natalia Molina-Pinzon, Guillermo Luigui Nieto, Carol Torres-Urrea,
and Juan Rodriguez-Velasquez

Fundación Universitaria Konrad Lorenz, Carrera 9Bis # 62-43 110231, Bogotá, Colombia
`{jorge.bacca,myriamc.sierrap,cecilia.avilag,natalia.molinap,`
`guillermol.nietoa,carolv.torresu,`
`juanc.rodriguezv}@konradlorenz.edu.co`

Abstract. Virtual Reality environments have been used to build empathy in different contexts. However, research on empathy-driven virtual reality experiences for building empathy with migrants is still in its childhood. In this paper, we present the results of a comparative study between two virtual reality environments that show stories about migrants in Colombia (South America). In total, 47 university students participated in this study and a self-reported instrument was used to collect information about emotional empathy, cognitive empathy, enjoyment and perceived ease of use. The results suggest that virtual reality improves emotional empathy but not cognitive empathy. In particular, students of psychology show higher levels of emotional empathy than students of engineering. Moreover, enjoyment and ease of use are higher in immersive VR environments to build empathy when compared to less immersive VR environments.

Keywords: Cognitive Empathy · Emotional Empathy · Virtual Reality · Migration · Enjoyment

1 Introduction

Empathy is a construct and according to Moya-Albiol, Herrera & Bernal it is understood as "the ability to vicariously experience the emotional states of others, and it is crucial in many forms of adaptive social interaction." [1] Empathy is the ability to recognize the emotions of others and to share them while distinguishing between self and the other ([2] cited in [3]). These definitions refer to the fact that empathy is the ability to reflect emotions between peers, a relevant aspect for prosocial behaviors and human interaction, since empathic response involves the individuals' ability to understand others, based on what is observed, information obtained either verbally or from memory, as well as the affective reaction of sharing the emotional state, which can cause sadness, anger, discomfort or anxiety [4].

© The Author(s), under exclusive license to Springer Nature Switzerland AG 2024
M.-L. Bourguet et al. (Eds.): iLRN 2023, CCIS 1904, pp. 533–542, 2024.
https://doi.org/10.1007/978-3-031-47328-9_38

Empathy is a concept that refers to several interrelated processes (see [2]), which can be divided into two main components. On the one hand, emotional empathy or the human ability to share the emotions of others, that is to say, the possibility of experiencing an emotion similar to that of another person, even if the event that caused the emotion did not occur directly [2]; on the other hand, there is cognitive empathy, also called affective theory of mind (TOM) or affective perspective-taking ([2, 5] cited in [3]). This component refers to understanding the emotion and feelings reported by other people, after exposure to various signals.

Previous studies have used virtual reality to generate empathy in different areas. However, the impact of virtual reality for creating empathy toward migrants is analyzed only in a few studies. To contribute to fill this gap in the literature, in this paper we report a study on the effect of virtual reality environment to create empathy about migrants in university students in Colombia. In this paper, we introduce two virtual reality applications designed and developed to generate empathy toward the migrant population and reports the results of an initial exploratory study comparing the effect of an immersive virtual reality environment and a non-immersive one on emotional and cognitive empathy. Additionally, the perceived ease of use and enjoyment of both environments is compared to determine the user experience level.

One of the most commonly used instruments to assess both emotional and cognitive empathy is the Interpersonal Reactivity Index (IRI) ([5, 6], cited in [4]), which is a 28-item scale distributed in four 7-item subscales that measure the following four global dimensions of the concept of empathy: 1) Perspective Taking (PT), which indicates the individual's spontaneous attempts to adopt the perspective of others in real life; 2) Fantasy (FS), which evaluates the individual's imaginative capacity to transpose himself into fictional situations; 3) Empathic Concern (EC), which measures feelings of compassion, concern and affection caused by the discomfort of others, and 4) Personal Distress (PD), which focuses on the feelings of discomfort and anxiety experienced by an individual when observing the negative experiences of others. The PT and FS subscales assess cognitive processes, while the EC and PD subscales measure the individuals' emotional reaction ([6, 7] cited in [4]). The items proposed in this study are based on these subscales.

The rest of this article is outlined as follows: Sect. 2 addresses related literature, Sect. 3 presents the two virtual reality applications that were developed, Sect. 4 describes the methodology, and Sect. 5 describes the results obtained. Finally, the results are discussed in Sect. 6, and the conclusions and future work are presented in Sect. 7.

2   Related Work

Previous research has analyzed the impact of virtual reality on the generation of empathy because so far virtual reality is one of the technologies that provides a higher level of immersion and would therefore allow someone to be in someone else's shoes. In previous studies, 360° videos have been used because they could provide higher levels of empathy as they achieve higher levels of presence [8]. Among these research papers the study by Jones and Sommer [9] can be mentioned, as it compared a virtual reality immigration environment at the US-Mexico border to reading an article on the same topic. However, the results did not show significant differences between the use of virtual reality and a printed text on the subject.

Schutte and Stilinović [10] conclude that a 360° video showing the documentary "Clouds Over Sidra" through virtual reality generates higher levels of empathy than traditional video (different from 360°). Similarly, Martingano [11] concluded that 360° virtual reality videos have a positive short-term effect on emotional empathy when compared to control conditions, which consist of reading stories similar to those shown on the 360° video only through text. However, the authors did not find a significant effect on cognitive empathy. On the other hand, Gitau [12] developed a virtual reality environment called EmbodiMap where a group of refugees can register their feelings and emotions in a creative and innovative way.

3   Virtual Reality Applications

Two virtual reality apps for the Meta Quest VR headset were developed for this study in the Unity video game engine. These applications were developed as a first exploratory prototype to initiate an XR resources co-creation process such as the one described in Varella et al. [13] and from the basics described in [14]. One of the applications shows an environment consisting of a small gallery with two rooms (See Fig. 1) where photos alluding to migration can be seen on the walls. In addition, the gallery has two large screens (one in each room) where two 3-min long videos can be watched (one per screen) with stories of people who had to migrate from Venezuela to Colombia. In this application, the participant can move freely across the two gallery rooms by using teleportation through the virtual reality glasses controls. Participants can also play or pause the videos whenever they want. The gallery tour experience takes about 14 min for participant. This environment will be called *immersive virtual reality environment hereinafter*. It has been given this name because the participant has greater freedom to move and interact with the gallery screens.

Additionally, a virtual reality environment was developed where a single room is shown and a text box allows the participant to read both migration stories, which were obtained from the transcription of the migration videos (See Fig. 2). In this virtual reality environment, participants cannot teleport themselves. Within the framework of this study, this environment has been called *non-immersive virtual reality environment* because it does not have interactive elements such as video screens and does not offer the possibility of moving around the room. The objective is to be able to compare which of the scenarios generates more empathy in the students when it comes to migration, and also to establish which of the scenarios is easier to use and which one generates a greater enjoyment of the virtual reality experience.

The reason why another means such as a mobile or a PC was not chosen to be compared to the virtual reality environment is that comparisons between different means to present the information should be avoided, in order to isolate variables that are not controlled in the experiment as suggested in [15]. This pilot study with both virtual reality applications will serve as reference to identify the aspects that must be considered when developing virtual reality environments that generate empathy towards Venezuelan migration in Colombia.

Fig. 1. Immersive Virtual Reality Environment – top view.

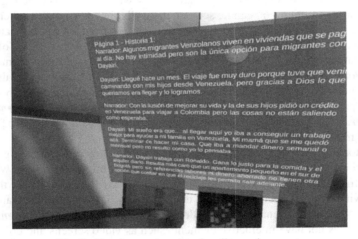

Fig. 2. Non-immersive virtual reality environment.

4   Methodology

A quasi-experimental research design was used in this study. Participants were 47 students, out of which 25 belonged to the Systems Engineering, Industrial Engineering and Mathematics programs, and 22 to the Psychology program, with an average age of 20.2 years. 27 participants are female and 20 are male. Participants were chosen through intentional sampling and participation was voluntary. Students who had experienced a personal or family migration process were excluded in order to reduce potential biases caused by previous experiences. All the participants signed an informed consent including the objectives and the low risk of their participation in this study.

To collect the information, an 18-item Likert scale instrument was designed, distributed as follows: five items assessed cognitive empathy and five items that were adapted from the Interpersonal Reactivity Index assessed emotional empathy [6]. In addition, five adapted items from the technology acceptance instrument [16] were used to assess perceived ease of use as well as three adapted items from the McLean & Wilson [17] published instrument to assess experience enjoyment.

5 Results

The aim of the study is to determine the effect of an immersive and non-immersive virtual reality environment on emotional empathy, cognitive empathy, and the perceptions of enjoyment and usability in two groups of Engineering and Psychology students towards Venezuelan migration in Colombia.

First, the Shapiro-Wilk test was used to determine whether the dataset follows a normal distribution. The test result shows that the dataset follows a normal distribution: $W = 0.941$, p-value $= 0.53$ because the p-value is greater than 0.05. Additionally, homogeneity of variance was analyzed by means of an F test of variance comparison. The result shows that sample variance is homogeneous: $F = 1.986$, p-value $= 0.278$. From these results, an analysis of variance (ANOVA) was used but the result was not significant, so a Student's T-test was used to make the relevant comparisons in this study.

The first aspect analyzed was emotional empathy among the group of Engineering and Psychology students who used the immersive virtual reality environment. The T-test result shows that Psychology students have greater emotional empathy ($M = 2.89$) when compared to Engineering students ($M = 2.36$). The difference between both groups is significant: $t(24) = -2.12$; p-value $= 0.043$ with an effect size (Cohen's d) of 0.88, indicating a large effect. Figure 3 shows the box plot for emotional empathy values in both groups.

As a second aspect, cognitive empathy was analyzed in both groups but the T-test result was not significant, which indicates that there is no difference between Engineering and Psychology students in terms of cognitive empathy: $t(24) = -1.456$, p-value $= 0.15$.

Additional comparisons were made by using the T-test to identify significant differences between emotional and cognitive empathy when using the non-immersive virtual reality environment. However, the results were not significant.

Regarding enjoyment perceptions, the assumption of homogeneity of variance was analyzed to determine the possibility of using an analysis of variance (ANOVA). The Levene test was applied, which yielded an 0.08 p-value indicating that the assumption of homogeneity of variance is met. The ANOVA result was significant with a p-value of 0.019. Pair-wise comparisons were made by using the Tukey test.

As a result, a significant difference was found between Psychology students who used the immersive virtual reality environment and those who used the non-immersive one with a 0.02 p-value in the group of students who used the immersive environment. In addition, a significant difference was found in terms of enjoyment perception between the group of Psychology students who used the non-immersive virtual reality environment and Engineering students who used the immersive virtual reality environment with a 0.04 p-value. The other comparisons were not significant. Figure 4 shows the box plot graph

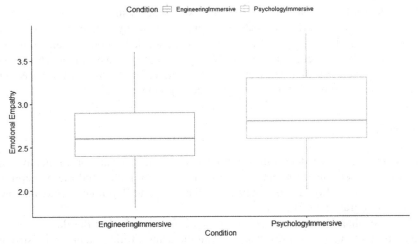

Fig. 3. Box plot graph for Emotional Empathy in Engineering and Psychology groups using the immersive application.

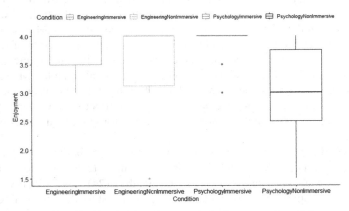

Fig. 4. Box plot graph for Enjoyment in both groups of participants.

that allows to compare experimental conditions in terms of enjoyment of the virtual reality experience.

In terms of ease of use of the application, normality of the dataset was analyzed by using a Shapiro-Wilk test that yielded a 0.0109 p-value indicating that the data do not follow a normal distribution so it is not possible to use a parametric test. As a result, it was decided to apply the continuity correction Wilcoxon test and the result shows that there is a significant difference between ease of use of the immersive application and the non-immersive one, as the immersive application obtained a p-value $= 0.027$. Figure 5 shows the ease of use box plot when comparing the groups of students that used the immersive and the non-immersive application.

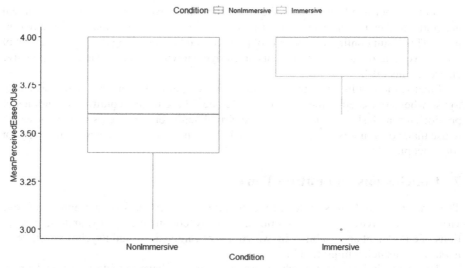

Fig. 5. Box plot comparison for perceived ease of use – immersive and non-immersive versions.

6 Discussion

The results of this study show that Psychology students show higher levels of emotional empathy when compared to Engineering students using a virtual reality environment with stories about Venezuelan migration to Colombia. One possible interpretation of this result is that Psychology's human science-focused background allows these students to be more empathic than Engineering students. This result also agrees with the findings of Schutte and Stilinović [10], who confirm that virtual reality has a positive impact on emotional empathy. Additionally, the results are consistent with the findings of the meta-analysis conducted by Martingano et al. [11] indicating that virtual reality has a positive impact on emotional empathy but not on cognitive empathy. On the other hand, the results confirm that there is no significant difference between the use of an immersive virtual reality environment and a non-immersive one (in which, for example, a text is read) in terms of the generation of emotional and cognitive empathy, which confirms the findings of the study reported in [9].

Virtual reality has been considered by some authors as "the ultimate empathy machine". However, there is controversy in this regard due to the potential implications of technology with respect to human communication. Virtual reality experiences like "Clouds over Sydra" could be effective for the generation of empathy. In this sense, more research that reveals the role of virtual reality in the generation of empathy and the potential of this technology to influence some aspects of empathy is required. Moreover, further research on the aspects that influence empathy in virtual reality can be useful to develop frameworks [18] on how to effectively design and develop virtual reality environments to create empathy about migrants.

On the other hand, the results show that the immersive virtual reality environment generates higher levels of enjoyment than the non-immersive virtual reality environment. This result confirms the results of previous studies regarding the positive effect of immersive virtual reality environments on enjoyment when compared to non-immersive environments [19].

Finally, the results show that the immersive virtual reality environment was easier to use when compared to the non-immersive one. These results confirm the findings of previous research showing that immersive virtual reality environments seem to be easier to use than non-immersive ones [20], even though virtual reality is a new technology for some people.

7 Conclusions and Future Work

The aim of the study was to determine the effect of an immersive and non-immersive virtual reality environment on emotional empathy, cognitive empathy, and the perceptions of enjoyment and usability in two groups of Engineering and Psychology students towards Venezuelan migration in Colombia.

The results indicate that Psychology students tend to have a greater emotional empathy than Engineering students. However, there is no significant difference in terms of cognitive empathy. Additionally, no significant differences were found when cognitive empathy was compared between participants who used the immersive and the non-immersive virtual reality environment. Regarding the perception of enjoyment, a significant difference was found in Psychology students who used the immersive virtual reality environment and the non-immersive one, with better results in the immersive virtual reality environment. Finally, the results show that the immersive virtual reality environment was perceived as easier to use when compared to the non-immersive one.

In previous studies on empathy, the use of virtual reality has been compared to other means such as computer, cell phone or print media, as in the study conducted by Jones and Sommer [9]. However, the means changes drastically, like when virtual reality is compared to printed media, therefore it is not possible to accurately determine whether the changes in empathy are due to the content itself or to the change in the means used to present the information. In this sense, we recommend that future research formulates experiments in which the means used to present the information are controlled to avoid introducing confounding variables in the study, as recommended in Buchner and Kerres [15].

The results of this study have provided key information for the next step in the research, which consists in co-creating virtual reality applications for the generation of empathy towards migration in Colombia based on migration stories collected through interviews with migrants. Another aspect that requires further research has to do with the reasons why no positive results have been found around the effect of virtual reality on cognitive empathy. Furthermore, policy development for the inclusion of migrants might be supported by technology to facilitate dissemination. Handbooks for inclusive learning such as the one reported in [21] might be a good starting point to contribute to the inclusion of migrants. Finally, another avenue of future research is to compare the levels of cognitive and emotional empathy with different stimuli in VR to determine the aspects that create empathy about migrants in VR.

Acknowledgments. This project was funded by the COMISIÓN DE REGULACIÓN DE COMU-NICACIONES – CRC and MINISTERIO DE CIENCIA, TECNOLOGIA E INNOVACIÓN in Colombia. This paper is one of the deliverables of the research project entitled "Co-creación de narrativas inmersivas sobre migración en Colombia: una propuesta metodológica" presented and approved under the research call 908 from MINCIENCIAS "Nuevo conocimiento, desarrollo tecnológico e innovación para el fortalecimiento de los sectores de TIC, postal y de contenidos audiovisuales".

References

1. Moya-Albiol, L., Herrero, N., Bernal, M.: Bases neuronales de la empatía. RevNeurol. **50**, 89–100 (2010). https://doi.org/10.33588/rn.5002.2009111
2. Uzefovsky, F., Knafo-Noam, A.: Empathy development throughout the life span. In: Sommerville, J., Decety, J. (eds.) Social cognition: Development Across the Life Span, pp. 71–97. Routledge/Taylor & Francis Group, New York, NY, US (2017)
3. Abramson, L., Uzefovsky, F., Toccaceli, V., Knafo-Noam, A.: The genetic and environmental origins of emotional and cognitive empathy: review and meta-analyses of twin studies. Neurosci. Biobehav. Rev. **114**, 113–133 (2020). https://doi.org/10.1016/j.neubiorev.2020.03.023
4. Mestre, V., Frías, M., Samper, P.: La medida de la empatía: análisis del Interpersonal Reactivity Index. Psicothema **16**, 255–260 (2004)
5. Davis, M.: A multidimensional approach to individual differences in empathy. JSAS Catalog Sel. Doc. Psychol. **10**, 85–104 (1980)
6. Davis, M.: Measuring individual differences in empathy: evidence for a multidimensional approach. J. Pers. Soc. Psychol. **44**(113), 126 (1983). https://doi.org/10.1037/0022-3514.44.1.113
7. Olivera, J., Braun, M., Roussos, A.J.: Instrumentos Para la Evaluación de la Empatía en Psicoterapia. Revista Argentina de Clínica Psicológica **XX**, 121–132 (2011)
8. Hollick, M., Acheampong, C., Ahmed, M., Economou, D., Ferguson, J.: Work-in-progress-360-degree immersive storytelling video to create empathetic response. In: 2021 7th International Conference of the Immersive Learning Research Network (iLRN), pp. 1–3. Eureka, CA (2021). https://doi.org/10.23919/iLRN52045.2021.9459340
9. Jones, J., Sommer, J.: Is Virtual Reality Uniquely Effective in Eliciting Empathy? (2018). https://osf.io/preprints/socarxiv/bgc5n/ https://doi.org/10.31235/osf.io/bgc5n
10. Schutte, N., Stilinović, E.: Facilitating empathy through virtual reality. Motiv. Emot. **41**, 708–712 (2017). https://doi.org/10.1007/s11031-017-9641-7
11. Martingano, A., Hererra, F., Konrath, S.: Virtual reality improves emotional but not cognitive empathy: a meta-analysis. Technol. Mind Behav. **2**, 1–15 (2021). https://doi.org/10.1037/tmb0000034
12. Gitau, L., et al.: Pre-engagement as method: an EmbodiMap TM VR experience to explore lived experience of people from south sudanese refugee background. Int J Qual Methods **21**, 160940692211231 (2022). https://doi.org/10.1177/16094069221123167
13. Varella, A., Antoniou, P., Pickering, J., Chatzimallis, C., Bamidis, P.: Evaluating co-creative XR resource design and development; observations from the field. In: 2022 8th International Conference of the Immersive Learning Research Network (iLRN), pp. 187–191. IEEE, Vienna (2022). https://doi.org/10.23919/iLRN55037.2022.9815915

14. Antoniou, P., Chondrokostas, E., Bratsas, C., Filippidis, P.-M., Bamidis, P.: A medical ontology informed user experience taxonomy to support co-creative workflows for authoring mixed reality medical education spaces. In: 2021 7th International Conference of the Immersive Learning Research Network (iLRN), pp. 1–9 (2021). https://doi.org/10.23919/iLRN52045.2021.9459388

15. Buchner, J., Kerres, M.: Media comparison studies dominate comparative research on augmented reality in education. Comput. duc. **195**, 104711 (2023). https://doi.org/10.1016/j.compedu.2022.104711

16. Davis, F.D.: Perceived usefulness, perceived ease of use, and user acceptance of information technology. MIS Q. **13**, 319–340 (1989). https://doi.org/10.2307/249008

17. McLean, G., Wilson, A.: Shopping in the digital world: examining customer engagement through augmented reality mobile applications. Comput. Hum. Behav. **101**, 210–224 (2019). https://doi.org/10.1016/j.chb.2019.07.002

18. Bacca, J.: Framework for the design and development of motivational augmented reality learning experiences in vocational education and training (2017). https://dialnet.unirioja.es/servlet/tesis?codigo=136816

19. Tang, Q., Wang, Y., Liu, H., Liu, Q., Jiang, S.: Experiencing an art education program through immersive virtual reality or iPad: examining the mediating effects of sense of presence and extraneous cognitive load on enjoyment, attention, and retention. Front. Psychol. **13**, 957037 (2022)

20. Omlor, A., et al.: Comparison of immersive and non-immersive virtual reality videos as substitute for in-hospital teaching during coronavirus lockdown: a survey with graduate medical students in Germany. Med. Educ. Online **27**, 2101417 (2022). https://doi.org/10.1080/10872981.2022.2101417

21. Politis, Y., et al.: Introducing the inclusive learning handbook: an OER for teachers and policy makers. In: EDULEARN14 Proceedings, pp. 5463–5469. IATED, Barcelona (2014)

A Review of Immersivity in Distance Higher Education STEM Subjects

André Roberto Guerra[1]([✉]) [iD], Luciano Frontino de Medeiros[1] [iD],
and Manuel Gericota[2] [iD]

[1] PPGENT – Postgraduate Program in Education and New Technologies, Centro Universitário Internacional UNINTER, Curitiba, Paraná, Brasil
andre.gu@uninter.com
[2] ISEP/IPP – School of Engineering, Polytechnic University of Porto, Porto, Portugal

Abstract. Immersive augmented reality, in practical terms, is a real-time, immersive processing experience which bind together elements of real life with the images presented. The study is a systematic literature review that aims to analyze the main methods and projects for the development of virtual learning environments (VLEs), especially in STEM disciplines, with immersive scenarios in the field of distance higher education. The analyzed scientific productions underwent revision on the search strings, which presented a high growth in the application of Virtual Reality, Augmented Reality, Mixed Reality and Extended Reality in education. The studies revealed that the use of Immersive Augmented Reality in education is able to increase students' motivation and interest in studies, mainly due to the teaching and learning environment becoming more dynamic. Additionally, it enables students in the immersive environment to interact and achieve effective learning.

Keywords: Immersive Learning · Virtual Reality · Augmented Reality · Virtual Learning Environments · STEM Subjects

1 Introduction

Currently, the new technologies in the field of education stand out for the diversity of applications and devices used, which contribute in an innovative and diversified way to the teaching and learning processes [1]. Virtual Reality (VR), for example, is one of the most well-known and widely used contemporary technologies in the videogame industry, although it is not restricted to this field alone, once its use is present in other areas of science, such as in education and/or in medicine [2, 3]. Higher Education Institutions (HEIs), by incorporating new technologies in education, provide learners with greater interest in their studies and demonstrate understanding on the relevance of immersive learning tools.

The study aimed to analyze the main methods and projects for the development of virtual learning environments (VLEs), especially in STEM disciplines with immersive scenarios, in the field of distance higher education. The study was carried out through the use of Systematic Literature Review (SLR), with scientific productions comprised between the period of 2018 to 2022. The SLR is one of the types of literature review which synthesizes all existing information about a phenomenon in an impartial and complete way [4, 5]. Unlike the unsystematic process, the systematic review is done in the most detailed manner.

Hence, it establishes a careful and well-defined sequence of steps [4]. The methodological procedures follow aspects of quali-quantitative and basic research, inspired by the use and assumptions of Design Science Research (DSR). Solutions for the development (construction) of computer-altered reality environments, through immersive virtual reality devices (hardware), development tools (software) and connectivity, with application in teaching and learning scenarios, are presented by scientific productions [7].

The study is structured as follows: in Sect. 2 the methodology used to carry out this work is presented, in Sect. 3 the results of the research are described, in Sect. 4 the conclusions are derived, and in the final section bibliographical references are made.

2   Methodology

The use of the Systematic Literature Review (SLR) is validated by the fact that it is done in a meticulous manner, that is, its process seeks to exhaust all information relevant to the objective outlined in a given study, and therefore it is possible to develop even further the scientific production.

According to the SLR process, the following steps were taken to prepare the study, considering the work methodology [4–6]:

2.1   The SLR Elements

The elements considered in the SLR for carrying out the research are presented in Table 1.

Table 1.   SLR elements (adap. [4, 7]).

Elements	Task/Target
Analyze	Theses and scientific publications
with the purpose of	Characterizing and analyzing
in relation to	Conduct a survey of existing research on digital bibliographic databases on the elaborate search string
from the point of view of	Researchers
in context of	Academic and Scientific

Using SLR as a method, applied to identify, evaluate and analyze relevant works for this study, the following keyword search strings (main findings) were elaborated for Table 2.

Table 2. Keywords.

Keywords	Immersive Learning; Virtual Reality (VR); Augmented Reality (AR); Mixed Reality (MR); Extended Reality (XR); 3DVLE (Virtual Learning Environment); STEM Subjects

The search strings (key findings) are based on the keywords: Immersive Learning; Virtual Reality (VR); Augmented Reality (AR); Mixed Reality (MR); Extended Reality (XR); 3DVLE (Virtual Learning Environment), STEM Subjects, seeking scientific documents and productions published in the bibliographic databases. The keyword Immersive Learning is justified by having greater grasp to the area of concentration, Education and New Technologies.

2.2   Flow of the Search Strings Development Process

Figure 1 illustrates the flow of the search strings development process. Truncation operators are used to insert "wildcard" characters and use only the stem of the word (without having to repeat singular/plural, amongst other). E.g. "robot". Boolean operators are the AND to link keywords, and the OR operator to enclose synonyms (using parentheses).

Figure 1 shows flow of the search strings elaboration process.

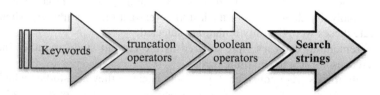

Fig. 1. Search strings elaboration process (adapt. From [4, 7]).

By using the aforementioned process, and considering the definitions of the Boolean operators, where AND is disjunctive and OR is connective, the following search string was elaborated: ("Education" OR "Immersive Learning") AND ("Virtual Reality" OR "Augmented Reality" OR "Mixed Reality" OR "Extended Reality") OR ("3DVLE" OR "Virtual Learning Environment").

For the IEEE Xplore the following string was used: ((("Author Keywords":"virtual reality" OR "Author Keywords":"VR" OR "Author Keywords":"Augmented Reality" OR "Author Keywords":"AR" OR "Author Keywords":"Mixed Reality" OR "Author Keywords":"MR" OR "Author Keywords":"Extended Reality" OR "Author Keywords":"XR") OR ("Author Keywords":3DVLE OR "Author Keywords":learning) AND ("Author Keywords":educat* OR "Author Keywords":learning) OR ("Index

Terms":"virtual reality" OR "Index Terms":"VR" OR "Index Terms":"Augmented Reality" OR "Index Terms":"AR" OR "Index Terms":"Mixed Reality" OR "Index Terms":"MR" OR "Index Terms":"eXtended Reality" OR "Index Terms":"XR") OR ("Index Terms":learning OR "Index Terms":educat*) OR ("Index Terms":3DVLE OR Virtual Learning Environments)) AND ("Full Text Only":"distance education").

The chosen scientific digital libraries are listed in Table 3.

Table 3. Scientific digital libraries selected.

Digital library	Link
SciELO – Scientific Electronic Library Online	https://scielo.org/
Science Direct	https://www.sciencedirect.com/
Google Scholar	https://scholar.google.com
IEEE	http://ieeexplore.ieee.org/Xplore/home.jsp
CAPES Periodicals (Higher Education Personnel Improvement Coordination)	https://www-periodicos-capes-gov-br.ez485.per iodicos.capes.gov.br/index.php

The selection of the scientific articles derived from the initial research, and, from the searches carried out in the aforementioned database, resulted in more than 5000 found and analyzed publications. After applying the selection filters, analysis of the inclusion/exclusion criteria which are described in 2.3 (below), articles published in the subareas were selected by the keywords Computer Science and Education, reducing significantly the number to only 42 results, all available for download, which, after reading and analyzing their abstracts, the last filter (extraction) was applied, when finally the doctorate theses were the only remaining selected.

The aforementioned theses were utilized as the current study is rather incipient, where references are scarce and quite recent.

Thus, only theses were considered, precisely because they are studies which relate to the theme proposed in this study, as well as because they are more robust references. It is worth mentioning that these are recent references, which are justified both by the fact that the respective topic is current and by the fact there is not a lot of published material on this subject.

2.3 Inclusion and Exclusion Criteria

The relevance of the selected theses is justified because they present a great theoretical-practical contribution, which served as the basis for the present study. Scientific productions result in significant experiences that contribute to the continuity of other studies, as well as the qualification of new experiences related to virtual reality for learning.

The teaching of STEM subjects; augmented reality for educators; the effects of immersion on learning in educational virtual environments; immersive environments for teaching computer science and among others.

The inclusion and exclusion criteria applied are as follows:

1. **Empirical/Conceptual**: Empirical – theses that present empirical experiments on teaching/learning environments. Conceptual – theses that present theoretical discussions related to the teaching/learning of STEM disciplines in computer science courses in distance learning.
2. **Target audience**: identify the target audience of the studies, such as teachers, students and other education professionals, especially in STEM courses.
3. **Research tools**: identify which research instruments were utilized to produce data from the selected papers.
4. **Research approach**: identify whether it was qualitative, quantitative or mixed approach used.
5. **Origin of studies**: countries of origin of the studies analyzed.

After reading and analyzing the documents and applying all filters, 3 theses were selected for the full reading of the final sample. Table 4 shows a preliminary survey of the current surveys with the amount of results obtained in each of the databases before and after the application of the exclusion criteria.

Table 4. Results obtained from search strings in databases.

Source	Execution	Selection	Extraction
SciELO	75	2	0
Science Direct	73	8	1
Google Scholar	1643	18	1
IEEE	4886	0	0
CAPES Periodicals	735	5	1

3 Results and Theses Chosen

The analyzed productions showed that VR can promote new learning possibilities in distance higher education institutions. It also allows designing, delivering, and evaluating different forms and strategies for the teaching and learning process. The VR-based educational process is capable of filling gaps between practical applications and theoretical discussions about the value of using immersive VR for education in the context of distance higher education [3].

Augmented reality tools effectively promote students' development in STEM-based learning. Through the indication of a change in the ability of organizations to infuse technology integration with STEM-based learning, it is feasible to feed back on the action of teachers, as they demonstrate flexibility and refinement in their craft and, consequently, grow more and more as educators [1].

Researchers and/or educators which work with immersive technology is significant for feedback from the educational field, especially due the fact that learning is not a sterile future science to be kept away in hiding in laboratories. Therefore, immersive technology is an approach that can qualify teaching and learning processes in a truly immersive and engaging way [5].

Figure 2 is the Research Model for Investigating the Influence of VR Characteristics on Learning Outcomes (yellow: supplied media and media effects; blue: learner's traits and trait effects; green: learner's states and state effects; purple: learner's outcomes).

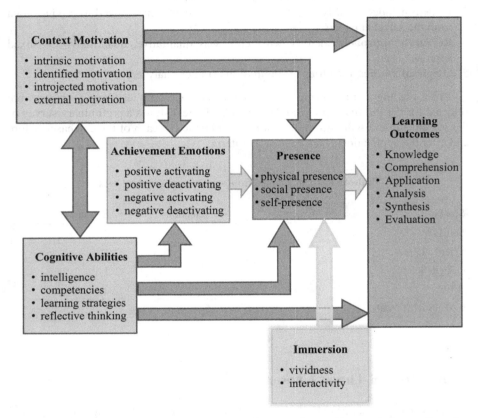

Fig. 2. Research Model for Investigating the Influence of VR Characteristics on Learning Outcomes (adapt. From [5]).

In summary, the teaching and learning processes in higher education combined with available technologies can provide capital knowledge and skills which then allow students and educators to create safe bases through the use of proven active learning methods [8, 9].

The next Table 5 shows chosen theses.

Table 5. Chosen theses.

Author	Title	Problems addressed
S. BACEVICIUTE	Designing Virtual Reality for Learning [3]	How we can combine knowledge from human cognition, psychology and behavioral insights to understand the efficacy of learning in VR Use this knowledge to guide the design of VR applications which improve learning and training
R.S BOOKHAMER	STEM in Elementary School Education: Evaluating a STEM and Augmented Reality Professional Development Workshop for Educators [1]	What are the educator's perspectives of STEM education? Based on the professional development workshops, what is the educators understanding of STEM principles and the 21st century skills after completing the workshops? Based on the professional development workshops, how are educators prepared and adapt to effectively integrating augmented reality tools into STEM-based instruction?
A. DENGEL	Effects of Immersion and Presence on Learning Outcomes in Immersive Educational Virtual Environments for Computer Science Education [5]	What are the effects of technological and person-specific factors on learning outcomes in Educational Virtual Environments for learning Computer Science?

4 Conclusions

The analyzes of scientific productions demonstrated the substantiality of the use of immersive virtual, augmented and extended reality in teaching and learning in STEM disciplines for distance learning of informatics. Innovation in the field of education is so vitally fundamental, as it enables students and educators to broaden their perspectives on the different processes and perspectives as to guarantee teaching and learning, considering the wide range of technological means available.

Virtual, augmented and extended immersive reality proves unpaired relevance in the context of teaching and learning STEM subjects for computer science in distance higher education, impacting on educational, practical, and theoretical processes in a dynamic way, reassessing how technological means are fundamental in the field of education, adding great value to teaching and learning. Having thus in mind, an SLR was elaborated to dig deeper in the concepts as to obtain a clear overview of the research which undergoing in this area.

In the aftermath, the great benefits of the technology and resources in the context of education through augmented immersive reality, provide a real sense of "being there", also identified as presence, whereas the learners engage at real time, with objects and contextualized environment perceived as 'real', therefore they do not necessarily have to be real physically [5].

Furthermore, the use of these technologies has the potential to revolutionize the way we approach education, providing new opportunities for interactive and engaging learning experiences. By harnessing the power of immersive virtual, augmented, and extended reality, we can create dynamic and personalized learning environments that cater to the individual needs of each student. This not only enhances the learning experience but also helps to bridge the gap between theory and practice, providing students with a deeper understanding of the subject matter. As such, it is essential that we continue to explore and develop these technologies to ensure that we are providing the best possible education for future generations.

Acknowledgements. I would like to express my sincere gratitude to my advisors, Prof. Luciano Frontino de Medeiros and Prof. Manuel Gradin de Oliveira Gericota, for their continuous support, valuable guidance and constructive feedback. They inspired me to pursue academic excellence and to contribute to the advancement of knowledge in Immersive Learning. Special thanks to Prof. Gericota for the welcome and guidance of the international doctoral internship carried out at ISEP – Porto.

References

1. Bookhamer, R.S.: STEM in Elementary School Education: Evaluating a STEM and Augmented Reality Professional Development Workshop for Educators. University of Pittsburgh (2022). http://d-scholarship.pitt.edu/43529/1/bookhamerRyan_etd.pdf
2. Reisoğlu, I., Topu, B., Yılmaz, R.: 3D virtual learning environments in education: a meta-review. Asia Pacific Educ. Rev. **18**, 81–100 (2017). https://doi.org/10.1007/s12564-016-9467-0
3. Baceviciute, S.: Designing Virtual Reality for Learning. University of Copenhagen (2020). https://www.researchgate.net/publication/349313006
4. De-la-Torre-Ugarte-Guanilo, M.C., Takahashi, R.F., Bertolozzi, M.R.: Revisão sistemática: noções gerais. J. School Nurs. – Univ. São Paulo (2011). https://doi.org/10.1590/S0080-623 42011000500033/
5. Dengel, A.: Effects of Immersion and Presence on Learning Outcomes in Immersive Educational Virtual Environments for Computer Science Education, University of Passau (2020). https://opus4.kobv.de/opus4-uni-passau/files/841/Dengel_Andreas_VirtualReality
6. Kitchenham, B., Charters, S.: Guidelines for performing systematic literature reviews in software engineering. Technical Report EBSE 2007-001, Keele University and Durham University Joint Report (2007). https://userpages.uni-koblenz.de/~laemmel/esecourse/slides/slr.pdf
7. Lacerda, D.P.: Design Science Research: research method for production engineering. Manag. Product. **20**, 741–761 (2013). https://www.scielo.br/j/gp/a/3CZmL4JJxLmxCv6b3pnQ8pq
8. Morillo, D.: Assessment in 3D virtual worlds: QTI in Wonderland. In: Sánchez, J. (Ed.): Congreso Iberoamericano de Informática Educativa, vol. 1, pp. 410–417. Santiago de Chile (2010). http://www.tise.cl/volumen6/TISE2010/Documento60.pdf
9. Ijsselsteijn, W.A.: Presence in depth. Phd Thesis, Industrial Engineering and Innovation Sciences. Technische Universiteit Eindhoven (2004). https://doi.org/10.6100/IR581425

Author Index

M.-L. Bourguet et al. (Eds.): iLRN 2023, CCIS 1904, pp. 551–553, 2024.
https://doi.org/10.1007/978-3-031-47328-9